Programming in HTML5 with JavaScript and CSS3

Training Guide

Glenn Johnson

PUBLISHED BY
Microsoft Press
A Division of Microsoft Corporation
One Microsoft Way
Redmond, Washington 98052-6399

Library of Congress Control Number: 2013933428
ISBN: 978-0-7356-7438-7

Printed and bound in the United States of America.

Fifth Printing: October 2015

Microsoft Press books are available through booksellers and distributors worldwide. If you need support related to this book, email Microsoft Press Book Support at mspinput@microsoft.com. Please tell us what you think of this book at http://www.microsoft.com/learning/booksurvey.

Microsoft and the trademarks listed at http://www.microsoft.com/about/legal/en/us/IntellectualProperty /Trademarks/EN-US.aspx are trademarks of the Microsoft group of companies. All other marks are property of their respective owners.

The example companies, organizations, products, domain names, email addresses, logos, people, places, and events depicted herein are fictitious. No association with any real company, organization, product, domain name, email address, logo, person, place, or event is intended or should be inferred.

Acquisitions Editor: Devon Musgrave
Developmental Editor: Devon Musgrave
Project Editor: Carol Dillingham
Editorial Production: nSight, Inc.
Technical Reviewer: Pierce Bizzaca; Technical Review services provided by Content Master, a member of CM Group, Ltd.
Copyeditor: Kerin Forsyth
Indexer: Lucie Haskins
Cover: Twist Creative • Seattle

Contents at a glance

Contents

What do you think of this book? We want to hear from you!

Microsoft is interested in hearing your feedback so we can continually improve our
books and learning resources for you. To participate in a brief online survey, please visit:

www.microsoft.com/learning/booksurvey/

Chapter 9   Asynchronous operations   393

Chapter 10   WebSocket communications   415

Chapter 15 Local data with web storage   555

Chapter 16 Offline web applications   581

What do you think of this book? We want to hear from you!

Microsoft is interested in hearing your feedback so we can continually improve our books and learning resources for you. To participate in a brief online survey, please visit:

www.microsoft.com/learning/booksurvey/

Introduction

This training guide is designed for information technology (IT) professionals who develop or plan to develop HTML documents such as webpages or Windows Store applications. It is assumed that, before you begin using this guide, you are familiar with web development and common Internet technologies.

This book covers some of the topics and skills that are the subject of the Microsoft certification exam 70-480. If you are using this book to complement your study materials, you might find this information useful. Note that this book is designed to help you in the job role; it might not cover all exam topics. If you are preparing for the exam, you should use additional study materials to help bolster your real-world experience. For your reference, a mapping of the topics in this book to the exam objectives is included in the back of the book.

By using this training guide, you will learn how to do the following.

- Create a project using Visual Studio Express 2012 for Web.
- Create a project using Blend for Visual Studio 2012.
- Create a project using Visual Studio Express 2012 for Windows 8.
- Create an HTML document using semantic markup.
- Implement JavaScript functionality with your HTML documents.
- Use test-driven development techniques for writing JavaScript code.
- Create Cascading Style Sheets (CSS) that visually format your HTML document.
- Create HTML tables.
- Create JavaScript objects.
- Use jQuery to simplify JavaScript programming.
- Create HTML forms with validation.
- Create a Node.js website and web service.
- Call web services from JavaScript.
- Perform asynchronous JavaScript operations.
- Perform WebSocket communications.
- Play audio and video on a webpage.
- Draw with an HTML5 canvas.
- Use SVG image files.
- Perform drag and drop operations.
- Make your HTML location aware.
- Persist data on the browser client.

Backward compatibility and cross-browser compatibility

This book does not attempt to cover every difference between every version of every browser. Such a comprehensive discussion could easily yield a library of books.

Most of the code in this book is written using Internet Explorer 10, which is installed with Windows 8. In addition, many but not all the code examples were tested using the following browsers.

- Firefox 17.0.1
- Google Chrome 23.0.1271.97 m
- Opera 12.11
- Apple Safari 5.1.7

In most cases, if the other browsers were not compatible, there is a note stating so. This is especially true in the last chapters because web storage is still relatively new, and the requirements are still fluid.

The best way to see which features are available among browsers is to visit a website that is updated when new browser versions are released and HTML5 features are updated. The website *http://caniuse.com* is particularly good.

System requirements

The following are the minimum system requirements your computer needs to meet to complete the practice exercises in this book.

- Windows 8 or newer. If you want to develop Windows Store applications, you need Windows 8 on your development computer.

Hardware requirements

This section presents the hardware requirements for using Visual Studio 2012.

- 1.6 GHz or faster processor
- 1 GB of RAM (more is always recommended)
- 10 GB (NTFS) of available hard disk space
- 5400 RPM hard drive
- DirectX 9–capable video card running at 1024 × 768 or higher display resolution.
- Internet connectivity

Software requirements

The following software is required to complete the practice exercises.

- Visual Studio 2012 Professional, Visual Studio 2012 Premium, or Visual Studio 2012 Ultimate. You must pay for these versions, but in lieu of one of these versions, you can install the following free express versions.
  - Visual Studio Express 2012 for Web. Available from *http://www.microsoft.com /visualstudio/eng/downloads#d-express-web*.
  - Visual Studio Express 2012 for Windows 8. This installation also installs Blend for Visual Studio 2012. Available from *http://www.microsoft.com/visualstudio/eng /downloads#d-express-web*.

Practice exercises

This book features practices exercises to reinforce the topics you've learned. These exercises are organized by chapter, and you can download them from *http://aka.ms /TGProgHTML5/files*.

Acknowledgments

Thanks go to the following people for making this book a reality.

- To Carol Dillingham for your constructive feedback throughout the entire process of writing this book. Thanks for also having patience while the winter holiday months were passing, and my desire and ability to write was constantly interrupted.
- To Devon Musgrave for providing me the opportunity to write this book.
- To Kerin Forsyth for your hard work in making this book consistent with other Microsoft Press books and helping me with the delivery of this book.
- To Pierce Bizzaca for your technical reviewing skills.

To all the other editors and artists who played a role in getting my book to the public, thank you for your hard work and thanks for making this book venture a positive experience for me.

Errata and book support

We've made every effort to ensure the accuracy of this book and its companion content. Any errors that have been reported since this book was published are listed on our Microsoft Press site:

http://aka.ms/TGProgHTML5/errata

If you find an error that is not already listed, you can report it to us through the same page.

If you need additional support, send an email to Microsoft Press Book Support at *mspinput@microsoft.com.*

Please note that product support for Microsoft software is not offered through the preceding addresses.

We want to hear from you

At Microsoft Press, your satisfaction is our top priority and your feedback our most valuable asset. Please tell us what you think of this book at:

http://aka.ms/tellpress

The survey is short, and we read every one of your comments and ideas. Thanks in advance for your input!

Stay in touch

Let's keep the conversation going! We're on Twitter at *http://twitter.com/MicrosoftPress.*

Getting started with Visual Studio 2012 and Blend for Visual Studio 2012

Welcome to the world of HTML5, CSS3, and JavaScript! These technologies, commonly referred to as simply HTML5, can be used to develop applications for Windows and the web.

This chapter introduces you to the primary tools you need, Microsoft Visual Studio 2012 and Blend for Visual Studio 2012, which are used in the book's lessons. Visual Studio 2012 provides exciting new features. The chapters that follow introduce you to many features in Visual Studio 2012 and Blend.

Lessons in this chapter:

Before you begin

To complete this book, you must have some understanding of web development. This chapter requires the hardware and software listed in the "System requirements" section in the book's Introduction.

> ### *REAL WORLD*   A CAREER OPPORTUNITY
>
> You're looking for a career in computer programming, but you don't know what technology to pursue. You want to learn a technology you can use at many companies to make yourself more marketable and to give you the flexibility to move between companies. What technology would you choose to give you this flexibility?
>
> The Internet has exploded. Nearly every company has a website, so why not learn the web technologies?

HTML, CSS, and JavaScript are three closely coupled core web technologies that you can learn to increase your marketability and give you flexibility to choose the company for which you want to work. This is the beginning of your path toward your future career. Learn these technologies well, and you can expand into other programming technologies such as Silverlight, Flash, C#, and Visual Basic.

Lesson 1: Visual Studio 2012

Visual Studio 2012 is a highly useful tool for application development. Depending on the edition of Visual Studio you have, it can provide you with an integrated development environment (IDE) you can use for the entire project life cycle.

After this lesson, you will be able to:
- Identify the available versions of Visual Studio 2012 and the features of each.
- Start a project by using Visual Studio Express 2012 for Web.
- Start a project by using Visual Studio Express 2012 for Windows 8.

Estimated lesson time: 40 minutes

Visual Studio 2012 editions

The following is a list with short descriptions of the editions of Visual Studio that Microsoft offers.

- **Visual Studio Test Professional 2012**   Provides team collaboration tools but not a full development IDE. This is ideal for testers, business analysts, product managers, and other stakeholders, but this is not an ideal edition for developers.

- **Visual Studio Professional 2012**   Provides a unified development experience that enables developers to create multitier applications across the web, the cloud, and devices. This is an ideal edition for a lone developer or a small team of developers who will be developing a wide range of web, Windows, phone, and cloud applications.

- **Visual Studio Premium 2012**   Provides an integrated application lifecycle management (ALM) solution and software development functions to deliver compelling applications for a unified team of developers, testers, and business analysts.

- **Visual Studio Ultimate 2012**   Provides a comprehensive ALM offering for organizations developing, distributing, and operating a wide range of highly scalable software applications and services.

- **Visual Studio Team Foundation Server Express 2012**   Provides the collaboration hub at the center of the ALM solution that enables small teams of up to five developers to be more agile, collaborate more effectively, and deliver better software more quickly. Includes source code control, work item tracking, and build automation for software projects to deliver predictable results. This is free.

- **Visual Studio Express 2012 for Web**   Provides the tools and resources to build and test HTML5, CSS3, ASP.NET, and JavaScript code and to deploy it on web servers or to the cloud by using Windows Azure. Best of all, it's free.

- **Visual Studio Express 2012 for Windows 8**   Provides the core tools required to build Windows Store apps, using XAML and your choice of .NET language or HTML5, CSS3, and JavaScript. This is also free.

If you use Visual Studio Express 2012 for Web, you can work on web projects only, and you must choose a .NET language to start with, such as Visual Basic or C#. If you use Visual Studio Express 2012 for Windows 8, you can work on Windows Store applications only, but you can start with a JavaScript project, and you don't need to set up a website to create small applications. Blend for Visual Studio 2012 also provides the ability to create Windows Store applications with a JavaScript project.

The Visual Studio Express 2012 products are available free on the Microsoft website. You should download and install both Visual Studio Express 2012 for Windows 8 and Visual Studio Express 2012 for Web.

Visual Studio 2012 support for HTML5

Visual Studio .NET 2012 contains a new HTML editor that provides full support for HTML5 elements and snippets. Here is a list of some of the Visual Studio 2012 features that will make your development experience more enjoyable and productive. The new features will be demonstrated and explained later in this book when appropriate.

- **Testing**   You can easily test your webpage, application, or site with a variety of browsers. Beside the Start Debugging button in Visual Studio 2012, you will find a list of all installed browsers. Just select the desired browser from the list when you are ready to test.

- **Finding the source of rendered markup**   By using the new Page Inspector feature, you can quickly find the source of rendered markup. The Page Inspector renders a webpage directly within the Visual Studio IDE, so you can choose a rendered element, and Page Inspector will open the file in which the markup was generated and highlight the source.

- **Improved IntelliSense**   Quickly find snippets and code elements. In the HTML and CSS editors, IntelliSense filters the display list as you enter text. This feature shows strings that match the typed text in their beginning, middle, or end. It also matches against initial letters. For example, "bw" will match "border-width."

- **Reusable Markup**   You can easily create reusable markup by selecting the markup and extracting it to a user control.

- **Automatic Renaming**   When you rename an opening or closing HTML tag, the corresponding tag is renamed automatically.

CSS3 support

Visual Studio .NET 2012 provides a new CSS editor that offers full support for CSS3, including support for cascading style sheets (CSS), hacks, and snippets for vendor-specific extensions to CSS.

- **Expandable Sections**   Use the CSS editor to expand and collapse sections by clicking the plus or minus sign that is displayed to the left of each style entry.
- **Hierarchical Indentation**   The CSS editor displays nested styles in a hierarchical fashion, which makes it much easier to read and understand the styles.
- **Add Comments**   You can easily comment and uncomment blocks.
- **Color Selector**   The CSS editor now has a color selector like the HTML editor.

JavaScript support

Visual Studio 2012 provides many new features to make the JavaScript developer experience more enjoyable and productive. The following is a list of some of the new features and enhancements.

- **Standards-based**   Visual Studio 2012 incorporates the JavaScript features of ECMAScript 5 and the HTML5 document object model (DOM).
- **Improved IntelliSense**   You can receive improved IntelliSense information for functions and variables by using new elements supported in triple-slash (///) code comments. New elements include *<var>* and *<signature>*. You can also view function signatures on the right side of the statement completion list.
- **Improved editor**   JavaScript Editor implements smart indenting, brace matching, and outlining as you write code. For example, if you position your cursor to the left of an open curly brace, the open and closed curly braces are highlighted. This works with curly braces, square brackets, angle brackets, and parentheses.
- **Go To Definition**   To locate function definitions in source code, you just right-click a function and then click Go To Definition. You can also put the cursor in the function, and then press the F12 key to open the JavaScript source file at the location in the file where the function is defined. (This feature isn't supported for generated files.)
- **IntelliSense from JavaScript comments**   The new IntelliSense extensibility mechanism automatically provides IntelliSense when you use standard JavaScript comment tags (//).
- **Breakpoints**   You now have more flexibility when setting a breakpoint. When a single line contains multiple statements, you can now break on a single statement.

- **Reference Groups**   You can control which objects are available in global scope by using Reference Groups. Reference Groups is configured on the menu bar by navigating to Tools | Options | Text Editor | JavaScript | IntelliSense | References.
- **Drag-and-drop references**   You can drag JavaScript files that have the .js extension from Solution Explorer to the JavaScript code editor, where they are added as references for Visual Studio to use to provide IntelliSense. When adding references by dragging and dropping, they are put at the top of the page in the code editor.

Exploring Visual Studio Express 2012 for Windows 8

When you start Visual Studio Express 2012 for Windows 8, the Start Page screen is displayed. Figure 1-1 shows the Start Page screen, which contains helpful information and links to learning and development resources. On the left side of the Start page are links to create a new project or open a new project. After you create at least one project, you'll see shortcut links to open any of your recent projects.

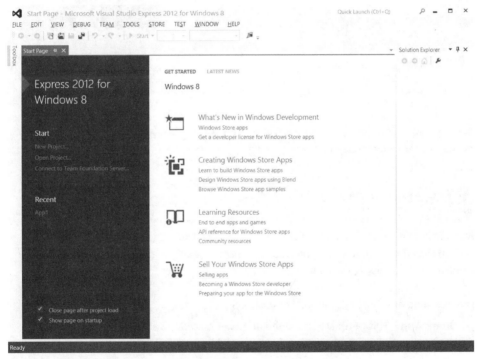

FIGURE 1-1 Visual Studio Express 2012 for Windows 8 Start page

In addition to clicking the New Project link on the Start page, you can start a new project by clicking File and choosing New Project. Figure 1-2 shows the New Project screen, which displays a list of starting templates from which you can choose to start on your new application quickly. You can think of a template as a project on which someone completed the mundane tasks that would be common to all applications of that type and then saved as a framework that you can use to get started.

On the left side of the New Project screen, you can select from recent project templates that you've used or from the complete list of installed templates, or you can go online to select a template. You'll find that the installed templates are divided according to programming language. Figure 1-2 shows the templates that are installed for JavaScript.

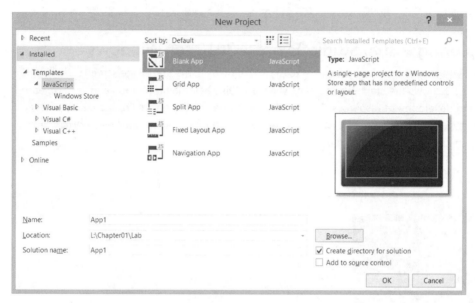

FIGURE 1-2 The New Project screen with the JavaScript project templates

The following are short descriptions of each template.

- **Blank App**   This template isn't quite empty. It provides a single-page project for a Windows app, but it has no predefined controls on the page.
- **Grid App**   This template provides an application that contains multiple pages and enables you to navigate among groups of items.
- **Split App**   This template creates a two-page project in which the first page contains a group of items, and the second page contains an item list with details of the selected item to the right of the list.

- **Fixed Layout App** This template provides a single page with a fixed aspect ratio layout that scales to fit the screen.
- **Navigation App** This template provides a single-page application containing controls for navigation.

Selecting a template causes a copy of the template to be opened in the Solution Explorer window. By default, the Solution Explorer window is on the right side, although windows can be dragged to any location on the screen. Solution Explorer contains a tree representation of all projects that are loaded into the current solution.

Under the Solution Explorer window is the Properties window, which is context-sensitive and contains the properties of the currently selected item. The properties are visible in this window, and most are also configurable.

On the left side of the screen is the toolbox. By default, the toolbox is a tab that you can point to to open the window. The toolbox is also context-sensitive, so different tools are available based on what is being displayed in the center window.

 Quick check

- You want to create a Windows Store application. Which edition of Visual Studio 2012 will you use, and is there an operating system requirement for your system to develop Windows Store application applications?

Quick check answer

- You must use Visual Studio Express 2012 for Windows 8 and have Windows 8 installed to develop Windows Store applications.

Examining the Blank App template

When the Blank App template is selected, a new solution containing one project is created. The new project won't be totally blank. As shown in Figure 1-3, there are several files and folders in this new project. At the outset, default.js was created, and it's currently displayed in the JavaScript editor window.

The default.js file is in the js folder, which is where you can add your own JavaScript files. This default.js file currently contains a small amount of code, which Chapter 3, "Getting started with JavaScript," revisits in more detail. Here is a general overview of what it does. The use of function on the third line creates a naming scope for variables and functions in your application. In the middle of the code are TODO comments that provide a place to put your own code to be executed when the application is launched or reactivated after being suspended or when the application is being suspended.

FIGURE 1-3 Blank App template with preliminary coding

Blank App also contains other files that you will want to explore. If you open the default.html file, you'll see the following HTML.

```html
<!DOCTYPE html>
<html>
<head>
    <meta charset="utf-8" />
    <title>App1</title>

    <!-- WinJS references -->
    <link href="//Microsoft.WinJS.1.0/css/ui-dark.css" rel="stylesheet" />
    <script src="//Microsoft.WinJS.1.0/js/base.js"></script>
    <script src="//Microsoft.WinJS.1.0/js/ui.js"></script>

    <!-- App1 references -->
    <link href="/css/default.css" rel="stylesheet" />
    <script src="/js/default.js"></script>
</head>
<body>
    <p>Content goes here</p>
</body>
</html>
```

The first line contains <!DOCTYPE html>, which is a declaration to the web browser that describes the version of HTML in which the page is written. It's not an HTML element; it's a special instruction. In HTML5, this special instruction must be the first thing the browser reads on the page. This instruction is not mandatory, but it is considered a best practice to have it.

Next is the *<html>* element that consists of the starting tag at the top and ending tag, </html>, at the bottom. This is considered the root element of the page, and all other elements are contained within the html element.

Inside the html element are the head and body elements. The head element typically contains metadata and page-related instructions. The body element contains content that will be displayed to the user. In this example, the head element contains a meta element that describes the character set being used (utf-8), a title that will be displayed in the browser title bar, links tags that reference CSS files, and script tags that reference JavaScript files. These references are instructions to the browser to load these files when the page loads. The body element contains a paragraph element with the message "Content goes here." This message appears when the application is executed.

The References folder contains a folder called Windows Library for JavaScript 1.0, which contains subdirectories that Microsoft provides and maintains. You should not modify files in this directory structure, but you should explore the files in this folder structure and learn as much as possible about these files. Of particular importance is the css folder that contains the ui-dark.css and ui-light.css files. These files set the primary theme for your application to either a light or dark theme.

> **MORE INFO** **LIGHT AND DARK BACKGROUNDS**
>
> The default.html file has a reference to the ui-dark.css file. If you run the application, the application displays the "Content goes here" message on a screen that has a dark background. If you change the reference to the ui-light.css file, you'll see a light background.

The css folder contains cascading style sheets for your application. Currently, the default.html file references a single file called default.css. The CSS file contains instructions for presenting your HTML file and will be covered in more detail in Chapter 4, "Getting started with CSS3."

The images folder contains blank images that are set to the best size for presentation to the user. You would typically edit these files as part of your finished application.

In the root directory of your application is a file with a .pfx extension that provides a security key for deployment and an appmanifest file that contains deployment metadata.

Exploring Visual Studio Express 2012 for Web

When you start Visual Studio Express 2012 for Web, the same Start Page screen is displayed as shown in Figure 1-1 and described in the previous section. In the installed templates, you'll find that they are divided according to .NET programming language, Visual Basic and Visual C#. Figure 1-4 shows the templates that are installed for Visual Basic.

FIGURE 1-4 The New Project screen with Visual Basic and Visual C# project templates

Your new project might differ based on the software installed on your computer. For example, the template shown here is the Get Windows Azure SDK For .NET template that was installed when the Azure SDK was installed.

All these templates are for web-related applications; none of them can be used to create a Windows 8 application. Note that none of the templates support the use of JavaScript as a server-side language, but you can select a Visual Basic or C# web project template and use client-side (on the browser) JavaScript. Remember that you can use HTML5, CSS3, and JavaScript as client-side technologies with any of the web application templates.

Under one of the languages, you can click the Web node to see a list of available web application templates. You can select a template called ASP.NET Empty Web Application to begin with a nearly empty startup project.

Examining ASP.NET Empty Web Application

After selecting ASP.NET Empty Web Application, a copy of the template is opened in the Solution Explorer window on the upper right, as shown in Figure 1-5. This window contains a node for the project (WebApplication1); a node that references the project settings, called My Project; and a node that references the project's configuration file, called Web.config. This project is almost empty. If you press F5 to build and run the web application, it won't run. You must add a webpage to the project first.

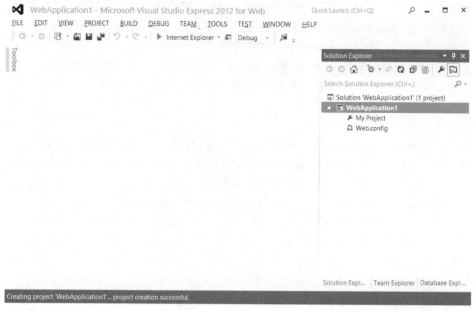

FIGURE 1-5 Almost empty ASP.NET Empty Web Application

By default, the Solution Explorer window is on the right side. Under the Solution Explorer window is the Properties window. The Properties window is context-sensitive and contains the properties of the currently selected item. The properties are visible in this window, and most are also configurable.

On the left side of the screen is the toolbox. By default, the toolbox is a tab that you can point to to open the window. The toolbox is also context-sensitive, so different tools are available based on what is being displayed in the center window.

You can add a webpage to the project by right-clicking the project node (WebApplication1) and then navigating to Add | New Item | HTML Page. If you name the page **default.html**, the web server automatically delivers the page to a browser that navigates to your website but doesn't specify the name of a webpage to retrieve. After adding the webpage, you can enter some text, such as a Hello World message, into the body of the webpage. When you press F5, you see the message in the browser.

Lesson summary

- The free editions of Visual Studio 2012 are the Express editions: Visual Studio Express 2012 for Web and Visual Studio Express 2012 for Windows 8. You can use the Express editions to work with HTML5, CSS3, and JavaScript.

- Use Visual Studio Express 2012 for Web to develop web applications. Use Visual Studio Express 2012 for Windows 8 to develop Windows 8 applications.

- Visual Studio Express 2012 for Windows 8 comes with Blend for Visual Studio 2012.

- Blend for Visual Studio 2012 drives the user interface design and must be run on Windows 8 to develop Windows 8 applications.

- You can change the style sheet reference from a dark theme to a light theme by changing the ui-dark.css reference in the default.html file to ui-light.css.

Lesson review

Answer the following questions to test your knowledge of the information in this lesson. You can find the answers to these questions and explanations of why each answer choice is correct or incorrect in the "Answers" section at the end of this chapter.

1. You would like to create a web application by using HTML5, JavaScript, and CSS3. Which of the following Visual Studio 2012 editions can you use? (Choose all that apply.)

   A. Visual Studio Professional 2012

   B. Visual Studio Premium 2012

   C. Visual Studio Ultimate 2012

   D. Visual Studio Express 2012 for Web

   E. Visual Studio Express 2012 for Windows 8

2. You would like to create a Windows 8 application by using HTML5, JavaScript, and CSS3. Which of the following Visual Studio 2012 editions can you use? (Choose all that apply.)

   A. Visual Studio Professional 2012

   B. Visual Studio Premium 2012

   C. Visual Studio Ultimate 2012

   D. Visual Studio Express 2012 for Web

   E. Visual Studio Express 2012 for Windows 8

3. You would like to create web applications and Windows 8 Windows Store applications by using HTML5, JavaScript, and CSS3, but while you're learning, you don't want to buy Visual Studio 2012. Which of the following Visual Studio 2012 editions can you use for free to accomplish your goal?

   A. Visual Studio Professional 2012

   B. Visual Studio Premium 2012

   C. Visual Studio Ultimate 2012

   D. Visual Studio Express 2012 for Web and Visual Studio Express 2012 for Windows 8

Lesson 2: Blend for Visual Studio 2012

Blend is included with Visual Studio 2012 Express for Windows 8 and helps you design your user interface. Blend is a design complement for Visual Studio and does for design what Visual Studio does for code. The following are some key features of Blend.

- **Visual design**   Edit HTML, CSS, and Windows Store controls in a "what you see is what you get" (WYSIWYG) environment. What you see in Blend is what users will see in Windows 8.

- **Interactive mode**   Design your app by changing states and setting styles. You don't need to compile and run continuously. Blend provides the ability to use interactive mode so the developer can run the application on the design surface until the desired state is reached. The developer can pause the application and then style the application for the new state.

- **App building**   Windows Store controls can be dragged and dropped onto the design surface. After that, just set the properties and styles.

- **Powerful code generation**   Blend takes care of all the syntax by generating concise, reliable, predictable code when you add a style or element to your application.

- **Debugging**   Blend offers visual debugging of HTML and CSS. It has a virtual rule called Winning Properties that shows you how an element obtained its effective style from the CSS inheritance and cascade.

After this lesson, you will be able to:

- Identify the key features of Blend.
- Start a project by using Blend.

Estimated lesson time: 25 minutes

Exploring Blend

Blend is an exciting tool for designers and developers who will be using HTML5, CSS3, and JavaScript to develop Windows 8 applications. Blend also supports the creation of Windows 8 Windows Store applications by using XAML with your choice of .NET programming language. Figure 1-6 shows the New Project screen, which has the same new project templates as Visual Studio Express 2012 for Windows 8.

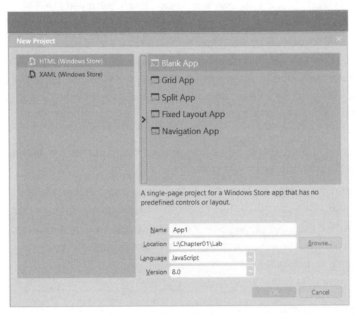

FIGURE 1-6 The Blend New Project screen with the JavaScript project templates

Selecting Blank App creates the same Blank App that was discussed in the previous section. Note the screen layout. Figure 1-7 shows the Blend screen layout. On the left is the Tools panel, where you can point to each icon to see a tooltip that displays the name of the command. Just to the right of the Tools panel is a column with two windows, one over the other. These windows have tabs that can be selected to show more information. The upper-left window contains the following tabs.

- **Projects** Contains a tree-based representation of your solution, which can contain many projects, each project containing resources such as files and folders.
- **Assets** Contains a library of resources such as HTML elements, JavaScript controls, and media that you will use within your application.
- **Style Rules** Contains a list of cascading style sheets that are referenced in your project.

Under Style Rules is the Live DOM window, which shows a dynamic representation of your HTML page.

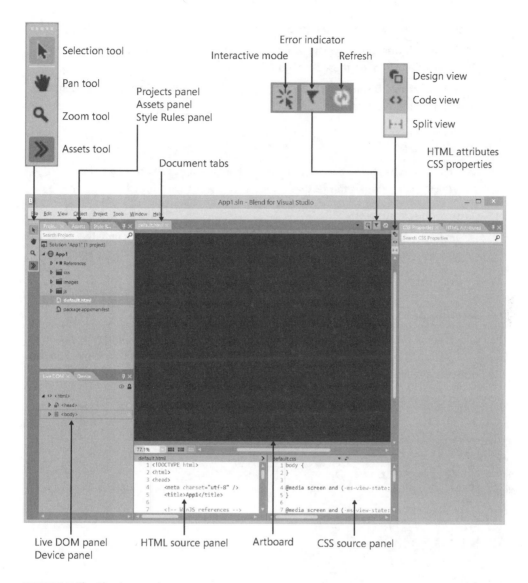

Selection tool

Pan tool

Zoom tool

Assets tool

Projects panel
Assets panel
Style Rules panel

Document tabs

Error indicator

Interactive mode

Refresh

Design view

Code view

Split view

HTML attributes
CSS properties

Live DOM panel
Device panel

HTML source panel

Artboard

CSS source panel

FIGURE 1-7 The Blend screen layout

In the middle of the screen is your primary workspace, the *artboard*. At the top of the artboard is a tabbed list of documents that are open. By default, this window displays the rendered page. Note that there are buttons in the upper-right corner that can be used to change the view.

The bottom center displays the default.html and the default.css sources. This makes it easy for you to change the files and see the rendered output. Also, as you use the other windows to modify the rendered page, you see the changes reflected in these files.

The rightmost window contains the following two tabs.

- **HTML Attributes** Displays the properties for the currently selected HTML element. You can view or change these settings.

- **CSS Properties** Displays the style settings for the currently selected HTML element. You can set these properties.

 Quick check

- You want to be able to design your app by changing states and setting styles. Which mode provides this feature?

Quick check answer

- Interactive mode. You can run the application on the design surface until the desired state is reached. You can pause the application and then style the application for the new state.

Projects panel

The Projects panel provides a file and folder view of the projects in your solution, as shown in Figure 1-8. You can use this panel to open files for editing by double-clicking the file. You can also right-click any file or folder to see options such as Copy, Delete, and Rename.

FIGURE 1-8 The Projects panel

Notice the different icons for the solution, project, references, folders, and files and note that the default.html file is underlined to indicate that it is the startup file when you run the application. At the top of the Projects panel is a Search Projects text box in which you can type the name of a file or folder you want to find. In the project is a virtual folder called

References. This is where you add references to CSS and JavaScript. The project also contains the package.manifest file, which contains all the settings for the project, including the setting for the Start page.

Assets panel

The Assets panel lists all the HTML elements, controls, and media that you can add to an HTML page that is open in the artboard, as shown in Figure 1-9. Although the Assets panel lists all the available controls in your Blend project, the most recently used controls appear in the Tools panel.

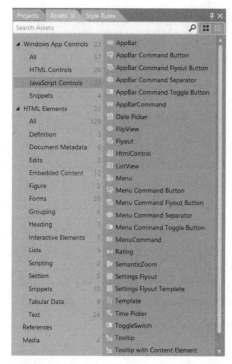

FIGURE 1-9 The Assets panel shown when building a Windows Store application with HTML

Open the Assets panel either by clicking the Assets icon at the bottom of the Tools panel or by clicking Assets in the Windows menu.

Device panel

Use the Device panel to configure your display so that you can visualize your application accurately on a variety of displays, as shown in Figure 1-10. You can select the following display options for your application.

- **View** The rendering mode when the application is run. Choices are landscape, filled, snapped, and portrait.

- **Display** The display size and resolution at which to render. Use this to simulate rendering on larger or smaller screens to see whether your application renders properly.
- **Show chrome** When selected, shows a simulated tablet screen around the edge of the application.
- **Override scaling** When selected, emulates the built-in display scaling of the device.
- **Deploy target** The device to which to deploy when the application is run.

FIGURE 1-10 The Device panel

Style Rules panel

The Style Rules panel, shown in Figure 1-11, lists all the style sheets attached to the current document. Within each style sheet is a list of all the defined styles. In addition, the Style Rules panel contains a text box in which you can enter search criteria when locating a style.

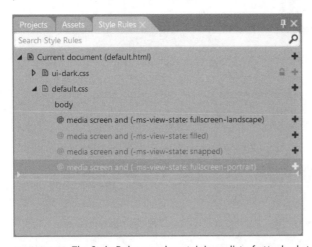

FIGURE 1-11 The Style Rules panel containing a list of attached style sheets

You can click the plus signs on the right side of the panel to add a new style rule at that location. The yellow line indicates where new styles will be created if a location is not specified. Style rules that are dimmed are defined but not used in the current document.

Live DOM panel

The Live DOM panel displays the structure of the current document as a hierarchical representation, as shown in Figure 1-12. With the Live DOM panel, you can select elements and adjust their style rules. The Live DOM view provides automatic updating as the state of the app changes.

FIGURE 1-12 The Live DOM panel displaying a hierarchical representation of the current document

The Live DOM panel displays nodes by using their ID if an ID is assigned or by using the tag name if no ID is assigned. You can control the visibility of any node by clicking the eye icon on the right side of the panel. This can be helpful when you have layers of elements stacked on top of each other.

As with Visual Studio, you can press F5 to run the application. Blend has many features that you can learn about by using the built-in help.

Lesson summary

- The interactive mode enables you to run the application to build to the desired state and then pause the application and set the styles of the application based on the current state.
- The Assets panel contains a list of all available assets in the project.
- The Projects panel contains a file and folder view of the projects in the current solution.
- The Style Rules panel contains a list of all style sheets attached to the current document.

- The Device panel enables you to run the application by using simulations of different screen sizes and orientations.

- The Live DOM panel enables you to select an element and apply style rules to it.

Lesson review

Answer the following questions to test your knowledge of the information in this lesson. You can find the answers to these questions and explanations of why each answer choice is correct or incorrect in the "Answers" section at the end of this chapter.

1. You would like to create a Windows 8 application by using Blend and HTML5, JavaScript, and CSS3. Which feature of Blend enables you to pause an application when it reaches a desired state so you can set the style rules for the page and its controls while in this state? (Choose all that apply.)

    A. Assets panel

    B. Projects panel

    C. Visual Design

    D. Interactive mode

2. On which panel can you see a hierarchically structured view of the DOM?

    A. Live DOM

    B. Projects

    C. Assets

    D. Device

3. Which panel can you use to access a list of the HTML elements, controls, and media that can be added to an HTML page that is open in the artboard?

    A. Projects

    B. Assets

    C. Device

    D. Live DOM

Practice exercises

If you encounter a problem completing any of these exercises, the completed projects can be installed from the Practice Exercises folder that is provided with the companion content.

Exercise 1: Hello World with Visual Studio Express 2012 for Windows 8

In this exercise, you create a simple HTML5 and JavaScript Hello World application by using Visual Studio Express 2012 for Windows 8. This practice, like all Hello World applications, is intended to get you started by creating a minimal application. In later exercises, you get more exposure to Visual Studio. In this exercise, you use HTML5 to display "Hello Visual Studio for Windows 8" on the screen.

1. If you haven't installed Visual Studio Express 2012 for Windows 8, do so now. You can download this from the Microsoft website.

2. Start Visual Studio. Click File and choose New Project to display the New Project dialog box. Navigate to Installed | Templates | JavaScript | Windows Store. Select Blank App.

3. Set the name of your application to **HelloVisualStudioForWin8**.

4. Select a location for your application.

5. Set the solution name to **HelloVisualStudioForWin8Solution**.

6. Be sure to keep the Create Directory For Solution check box selected.

7. Click OK to create your new project.

8. When the application is created, the default.js file is displayed with some template code.

   This code is covered later, and there is no need to alter it now.

9. Open the default.html file.

   It contains HTML from the template.

10. To see the default content, press F5 to start debugging the application.

    You should see a black screen and, in the upper-left corner, a message stating, "Content goes here."

11. Switch back to Visual Studio by pressing Alt+Tab.

    The title bar says (Running).

12. Press Shift+F5 to stop debugging.

    Shift+F5 works only when Visual Studio has the focus; it does not work when the running application has the focus.

13. In the default.html file, replace the "Content goes here" message with **Hello Visual Studio for Windows 8**.

14. Replace the reference to ui-dark.css with ui-light.css.

    Your HTML should look like the following.

```
<!DOCTYPE html>
<html>
<head>
    <meta charset="utf-8" />
    <title>HelloWorldForWin8</title>
```

```
<!-- WinJS references -->
<link href="//Microsoft.WinJS.1.0/css/ui-light.css" rel="stylesheet" />
<script src="//Microsoft.WinJS.1.0/js/base.js"></script>
<script src="//Microsoft.WinJS.1.0/js/ui.js"></script>

<!-- HelloWorld references -->
<link href="/css/default.css" rel="stylesheet" />
<script src="/js/default.js"></script>
</head>
<body>
    <p>Hello Visual Studio for Windows 8</p>
</body>
</html>
```

15. Press F5 to start debugging.

    The screen is white because you now reference the ui-light.css file instead of the ui-dark.css file. The screen also displays Hello Visual Studio For Windows 8. Congratulations—you have written your first Windows 8 application by using HTML5 technologies!

Exercise 2: Hello World with Visual Studio Express 2012 for Web

In this exercise, you create a simple HTML5 and JavaScript Hello World application by using Visual Studio Express 2012 for Web. This practice, like all Hello World applications, is intended to get you started by creating a minimal application. In later exercises, you get more exposure to Visual Studio. In this exercise, you create a new project in Visual Studio Express 2012 for Web and use HTML5 to display "Hello Visual Studio for Web" on the screen.

> **NOTE NO SERVER CODE IN THIS EXERCISE**
>
> You will not be writing any server code in this exercise, so it doesn't matter whether you select Visual Basic or Visual C# when starting the new project.

1. If you haven't installed Visual Studio Express 2012 for Web, do so now. You can download this from the Microsoft website.

2. Start Visual Studio. Click File and choose New Project to display the New Project dialog box. Navigate to Installed | Templates | Visual Basic | Web. Select the ASP.NET Web Form Application.

3. Set the name of your application to **HelloVisualStudioForWeb**.

4. Select a location for your application.

5. Set the solution name to **HelloVisualStudioForWeb Solution**.

6. Be sure to keep the Create Directory For Solution check box selected.

7. Click OK to create your new project.

8. When the application is created, the default.aspx page will be displayed with some template code.

9. In the Solution Explorer window, build the project by right-clicking the project node and choosing Build.

10. To see this template's default content, press F5 to start debugging the application.

    You should see a fancy screen with information on how to get started plus other useful information.

11. Switch back to Visual Studio by pressing Alt+Tab.

    The title bar says (Running).

12. Press Shift+F5 to stop debugging.

    Note that Shift+F5 works only when Visual Studio has the focus. Shift+F5 does not work when the running application has the focus.

13. Delete the default.aspx file by right-clicking this file in the Solution Explorer window, choosing Delete, and then clicking OK.

14. In the Solution Explorer window, add a default.html file by right-clicking the project node. Click Add and then choose HTML. Name the page **default.html**.

15. In the default.html file, place the text **Hello Visual Studio for Web** between the *<body>* and *</body>* tags.

16. In the default.html file, place the text **HelloVisualStudioForWeb** between the *<title>* and *</title>* tags.

    Your HTML should look like the following.

    ```
    <!DOCTYPE html>
    <html xmlns="http://www.w3.org/1999/xhtml">
    <head>
    <title>HelloVisualStudioForWeb</title>
    </head>
    <body>
        Hello Visual Studio for Web
    </body>
    </html>
    ```

17. In the Solution Explorer window, set the default.html file as the startup file by right-clicking the default.html file and choosing Set As Start Page.

18. Press F5 to start debugging.

    The screen now displays Hello Visual Studio For Web. Congratulations—you have written your first web application using HTML5 technologies!

Exercise 3: Hello World with Blend

In this exercise, you create a simple HTML5 and JavaScript Hello World application by using Blend. This practice, like all Hello World applications, is intended to get you started by creating a minimal application. In later exercises, you get more exposure to Blend. In this exercise, you create a new project in Blend and use HTML5 to display "Hello World" on the screen.

1. If you haven't installed Blend, do so now. Remember that Blend is installed automatically when you install Visual Studio Express 2012 for Windows 8. You can download this from the Microsoft website.

2. To start Blend, click New Project to display the New Project dialog box. Select the HTML (Windows Store) category in the left pane and select Blank App in the right pane.

3. Set the name of your application to **HelloBlend**.

4. Select a location for your application.

5. Click OK to create your new project.

   When the application is created, the default.html file is displayed.

6. To see the default content, press F5 to start debugging the application.

   You should see a black screen and, in the upper-left corner, a message stating, "Content goes here."

7. Close the running application by pressing Alt+F4.

8. If Blend is not displayed, return to Blend by pressing Alt+Tab.

9. In the default.html file, double-click the "Content Goes Here" message and replace the text with **Hello from Blend**.

   You see the change in the default.html source view window at the bottom of the screen.

10. Replace the reference to ui-dark.css with ui-light.css.

    Your HTML should look like the following.

```
<!DOCTYPE html>
<html>
<head>
    <meta charset="utf-8" />
    <title>HelloBlend</title>

    <!-- WinJS references -->
    <link href="//Microsoft.WinJS.1.0/css/ui-light.css" rel="stylesheet" />
    <script src="//Microsoft.WinJS.1.0/js/base.js"></script>
    <script src="//Microsoft.WinJS.1.0/js/ui.js"></script>

    <!-- HelloBlend references -->
    <link href="/css/default.css" rel="stylesheet" />
    <script src="/js/default.js"></script>
</head>
<body>
```

```
    <p>Hello from Blend</p>
</body>
</html>
```

11. Press F5 to start the application.

    Notice that the screen is white because you now reference the ui-light.css file instead of the ui-dark.css file. The screen now displays Hello From Blend. Congratulations—you have written a Windows 8 application by using HTML5 technologies with Blend!

Suggested practice exercises

The following additional exercises are designed to give you more opportunities to practice what you've learned and to help you successfully master the lessons presented in this chapter.

- **Exercise 1**   Learn more about Visual Studio Express 2012 for Web by creating new projects from each of the included project templates. After creating each project, try adding Hello World and run the application to see how the project looks and behaves.

- **Exercise 2**   Learn more about Visual Studio Express 2012 for Windows 8 by creating new projects from each of the included project templates. After creating each project, try adding Hello World and run the application to see how the project looks and behaves.

- **Exercise 3**   Learn more about Blend by creating new projects from each of the included project templates. After creating each project, try adding Hello World and run the application to see how the project looks and behaves.

Answers

This section contains the answers to the lesson review questions in this chapter.

Lesson 1

1. **Correct answers: A, B, C, and D**

    A. **Correct:** Visual Studio Professional 2012 provides web templates for creating web applications.

    B. **Correct:** Visual Studio Premium 2012 provides web templates for creating web applications.

    C. **Correct:** Visual Studio Ultimate 2012 provides web templates for creating web applications.

    D. **Correct:** Visual Studio Express 2012 for Web provides web templates for creating web applications only.

    E. **Incorrect:** Visual Studio Express 2012 for Windows 8 provides templates for building Windows 8 applications only.

2. **Correct answers: A, B, C, and E**

    A. **Correct:** Visual Studio Professional 2012 provides web templates for creating Windows 8 applications.

    B. **Correct:** Visual Studio Premium 2012 provides web templates for creating Windows 8 applications.

    C. **Correct:** Visual Studio Ultimate 2012 provides web templates for creating Windows 8 applications.

    D. **Incorrect:** Visual Studio Express 2012 for Web provides web templates for creating web applications only.

    E. **Correct:** Visual Studio Express 2012 for Windows 8 provides templates for building Windows 8 applications only.

3. **Correct answer: D**

    A. **Incorrect:** Visual Studio Professional 2012 enables you to create web and Windows 8 applications, but it is not free.

    B. **Incorrect:** Visual Studio Premium 2012 enables you to create web and Windows 8 applications, but it is not free.

    C. **Incorrect:** Visual Studio Ultimate 2012 enables you to create web and Windows 8 applications, but it is not free.

    D. **Correct:** Visual Studio Express 2012 for Web provides web templates for creating web applications, and Visual Studio Express 2012 for Windows 8 provides templates for creating Windows 8 applications. Both are free.

Lesson 2

1. **Correct answers: C and D**

   A. Incorrect: The Assets panel enables you to access a list of the HTML elements, controls, and media that can be added to an HTML page that is open in the artboard.

   B. Incorrect: The Projects panel provides a file and folder view of the projects in the current solution.

   C. Correct: With Visual Design, what you see in Blend is what users will see in Windows 8.

   D. Correct: Interactive mode enables you to run the application on the design surface until the desired state is reached. You can pause the application and then style the application for the new state.

2. **Correct answer: A**

   A. Correct: Live DOM displays the structure of the current document as a hierarchical representation. You can use the Live DOM panel to select elements and adjust their style rules.

   B. Incorrect: The Projects panel provides a file and folder view of the projects in your solution.

   C. Incorrect: The Assets panel lists all the HTML elements, controls, and media that you can add to an HTML page that is open in the artboard.

   D. Incorrect: The Device panel enables you to configure your display so that you can visualize your application accurately on a variety of displays.

3. **Correct answer: B**

   A. Incorrect: The Projects panel provides a file and folder view of the projects in your solution.

   B. Correct: The Assets panel lists all the HTML elements, controls, and media that you can add to an HTML page that is open in the artboard.

   C. Incorrect: The Device panel enables you to configure your display so that you can visualize your application accurately on a variety of displays.

   D. Incorrect: The Live DOM panel displays the structure of the current document as a hierarchical representation. You can use the Live DOM panel to select elements and adjust their style rules.

## CHAPTER 2

Getting started with HTML5

Welcome to the world of HTML5, JavaScript, and CSS3! This chapter gets you started with HTML5. The next chapter does the same with JavaScript, and the following chapter familiarizes you with CSS3.

Now that you've installed Visual Studio 2012 and Blend, you're ready to build your knowledge foundation by learning some basic HTML. This chapter presents a great deal of HTML content. Although much of the content in this chapter exists in previous releases of HTML, all content in this chapter is part of the HTML5 specification.

Lessons in this chapter:

Before you begin

To complete this book, you must have some understanding of web development. This chapter requires the hardware and software listed in the "System requirements" section in the book's Introduction.

Lesson 1: Introducing HTML5

Chapter 1, "Getting Started with Visual Studio 2012 and Blend for Visual Studio 2012," presented a very brief overview of the Visual Studio editions and Blend. This was necessary to introduce you to the tools that will be used in this book. This lesson presents a rather detailed overview of HTML5 and covers many of the fundamentals of HTML that existed prior to HTML5 but are still part of the HTML5 specification.

After this lesson, you will be able to:

- Understand the history of HTML5.
- Create an HTML5 document and add elements and attributes to it.
- Add comments to an HTML5 document.
- Use special characters in your HTML document.

Estimated lesson time: 30 minutes

Understanding HTML, XHTML, and HTML5

 HTML is an acronym for Hypertext Markup Language, which is the language we have used to create webpages since the first webpages arrived on the web. HTML roots are from an older markup language that was used in document publishing, called SGML (Standard Generalized Markup Language). Like SGML, HTML uses *tags* to provide formatting features such as **this is bold**, which would cause the text within the starting b tag and ending b tag to render as bolded text. Notice the difference between the first and second tag; the second tag has a slash (/) to indicate that it's an ending tag. Many but not all HTML tags have a matching end tag. HTML tags such as *
* and *<img>* did not have ending tags because the *
* just rendered a line break, and the *<img>* tag just rendered an image.

One interesting aspect of HTML and its relationship with browsers was that browsers were designed to be backward compatible and forward compatible. Creating a browser that is backward compatible is relatively easy because the problem domain is known, but how is forward compatibility accomplished? Browsers were created to ignore tags that they didn't recognize. For example, if a browser came across a *<xyz>* tag that it didn't recognize, it would skip over the tag as though it didn't exist.

Although HTML served its purpose for quite some time, people wanted more. Another evolving technology, called XML (eXtensible Markup Language), was becoming popular. XML looks a lot like HTML because both languages use tags. However, there are several big differences. First, XML always requires matching end tags for every tag, although you can use a shortcut notation to denote a starting tag and ending tag together. Another difference is that HTML has a very specific set of tag names, and each of these tags denotes a formatting feature that is to be applied to the rendered webpage. XML doesn't have a defined set of tag names, so you create your own tag names, and the tags can represent anything. XML tags are typically metadata tags: tags that describe the data that is within the tag. Although there are many other differences, one other large difference is that XML uses XML Schema Definition (XSD) technology, which validates the format of an XML document to ensure that all aspects of a document are valid before processing the XML document. HTML's lack of rigid structure prevented the creation of a technology such as XSD that could validate HTML documents.

 The *World Wide Web Consortium*, also known as *W3C* (*http://ww.w3c.org*), is responsible for developing open standards for the web. The W3C introduced XHTML to solve the problems in HTML, which was up to version 4. *XHTML* is an XML-based specification that tightened the HTML specification to make HTML adhere to the XML rules that describe a well-formed document, such as having a matching end tag for each starting tag. This meant that XHTML documents could be validated by using XSD files and could be edited by using XML tools.

Although XHTML solved some problems, other problems still needed a solution. There was a need for an increasing amount of multimedia on the web. Companies wanted the flashiest (pun intended) website. Cascading Style Sheets (CSS) provided support for adding styles such as colors and fonts consistently across a website, but companies wanted more. They wanted their webpages to be highly interactive, with video and animations. Browsers added programmable support by providing JavaScript, but early versions of JavaScript were slow and difficult to program. The browsers became extensible by providing an application programming interface (API) that would allow third parties to create *plug-ins* that could run in the browser's environment. One such plug-in is Flash, which has a very large installed base. Flash provides a development environment that can be used to create a rich user experience. Although third-party plug-ins solved the immediate need for technology to create flashy websites, there was still a need for tighter integration of multimedia with the browser, especially on small devices.

HTML5 does not originate from XHTML; HTML5 originates from HTML 4.01. As a rule, however, applying XHTML rules to your HTML5 will make your webpage more compliant with a wider variety of browsers and webpage readers, generators, and validators. This book attempts to be most compliant with the most technologies.

HTML5 represents a reinvented HTML, CSS, and JavaScript in a way that solves the need for rich, interactive websites that can play audio and video and support animations from within the browser without the need for plug-ins. HTML5 contains most of the tags from HTML 4.01, but many of the tags have been redefined to be semantic tags.

Introducing semantic markup

HTML5 stresses separating structure, presentation, and behavior, a good practice to adhere to. *Semantic* is defined as the study of meaning of linguistic expressions. In the context of HTML, that means that tags provide meaning to the content in the HTML document. Tags do not provide presentation; they provide meaning.

HTML tags provide a meaningful structure, but do not provide presentation. Remember that separation is accomplished by providing structure in your HTML5 document, maintaining presentation in your CSS3 style sheet, and maintaining behavior in your JavaScript file.

How can you maintain separation when tags such as *<b>* (bold) and *<i>* (italic) exist? After all, these tags have presentation in their definitions. The W3C now defines the *<b>* tag as "a span of text offset from its surrounding content without conveying any extra emphasis or importance, and for which the conventional typographic presentation is bold text; for example, keywords in a document abstract, or product names in a review." The W3C now defines the *<i>* tag as "a span of text offset from its surrounding content without conveying any extra emphasis or importance, and for which the conventional typographic presentation is italic text; for example, a taxonomic designation, a technical term, an idiomatic phrase from another language, a thought, or a ship name." Do these tags need to render as bold and italic? Not at all, and the new definitions of these tags attempt to specify this.

Chapter 5, "More HTML5," revisits the notion of semantic markup. For now, remember that your HTML tags should be used to provide structure, not presentation. Presentation is the cascading style sheet's job.

Working with elements

An *element* is composed of a beginning tag, an ending tag, and the content between the tags. Consider the following HTML fragment.

```
<div>
    The quick brown <b>fox</b> jumps over the lazy dog
</div>
```

In this sample, the *<div>* tag is just the beginning tag on the first line. The *<div>* element is the complete sample, which includes content that also contains a *<b>* element. The *<b>* element consists of the beginning *<b>* tag, the content, which is the word "fox," and the ending *</b>* tag.

The *<div>* element creates a section in your document. It's common to use *<div>* elements to denote a section to which you will attach a style. You'll see many uses of the *<div>* element in this book and on most websites.

HTML tag names are not case sensitive. If you're working on an older webpage, you might notice that it was written using uppercase tag names. Browsers will treat a *<b>* tag and a *<B>* tag the same.

To comply with as many standards as possible, consider using lowercase tag names for any webpages you create by convention because the W3C recommends lowercase tag names in HTML 4.01 and requires lowercase tag names in XHTML. Although HTML5 does not mandate lowercase tag names, lowercase tag names are recommended.

Element reference

HTML5 has more than 100 defined elements that you can use to create rich webpages and applications. The W3C defines the following list of these elements with a brief description. Note that brevity is a substitute for 100 percent accuracy in these descriptions.

- **<a>** Hyperlink
- **<abbr>** Abbreviation
- **<address>** Contact information
- **<area>** Image map region
- **<article>** Independent section
- **<aside>** Auxiliary section
- **<audio>** Audio stream

- **<b>** Bold text
- **<base>** Document base URI
- **<bb>** Browser button
- **<bdo>** Bi-directional text override
- **<blockquote>** Long quotation
- **<body>** Main content
- **
** Line break
- **<button>** Push button control
- **<canvas>** Bitmap canvas
- **<caption>** Table caption
- **<cite>** Citation
- **<code>** Code fragment
- **<col>** Table column
- **<colgroup>** Table column group
- **<command>** Command that a user can invoke
- **<datagrid>** Interactive tree, list, or tabular data
- **<datalist>** Predefined control values
- **<dd>** Definition description
- **<del>** Deletion
- **<details>** Additional information
- **<dfn>** Defining instance of a term
- **<dialog>** Conversation
- **<div>** Generic division
- **<dl>** Description list
- **<dt>** Description term
- **<em>** Stress emphasis
- **<embed>** Embedded application
- **<fieldset>** Form control group
- **<figure>** A figure with a caption
- **<footer>** Section footer
- **<form>** Form
- **<h1>** Heading level 1
- **<h2>** Heading level 2
- **<h3>** Heading level 3
- **<h4>** Heading level 4

- **<h5>** Heading level 5
- **<h6>** Heading level 6
- **<head>** Document head
- **<header>** Section header
- **<hr>** Separator
- **<html>** Document root
- **<i>** Italic text
- **<iframe>** Inline frame
- **<img>** Image
- **<input>** Form control
- **<ins>** Insertion
- **<kbd>** User input
- **<label>** Form control label
- **<legend>** Explanatory title or caption
- **<li>** List item
- **<link>** Link to resources
- **<map>** Client-side image map
- **<mark>** Marked or highlighted text
- **<menu>** Command menu
- **<meta>** Metadata
- **<meter>** Scalar measurement
- **<nav>** Navigation
- **<noscript>** Alternative content for no script support
- **<object>** Generic embedded resource
- **<ol>** Ordered list
- **<optgroup>** Option group
- **<option>** Selection choice
- **<output>** Output control
- **<p>** Paragraph
- **<param>** Plug-in parameter
- **<pre>** Preformatted text
- **<progress>** Progress of a task
- **<q>** Inline quotation
- **<rp>** Ruby parenthesis
- **<rt>** Ruby text

- **<ruby>** Ruby annotation
- **<samp>** Sample output
- **<script>** Linked or embedded script
- **<section>** Document section
- **<select>** Selection control
- **<small>** Small print
- **<source>** Media resource
- **<span>** Generic inline container
- **<strong>** Strong importance
- **<style>** Embedded style sheet
- **<sub>** Subscript
- **<sup>** Superscript
- **<table>** Table
- **<tbody>** Table body
- **<td>** Table cell
- **<textarea>** Multiline text control
- **<tfoot>** Table footer
- **<th>** Table header cell
- **<thead>** Table head
- **<time>** Date and/or time
- **<title>** Document title
- **<tr>** Table row
- **<ul>** Unordered list
- **<var>** Variable
- **<video>** Video or movie
- **<wbr>** Optionally break up a large word at this element

Many of these elements are discussed in more detail later in this book.

Adding attributes to elements

The begin tag can contain additional data in the form of an attribute. An *attribute* is a name="value" pair in which name is unique within the tag and value is always enclosed within either single quotes or double quotes. You can add many attributes to the begin tag. You can also alternate using single quotes and double quotes, which is especially beneficial when you need to embed single or double quotes within the value of the attribute. You can also have Boolean attributes that contain the attribute name but no value.

Here is an example of an element that has attributes.

```
<div id="main" class='mainContent'></div>
```

In this example, id and class are attributes. The id attribute uniquely identifies an element within an HTML document. The class attribute specifies a named CSS style that should be applied to the element.

Working with Boolean attributes

 Some attributes are *Boolean* attributes, which means that the mere presence of the attribute indicates that an option is set.

Some examples of Boolean attributes are as follows.

- **checked**   Used with the check box and option button to indicate selection
- **selected**   Used to indicate which option is selected in a drop-down or select list
- **disabled**   Used to disable input, text area, button, select, option, or opt group
- **readonly**   Used to prevent the user from typing data into a text box, password, or text area

There are different ways to indicate a Boolean attribute. One way is to use the minimized form, by which you just add the attribute name into the starting tag but don't provide a value. Here is an example of minimized form when setting a check box to selected.

```
<input type="checkbox" name="fruit" value="Apple" checked />
```

Another way to indicate a Boolean attribute is to use quoted form, in which you provide either an empty value or the name of the attribute as its value. Here are examples of both.

```
<input type="checkbox" name="fruit" value="Apple" checked='' />
<input type="checkbox" name="fruit" value="Apple" checked='checked' />
```

The latter seems redundant but is usually considered to be the preferred way to represent the Boolean attribute. If you use jQuery, which is a third-party JavaScript toolset, you'll find that it works best with that redundant example.

 Quick check

- You are using a *<button>* element, and you want it to be disabled until some criteria is met. What is the best way to disable the *<button>* element when the page is loaded?

Quick check answer

- Write the *<button>* element using quoted syntax and assign the attribute name to the attribute as follows.

```
<button type='button' id='myButton' disabled='disabled'>Button</button>
```

HTML5 global attribute reference

HTML5 defines a set of named attributes that can be applied to any HTML5 element. These elements are called global attributes, and each has a very specific meaning, as follows.

- **accesskey** Enables you to either specify a shortcut key to which to jump or to set focus to an element. As a rule, you shouldn't use this because it can cause problems with other technologies.

- **class** Used with CSS to specify one or more class names for an element.

- **contenteditable** Specifies that the content within the tag can be edited.

- **contextmenu** User can right-click an element to display a menu. At the time of this writing, no browser supports this attribute.

- **dir** Enables you to specify left-to-right or right-to-left text direction for the content in an element.

- **draggable** Specifies whether an element is draggable.

- **dropzone** Enables you to specify the behavior of the dragged data when it's dropped. Data can be copied, moved, or linked.

- **hidden** Specifies that an element is not relevant.

- **id** Specifies a unique id for an element.

- **lang** Specifies the language (English, French, German, and so on) of the element's content.

- **spellcheck** Used with the lang attribute to enable you to indicate whether the element is to have its spelling and grammar checked.

- **style** Specifies an inline CSS style for the element.

- **tabindex** Sets the tabbing order of the element.

- **title** Provides extra information about the element.

You'll see many examples of these global attributes in this book.

Working with self-closing tags

You can represent any element that contains no content as a self-closing tag. A *self-closing tag* is a beginning tag and an ending tag in one. You end the starting tag with a space, slash, and greater-than symbol. For example, the *
* element cannot have any content, so here is the beginning and ending tag in one: *
*.

In XML, any empty element can be written with a self-closing tag, but in HTML5, this can cause problems in different browsers. The rule of thumb is to use self-closing tags for tags that cannot have content, such as the *
* tag. Empty elements that are capable of having content but currently don't have content should have separate end tags. An example is *<div></div>*; there is no content, but the beginning and ending tags still exist.

Quick Check

- You want to use the *<script>* element to include a JavaScript file named MyCode.js in the scripts folder. What is the proper syntax?

Quick Check Answer:

- <script src="/Scripts/MyCode.js"></script>

Working with void elements

 Most but not all elements can have content, and the content can include elements with content. Elements are not required to have content, but some elements cannot have content. These are called *void elements*. For example, the *
* tag represents a line break and cannot have any content.

The following is a list of void elements in HTML5.

- **<area>** Defines a hyperlink area with some text in an image map
- **<base>** Specifies the document's base URL or target for all relative URLs in the document
- **
** Represents a line break
- **<col>** Defines the properties of one or more columns within a *<colgroup>* element
- **<command>** Defines a command that can be invoked by a user
- **<hr>** Specifies a thematic change in content
- **<img>** Defines an image
- **<input>** Defines a typed data field that allows the user to edit the data
- **<link>** Defines a relationship between a document and an external resource such as a cascading style sheet
- **<keygen>** Defines a key-pair generator control for forms that is used to encrypt data that will be passed to the server
- **<meta>** Defines metadata that describes the HTML document

- **<param>** Defines a parameter for an object
- **<source>** Defines a multimedia resource for a *<video>* or *<audio>* element
- **<wbr>** Optionally breaks up a large word at this element

In earlier versions of HTML, you just used the *
* tag with no ending tag to indicate that you wanted to start a new line on the webpage. With XHTML, this was a problem because all beginning tags are required to have matching end tags. HTML5 allows you to use a beginning tag with no end tag, but a better solution is to use self-closing tags.

Adding expando attributes

Expando attributes are attributes that you define. Expando attributes are also known as author-defined attributes or simply as custom attributes. Any time you want to attach data to an HTML tag, you can just create an attribute with the name of your choice and assign the data. However, the name you create might conflict with either an existing W3C-defined attribute name or a future W3C-defined attribute name. To ensure that you have no existing or future naming conflict, assign a name that is prefixed with "data-".

 Quick check
- You have a webpage with a *<span>* element that contains the customer's name. Along with the name, you want to include the customer number on the *<span>* element, but you don't want to display the customer number. How can you write the *<span>* element for a customer called Contoso Ltd with customer number 123?

Quick check answer
- Use an expando attribute to hold the customer number as follows.

```
<span data-customerNumber='123'>Contoso Ltd</span>
```

Adding comments

You can add comments to your HTML source by using the following syntax.

```
<!--comment here -->
```

Comments are not displayed on the rendered browser page but are sent to the browser. Comments can help document your source.

No spaces are allowed between the <! characters and the -- characters at the beginning of the comment, but spaces are allowed between the -- characters and the > character at the end of the comment tag. This seemingly weird behavior means that you cannot have back-to-back dashes (--) in your comment because this combination causes HTML syntax errors. In addition, you cannot end a comment with three dashes, such as <!-- and then it happened---> because this also generates a syntax error.

Adding conditional comments

Only Internet Explorer recognizes *conditional comments*, which enable you to add a browser-specific source that executes if the browser is Internet Explorer but is treated as a comment by other browsers. You can add conditional comments to your HTML document by using the following syntax.

```
<!--[if lte IE 7]>   <html class="no-js ie6" lang="en"> <![endif]-->
<!--[if lt IE 7]>    <html class="no-js ie6" lang="en"> <![endif]-->
<!--[if IE 8]>       <html class="no-js ie8" lang="en"> <![endif]-->
<!--[if gt IE 8]>    <html class="no-js" lang="en">      <![endif]-->
<!--[if gte IE 9]>   <html class="no-js" lang="en">      <![endif]-->
<!--[if !IE]> -->    This is not Internet Explorer!<br />            <!-- <![endif]-->
```

The first conditional comment checks whether the browser is Internet Explorer and the version is earlier than or equal to 7. The next conditional comment checks whether the browser is Internet Explorer and the version is earlier than 7. The next conditional comment checks whether the browser is Internet Explorer and the version is 8. The next conditional comment checks whether the browser is Internet Explorer and the version is later than 8, followed by a check to see whether the browser is Internet Explorer and the version is later than or equal to 9. The last line checks whether the browser is not Internet Explorer. Note that the syntax of the last line is different from the others.

Creating an HTML document

Now that you've seen the various elements and attributes, it's time to group them in a meaningful way to create an HTML document. The HTML document contains an outer structure, metadata, and some content.

Basic document structure

Every HTML document should have a basic structure that consists of a *<!DOCTYPE html>* declaration, which historically has indicated the version of HTML to the browser. In HTML5, this indicates to the browser that it should be in no-quirks mode. *No-quirks mode* causes the browser to operate in an HTML5-compliant manner. Next is the root *<html>* element, which contains the *<head>* element and the *<body>* element.

The *<head>* element contains hidden information such as metadata that describes the HTML document and instructions. The following is an example of metadata in the *<head>* element.

```
<!DOCTYPE html>
<html>
  <head>
    <meta charset="utf-8" />
    <title>title here</title>
  </head>
  <body>
    content here
```

```
    </body>
</html>
```

In this example, the *<meta>* element describes the character set as *utf-8*, which is an effi-cient form of unicode in which the English language characters (ASCII) require only a single byte to be represented, and in which other languages can have characters that are repre-sented with up to 4 bytes. This is the most common character set used in HTML and XML documents.

This example also contains a *<title>* element, which is important because it serves the fol-lowing purposes.

- Displays in the browser toolbar
- Provides the default name for the page when it is added to favorites
- Displays the title when a search engine displays the page in the search results

The *<body>* tag contains the displayable contents.

Using special characters (HTML entities)

You might want to display the < and > characters on your webpage, but you've seen that the less-than and greater-than characters define tags. These characters can be displayed in your content by using either the entity name or entity number as follows.

&entity_name;

or

&#entity_number;

There are many HTML entities, but Table 1-1 lists the most common HTML entities you will use in your HTML document.

TABLE 1-1 Reference to common entities

Display	Entity Name	Entity Number	Description
&	&	&	Ampersand
>	>	>	Greater-than sign
<	<	<	Less-than sign
"	"	"	Double quotation
©	©	©	Copyright
®	®	®	Registered trademark
™	™	™	Trademark
		$#160;	Nonbreaking space

NONBREAKING SPACE

If you try to embed a series of spaces into your HTML document, the browser normalizes contiguous white-space characters (such as spaces, tabs, and line breaks) and renders only a single space. This is usually a desirable feature because it enables you to format your HTML source content in a manner that is most readable in source mode while eliminating white-space in the rendered output.

When you want to display several spaces, you can use the nonbreaking space character. Nonbreaking space is also known as nonbreak space, nonbreakable space, and hard space. In addition to preventing the collapse of contiguous whitespace, the *nonbreaking space* prevents the automatic line break between words that you want to keep together on the same line.

Consider an HTML document in which you want to display 10 mph, where there is a space between the number 10 and the mph. You want to ensure that mph will not be separated from the number 10 by being moved to the next line. In your HTML document, use 10 mph to keep the number 10 and mph together.

Lesson summary

- An element is composed of a starting tag, inner content, and an ending tag.
- Browsers ignore tags that are not recognized.
- HTML5 originates from HTML 4.01, not from XHTML.
- The W3C is responsible for developing open standards for the web.
- HTML elements provide structure, CSS style sheets provide presentation, and JavaScript provides behavior.
- Use lowercase tag names.
- Attribute values should always be quoted using either single quotes or double quotes.
- Boolean attributes are attributes whose mere presence on the starting tag indicates that the option is set.
- HTML5 defines global attributes, which are the set of attributes that can appear on any HTML5 element.
- Self-closing tags are tags whose beginning and ending tags are together to create an element with no content. Self-closing tags should be used only with elements that cannot have content.
- Void elements cannot have content. They should be created by using self-closing tags.
- Expando attributes are attributes that you define and are also known as author-defined attributes or custom attributes. Prefix these attributes with "data-".
- You can use conditional comments to add a browser-specific source that will work with Internet Explorer but be treated as a comment by other browsers.

- HTML entities are special characters and can be embedded in your HTML document by using the ampersand (&), the entity name, and a semicolon (;). You can also use the ampersand (&), the hash symbol (#), the entity number, and the semicolon (;).

- Nonbreaking spaces can be used to render several contiguous spaces. You can also use nonbreaking spaces to keep two words from being separated by a line break.

- The id attribute specifies a unique identifier for an element.

Lesson review

Answer the following questions to test your knowledge of the information in this lesson. You can find the answers to these questions and explanations of why each answer choice is correct or incorrect in the "Answers" section at the end of this chapter.

1. You want to create an expando attribute on several *<h3>* tags that display vehicles for sale. The expando attribute will store the VIN (vehicle identification number) of the vehicle for sale. Which of the following is the most appropriate example of creating the expando attribute?

    A. *<h3 vin='current VIN here'>1965 VW Beetle</h3>*

    B. *<h3 id='current VIN here'>1965 VW Beetle</h3>*

    C. *<h3 data-vin='current VIN here'>1965 VW Beetle</h3>*

    D. *<h3 datavin='current VIN here'>1965 VW Beetle</h3>*

2. Which technology is HTML5 preceded by and derived from?

    A. HTML 4.01

    B. SGML

    C. XHTML 1.0

    D. XML

3. How should you start each HTML5 document?

    A. *<html>*

    B. *<head>*

    C. *<title>*

    D. *<!DOCTYPE html>*

4. You want to use the disabled Boolean attribute on a text box. How can you accomplish this? (Choose all that apply.)

    A. <input name='firstName' type='text' disabled />

    B. <input name='firstName' type='text' disabled='' />

    C. <input name='firstName' type='text' disabled='true' />

    D. <input name='firstName' type='text' disabled='disabled' />

Lesson 2: Embedding content

Soon, you will want to embed content in your HTML document. The content might be from an existing webpage, or you might embed images in your HTML document. You might also embed Adobe Flash applications. You can embed many interesting elements, and this lesson covers many of the ways to embed content.

> **After this lesson, you will be able to:**
> - Embed HTML documents in another HTML document by using inline frames.
> - Create hyperlinks to remote or local HTML documents.
> - Add images and image maps to the current HTML5 document.
> - Embed plug-in content.
>
> **Estimated lesson time: 30 minutes**

Embedding HTML by using inline frames

You can use the *<iframe>* element to embed an inline frame that contains an HTML document within the current HTML document. This can be useful when you want to create reuse functionality on your site; for example, when you want to create a common header that will show on all pages of your website. This can also be useful when you want to include an HTML page from another website on your page.

The *<iframe>* element creates a nested browser context into which another HTML document can be loaded. Loading an HTML document creates a browsing context for that document. The document that contains an *<iframe>* is contained within the parent browser context, where the document that is loaded into the *<iframe>* element is within the nested browser context.

You can navigate nested browsing contexts by using the following properties of the window object.

- **window.top**   A WindowProxy object representing the top-level browsing context
- **window.parent**   A WindowProxy object representing the parent browsing context
- **window.frameElement**   An element that represents the browsing context container but returns null if there isn't one

The *<iframe>* element has a src (source) attribute and a name attribute. The src attribute can be set to the absolute or relative URL of the HTML document that you want to include, as shown in the following sample.

```
<iframe src="menu.html"></iframe>
```

The name attribute sets the browsing context name, which is useful when you need to reference the *<iframe>* element, possibly as the target of a hyperlink, as described in the

"Working with hyperlinks" section that follows. A valid browsing context name is any string with at least one character that does not start with an underscore because the underscore is used for these special key names: _blank, _self, _parent, and _top.

Sandboxing embedded content

Sandboxing is a means for preventing malware and annoyances such as pop-ups from being introduced when the content is embedded on your HTML page. The *<iframe>* element provides the sandbox attribute for this purpose.

The sandbox attribute places a set of extra restrictions on any content hosted by the iframe. When the sandbox attribute is set, the content is treated as being from a unique and potentially dangerous origin. Forms and scripts are disabled, and links are prevented from targeting other browsing contexts. Consider the following example.

```
<iframe sandbox src="http://someOtherDomain.net/content">
</iframe>
```

In the example, the source is referencing potentially hostile content in a different domain. This content will be affected by all the normal cross-site restrictions. In addition, the content will have scripting, plug-ins, and forms disabled. The content cannot navigate any frames or windows other than itself.

The restrictions can be overridden by space-separating any of the following.

- **allow-forms**   Enables forms
- **allow-same-origin**   Allows the content to be treated as being from the same origin instead of forcing it into a unique origin
- **allow-scripts**   Enables scripts except pop-ups
- **allow-top-navigation**   Allows the content to navigate its top-level browsing context

In the following example, allow-same-origin, allow-forms, and allow-scripts are enabled. On the surface, it might seem that the sandbox is not providing any protection, but the sandbox still disabling plug-ins and pop-ups.

```
<iframe sandbox="allow-same-origin allow-forms allow-scripts"
    src="http://otherContent.com/content.html"></iframe>
```

Seamless content embedding

The *<iframe>* tag has a seamless attribute that indicates that the source content is to appear as though it's part of the containing document. This means that the *<iframe>* element will not have borders and scrollbars. The seamless attribute is a Boolean attribute, so its presence on the *<iframe>* tag indicates that you want this option, but there are three ways to set a Boolean attribute. Here are three ways to specify seamless embedding of content.

```
<iframe seamless="seamless" src="http://otherContent.com/content.html"></iframe>
<iframe seamless="" src="http://otherContent.com/content.html"></iframe>
<iframe seamless src="http://otherContent.com/content.html"></iframe>
```

At the time of this writing, the seamless attribute is not supported on any browsers, but its intent is to blend the external content into the current HTML document so the HTML page does not look like it has embedded content. The alternative is to use CSS to obtain a similar presentation.

Working with hyperlinks

The *<a>* element creates a link to an external HTML document (external link) or jumps to a location in the current HTML document (internal link). The content of the *<a>* element is displayed in the browser with the following default appearance.

- **Unvisited link** Underlined and blue
- **Visited link** Underlined and purple
- **Active link** Underlined and red

The *<a>* element has the href attribute, which you usually use to specify the link destination. If the link is external, the href can be populated with either a relative or absolute URL as follows.

```
<a href="ExpenseReports.html">Expense Report Page</a>
<a href="http://www.contoso.com/SalesReports.html">Sales Report Page</a>
```

If the link is internal, the href will contain the hash (#) symbol followed by the id of the tag that you want to jump to. If you use only the hash symbol, clicking the link takes you to the top of the HTML document. Here are two examples.

```
<a href="#">Top</a>
<a href="#BillingAddress">Go To Billing Address</a>
```

Specifying the hyperlink target

When you're on a webpage and you click a hyperlink to an external resource, the external resource opens in the current browser window. If the external link is to a page on your website, this behavior probably makes sense. If the external link is to a different website, you might want to open a new browser window. By using the target attribute, you can control the link behavior by assigning one of the following.

- **_blank** Open in a new browser window
- **_parent** Open in the parent frame or window
- **_self** Open in the current window or frame (default)
- **_top** Open in the topmost frame, thus replacing the contents of the window
- **<iframe_name>** Open in the *<iframe>* element with matching name attribute

When you have a menu with hyperlinks that shows on every page, you might want to create an *<iframe>* element with its name attribute set to content and then set the target of all menu links to be content so the pages load into the *<iframe>* element as shown in the following example.

```
Main Menu<br />
<a href="Calendar.html" target="content">Calendar</a><br />
<a href="HumanResources.html" target="content">Human Resources</a><br />
<a href="ExpenseReports.html" target="content">Expenses</a><br />
<a href="Commissions.html" target="content">Commissions</a><br />
<br />
<iframe name="content"></iframe>
```

Sending email with hyperlinks

You can use mailto protocol to send email messages. The mailto URL accepts the following parameters: subject, cc, bcc, and body. The parameters can be entered in any order by adding a question mark (?) after the email address and separating the parameters with the ampersand (&). Some examples of an email hyperlink are as follows.

```
<!-- basic mailto -->
<a href="mailto:sales@contoso.com">Contact Sales</a>

<!-- add the name, notice that email is wrapped with &lt; and &gt; -->
<a href="mailto:Joe&lt;sales@contoso.com&gt;">Contact Joe in Sales</a>

<!-- multiple recipients comma separated -->
<a href="mailto:sales@contoso.com,service@contoso.com">Contact Sales and Service</a>

<!-- add carbon copy -->
<a href="mailto:sales@contoso.com?cc=service@contoso.com">Contact Sales cc Service</a>

<!-- add blind carbon copy -->
<a href="mailto:sales@contoso.com?bcc=service@contoso.com">Contact Sales</a>

<!-- basic mailto with message -->
<a href="mailto:sales@contoso.com?body=call me.">Contact Sales with call me message</a>

<!-- basic mailto with multi line message -->
<a href="mailto:sales@contoso.com?body=call me.%0AThanks">Contact Sales with multi line
message</a>

<!-- basic mailto with subject and message -->
<a href="mailto:sales@contoso.com?subject=hi&body=call me.">Contact Sales with hi
subject
 and call me message</a>
```

Adding images to your HTML document

When you want to embed an image in your HTML document, use the *<img>* element. The *<img>* element does not have an ending tag; it's a void element. The *<img>* element has required attributes of src (abbreviation for source) and alt (abbreviation for alternate). Use the src attribute to provide an absolute or relative URL reference to the image that is to be displayed. Use the alt attribute to provide alternate text to be displayed when the image is not available due to slow connection or other mishap. The following is an example of the *<img>* element.

```
<img src="/images/logo.png" alt="logo" />
<img src="http://search.microsoft.com/global/search/en-
us/PublishingImages/bing_logo.png" alt="Bing Logo" />
```

It's important to understand that the image is not embedded in the HTML document. Instead, you provide a reference to the image file. When the browser reads your HTML document, the browser will reach your *<img>* element and retrieve the image based on the src attribute. When the image is retrieved, the browser will merge the image into the final rendering that is displayed into the browser window. If the browser cannot display the image, it will display the alternate text.

Image file types

When using the *<img>* element, you can supply JPEG (.jpg or .jpeg), GIF (.gif), PNG (.png), or SVG (.svg) files. The following is a brief description of each file type that should help you decide which file type to use for your application.

- **JPG**   Also known as JPEG, this is best for photographs because it offers high compression and up to 16.8 million color combinations, but the compression algorithm is lossy, meaning that you lose detail every time you save the file.

- **GIF**   GIF is great to use on small images that have a fixed number of colors. GIF also supports transparent color. GIF uses lossless compression and is best for logos and worst for photos. GIF also supports the ability to encapsulate multiple images in one file, which is commonly used to provide animated GIFs.

- **PNG**   PNG is a great all-around file type due to its lossless high compression. PNG files can be 48-bit true color or 16-bit grayscale. PNG not only supports transparent color but also offers variable transparency. Photos aren't compressed to be as small as JPG photos, but being lossless makes it worth the extra size in many scenarios. You might use PNG as your storage type for photos that you want to edit, but when displaying them on the web, you might want to save the PNG as JPG to achieve the best compression.

- **SVG**   SVG is Scalable Vector Graphics and is great for drawings but not for photos. SVG images can be scaled up or down without losing detail because the file contains the instructions to draw the image, as opposed to the other file types that contain a raster-based image. Raster-based images are composed of color dots that make up the image. If you need to scale a raster-based image up or down, you will see that in color, dots are re-sampled, and the image typically ends up looking blocky.

Quick check

- You are creating several small icons that will be displayed on your webpage. These icons will render as different shapes and will use transparent color. Each icon uses a small number of colors. Which would be the best image file type for this application?

Quick check answer

- Use the GIF format because it has transparent color support and because it requires small numbers of colors.

Creating image links

If you create a hyperlink and the hyperlink's content is an *<img>* element, you have created an image that can be clicked—an image link. Here is an example of an image link.

```
<a href="Investments.html"><img src="CurrencySymbol.png" /></a>
```

Creating an image map

You can create a clickable image map on your HTML document by using the *<map>* element. It contains *<area>* elements that define clickable regions on the image.

The *<map>* element has a name attribute that must be set. On an *<img>* element, set the usemap attribute to the *<map>* element's name to create a relationship between the image and the map.

In the *<map>* element, you define *<area>* elements by using the shape, coords, href, and alt attributes. The *<area>* element is a void element, so you use a self-closing tag. The shape attribute is set to rect, circle, poly, or default, where default is an *<area>* element whose size is the same as the image and is triggered if no specific *<area>* is defined for coordinates where you clicked.

The coords attribute will contain *x* and *y* coordinates where 0, 0 is the top-left corner of the image. The coords attribute is set according to the shape as follows.

- **rect** $x1, y1, x2$, and $y2$ specify the coordinates of the left, top, right, and bottom.
- **circle** x, y, and *radius* specify the coordinates of the center and the radius.
- **poly** $x1, y1, x2, y2,.., xn$, and yn specify the coordinates of the edges. The first and last coordinate pairs should be the same to close the polygon, but if they aren't the same, the browser will add a closing pair.

The href attribute is the same as the href attribute on the *<a>* element and can be set to an absolute or relative URL.

The alt attribute is set to alternate text to be displayed and is required when the href attribute is set.

The following is an example of creating an image map with its areas and assigning the image map to an image.

```html
<img src ="worldmap.gif" width="145" height="126"
   alt="World Map" usemap ="#countries" />

<map name="countries">
   <area shape="rect" coords="10,15,30,25"
      href="USA.html" alt="USA" />
   <area shape="circle" coords="95,40,20"
      href="China.html" alt="China" />
   <area shape="poly" coords="97,76,115,76,113,83,105,90,97,76"
      href="Australia.html" alt="Australia" />
   <area shape="default" href="InvalidChoice.html" alt="Invalid" />
</map>
```

Embedding plug-in content

You can use the *<object>* and *<embed>* elements to embed content from plugins. Why are there two tags for the same purpose? The reason is the differences in browsers over the years. Originally, Netscape created the *<embed>* tag for Netscape-style plug-ins, and Internet Explorer added support for the *<embed>* tag. The *<object>* tag was added to HTML 4.0 with the benefit of supporting Internet component downloads so that the plug-in could be automatically downloaded and installed.

The *<embed>* tag

Although the HTML 4.01 specification did not support the *<embed>* tag, most browsers continued support due to the installed base and the ease of use. In HTML5, both tags exist. The *<object>* tag provides more functionality, whereas the *<embed>* tag is easier to use. For example, if you want to play a Flash file, you can use the *<embed>* tag as follows.

```html
<embed src="myFlashFile.swf" >
</embed>
```

The *<embed>* tag has the following attributes.

- **height** Specifies the height in pixels of the embedded content
- **src** Specifies the URL of the external file to embed
- **type** Specifies the MIME type of the embedded content
- **width** Specifies the width in pixels of the embedded content

For browsers that don't support the *<embed>* tag, you can add fallback content into the element as follows.

```html
<embed src="myFlashFile.swf" >
 <a href="/go/getflashplayer/">
   <img src=http://www.adobe.com/images/shared/download_buttons/get_flash_player.gif
      alt="Get Adobe Flash player" />
 </a>
</embed>
```

The *<object>* tag

The *<object>* tag embeds an object within an HTML document. You can embed multimedia such as audio, video, Java applets, ActiveX, PDF, and Flash in your webpages. The *<object>* tag contains the following attributes.

- **data** Supplies the URL of the resource to be used by the object
- **form** Indicates one or more form ids to which the object belongs
- **height** Specifies the height in pixels of the object
- **name** Defines the name of the object
- **type** Defines the MIME type of data specified in the data attribute
- **usemap** Indicates the name of a client-side image map to be used with the object
- **width** Specifies the width in pixels of the object

IMPORTANT **AT A MINIMUM**

At a minimum, you must define either the data or type attribute.

The *<object>* tag can be used within the *<body>* element only. You might find *<object>* examples that implement many more attributes than are defined in this list because older versions of HTML supported other attributes, but HTML5 supports only the attributes that are listed plus the global attributes.

You can also use the *<object>* tag to embed another webpage in your HTML document. The following is an example of using the *<object>* element to embed a webpage in your HTML document.

```
<object id="headerContent" standby="loading header..."
    title="loading header..." width="100%" height="15%"
    type="text/html" data="Header.aspx"></object>
```

As a rule, consider using the *<iframe>* tag when embedding a webpage from another domain into your HTML document by using sandboxing. It's made for that purpose, whereas the *<object>* tag is a more general-purpose tag. The *<object>* tag behaves differently with different browsers, and you might find that features such as tooltips work only with the *<iframe>* tag and not with the *<object>* tag.

It is possible to embed images and image maps in your HTML document by using the *<object>* tag, but you should avoid doing so. It's best to use the *<img>* tag to embed images.

The text within the *<object>* element is alternate text to be displayed for browsers that do not support the *<object>* tag.

Passing parameters to an object

Because the *<object>* tag can represent any object, the *<param>* tag enables you to pass data to the object. You can use one or more *<param>* tags to pass parameters to plug-ins that have been embedded with the *<object>* tag. The *<param>* tags must be before any alternate text that is within the *<object>* element.

The *<param>* tag has a name and a value attribute, and both are required for each *<param>* tag. The following is an example of using a *<param>* tag with an audio file to keep the audio file from automatically playing when the page is loaded.

```
<object data="tada.wav">
   <param name="autoplay" value="false" />
</object>
```

Using the object tag to create a browser context

In addition to using the *<iframe>* tag to create a nested browser context, you can use the *<object>* tag, but this is not supported on all browsers, so you should use the *<iframe>* tag.

Lesson summary

- You can use the *<iframe>* element to provide reuse of HTML by embedding an HTML document in your current HTML document.
- Use the sandbox attribute on the *<iframe>* tag to help prevent malware and annoyances such as pop-ups from being introduced when the content is embedded in your HTML page.
- Use the seamless attribute on the *<iframe>* tag to indicate that the source content is to be rendered to appear as though it's part of the containing document.
- The *<a>* tag creates a hyperlink to either an external HTML document or an internal location in the current document. The *<a>* tag can also be used to send email messages.
- The *<img>* element is a void element and is used to add an image reference to your HTML document.
- JPG is best for displaying photos on HTML pages due to its compression, GIF is best for small images with transparency and embedded animations, PNG is best for storage due to lossless compression during editing sessions, and SVG is best for drawings due to its vector drawing scalability.
- You can create a clickable image map by using the *<map>* and *<area>* elements.
- You can use the *<embed>* tag to provide simple content embedding.
- You can use the *<object>* tag to provide content embedding with greater flexibility because it can have nested *<param>* elements.

Lesson review

Answer the following questions to test your knowledge of the information in this lesson. You can find the answers to these questions and explanations of why each answer choice is correct or incorrect in the "Answers" section at the end of this chapter.

1. You want to embed a Flash file called myFlash.swf in your HTML document. Which is the most appropriate code?

    A. *<a href="myFlash.swf" ></a>*

    B. *<iframe src="myFlash.swf" ></iframe>*

    C. *<img src="myFlash.swf" />*

    D. *<embed src="myFlash.swf" ></embed>*

2. You want to create a drawing of a machine that Contoso, Ltd., will be selling on its website. The drawing will be embedded in your HTML document, and you want it to maintain its quality when resized. Which is the most appropriate file type to use?

    A. SVG

    B. GIF

    C. JPG

    D. PNG

Practice exercises

You've learned a bit about HTML elements and attributes, and it's time to create a website. In Exercise 1, you create a website for a fictitious company, Contoso, Ltd., and add a home page. In Exercise 2, you add the expense reports, human resources, and main content pages.

If you encounter a problem completing an exercise, the completed projects can be installed from the Practice Exercises folder that is provided with the companion content.

Exercise 1: Create a simple website by using Visual Studio Express for Web

In this practice, you create a simple website by using Visual Studio Express 2012 for Web. The quality of the webpages produced will be less than desirable because CSS hasn't been discussed yet. The goal of this practice is to use many of the tags that have been described in this lesson.

You start by creating an ASP.NET website by using Visual Studio Express 2012 for Web, and then you add to and modify the home page.

1. If you haven't installed Visual Studio Express 2012 for Web, do so now. You can download this from the Microsoft website.

2. Start Visual Studio Express 2012 for Web. Navigate to file and choose New Project. Navigate to Installed | Templates | Visual Basic | Web and select ASP.NET Empty Web Application.

3. Set the name of your application to **ContosoWebSite**.

4. Select a location for your application.

5. Set the solution name to **ContosoWebSiteSolution**.

6. Be sure to keep the Create Directory For Solution check box selected.

7. Click OK to create your new project.

8. When the application is created, click Debug and select Start Debugging. (The shortcut key is usually F5 but can vary based on your installation settings.)

   The ASP.NET Empty Web Application doesn't include a home page, so an error page is displayed, showing an HTTP Error 403.14 - Forbidden error. The error page indicates (in a rather indirect way) that you don't have a default page on your website, so the web server tries to display a list of all files in the directory. However, the security settings on the website will not permit directory browsing to display the directory contents.

9. Close the error page, which should automatically stop debugging. If you need to, you can stop debugging by clicking Debug and choosing Stop Debugging (or pressing Shift+F5).

10. Add a home page. In the Solution Explorer window, right-click the ContosoWebSite project, choose Add, and select HTML Page. Set the name to **default.html** and click OK.

    The home page is added to your website and contains the following HTML.

```
<!DOCTYPE html>
<html xmlns="http://www.w3.org/1999/xhtml">
<head>
    <title></title>
</head>
<body>

</body>
</html>
```

11. In the *<title>* element, set the title to **Contoso Ltd. Home Page**.

12. In the Solution Explorer window, right-click the project, choose Add, select New Folder, and name the folder **Images**.

13. In the Solution Explorer window, right-click the Images folder that you just added, choose Add, select Existing Item, and select the ContosoLogo.jpg file that is located in the Chapter02 Resources folder.

14. In the *<body>* element, add a comment and set the text to **Add <img> with Contoso logo**.

    The <img> element is covered in Lesson 2.

15. Using the *<h1>* element to create a heading, add the **Welcome to Contoso Ltd.** heading to the body after the comment.

16. After the *<h1>* element, add a comment. Set the comment text to **Add <iframe> here**.

The *<iframe>* element is discussed in Lesson 2. Your default.html page should look like the following.

```
<!DOCTYPE html>
<html xmlns="http://www.w3.org/1999/xhtml">
<head>
    <title>Contoso Ltd. Home Page</title>
</head>
<body>
    <!--Add <img> with Contoso logo-->
    <h1>Welcome to Contoso Ltd.</h1>
    <!--Add <iframe> here-->
</body>
</html>
```

17. In the Solution Explorer window, right-click the default.html page and choose Set As Start Page.

18. Click Debug and choose Start Debugging (F5).

You should see the rendered screen, as shown in Figure 2-1. Using the *<h1>* element produced a heading with a large font. Notice that comments are not displayed, but if you right-click the page and choose View Source, you see the HTML source, which has the comments. The text in the browser tab contains Contoso Ltd. Home Page, which is the text that you entered in the <title> element.

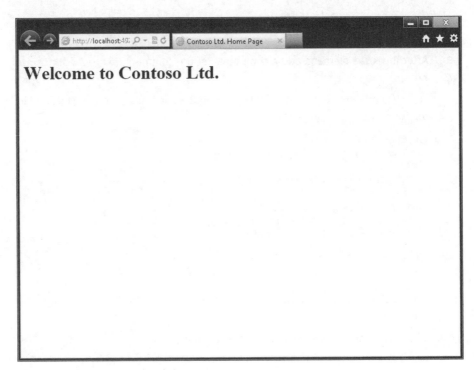

FIGURE 2-1 The Contoso Ltd. website

Exercise 2: Create additional pages

In this exercise, you add pages to the website you created in Exercise 1. If you didn't per-form Exercise 1, you can use the files in the Exercise2\LabStart folder to start. You won't be able to get to the new pages from the home page yet because you add that functionality in Exercise 3.

1. In the Solution Explorer window, right-click the project, choose Add, and select HTML Page. Set the name to **MainContent.html** and click OK.

   The content will be kept simple.

2. In the *<body>* element of the MainContent.html page, add the following text: **Here is the main content for the home page**. Set the title to **Main Content**.

   Your HTML should look like the following.

```
<!DOCTYPE html>
<html xmlns="http://www.w3.org/1999/xhtml">
<head>
    <title>Main Content</title>
</head>
<body>
    Here is the main content for the home page.
</body>
</html>
```

3. To view this page, right-click the middle of the source and choose View In Browser (Internet Explorer).

You should see the rendered screen, as shown in Figure 2-2. Note that almost nothing is on this page. It doesn't have a heading or logo. In Exercise 3 you combine this content with the home page to obtain the header and logo.

Here is the main content for the home page.

FIGURE 2-2 The rendered main content page

4. Close the browser window.

5. Add a new HTML file and name it **HumanResources.html**. In the *<body>* element, add the following text: **Human Resource content here**.

6. Right-click the middle of the source and choose View In Browser (Internet Explorer).

You should see the rendered screen with the text you entered.

7. Add another HTML file and name it **ExpenseReports.html**. In the *<body>* element, add the following text: **Expense Report content here**.

8. Right-click the middle of the source and choose View In Browser (Internet Explorer).

You should see the rendered screen with the text you entered.

Exercise 3: Embedding Content

You learned about embedding content in Lesson 2; this exercise uses this information to connect the pages of the Contoso, Ltd., website by embedding the pages in the home page, using an inline frame.

In this practice, you extend the Contoso, Ltd., website that you created in Exercise 1 by linking the pages and displaying pages in an inline frame. If you didn't perform Exercise 1, you can use the files in the Exercise3Start folder to start.

1. Open the default.html file and locate the comment that states that an *<img>* tag is to be added. Add an *<img>* tag after the comment. Set the src attribute to **Images/ContosoLogo.jpg**.

2. Locate the comment that states that an *<iframe>* tag is to be added. Add an *<iframe>* element with a name attribute set to **iframeContent** and an src attribute set to **MainContent.html**.

   Your default.html page should look like the following.

   ```
   <!DOCTYPE html>
   <html xmlns="http://www.w3.org/1999/xhtml">
   <head>
       <title>Contoso Ltd. Home Page</title>
   </head>
   <body>
       <!--Add <img> with Contoso logo-->
       <img src="Images/ContosoLogo.jpg" />
       <h1>Welcome to Contoso Ltd.</h1>
       <!--Add <iframe> here-->
       <iframe name="iframeContent" src="MainContent.html"></iframe>
   </body>
   </html>
   ```

3. Click Debug and choose Start Debugging (F5).

   You should see the Contoso logo, and the MainContent.html file is now included on the page. The rendered screen is shown in Figure 2-3.

FIGURE 2-3 The rendered home page with the MainContent.html page embedded

4. Stop debugging.

5. On the default.html page, after the *<h1>* element, add a hyperlink for Human Resources that references the HumanResources.html file and targets the *<iframe>* element called iframeContent.

6. After the Human Resources hyperlink, add a hyperlink for Expense Reports that references the ExpenseReports.html file and targets the *<iframe>* element called iframeContent.

7. Add a *
* element after the Expense Reports hyperlink.

   The completed default.html file should look like the following.

```
<!DOCTYPE html>
<html xmlns="http://www.w3.org/1999/xhtml">
<head>
    <title>Contoso Ltd. Home Page</title>
</head>
<body>
    <!--Add <img> with Contoso logo-->
    <img src="Images/ContosoLogo.jpg" />
    <h1>Welcome to Contoso Ltd.</h1>
    <a href="HumanResources.html" target="iframeContent">Human Resources</a>
    <a href="ExpenseReports.html" target="iframeContent">Expense Reports</a>
    <br />
    <!--Add <iframe> here-->
```

```
    <iframe name="iframeContent" src="MainContent.html"></iframe>
</body>
</html>
```

8. In the HumanResources.html and ExpenseReports.html files, add a <br /> tag to the end of the body text, and then add a hyperlink to the home page that references MainContent.html.

Note that you don't need to target the current frame because the default behavior of the hyperlink is to replace the current page with the new page. The following is an example of the completed ExpenseReports.html file.

```
<!DOCTYPE html>
<html xmlns="http://www.w3.org/1999/xhtml">
<head>
    <title></title>
</head>
<body>
    Expense Reports content here.
    <br />
    <a href="MainContent.html" >Home</a>
</body>
</html>
```

9. Click Debug and choose Start Debugging (F5).

You should see the new home page with hyperlinks. If you click the Human Resources hyperlink, you should see the HumanResources.html content load into the *<iframe>* element, as shown in Figure 2-4. In the *<iframe>* content, you should see a hyperlink to the home page that you can click to reload the MainContent.html file into the *<iframe>* element.

> **NOTE**   **CLICK REFRESH TO SEE THE HOME HYPERLINK**
>
> You might not see the Home hyperlink because the original page might be cached. Right-click in the *<iframe>* and click Refresh.

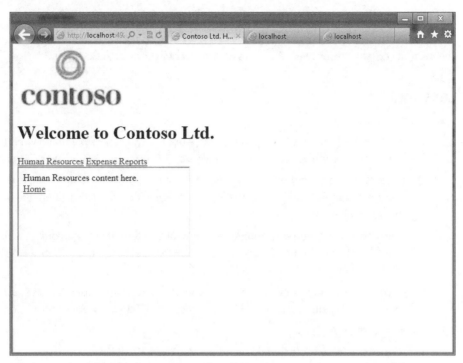

FIGURE 2-4 The default.html page shown after clicking the Human Resources hyperlink

Suggested practice exercises

The following additional practices are designed to give you more opportunities to practice what you've learned and to help you successfully master the lessons presented in this chapter.

- **Exercise 1** Learn more about each of the HTML tags that are part of the HTML5 specification by using each in an HTML document.

- **Exercise 2** Learn more about embedding content by adding images and image maps to an HTML document.

Answers

This section contains the answers to the lesson review questions in this chapter.

Lesson 1

1. **Correct answer: C**

   A. **Incorrect:** Although this example would work today, it's possible that a vin attribute could be introduced by a future version of HTML that would cause a conflict.

   B. **Incorrect:** You cannot use the id attribute as an expando attribute because the id attribute is already defined by the HTML5 specification to provide a unique identifier to an element.

   C. **Correct:** This is a properly defined expando attribute that will not conflict with attributes introduced by future versions of HTML because the attribute name is prefixed with "data-" as required by the HTML specification.

   D. **Incorrect:** Although this example would work today, it's possible that a vin attribute could be introduced by a future version of HTML that would cause a conflict.

2. **Correct answer: A**

   A. **Correct:** HTML5 is preceded by and derived from HTML 4.01.

   B. **Incorrect:** Although HTML's root is SGML, which means that HTML5 is derived from SGML, HTML5 is preceded by HTML 4.01.

   C. **Incorrect:** Although XHTML 1.0 was released after HTML 4.01, HTML5 does not inherit from XHTML1.0.

   D. **Incorrect:** Although XHTML1.0 inherits from XML, HTML5 does not.

3. **Correct answer: D**

   A. **Incorrect:** The *<html>* element is the root element for your HTML5 document, but it should be listed after you indicate the document type to the browser.

   B. **Incorrect:** The *<head>* tag must be contained within the *<html>* element, so it cannot be located at the beginning of the HTML5 document.

   C. **Incorrect:** The *<title>* tag must be contained within the *<head>* element, so it cannot be located at the beginning of the HTML5 document.

   D. **Correct:** The <!DOCTYPE html> indicates to the browser that this is an HTML5 document.

4. **Correct answers: A, B, and D**

   A. **Correct:** The use of disabled by itself, with no value, is the minimized method for implementing Boolean attributes.

   B. **Correct:** The use of disabled with an empty value is one way to implement Boolean attributes by using quoted form.

    C.   **Incorrect:** The use of disabled with a value of true is not an acceptable way to implement Boolean attributes.

    D.   **Correct:** The use of disabled with a value that is the same as the attribute name is one way to implement Boolean attributes by using quoted form.

Lesson 2

1.   **Correct answer: D**

    A.   **Incorrect:** The *<a>* element creates a hyperlink.

    B.   **Incorrect:** The *<iframe>* element creates an inline frame that references another HTML document.

    C.   **Incorrect:** The *<img>* element embeds an image in the current HTML document.

    D.   **Correct:** The *<embed>* element embeds an object such as a Flash file in the current HTML document.

2.   **Correct answer: A**

    A.   **Correct:** The SVG file type is used to create Scalable Vector Graphics, which scale well while maintaining quality.

    B.   **Incorrect:** The GIF file type is best for small images with limited colors, but it is raster-based and does not scale well.

    C.   **Incorrect:** The JPG file type is best for photos when millions of colors are used and high compression is desirable, but it is raster-based and does not scale well.

    D.   **Incorrect:** The PNG file type is best for photos when millions of colors are used and medium no-loss compression is desirable, but it is raster-based and does not scale well.

Getting started with JavaScript

When you create HTML documents, you'll almost always add behavior to make the document more interactive. You might have animations or buttons that perform various actions. Maybe you need to retrieve data from the server as a user is typing in a text box. You can use JavaScript to accomplish these tasks because JavaScript is the programming language of the web.

This chapter starts by introducing you to JavaScript and then examines the JavaScript testing environment and test-driven development (TDD). As soon as you understand what JavaScript is, you'll want to start writing some code to see whether it runs the way you think it should run. You'll want to test your knowledge. You'll want to write code for HTML documents with which you're working.

By setting up a testing environment, you can write code and test it without requiring the production HTML document. You want to have as much separation as possible between your JavaScript code and your HTML document so you can write the JavaScript code independently from the HTML document. The sooner you have a testing environment set up, the sooner you'll be able to start writing JavaScript code.

Lessons in this chapter:

Before you begin

To complete this book, you must have some understanding of web development. This chapter requires the hardware and software listed in the "System requirements" section in the book's Introduction.

Lesson 1: Introducing JavaScript

This lesson presents a great deal of the JavaScript language. Although much of the content exists in previous releases of JavaScript, all content in this chapter is part of the latest JavaScript specification.

After this lesson, you will be able to:

- Define JavaScript variables.
- Create JavaScript statements.
- Create function declarations.
- Create function expressions.
- Convert objects to a different type.
- Write conditional statements.
- Write looping statements.
- Handle errors.

Estimated lesson time: 60 minutes

Understanding JavaScript

JavaScript is not related to Java, although it is a curly-brace language like Java, C#, C++, and many other programming languages. JavaScript is related to ECMAScript, however. Ecma International, working with other organizations, created this standardized scripting language in the ECMA-262 specification and ISO/IEC 16262. The language is widely used for client-side scripting on the web, and you commonly see several well-known variations of ECMAScript such as JavaScript, JScript, and ActionScript. The current release is ECMAScript Edition 5.1 and most common browsers support ECMAScript Edition 5.0 or newer.

JavaScript is untyped, which means that when you create a variable, you don't need to specify its type. This might seem like a feature because you declare a variable with the var keyword and assign a string to the variable, and later, you can assign a number to the same variable. However, it's difficult to apply Microsoft IntelliSense to untyped languages. It's also difficult to maintain the code because it's difficult to know the variable's type. This might cause you to develop an immediate dislike for the language, but persevere and work with the language. You'll be amazed at the power of JavaScript. Although you might never want to trade in Visual Basic .NET or C#, you'll find that the more time you spend with JavaScript, the more respect you'll develop for this language.

One way to ease the pain of learning JavaScript is to make sure you are using tools that can help you. The latest release of Visual Studio 2012 adds more IntelliSense to JavaScript and adds the JavaScript Console, which can simplify debugging. Search the web for other tools such as Resharper by JetBrains. This tool has many features that can help you with writing JavaScript code.

Understanding the role of data

When you want to create a program, you typically find that the program must access and manipulate data because data is at the root of all systems. You collect data, manipulate data, store data, retrieve data, display data, and so on.

The data will be in different forms, but most data can be broken into smaller pieces called *values*. JavaScript defines a *value type* as an object, a primitive value, or a function. A *primitive value* is a datum that is represented at its lowest level of the language implementation and, in JavaScript, is one of the following types: undefined, null, Boolean, number, or string. A *function* is a callable object, and a function that is a member of an object is called a *method*.

JavaScript also defines the following built-in objects: the global object, the Object object, the Function object, the Array object, the String object, the Boolean object, the Number object, the Math object, the Date object, the RegExp object, the JSON object, and several variations of Error objects.

Using expressions to produce data

An *expression* is a piece of code that produces a value. An expression can be a simple value, or it can contain operands and operators. Mathematical symbols, such as the plus, minus, divide, and multiply signs, are examples of operators. Numbers are operands. The operators cause an operation to be executed by using the operands on each side of the operator. Note that an operand can be a value, or it can be another expression.

Understanding the number type

Numbers are one of the primitive types defined in JavaScript. A numeric value is a member of the number type and corresponds to a double-precision, 64-bit binary format, IEEE 754 value. In JavaScript, all numeric values are internally represented as floating point values. The 64-bit number is divided into three components: the fraction is 52 bits (bits 0 to 51), the exponent is 11 bits (bits 52 to 62), and the sign is a single bit (bit 63).

The highest integer number that can be represented internally is 2^{53}, which is 9,007,199,254,740,994. After that, numbers are stored as a fraction times $2^{exponent}$. When performing integer calculations, the results are always precise, but when working with fractions, problems can arise. A calculation such as 0.1 + 0.2 will not result in 0.3 due to the manner in which fractions are stored. The result will be 0.30000000000000004 because 0.1 and 0.2 cannot easily be stored as a binary fraction value. For situations like this, you might need to round your results to truncate the fraction to a fixed number of decimal places.

SPECIAL VALUES

The number type supports the following special values:

- *NaN*   Not a number indicator. Performing any mathematical operation with *NaN* will produce a result of *NaN*.

- **Infinity**   Represents positive infinity when your value exceeds 1.7976931348623157E + 10308.

- **-Infinity**   Represents negative infinity when your value exceeds -1.7976931348623157E + 10308.

- **undefined**   No value has been assigned.

ARITHMETIC

We need numbers to perform arithmetic operations. Many arithmetic operations, such as addition, subtraction, multiplication, and division, perform an operation on two numeric values to produce a resultant numeric value. In JavaScript, you might write an expression to do something like this:

```
7 + 3 * 8
```

This is an expression with operands and operators. The plus sign (+) and multiplication sign (*) are operators. The numbers are operands. The operators cause an operation to be executed, using the operands on each side of the operator.

OPERATOR PRECEDENCE

In this expression, you do not add 7 and 3 to get 10 and then multiply 10 by 8 to get 80. JavaScript supports operator precedence, the assignment of a precedence, or priority, to each operator. In this expression, the multiplication sign has a higher precedence than the addition sign, so 3 is first multiplied by 8 to give 24, and then 7 is added to 24 to get 31, which is different from the previous result of 80. The addition sign (+) and subtraction sign (–) have the same precedence. The multiplication sign (*) and division sign (/) have the same precedence, which is higher than the addition and subtraction signs. If you are working with an expression in which multiple operators have the same precedence, you just apply the operators from left to right.

In this example, the plus and multiplication signs are operators. The multiplication sign has 3 and 8 as operands that produce an expression. The plus sign has 7 and the result of 3 times 8 as operands. In the latter case, the second operand is an expression.

In the previous example, what would you do if you actually wanted to add 7 and 3 first? You can use parentheses to indicate the order of precedence. Parentheses have the highest precedence, so the expression within the parentheses will be executed first. Here is the modified expression:

```
(7 + 3) * 8
```

Thus, you don't necessarily need to memorize the precedence for each operator because you can override the precedence order by using parentheses.

MODULO

The modulo (%) operator performs an implied division and returns the remainder. For example, 25 % 7 produces a result of 4, which is the remainder after dividing 25 by 7.

Understanding the string type

A string is a collection of characters and is used to represent text. You can create a string by enclosing in single or double quotes. It doesn't matter whether you use single or double quotes as long as the starting and ending delimiters match, as in the following examples:

```
"Every good boy deserves fudge"
'The quick brown fox jumps over the lazy dog'
'The doctor said "Today is your lucky day!" '
"I'm going to be happy when you give me the news!"
```

Notice that the third example demonstrates the use of single quotes when you need to embed double quotes within the string. The fourth example demonstrates the use of double quotes when you need to embed a single quote within the string. If you need to embed double or single quotes into the string, you can use the backslash (\) character to escape the single or double quote, as shown in the following example:

```
'The doctor said "I\'m pleased to announce that it\'s a girl!" '
"The doctor said \"I'm pleased to announce that it's a girl!\" "
```

In the first example, the backslash is used to escape the single quote so it's not interpreted as being the end of the string. In the second example, the backslash is used to escape the double quotes so they aren't interpreted as being the end of the string.

Some other common escape sequences are \t to embed a tab and \n to embed a new line. You can also use \uHHHH where HHHH is a 4-digit hexadecimal code to embed a unicode string.

You can use the plus sign to represent string concatenation. The following is an example in which several strings are concatenated to produce one large string:

```
'Hickory Dickory Dock.' + "The mouse ran up the clock." + 'The clock struck one...'
```

You probably wouldn't do this because this example could have been easily written as a single large string, but you might want to continue a string over several lines, like the following:

```
'Hickory Dickory Dock.' +
"The mouse ran up the clock." +
'The clock struck one...'
```

Using unary operators

When an operator requires two operands, it's a binary operator. Examples of binary operators are plus, minus, multiply, divide, and modulo. Some operators, called unary operators, require only a single operand. One unary operator is the typeof operator, which requires a single operand and returns a string that indicates the operand's type, as follows:

```
typeof 'Hello World'
typeof 19.5
typeof true
```

In the three examples, the first example returns 'string', the second example returns 'number', and the third example returns 'Boolean'.

In addition to being binary operators, the plus and minus signs can also be used as unary operators, as in the following examples:

```
+23
-49
```

In these examples, the plus and minus signs are being used as unary operators to specify the signs of the numbers.

Understanding the Boolean type

The Boolean type can contain the values true and false. Although you can use these values directly, it's more common to produce a true or false value by comparing two values, as shown in the following examples that use the less-than (<) and greater-than (>) signs:

```
10 < 9
20 > 3
```

The first example produces a false value, whereas the second example produces a true value. The next examples use the less-than-or-equal-to (<=) sign and the greater-than-or-equal-to (>=) sign:

```
5 <= 4
7 >= 8
```

The first expression evaluates to false, and the second expression evaluates to false. You can also use the equals (==) and not equals (!=) operators, as shown in the following example:

```
'Apples' != 'Oranges'
10 == 13 - 3
```

Both of these expressions evaluate to true.

LOGICAL OPERATORS

JavaScript provides three logical operators: and (&&), or (||), and not (!). These operators can be used in expressions to produce a Boolean value. The and operator will produce a true value if both operands evaluate to true; else it produces a false value. The or operator will produce a true value if either operand evaluates to true; else it produces a false value. The not operator is a unary operator that will invert the operand, so if the operand evaluates to true, the result is false, and vice versa. Consider the following examples:

```
'Apples' == 'Oranges' && 5 > 3
5 > 10 || 4 < 2
3 < 10 && 10 > 8
7 > 5 || 1 > 2
!(7 > 5 || 1 > 2)
```

The first example uses the and operator and produces a false result because the first operand evaluates to false. The second example uses the or operator and produces a false result because neither operand evaluates to true. The third example uses the and operator and produces a true result because both operands evaluate to true. The fourth example uses the or operator and produces a true result because the first operand (7 > 5) evaluates to true. The fifth example uses the or operator and the not operator. Inside the parentheses, the expression evaluates to true, but the not operator inverts the true to produce a false result.

SHORT-CIRCUITING OPERATORS

In the previous JavaScript example, the first line produced a false value because both the operands did not evaluate to true, but there's more: because the first operand evaluated to false, JavaScript made no attempt to evaluate the second operand. This is known as short-circuit evaluation. In the fourth example, the result is true because the first operand evaluated to true. JavaScript needed only one operand to be true to produce a true result; no time was wasted evaluating the second operand.

Using statements

In JavaScript, a statement is a command that is terminated with a semicolon. A statement is different from an expression because an expression just produces a value, and then JavaScript discards the value. A statement tells the JavaScript host what to do. The host could be the browser or Windows 8. A statement can be a command to store the result of an expression so it can be reused in other statements.

Using variables

One way to store the results of an expression is to assign the results to a variable. A *variable* is a named reference to a location in memory for storing data. To create a variable, use the JavaScript keyword var, as in the following example:

```
var totalCost = 3 * 21.15;
```

In this example, a variable named *totalCost* is created, and the result of 3 * 21.15 is assigned to the *totalCost* variable. After this variable is created, it can be an operand in other expressions, such as the following:

```
var totalCost = 3 * 21.15;
var tax = totalCost * .05;
```

In this example, another statement was added to the statement from the previous example. This statement contains an expression that uses the *totalCost* variable to calculate the tax and store it in another variable called *tax*.

Note that you can declare the variable in one statement and initialize it in a different statement, as follows:

```
var totalCost;
var tax;
totalCost = 3 * 21.15;
tax = totalCost * .05;
```

This example shows you how you could declare all your variables first and then initialize the variables later in the program.

The value you assign to a variable is not permanent; it is called a variable because you can change it. The following examples modify the *totalCost* variable:

```
var totalCost = 3 * 21.15;
totalCost = totalCost * .1;
totalCost *= .1;
```

The first example initializes the *totalCost* variable. The second example reads the value of *totalCost*, multiplies the value by .1, and stores the result back into *totalCost*. This overwrites the old value with the new value. The third example is a shortcut for the action in the second example. It uses the *= syntax to indicate that you want to multiply the existing value by .1 and store the result in the same variable:

Rules for naming variables

Every programming language has rules for naming variables, and JavaScript is no exception. You must adhere to the following rules when naming JavaScript variables.

- A variable name can contain numbers, but they cannot begin with a number. Legal examples are *x1*, *y2*, *gift4you*. Illegal examples are *4YourEyes*, *2give*, *1ForAll*.

- Variable names must not contain mathematical or logical operators. Illegal examples are *monday-friday*, *boxes+bags*, *cost*5*.

- Variable names must not contain any punctuation marks of any kind other than the underscore (_) and dollar sign ($). Legal examples are *vehicle_identification*, *first_name*, *last_name*, *$cost*, *total$*. Illegal examples are *thisDoesn'tWork*, *begin;end*, *Many#s*.

- Variable names must not contain any spaces.

- Variable names must not be JavaScript keywords, but they can contain keywords. Illegal examples are function, char, class, for, var. Legal examples are *theFunction*, *forLoop*, *myVar*.

- Variable names are case-sensitive. Examples of different-case variables are *MyData*, *myData*, *mydata*, *MYDATA*.

Naming variables

When you create a variable, give the variable a name that is descriptive enough that you don't need a comment to describe what it is. If you need to add a comment to describe the variable usage, the comment will be at the declaration only. If you name the variable in a way that does not require a comment, the meaningful name will be readable throughout your code. Here are some good and bad examples of variable naming:

```
//bad examples
var last;       //last accessed date
var current;    //current vehicle
var changed;    //the vehicle make was changed
```

```
//good examples
var lastAccessedDate;
var currentVehicle;
var vehicleMakeWasChanged;
```

Notice the casing that is used in the good examples. The recommended naming convention for JavaScript variables is to use camel casing, which means you start a variable name in lowercase and then capitalize the first letter of each subsequent word that makes up the variable name.

Although a variable name can contain the dollar sign and the underscore, it's usually preferable not to use them. The exception is when assigning jQuery objects (discussed in Chapter 6, "Essential JavaScript and jQuery") to variables, when you might want to begin the variable name with the dollar sign.

Creating the environment

The collection of all variables and their values is commonly referred to as the *environment*. When the environment is created, it contains many standard variables plus the variables you create.

In a web application, each time a webpage is loaded into the browser, a new environment is created, and the old environment is destroyed. Any variables that you create are accessible until a new webpage is loaded.

In a Windows 8 program, an environment is created when the application starts, and the environment is destroyed when the application ends. A variable is accessible as long as your program is running.

Working with functions

A *function* is a grouping of statements that are executed when you call the function. Functions promote code reuse because you can call the function many times from within your code. Functions can have parameters, which enable you to pass data into the function. Functions can also have a return value, so you can return the results of the function to the caller.

Using function declarations

A function can be declared by using the function keyword and then providing a name (also known as an *identifier*), the optional list of parameters enclosed in parentheses, and a set of curly braces with the grouping of statements, as follows:

```
function Add(x, y) {
    return x + y;
}
```

This is an example of a *function declaration*, in which the function is called Add and has two parameters, *x* and *y*. The function has a grouping of statements, denoted by the curly braces (also known as a *code block*). This function has only one statement, but it could have many statements.

When you *call* the function from your code, you are *invoking* or *applying* the function. An example of calling, invoking, or applying the Add function is as follows:

```
var a = 5;
var b = 10;
var c = Add(a, b);
```

In this example, three variables are declared. Variables *a* and *b* are initialized with data to be passed as *arguments* to the Add function. Variable *c* will contain the return value of the Add function. The Add function will receive the arguments into its *x* and *y* parameters. Finally, the return statement will add *x* and *y* and return the result, which is assigned to variable *c*.

> **NOTE   DISTINGUISHING "ARGUMENT" AND "PARAMETER"**
>
> Many people use the terms "argument" and "parameter" synonymously, but these terms are different. Arguments represent the values you pass to the function (variables *a* and *b* in the previous example), whereas the parameters represent the values received from the caller (variables *x* and *y* in the previous example).

Function declarations may be called before the function declaration is declared because the function declarations are resolved when the JavaScript is parsed. The following example will run properly even though the call to the Add function is before the Add function:

```
var a = 5;
var b = 10;
var c = Add(a, b);

function Add(x, y) {
    return x + y;
}
```

Using function expressions

A function expression produces a value of type function. You can assign function expressions to variables or execute them directly. Here is an example of a function expression being created and assigned to a variable:

```
var addFunction = function(x, y){
    return x + y;
};

var c = addFunction(5, 10);
```

First, notice that *addFunction* is called after the function expression is assigned to the *addFunction* variable. If you tried to call *addFunction* before the assignment of the function expression to the *addFunction* variable, an exception would be thrown.

The *addFunction* variable is of type *function*, in which the function expression is created by using the function keyword to create a function with no name (also known as an *anonymous function*), and then the function expression is assigned to the variable. An anonymous function has no name or identifier. Although function expressions can be named or anonymous, it's considered better to leave the function anonymous to minimize confusion.

Function expressions can be beneficial when you want to determine the code conditionally to be executed at runtime. Here is an example of when you might add two values or subtract one value from the other:

```
var myFunction = function(x, y){
    return x + y;
};
//lots of code
var c = myFunction(10, 5);
//lots of code
myFunction = function(x, y){
    return x - y;
};
//lots of code;
var d = myFunction(10,5);
```

In this example, variable *c* will be assigned a value of 15 because *myFunction* was declared and assigned code that adds *x* and *y*. Variable *d* is assigned the value of 5 because *myFunction* was assigned new code that subtracts *y* from *x*.

Deciding which arguments

JavaScript is very loose when passing arguments to functions. If you have too many arguments, JavaScript just discards the extras. If you don't have enough arguments, the parameter values for missing arguments will be undefined.

The biggest benefit of this loose behavior is that you can add parameters to a method that has already been created and is already being called. The added parameters might provide extra functionality that can be accessed, but existing callers continue to work.

The drawback of this loose behavior is that you might inadvertently pass an incorrect quantity of arguments to the function, and you get no indication of a problem.

Using the browser's built-in alert, prompt, and confirm functions

When writing web applications, the browser provides the following functions that can present data to and collect data from the user:

- **alert**   Used to display a message to the user in a modal window. The user clicks the OK button to close the message window. The following code produces the alert window in Figure 3-1:

```
alert('Here is an alert');
```

FIGURE 3-1 The alert window showing a message and an OK button

- **prompt**   Used to query the user for input by displaying a modal message prompt and a text box for the user to enter data into. The text box can be supplied a default value that allows the user just to press Enter or click the OK button to accept the default value. The user can close the window by clicking the OK or Cancel button. The prompt function returns the data that the user typed in the text box. The following code produces the prompt in Figure 3-2:

```
var promptResult = prompt('This is a prompt for information', 'default value');
```

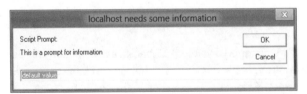

FIGURE 3-2 The prompt window collecting text

- **confirm**   Used to query the user for OK or Cancel by displaying a modal message window. The user can close the window by clicking the OK or Cancel button. The confirm function returns either true (when the OK button is clicked) or false (when the Cancel button is clicked):

```
var confirmResult = confirm('Do you confirm?');
```

FIGURE 3-3 The confirm window presents a message and OK and Cancel buttons

These built-in functions, and any functions you write, can be overwritten very easily because the function name is a variable. Consider the following scenario, in which a different function is assigned to the prompt function:

```
prompt = function(){
    return 'hello again';
};
```

This code replaces the behavior of the prompt function with a function that always returns the string, 'hello again'. The function name is represented by a variable, and you can change its value dynamically. This is the same for function declarations and function expressions.

Scoping variables

Scoping is the context within a computer program in which a variable name is valid and can be used to access the variable. Outside the scope of a variable name, the variable's value might still be stored and might even be accessible in some way, but the name cannot access the value.

In JavaScript, there are essentially two scopes, global and local. A variable with a global scope is accessible from anywhere in the program. A variable with a local scope is accessible only from within the function in which the variable is defined, so you can think of local scope as being function scope.

The fact that local scope is limited to a function is very different from many other languages, in which a new local scope is created for each set of curly braces. This means that in many other languages, conditional and looping statements that have curly braces also start a new local context. This is not the case for JavaScript, in which the only local scope is at the function. Variables that are declared anywhere inside the function will have a local function scope. To avoid confusion, you should declare all function variables at the top of the function.

> **NOTE BE CAREFUL NOT TO CREATE GLOBAL VARIABLES IMPLICITLY**
>
> If you do not use the var keyword when you declare a variable, the variable is automatically created, but it will have a global scope. Consider the following code example:
>
> ```
> totalCost = 3 * 21.15;
> tax = totalCost * 1.05;
> ```

If this code were inside a function, you might have thought that *totalCost* and *tax* would be automatically created with a local scope, but that's not the case. As it turns out, *totalCost* and *tax* will always be created with a global scope, and these variables will be accessible from anywhere in the program. You should always declare variables by using the var keyword.

Nesting functions and nested local variable scoping

There's more to local scoping that you need to know. In JavaScript, you can nest function declarations inside function declarations. JavaScript allows multiple levels of function declaration nesting. Remember that a function produces a local scope, so you can get additional scopes by using this function-nesting trick.

Nested functions are private to the function in which they are defined. Nested functions also start their own local context, whereas defined variables are accessible within this function only. In addition, a nested function can access variables defined in the parent function's local context, the grandparent function's local context, and so on. Here is an example of using a nested function to get a nested local scope:

```
function areaOfPizzaSlice(diameter, slicesPerPizza) {
    return areaOfPizza(diameter) / slicesPerPizza;
    function areaOfPizza(diameter) {
        var radius = diameter / 2;
        return 3.141592 * radius * radius;
    }
}
```

In this example, the areaOfPizza function is nested in the areaOfPizzaSlice function, which means that the areaOfPizza function is declared inside the areaOfPizzaSlice function's local scope. The areaOfPizza function is not accessible outside the areaOfPizzaSlice function. The radius variable is declared inside the nested local scope and is accessible only from within the areaOfPizza function. There are two diameter variables, one in the local scope of areaOfPizzaSlice and one in the areaOfPizza. When in the areaOfPizza function, the diameter variable that is defined in that local context is accessible. When in the areaOfPizzaSlice function, the diameter variable that is defined in that local scope is accessible. The *slicesPerPizza* variable is accessible in both functions because parent variables are accessible to the children as long as they are not hidden by local variables with the same name.

Converting to a different type

In many scenarios, you will want to convert a variable from one type to another. For example, the prompt function always returns a string, but you have prompted the user to enter a number. For conversions, you can use the Number and String functions.

Using the Number function

The Number function attempts to convert the object argument that is passed into the function to a number. If the object argument cannot be converted to a number, a value of *NaN* (not a number) is returned.

Consider the following example, in which the user is prompted to enter his or her age, the age is incremented, and a message is displayed, using the new age:

```
var age = prompt('Enter age', '');
alert('You will soon be ' + age + 1 + ' years old!');
```

When you run this code and input a number such as 20, the message displays as You Will Soon Be 201 Years Old! because age is a string, so the plus sign automatically converts the number 1 to a string and concatenates to the age, resulting in an age of 201.

By using the Number function, you can convert the age to a number and then add 1, as shown in the following example:

```
var age = prompt('Enter age', '');
alert('You will soon be ' + Number(age) + 1 + ' years old!');
```

If you try to run this code, you get the same age response of 201 years old. What happened? The first plus sign has a string on the left side and the Number function on the right. Although you converted to a number, the first plus sign automatically converted the number back to a string and returned the same value of 201.

To solve the problem, put parentheses around the math to ensure that age receives the proper value before being converted to a string and concatenated as follows:

```
var age = prompt('Enter age', '');
alert('You will soon be ' + (Number(age) + 1) + ' years old!');
```

When you run this code, you get a response of You Will Soon Be 21 Years Old! because the age is converted to a number and incremented before any of the string concatenation occurs.

 Quick check

- You prompt the user for the year of his or her vehicle and place the result in a *vehicleYear* variable. The current year is stored in a *currentYear* variable. You want to display a message that states, "Your vehicle is xx years old!" where xx is the age of the vehicle. What will this line of code be?

Quick check answer

- You can use the alert function to display the message and the Number function to convert the *vehicleYear* variable to numeric as follows:

```
alert('Your vehicle is ' + (currentYear - Number(vehicleYear)) + ' years old!');
```

Using the String function

The String function attempts to convert the object argument that is passed into the function into a string. Consider the scenario in which you have two numbers such as 10 and 20, and you want to concatenate them like strings and display the resulting string of 1020. You might try the following code:

```
var x = 10;
var y = 20;
alert(x + y);
```

This example will display a value of 30 because the plus sign added the values instead of concatenating them as strings. To solve the problem, you can use the String function to convert the numbers to strings as follows:

```
var x = 10;
var y = 20;
alert(String(x) + String(y));
```

This example will display a value of 1020 because the numbers were converted to strings, and then the plus sign concatenated the values.

Conditional programming

You will often need to execute certain code when an expression evaluates as true and execute different code when the expression evaluates to false. This is when the *if* and *switch* keywords can help.

Using the if/else keywords

Consider the scenario in which the user is prompted to enter his or her age, one is added to the age, and a message is displayed. Here is the code that was used earlier when the built-in prompt function was discussed:

```
var age = prompt('Enter age', '');
alert('You will soon be ' + (Number(age) + 1) + ' years old!');
```

What happens if someone enters I Don't Know for the age? This string is not numeric, and the displayed message will be You Will Soon Be NaN Years Old, where *NaN* means *Not a Number*. You might want to provide a more specific message when the user input is not a number. This can be accomplished by using the *if/else* keywords with a built-in function called isNaN, as follows:

```
var age = prompt('Enter age', '');
if(isNaN(age))
    alert('You need to enter a valid number');
else
    alert('You will soon be ' + (Number(age) + 1) + ' years old!');
```

The isNaN function accepts one object argument and tests this object to see whether it is numeric. The isNaN function returns true if the object is not numeric and false if it is numeric.

The if keyword is used with an expression that is surrounded by parentheses and evaluates to a Boolean value. This expression is used in your code to steer the program flow based on the result of the isNaN function, which, when true, displays the message, You Need To Enter A Valid Number. Notice that the if keyword has a corresponding else keyword that is used to provide an alternate program flow when the if expression evaluates to false. The else keyword is optional.

The previous example executes a single statement when true and a single statement when false. If you need to execute multiple statements when true or false, you must surround the statements with curly braces to indicate that you have a code block to execute as follows:

```
var age = prompt('Enter age', '');
if(isNaN(age)){
   age = 0;
   alert('You need to enter a valid number');
}
else {
   age = Number(age) + 1;
   alert('You will soon be ' + age + ' years old!');
}
```

As a rule, you should consider using curly braces all the time. This enables a user to add code into the code block without having to think about whether the curly braces exist.

You can also create chained (also known as cascading) if statements by adding another if after the else keyword. Here is an example of a cascading if:

```
var age = prompt('Enter age', '');
if(isNaN(age)){
   age = 0;
   alert('You need to enter a valid number');
}
else if(Number(age) >= 50) {
   age = Number(age) + 1;
   alert('You're old! You will soon be ' + age + ' years old!');
}
else if(Number(age) <= 20) {
   age = Number(age) + 1;
   alert('You're a baby! You will soon be ' + age + ' years old!');
}
else
{
   alert('You will soon be ' + (Number(age) + 1) + ' years old!');
}
```

In this example, the first conditional test checks to see whether the age is not a number. The else condition is checking to see whether the age is greater than or equal to 50. The next else condition is checking to see whether the age is less than or equal to 20. Finally, the last else condition is just displaying a default message.

Using the switch keyword

The switch keyword can be used when a single value is to be examined and, based on its value, there could be several outcomes. Consider the following example that uses the switch keyword, in which the user is prompted to select a color for the car that he or she is purchasing:

```
var carColor = prompt('What color car would you like to buy?', 'white');
switch (carColor) {
   case 'red':
      alert('Red is a fancy choice!');
      break;
   case 'black':
      alert('Black looks nice, but you need to wash often!');
      break;
   case 'white':
      alert('White is in stock and you get a discount!');
      break;
   default:
      alert('The color:' + carColor + ' is not known.');
break;
};
```

In this example, the user is prompted to enter a car color and presented with a default value of white. The switch keyword examines *carColor* to see whether its value matches any of the values provided in the cases. If there is a match, the code within the case is executed until the code reaches either a break or a return keyword. If there is no break or return, the code continues into the next case or default.

How do you use the switch with numeric ranges? Many people would say that you can't work with numeric ranges because the switch is looking for an exact match to a case value, but there is a trick to solving this problem. Consider the cascading if example, covered earlier, when the program produced a different message based on the user's age response. Four different categories of responses—if the age was not a number, if it was greater than or equal to 50, if it was less than or equal to 20, or if it was any other number—received four different messages. The following is a rewrite of the cascading if as a switch:

```
var age = prompt('Enter your age', '');
age = Number(age);
switch (true) {
   case isNaN(age):
      age = 0;
      alert('You need to enter a valid number');
      break;
   case (age >= 50):
      age = Number(age) + 1;
      alert("You're old! You will soon be " + age + " years old!");
      break;
   case (age <= 20):
      age = Number(age) + 1;
```

```
        alert("You're a baby! You will soon be " + age + " years old!");
        break;
    default:
        alert('You will soon be ' + (Number(age) + 1) + ' years old!');
        break;
};
```

In this example, the trick is to use *switch(true)*, which enables you to use conditional statements with each case that evaluates as true or false.

Determining whether a variable has a value

You will often want to determine whether a variable has a value. You can use the if keyword to determine this. The if keyword evaluates as true if the variable has a value; it evaluates as false when the variable is either *undefined* or *null*. The difference between undefined and *null* is minimal, but there is a difference. A variable whose value is undefined has never been initialized. A variable whose value is null was explicitly given a value of null, which means that the variable was explicitly set to have no value. If you compare undefined and null by using the null==undefined expression, they will be equal.

Consider the following example, in which you want to determine whether *myVar* has a value:

```
if(myVar){
    alert('myVar has a value');
}
else {
    alert('myVar does not have a value');
}
```

If *myVar* is 0, *NaN*, empty string, null, or undefined, a message is displayed, stating that *myVar* does not have a value. If *myVar* contains any other value, a message is displayed stating that *myVar* has a value.

No value coalescing operators

Often, you want to check a variable to see whether it has a value and, if the variable has a value, use either the variable or a default value. JavaScript offers a rather simple way to accomplish this: use the || (or) operator.

The following is an example of using the or operator to accomplish this task:

```
var customer = prompt('Please enter your name');
alert('Hello ' + (customer || 'Valued Customer'));
```

In this example, if customer has a value, the or operator will be evaluated as true, and the actual value is returned. Because the or operator is short-circuiting, there is no evaluation of the second operand. If customer has no value, the or operator returns the second operand, even if it's null.

It's interesting to note that or operators can be chained, as shown in this example, in which the user is prompted for a name and then prompted for a company name:

```
var customer = prompt('Please enter your name');
var companyName = prompt('Please enter your company name');
alert('Hello ' + (customer || companyName || 'Valued Customer'));
```

In this example, the alert message will contain the value of the first variable that has a value or Valued Customer if none of the variables has a value.

The && (and) operator exhibits similar behavior but returns the first empty value instead of the first non-empty value. If all variables have a value, Valued Customer is returned. There isn't much real-world value to this behavior, but it is a tool in your JavaScript toolbox.

Determining whether two values have the same type and are equal

When JavaScript evaluates the following expressions, they all evaluate as true:

```
null == undefined
false == 0;
'' == 0;
'123' == 123
```

JavaScript attempts to convert the operands to types that are compatible before performing the equality check. However, you might want these expressions to evaluate as false because the types are different.

To perform a type and equality comparison, JavaScript provides the === and the !=== operators. The following expressions evaluate as false:

```
null === undefined
false === 0;
'' === 0;
'123' === 123
```

Implementing code loops

Code loops are an important part of every programming language because many programs need to repeat a sequence a given number of times or repeat a sequence until some value has changed. JavaScript gives us the *while, do,* and *for* keywords to perform looping operations.

Implementing the while loop

The *while* keyword can be used to create a loop that accepts a loop expression enclosed within parentheses. The loop can contain a single statement or a code block that executes as long as the loop expression evaluates as true. Here is an example of the while loop:

```
var x = 10;
while(x > 0) {
    x--;
    alert("The value of x is " + x);
}
```

In this example, as long as the loop expression evaluates as true, the loop continues. Each time through the loop, x is decremented, using the x-- statement. After x is decremented, an alert message is displayed that shows the current value of x. Note that the code block can execute zero to many times, based on the value of x when the program pointer reaches the while loop. If x were initialized to zero, the loop would not execute.

Implementing the do loop

The *do* keyword can be used to create a loop that executes one to many times. The do statement starts with the word "*do*," followed by a mandatory set of curly braces containing a code block that will be executed each time the loop executes, followed by the while keyword and a loop expression that is enclosed in parentheses.

The most compelling reason to use the do loop is that it executes at least once because the loop expression is evaluated after the loop executes. It can be difficult to think of a real-world implementation of this loop, but consider when a login screen needs to be displayed to collect the user name and password, and the login screen will be redisplayed if the login credentials are not correct. The following example should provide some clarity to this implementation:

```
var retries = 0;
do{
    retries++;
    showLoginScreen();
} while(!authenticated() && retries < 3);
if(retries==3){
    alert('Too many tries');
    return;
}
```

In this example, a *retries* variable is first created and initialized to zero. Next, the do loop executes. Inside the loop's code block, the *retries* variable is incremented, and a call is made to a showLoginScreen function, which will display a login screen that prompts for a user name and password. After the user enters the appropriate information and closes the login screen, the loop expression is evaluated. The authenticated function checks the user name and password and returns true if the user should be authenticated. The loop will continue as long as the user is not authenticated and the *retries* count is less than three.

Implementing the for loop

The *for* loop is typically used when you know how many times the loop will execute, and you want a *loop counter* variable. The for loop uses the following syntax:

```
for (var variable=startvalue; variable < endvalue; variable = variable + increment)
{
    code to be executed
}
```

Within the parentheses are three sections, separated by semicolons. The two semicolons must exist, even if you leave a section empty. The first section enables you to declare and initialize a loop variable. This section executes once when the program reaches this loop. The second section is the loop expression, which is called prior to executing the loop code, to determine whether the loop should execute. If the loop expression evaluates as true, the loop code executes. The third section is the loop modification section. This is when you might want to increment (or decrement) the loop variable. This section is executed after the loop code executes for each loop.

You might use the for loop when you know that you want to loop a specific number of times and, in the loop code, you want to access a *counter* variable, as shown in the following example:

```
for (var counter = 0; counter < 10; counter++){
    alert('The counter is now set to ' + counter);
}
```

In this example, a *counter* variable is created with the var keyword. Be careful to use the var keyword to avoid creating a global variable by mistake. The loop will continue as long as the counter variable is less than 10. Each time the loop executes, the counter is incremented, using the counter++ syntax. The *counter* variable is used in the loop code to display a message, but the counter could certainly be used for more elegant tasks.

Breaking out of a loop

As your loop logic becomes complicated, you might find that you need a way to exit the loop by using a conditional check within the loop code. For scenarios such as this, you can use the break keyword to exit the immediate loop. Note that the break keyword will exit only from the current loop. If you are in a nested loop, you will exit only one level.

In the following scenario, a loop is created to determine whether a number is a prime number, and the break keyword is used to exit the loop if the number to test is determined not to be a prime number:

```
var numberToTest = prompt('Type number here.', '');
var index = 2;
var isPrime = true;
while (index < numberToTest) {
    if (numberToTest % index == 0) {
        isPrime = false;
        break;
    }
    index++;
}
if (isPrime) {
    alert(numberToTest + ' is a prime number');
}
else {
    alert(numberToTest + ' is not a prime number because it is divisible by ' + index);
}
```

In this example, the modulo (%) operator determines whether index can be divided into the number to test without producing a remainder. If so, the number to test is not a prime number. As soon as a number is found to be nonprime, there is no need to continue looping, so the break keyword is used to exit the loop.

Handling errors

When writing code, you always want to make sure that your code does not cause an *exception*. An *exception* is an error that occurs at runtime due to an illegal operation during execution. You should validate your variables preemptively before performing an operation that could throw an exception. For example, before you divide one variable (numerator) by another variable (denominator), verify that the denominator is not zero so you don't throw a divide-by-zero exception.

Sometimes, you can't preemptively check for a potential error. For example, you are reading from a network stream when the network connection is abruptly lost. For situations like this, you can use the *try (try block)*, *catch (catch block)*, or *finally (finally block)* keywords.

The try block is used with a code block that contains the code that might fail. You want to *try* to execute the code block. The try block requires a catch block, a finally block, or both.

The catch block will have the exception passed to it, so you have access to the exception within your code. The catch block is automatically executed if the code in the try block throws an exception. In that case, program execution immediately jumps to the catch block without executing further statements in the try block.

The finally block is executed after the try block successfully completes or the catch block completes. The intent of the finally block is to provide a place for cleanup code because the finally block executes regardless of whether an exception was thrown.

The following code example illustrates the use of try, catch, and finally blocks:

```
try{
    undefinedFunction()
    alert('Made it, so undefinedFunction exists')
}
catch(ex){
    alert('The following error occurred: ' + ex.message)
}
finally{
    alert('Finally block executed')
}
```

In this example, if the undefinedFunction function exists and doesn't throw an exception, you get two alerts the first alert is Made It, So undefinedFunction Exists, and the second alert is Finally Block Executed.

If the undefinedFunction function does not exist, an exception is thrown, and you receive two alerts: the first alert is The Following Error Occurred, and the second alert is Finally Block Executed. An exception was thrown because undefinedFunction didn't exist, and the program immediately jumped to the catch block without executing the rest of the try block.

Remember that the finally block always executes either after the try block completes successfully or after the catch block executes. If the catch block throws an exception, the finally block executes before the exception is passed to the calling routine.

Lesson summary

- JavaScript is untyped, so when you create a variable, you don't need to specify its type.
- JavaScript defines the following built-in objects: the global object, the Object object, the Function object, the Array object, the String object, the Boolean object, the Number object, the Math object, the Date object, the RegExp object, the JSON object, and several types of Error objects.
- In JavaScript, all numeric values are internally represented as floating point values.
- The typeof operator is a unary operator that returns a string that indicates the operand's type.
- The && and || operators are short-circuiting operators.
- Use camel casing for variable names.
- Scoping is the context within a computer program in which a variable name is valid and can be used to access the variable.
- In JavaScript, there are essentially two scopes, global and local, but you can create nested local scopes by nesting functions.
- For no value coalescing, use the || operator.
- Use two equal signs (==) to test for equality, and use three equal signs (===) to test for same type and equality.
- The while loop executes zero to many times, and the do loop executes one to many times.
- The for loop executes zero to many times and has a *counter* variable.
- Use the break keyword to exit from the current loop.
- Use the try, catch, and finally keywords to handle exceptions.

Lesson review

Answer the following questions to test your knowledge of the information in this lesson. You can find the answers to these questions and explanations of why each answer choice is correct or incorrect in the "Answers" section at the end of this chapter.

1. Your application prompts the user to enter his or her age, which is placed in an *age* variable. A user ran the application and entered I Don't Know for the age. The application then multiplies age by two. What is the result?

   A. undefined
   B. null

    C. NaN

    D. infinity

2. Which of the following represent valid variable declarations? (Choose all that apply.)

    A. *var switch;*

    B. *var myChar;*

    C. *var $cost;*

    D. *var _total;*

    E. *var 1to1;*

    F. *var tooGood4u;*

3. In your application, you want to display a personalized message to the user, if the user's name is populated, in the *userName* variable, but if *userName* is empty, you want to use Valued User instead. How can you accomplish this most efficiently?

    A. var personalized = 'Hello ' + (userName ?? 'Valued User');

    B. var personalized = 'Hello ' + (userName || 'Valued User');

    C. var personalized = 'Hello ' + (userName && 'Valued User');

    D. var personalized = 'Hello ' + (userName + 'Valued User');

Lesson 2: Writing, testing, and debugging JavaScript

The previous lesson presented an in-depth introduction to JavaScript, and you're probably ready to start writing some code, which is what this lesson explains. It starts with writing code, using test-driven development practices. Along the way, a new project is created, and a JavaScript file is added, using the *<script>* element. Finally, this lesson covers the JavaScript debugging features in Visual Studio.

When working with a programming language, you'll probably want to create a Hello World program so you can see what is required to get a simple program to run. Although a Hello World program was created previously, it was created by using HTML. This time, you create a JavaScript version of the Hello World program.

After this lesson, you will be able to:

- Describe test-driven development (TDD).
- Set up a web application for TDD.
- Set up a Windows 8 application for TDD.
- Debug JavaScript code.

Estimated lesson time: 45 minutes

Hello World from JavaScript

There are several ways to write a Hello World program, and they differ primarily in how you want to display the Hello World message. For example, you can programmatically make the Hello World text visible or invisible on an HTML page, or you can display an alert message with Hello World in it. These are good examples, but it would be better if the first example started you on the correct way of writing JavaScript code. Try doing the Hello World from a test-driven perspective.

Writing test-driven code

Test-driven development (TDD) is a great way to write code and learn about code. One of the benefits is that you can write your test without having to write a user interface. It's also easy to prototype code. TDD makes it easy to write a bit of code to see whether the code works the way you expected. Best of all, it's easy to get started.

There are many add-ins for writing test-driven code, but the choices are relatively few for test-driven JavaScript code. Probably the most common tool is QUnit, which can be used with ASP.NET web applications; for Windows 8 applications, a variant to QUnit is QUnit-Metro.

Setting up QUnit with ASP.NET applications

To set up QUnit with an ASP.NET application, you must first start Visual Studio Express 2012 for Web and create a web application. In this example, the ASP.NET Empty Web Application is created.

In the Solution Explorer window, right-click the project node and click Manage NuGet Packages. This displays the Manage NuGet Packages window. NuGet is an open-source package-management system for the .NET platform that simplifies the addition of third-party libraries into your code. Click the Online node, and then, in the Search Online text box, type **QUnit** and click the magnifying glass to perform the search. The results display similar to Figure 3-4. Keep in mind that your result screen might be different due to the many new packages that are being released, so be sure to look for the QUnit for ASP.NET MVC package.

Click QUnit For ASP.NET MVC; you should see an Install button. Click the Install button to install QUnit For ASP.NET MVC into your project. After the package is installed, you should see a check mark where the Install button was located. Click the Close button to close the Manage NuGet Packages screen. Note that this QUnit for ASP.NET MVC package works with both model, view, controller (MVC) applications and ASP.NET web applications, although the cascading style sheet that is added is not in the standard style sheet location for ASP.NET applications. (For the time being, we'll leave the style sheet alone.)

After the QUnit for ASP.NET MVC package has been added, you see a packages.config file, which contains a reference to your package. The Scripts folder contains a file called qunit.js, which contains the QUnit source code. The Content folder contains a qunit.css file, which contains the cascading style sheet for QUnit.

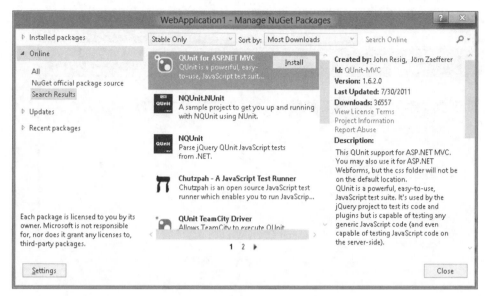

FIGURE 3-4 The NuGet search results containing QUnit For ASP.NET MVC

Next, add a default.html page by right-clicking the project node (in the Solution Explorer window) and click Add; choose HTML Page. Name the file **default.html** and click OK. Make the default.html file your startup page by right-clicking the default.html file and choosing Set As Start Page. Modify the default.html file to look like the following example, in which the inserted lines are in bold:

```
<!DOCTYPE html>
<html xmlns="http://www.w3.org/1999/xhtml">
<head>
    <title></title>
    <link rel="stylesheet" type="text/css" href="Content/qunit.css" />
    <script type="text/javascript" src="Scripts/qunit.js"></script>
</head>
<body>
    <h1 id="qunit-header">QUnit example</h1>
    <h2 id="qunit-banner"></h2>
    <div id="qunit-testrunner-toolbar"></div>
    <h2 id="qunit-userAgent"></h2>
    <ol id="qunit-tests"></ol>
    <div id="qunit-fixture">test markup, will be hidden</div>
</body>
</html>
```

The QUnit setup is done, but in this file, you still need to add references to the code that will be tested and the actual tests. Your code and your tests should be in separate files, so you will be adding at least two references. Navigating to Debug and choosing Start Debugging causes the QUnit summary screen to be displayed, as shown in Figure 3-5.

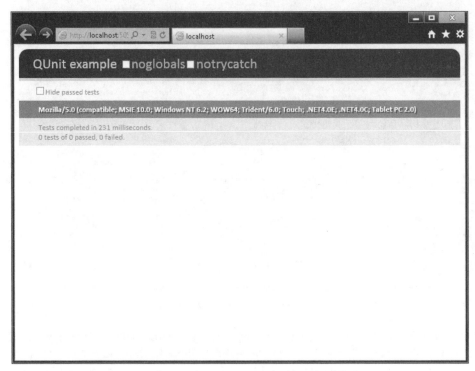

FIGURE 3-5 The QUnit summary screen showing 0 tests of 0 passed, 0 failed

This screen is showing that no tests have passed and no tests have failed because you have no tests yet. It's time to add a Hello World test to the application.

A default.js file and a tests.js file need to be added to the Scripts folder by right-clicking the Scripts folder and choosing Add. Choose the JavaScript file. Name the file **default.js** and click OK. Do the same for the tests.js file.

A reference to these files needs to be added to the default.html file. With the default.html file open, drag the default.js file out to the source of the default.html file and drop the file right after the last ending script tag (</script>). Drag the tests.js file out and drop it after the last ending script tag. Your results should look like the following, in which the inserted lines are bold:

```
<!DOCTYPE html>
<html xmlns="http://www.w3.org/1999/xhtml">
<head>
    <title></title>
    <link rel="stylesheet" type="text/css" href="Content/qunit.css" />
    <script  src="Scripts/qunit.js"></script>
    <script  src="Scripts/default.js"></script>
    <script  src="Scripts/tests.js"></script>
</head>
<body>
    <h1 id="qunit-header">QUnit example</h1>
```

```
    <h2 id="qunit-banner"></h2>
    <div id="qunit-testrunner-toolbar"></div>
    <h2 id="qunit-userAgent"></h2>
    <ol id="qunit-tests"></ol>
    <div id="qunit-fixture">test markup, will be hidden</div>
</body>
</html>
```

Now write the first test. When using TDD, always write the test first, run it to see the test fail, and then add code to make the test pass. In the tests.js file, add the following test to see whether a *greeting* variable contains Hello World:

```
test("A Hello World Test", 1, function () {
    equal(greeting, "Hello World", "Expect greeting of Hello World");
});
```

Here is an overview of what's happening with this code. The code is calling a test function, which is included in the QUnit source code. A function is a block of code that you can call to perform one or more actions. The test function requires three parameters. The first parameter is a freeform description of the test, which is A Hello World Test. The description of the test is displayed in the QUnit summary screen when you run the tests. The second parameter, which has a value of one, represents the quantity of assertions that you expect to perform within the test function. The third parameter is an anonymous function. An *anonymous function* is a block of code that has no name and can perform one or more actions. This is where you add any code to execute, and then you perform assertions to verify that the test is successful. In this anonymous function, the equal function is being called to see whether the *greeting* variable contains Hello World. The equal function takes three parameters. The first parameter is the actual value, in this case, the *greeting* variable. The second parameter is the expected value, Hello World. The third parameter is a message that you want to display, in this case, Expect Greeting Of Hello World.

Because you have not created a *greeting* variable, this test should fail. When you run the tests (click Debug and choose Start Debugging), you should see the failed test with a red indicator. Figure 3-6 shows the QUnit summary screen with the failed test.

The test failed with a message that states that "greeting" is undefined. Now, to make the test pass, add the following code, which declares a greeting variable and assigns a value of Hello World in the default.js file:

```
var greeting = 'Hello World';
```

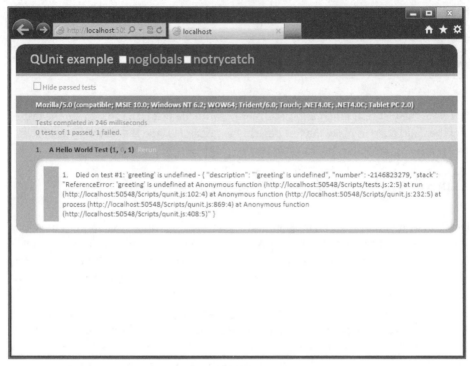

FIGURE 3-6 The QUnit summary screen showing a failed test

Save all files by navigating to File and choosing Save All (or Ctrl+Shift+S) and then run the application again. If you see the same error, try pressing Ctrl+F5 in the browser window to clear the browser cache. You should see that the test now passes because *greeting* is defined and initialized to Hello World. In the QUnit summary screen, you should see a message that states 1 Tests Of 1 Passed, 0 Failed. If you click the test, you should see the test showing a green indicator, as shown in Figure 3-7.

As you add more features to your application, just add another test that defines or helps shape each feature, and then write the code to make the test pass.

FIGURE 3-7 QUnit summary screen showing the successful Hello World test

Setting up QUnit-Metro with Windows 8 applications

To set up QUnit with a Windows 8 application, you must first start Visual Studio Express 2012 for Windows 8 and create a JavaScript | Windows Store application. In this example, Blank App is created.

In the Solution Explorer window, right-click the project node and click Manage NuGet Packages. This displays the Manage NuGet Packages window. NuGet is an open-source package management system for the .NET platform that simplifies the addition of third-party libraries to your code. Click the Online node and then, in the Search Online text box, enter **QUnit-Metro** and click the magnifying glass to perform the search. The results display, similar to Figure 3-8. Your result screen might be different due to the many new packages that are being released, so be sure to look for the QUnit-Metro package.

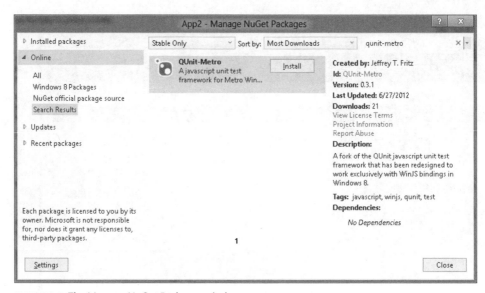

FIGURE 3-8 The Manage NuGet Packages window

Click the QUnit-Metro package; you should see an Install button. Click the Install button to install QUnit-Metro in your project. After the package is installed, you should see a check mark where the Install button was located. Click the Close button to close the Manage NuGet Packages screen.

After the QUnit-Metro package has been added, you see a packages.config file that contains a reference to your package. The js folder contains a new file, qunitmetro.js, which contains the QUnit-Metro source code. The css folder contains new cascading style sheets, called qunitmetro.css, qunitmetro-dark.css, and qunitmetro-light.css. You use the qunitmetro.css to get the default presentation, but you can add either the qunitmetro-dark.css or the qunitmetro-light.css file to your test page to make the QUnit-Metro screen look more like a Windows 8 application.

Blank App already has a default.html page. Modify the default.html file to look like the following example, in which the inserted lines are in bold:

```
<!DOCTYPE html>
<html>
<head>
    <meta charset="utf-8" />
    <title>App2</title>

    <!-- WinJS references -->
    <link href="//Microsoft.WinJS.1.0/css/ui-dark.css" rel="stylesheet" />
    <script src="//Microsoft.WinJS.1.0/js/base.js"></script>
    <script src="//Microsoft.WinJS.1.0/js/ui.js"></script>

    <!-- App2 references -->
    <link href="/css/default.css" rel="stylesheet" />
    <script src="/js/default.js"></script>
```

```
<!--QUnit-Metro references-->
<link rel="stylesheet" type="text/css" href="css/qunitmetro.css" />
<link rel="stylesheet" type="text/css" href="css/qunitmetro-dark.css" />
<script type="text/javascript" src="js/qunitmetro.js"></script>

</head>
<body>
    <h1>Tests</h1>
    <div id="appBar" data-win-control="WinJS.UI.AppBar" data-win-options=""></div>
</body>
</html>
```

The QUnit-Metro setup is done, but in this file, you still need to add a reference to the test code file. Your code and your tests should be in separate files. You already have a reference to the default.js file, so you will be adding one more reference. Navigating to Debug and choosing Start Debugging displays the default.html file. Right-click the screen to display the application bar at the bottom and click Run Tests. The QUnit summary screen is displayed, as shown in Figure 3-9.

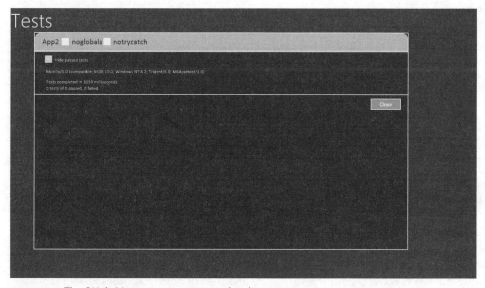

FIGURE 3-9 The QUnit-Metro summary screen showing no tests run

This screen is showing that no tests have passed and no tests have failed because you have no tests yet. Now, add a Hello World test to the application.

A tests.js file must be added to the js folder by right-clicking the js folder and navigating to Add | New Item | JavaScript File. Name the file **tests.js** and click OK.

Next, a reference to this file must be added to the default.html file. With the default.html file open, drag the tests.js file out to the source of the default.html file and drop the file right after the last ending script tag (</script>). Your results should look like the following, in which the inserted line is bold:

```
<!DOCTYPE html>
<html>
<head>
    <meta charset="utf-8" />
    <title>App2</title>

    <!-- WinJS references -->
    <link href="//Microsoft.WinJS.1.0/css/ui-dark.css" rel="stylesheet" />
    <script src="//Microsoft.WinJS.1.0/js/base.js"></script>
    <script src="//Microsoft.WinJS.1.0/js/ui.js"></script>

    <!-- App2 references -->
    <link href="/css/default.css" rel="stylesheet" />
    <script src="/js/default.js"></script>

    <!--QUnit-Metro references-->
    <link rel="stylesheet" type="text/css" href="css/qunitmetro.css" />
    <link rel="stylesheet" type="text/css" href="css/qunitmetro-dark.css" />
    <script src="js/qunitmetro.js"></script>
    <script src="js/tests.js"></script>

</head>
<body>
    <h1>Tests</h1>
    <div id="appBar" data-win-control="WinJS.UI.AppBar" data-win-options=""></div>
</body>
</html>
```

Now you can write the first test. When using TDD, always write the test first, run it to see the test fail, and then add code to make the test pass. In the tests.js file, add the following test to see whether a *greeting* variable contains Hello World:

```
test("A Hello World Test", function () {
    equal(greeting, "Hello World", "Expect greeting of Hello World");
});
```

Here is an overview of what's happening with this code. The code is calling a test function, which is included in the QUnit source code and requires two parameters. The first parameter is the name of the test, which is A Hello World Test. The name of the test is displayed in the QUnit summary screen when you run the tests. The second parameter is an anonymous function, in which you add any code to execute and then perform assertions to verify that the test is successful. In this anonymous function, the equal function is called to see whether the *greeting* variable contains Hello World. The equal function takes three parameters. The first parameter is the actual value, in this case, the *greeting* variable. The second parameter is the expected value, Hello World. The third parameter is a message you want to display, in this case, Expect Greeting Of Hello World.

Because you have not created a *greeting* variable, this test should fail. When you run the tests (click Debug, choose Start Debugging, right-click the screen, and choose Run Tests), you should see the failed test with a red indicator. Figure 3-10 shows the QUnit summary screen with the failed test.

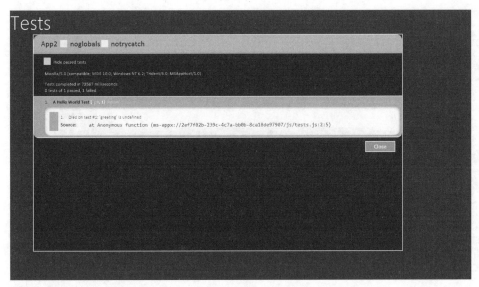

FIGURE 3-10 The QUnit-Metro summary screen showing the failed test

The test failed with a message that states that greeting is undefined. Now, you make the test pass. In the bottom of the default.js file, add the following code that declares a *greeting* variable and assigns a value of Hello World:

```
var greeting = 'Hello World';
```

Save all files by clicking File and choosing Save All (or pressing Ctrl+Shift+S) and then run the application again. You should see that the test now passes because greeting is defined and initialized to Hello World. In the QUnit-Metro summary screen, you should see a message that states 1 Tests Of 1 Passed, 0 Failed. If you click the test, you should see a green indicator, as shown in Figure 3-11.

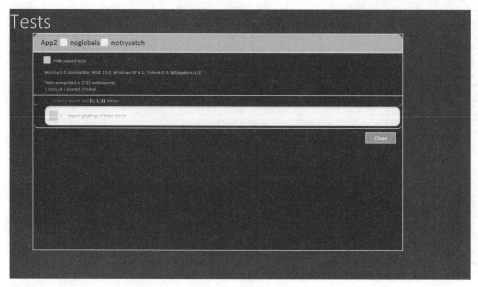

FIGURE 3-11 The QUnit-Metro summary screen showing the passing test

As you add more features to your application, you add another test that defines or helps shape each feature, and then write the code to make the test pass.

Using the script tag

In the previous sections, links to JavaScript files were added to HTML documents by dragging the JavaScript file from the Solution Explorer window and dropping it on the HTML document. Upon dropping, a *<script>* element is added that references the JavaScript file.

The *<script>* element can define a JavaScript code block or load an external JavaScript file, but not both.

The following is an example of using the *<script>* element to define a JavaScript code block within the HTML document:

```
<script type="text/javascript">
<!--
    function Add(x, y) {
        return x + y;
    }
    alert(Add(3, 2));
//-->
</script>
```

The type attribute specifies the MIME type, which was required in earlier versions of HTML but is optional in HTML5.

Next is the beginning of an HTML comment. Notice that the bottom contains a JavaScript comment and an HTML end comment. This is the recommended method for dealing with browsers that don't support the script element. Without the comment, the browser would just render the JavaScript source to the screen.

This script defines an add function. An alert is executed that calls the add function and sends the results to the alert function. Notice that the call to the alert function is not within a function; this call is inline. As this HTML document is being loaded, the browser reaches the alert call and, because it's inline, the alert call is immediately executed.

The following is an example of a *<script>* element referencing an external JavaScript file:

```
<script type="text/javascript" src="Scripts/tests.js"></script>
```

The src attribute references the external JavaScript file. When the src attribute is included, the content of the *<script>* element must be empty. It's important to use an explicit end tag to prevent problems in some browsers.

For external JavaScript files, the following attributes can also be used:

- **async** A Boolean attribute specifying that the script is executed asynchronously while the page continues the parsing.
- **defer** A Boolean attribute specifying that the script is executed after the page has finished parsing.

If async and defer are not present, the script is fetched when the HTML parser reaches the script element and is executed immediately, before the browser continues parsing the page. For large HTML documents and large JavaScript files, the result is that the page takes much longer to render.

> **NOTE** **USING ASYNC AND DEFER**
>
> Be careful when using async and defer. First, not all browsers support these attributes yet. Second, when you are loading many external JavaScript files that depend on one another, using these attributes can change the execution order.

Handling browsers that don't support JavaScript

In addition to placing HTML comments around script blocks to keep your JavaScript source from being rendered to the screen when a browser does not support the *<script>* element, you can use the *<noscript>* element to specify alternate content to display. The following is an example of the *<noscript>* element:

```
<script type="text/javascript">
<!--
    function Add(x, y) {
        return x + y;
    }
```

```
    alert(Add(3, 2));
//-->
</script>
<noscript>Your browser does not support JavaScript so page functionality will be
significantly reduced.</noscript>
```

Inline JavaScript vs. external JavaScript files

Placing your JavaScript in the HTML file as inline code is generally undesirable because it limits the amount of reuse you can get from the code. Your goal should be to have unobtrusive JavaScript—good separation of HTML and JavaScript by placing them in separate files.

Is there any benefit of using inline versus external files? As the size of the HTML and JavaScript code increases, you will see a large performance gain by placing JavaScript in external files because most browsers cache the JavaScript files.

 Quick check

- You are creating a webpage that will require a lot of JavaScript code. Is it better to put all the JavaScript in your HTML file or to put it in a separate JavaScript file?

Quick check answer

- It is better to place the JavaScript code in a separate JavaScript file because the JavaScript file will be cached, and it's best to provide unobtrusive JavaScript.

Placing your script elements

In many of the HTML documents you examine, you will see that the *<script>* elements are typically within the *<head>* element, primarily because that's where everyone was told to put them. The *<head>* element is for things that should not show on the rendered page, right?

From a performance perspective, it's unproductive to put *<script>* elements in the *<head>* element because the browser will stop parsing, retrieve the JavaScript file, and execute the JavaScript before continuing to parse the rest of the HTML document. Nothing has been displayed yet because the parser is in the *<head>* element and hasn't reached the *<body>* element. The result is that you see an empty browser window while the JavaScript files are being loaded.

Put JavaScript script tags at the end of the HTML document unless you have a compelling reason not to do so.

One such reason for placing a *<script>* element in the *<head>* element is that you might have JavaScript that must exist early so the page can render properly. If so, move as little as possible to the *<head>* element to minimize the performance cost. Also, place these external references after your style sheet references so the browser attempts to load both at the same time.

When placing your *<script>* elements at the bottom of the HTML document, they should be just before the *</body>* tag. This guarantees that the document object model (DOM) has loaded and is visible to the waiting user. This also means that any elements referenced in the JavaScript will be present on the page.

Using the Visual Studio .NET JavaScript debugger

The best developers are those who know how to run the debugger. You can learn much about an application by pausing the execution of an application and exploring the application variables. If you can step through the application while troubleshooting, you can understand how the program works and find problems quickly.

Visual Studio 2012 supports debugging JavaScript better than any previous version of Visual Studio. This section introduces you to JavaScript debugging.

The previous lesson covered nested functions, and the example was a nested function to calculate the area of a slice of pizza. If you know the formula for this calculation, you can calculate the area of an 18-inch pizza and divide by 8 because there will be eight pieces per pizza. The formula is areaPerPiece = (pi x (*pizzaRadius*) x (*pizzaRadius*))/*piecesPerPizza*. To get the *pizzaRadius*, divide the *pizzaDiameter* (18 inches) by 2 to get a *pizzaRadius* of 9 inches. Therefore, the formula is (3.141592 * 9 * 9)/8, which equals 31.808619 square inches. The test should look like the following:

```
test('Area of Pizza Slice', 1, function(){
    equal(areaOfPizzaSlice(18,8), 31.808619, 'Expected 31.808619');
});
```

When you run the test, it will fail with the message 'areaOfPizzaSlice' is undefined, so you add the areaOfPizzaSlice code as follows:

```
function areaOfPizzaSlice(diameter, slicesPerPizza) {
    return areaOfPizza(diameter) / slicesPerPizza;
    function areaOfPizza(diameter) {
        var radius = diameter / 2;
        return 3.141592 * radius * radius;
    }
}
```

Next, run the test. It should pass. You now have some code that you can step through and debug.

Setting a breakpoint

You can set a breakpoint in your JavaScript by clicking the line of code and pressing F9 or by clicking Debug and choosing Toggle Breakpoint. If you set a breakpoint on the second line of the areaOfPizzaSlice function, you should see a burgundy-colored dot to the left of the line, and all or part of the line will also be burgundy-colored, depending on where your cursor was when you set the breakpoint. Figure 3-12 shows the code with the breakpoint set. You can also click the gray vertical bar (where the breakpoint is showing in Figure 3-12) to set a breakpoint.

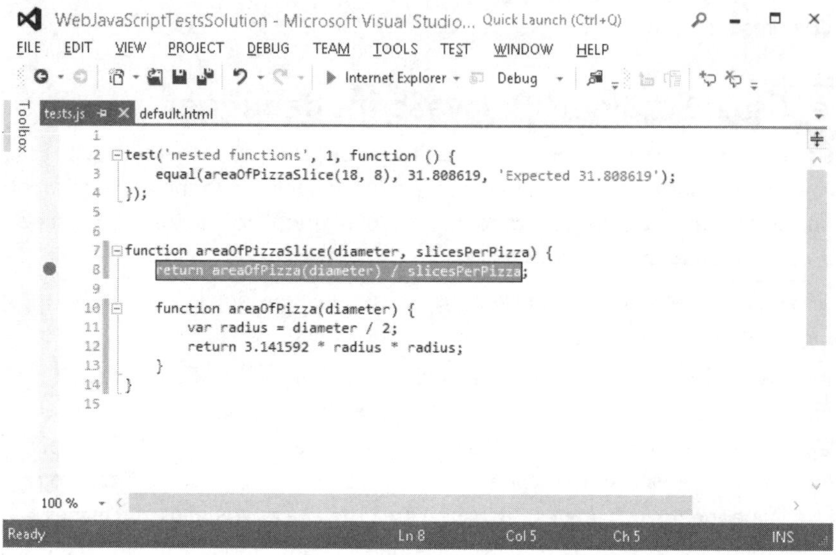

FIGURE 3-12 Press F9 to set a breakpoint

Now that you have set a breakpoint, if you press F5 (Debug | Start Debugging) to run the test, you should hit the breakpoint. When you hit the breakpoint, the program pointer is displayed in yellow on that line. Now that you're in break mode, you can examine the variables.

Examining variables

One of the easiest ways to examine variables when in break mode is just to use your mouse cursor to point to the variable. This causes a ToolTip to display with the variable information, as shown in Figure 3-13.

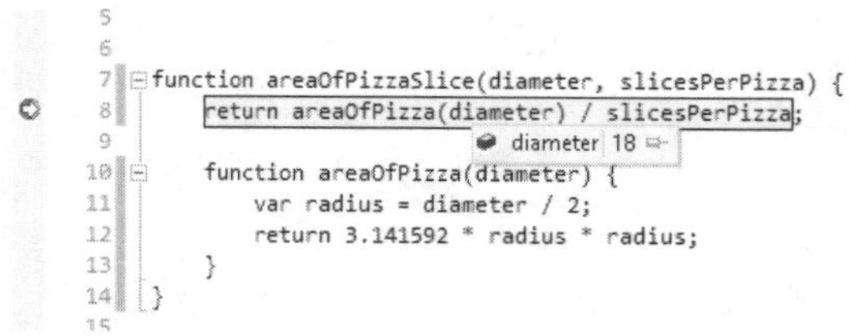

FIGURE 3-13 In break mode, pointing to a variable to get its information

In the figure, you can see that the diameter was pointed to, and the tooltip was displayed, showing its value of 18. If you point to slicesPerPizza, you see a tooltip displaying the value of 8.

Another way to explore the variables is to view the Locals window, which displays all variables that are in scope, including the special *this* variable, which is the current object.

Normally, when you are in break mode, you see the Locals window on the lower right of the Visual Studio window. If the Locals window is not visible and you are in break mode, you can display the Locals window by navigating to Debug | Windows | Locals. You should see the Locals window, as shown in Figure 3-14.

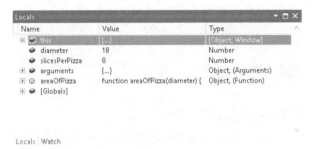

FIGURE 3-14 The Locals window displaying all variables that are in scope

As a program grows, the Locals window fills with variables that might not interest you, but you might see several variables you want to keep watching. In Figure 3-14, the Watch tab is in the lower-left corner. If you click this tab, you see the Watch window. This window enables you to add the variables that interest you. You can click the empty line, type the name of the variable, and press Enter, or, in the code window, you can highlight the variable (usually by double-clicking it) and drag and drop it into the Watch window. Figure 3-15 shows the use of the Watch window.

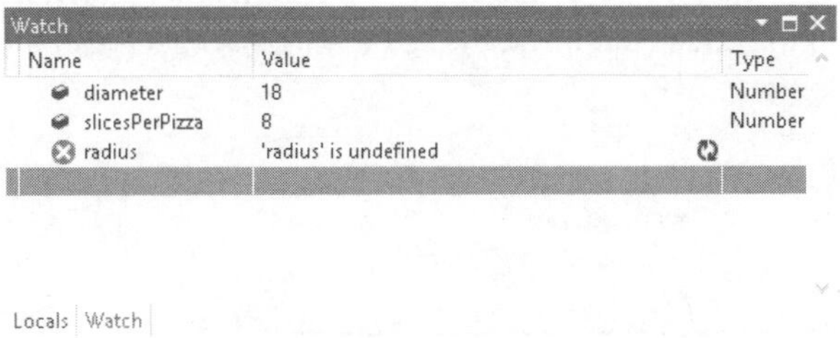

FIGURE 3-15 Using the Watch window to add the variables that interest you

Notice in Figure 3-15 that the radius is listed as undefined. This is because the program hasn't reached the nested function where radius is declared and set.

Stepping through the code

Now that you're in break mode, you can step through the code by pressing F11 (Debug | Step Into), F10 (Debug | Step Over), or Shift+F11 (Debug | Step Out). These options are also on the toolbar. The current line of code returns the area of the pizza slice if you press F10 because stepping over means that you want to execute all the code in the current statement and then go back to break mode on the next statement.

By pressing F11, you step into the areaOfPizza function. When you're in the function, press F11 again to set the radius. You should be able to point to the radius to see that the value was set to 9 and, in the Locals window, radius is displaying a value of 9. The color is red, which indicates that this value has changed since the last time you were in break mode.

If you swipe across 3.141592 * radius * radius and then right-click the selection, you can add Watch, which adds this expression to the Watch window. You can also add Parallel Watch, which, in a multithreaded application, displays the Watch expression with its value for each thread that has a value. Figure 3-16 shows the Parallel Watch window, which is visible after you add a parallel watch.

FIGURE 3-16 The Parallel Watch window showing the value of the expression for each thread that has a value

In Figure 3-16, the window is presented as a grid in which the first row contains the column headings and each additional row represents a thread with a value. Each expression that's added will add another column to the grid.

When right-clicking the expression, you can Pin To Source, which pins a tooltip on the source window that shows the value of the expression, as shown in Figure 3-17. After pinning, you can drag the tooltip to anywhere in the code editor, and the value will be at that location until you click the X in the upper-left corner.

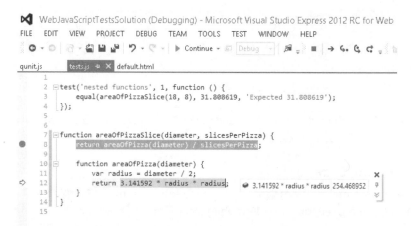

FIGURE 3-17 The Pin To Source option that pins a ToolTip to the code

You can click the chevron symbol (bottom symbol with double v) to add a comment to this expression, too.

When you're ready to run the application at full speed, you can press F5 (Debug | Continue).

Lesson summary

- TDD provides a great way to write code and learn about code.
- QUnit can be used to perform TDD with web applications.
- QUnit-Metro can be used to perform TDD with Windows 8 applications.
- NuGet is an open-source package management system for the .NET platform that simplifies the addition of third-party libraries into your code.
- When creating tests, always create a failing test first, and then add code to make the test pass.
- Always try to keep your JavaScript code separate from your HTML.
- For best performance, place the *<script>* elements at the bottom of the HTML document, before the *</body>* tag.
- You can set a breakpoint in your JavaScript by clicking the statement and pressing F9 (Debug | Toggle Breakpoint).
- You can step through code by pressing F11 (Debug | Step Into), F10 (Debug | Step Over), or Shift+F11 (Debug | Step Out).

Lesson review

Answer the following questions to test your knowledge of the information in this lesson. You can find the answers to these questions and explanations of why each answer choice is correct or incorrect in the "Answers" section at the end of this chapter.

1. You are creating a new Windows 8 application, and you want to set up TDD for your JavaScript code. Which testing framework will you use?

   A. QUnit

   B. QUnit-Metro

   C. Microsoft Test

   D. NUnit

2. What are the steps for TDD?

   A. Write the passing test, write the code, run the test again to validate that it still passes.

   B. Write the failing test, write the code, run the test again to validate that it passes.

   C. Write the code, write the test to validate that it passes, run the test again to validate that it still passes.

   D. Write the passing test, write the code, break the code, run the test again to validate that it fails.

3. Where should your JavaScript code be placed?

   A. In the <head> element of your HTML document.

   B. Just before the </body> tag.

   C. You should always place your JavaScript code in separate files, external to your HTML document.

   D. Inside the <body> element, at the top.

Lesson 3: Working with objects

In this chapter, you've seen a lot of JavaScript basics, but some elements haven't been discussed. You still need to know how to access existing objects and how to create and use an array, which is a special JavaScript object. You also need to know how to be notified when something changes on an object. Creating your own custom objects is covered in Chapter 6, "Essential JavaScript and jQuery."

This lesson explains arrays, the document object model (DOM), and how you can access the DOM by using JavaScript. The lesson goes on to describe event notifications, which enable you to subscribe to DOM events.

After this lesson, you will be able to:

- Create and modify an array of items.
- Navigate the DOM by using JavaScript.
- Subscribe to DOM events.

Estimated lesson time: 60 minutes

Working with arrays

 An *array* is a collection object that has a sequence of items you can access and modify. The array is assigned to a variable, and you can access its items by using its indexer, which is square brackets ([ ]). Because the collection of items is in one variable, you can easily pass the array to a function. You can also loop through the items in the array as needed.

Creating and populating an array

There are three ways to create an array. It doesn't matter which method you choose, although your choice typically will be based on the array implementation in the program:

- **Inserting items with the indexer** The array is created by using the *new* keyword, which creates an instance of the Array object. After the array is created and assigned to a variable, items are added to the array by using the index number, which is zero-based. For inserting new items, the index number must be the size of the array.

For example, after the array is created, its size is zero, so zero is used to insert the first item. Using this method, items can be added anywhere in the program. Note that if you use an index number that is higher than the quantity of items that currently exist, you add empty items to the array. For example, if you currently have only one item in the array but specify an index number of 2, you will add your item with an index number of 2, and an empty item will be added at index number 1. The following is an example of creating the array and adding items:

```
var pizzaParts = new Array();
pizzaParts[0] = 'pepperoni';
pizzaParts[1] = 'onion';
pizzaParts[2] = 'bacon';
```

- **Condensed array** The array is created by using the *new* keyword, which creates an instance of the Array object, and all items are passed into the Array object's constructor. The condensed method is convenient, but you need to know all items at the time you create the array. The following is an example of creating the populated array:

```
var pizzaParts = new Array('pepperoni', 'onion', 'bacon');
```

- **Literal array** The array is created by supplying the item list, enclosed in square brackets. This is very similar to the condensed array; it just requires less typing. The following is an example of the literal array:

```
var pizzaParts = ['pepperoni', 'onion', 'bacon'];
```

Accessing the array items

To access the items in the array, use the indexer. Remember that the array is zero-based, and if you try using a number that's greater than the quantity of items in the array, a value of undefined is returned. The following example retrieves the onion:

```
var secondItem = pizzaParts[1];
```

Modifying the array items

You also use the indexer when you want to modify the items in the array. If you try using a number that's greater than the quantity of items in the array, no exception is thrown. Instead, the item is added to the array, and the array size grows to the number you used plus one. The following example modifies the onion by setting its value to cheese:

```
pizzaParts[1] = 'cheese';
```

Understanding array properties

Each piece of data objects can hold is called a *property*. Some properties are read-only, whereas others are readable and writeable. The Array object has one property that you'll use often, the *length* property. This property is read-only and returns the quantity of items in the array. For example, an array with two items returns 2. The length property is useful when looping through the items in the array. The following example code demonstrates the length property:

```
for(var i=0; i < pizzaParts.length; i++){
   alert(pizzaParts[i]);
}
```

Using array methods

Objects can have their own functions; each object function is called a *method*. The Array object has the following useful methods:

- **concat**   Joins two or more arrays and returns a new array with all the items, as shown in the following example:

```
var pizzaMeatParts = ['pepperoni', 'ham', 'bacon'];
var pizzaVegetableParts = ['pepper', 'onion'];
var pizzaParts = pizzaMeatParts.concat(pizzaVegetableParts);
```

- **indexOf**   Locates the item in the array and returns its index, as shown in the following example, in which the *baconIndex* variable will be set to 2:

```
var pizzaMeatParts = ['pepperoni', 'ham', 'bacon'];
var baconIndex = pizzaMeatParts.indexOf('bacon');
```

- **join**   Creates a string from the items in the array. The items are comma-delimited by default, but you can pass an alternate separator. The following assigns a string containing 'pepperoni, ham, bacon' to the *meatParts* variable:

```
var pizzaMeatParts = ['pepperoni', 'ham', 'bacon'];
var meatParts = pizzaMeatParts.join();
```

- **lastIndexOf**   Searches from the end of the array for the last item in the array that meets the search criteria and returns its index, as shown in the following example, in which the *lastHamIndex* variable will be set to 3:

```
var pizzaMeatParts = ['pepperoni', 'ham', 'bacon', 'ham', 'prosciutto'];
var lastHamIndex = pizzaMeatParts.lastIndexOf('ham');
```

- **pop**   Removes and returns the last element of the array. This reduces the length of the array by one. The following example assigns 'bacon' to the *lastItem* variable:

```
var pizzaMeatParts = ['pepperoni', 'ham', 'bacon'];
var lastItem = pizzaMeatParts.pop();
```

- **push**   Adds a new item to the end of an array and returns the new length, as shown in the following example, in which 'prosciutto' is added to the end of the array and 4 is assigned to the *newLength* variable:

```
var pizzaMeatParts = ['pepperoni', 'ham', 'bacon'];
var newLength = pizzaMeatParts.push('prosciutto');
```

- **reverse** Reverses the order of the items in an array and returns a reference (not a new array) to the reversed array, so the original array is modified. The following example reverses the order of the array:

```
var pizzaMeatParts = ['pepperoni', 'ham', 'bacon', 'prosciutto'];
pizzaMeatParts.reverse();
```

- **shift** Removes and returns the first item in the array. If no items are in the array, the return value is undefined. The following example removes 'pepperoni' from the array and assigns it to the *firstItem* variable:

```
var pizzaMeatParts = ['pepperoni', 'ham', 'bacon'];
var firstItem = pizzaMeatParts.shift();
```

- **slice** Returns a new array that represents part of the existing array. The slice method has two parameters: *start* and *end*. The start parameter is the index of the first item to include in the result. The end parameter is the index of the item that you don't want included in the result. In the following example, the *mySlice* variable will be assigned 'ham' and 'bacon'. Note that 'meatball' is not included in the result, and the original array is not changed:

```
var pizzaMeatParts = ['pepperoni', 'ham', 'bacon', 'meatball', 'prosciutto'];
var mySlice = pizzaMeatParts.slice(1,3);
```

- **sort** Sorts the items in an array and returns a reference to the array. The original array is modified. The following example sorts the array. After sorting, pizzaMeatParts will contain 'bacon', 'ham', 'meatball', 'pepperoni', 'prosciutto':

```
var pizzaMeatParts = ['pepperoni', 'ham', 'bacon', 'meatball', 'prosciutto'];
pizzaMeatParts.sort();
```

- **splice** Adds and removes items from an array and returns the removed items. The original array is modified to contain the result. The splice method's first parameter is the starting index of where to start adding or deleting. The second parameter indicates how many items to remove. If 0 is passed as the second parameter, no items are removed. If the second parameter is larger than the quantity of items available for removal, all items from the starting index to the end of the array are removed. After the first two parameters, you can specify as many items as you want to add. The following example removes 'ham' and 'bacon' from the original array and assigns 'ham' and 'bacon' to *mySlice*. In addition, 'spam' is inserted in pizzaMeatParts, which results in pizzaMeatParts containing 'pepperoni', 'spam', 'meatball', 'prosciutto':

```
var pizzaMeatParts = ['pepperoni', 'ham', 'bacon', 'meatball', 'prosciutto'];
var mySlice = pizzaMeatParts.splice(1,2,'spam');
```

- **toString** All objects have a toString method. For the Array object, toString creates a string from the items in the array. The items are comma-delimited, but if you want a different delimiter, you can use the join method and specify an alternate separator. The following assigns a string containing 'pepperoni,ham,bacon' to the *meatParts* variable:

```
var pizzaMeatParts = ['pepperoni', 'ham', 'bacon'];
var meatParts = pizzaMeatParts.toString();
```

- **unshift**   Adds a new item to the beginning of an array and returns the new length, as shown in the following example, in which 'prosciutto' is added to the beginning of the array and 4 is assigned to the *newLength* variable:

```
var pizzaMeatParts = ['pepperoni', 'ham', 'bacon'];
var newLength = pizzaMeatParts.unshift('prosciutto');
```

- **valueOf**   All objects have a valueOf method. For the Array object, valueOf returns the primitive values of the array as a comma-delimited string, as shown in the following example, which assigns a string containing 'pepperoni,ham,bacon' to the *meatParts* variable:

```
var pizzaMeatParts = ['pepperoni', 'ham', 'bacon'];
var meatParts = pizzaMeatParts.valueOf();
```

 Quick check

- You want to retrieve a new array that is part of an existing array. Which array method should you use?

Quick check answer

- Use the slice method.

Accessing DOM objects

When building an application, the primary objects you must access are the objects that make up the DOM, which represents the HTML document. You need to access the DOM to control the behavior of your HTML document and to be notified when something happens on the page.

Navigating the DOM

The DOM represents a hierarchy of objects, forming a model of your HTML document. To retrieve elements from the DOM, use the built-in *document* variable, which references the DOM, and perform one of the search methods.

 Some of the search methods return a single element, whereas others return an array of elements. The methods that return an array return either a *live NodeList* or a *static NodeList*. The live NodeList represents an array of elements that is continuously updated as the DOM changes, whereas the static NodeList represents a snapshot of elements that doesn't change as the DOM changes. From a performance perspective, it takes longer to create the static

NodeList, so consider working with the search methods that return a live NodeList if you want the best performance. It's important to understand this difference because it can affect your choice of search method.

The following is a list of the DOM search methods with a short description and example:

- **getElementById**   Returns a reference to the first object with specified id, as shown in the following example, which retrieves a reference to the button with the id of btnSave:

```
var btn = document.getElementById('btnSave');
```

- **getElementsByTagName**   Returns a live NodeList, which is a special array of all elements with the specified tag name. The live NodeList automatically updates if you add, delete, or modify elements. The following example returns an array of all images:

```
var images = document.getElementsByTagName('img');
```

- **getElementsByName**   Returns a live NodeList of all elements with the specified name. This works well with option buttons when all their options typically have the same name. The following example retrieves an array of all elements with the name pizzaSize:

```
var pizzaSizes = document.getElementsByName('pizzaSize');
```

- **getElementsByClass**   Not supported in Internet Explorer 8 and earlier. Returns a live NodeList of all elements with the specified CSS class name. CSS classes are examined in more detail in Chapter 4, "Getting started with CSS3." This works well when you have many elements, but you need to group them, possibly to make the elements visible or hidden. The following example retrieves an array of all elements with the class name pizzaPart:

```
var pizzaParts= document.getElementsByClass('pizzaPart');
```

- **querySelector**   Not supported in Internet Explorer 7 and earlier. Accepts a CSS selector as its parameter. Because CSS is described in detail in Chapter 4, this example is simplified. The querySelector method returns the first matched element if one-to-many exist or null if there is no match. In addition to being supported on the document object, the querySelector method exists on the Element object, so you can query either the entire DOM or just an element's content. In the following example, the pound symbol (#) indicates a search for an id. This example returns a reference to the button whose id is btnSave:

```
var btn = document.querySelector('#btnSave');
```

- **querySelectorAll**   Not supported on Internet Explorer 7 and earlier. Accepts a CSS selector as its parameter. Again, because CSS is described in detail in Chapter 4, this example is simplified. The querySelectorAll method returns a static NodeList of all elements that match or an empty array if there is no match. In addition to being supported on the document object, the querySelector method exists on the Element object, so you can query either the entire DOM or just an element's content. In the following example, the period (.) indicates a search for a CSS class name. This example returns a reference to the elements whose CSS class name is pizzaPart:

```
var btn = document.querySelector('.pizzaPart');
```

Working with events

Events provide the spark to the JavaScript engine. An *event* takes place at a point in time. For JavaScript, an event most commonly occurs with user interaction but also occurs when something changes state, such as a video starting or stopping. For example, the user points to an image, clicks a button, or tabs from one text box to another. The DOM provides events to give the developer the ability to subscribe to the event and execute code.

Events are based on the publisher-subscriber design pattern. When an object is created, the developer of the object can expose, or publish, events related to the object. When the object is used, the developer can add event handlers for, or subscribe to, the object's events. Adding an event handler requires the developer to supply a function that is called when the event is triggered. When the event is triggered, all the event subscribers are notified by executing the event handler function.

When an event is triggered, an Event object is passed to the event handler function, which provides information about the event and what was happening at the time, such as the location of the mouse for mouse-related events or the key that was pressed for keyboard events.

Event capturing and event bubbling

If the click event is triggered on a button, and the button is inside a hyperlink, as shown in Figure 3-18, does the hyperlink automatically trigger a click event? If so, which event is triggered first (hyperlink click or button click)?

When a child element is nested within a parent element and the child element triggers a click event, the event is passed down the DOM hierarchy, starting from the document object, which is denoted in Figure 3-18 as #document. This is called *event capturing*. After the event reaches the element that triggered the event, the event is passed back up the hierarchy, which is called *event bubbling*. Figure 3-18 shows capturing and bubbling. Passing the event down and back up the hierarchy gives the developer the opportunity to subscribe on the way down the DOM (capturing), or on the way up (bubbling). The developer can also cancel the event propagation.

Refer to Figure 3-18, in which a button is nested within a hyperlink. When the button is clicked, the capture process takes place where the click event is triggered on the document object, the html object, the body object, the hyperlink, and, finally, on the button object. Next, the bubble process takes place where the click event is triggered on the hyperlink object, the body object, the html object, and, finally, on the document object.

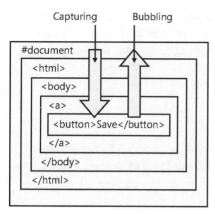

FIGURE 3-18 Events captured down and bubbled up the DOM hierarchy

Subscribing to an event

To subscribe to an event, you can use the addEventListener function, which has three parameters. The first parameter is the event to which you want to subscribe. The second parameter is the function you want to execute when the event is triggered. The third parameter is a Boolean value to specify when your function will execute, where true indicates to execute on event capture and false indicates to execute on event bubble. It's typically preferred to set this parameter to false. The following is an example of subscribing to the click event of a button whose id is btnSave when the saveData function is called during the bubbling of the click event:

```
var btn = document.getElementById('btnSave');
btn.addEventListener('click', saveData, false);
```

When you subscribe to an event by calling addEventListener, existing event listeners are unaffected, meaning that any existing functions that were added will still be executed. In the previous example, if you execute the second line twice, you add a second call to the saveData function, and this function will execute twice when you click the button.

The previous example is the preferred way to subscribe to an event because it is the *W3C-specified* subscription, and this code would be in your JavaScript file. However, you can also subscribe to an event by adding an *inline* subscription to the HTML tag. This is the oldest way to subscribe to events and is compatible with all browsers. When adding to the HTML tag, you must add the prefix "on" to the event name to create the proper attribute name, as shown in the following example, which is equivalent to the previous example, in which the event subscription is added to the bubbling process:

```
<button id='btnSave' onclick='saveData();' >Save</button>
```

A variation of the inline method of subscribing to an event is the *traditional* subscription, which enables you to subscribe to an event in your JavaScript code by using the attribute name, which also adds the event to the bubbling process, as shown in the following example:

```
var btn = document.getElementById('btnSave');
btn.onclick = saveData;
```

Unsubscribing from an event

To unsubscribe from an event, use the removeEventListener function, which has the same three parameters as the addEventListener function. The following is an example of removing the saveData function from the click event of the button whose id is btnSave:

```
var btn = document.getElementById('btnSave');
btn.removeEventListener('click', saveData, false);
```

Canceling event propagation

At any time during the event capture or event bubble process, you might want to stop the propagation of the event. You might have a global event handler assigned at the document object on bubbling of the click event and, after you handled the click event specifically on a button, you don't want the global click event handler to be triggered. To cancel event propagation, use the stopPropagation function on the Event object. The Event object is passed to your event handler function, as shown in the following example:

```
var btn = document.getElementById('btnSave');
btn.addEventListener('click', saveData, false);
function saveData(e){
    //save the data
    e.stopPropagation();
}
```

In this example, if any capture event handler functions existed, they would still execute. When the event reaches the button, saveData uses the passed in Event object to call the stopPropagation function. No bubble event handler functions will execute.

Preventing the default operation

When you click a check box or option button, they have built-in functionality to change their visual appearance to be selected or cleared. When you click a hyperlink, the built-in functionality navigates to the href location. Even if you add a click event for these objects, they still provide their default behavior. To stop the default behavior, you can call the preventDefault method on the Event object, as shown in the following example, which stops the navigation to the href location on the hyperlink:

```
var hyperlink = document.getElementById('lnkSave');
hyperlink.addEventListener('click', saveData, false);
function saveData(e){
    //save the data
    e.preventDefault();
}
```

Working with "this"

When working with events, you will frequently want to access the object that caused the event. In addition, you will want to access the object in a generic way so you can call the same code from the click event of several buttons.

JavaScript provides the *this* keyword. The *this* keyword references the object that caused the event. More explicitly, the *this* keyword provides a reference to the owner of the function. If you assign the function to the click event of a button, the button is the owner of the function. If you assign the function to another button, that button owns the function when that button is clicked.

Window event reference

The built-in *window* variable is an instance of the Window object, which represents the current browser window. The Window object has the following events, which can be applied to the *<body>* tag by adding the "on" prefix:

- **afterprint**   Triggered after the document is printed
- **beforeprint**   Triggered before the document is printed
- **beforeonload**   Triggered before the document loads
- **blur**   Triggered when the window loses focus
- **error**   Triggered when an error occurs
- **focus**   Triggered when the window receives focus
- **haschange**   Triggered when the document has changed
- **load**   Triggered when the document loads
- **message**   Triggered when the message is triggered
- **offline**   Triggered when the document goes offline
- **online**   Triggered when the document comes online
- **pagehide**   Triggered when the window is hidden
- **pageshow**   Triggered when the window becomes visible
- **popstate**   Triggered when the window's history changes
- **redo**   Triggered when the document performs a redo
- **resize**   Triggered when the window is resized
- **storage**   Triggered when a web storage area is updated
- **undo**   Triggered when the document performs an undo
- **unload**   Triggered when the user leaves the document

The following is an example of subscribing to a Window event:

```
window.addEventListener('load', winEvent, false);
function winEvent (e){
    alert('Window Load');
}
```

Form event reference

The following events are triggered by actions inside an HTML form. Although these events apply to all HTML5 elements, they are most common in form elements:

- **blur**   Triggered when an element loses focus
- **change**   Triggered when an element changes
- **contextmenu**   Triggered when a context menu is triggered
- **focus**   Triggered when an element receives focus
- **formchange**   Triggered when a form changes
- **forminput**   Triggered when a form receives user input
- **input**   Triggered when an element receives user input
- **invalid**   Triggered when an element is invalid
- **select**   Triggered when an element is selected
- **submit**   Triggered when a form is submitted

The following is an example of subscribing to a form event:

```
var lastName = document.getElementById('txtLastName');
lastName.addEventListener('focus', gotFocus, false);
function gotFocus (e){
   alert('last name has focus');
}
```

Keyboard event reference

The following events are triggered by the keyboard, and these events apply to all HTML5 elements:

- **keydown**   Triggered when a key is pressed
- **keypress**   Triggered when a key is pressed and released
- **keyup**   Triggered when a key is released

The following is an example of subscribing to a keyboard event. Notice that the keyboard event object has the *which* property that contains the char code of the key that was pressed, and you can convert that to a string as needed:

```
lastName.addEventListener('keypress', keyGotPressed, false);
function keyGotPressed (e){
      var charCode = e.which;
      var charStr = String.fromCharCode(charCode);
      alert(charStr);
}
```

Mouse event reference

The following events are triggered by a mouse or similar user actions, and these events apply to all HTML5 elements:

- **click**   Triggered on a mouse click
- **dblclick**   Triggered on a mouse double-click
- **drag**   Triggered when an element is dragged
- **dragend**   Triggered at the end of a drag operation
- **dragenter**   Triggered when an element has been dragged to a valid drop target
- **dragleave**   Triggered when an element leaves a valid drop target
- **dragover**   Triggered when an element is being dragged over a valid drop target
- **dragstart**   Triggered at the start of a drag operation
- **drop**   Triggered when the dragged element is being dropped
- **mousedown**   Triggered when a mouse button is pressed
- **mousemove**   Triggered when the mouse pointer moves
- **mouseout**   Triggered when the mouse pointer moves out of an element
- **mouseover**   Triggered when the mouse pointer moves over an element
- **mouseup**   Triggered when a mouse button is released
- **mousewheel**   Triggered when the mouse wheel is being rotated
- **scroll**   Triggered when an element's scrollbar is being scrolled

The following is an example of subscribing to a mouse event on the lastName text box:

```
lastName.addEventListener('click', gotClicked, false);
function gotClicked (e){
      alert('Got Clicked');
}
```

Media event reference

The following events are triggered by media such as videos, images, and audio. These events apply to all HTML5 elements, but are most common in media elements such as *<audio>*, *<embed>*, *<img>*, *<object>*, and *<video>*:

- **abort**   Triggered on abort
- **canplay**   Triggered when a file is ready to start playing, which is when it has buffered enough to begin
- **canplaythrough**   Triggered when a file can be played all the way to the end without pausing for buffering
- **durationchange**   Triggered when the length of the media changes
- **emptied**   Triggered when something bad happens and the file is suddenly unavailable, such as when it unexpectedly disconnects
- **ended**   Triggered when the media has reached the end, which is a useful event for messages such as "thanks for listening"
- **error**   Triggered when an error occurs while the file is being loaded

- **loadeddata**   Triggered when media data is loaded

- **loadedmetadata**   Triggered when metadata (such as dimensions and duration) is loaded

- **loadstart**   Triggered just as the file begins to load before anything is actually loaded

- **pause**   Triggered when the media is paused either programmatically or by the user

- **play**   Triggered when the media is ready to start playing

- **playing**   Triggered when the media actually has started playing

- **progress**   Triggered when the browser is in the process of getting the media data

- **ratechange**   Triggered each time the playback rate changes, such as when a user switches to a slow-motion or fast-forward mode

- **readystatechange**   Triggered each time the ready state changes when the ready state tracks the state of the media data

- **seeked**   Triggered when the seeking attribute is set to false, indicating that seeking has ended

- **seeking**   Triggered when the seeking attribute is set to true, indicating that seeking is active

- **stalled**   Triggered when the browser is unable to fetch the media data for any reason

- **suspend**   Triggered when fetching the media data is stopped before it is completely loaded for any reason

- **timeupdate**   Triggered when the playing position has changed, such as when the user fast-forwards to a different point in the media

- **volumechange**   Triggered each time the volume is changed, which includes setting the volume to "mute"

- **waiting**   Triggered when the media has paused but is expected to resume, such as when the media pauses to buffer more data

The following is an example of subscribing to a media event on the *<video>* element:

```
var video = document.getElementById('video');
video.addEventListener('play', playing, false);

function playing(e) {
    alert('Playing');
}
```

Lesson summary

- An *array* is a collection object that has a sequence of items that you can access and modify. You can use the indexer to access items in an array. Use the length property on the array to retrieve the size of the array.

- A function that is defined on an object is called a *method*.

- The Array object has many methods.

- The DOM represents a hierarchy of objects, forming a model of your HTML document.

- An *event* takes place at a point in time.

- Events are based on the publisher or subscriber pattern.

- To subscribe to an event, you can use the addEventListener function. To cancel event propagation, use the stopPropagation function on the Event object. To unsubscribe from an event, use the removeEventListener function. To stop default behavior, call the preventDefault method on the Event object.

- To add an event subscription on an HTML element, add the "on" prefix to the event name to get the name of the attribute you will add to the start tag of the element.

Lesson review

Answer the following questions to test your knowledge of the information in this lesson. You can find the answers to these questions and explanations of why each answer choice is correct or incorrect in the "Answers" section at the end of this chapter.

1. You have two arrays of strings, customers and employees, and you want to combine them to create a contacts array. Which method would be most suitable for this task?

   A. concat

   B. join

   C. push

   D. splice

2. You want to obtain a list of all elements whose tag name is div, and you need to retrieve this list as quickly as possible. Which function is most appropriate for this task?

   A. getElementsByName

   B. querySelectorAll

   C. getElementsByTagName

   D. getElementsByClass

Practice exercises

If you encounter a problem completing any of these exercises, the completed projects can be installed from the Practice Exercises folder that is provided with the companion content.

Exercise 1: Create a calculator webpage

In this exercise, you practice your JavaScript knowledge by creating a website with a single webpage that contains a calculator. The webpage itself will be somewhat basic until CSS is discussed in Chapter 4.

1. If you haven't installed Visual Studio Express 2012 for Web, do so now. You can download this from the Microsoft website.

2. Start Visual Studio. Click File and choose New Project. Navigate to Installed | Templates | Visual Basic or Visual C# | ASP.NET Empty Web Application.

3. Set the name of your application to **WebCalculator**.

4. Select a location for your applications.

5. Set the solution name to **WebCalculatorSolution**.

6. Be sure to keep the Create Directory For Solution check box selected.

7. Click OK to create your new project.

   When the application is created, you will have an empty project.

8. In the Solution Explorer window, add a home page by right-clicking the project node. Click Add, and then choose HTML Page. Name the page **default.html** and click OK.

9. In the Solution Explorer window, right-click the default.html file and choose Set As Start Page.

10. Open the default.html page and enter **Web Calculator** into the *<title>* element.

11. Enter the following HTML into the *<body>* element to provide a basic user interface for the calculator:

```
<input id="txtResult" type="text" readonly="readonly" /><br />
<input id="txtInput" type="text" /><br />
<button id="btn7">7</button>
<button id="btn8">8</button>
<button id="btn9">9</button><br />
<button id="btn4">4</button>
<button id="btn5">5</button>
<button id="btn6">6</button><br />
<button id="btn1">1</button>
<button id="btn2">2</button>
<button id="btn3">3</button><br />
<button id="btnClear">C</button>
<button id="btn0">0</button>
<button id="btnClearEntry">CE</button><br />
<button id="btnPlus">+</button>
<button id="btnMinus">-</button>
```

12. In the Solution Explorer window, add a JavaScript file for your code by right-clicking the Scripts folder; click Add and choose JavaScript File. Set name to **CalculatorLibrary.js,** and click OK.

13. To see what you have so far, press F5 to start debugging the application. You should see a white screen with a crude calculator interface, as shown in Figure 3-19.

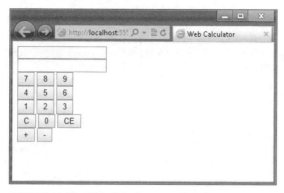

FIGURE 3-19 The Web Calculator user interface

14. Switch back to Visual Studio by pressing Alt+Tab. Notice that the title bar says (Running).

15. Press Shift+F5 to stop debugging. Note that Shift+F5 works only when Visual Studio has the focus. It does not work when the running application has the focus.

Exercise 2: Add the QUnit testing framework

In this exercise, you continue with the project from Exercise 1 and add the QUnit test framework, which will help you with your JavaScript development for the calculator.

1. Open the project from Exercise 1.

If you didn't perform Exercise 1, you can use the project located in the Exercise 2 Start folder.

2. In the Solution Explorer window, add QUnit by right-clicking the WebCalculator node. Click Manage NuGet Packages, choose Online, and type **QUnit** in the search box. Install QUnit for ASP.NET MVC.

3. In the Solution Explorer window, add a JavaScript file for your JavaScript tests by right-clicking the Scripts folder. Click Add and choose JavaScript File. Set name to **tests.js** and click OK.

4. In the Solution Explorer window, add an HTML test page by right-clicking the WebCalculator project node. Click Add and choose HTML Page. Name the page **CalculatorTests.html** and click OK.

5. Add markup in the *<head>* element of the CalculatorTests.html file that adds references to the QUnit.css file, QUnit.js file, CalculatorLibrary.js file, and tests.js file.

6. To complete the QUnit framework setup, add markup in the *<body>* element for the QUnit header, banner, toolbar, user agent tests, and fixture. Your HTML source should look like the following:

```
<!DOCTYPE html>
<html xmlns="http://www.w3.org/1999/xhtml">
<head>
```

```
    <title></title>
    <link rel="stylesheet" type="text/css" href="Content/qunit.css" />
    <script type="text/javascript" src="Scripts/qunit.js"></script>
    <script type="text/javascript" src="Scripts/CalculatorLibrary.js"></script>
    <script type="text/javascript" src="Scripts/tests.js"></script>
</head>
<body>
    <h1 id="qunit-header">QUnit example</h1>
    <h2 id="qunit-banner"></h2>
    <div id="qunit-testrunner-toolbar"></div>
    <h2 id="qunit-userAgent"></h2>
    <ol id="qunit-tests"></ol>
    <div id="qunit-fixture">
        test markup, will be hidden
    </div>
</body>
</html>
```

7. Notice that the *<div>* element for the QUint fixture is a placeholder for HTML markup that you want to access in your tests, where this markup should not render. Copy the HTML markup that is in the default.html file and paste it in the QUnit fixture.

Your HTML source should now look like the following:

```
<!DOCTYPE html>
<html xmlns="http://www.w3.org/1999/xhtml">
<head>
    <title></title>
    <link rel="stylesheet" type="text/css" href="Content/qunit.css" />
    <script type="text/javascript" src="Scripts/qunit.js"></script>
    <script type="text/javascript" src="Scripts/CalculatorLibrary.js">
    </script>
    <script type="text/javascript" src="Scripts/tests.js"></script>
</head>
<body>
    <h1 id="qunit-header">QUnit example</h1>
    <h2 id="qunit-banner"></h2>
    <div id="qunit-testrunner-toolbar"></div>
    <h2 id="qunit-userAgent"></h2>
    <ol id="qunit-tests"></ol>
    <div id="qunit-fixture">
        test markup, will be hidden
        <input id="txtResult" type="text" readonly="readonly" /><br />
        <input id="txtInput" type="text" /><br />
        <button id="btn7">7</button>
        <button id="btn8">8</button>
        <button id="btn9">9</button><br />
        <button id="btn4">4</button>
        <button id="btn5">5</button>
        <button id="btn6">6</button><br />
        <button id="btn1">1</button>
        <button id="btn2">2</button>
        <button id="btn3">3</button><br />
        <button id="btnClear">C</button>
        <button id="btn0">0</button>
```

```
            <button id="btnClearEntry">CE</button><br />
            <button id="btnPlus">+</button>
            <button id="btnMinus">-</button>
        </div>
    </body>
</html>
```

8. Right-click the CalculatorTests.html file and choose Set As Start Page.

It's time to add the first test. The goal of the test is to add a 5 in the txtInput text box when btn5 is clicked. Btn5 is arbitrarily picked, which doesn't matter because you will add code to make all the buttons work. The QUnit object has a trigger method event that can be used to simulate a click on btn5. In the tests.js file, add the following test:

```
test("Btn5 Click Test", function () {
    expect(1);
    var btn = document.getElementById('btn5');
    QUnit.triggerEvent(btn, "click");
    var result = txtInput.value;
    var expected = '5';
    equal(result, expected, 'Expected value: ' + expected + ' Actual value: ' +
result);
});
```

In the previous code example, a txtInput variable is being referenced, but the variable hasn't been declared.

9. In the CalculatorLibrary.js file, add a statement that declares the variable and an initialize function that can be called when each test is run but will be called by the default.html page when it runs the finished code.

10. In the initialize function, add a statement that locates the txtInput text box and assign the result to the *txtInput* variable. Your code should look like the following:

```
var txtInput;

function initialize() {
    txtInput = document.getElementById('txtInput');
}
```

You must modify the tests.js file to call the initialize function as part of a setup function that will run before each test function. Do this by defining a module at the top of the tests.

11. Add the following code to the top of the tests.js file:

```
module('Calculator Test Suite', { setup: function () { initialize(); } });
```

The first parameter of the module definition is the name of the module. The second parameter defines an object that has a setup property. The setup property is assigned a function expression that calls the initialize function before each test.

12. Press F5 to run the test, which should fail, as shown in Figure 3-20, because you don't have any code yet. Notice that the failure states that "5" was expected but actual was "".

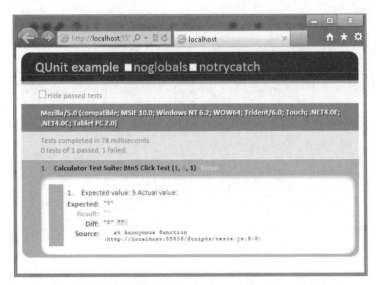

FIGURE 3-20 The failed QUnit test because no code has been added yet

13. In the CalculatorLibrary.js file, add a numberClick function that reads the innerText (textual content of the element) property of the button that was clicked and appends the innerText property to the *txtInput* text box value.

However, if *txtInput* has a value of zero, you should replace its value with the new value so you don't end up with leading zeros in the text box. Your code should look like the following:

```
function numberClick() {
    txtInput.value = txtInput.value =='0' ?
        this.innerText : txtInput.value + this.innerText;
}
```

14. In the initialize function, add JavaScript code to subscribe to the click event of btn5, which will call the numberClick function when btn5 is clicked. The code should look like the following:

```
document.getElementById('btn5').addEventListener('click', numberClick, false);
```

15. Press F5 to run the test, which should pass. Click the test to expand it and see the green indicator, as shown in Figure 3-21.

FIGURE 3-21 The passing test

16. Modify the test by adding a loop to test all the number buttons. Rename the test to **Button Click Test**.

Remember that you are appending to *txtInput*, so you need to test the last character to see whether you got the correct result. You should also add another assertion to the length of the string as you append to *txtInput*. Don't forget that you added code to numberClick to remove leading zeros, and this loop starts by triggering btn0, so your assertion on the length must take that into account. Your test should look like the following:

```
test("Button Click Test", function () {
    var buttonQuantity = 10;
    expect(buttonQuantity * 2);
    for (var i = 0; i < buttonQuantity; i++) {
        var btn = document.getElementById('btn' + i);
        QUnit.triggerEvent(btn, "click");
        var result = txtInput.value[txtInput.value.length-1];
        var expected = String(i);
        equal(result, expected, 'Expected value: ' + expected +
            ' Actual value: ' + result);
        var expectedLength = i < 2 ? 1 : i;
        equal(txtInput.value.length, expectedLength,
            'Expected string length: ' + expectedLength +
            ' Actual value: ' + txtInput.value.length);
    }
});
```

This test sets the *buttonQuantity* variable to 10, and *buttonQuantity* calls the expect function to set the quantity of assertions to expect. There are two assertions per button. The for loop executes 10 times to obtain a reference to the appropriate button, trigger the click event, retrieve the result, perform an assertion that checks the last character of *txtInput*, and perform an assertion that checks the length of *txtInput*.

17. Press F5 to run the test, and all 10 tests will fail. Look closely at each test to understand why each test failed.

You must add code to subscribe to the click event of the number buttons.

18. Fix the failing tests by adding looping code to the initialize function that subscribes to the click event of all ten number buttons.

Your code should look like the following:

```
for (var i = 0; i < 10; i++) {
    document.getElementById('btn'+i).addEventListener('click',
        numberClick, false);
}
```

19. Press F5 to run the test, which should pass.

When btnPlus is clicked, the value in *txtInput* will be added to the value in *txtResult*.

20. In the tests.js file, add a new test to check btnPlus when it's clicked.

Your test code should look like the following:

```
test("Add Test", function () {
    expect(1);
    txtInput.value = '10';
    txtResult.value = '20';
    var btnPlus = document.getElementById('btnPlus');
    QUnit.triggerEvent(btnPlus, "click");
    var expected = '30';
    equal(txtResult.value, expected, 'Expected value: ' + expected +
        ' Actual value: ' + txtResult.value);
});
```

21. Press F5 to run the test and verify that the test fails because you haven't subscribed to the click event of btnPlus.

22. In the initialize function, add code to obtain a reference to the *txtResult* text box and assign it to a new global *txtResult* variable. Add code in the initialize function to subscribe to btnPlus and call the plusClick function. Add the plusClick function with code to add *txtInput* to *txtResult*.

Your code should look like the following:

```
var txtInput;
var txtResult;

function initialize() {
    for (var i = 0; i < 10; i++) {
        document.getElementById('btn'+i).addEventListener('click',
            numberClick, false);
    }
    txtInput = document.getElementById('txtInput');
    txtResult = document.getElementById('txtResult');

    document.getElementById('btnPlus')
        .addEventListener('click', plusClick, false);
}
```

```
function plusClick() {
    txtResult.value = Number(txtResult.value) + Number(txtInput.value);
}
```

23. Press F5 to run the test, which should pass.

When btnMinus is clicked, the value in *txtInput* will be subtracted from the value in *txtResult*.

24. In the tests.js file, add a new test to check btnMinus when it's clicked.

Your test code should look like the following:

```
test("Subtract Test", function () {
    expect(1);
    txtInput.value = '10';
    txtResult.value = '20';
    var btnMinus = document.getElementById('btnMinus');
    Qunit.triggerEvent(btnMinus, "click");
    var expected = '10';
    equal(txtResult.value, expected, 'Expected value: ' + expected +
    ' Actual value: ' + txtResult.value);
});
```

25. Press F5 to run the test and verify that the test fails because you haven't subscribed to the click event of btnMinus.

26. In the initialize function, add code to subscribe to btnMinus and call the minusClick function. Add the minusClick function with code to subtract *txtInput* from *txtResult*.

Your code should look like the following:

```
function initialize() {
    for (var i = 0; i < 10; i++) {
        document.getElementById('btn'+i).addEventListener('click',
            numberClick, false);
    }
    txtInput = document.getElementById('txtInput');
    txtResult = document.getElementById('txtResult');

    document.getElementById('btnPlus')
        .addEventListener('click', plusClick, false);
    document.getElementById('btnMinus')
        .addEventListener('click', minusClick, false);
}

function minusClick() {
    txtResult.value = Number(txtResult.value) - Number(txtInput.value);
}
```

27. Press F5 to run the test, which should pass.

When btnClearEntry is clicked, the value in *txtInput* will be set to zero.

28. In the tests.js file, add a new test to check btnClearEntry when it's clicked.

Your test code should look like the following:

```
test("Clear Entry Test", function () {
    expect(1);
```

```
        txtInput.value = '10';
        QUnit.triggerEvent(btnClearEntry, "click");
        var expected = '0';
        equal(txtInput.value, expected, 'Expected value: ' + expected +
            ' Actual value: ' + txtInput.value);
    });
```

29. Press F5 to run the test and verify that the test fails because you haven't subscribed to the click event of btnClearEntry.

30. In the initialize function, add code to subscribe to btnClearEntry and call the clearEntry function. Add the clearEntry function with code to reset *txtInput* to zero.

    Your code should look like the following:

```
function initialize() {
    for (var i = 0; i < 10; i++) {
        document.getElementById('btn'+i).addEventListener('click', numberClick,
false);
    }
    txtInput = document.getElementById('txtInput');
    txtResult = document.getElementById('txtResult');

    document.getElementById('btnPlus')
        .addEventListener('click', plusClick, false);
    document.getElementById('btnMinus')
        .addEventListener('click', minusClick, false);
    document.getElementById('btnClearEntry')
        .addEventListener('click', clearEntry, false);
}

function clearEntry() {
    txtInput.value = '0';
}
```

31. Press F5 to run the test, which should pass.

    When btnClear is clicked, the value in txtInput and *txtResult* will be set to zero.

32. In the tests.js file, add a new test to check btnClear when it's clicked.

    Your test code should look like the following:

```
test("Clear Test", function () {
    expect(2);
    txtInput.value = '10';
    txtResult.value = '20';
    QUnit.triggerEvent(btnClear, "click");
    var expected = '0';
    equal(txtInput.value, expected, 'Expected value: ' + expected +
        ' Actual value: ' + txtInput.value);
    equal(txtResult.value, expected, 'Expected value: ' + expected +
        ' Actual value: ' + txtResult.value);
});
```

33. Press F5 to run the test and verify that the test fails because you haven't subscribed to the click event of btnClear.

34. In the initialize function, add code to subscribe to btnClear and call the clear function. Add the clear function with code to reset *txtInput* and *txtResult* to zero.

Your code should look like the following:

```
function initialize() {
    for (var i = 0; i < 10; i++) {
        document.getElementById('btn'+i)
            .addEventListener('click', numberClick, false);
    }
    txtInput = document.getElementById('txtInput');
    txtResult = document.getElementById('txtResult');

    document.getElementById('btnPlus')
        .addEventListener('click', plusClick, false);
    document.getElementById('btnMinus')
        .addEventListener('click', minusClick, false);
    document.getElementById('btnClearEntry')
        .addEventListener('click', clearEntry, false);
    document.getElementById('btnClear')
        .addEventListener('click', clear, false);
}

function clear() {
    txtInput.value = '0';
    txtResult.value = '0';
}
```

35. Press F5 to run the test, which should pass.

After btnPlus or btnMinus is clicked and the mathematical operation is performed, *txtInput* should be reset to zero.

36. In the tests.js file, modify the add test and the subtract test to assert that *txtInput* was reset to zero.

Your test code should look like the following:

```
test("Add Test", function () {
    expect(2);
    txtInput.value = '10';
    txtResult.value = '20';
    QUnit.triggerEvent(btnPlus, "click");
    var expected = '30';
    equal(txtResult.value, expected, 'Expected value: ' + expected +
        ' Actual value: ' + txtResult.value);
    expected = '0';
    equal(txtInput.value, expected, 'Expected value: ' + expected +
        ' Actual value: ' + txtInput.value);
});

test("Subtract Test", function () {
    expect(2);
    txtInput.value = '10';
    txtResult.value = '20';
    QUnit.triggerEvent(btnMinus, "click");
```

```
        var expected = '10';
        equal(txtResult.value, expected, 'Expected value: ' + expected +
            ' Actual value: ' + txtResult.value);
        expected = '0';
        equal(txtInput.value, expected, 'Expected value: ' + expected +
            ' Actual value: ' + txtInput.value);

});
```

Notice that in these tests, the expect function call is passed a value of two because you now have two assertions.

37. Press F5 to run the test and verify that the test fails because you haven't added code to the plusClick and minusClick functions that will reset *txtInput*.

38. At the bottom of the plusClick and minusClick functions, call the clearEntry function.

Your code should look like the following:

```
function plusClick() {
    txtResult.value = Number(txtResult.value) + Number(txtInput.value);
    clearEntry();
}

function minusClick() {
    txtResult.value = Number(txtResult.value) - Number(txtInput.value);
    clearEntry();
}
```

39. Press F5 to run the test, which should pass.

When the application starts, *txtInput* and *txtResult* should be initially set to zero.

40. Add a test to the top of tests.js that checks *txtInput* and *txtResult*.

Your test code should look like the following:

```
test("Initialize Test", function () {
    expect(2);
    txtInput.value = '';
    txtResult.value = '';
    var expected = '0';
    equal(txtInput.value, expected, 'Expected value: ' + expected +
        ' Actual value: ' + txtInput.value);
    equal(txtResult.value, expected, 'Expected value: ' + expected +
        ' Actual value: ' + txtResult.value);
});
```

41. Press F5 to run the test and verify that the test fails because you haven't added code to the initialize function to initialize *txtInput* and *txtResult*.

42. At the bottom of the initialize function, add a call to the clear function to initialize *txtInput* and *txtResult*.

Your code should look like the following:

```
function initialize() {
    for (var i = 0; i < 10; i++) {
```

```
                document.getElementById('btn'+i)
                    .addEventListener('click', numberClick, false);
            }
            txtInput = document.getElementById('txtInput');
            txtResult = document.getElementById('txtResult');

            document.getElementById('btnPlus')
                    .addEventListener('click', plusClick, false);
            document.getElementById('btnMinus')
                    .addEventListener('click', minusClick, false);
            document.getElementById('btnClearEntry')
                    .addEventListener('click', clearEntry, false);
            document.getElementById('btnClear').addEventListener('click', clear, false);
            clear();
        }
```

43. Press F5 to run the test, which should pass.

Now that all tests pass, you are almost ready to run the application, but you need to add code to the default.html file to call the initialize function when the page is loaded.

44. Open the default.html file and add the following inline script block to the bottom of the *<body>* element:

```
<script type="text/javascript">
    window.addEventListener('load', initialize, false);
</script>
```

45. In the Solution Explorer window, set the default.html file as the startup file by right-clicking the default.html file. Click Set As Start Page.

46. Press F5 to start debugging. Try clicking the number buttons to enter a number and try the plus and minus buttons, while observing the results. Try clicking the clear entry button after you enter a number. Try clicking the clear button to see the input and result clear.

Suggested practice exercises

The following additional exercises are designed to give you more opportunities to practice what you've learned and to help you successfully master the lessons presented in this chapter.

- **Exercise 1** Learn more about objects and events by adding more functionality to the calculator. You might consider adding multiplication and division.

- **Exercise 2** Learn more about QUnit and TDD by adding more tests, and then add the code to make the tests pass.

- **Exercise 3** Learn more about event bubbling by adding a *<div>* element that encompasses the buttons, and then add a click event to the *<div>* element so that all click events bubble to the *<div>* element.

Answers

This section contains the answers to the lesson review questions in this chapter.

Lesson 1

1. **Correct answer: C**

    A. **Incorrect:** The undefined value means that the variable has never been initialized.

    B. **Incorrect:** The null value means that the variable was explicitly set to have no value.

    C. **Correct:** When performing a mathematical operation on a nonnumeric value, NaN (not a number) will result.

    D. **Incorrect:** The Infinity value will result when your value exceeds 1.7976931348623157E + 10308.

2. **Correct answers: B, C, D, and F**

    A. **Incorrect:** You cannot use a JavaScript keyword for a variable name, and switch is a JavaScript keyword.

    B. **Correct:** The myChar variable name is valid.

    C. **Correct:** JavaScript allows a variable name to contain the dollar sign, so the $cost variable name is valid.

    D. **Correct:** JavaScript allows a variable name to contain the underscore, so the _total variable name is valid.

    E. **Incorrect:** Variable names cannot begin with a number.

    F. **Correct:** Variable names can contain numbers but cannot begin with a number.

3. **Correct answer: B**

    A. **Incorrect:** The use of ?? causes a syntax error.

    B. **Correct:** The use of || causes Valid User to be displayed if userName has no value.

    C. **Incorrect:** The use of && displays nothing if userName has no value.

    D. **Incorrect:** The use of + causes Valid User to be displayed if userName has no value, but it also displays the userName and Valid User together when the userName has a value.

Lesson 2

1. **Correct answer: B**

    A. **Incorrect:** QUnit is for testing JavaScript for the web, not Windows 8.

    B. **Correct:** QUnit-Metro is a variation of QUint, which supports Windows 8.

C. Incorrect: Microsoft Test does not support JavaScript.

D. Incorrect: NUnit does not support JavaScript.

2. **Correct answer: B**

   A. Incorrect: You need to write a failing test first so you can see the test pass after you write the code.

   B. Correct: You write a failing test and then write code that makes the test pass; then run the test again to validate that it passes.

   C. Incorrect: You should never write code without first writing a test that fails.

   D. Incorrect: If you write a passing test first, the code cannot be tested for success.

3. **Correct answer: C**

   A. Incorrect: Placing your JavaScript code in the <head> element does not promote reuse, and inline code might reference elements that are not yet loaded.

   B. Incorrect: Placing your JavaScript code in the </body> tag does not promote reuse.

   C. Correct: Placing your JavaScript code in separate files, external to your HTML document, promotes reuse.

   D. Incorrect: Placing your JavaScript code in the <body> element does not promote reuse, and inline code might reference elements that are not yet loaded.

Lesson 3

1. **Correct answer: A**

   A. Correct: Concat concatenates multiple arrays and produces a resultant array.

   B. Incorrect: Join creates a string from the items in the array.

   C. Incorrect: Push adds a single item to the end of the array.

   D. Incorrect: Splice adds and removes items from an array and produces a resultant array, but you must add the items one by one, not as an array.

2. **Correct answer: C**

   A. Incorrect: getElementsByName retrieves a live NodeList of elements based on the element's name attribute, not on the tag name.

   B. Incorrect: querySelectorAll is capable of retrieving the elements by tag name, but returns a static NodeList, which does not perform as well as functions that return a live NodeList.

   C. Correct: getElementsByTagName retrieves a live NodeList of elements based on the element's tag name.

   D. Incorrect: getElementsByClass retrieves a live NodeList of elements based on the CSS class name.

Getting started with CSS3

You've learned that HTML provides the structure, and JavaScript provides the behavior to your HTML document. In this chapter, you learn how Cascading Style Sheets (CSS) provide the presentation to your HTML document. CSS provides the tool to design and create a great-looking web or Windows 8 application with reusability across all pages.

CSS offers far more choices for rendering a document than are available if you just use HTML to provide formatting, and CSS is compact and fast. CSS also simplifies site updates, so you can modify the styles to change the look completely of all HTML documents in your web or Windows 8 application.

This chapter introduces CSS history briefly and then discusses CSS selectors and properties in depth.

Lessons in this chapter:

Before you begin

To complete this chapter, you must have some understanding of web development. This chapter requires the hardware and software listed in the "System requirements" section in the book's Introduction.

Lesson 1: Introducing CSS3

The principle of Cascading Style Sheets (CSS) has roots in Standardized Generalized Markup Language (SGML) from the 1980s. Its goals are to create a consistent look across many webpages and to separate structure from presentation so you can provide different style sheets for printing, browsing, or other scenarios.

The World Wide Web Consortium (W3C) published CSS Level 1 recommendations in December 1996, and then started working on CSS Level 2. (The word recommendation means a formal release of the publication.) In May 1998, CSS Level 2 was published, and the W3C started working on various modules of CSS Level 3 (CSS3). Rather than creating one large publication for CSS3, the W3C separated CSS3 into modules that could be published independently.

In 2005, the W3C became stricter with enforcement of the requirements for standards, and already-published standards such as CSS Level 2 Revision 1 (CSS 2.1), CSS3 Selectors, and CSS3 Text were pulled back from Candidate Recommendation to Working Draft level. It wasn't until June 2011 that the CSS 2.1 recommendation was published.

Because CSS3 is modular, the stability of each module differs, and its status differs. More than 50 modules are published from the W3C's CSS Working Group. At the time of this writing, the following four modules have reached recommendation status.

- **Media Queries** Adapts the rendering of HTML documents based on conditions such as screen resolution and orientation to accommodate different devices such as smart phones and tablets.

- **Namespaces** XML-based formats that can use namespaces to distinguish multiple uses of the same element name from one another within the same document. This publication explains how CSS selectors can be extended to select those elements based on their namespace and on their local name.

- **Selectors Level 3** Describes the element selectors used in CSS when selectors are used to select elements in an HTML or XML document to attach style properties.

- **Color** Specifies the color-related aspects of CSS, including transparency and the various representations of the *<color>* value type.

CSS 2.1 is included in CSS3 because CSS3 is being designed to be backward compatible with the CSS 2.1 recommendation. This chapter introduces you to CSS3 by covering many aspects of CSS 2.1.

Cascading style sheets provide a means to apply a presentation to an HTML structure by defining how HTML elements are displayed. By using CSS, you can set background and foreground colors, margins, borders, fonts, positions, and much more. You have creative control of the HTML elements, so you can decide what the elements look like and where they display on the screen.

If you have worked with a word processing application such as Microsoft Word, you might have applied a style to change the font size of a word or paragraph. This is similar to CSS, in which you can apply a style to an element that causes it to render differently. A *style* is a rule that describes how to format a specific part of an HTML document. A *style sheet* is a set of style rules.

You can create a style and apply it to many elements based on a selector. You use a *selector* to locate and select elements based on tag name, class name, ID, and more. You can create a style that works with images, and you can create a style that works only with hyperlinks. You can also create a named style that you can apply to any element. The reusability is powerful.

Probably the most powerful feature of CSS is *cascading*. To understand cascading, think about the browser's role in resolving the effective style of an element. The browser could be reading multiple style sheets for an HTML page, in which each style sheet could have style rules that affect the effective style of the element. As each style is read, it modifies the effective style of the element. Style settings that were applied from one style sheet can be overwritten by styles that are subsequently evaluated. The effective style cascades from one style sheet to the next style sheet, possibly being overwritten along the way. Cascading is explained in more detail in Lesson 2, "Understanding selectors, specificity, and cascading."

Defining and applying a style

 A style rule, or style, is composed of two parts: the *selector,* which locates the elements in the HTML document that will be styled, and the *declaration block*, which contains the formatting instructions (declarations). Multiple declarations are always separated with a semicolon. A declaration comprises a CSS property, followed by a colon, followed by a value. The following is an example of a style rule that locates the *<body>* element and sets the background color to white and the font color to gray.

```
body {
    background-color: white;
    color: gray;
}
```

In this example, the selector is body and the declaration block is contained within the curly braces. There are two declarations, each terminated with a semicolon. The first declaration specifies the CSS *background-color* property followed by a colon separator and the property value of *white*.

Selectors can be much more complex, and declaration blocks can contain many more declarations, as you see later in this chapter.

Adding comments within a style sheet

You can add comments within a style sheet by using the /* characters to start the comment and the */ characters to end the comment. Comments may also span multiple lines, as shown in the following example.

```
/* This is the style
   for the body element */
body {
    background-color: white; /* The rgb value is #ffffff */
    color: gray; /* This is the font color */
}
```

Creating an inline style

All elements have a global attribute called style that can be used to provide an *inline style*. Because an inline style is defined on the element to which you wish to add styling, you don't need a selector; you just need to specify the declaration block. The following is an example of an inline style on the *<body>* element that sets the background color to white and the font color to gray.

```
<body style='background-color: white; color: gray;'>
</body>
```

In this example, you don't need an external style sheet because you defined the style on the actual *<body>* element. You should try to avoid this technique; it violates the primary goal of separation between structure and presentation and doesn't create any reusability because you will need to copy this style to each HTML document you add to your application. An advantage of using an inline style is that it always overrides styles that are defined else-where because the inline styles are specific to the element on which the inline style is defined. This specificity can solve isolated problems when a style is applied globally in an external style sheet, but one element needs to be styled differently. Even then, it's preferable to maintain separation of structure and presentation, so you should avoid this approach.

Creating an embedded style

Instead of creating inline styles by using the global style attribute, you can use the *<style>* element to create an embedded style sheet within your HTML document. You must use CSS selectors to assign the style definitions to elements on the page. The following is an example of an embedded style sheet with a style rule that locates the *<body>* element and sets the background color to white and the font color to gray.

```
<!DOCTYPE html>
<html xmlns='http://www.w3.org/1999/xhtml'>
<head>
    <title></title>
    <style>
        body {
            background-color: white;
            color: gray;
        }
    </style>
</head>
<body>

</body>
</html>
```

Notice that the embedded style is located within the *<head>* element. Within the *<style>* element, you can add as many style rules as you need. As a rule, you should not use this technique, however. Although this technique separates the structure of the body of the HTML document from the style, it does not provide file separation. It provides reuse within the files, but it does not promote reuse across HTML documents. You might use this approach when you want to have a single, stand-alone HTML document that contains everything needed to render.

Creating an external style sheet

Instead of creating the same embedded styles in every HTML document, the best approach is to create an external style sheet file that you can link to all your pages. You can use the *<link>* element, as shown in the following example.

```
<!DOCTYPE html>
<html xmlns='http://www.w3.org/1999/xhtml'>
<head>
    <title></title>
    <link rel='stylesheet' type='text/css' href='Content/default.css' />
</head>
<body>

</body>
</html>
```

In this example, the *<link>* element contains the *rel* attribute, which specifies the relationship between the current HTML document and the external file as a style sheet. The *type* attribute specifies the MIME type of the external file as a text-based cascading style sheet. The href attribute specifies the relative location of the external CSS file, which is the default.css file located in the Content folder. If you want a style rule that locates the *<body>* element and sets the background color to white and the font color to gray, you would open the default.css file and add the following.

```
body {
    background-color: white;
    color: gray;
}
```

A style sheet file can have as many style rules as you need. Using an external style sheet is considered the best way to implement your styles. You can also link many external style sheets to an HTML document. For example, your company might create a corporate style sheet that it expects to be used on all websites that are exposed to the public. In addition to using the corporate style sheet, you might also create your own style sheet to address specific needs that your department is working on. In your webpages, you can add a *<link>* element for each style sheet.

Using media to specify the target device

The *<link>* element also has a *media* attribute that can specify the target device. By using the media attribute, you can create a CSS file for each device type and link all the CSS files into your HTML documents. When the HTML document is rendered, the browser determines the media type and uses the appropriate CSS file. The browser can select only one media type for the rendering of an HTML document. The following is a list of the media types that are available for use.

- **all** Renders to all devices
- **braille** Renders to braille tactile feedback devices
- **embossed** Renders to paged braille printers
- **handheld** Renders to handheld devices that typically have small, low-resolution screens and limited bandwidth
- **print** Renders paged material and documents viewed on screen in print preview mode
- **screen** Renders to color computer screens
- **speech** Renders to speech synthesizers
- **tty** Renders to media, using a fixed-pitch character grid such as teletypes, terminals, and portable devices with limited display capabilities
- **tv** Renders to television-type devices that typically have low-resolution color screens with limited ability to scroll and have sound

The following is an example of an HTML document that contains *<link>* elements for screen styles and print styles.

```
<!DOCTYPE html>
<html xmlns='http://www.w3.org/1999/xhtml'>
<head>
  <title></title>
  <link rel='stylesheet' type='text/css' href='Content/screen.css' media='screen' />
  <link rel='stylesheet' type='text/css' href='Content/printer.css' media='print' />

</head>
<body>

</body>
</html>
```

You can specify a CSS file as being applicable to multiple device types by comma separating each device type within the quotes.

 Quick check

- You want to provide a separate style sheet file for styles that are to be used when a webpage is rendered to the printer. Which media attribute setting should be set with the *<link>* element?

Quick check answer

- media = 'print'

Specifying the character encoding of the style sheet

To specify the character encoding of the style sheet text, use the @charset rule at the top of your style sheet. To be compatible with all browsers, be sure to place this on the first line of your CSS file. The following is an example of a CSS file that sets the character set to UTF-8, which is the most common character set that is usable with Unicode characters.

```
@charset 'UTF-8';
body {
    background-color: white;
    color: gray;
}
```

Note that if your HTML document has a *<meta>* element that describes the character set of the HTML document, that setting overrides the @charset setting in the CSS file. The following is an example of using the *<meta>* element in an HTML document.

```
<html xmlns="http://www.w3.org/1999/xhtml">
<head>
  <title></title>
  <meta http-equiv='Content-Type' content='text/html;charset=UTF-8' >
  <link rel='stylesheet' type='text/css' href='Content/default.css' />
</head>
<body>

</body>
</html>
```

If all your HTML documents specify the *<meta>* element with the @charset setting, you don't need the @charset rule in the CSS file. If the CSS file will be shared and you want to ensure that the style sheet character set is correct, you should specify the @charset rule.

Imported style sheets from other style sheets

As your style sheet grows, you will want to break it into smaller, more manageable files. The @import rule enables you to import a CSS file to the current style sheet. You can specify as many @import rules as you need, but the @import rules must be at the top of your style sheet, before any other content except the @charset rule. If you even have a comment above the @import rules, they will not work properly.

The following is an example of creating a main style sheet file that combines several other style sheet files.

```
@charset 'UTF-8';
@import url('/Content/header.css');
@import url('/Content/menu.css');
@import url('/Content/sidebar.css');
@import url('/Content/mainContent.css');
@import url('/Content/footer.css');
body {
    background-color: white;
    color: gray;
}
```

You can still have content in the CSS file, as shown in the example, but it must follow the @import rules. You can also specify the media type for each @import rule, as shown in the following example that specifies screen and print types.

```
@charset 'UTF-8';
@import url('/Content/header.css'); screen
@import url('/Content/menu.css'); screen
@import url('/Content/sidebar.css'); screen
@import url('/Content/mainContent.css');
@import url('/Content/footer.css'); print
body {
    background-color: white;
    color: gray;
}
```

Notice that the @import rule for the mainContent.css file is missing the media type, which means that the default media type of *all* is applicable, and this CSS file will be used for the screen and the printer.

Using @font-face rule to import fonts

You might want to use a specific font, but you know that many users will not have that font on their computer. To solve this problem, you can provide a link to the font so it can be downloaded and used in your style sheet. The following is an example of specifying the @font-face rule to define the myFont font, which will be loaded from a file on the current website, Fancy_Light.ttf or Fancy_Light.eot.

```
@font-face {
    font-family: myFont;
    src: url('Fancy_Light.ttf'),
         url('Fancy_Light.eot'); /* IE9 */
}
```

Starting with Internet Explorer 9, support was added for Embedded Open Type (.eot) files only, which Microsoft developed for web use. These font files can be created from existing TrueType font files by using the Microsoft Web Embedding Fonts Tool (WEFT). Firefox, Chrome, Safari, and Opera support True Type Files (*.ttf*) files, so you must specify both file types to be compatible with most browsers.

> ***NOTE*** **FONT LICENSING**
>
> **Fonts are intellectual property, just like software, music, and video. Be sure to have the proper license to use any font with the @font-face rule.**

Lesson summary

- A style rule, or style, is composed of two parts: the *selector* and the *declaration block*.
- The *selector* locates the elements in the HTML document to be styled.

- The *declaration block* contains the formatting instructions (declarations).
- Styles can be inline, embedded, or external.
- To maintain separation between structure and presentation, use external style sheets.
- Use the media attribute of the *<link>* element to specify the target device for a style sheet.

Lesson review

Answer the following questions to test your knowledge of the information in this lesson. You can find the answers to these questions and explanations of why each answer choice is correct or incorrect in the "Answers" section at the end of this chapter.

1. You want to add a comment to your style sheet that says "temporary." Which is the proper line to add to the CSS file?

   A. //temporary

   B. --temporary

   C. /* temporary */

   D. rem temporary

2. You want to maintain separation between structure and presentation. How do you create your style rules?

   A. Use inline styles.

   B. Use embedded styles.

   C. Use external style sheets.

   D. In the HTML document, specify @import to load style sheets.

3. You want your printer.css style sheet to target printers. How would you set up the style sheet link?

   A. <link rel='printer' type='text/css' href='Content/printer.css' />

   B. <link rel='stylesheet' type='text/css' href='Content/printer.css' media='print' />

   C. <link rel='stylesheet' type='text/css' href='Content/printer.css' />

   D. <link rel='stylesheet' type='text/css' href='Content/printer.css' target='print' />

Lesson 2: Understanding selectors, specificity, and cascading

This lesson covers the most important parts of CSS, starting with selectors, which connect the style rule to your HTML. This lesson then discusses some of the ways you can end up with multiple style rules for the same HTML and how to determine which selector is most specific. Finally, this lesson discusses the meaning and value of cascading.

Defining selectors

When defining a selector, you can create element selectors, id selectors, and class selectors. This section examines these common selector types and many of the common selector variations.

Creating an element type selector

 An *element type selector* is based on the name of the tag. In the previous example, the tag name (body) is the selector. There is only one *<body>* element in an HTML document, but what would happen if the selector were set to button, as shown in the following example?

```
button {
    background-color: white;
    color: gray;
}
```

If your HTML document contains 50 buttons, the style of all 50 buttons would be set. This is desirable in some scenarios, but in other scenarios, you might have wanted to set the style on a single button or a subset of buttons.

Creating an id selector

 An *id selector* is based on the id of the element. To set the style on a single button, you can assign an id to the button and then specify the id as the selector, prefixed with the hash (#) symbol. The following example sets the style on an element whose id is btnSave.

```
#btnSave {
    background-color: white;
    color: gray;
}
```

In this example, it doesn't matter which type of element is being accessed; all that matters is that the id is btnSave. Because the id must be unique across the HTML document, using this approach to set a style limits the reusability on a page, but across webpages, this sets the style of any element whose id is btnSave.

Creating a class selector

 A *class selector* is a style with a class name of your choice, prefixed with the period (.) symbol. This is also called a *named style*. The class name can be assigned to any element through the class attribute. In the following example, a style is created with a class name of myStyle.

```
.myStyle {
    background-color: white;
    color: gray;
}
```

This style won't apply to any elements until you specify the class name by using the class attribute, as shown in the following example.

```
<!DOCTYPE html>
<html xmlns='http://www.w3.org/1999/xhtml'>
<head>
    <title></title>
    <link rel='stylesheet' type='text/css' href='Content/default.css' />
</head>
<body>
   <input id='txtName' name='txtName' type='text' class='myStyle' />
   <button id='btnOk' class='myStyle'>Ok</button>
   <button id='btnSave'>Save</button>
   <button id='btnCancel' class='myStyle'>Cancel</button>
</body>
</html>
```

In this example, the class attribute specifies the myStyle style on the text box and two of the buttons. Named styles promote reuse because they can be used on any element as needed.

Using the universal selector

If you want to apply a style to every element, you can use the asterisk (*) symbol. The following example applies the style to every element in the HTML document.

```
* {
    background-color: white;
    color: gray;
}
```

You should avoid using the universal selector because of the performance cost.

Using descendant selectors

You might want to change the style of elements only if the elements are descendants of another element. For example, you might want to remove the underline from hyperlinks if they are presented in a list item. This can be done by specifying a *selector chain*, which is a group of selectors that specify a path to the elements that interest you. The selector chain specifies an ancestor element, followed by a space, and then specifies the descendant element, as shown in the following example.

```
li a {
    text-decoration: none;
}
```

This example removes the underline from every hyperlink that is a descendant of a list item, regardless of whether the hyperlink is a child, grandchild, or distant descendant. You can specify a selector chain with many descendant levels to provide a path to the elements you wish to style. The following demonstrates multiple descendant levels; the underline is removed from a hyperlink if it has an ancestor that is a list item, the list item has an ancestor that is an ordered list, and the ordered list has an ancestor that is a division.

```
div ol li a {
    text-decoration: none;
}
```

In large HTML documents, using descendant selectors can cause performance problems due to the amount of searching required. Try to implement a selector that is more specific, such as the child selector that's discussed next.

Using child selectors

You might want to change the style of elements only if the elements are direct children of another element. For example, you might want to remove the underline from hyperlinks if they are children of a list item. You can do this by specifying a parent element, followed by a greater-than symbol (>), and then specifying the child element, as shown in the following example.

```
li > a {
    text-decoration: none;
}
```

This example removes the underline from hyperlinks that are children of a list item, but it will not remove the underline of grandchildren or distant descendants. You can specify many child levels to provide a path to the element you wish to style. The following demonstrates multiple child levels; the underline is removed from a hyperlink if it has a parent that is a list item, the list item has a parent that is an ordered list, and the ordered list has a parent that is a division.

```
div > ol > li > a {
    text-decoration: none;
}
```

Using pseudo-class and pseudo-element selectors

Styles are generally attached to an element based on locating the element in the document object model (DOM) tree. Although this usually works fine, sometimes you want to apply a style to something more granular than an element. How do you assign a style to the first line of a paragraph? How do you assign a style to a hyperlink that has been visited?

To access information that is either outside the DOM tree or difficult to access in the DOM tree, you can use pseudo classes and pseudo elements.

 Pseudo classes classify elements based on something other than name, attributes, or content and, usually, something that cannot be deduced from the DOM tree. Exceptions to the rule are :first-child, which can be deduced from the DOM tree, and :lang(), which can sometimes be deduced from the DOM tree. You can use the pseudo classes anywhere in your selector chain to help you locate elements when the identified state is true. You can also use pseudo classes at the end of the selector chain to set the style of the element when the identified state is true. The following is a list of pseudo classes.

- **:link**   Denotes an unvisited link where a:link selects all unvisited links.

- **:visited**   Denotes visited links where a:visited selects all visited links.

- **:active**   Denotes an active link when active means that the mouse button is pressed down and a:active selects all active links.

- **:hover**   Denotes a link the mouse cursor is over when a:hover selects the link the mouse is over.

- **:focus**   Denotes an element that has focus when input:focus selects the input that has focus.

- **:checked**   Denotes an option button or check box element whose checked attribute is set, where input[type='checkbox']:checked selects all check boxes that are selected.

- **:lang(language)**   Denotes an element whose lang attribute is set to language when p:lang(en) selects all paragraphs and the lang attribute starts with en.

- **:not**   Provides negation when div:not("#mainContainer") selects all *<div>* elements except the *<div>* element whose id is mainContainer.

- **:nth-child(formula)**   Selects the *n*th child of a parent if the formula is an integer value. For example, li:nthchild(3) selects the third list item. Note that the number is one-based, not zero-based. This pseudo class is powerful.

  You can provide a formula based on *an + b* when *a* is cycle count and *n* is a counter variable, and *b* represents the element within the cycle that you want to select. For example, li:nthchild(10n + 3) selects the third element of every 10 elements, so if a *<ul>* element contains 45 *<li>* elements, elements 3, 13, 23, 33, and 43 will be selected.

  You can also use the keywords *odd* and *even* to select odd and even child elements. For example, li:nth-child(odd) selects elements 1, 3, 5, 7, and so on.

- **:nth-last-child(n)**   Selects the *n*th child of a parent if the formula is an integer value. For example, li:nth-last-child(3) selects the third list item from the end of the list. Note that the number is one-based, not zero-based.

- **:only-child**   Selects elements that are the only child of the parent.

- **:only-of-type**   Selects elements that are the only child of the parent and have the specified type.

- **:first-of-type**   Selects the first element of the specified type.

Pseudo elements are abstractions of the document tree that provide access to information that is not directly available in the DOM tree. You cannot group pseudo elements in the same selector as you can, for example, pseudo classes, in which you might combine a:hover and a:active as a:hover:active. You cannot use pseudo elements in inline styles. You cannot use pseudo elements in the selector chain to help you find other elements such as descendants.

You can use pseudo elements only at the end of the selector chain to set the style of the pseudo element. The following is a list of pseudo elements.

- **::first-line**   Selects the first line where p::first-line selects the first line of each paragraph. You can apply a different style to the first line of a paragraph.

- **::first-letter**   Selects the first letter where p::first-letter selects the first letter of each paragraph. You can apply a different style to the first letter of a paragraph. This option is useful when you want to create a large first letter.

- **::before**   Inserts generated textual content inside the element where p::before{ content: "Note: "; } inserts "Note: " into each paragraph directly before the existing content. In addition to adding the textual content, you can provide a style for the content when p::before{ content: "Note: "; color: red;} sets the color of "Note: " to red.

- **::after**   Inserts generated textual content inside each element when p::after{ content: "Done!"; } inserts "Done!" into each paragraph directly after the existing content. In addition to adding the textual content, you can provide a style for the textual content when p::after{ content: "Done!"; color: red;} sets the color of "Done!" to red.

> **NOTE**   **ONE OR TWO COLONS BEFORE PSEUDO ELEMENTS**
> CSS3 recommends one colon (:) before pseudo classes and two colons (::) before pseudo elements as a way to tell the difference between the two. CSS3 also allows one-colon usage on existing rules to be backward compatible with existing browsers, so most people will continue to use one colon to be backward compatible with older browsers. All new pseudo elements are required to have two colons.

Grouping selectors

You can group selectors when you will be applying the same style by separating each selector with a comma. Consider the following example, in which the two style rules have the same declaration blocks.

```
button {
    background-color: white;
    color: gray;
}
p {
    background-color: white;
    color: gray;
}
```

In this scenario, you can condense the two style rules into a single style rule as shown in the following example, which applies the same style to all button and paragraph elements.

```
button, p {
    background-color: white;
```

```
    color: gray;
}
```

Using subsequent adjacent sibling selectors

An *adjacent selector* can be used to select an element if it is preceded by a specific element. The plus (+) sign denotes an adjacent selector. For example, div + h1 selects the *<h1>* element that immediately follows a *<div>* element.

In the following example, div + h1 set the heading to a background color of yellow if the heading is preceded by a *<div>* element as the previous sibling.

```
div + h1 {
    background-color: yellow;
}
```

Consider the following HTML document, which has two *<div>* elements and various *<h1>* elements.

```
<!DOCTYPE html>
<html xmlns="http://www.w3.org/1999/xhtml">
<head>
    <title></title>
    <link href="default.css" rel="stylesheet" />
</head>
<body>
    <h1>The h1 child before the first div
    </h1>
    <div>
        some child content
        <h1>This is the first h1 child
        </h1>
        <div>another div here</div>
        some text after the div
        <h1>This is the second h1 child
        </h1>
        <h1>This is the third h1 child
        </h1>
    </div>
    some following content
    <span>here is a span</span>
    <h1>This the first h1 that follows the paragraph
    </h1>
    <h1>This the second h1 that follows the paragraph
    </h1>
    <h1>This the third h1 that follows the paragraph
    </h1>
</body>
</html>
```

The first *<div>* element has child *<h1>* elements, but they are children, not adjacent elements. The adjacent element that follows the first *<div>* element is the *<span>* element, which means that the first *<div>* element does not play a role in changing an *<h1>* element's background to yellow. The second *<div>* element is followed by some textual content, but the first element that follows the second *<div>* element is an *<h1>* element, so that *<h1>* element will have a yellow background. The result is shown in Figure 4-1.

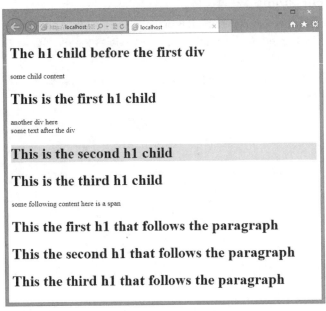

FIGURE 4-1 Only one *<h1>* element background color set to yellow

Using the subsequent sibling selector

The *subsequent sibling selector* is similar to the adjacent sibling selector, but its search for the sibling match doesn't stop at the first match. The tilde (~) character denotes the sibling selector. For example, div ~ h1 selects all *<h1>* elements that follow a *<div>* element.

In the following example, div ~ h1 sets the heading to a background color of yellow if the heading is preceded by a *<div>* element as a previous sibling.

```
div ~ h1 {
    background-color: yellow;
}
```

Using the HTML document from the adjacent sibling selector example, the first *<div>* element has child *<h1>* elements, but they are children, not adjacent elements. The adjacent element that follows the first *<div>* element is the *<span>* element, but sibling *<h1>* elements follow, and their backgrounds are changed to yellow. The second *<div>* element is followed by some textual content, and two *<h1>* elements follow the second *<div>* element; they will have a yellow background. Notice that with both *<div>* elements, there is an *<h1>* element before the *<div>* element, and their background color is not set to yellow because although they are siblings, they are prior siblings. The result is shown in Figure 4-2.

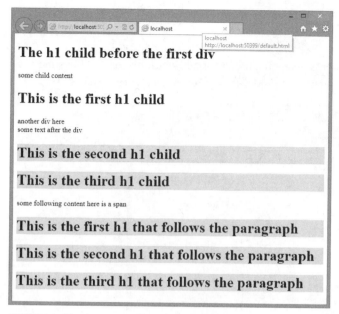

FIGURE 4-2 All subsequent *<h1>* elements background color set to yellow

Using an attribute selector

An *attribute selector* selects elements based on the existence of the specified attribute. For example, a[title] selects all hyperlinks whose title attribute is defined.

The following example demonstrates the use of an attribute selector to locate all hyperlinks whose href attribute is defined. This example also demonstrates combining the attribute selector with the :hover pseudo class and the :after pseudo element to display the href in parentheses when the link is hovered over. Notice the use of the attr( ) function to retrieve the value of an attribute.

```
a[href]:hover:after {
    content: " (" attr(href) ")";
    background-color: yellow;
}
```

Consider the following HTML document that has is three *<a>* elements, two of which define the href attribute.

```
<!DOCTYPE html>
<html xmlns="http://www.w3.org/1999/xhtml">
<head>
    <title></title>
    <link href="default.css" rel="stylesheet" />
</head>
<body>
    <a  href='http://contoso.com' >Link 1</a><br />
    <a>Link 2</a><br />
```

```
    <a  href='http://microsoft.com' >Link 3</a><br />
</body>
</html>
```

The first and third *<a>* elements define the href attribute, which means that hovering over either of these causes the hyperlink to be displayed. The result is shown in Figure 4-3.

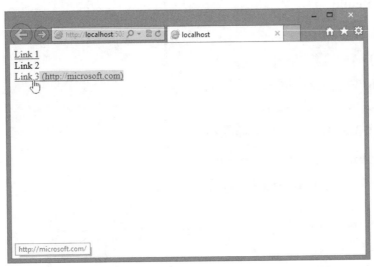

FIGURE 4-3 Hovering over a link whose href attribute is defined, causing the href value to be displayed

Using an attribute value selector

An *attribute value selector* selects all elements where the specified attribute has the specified value. For example, a[href='http://contoso.com'] selects all hyperlinks where the href attribute is set to http://contoso.com.

The following example demonstrates the use of the attribute value selector to locate all hyperlinks that have the href attribute set to http://contoso.com. This example also demonstrates combining the attribute selector with the :hover pseudo class.

```
a[href='http://contoso.com']:hover {
    background-color: yellow;
}
```

Consider the following HTML document, which has three *<a>* elements, one of which has the href attribute set to http://contoso.com.

```
<!DOCTYPE html>
<html xmlns="http://www.w3.org/1999/xhtml">
<head>
    <title></title>
    <link href="default.css" rel="stylesheet" />
</head>
```

```
<body>
    <a  href='http://contoso.com' >Link 1</a><br />
    <a>Link 2</a><br />
    <a  href='http://www.contoso.com' >Link 3</a><br />
</body>
</html>
```

The first *<a>* element sets the href attribute to http://contoso.com, so hovering over this link causes the hyperlink to be displayed with a yellow background, as shown in Figure 4-4. The other hyperlinks remain unaffected.

FIGURE 4-4 Hovering over a link whose href attribute is set to http://contoso.com causes the href value to be displayed

A potential problem with this approach is that the value must match exactly to work. To solve this problem, use the attribute contains value selector.

Using the attribute contains value selector

The *attribute contains value selector* selects all elements that contain the specified attribute value within the specified attribute. This is similar to the attribute value selector, but it is more flexible because you don't need to provide an exact match. To specify the attribute contains value selector, add an asterisk (*) suffix to the attribute name.

The following example demonstrates the use of the attribute contains value selector to locate all hyperlinks that have an href attribute value that contains contoso.com. This example also demonstrates combining the attribute selector with the :hover pseudo class.

```
a[href*='contoso.com']:hover {
    background-color: yellow;
}
```

Consider the following HTML document, which has three *<a>* elements, one of which sets the href attribute to http://contoso.com.

```
<!DOCTYPE html>
<html xmlns="http://www.w3.org/1999/xhtml">
<head>
    <title></title>
    <link href="default.css" rel="stylesheet" />
</head>
<body>
    <a  href='http://contoso.com' >Link 1</a><br />
    <a href='http://microsoft.com'>Link 2</a><br />
    <a  href='http://www.contoso.com/default.html' >Link 3</a><br />
</body>
</html>
```

The first and third hyperlinks have href attributes that contain contoso.com, so hovering over these hyperlinks causes the hyperlink to be displayed with a yellow background.

Using the attribute value starts with selector

An *attribute value starts with selector* selects all elements whose specified attributes value starts with the specified value. To specify the attribute value starts with selector, add a caret (^) suffix to the attribute name.

The following example demonstrates the use of the attribute value starts with selector to locate all hyperlinks that reference external sites by looking for href values that start with http. This automatically includes hrefs that start with https.

```
a[href^='http']:hover {
    background-color: yellow;
}
```

Consider the following HTML document that has three *<a>* elements, one of which sets the href attribute to http://microsoft.com.

```
<!DOCTYPE html>
<html xmlns="http://www.w3.org/1999/xhtml">
<head>
    <title></title>
    <link href="default.css" rel="stylesheet" />
</head>
<body>
    <a  href='sales/default.html' >Link 1</a><br />
    <a href='http://microsoft.com'>Link 2</a><br />
    <a  href='default.html' >Link 3</a><br />
</body>
</html>
```

The first and third hyperlinks have href attributes that don't start with http, so hovering over these hyperlinks does not cause the hyperlink to be displayed with a yellow background. Hovering over the second hyperlink does cause the hyperlink to display with a yellow background.

Using the attribute value ends with selector

An *attribute value ends with selector* selects all elements whose specified attributes value ends with the specified value. To specify the attribute value ends with selector, add a dollar sign ($) suffix to the attribute name.

The following example demonstrates the use of the attribute value ends with selector to locate all hyperlinks that reference jpg files.

```
a[href$='jpg']:hover {
    background-color: yellow;
}
```

Consider the following HTML document that has is three <a> elements, one of which sets the href attribute to http://microsoft.com.

```
<!DOCTYPE html>
<html xmlns="http://www.w3.org/1999/xhtml">
<head>
    <title></title>
    <link href="default.css" rel="stylesheet" />
</head>
<body>
    <a  href='sales/default.html' >Link 1</a><br />
    <a href='logo.jpg'>Link 2</a><br />
    <a  href='default.html' >Link 3</a><br />
</body>
</html>
```

The first and third hyperlinks have href attributes that don't end with jpg, so hovering over these hyperlinks does not cause the hyperlink to be displayed with a yellow background. Hovering over the second hyperlink does cause the hyperlink to display with a yellow background.

Using the attribute contains value in list selector

An attribute contains value in list selector selects all elements whose specified attribute contains the specified value when the attribute has a space-delimited list of values and there is a match to one of the values. This works well with custom attributes when you might want to specify a list of values in one attribute. For example, you might have a hyperlink that has a datalinktype attribute that contains a list of values that describe the type of link, such as *secure, externalLink, internalLInk, imageFile, zipFile*. When the link is rendered to the browser, it includes the datalinktype attribute with the appropriate values. You want to add different styles to the hyperlink based on these values, as follows.

```
a[data-linktype ~='externalLink'] {
    background-color: yellow;
}

a[data-linktype ~='internalLink'] {
    background-color: lime;
}
```

```
a[data-linktype ~='imageFile']:after {
    content: '(img)';
}

a[data-linktype ~='zipFile']:after {
    content: '(zip)';
}}
```

Consider the following HTML document that has three *<a>* elements where there is a mix of values and the appropriate styles must be applied based on the datalinktype attribute.

```
<!DOCTYPE html>
<html xmlns="http://www.w3.org/1999/xhtml">
<head>
    <title></title>
    <link href="default.css" rel="stylesheet" />
</head>
<body>
    <a  href='http://contoso.com' data-linktype="externalLink zipFile">Link 1</a><br />
    <a  href='default.html' data-linktype="internalLink zipFile">Link 2</a><br />
    <a  href='http://microsoft.com/logo.jpg' data-linktype="externalLink imageFile">Link
3</a><br />
</body>
</html>
```

The first and third hyperlinks are external links, so they have a background color of yellow. The second hyperlink is an internal link, so it has a background color of lime. The first and second hyperlinks are links to zip files, so '(zip)' is appended to the content. The third hyperlink is a link to an image so '(img)' is appended to the content. The rendered HTML document is shown in Figure 4-5.

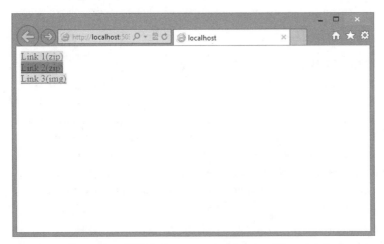

FIGURE 4-5 The rendered HTML document showing the different styles based on matching to an item in the datalinktype attribute

Understanding the browser's built-in styles

Even if you don't define any styles for your HTML documents, at least one style sheet will be used to calculate the effective style for the elements within the document. Each browser has a built-in default style sheet, which is applied to all HTML documents before any other style sheets are applied.

You cannot access the browser's style sheet directly, and be aware that there can be differences among browsers.

Extending browser styles with user styles

You can extend the browser's styles by adding a user-defined style sheet to the browser. This is done differently based on the browser. To add a user-defined style sheet in Internet Explorer, navigate to Tools | Internet Options | General | Accessibility. The Accessibility window is displayed, as shown in Figure 4-6.

FIGURE 4-6 The user style sheet if set to the myUser.css file

User styles are applicable only to that browser on that computer, so if you launch a different browser on the same computer, your user-defined style sheet won't work. In addition, if you run the same browser on a different computer, your user-defined style sheet won't work.

Working with important styles

When you add styles to a user-defined style sheet, the styles typically don't work because the user-defined styles are read, and then the HTML document's styles are read. If the browser has a style rule setting from the user-defined style sheet, and then the HTML document's style sheet reads a different style rule setting, the user-defined style is overridden by the HTML document's style sheet. In the example, the problem is that the user might have difficulty reading webpage text and want to increase the font size on all webpages.

To solve this problem, in the user-defined style sheet, you can add the "!important" modifier after the CSS value to increase its priority. The "!important" modifier in the user-defined style sheet overrides any value from the HTML document's style sheet, even if the "!important" modifier is used in the HTML document's style sheet. This is the most appropriate use of the "!important" modifier.

Although you can use the "!important" modifier with your HTML document's style sheets, it's not good practice to do so. It's equivalent to using a jackhammer on a finish nail.

The following is an example of a user-defined CSS file that overrides the background color and text color of the body element.

```
@charset 'UTF-8';
body {
    background-color: white !important;
    color: black !important;
}
```

Remember that the user-defined style sheet settings have a lower priority than the HTML document's style sheets except when the "!important" modifier is used in the user-defined style sheet. In this case, the user-defined style has the highest priority.

How do styles cascade?

It's important to understand how styles are resolved by the browser when style rules conflict. The following is the order of precedence the browser uses to calculate the effective style of an element.

1. **Important**   The browser must determine whether the "!important" modifier has been used. This has the highest priority, so if the "!important" modifier is found, it takes precedence over the specificity or textual order.

2. **Specificity**   The browser determines which rule is most specific and, if the browser can determine which rule is most specific, there is no need to examine the textual order.

3. **Textual Order**   The browser determines the textual order of the style rules where the last style rule in textual order has precedence over prior style rules.

Style rules can be defined in several style sheets, and it's important to understand these style sheets, especially their relationship to the textual order. The following list describes the evaluation order of the various style sheets.

1. Browser's built-in style sheet

2. User's normal declarations in the user style sheet

3. Author's normal declarations in the author style sheet

4. Author's important declarations in the author style sheet

5. User's important declarations in the user style sheet

The author of the page can provide normal style declarations that override the user's defined styles, based on the evaluation order. The user can have the final word by overriding the author's declarations by using the "!important" modifier. This is probably the best implementation of the "!important" modifier.

 Quick check

- What is the order of precedence for calculating the effective style of an element?

Quick check answer

- (1) Important, (2) Specificity, (3) Textual Order

Using specificity

Probably the most confusing aspect of determining the effective style of an element is determining the victor of conflicting styles when specificity is different among them. The rule with the most specific selector will prevail, but how do you determine which rule is most specific?

To calculate the selector's specificity, start by recording three values, known as a, b, and c, as follows.

- a Record the number of id attributes in the selector.
- b Record the quantity of class selectors, attributes selectors, and pseudo classes.
- c Record the quantity of element names in the selector.

Although pseudo classes are counted, pseudo elements are not counted in the specificity calculation. In addition, if you use the negation pseudo class, the selectors within it are counted, but the negation pseudo class is not counted. Last, the universal selector (*) is never included in calculations.

After recording the values of a, b, and c, concatenate the three numbers to form a specificity value so that a has the highest value, then b, and c has the lowest value. Figure 4-7 demonstrates the calculation of various selectors, from the lowest specificity value to the highest specificity value.

Lowest Precedence			

Selector	a	b	c
*	0	0	0
li	0	0	1
ol + li	0	0	2
div ol + li	0	0	3
div .content	0	1	1
div .content ol + li	0	1	3
div .content ol + li .selected	0	2	3
#main	1	0	0
#main .selected	1	1	0
#main ul + li .selected	1	1	2

Highest Precedence	

FIGURE 4-7 Specificity value calculation examples, sorted from lowest to highest value

If you have conflicting style rules and you calculate the specificity value of each, if the values are the same, which style rule is used? Textual order becomes the tie breaker. The later of the style rules will be the effective style.

Understanding inheritance

An element can get its style from a parent element when no other styles are defined that are more specific, but it's important to understand that the element only inherits a style from a parent when no style is defined for the prospective element property. Consider the scenario in which you want all text in your HTML document to be sized to extra-large. Rather than define a style for *<input>* elements, another style for *<div>* elements, and so on, you can just set the font of the *<body>* element as follows.

```
body {
    font-size: x-large;
}
```

In this example, all elements within the *<body>* element inherit the font size, but if an element is assigned a font size, the assigned font size overrides the inherited size.

Using the inherit value

The previous example was rather simple because elements typically have their properties set to inherit by default. What would you do if you have an element whose background color is set, but you want to reset the element to inherit from its parent? You could assign the inherit value to the background color, as shown in the following example.

```
body {
    font-size: x-large;
}
li:nth-child(even) {
    font-size: small;
}
li:nth-child(4) {
    font-size: inherit;
}
```

In this example, the *<body>* element font size is set to extra-large, and all child elements can inherit this setting. The next style rule selects even-numbered *<li>* elements and sets the font size to small. The last style rule resets the font size back to inherit for the fourth child *<li>* element.

Lesson summary

- A style rule, or style, is composed of two parts: the *selector* and the *declaration block*. The *selector* locates the elements in the HTML document that will be styled. The *declaration block* contains the formatting instructions (declarations).
- Styles can be inline, embedded, or external.
- To maintain separation between structure and presentation, use external style sheets.
- Use the media attribute of the *<link>* element to specify the target device for a style sheet.
- Pseudo classes provide another way to select elements. Pseudo elements provide access to information that is not available from the DOM. Use two colons (::) to denote pseudo elements.
- Use the "!important" modifier with user-defined styles to override author-defined styles.
- Cascading precedence is by importance, specificity, and then textual order.
- The evaluation order of style sheets is the browser's built-in style sheet, the user-defined style sheet, the author's normal style sheet, the author's important style sheet, and the user's important style sheet.
- Calculating the specificity of a selector is based on three levels of magnitude.
- Element styles that are not assigned can inherit their style from a parent element.

Lesson review

Answer the following questions to test your knowledge of the information in this lesson. You can find the answers to these questions and explanations of why each answer choice is correct or incorrect in the "Answers" section at the end of this chapter.

1. You want to set the style of the first letter of every paragraph in a *<div>* element whose id is readingPane. Which style selector is most appropriate?

   A. #readingPane p::first-letter

   B. #readingPane::first-letter

   C. #readingPane p:first-child

   D. #readingPane:first-child

2. The following style sheet rule is defined in Corporate.css.

   ```
   div p.highlight{
       font-size: xx-large;
       background-color: yellow;
   }
   ```

   In Department.css, the following style sheet rule is defined.

   ```
   div p {
       background-color: blue;
   }
   ```

   Your HTML document contains the following.

   ```
   <!DOCTYPE html>
   <html xmlns="http://www.w3.org/1999/xhtml">
   <head>
       <title></title>
       <link href="Corporate.css" rel="stylesheet" />
       <link href="Department.css" rel="stylesheet" />
   </head>
   <body>
       <div id="readingPane">
           <p class='highlight'>
               Here is a test to see what the background color of a paragraph
               will be blue or yellow.
           </p>
       </div>
       </body>
   </html>
   ```

   What will be the rendered background color of the paragraph?

   A. Yellow

   B. Blue

   C. Transparent

   D. White

3. The following style sheet rule is defined in Corporate.css.

```
div p.highlight{
    font-size: xx-large;
    background-color: yellow;
}
```

In Department.css, the following style sheet rule is defined.

```
div p:first-of-type. {
    background-color: blue;
}
```

Your HTML document contains the following.

```
<!DOCTYPE html>
<html xmlns="http://www.w3.org/1999/xhtml">
<head>
    <title></title>
    <link href="Corporate.css" rel="stylesheet" />
    <link href="Department.css" rel="stylesheet" />
</head>
<body>
    <div id="readingPane">
        <p class='highlight'>
            Here is a test to see what the background color of a paragraph
            will be blue or yellow.
        </p>
    </div>
    </body>
</html>
```

What will be the rendered background color of the paragraph?

A. Yellow

B. Blue

C. Transparent

D. White

Lesson 3: Working with CSS properties

Now that you know how to use CSS selectors, you can work with CSS properties. There are many CSS properties, and this lesson discusses the basic CSS properties that you need to know to provide a page layout.

Colors are explained in detail, followed by measurements and the CSS box model.

After this lesson, you will be able to:

- Set CSS colors.
- Implement a layout by using the CSS box model.
- Position *<div>* elements.

Estimated lesson time: 30 minutes

Working with CSS colors

With CSS, colors can be specified in several ways, such as by color names, RGB color values, and ARGB color values. You can set the transparency or opacity.

RGB values have been available since the earliest version of CSS. The RGB value is a six-character field that represents a two-character hexadecimal value for the amount of red, then green, and then blue, and is prefixed with the pound (#) symbol. A value of 00 (two zeros) is the minimum value, and ff represents the maximum value for that color. This represents 0–255 in decimal. The following are examples of RGB values.

- **black** #000000
- **white** #ffffff
- **red** #ff0000
- **green** #008000
- **lime** #00ff00
- **blue** #0000ff
- **yellow** #ffff00
- **gray** #808080

An example of setting the background color of an HTML document to yellow is as follows.

```
body {
    background-color: #ffff00;
}
```

> **NOTE** **SHORTCUT FOR SETTING THE VALUE OF COLORS**
>
> Instead of representing the RGB value as #rrggbb, you might be able to represent the RGB value as #rgb. If the two-character codes for red, green, and blue are the same, you can use a single character for each to reduce the six-character value to a three-character value. For example, yellow is #ffff00 where the red component's characters are the same, the green component's characters are the same, and the blue component's characters are the same. Therefore, yellow can be represented as three-character #ff0. This is a shortcut, and can only be used to represent the value as three characters. When the browser reads the color value as three characters, it will expand each character to be two of the same character. A color of #123 is the same as #112233, *not* #000123.

Most colors can be represented by using this combination of red, green, and blue, but you don't need to remember the RGB values if you take advantage of the CSS ability to use color names when making color assignments to properties. Table 4-1 contains a list of the color names with their corresponding RGB values.

TABLE 4-1 Color names with corresponding hex and decimal values

Color Name	Hex Value	Decimal Value
aliceblue	#f0f8ff	240,248,255
antiquewhite	#faebd7	250,235,215
aqua	#00ffff	0,255,255
aquamarine	#7fffd4	127,255,212
azure	#f0ffff	240,255,255
beige	#f5f5dc	245,245,220
bisque	#ffe4c4	255,228,196
black	#000000	0,0,0
blanchedalmond	#ffebcd	255,235,205
blue	#0000ff	0,0,255
blueviolet	#8a2be2	138,43,226
brown	#a52a2a	165,42,42
burlywood	#deb887	222,184,135
cadetblue	#5f9ea0	95,158,160
chartreuse	#7fff00	127,255,0
chocolate	#d2691e	210,105,30
coral	#ff7f50	255,127,80
cornflowerblue	#6495ed	100,149,237
cornsilk	#fff8dc	255,248,220
crimson	#dc143c	220,20,60
cyan	#00ffff	0,255,255
darkblue	#00008b	0,0,139
darkcyan	#008b8b	0,139,139
darkgoldenrod	#b8860b	184,134,11
darkgray	#a9a9a9	169,169,169
darkgreen	#006400	0,100,0
darkgrey	#a9a9a9	169,169,169
darkkhaki	#bdb76b	189,183,107

Color Name	Hex Value	Decimal Value
darkmagenta	#8b008b	139,0,139
darkolivegreen	#556b2f	85,107,47
darkorange	#ff8c00	255,140,0
darkorchid	#9932cc	153,50,204
darkred	#8b0000	139,0,0
darksalmon	#e9967a	233,150,122
darkseagreen	#8fbc8f	143,188,143
darkslateblue	#483d8b	72,61,139
darkslategray	#2f4f4f	47,79,79
darkslategrey	#2f4f4f	47,79,79
darkturquoise	#00ced1	0,206,209
darkviolet	#9400d3	148,0,211
deeppink	#ff1493	255,20,147
deepskyblue	#00bfff	0,191,255
dimgray	#696969	105,105,105
dimgrey	#696969	105,105,105
dodgerblue	#1e90ff	30,144,255
firebrick	#b22222	178,34,34
floralwhite	#fffaf0	255,250,240
forestgreen	#228b22	34,139,34
fuchsia	#ff00ff	255,0,255
gainsboro	#dcdcdc	220,220,220
ghostwhite	#f8f8ff	248,248,255
gold	#ffd700	255,215,0
goldenrod	#daa520	218,165,32
gray	#808080	128,128,128
green	#008000	0,128,0
greenyellow	#adff2f	173,255,47
grey	#808080	128,128,128
honeydew	#f0fff0	240,255,240
hotpink	#ff69b4	255,105,180
indianred	#cd5c5c	205,92,92
indigo	#4b0082	75,0,130

Color Name	Hex Value	Decimal Value
ivory	#fffff0	255,255,240
khaki	#f0e68c	240,230,140
lavender	#e6e6fa	230,230,250
lavenderblush	#fff0f5	255,240,245
lawngreen	#7cfc00	124,252,0
lemonchiffon	#fffacd	255,250,205
lightblue	#add8e6	173,216,230
lightcoral	#f08080	240,128,128
lightcyan	#e0ffff	224,255,255
lightgoldenrodyellow	#fafad2	250,250,210
lightgray	#d3d3d3	211,211,211
lightgreen	#90ee90	144,238,144
lightgrey	#d3d3d3	211,211,211
lightpink	#ffb6c1	255,182,193
lightsalmon	#ffa07a	255,160,122
lightseagreen	#20b2aa	32,178,170
lightskyblue	#87cefa	135,206,250
lightslategray	#778899	119,136,153
lightslategrey	#778899	119,136,153
lightsteelblue	#b0c4de	176,196,222
lightyellow	#ffffe0	255,255,224
lime	#00ff00	0,255,0
limegreen	#32cd32	50,205,50
linen	#faf0e6	250,240,230
magenta	#ff00ff	255,0,255
maroon	#800000	128,0,0
mediumaquamarine	#66cdaa	102,205,170
mediumblue	#0000cd	0,0,205
mediumorchid	#ba55d3	186,85,211
mediumpurple	#9370db	147,112,219
mediumseagreen	#3cb371	60,179,113
mediumslateblue	#7b68ee	123,104,238
mediumspringgreen	#00fa9a	0,250,154

Color Name	Hex Value	Decimal Value
mediumturquoise	#48d1cc	72,209,204
mediumvioletred	#c71585	199,21,133
midnightblue	#191970	25,25,112
mintcream	#f5fffa	245,255,250
mistyrose	#ffe4e1	255,228,225
moccasin	#ffe4b5	255,228,181
navajowhite	#ffdead	255,222,173
navy	#000080	0,0,128
oldlace	#fdf5e6	253,245,230
olive	#808000	128,128,0
olivedrab	#6b8e23	107,142,35
orange	#ffa500	255,165,0
orangered	#ff4500	255,69,0
orchid	#da70d6	218,112,214
palegoldenrod	#eee8aa	238,232,170
palegreen	#98fb98	152,251,152
paleturquoise	#afeeee	175,238,238
palevioletred	#db7093	219,112,147
papayawhip	#ffefd5	255,239,213
peachpuff	#ffdab9	255,218,185
peru	#cd853f	205,133,63
pink	#ffc0cb	255,192,203
plum	#dda0dd	221,160,221
powderblue	#b0e0e6	176,224,230
purple	#800080	128,0,128
red	#ff0000	255,0,0
rosybrown	#bc8f8f	188,143,143
royalblue	#4169e1	65,105,225
saddlebrown	#8b4513	139,69,19
salmon	#fa8072	250,128,114
sandybrown	#f4a460	244,164,96
seagreen	#2e8b57	46,139,87
seashell	#fff5ee	255,245,238

Color Name	Hex Value	Decimal Value
sienna	#a0522d	160,82,45
silver	#c0c0c0	192,192,192
skyblue	#87ceeb	135,206,235
slateblue	#6a5acd	106,90,205
slategray	#708090	112,128,144
slategrey	#708090	112,128,144
snow	#fffafa	255,250,250
springgreen	#00ff7f	0,255,127
steelblue	#4682b4	70,130,180
tan	#d2b48c	210,180,140
teal	#008080	0,128,128
thistle	#d8bfd8	216,191,216
tomato	#ff6347	255,99,71
turquoise	#40e0d0	64,224,208
violet	#ee82ee	238,130,238
wheat	#f5deb3	245,222,179
white	#ffffff	255,255,255
whitesmoke	#f5f5f5	245,245,245
yellow	#ffff00	255,255,0
yellowgreen	#9acd32	154,205,50

An example of using a color name to set the background color of an HTML document to yellow is as follows.

```
body {
    background-color: yellow;
}
```

Using the rgb function

Another way to represent RGB colors is to use the rgb function. This function accepts the three R, G, and B parameters, either as an integer or as a percentage. If the integer value is above or below the valid 0–255 range, the value is automatically interpreted as the minimum or maximum value. The following are examples of the rgb function.

```
h1 { background-color: rgb(255,0,0); }
h1 { background-color: rgb(-100,500,0); } /*interpreted as 0,255,0 */
h1 { background-color: rgb(20%,150%,0%); } /*interpreted as 20%,100%,0% */
```

Using transparency

You can set the CSS *opacity* property to control the amount of transparency an element has. This is especially useful when content is placed over an image and you still want to see the image. The opacity must be a value between 0.0 and 1.0, where 0.0 is invisible and 1.0 is opaque. In the following example, the opacity of an element whose id is mainContent is set so the element is 50 percent see-through and anything under that element is still visible.

```
#mainContent {
    opacity: .5;
}
```

Using the rgba function

The rgba function is similar to the rgb function except it has an *alpha* parameter, which represents the amount of transparency to use. The alpha parameter value must be between 0.0 and 1.0, where 0.0 is invisible and 1.0 is fully opaque. The following are examples of using the rgba function.

```
h1 { background-color: rgba(255,0,0,0.5); }
h1 { background-color: rgba(0,255,0,1); }
h1 { background-color: rgba(20%,50%,0%, 0.2); }
```

Using the hsl function

Another way to represent a color in CSS3 is to use hue-saturation-lightness (HSL) colors. Like RGB colors, HSL colors use three numbers, but the numbers are for hue, saturation, and lightness. The hue is calculated as an angle of the color circle where red is 0 or 360 (degrees), and other colors are spread around the circle, as shown in Figure 4-8. As you look at the degrees in the circle, yellow can be represented as 60, as –240, or even as 420. You can normalize the value by using the (((x mod 360) + 360) mod 360) formula. The reason for adding 360 and performing a second modulus is to handle negative values.

The saturation and lightness values are represented in percentages. Saturation is the amount of color to provide, and lightness is the amount of lightening to provide. It's easy to produce matching colors by keeping the hue value the same and adjusting the saturation and lightness to get the desired colors. Primary colors typically have a saturation value of 100 percent and a lightness value of 50 percent. Some examples of HSL are as follows.

```
h2 { color: hsl(60, 100%, 50%); } /* yellow */
h2 { color: hsl(120, 100%, 25%); } /* dark green */
h2 { color: hsl(0, 100%, 50%); } /* red */
```

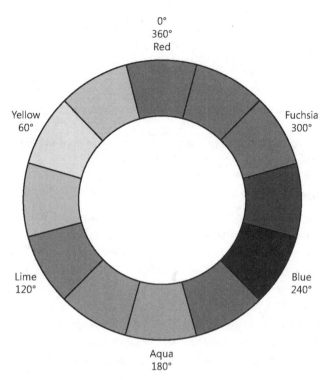

FIGURE 4-8 The HSL color wheel

Working with text

Formatting text is one of the most common CSS tasks. You set the font *typeface*, which is also known as the *font family*, such as Times New Roman. You then set the *font*, which is a specific member of the typeface, such as Times New Roman 12-point bold.

Font families belong to one of five groups.

- **serif**   Font families with serifs or curls at the top and bottom of characters, such as Times New Roman

- **sans serif**   Font families without serifs, such as Arial

- **monospace**   Font families in which all characters have the same width, such as Courier New

- **cursive**   Font families that imitate handwriting, such as Mistral

- **fantasy**   Font families that are decorative and used in titles, such as Impact

The most commonly used font families belong to one of three groups: serif, sans serif, or monospaced. Figure 4-9 shows an example of the three groups.

serif: Hello

sans-serif: **Hello**

monospaced: `Hello`

FIGURE 4-9 The serif, sans serif, and monospaced font families

Serif and sans serif font families have characters of proportional width, meaning that characters have different widths, unlike the monospaced font families.

Setting the font-family property

In your style rule, you can use the font-family property to set the typeface of the elements that match the selector. Be careful when specifying the font family because the one you specify must exist on the user's computer. If the font family doesn't exist, the browser will use its default font. To be safe, it's usually best to specify a common font family such as Arial, Courier New, Georgia, Times New Roman, or Verdana. Arial and Verdana are sans serif fonts that are easy to read and commonly used.

You can specify a list of font families in your style rule. The browser will attempt to use the first font family specified. If the browser doesn't have the first font family, it will attempt to use the second font family, and so on. The following example depicts multiple font families being specified.

```
h1 { font-family: arial, verdana, sans-serif; }
h1 { font-family: "times new roman", serif; }
h1 { font-family: "courier new", monospace; }
```

In this example, the last font family listed is actually the name of the generic group, which instructs the browser to use a font family from that group if the browser doesn't have the other font families that were first specified.

What other options do you have when you are trying to specify a font family that the user probably won't have? In the past, developers would create a GIF image that was a picture of the text and then use the image on the page. If you do this, you should always populate the alt attribute with the text. Remember that Lesson 1 covers the use of @font-face, which enables you to provide a link to the font you want to use.

Specifying the font size

To set the size of the font, you can set the font-size property. Font sizes can be specified by using absolute units or relative units, and there are many ways to set the size. The absolute length units are useful when the output environment is known because absolute length units are fixed in relation to one another and anchored to some physical measurement. The following is a list of the available measurement units.

- **em** A relative measurement multiplier of the parent element's computed font size
- **px** An absolute measurement pixel unit, 96 pixels per inch

- **pt**   An absolute measurement point unit, 72 points per inch
- **pc**   An absolute measurement pica unit, 12 points per pica
- **in**   An absolute measurement inch unit
- **mm**   An absolute measurement millimeter unit
- **cm**   An absolute measurement centimeter unit

There is also a set of absolute sizes whose size is controlled by the browser, but the recommended size is 1.2 em from the previous size. These sizes are xx-small, x-small, small, medium, large, x-large, and xx-large.

Similar to this, there is a set of relative sizes whose size is based on the parent element's size. These sizes are larger and smaller.

In addition to all the sizes already covered, you can use percentage values to size your font, which provides a size that's relative to the parent element's computed font size.

Here are some examples of using the various measurement units to set the font-size property.

```
h1 { font-size: 12px; }
h1 { font-size: 200%; }
h1 { font-size: 1.2em; }
h1 { font-size: 1in; }
h1 { font-size: 2cm; }
```

With all these measurement choices, what is the recommended measurement unit to use? For screen rendering, try to use the em or percentage measurements because these measurements scale well. For printer rendering, consider using any of the absolute font measurements such as point, pixels, picas, inches, centimeters, or millimeters.

Working with the CSS box model

Creating a nice layout for your webpage requires you to understand the CSS box model, which defines the spacing around boxes in your HTML document, as shown in Figure 4-10.

The margin is the space outside the border, between the border and the next element. The padding is the space inside the border, between the border and the content. If the border is being displayed, the margin and padding settings will have distinct effects. If the border is not being displayed, it can be difficult to differentiate margin and padding settings.

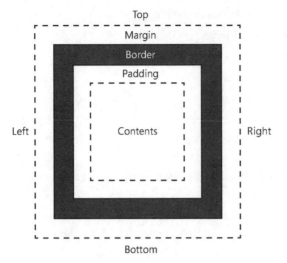

FIGURE 4-10 The CSS box model

Setting the border, padding, and margin properties

You can set the border, padding, and margin easily by assigning a value to the corresponding property, as shown in the following style sheet rule.

```
p {
    border: 10px;
    padding: 25px;
    margin: 15px;
    background-color: yellow;
    border-style: solid;
    border-color: green;
}
```

This style sheet rule sets the border width to 10 pixels on all four sides. The padding is set to 25 pixels on all four sides, and the margin is set to 15 pixels on all four sides. Now consider the following HTML document and how the style rule affects its rendering.

```
<!DOCTYPE html>
<html xmlns="http://www.w3.org/1999/xhtml">
<head>
    <title></title>
    <link href="default.css" rel="stylesheet" />
</head>
<body>
    <p>
        this is the third div - Lorem ipsum dolor sit amet, salutandi
        conceptam sea cu, eos id legimus percipit argumentum. Habeo
        ipsum mandamus sit an, aeterno pertinax vim ad, et cibo
        atomorum mea. Ad vis illum porro disputando, ei eligendi
        mandamus liberavisse sea. Sea debet comprehensam no, et
        blandit officiis eos, ut per ubique abhorreant
```

```
        </p>
    </body>
</html>
```

Figure 4-11 shows the rendered webpage. Notice the large gap between the text and the border, which is the padding. The border is rather thick with its width setting of 10 pixels. Outside the border, there is white space all around the paragraph, which is the margin property setting of 15 pixels.

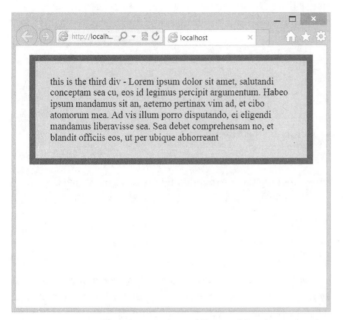

FIGURE 4-11 Controlling the margin, padding, and border properties

In addition to setting each of these properties to a value that controls all four sides, you can specify each side and the value. For example, you can assign a different value to each side of the border, as shown in the following style rule.

```
p {
    border-bottom: 10px;
    border-right: 5px;
    border-left: 1px;
    border-top: 0px;
    padding: 25px;
    margin: 15px;
    background-color: yellow;
    border-style: solid;
    border-color: green;
}
```

In this example, the top border is not displayed because its width is set to 0 pixels. You can also add -bottom, -top, -left, and -right to the padding and margin properties. There are also some shortcuts to specifying the settings for each side. You can set the properties by specifying top, right, bottom, and left by separating each value with a space as follows.

```
padding: 1px 2px 3px 4px ;
```

In this example, the top is set to 1 pixel, the right is set to 2 pixels, the bottom is set to 3 pixels, and the left is set to 4 pixels. In addition, if you know that you want the top and bottom to have the same values and the left and right to have the same values, you can assign the two values so that the first value is the top and bottom setting, and the second value is the left and right setting. The following example sets the top and bottom to 5 pixels and the left and right to 15 pixels.

```
padding: 5px 15px;
```

 Quick check

- From the element outward, describe the box model.

Quick check answer

- An element contains content immediately surrounded by the padding, which is then surrounded by the border, which is then surrounded by the margin.

Positioning *<div>* elements

 The *<div>* element has been the all-purpose element to use for creating page layouts. Although there is movement away from using the *<div>* element in favor of using semantic markup, the *<div>* element is still used when style needs to be applied to content that is not represented with semantic elements.

The *<div>* element represents a rectangular block of content. Consider the following HTML document.

```
<!DOCTYPE html>
<html xmlns="http://www.w3.org/1999/xhtml">
<head>
    <title></title>
    <link href="default.css" rel="stylesheet" />
</head>
<body>
    <div id="div1">
        <p>this is the first div</p>
    </div>
    <div id="div2">
        <p>this is the second div</p>
        <div id="div3">
            <p>
                this is the third div - Lorem ipsum dolor sit amet, salutandi
                conceptam sea cu, eos id legimus percipit argumentum. Habeo
                ipsum mandamus sit an, aeterno pertinax vim ad, et cibo
```

```
        atomorum mea. Ad vis illum porro disputando, ei eligendi
        mandamus liberavisse sea. Sea debet comprehensam no, et
        blandit officiis eos, ut per ubique abhorreant
    </p>
</div>
<div id="div4">
    <p>
        this is the fourth div - Ignota impetus sadipscing sed ut,
        sed ea alia menandri imperdiet. Te inani suscipiantur duo,
        ad mei utroque accusata. Has veri dolores assueverit cu,
        ad vocent fuisset expetenda quo. Vim id quot aliquid, ea
        iisque gloriatur mei, eos ea ludus graeci melius. Saepe
        accusam pericula cu usu, eos at alia everti.
    </p>
</div>
<div id="div5">
    <p>
        this is the fifth div - Ei duo viderer legendos, fastidii
        eligendi ad usu, audire accusamus te vel. Ullum referrentur
        mei at, qui tota reque neglegentur ne. Ius eu minim
        copiosae, malorum antiopam voluptaria te vel, nemore
        eruditi fastidii nec te. Eos id prima ridens, prompta
        alterum conclusionemque eu duo. Et vis elaboraret quaerendum.
        Repudiare interesset his ad, vis facete commune ne.
    </p>
</div>
</div>
<div id="div6">
    <p>
        this is the sixth div
    </p>
</div>
</body>
</html>
```

Notice that the *<div>* elements with id of div3, div4, and div5 are nested within div2. These elements contain dummy filler text. The default.css file contains the following style rule.

```
p {
    margin: 0px;
}

div {
    border: solid;
    border-color: black;
}

#div1 {
    background-color: yellow;
}

#div2 {
    background-color: cyan;
}
```

```
#div3 {
    background-color: lightpink;
}

#div4 {
    background-color: orange;
}

#div5 {
    background-color: lightblue;
}

#div6 {
    background-color: lightgray;
}
```

In the style rules, the *<p>* element margin is set to 0 pixels to keep the paragraph from inserting lots of space. Each *<div>* element background color is set to help differentiate each element. If you display this page in a browser, you will see something that looks like Figure 4-12.

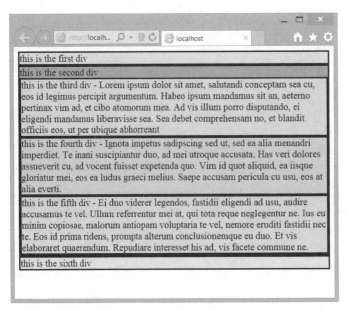

FIGURE 4-12 The *<div>* elements rendering below one another

The default behavior of the *<div>* element is such that it consumes the entire width of the screen, which forces the next *<div>* element to render on the next line. The borders touch one another, and the text is very close to the borders. You can see how div2 contains div3, div4, and div5 because the borders are contained within div2's border.

The first thing you might want to do is set the *<div>* elements to a fixed location and size to help you gain control of the placement of the *<div>* elements when you are creating your page layout. Use the *position* property, which should be set to static, relative, absolute, or fixed as follows.

Using the static position

The element is displayed where it would normally appear in the HTML flow. This is the default setting and is not usually used except to override settings that might have been applied.

Using the relative position

The element can be offset from where it normally appears in the HTML flow. In this example, div2 has the following style rule.

```
#div2 {
    background-color: cyan;
    position: relative;
    top: 15px;
    left: 30px;
}
```

With the top set to 15 pixels, div2 and its contents will be pushed down 15 pixels from its normal location. The left setting of 30 pixels will push div2 and its contents to the right by 30 pixels. The result is shown in Figure 4-13.

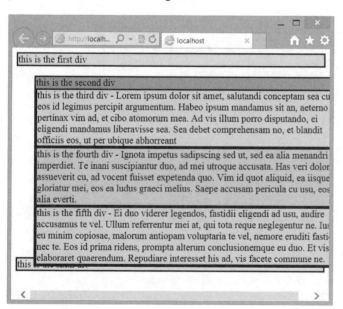

FIGURE 4-13 The use of relative positioning to move div2 and its contents

In this example, div2 and its contents maintained the original size and were cut off on the right side of the screen, and the last *<div>* element, div6, is still in its original location. The values for top and left can also be negative to move the element in the opposite direction.

Using the absolute position

The element is removed from the HTML flow and positioned within the first non-static element. If all parent elements are static (the default), then the element is positioned within the browser window. In this example, div2 has the following style rule, which sets the position to absolute, and no parent elements are non-static.

```
#div2 {
    background-color: cyan;
    position: absolute;
    top: 15px;
    left: 30px;
}
```

With the top set to 15 pixels, div2 and its contents will be pushed down 15 pixels, not from its normal location, but from the top of the browser window. The left setting of 30 pixels will push div2 and its contents to the right by 30 pixels, also not from its normal location, but from the left side of the browser window. The result is shown in Figure 4-14.

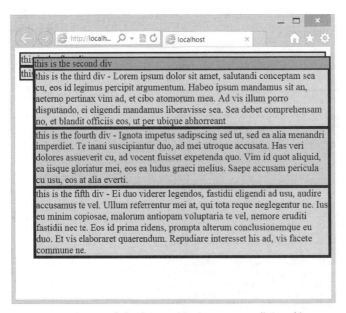

FIGURE 4-14 The use of absolute positioning to move div2 and its contents

In this example, div2 and its contents maintained the original size, and the last *<div>* element, div6, has moved from its original location and is now under div1 because div2 and its contents are no longer in the HTML document flow. Because there are no parent elements that are non-static, the positioning is relative to the browser window.

Now that div2 is non-static, what would happen if the position of one of its child elements were set to absolute? For example, suppose div5 has the following style rule.

```
#div5 {
    background-color: lightblue;
    position: absolute;
    top: 5px;
    left: 5px;
}
```

If div5 had no non-static parent elements, div5 would be positioned in the top-left corner of the browser window. Because div5 has div2 as a non-static parent, div5 will be positioned in the top-left corner of div2. The result is shown in Figure 4-15.

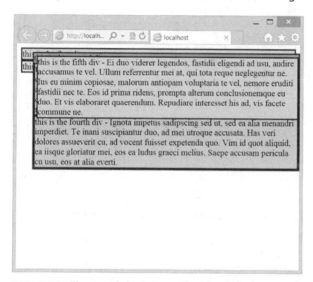

FIGURE 4-15 The use of absolute positioning within a non-static element

Notice that div5 is positioned relative to div2, not relative to the browser window. One of the benefits of this approach is that you can easily set up div3, div4, and div5 as columns within div2 by setting the top, left, right, and width properties for div3, div4, and div5, respectively. Before demonstrating this, what would you do if you wanted div5's position to be relative to the browser window? You can use fixed positioning instead of absolute positioning.

Using the fixed position

The element position is calculated much like it is with absolute positioning, but this is always in relation to the browser window.

From the previous example, the style rule for div5 is changed to the following.

```
#div5 {
    background-color: lightblue;
    position: fixed;
    top: 5px;
```

```
        left: 5px;
}
```

With the position set to fixed, div5 is positioned relative to the browser window, as shown in Figure 4-16.

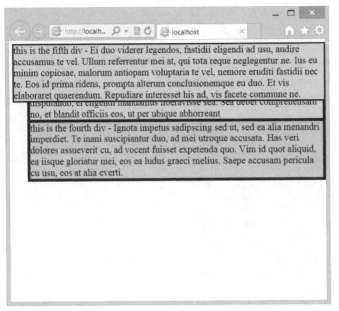

this is the fifth div - Ei duo viderer legendos, fastidii eligendi ad usu, audire accusamus te vel. Ullum referrentur mei at, qui tota reque neglegentur ne. Ius eu minim copiosae, malorum antiopam voluptaria te vel, nemore eruditi fastidii nec te. Eos id prima ridens, prompta alterum conclusionemque eu duo. Et vis elaboraret quaerendum. Repudiare interesset his ad, vis facete commune ne. disputando, ei eligendi mandamus noeravisse sea. Sea debet comprehensam no, et blandit officiis eos, ut per ubique abhorreant

this is the fourth div - Ignota impetus sadipscing sed ut, sed ea alia menandri imperdiet. Te inani suscipiantur duo, ad mei utroque accusata. Has veri dolores assueverit cu, ad vocent fuisset expetenda quo. Vim id quot aliquid, ea iisque gloriatur mei, eos ea ludus graeci melius. Saepe accusam pericula cu usu, eos at alia everti.

FIGURE 4-16 Setting the position to fixed to set the positioning relative to the browser window

More absolute positioning

Return now to absolute positioning. You can set the position, size, and location of div3, div4, and div5. The following is the contents of the default.css file.

```
p {
    margin: 0px;
}

div {
    border: solid;
    border-color: black;
}

#div1 {
    background-color: yellow;
}

#div2 {
    background-color: cyan;
    position: absolute;
    top: 15px;
```

```
        left: 30px;
        width: 450px;
        height:400px;
}

#div3 {
        background-color: lightpink;
        position: absolute;
        top:0px;
        left: 0px;
        width: 33%;
        height:100%;
}

#div4 {
        background-color: orange;
        position: absolute;
        top:0px;
        left:33%;
        width:33%;
        height:100%;
}

#div5 {
        background-color: lightblue;
        position: absolute;
        top: 0px;
        right: 0px;
        width:33%;
        height:100%;
}

#div6 {
        background-color: lightgray;
}
```

In this example, div2 has an explicit width set to 450 pixels, and its height is set to 400 pixels. The top and left properties of div3 are set to 0 pixels. These settings are relative to div2. The width of div3, div4, and div5 are set to 33 percent, which is relative to div2's width. The height of div3, div4, and div5 are set to 100 percent, which is relative to the height of div2. The left property of div4 is set to 33 percent instead of 150 pixels, which means that you can change the width of div2, and the columns will be automatically sized and positioned. The result is shown in Figure 4-17.

One of the problems with this solution is that the height of div2 is fixed at 400 pixels, and changes to the content of div3, div4, or div5 can result in a large gap at the bottom or clipping of the text at the bottom. This might be acceptable in some scenarios, but div6 is still at the top. You might want the columns to grow and shrink dynamically and div6 to be placed at the bottom of the columns, even as the column height changes. The use of the float property can solve this problem.

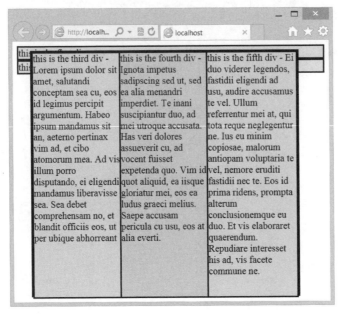

FIGURE 4-17 The use of absolute positioning to create columns

Using the float property

Absolute positioning can be a bit brittle when using absolute settings. In the previous example, it would be better if the *<div>* elements were not removed from the HTML document flow but, rather, could be sized and placed side by side to produce columns. If the *<div>* elements are not removed from the HTML document flow, div6 will automatically stay at the bottom.

The float property can be set to allow an element to float to the left or right. An element can be floated only horizontally, not vertically, and will float as far to the left or right as it can. Elements after the floating element flow around the floating element. Elements before the floating element are not affected.

To understand how the float property works, the same HTML document is used as in previous examples, and the following is the content of the default.css file.

```
p {
    margin: 0px;
}

div {
    border: solid;
    border-color: black;
}

#div1 {
    background-color: yellow;
```

```
}

#div2 {
    background-color: cyan;
}

#div3 {
    background-color: lightpink;
    float: left;
    width: 80%;
}

#div4 {
    background-color: orange;
}

#div5 {
    background-color: lightblue;
}

#div6 {
    background-color: lightgray;
}
```

In this example, the div3 float property is set to left, and the width is set to 80 percent. Figure 4-18 shows the rendered page.

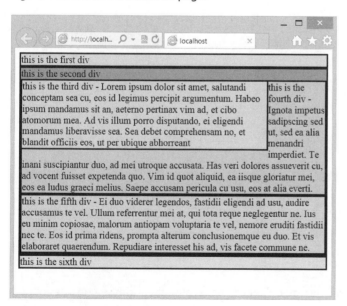

FIGURE 4-18 Floating elements with wrapping

In Figure 4-18, div3 width and float properties are set. The width is set to 80 percent, but what happens to the leftover 20 percent? In this example, div4 is placed right after div3, so div4 flows downward until div3 ends. At that point, div4's width becomes 100 percent. The net effect is that div4 wraps around div3. This technique is commonly used to insert pictures in an HTML document so that the text wraps around the image.

When multiple elements' float property is set to the same direction, the elements stack horizontally. This behavior can be used to create columns. In the following example, the float property of div3, div4, and div5 is set to left, and their width property is set to 33 percent, using the following style rules.

```
p {
    margin: 0px;
}

div {
    border: solid;
    border-color: black;
}

#div1 {
    background-color: yellow;
}

#div2 {
    background-color: cyan;
}

#div3 {
    background-color: lightpink;
    float: left;
    width: 32%;
}

#div4 {
    background-color: orange;
    float: left;
     width: 32%;
}

#div5 {
    background-color: lightblue;
    float: left;
     width: 32%;
}

#div6 {
    background-color: lightgray;
}
```

The width is set to 32 percent instead of 33 percent because the width setting does not include the border width, which is defaulting to 2 pixels. The result is shown in Figure 4-19.

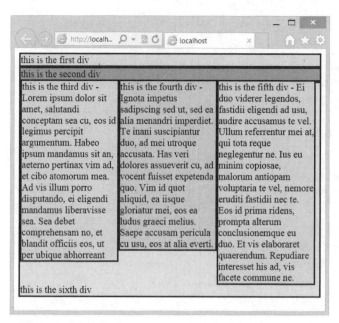

FIGURE 4-19 Using the float property to create columns

With all three columns rendering side by side and inside div2, borders use a total of 14 pixels. If the width is set to 33 percent, the last column won't fit and will be pushed under div3 because setting the width to 32 percent causes a sliver to be available on the right side, and div6 fills the void. How can div6 be styled to show just at the bottom? Use the clear property.

Using the clear property

The clear property instructs the browser to place the clear element after the floating elements. Set the clear property to both, as shown in the following style rule for div6.

```
#div6 {
    background-color: lightgray;
    clear: both;
}
```

Figure 4-20 shows the rendered page. Notice the location of div6. Using this approach keeps div6 from consuming space beside the columns.

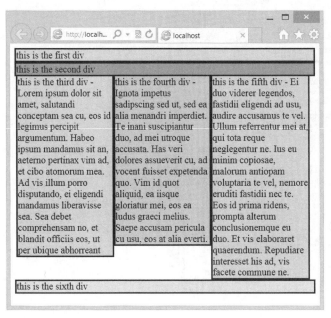

FIGURE 4-20 The clear property set to both

Using the box-sizing property

The previous example looks good except for the space on the right side. Many developers would play with the width settings on the three columns until they found settings that cause the third column to line up properly on the right. Remember that the reason for the gap on the right side is that the width of the columns is set to 32 percent because the width is based on the content of the element, not including the border.

To solve this problem, you can change the way the browser calculates the width by setting the box-sizing property on div3, div4, and div5. The box sizing has the following valid values.

- **content-box** The default setting; calculates the width based on the content width only.
- **border-box** Calculates the width based on the border, padding, and content width.
- **padding-box** Calculates the width based on the padding and content width.

In the following example, the columns' box sizing is set to border-box, and then the width of the columns is set to 33 percent, 34 percent, and 33 percent.

```
p {
    margin: 0px;
}

div {
    border: solid;
    border-color: black;
```

```
}

#div1 {
    background-color: yellow;
}

#div2 {
    background-color: cyan;
    clear: both;
}

#div3 {
    background-color: lightpink;
    box-sizing: border-box;
    float: left;
    width: 33%;
}

#div4 {
    background-color: orange;
    box-sizing: border-box;
    float: left;
    width: 34%;
}

#div5 {
    background-color: lightblue;
    box-sizing: border-box;
    float: left;
    width: 33%;
}

#div6 {
    background-color: lightgray;
    clear: both;
}
```

The rendered output is shown in Figure 4-21.

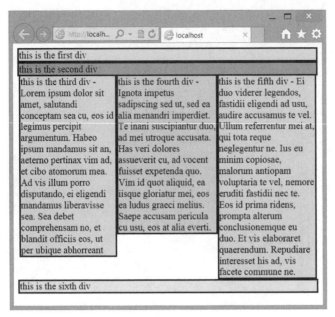

FIGURE 4-21 Using the box-sizing property to control width calculations

If you look closely at Figure 4-21, you might notice that on the left and right sides of the columns, there is a very small space. This is because div3, div4, and div5 are inside div2; they fit within the border of div2. If you need these columns to line up exactly with the border of div2, you can take div3, div4, and div5 out of div2.

 Quick check

- You want to set the width of an element based on its overall width. What should the box sizing be set to?

Quick check answer

- box-sizing: border-box;

Centering content in the browser window

Creating a page layout that looks great in any browser and continues to look good as the browser window is resized can be a daunting task. A common approach to solving this problem is to create a *<div>* element that contains your content and set the *<div>* to a fixed width, such as 800 pixels.

If you set the width to a fixed size, you'll probably want to center the *<div>* element in the browser window. You can do that by setting the left and right margins of the *<div>* element to *auto*. When both margins are set to auto and the width is set, the browser divides the excess margin space equally. The result is a centered *<div>* element. For example, if your content is in a *<div>* element whose id is set to "container", you can add the following style rule to center the container's contents.

```
#container {
    width: 600px;
    margin-left: auto;
    margin-right: auto;
}
```

The width must be set, or the centering will not work.

Lesson summary

- CSS colors can be set using color names; hexadecimal notation; or the rgb, rgba, and hsl functions.
- Use the opacity property to set the transparency.
- To format text, set the font-family property and then set the font properties.
- Font families that have curls at the top and bottom of characters belong to the serif font family group. Font families that don't have curls belong to the sans serif font family group. Font families whose characters are all the same width belong to the monospaced font family group. Font families that imitate handwriting belong to the cursive font family group. Font families that are decorative belong to the fantasy font family group.
- The CSS box model defines element content as surrounded by padding, which is then surrounded by the border, which is then surrounded by the margin.
- You can set all four sides of the margin, padding, and border by providing a single size to be applied to all sides, or you can set individual sides by adding -top, -bottom, -left, or -right to the property and assigning a value to each.
- The *<div>* element can be positioned by assigning a value of static, relative, absolute, or fixed to the position property.
- The float property can be used to create columns without removing the *<div>* element from HTML flow. This property can also be used to position images so that text flows around the image.

- Use the clear property to indicate when an element is to be positioned clear after the previous element.
- Use the box-sizing property to change the default width calculation from content to border.

Lesson review

Answer the following questions to test your knowledge of the information in this lesson. You can find the answers to these questions and explanations of why each answer choice is correct or incorrect in the "Answers" section at the end of this chapter.

1. You want to find three shades of a color to use on parts of your webpage. Which color function helps you accomplish this task?

   A. rgb( )

   B. rgba( )

   C. hsl( )

   D. color( )

2. A font that has curls at the top and bottom of its characters belongs to which font family group?

   A. monospace

   B. serif

   C. sans serif

   D. cursive

   E. fantasy

3. You want to position a *<div>* element in relation to the browser window. Which position setting do you use?

   A. static

   B. relative

   C. absolute

   D. fixed

Practice exercises

If you encounter a problem completing any of these exercises, the completed projects can be installed from the Practice Exercises folder that is provided with the companion content.

Exercise 1: Add a style sheet to the calculator project

In this exercise, you apply your CSS3 knowledge by adding a cascading style sheet to the WebCalculator project that you created in Chapter 3, "Getting started with JavaScript." You add style rules to improve the look of the webpage. The color scheme for this webpage will be purple-blue, and all colors will have the hue set to 255.

This exercise adds style rules with a minimum of modifications to the default.html file. In the next exercise, you make changes to the default.html file that the style rules can use to finish cleaning up the webpage.

1. Start Visual Studio Express 2012 for Web. Navigate to File | Open Project.

2. Navigate to the solution that you created in Chapter 3 and select the WebCalculator.sln file. Click Open. You can also navigate to File | Recent Projects and Solutions to select the solution.

   If you didn't complete the exercises in Chapter 3, you can use the solution in the Chapter 4 Exercise 1 Start folder.

3. In the Solution Explorer window, right-click the default.html file and choose Set As Start Page. Press F5 to verify that your home page is displayed.

4. In the Solution Explorer window, add a CSS file by right-clicking the Content folder in the project and navigating to Add | Style Sheet.

5. Name the page **default.css** and click OK.

6. Open the default.html page, drag the default.css file from the Solution Explorer window, and drop it just before the *<script>* element that loads the CalculatorLibrary.js file. The *<head>* element should look like the following.

   ```
   <head>
       <title>Web Calculator</title>
       <link href="Content/default.css" rel="stylesheet" />
       <script type="text/javascript" src="Scripts/CalculatorLibrary.js"></script>
   </head>
   ```

7. Open the default.css file and set the body background color with maximum saturation and half lightening as follows.

   ```
   body {
       background-color: hsl(255,100%,50%);
   }
   ```

8. Add a style rule that formats the text boxes.

   This style sets the height, width, text alignment, padding, and border style as follows.

   ```
   input {
       width: 446px;
       height: 35px;
       text-align: right;
       padding: 10px;
       border: inset;
   }
   ```

9. Add a style rule that formats the buttons.

   This style sets the background color, width, height, and border styles as follows.

   ```
   button {
       background-color: hsl(255, 50%, 80%);
       width: 150px;
       height: 50px;
       border: outset;
   }
   ```

10. Add a style rule that sets the format of the buttons when you hover over a button.

    This style sets the background color as follows.

    ```
    button:hover {
        background-color: hsl(255, 50%, 90%);
    }
    ```

11. Add a style rule that sets the format of the buttons when a button is clicked.

    This style sets the background color and the border style as follows.

    ```
    button:active {
        border: inset;
        border-width: thick;
        border-color: hsl(255, 100%, 100%);
        background-color: hsl(255, 50%, 50%);
    }
    ```

12. Add a style rule that provides common formatting for the buttons and text boxes.

    The selector should be for the *<input>* and the *<button>* elements and should set the font family, font size, border width, border color, and margin.

    ```
    input, button {
        font-family: Arial;
        font-size: 24pt;
        border-width: thick;
        border-color: hsl(255, 100%, 100%);
        margin: 5px;
    }
    ```

13. Add a style to the *txtResult* text box to indicate that this text box is read-only.

    The style sets the background color as follows.

    ```
    #txtResult {
        background-color: hsl(255, 50%, 80%);
    }
    ```

14. To see the results, press F5 to start debugging the application.

    You should see a nicer-looking calculator interface, as shown in Figure 4-22.

FIGURE 4-22 The web calculator user interface

15. Try entering data and clicking the plus and minus buttons.

The calculator should be working.

16. Switch back to Visual Studio by pressing Alt+Tab. Notice that the title bar says (Running).

17. Press Shift+F5 to stop debugging.

Shift+F5 works only when Visual Studio has the focus, not when the running application has the focus.

The only real change on the default.html page was to add the link to the style sheet. The calculator is left justified in the browser window, and too many settings have absolute values. In the next exercise, you clean up the rest of this webpage.

Exercise 2: Clean up the web calculator

In this exercise, you continue with the project from Exercise 1 and modify the default.html file to aid in formatting the webpage. You add *<div>* elements so you can center the calculator in the browser window. You also implement a read-only CSS class that can be used on any read-only text box.

1. Open the project from Exercise 1.

   If you didn't perform Exercise 1, you can use the project located in the Exercise 2 Start folder.

2. Open the default.html file.

3. Surround the inputs and buttons with a *<div>* element whose id is set to "calculator".

   This *<div>* element will be used to center the calculator and create a box around it. The default.html should look like the following.

```
<!DOCTYPE html>
<html xmlns="http://www.w3.org/1999/xhtml">
<head>
    <title>Web Calculator</title>
    <link href="Content/default.css" rel="stylesheet" />
    <script type="text/javascript" src="Scripts/CalculatorLibrary.js"></script>
</head>
<body>
    <div id="calculator">
        <input id="txtResult" type="text" readonly="readonly" /><br />
        <input id="txtInput" type="text" /><br />
        <button id="btn7">7</button>
        <button id="btn8">8</button>
        <button id="btn9">9</button><br />
        <button id="btn4">4</button>
        <button id="btn5">5</button>
        <button id="btn6">6</button><br />
        <button id="btn1">1</button>
        <button id="btn2">2</button>
        <button id="btn3">3</button><br />
        <button id="btnClear">C</button>
        <button id="btn0">0</button>
        <button id="btnClearEntry">CE</button><br />
        <button id="btnPlus">+</button>
        <button id="btnMinus">-</button>
    </div>
    <script type="text/javascript">
        window.addEventListener('load', initialize, false);
    </script>
</body>
</html>
```

4. Open the default.css file.

5. Insert, after the body style, a style rule for the *<div>* element whose id is "calculator". Set the style properties to put a border around the calculator. Set a fixed height and width. Center the contents and set the padding as follows.

```
#calculator {
    border: solid;
    background-color: hsl(255, 100%, 60%);
    width: 500px;
    height: 500px;
    margin-left: auto;
```

```
        margin-right: auto;
        text-align: center;
        padding: 10px;
    }
```

Now that you have a box with a fixed height and width, you can change the height and width settings on the input and button elements to be a percentage of the calculator size.

6. Change the style rules as follows.

```
input {
    width: 85%;
    height: 7%;
    text-align: right;
    padding: 10px;
    border: inset;
}

button {
    background-color: hsl(255, 50%, 80%);
    width: 25%;
    height: 10%;
    border: outset;
}
```

Instead of setting the style of *txtResult* by using its id, it would be better to change the selector to apply the style to any element whose read-only attribute is set.

7. Change the style rule as follows.

```
[readonly] {
    background-color: hsl(255, 50%, 80%);
}
```

Your completed default.css file should look like the following.

```
body {
    background-color: hsl(255,100%,50%);
}

#calculator {
    border: solid;
    background-color: hsl(255, 100%, 60%);
    width: 500px;
    height: 500px;
    margin-left: auto;
    margin-right: auto;
    text-align: center;
    padding: 10px;
}

input {
    width: 85%;
    height: 7%;
    text-align: right;
```

```
        padding: 10px;
        border: inset;
    }

button {
    background-color: hsl(255, 50%, 80%);
    width: 25%;
    height: 10%;
    border: outset;
}

    button:hover {
        background-color: hsl(255, 50%, 90%);
    }

    button:active {
        border: inset;
        border-width: thick;
        border-color: hsl(255, 100%, 100%);
        background-color: hsl(255, 50%, 50%);
    }

input, button {
    font-family: Arial;
    font-size: 24pt;
    border-width: thick;
    border-color: hsl(255, 100%, 100%);
    margin: 5px;
}

[readonly] {
    background-color: hsl(255, 50%, 80%);
}
```

8. Press F5 to run the application.

Figure 4-23 shows the completed calculator.

FIGURE 4-23 The completed web calculator

9. Try clicking the number buttons to choose numbers and try the plus and minus buttons while observing the result. Try clicking the clear-entry button after you enter a number. Try clicking the clear button to see the input and result clear.

Suggested practice exercises

The following additional exercises are designed to give you more opportunities to practice what you've learned and to help you successfully master the lessons presented in this chapter.

- **Exercise 1** Learn more about positioning by adding more *<div>* elements to the webpage to define a header and footer for the page. Use CSS style rules to set the position.

- **Exercise 2** Learn more about CSS selectors by adding more elements to the page and try setting the format by selecting the elements without using an id.

- **Exercise 3** Learn more about colors by changing the color scheme, using RGB values.

Answers

This section contains the answers to the lesson review questions in this chapter.

Lesson 1

1. **Correct answer: C**

   A. Incorrect: //temporary is a comment for programming languages such as C, C++, and C#, but it's not applicable in a style sheet.

   B. Incorrect: --temporary is a SQL Server comment, not a style sheet comment.

   C. Correct: The block comment syntax, /* temporary */, can make an entire block of text into a comment.

   D. Incorrect: rem temporary is a DOS batch file comment, but it's not applicable to style sheets.

2. **Correct answer: C**

   A. Incorrect: Inline styles do not provide any separation because they are defined on the HTML element.

   B. Incorrect: Embedded styles provide little separation because they are located in the HTML *<head>* element.

   C. Correct: External style sheets provide the best separation because the style rules are in a separate file from the HTML document.

   D. Incorrect: The @import statement is used in external style sheets to import styles into the style sheet. This provides reuse functionality. The @import statement cannot be used in the HTML document.

3. **Correct answer: B**

   A. Incorrect: The rel attribute specifies the relationship between the HTML document and the linked file.

   B. Correct: The media attribute is required to specify the style sheet usage.

   C. Incorrect: Using the printer.css name has no bearing on the usage of the file.

   D. Incorrect: The target attribute typically specifies the frame the link will target.

Lesson 2

1. **Correct answer: A**

   A. Correct: The first part of the selector locates the element with id of readingPane while the second part of the selector locates all paragraph elements, and then returns the first letter of each paragraph so the style can be applied to it.

B. **Incorrect:** The first part of the selector locates the element with id of readingPane while the second part of the selector returns the first letter of the *<div>* element, but not for each paragraph.

C. **Incorrect:** The first part of the selector locates the element with id of readingPane while the second part of the selector locates all paragraph elements and returns only the first paragraph. The style is applied to the entire paragraph.

D. **Incorrect:** The first part of the selector locates the element with id of readingPane while the second part of the selector returns the child of its parent, so the style is applied to the entire *<div>* element.

2. **Correct answer: A**

A. **Correct:** Specificity is the deciding factor in this example. The specificity value is 0,1,2 in the first style rule. The specificity value is 0,0,2 in the second style rule. The first value is higher; thus, yellow is displayed.

B. **Incorrect:** Remember that textual order comes into play only when the specificity values are the same.

C. **Incorrect:** There are selector matches that would keep the color from being transparent.

D. **Incorrect:** There are selector matches that would keep the color from being white.

3. **Correct answer: B**

A. **Incorrect:** Remember that if the specificity values are the same, textual order dictates the outcome.

B. **Correct:** The specificity value for both style rules is 0,1,2, so textual order dictates the outcome. The Department.css file is linked after the Corporate.css file, so the style rule in the Department.css file will be applied.

C. **Incorrect:** There are selector matches that would keep the color from being transparent.

D. **Incorrect:** There are selector matches that would keep the color from being white.

Lesson 3

1. **Correct answer: C**

A. **Incorrect:** The rgb function requires you to specify varying amounts of red, green, and blue for each color, so it's not easy to derive three colors that match.

B. **Incorrect:** The rgba function is the same as the rgb function, except that you need to specify the alpha (opacity) value, too.

C. **Correct:** By using the hsl function, you can set the hue value and then adjust the saturation and lightening values to derive other matching colors.

D. **Incorrect:** There is no color function that can be used in a style sheet to generate a color.

2. **Correct answer: B**

    A. **Incorrect:** The monospace font family characters are all the same width.

    B. **Correct:** The serif font family characters have serifs (curls) on the top and bottom of them.

    C. **Incorrect:** The sans serif font family characters do not have serifs (curls) on the top and bottom of them.

    D. **Incorrect:** The cursive font family characters imitate handwriting.

    E. **Incorrect:** The fantasy font family has decorative characters.

3. **Correct answer: D**

    A. **Incorrect:** Using static, the element is displayed where it would normally appear in the HTML flow. This is the default.

    B. **Incorrect:** Using relative, the element is displayed relative to where it would normally appear in the HTML flow.

    C. **Incorrect:** Using absolute, the element is removed from the HTML flow and positioned within the first non-static element. Although this could mean that the element is positioned within the browser window, it's not guaranteed.

    D. **Correct:** Using fixed, the element is removed from the HTML flow and positioned within the browser window.

CHAPTER 5

More HTML5

The previous chapters covered a lot of material you need to know. Much, but not all, of the content in the previous chapters existed before the HTML5 technologies came to be. This chapter provides a transition, moving you from old to new topics. Lesson 1, "Thinking HTML5 semantics," discusses many aspects of HTML5 semantics that are primarily new topics. Lesson 2, "Working with tables," explains tables, which is an older but relevant topic, and describes added features in HTML5.

Lessons in this chapter:

Before you begin

To complete this chapter, you must have some understanding of web development. This chapter requires the hardware and software listed in the "System requirements" section in the book's Introduction.

Lesson 1: Thinking HTML5 semantics

The previous chapter covered CSS positioning; all the examples used the *<div>* element. The *<div>* element has been the preferred element to use for positioning content when creating a page layout.

Many developers have also used the *<table>* element, but that element is much more difficult to use, especially to maintain a website. Lesson 2 explains the *<table>* element but doesn't use a *<table>* element for page layout.

This lesson provides a different approach to creating a page layout; it covers semantic elements and explains why you should use them.

Why semantic markup?

One of the problems with using *<div>* and *<span>* elements is that they have little meaning other than "I need to do something with this content." For *<div>* elements, you typically need to position the content on the page. For *<span>* elements, you need to apply special formatting to the content.

You might be wondering what kind of meaning the *<div>* and *<span>* elements can provide. For *<div>* elements, it might be better to have an element that represents the page header and can be positioned. You might want a different element that represents the page footer and can be positioned.

Are your users reading your HTML source? If the *<div>* element is the all-purpose tool to position elements, why use these new semantic elements?

These are good questions and thoughts. In fact, if you search the web for semantic markup, you'll see plenty of discussions, some quite heated, about this topic.

Developers have been using *<div>* elements for page layout, and the developer usually provides the meaning of each *<div>* element based on its id or CSS class. The W3C analyzed thousands of webpages and found the most common id and class names. Rather than start over, the W3C made these names into new elements. Obvious examples are the *<header>* and *<footer>* elements.

Browser support for HTML5

Your users typically don't read your HTML source when they browse to your website, but many machines are reading your HTML source with the goal of interpreting your webpage. Web crawlers are constantly surfing the Internet, reading webpages and building indexed searchable content that can be used to find your website. Many people have Nonvisual Desktop Access (NVDA) devices, which provide an alternate means of viewing, reading, and processing webpages. Some NVDA devices implement voice synthesis to read webpages to visually impaired people; others provide a Braille-like interface so the user can read your webpages by touch, as shown in Figure 5-1.

NVDA devices need your help to interpret your webpage content properly. They need you to use meaningful HTML tags that define the purpose of each element's contents. Doing so helps crawlers produce better matches to search queries, and NVDA devices that read your webpages to users can provide a more meaningful experience. For more information, visit *http://www.nvdaproject.org/.*

FIGURE 5-1 The refreshable Braille display

Creating semantic HTML5 documents

Now that you understand the importance of using semantic markup, you might decide that you'll never use a *<div>* or *<span>* element again. However, you will come across content that needs to be styled but doesn't clearly fit the meaning of any semantic elements. You can and should use *<div>* and *<span>* elements in these scenarios.

Throughout this book, you will find many HTML5 tags. As you create your HTML pages, you will be faced with the sometimes daunting task of providing meaning to your content by supplying semantic tags. Use semantics carefully so you use an element only for its intended purpose. If you need a custom element, use the *<div>* or *<span>* tag and add a class name or id that conveys the semantics you desire. Be pragmatic and not too much of a purist.

Creating an HTML5 layout container

The previous chapter showed many examples that demonstrate the use of *<div>* elements to provide positioning of content on a webpage. If you were creating a webpage to display blog posts, you might create a layout container for your page that looks like the example in Figure 5-2.

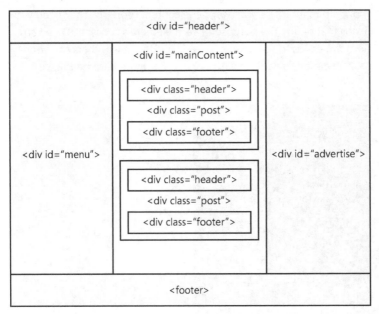

FIGURE 5-2 A blog site layout container using *<div>* elements

A *layout container* lays out its children in a way that is flexible and reusable. For the developer, the purpose of the *<div>* elements is easy to understand based on the id and CSS class names. How can the browser understand the elements? If you want the browser to give the user the ability to focus automatically on the first element in the main content when the page opens, how would you do this? If you want the browser to give the user special quick-launch buttons for the menu items, how could you accomplish this?

By using HTML5 semantic elements, you can create a layout container that uses elements that are meaningful to both the developer and the browser. The following are common elements by which to create an HTML5 layout container.

- **<header>**   Defines a section that provides a header. You can use the *<header>* element at the top of your HTML document as a page header. You can also use the *<header>* element in the *<article>* element.

- **<footer>**   Defines a section that provides a footer. You can use the *<footer>* element at the bottom of your HTML document as a page footer. You can also use the *<footer>* element in the *<article>* element.

- **<nav>**   Defines a section that houses a block of major navigational links.

- **<aside>**   Defines a section of content that is separate from the content the *<aside>* element is in. This is typically used for sidebars.

- **<section>**   Part of the whole that is typically named with an *<h1>* to *<h6>* element internal element.

- **<article>**   A unit of content that can stand on its own and can be copied to other locations. A blog post is a good example of an article.

Figure 5-3 shows how these elements might be applied to create a layout container.

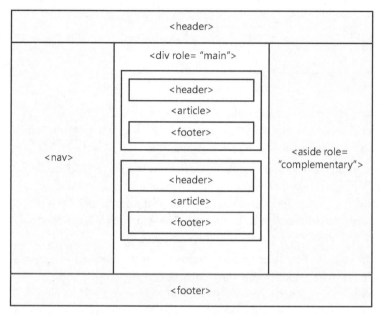

FIGURE 5-3 Layout container example, using the new HTML5 elements

In Figure 5-3, all *<div>* elements have been replaced with the new HTML5 elements.

Using the *<header>* element

The *<header>* elements in Figure 5-3 replace the *<div id="header">* elements in Figure 5-2, which cleans up the page a bit and provides a section meaning to browsers and other devices. Don't confuse the HTML5 *<header>* element that is within a *<body>* element, which is visible, with the HTML *<head>* element for the HTML document, which is invisible.

The *<header>* element should contain *<h1>* to *<h6>*, referred to as an *<hn>* moving forward element, containing your visible heading. You can also have other content with your *<header>* element, such as company logos and navigational links, as in the following example.

```
<header>
    <h1>Contoso Ltd.</h1>
    <img src="logo.jpg" alt="Company Logo" />
    <p>Other supplementary information</p>
</header>
```

You can have multiple *<header>* elements in an HTML document. There are multiple *<header>* elements within this layout container because each *<article>* element has a *<header>*.

The *<header>* element can also contain the *<hgroup>* element, which provides the ability to group one or more *<hn>* elements within a *<header>* element, as shown in the following code example.

```
<header>
    <hgroup>
        <h1>Primary Header</h1>
        <h2>seconday header</h2>
    </hgroup>
    <img src='logo.jpg' alt='Company Logo' />
</header>
```

The *<hgroup>* is a wrapper for one or more related header elements. The *<hgroup>* element can be in a *<header>* element but doesn't need to be in a *<header>* element. The *<hgroup>* is most commonly used for subtitles and alternative titles.

The biggest reason for using the *<hgroup>* element has to do with using HTML5 outliner tools. If you have an *<h1>* header element and an *<h2>* subheader element, and you don't use the *<hgroup>* to connect a header and subheader, the outline treats the *<h2>* as a second level, but you really want the subheading to be ignored. The *<hgroup>* will expose only the first element and hide the other *<hn>* elements in the *<hgroup>*.

If your header is just an *<hn>* and contains no other content, you don't need a *<header>* element. As soon as you have more than a single *<hn>*, such as *<img>* elements and *<p>* elements, wrap your content in a *<header>* element. When you have multiple *<hn>* elements, such as a header and subheader, wrap the *<hn>* elements in the *<hgroup>* element. A *<header>* element should not be nested inside a *<header>* element.

By looking at the difference between Figure 5-2 and Figure 5-3, you can see that the *<header>* element replaced the *<div id="header">* element. Be careful, because by default the *<header>* element on some browsers does not render as a rectangular block as the *<div>* element does. You can fix this by adding the following style rule to provide matching behavior.

```
header { display:block;}
```

Using the *<footer>* element

The *<footer>* elements in Figure 5-3 replace the *<div id="footer">* elements in Figure 5-2, which cleans up the page a bit and provides a section meaning to browsers and other devices.

The *<footer>* element typically contains information about the section it's in, such as who wrote it, copyright information, and links to related documents. The *<footer>* element is much like the *<header>* element except that it typically belongs at the bottom of a section instead of at the top. Like the *<header>* element, it can be used many times within an HTML document to provide ending content for the HTML document and ending content for articles and sections within the HTML document. The *<footer>* element should not be nested inside a *<footer>* element. The following is an example of a *<footer>* element.

```
<footer>
  <ul>
    <li>Copyright (C) 2012, Contoso Ltd., All rights reserved</li>
    <li><a href="default.html">Home</a></li>
  </ul>
</footer>
```

Using the *<nav>* element

The *<nav>* element in Figure 5-3 replaces the *<div id="menu">* element in Figure 5-2, which provides a section meaning to browsers and devices. The *<nav>* element wraps a group of major links that are on your page. Menus are the most common candidates for the *<nav>* element.

Like menus, footers commonly have groups of links, but you don't need to use the *<nav>* element if you are using the *<footer>* element, and the *<nav>* element is not required for links within your content. You can have many *<nav>* elements in an HTML document. For example, in addition to the menu that is normally on the left side or across the top of the page, you might have a group of links above the footer that link to the next page of blog posts or to other major areas of your site.

Think of a screen reader when implementing the *<nav>* element. It will be looking for the primary navigation area on the webpage so it can present these links to the user as menu items that have links to other areas within the current website. Links to off-site locations should not be part of the *<nav>* element. Footer links to secondary areas of your website also don't require a *<nav>* element.

Using the *<aside>* element

The *<aside>* element in Figure 5-3 replaces the *<div id="advertise">* element in Figure 5-2, which provides a section meaning to browsers and devices.

The *<aside>* element wraps secondary content when used for sidebars. In many cases, this is where the advertising and other site-related content goes. In addition, when the *<aside>* element is in an article, it should contain content tangentially related to the content within the article. The use of the *<aside>* element differs based on the context, as shown in the following example.

```
<body>
  <header>
    <h1>Blogging for fun</h1>
  </header>
  <article>
    <h1>Blog of the day</h1>
    <p>This is today's blog post. La, la, la, la, la,
    la, la, la, la, la, la</p>
    <aside>
      <!-- Inside the article, so it's related to the article -->
      <h1>What's this all about?</h1>
      <p>This article talks about la, la...</p>
    </aside>
```

```
    </article>
    <aside>
      <!-- Outside the article, so it's related to the sites -->
      <h2>Blog Advertising</h2>
      <p>You too can have your own blog...</p>
    </aside>
  </body>
```

The two meanings make sense when you consider that an article should be a complete unit that can be shared.

Using roles

In Figure 5-3, the *<aside>* element and the *<div>* element implement the role attribute, specified by the Web Accessible Initiative (WAI), which specifies the Accessible Rich Internet Applications (ARIA) suite, called WAI-ARIA.

 WAI-ARIA defines the role class hierarchy and how roles are used to provide specific meaning to screen readers for accessibility purposes. There are many parent role classes, and there are child role classes that inherit from role classes. One such parent role class is called the *landmark* role class, which represents regions of the page intended as navigational landmarks. The following are child classes of the landmark role class.

- **application** An area declared as a web application as opposed to a web document.

- **banner** An area on a webpage that has site-specific content, such as site name and logo, instead of page-specific content; maximum one per webpage, usually header content.

- **complementary** An area on a webpage that complements the page but still has meaning if separated from the page.

- **contentinfo** An area that contains information about the parent document such as copyright notices and links; maximum one per webpage, usually footer content.

- **form** An area on a webpage that contains a collection of input controls for gathering data to be sent to the web server; search forms should use the search role.

- **main** An area that contains the main content of the document; maximum one per webpage.

- **navigation** An area that contains navigational links.

- **search** An area on a webpage that contains a collection of input controls for entering and displaying search information.

You can use these roles to provide meaning to an area of the webpage, but the new HTML5 elements already provide meaning. However, the HTML5 elements don't provide a new element to identify the main content of the webpage. Instead, all known content is not the main content, and what's left over must be the main content. Furthermore, the *<aside>* element is used as a sidebar, and you might want to provide more meaning. Why not use the WAI-ARIA role to provide meaning to other developers and to assistive devices? That is what is illustrated in Figure 5-3.

Controlling format by using the *<div>* element

Don't forget that the *<div>* element can be placed around content, enabling you to control its format. The *<div>* element is invisible and has no meaning, so when using HTML5, it's generally better to use a semantic element such as article or section to provide context that has meaning. If all you need is formatting, the use of the *<div>* element is perfect.

Adding thematic breaks

Use the *<hr />* element to add a thematic break. It is a void element, so it cannot have any content. You can use the *<hr />* element to provide a thematic break when there is a scene change in a story or to denote a transition to another topic within a section of a reference book.

Annotating content

When annotating content by using HTML5 elements, be aware that the *<b>* and *<i>* elements that have been around since the beginning are still available but now have new meaning. This section describes the use of the *<b>* and *<i>* elements and many other elements that can be used to annotate content.

Using the *<b>* element

The *<b>* element was used to produce bold text, but now elements should have meaning, not style. To keep the *<b>* element but also have semantic elements, the meaning needed to change.

According to the W3C, the *<b>* element represents a span of text to which attention is being drawn for utilitarian purposes without conveying any extra importance and with no implication of an alternate voice or mood, such as keywords in a document abstract; product names in a review; actionable words in interactive, text-driven software; or an article lede. Therefore, you can apply any style you want to the *<b>* element, although keeping the bold style makes the most sense.

The *<b>* element is the element of last resort because headings should be denoted with the *<hn>* element, emphasized text should be denoted with the *<em>* element, important text should be denoted with the *<strong>* element, and marked or highlighted text should use the *<mark>* element. Refrain from using the *<b>* element except to denote product names in a review, keywords in a document extract, or an article lede, as shown in the following example.

```
<article>
   <h1>PolyWannaWidget Review</h1>
   The <b>PolyWannaWidget</b> is the best product
   to use for creating crackers from nothing
   other than a hammer.
</article>
```

Using the *<strong>* element

Closely related to the *<b>* element is the *<strong>* element, which represents strong importance for its contents. You can show relative importance by nesting *<strong>* elements within *<strong>* elements. Note that changing the importance of part of the text in a sentence does not change the meaning of the sentence. The following is an example that is in response to the question, "Should I take a left turn?"

```
<p>
   You need to turn <strong>right</strong>.
</p>
```

Note that the default styles for *<strong>* and *<b>* elements look the same.

Using the *<i>* element

The *<i>* element was used to produce italic text, but like the *<b>* element, the element should provide meaning, not style.

According to the W3C, the *<i>* element represents a span of text that is in an alternate voice or mood or is otherwise offset from the normal prose in a manner indicating a different quality of text, such as a taxonomic designation, a technical term, an idiomatic phrase from another language, a thought, or a ship name in Western texts.

This means that that you can apply any style to the *<i>* element, although, like the *<b>* element, you probably should keep the default style.

The *<em>* element

Use the *<em>* element for emphatic stress. Use it to designate text you'd pronounce somewhat differently, with emphasis. The following is an example that is in response to the question, "Can you find a developer?"

```
<p>
   I <em>am</em> a developer.
</p>
```

Note that the default styles for *<em>* and *<i>* elements look the same.

Using the *<abbr>* element for abbreviations and acronyms

In earlier versions of HTML, you could indicate an acronym by using the *<acronym>* element, but in HTML5, the *<acronym>* element is obsolete. Use the *<abbr>* element to indicate an abbreviation or acronym and use the title attribute to provide the full text.

The *<abbr>* element is an inline element and can be used with *<strong>* or other inline elements as necessary. The following is an example of denoting an abbreviation and acronym by using the *<abbr>* element.

```
<p>
   The <abbr title='radio detection and ranging'>radar</abbr>
   must be repaired <abbr title='as soon as possible'>ASAP</abbr>
```

```
    by Contoso, <abbr title='Incorporated'>Inc.</abbr>
</p>
```

Note that the title is not required, especially when you know that everyone will know the meanings of the abbreviations and acronyms.

The *<address>* element

Use the *<address>* element to define contact information for the author/owner of a document. You may include email address, postal address, or any contact address that references the author/owner of the document.

Be careful to use the *<address>* element only when referencing the author/owner of the document. Do not use it for arbitrary address information on your webpage. For example, if you are displaying your customer's address on a webpage, it should not be wrapped in an *<address>* element.

The following is an example of the use of the *<address>* element in the footer of a webpage.

```
<footer>
    Copyright (C) 2012
    <address>
        Contoso, Inc.
        <a href="email:WebMaster@Contoso.com">
            WebMaster@Contoso.com
        </a>
    </address>
</footer>
```

Quotations and citations

When it's time to start quoting, you can use the *<blockquote>* element to create a long, running quotation and the *<q>* element for an inline quotation. Both these elements have a *cite* attribute that names the source work of the quote.

The *<blockquote>* element is a block-level element; it can contain almost anything, including headers, footers, tables, and paragraphs. The *<blockquote>* element is a *sectioning root*, which means that any *<hn>* elements within the *<blockquote>* element will not be included in an outline of the HTML document. In addition, a single paragraph does not need to be included in a *<p>* element.

The *<blockquote>* and *<q>* elements have a *cite* attribute that names the source work, but as an attribute, this is hidden data. A better approach is to use the *<cite>* element, which you can place in the *<footer>* element of your *<blockquote>* and *<q>* elements. The citation should always contain the name of the work, not the author name. The following is an example of the *<blockquote>* element.

```
<blockquote>
    O Romeo, Romeo, wherefore art thou Romeo?<br />
    Deny thy father and refuse thy name;<br />
```

```
    Or if thou wilt not, be but sworn my love<br />
    And I'll no longer be a Capulet.<br />
    <footer>
      <p>
          by William Shakespeare,
          <cite>Romeo and Juliet</cite> Act 2, scene 2
      </p>
    </footer>
</blockquote>
```

The *<cite>* element contains only the name of the work, not the author or the location within the work.

When you want to add an inline quotation, use the *<q>* element instead of using quotation marks. The browser will insert the quotation marks for you. You can add the *cite* attribute to the *<q>* element, which should contain only the name of the work. Furthermore, the *<q>* element can be nested within another *<q>* element. The following is an example of the *<q>* element.

```
<p>
    John said to the audience <q>Sally was crying when she
    shouted <q>Leave me alone</q> and then she ran away.</q>
</p>
```

This example renders the first quotation by using double quotes and the second quotation by using single quotes.

Documenting code by using the *<code>* and *<samp>* elements

When you're documenting code and code examples in your HTML document, the *<code>* and *<samp>* elements provide a means for adding semantic meaning to your code and code output.

When you want to display source code of any type in the HTML document, use the *<code>* element, as shown in the following example.

```
<code class="keepWhiteSpace">
sayHello('Mom');
function sayHello(name)
{
    alert('Hello ' + name + '!');
}
</code>
```

After you run the sample code, you can document the output of the code by using the *<samp>* element, as shown in the following example.

```
<samp class="keepWhiteSpace">
   Hello Mom!
</samp>
```

Remember that the *<code>* and *<samp>* elements provide semantic meaning to the HTML, but they don't preserve the white space. For example, the preceding sample code will display on one line, but the keepWhiteSpace class preserves the white space by using the following style rule.

```
.keepWhiteSpace {
    white-space: pre;
}
```

This style rule is not compatible with all browsers, so you might want to use the *<pre>* element to prevent white space normalization, as described next.

Displaying preformatted content by using the *<pre>* element

The browser typically normalizes the HTML content by removing extra white space, line feeds, and paragraphs from the rendered page. You will often need to provide blocks of text where you want to maintain the existing format when it's rendered. Use the *<pre>* element to prevent the normalization of the HTML document, as shown in the following example.

```
<pre>
<code>
sayHello('Mom');
function sayHello(name)
{
    alert('Hello ' + name + '!');
}
</code>
</pre>
```

In this example, the *<code>* element provides semantic meaning to the content, and the *<pre>* element prevents white-space normalization.

Using the *<var>* element

The *<var>* element denotes a variable in a mathematical equation, as shown in the following example.

```
<p>
The resistance <var>r</var> of a piece of wire is equal to the voltage <var>v</var>
divided by the current <var>i</var>.
</p>
```

Using the *
* and *<wbr />* elements

The *
* and *<wbr />* elements are void elements, meaning that they cannot have any content and provide only a line break in your HTML document.

The *
* element provides an immediate line break, which continues the document flow on the next line of the browser.

The *<wbr />* element, which is a *word break*, provides an indication to the browser that it may insert a line break at this location. The browser decides whether to insert the break.

Using the *<dfn>* element to define a term

The *<dfn>* element denotes the definition of a term, also known as the defining instance of the term. The *<dfn>* element can contain a title attribute, which, if it exists, must contain the term being defined.

If the *<dfn>* element contains exactly one element child node and no child text nodes, and that child element is an *<abbr>* element with a title attribute, that attribute is the term being defined.

Consider the following example that uses the *<dfn>* element with the *<abbr>* element to provide a definition.

```
<p>
    A motor vehicle has a <dfn id="vin">
    <abbr title="Vehicle Identification Number">VIN</abbr></dfn>
    that is unique. Over the years, the
    <abbr title="Vehicle Identification Number">VIN</abbr>
    has had different formats,
    based on the vehicle manufacturer.
</p>
<p>
    In the United States, the <a href="#vin">
    <abbr title="Vehicle Identification Number">VIN</abbr></a>
    was standardized to a 17 character format where
    the 10th character of the
    <abbr title="Vehicle Identification Number">VIN</abbr>
    represents the year of the vehicle.
</p>
```

In this example, the *<dfn>* element is used once where the first instance of VIN is being presented. Inside the *<dfn>* element is an *<abbr>* element, which provides the meaning of VIN in its title attribute. The default style of the *<dfn>* element is italic text, as shown in Figure 5-4. The use of the *<a>* element provides a hyperlink to the definition.

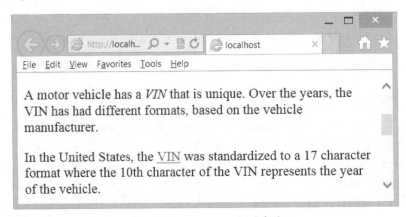

FIGURE 5-4 The *<dfn>* element italicizing its text by default

Working with figures

A *figure* is a unit of content that might have a caption and is referenced from the main document. Use the *<figure>* element to denote a figure that can be one or more photos, one or more drawings, one or more illustrations, or other content that is referred to as a unit. Use the *<figcaption>* element to denote an optional caption.

When using the *<figure>* element, remember that the figure is related to the main content of the page, and the figure's location is not important. This is different from the *<aside>* element, which is more related to the site than to the page's document. If placement is important, don't use the *<figure>* element; use the *<div>* element.

The following example shows the use of the *<figure>* and *<figcaption>* elements (bolded) to display an image that is referred to in the main document of the webpage.

```
<div role="main">
    <p>
        The peanut butter and jelly
        <abbr title="peanut butter and jelly">PB&J</abbr>
        sandwich has been a staple food of many families
        due to its health benefits, its cost, and its
        wonderful flavor.
    </p>
    <p>
        When assembling a peanut butter and jelly sandwich,
        you need to gather all the required materials as
        shown in <a href="#figure1">Figure 1</a>.
    </p>
    <figure id="figure1">
        <img src="/pbj.jpg" alt="peanut butter and jelly requirements" />
        <figcaption>Figure 1 The PB&J sandwich requirements.</figcaption>
    </figure>
</div>
```

Working with the *<summary>* and *<details>* elements

Use the *<details>* element with the *<summary>* element to create collapsible details content under the summary. The *<details>* and *<summary>* elements currently work with the Google Chrome browser only, but more support is expected.

In the *<details>* element, nest a *<summary>* element that contains the content that will always be displayed. The details content is placed inside the *<details>* element following the *<summary>* element. When the page is rendered, only the content of the *<summary>* element is displayed. Clicking the summary content causes the details content to be displayed. Clicking again causes the details content to be hidden.

```
<div role="main">
    <details>
        <summary>Make a peanut butter and jelly sandwich</summary>
        <p>
            The peanut butter and jelly
            <abbr title="peanut butter and jelly">PB&J</abbr>
```

```
        sandwich has been a staple food of many American families
        due to its health benefits, its cost, and its
        wonderful flavor.
    </p>
    <p>
        When assembling a peanut butter and jelly sandwich,
        you need to gather all the required materials as
        shown in <a href="#figure1">Figure 1</a>.
    </p>
    <figure id="figure1">
        <img src="/pbj.jpg" alt="peanut butter and jelly requirements" />
        <figcaption>The PB&J sandwich requirements.</figcaption>
    </figure>
</details>
</div>
```

In this example, the previous example content is placed in the *<details>* element, and the *<summary>* element contains a general description of the content. Clicking the summary content toggles the display of the details.

Understanding other annotations

In addition to the annotation elements already discussed, the following is a list of annotations you might use in your HTML document.

- **<s>**   Denotes strike-out text, text that is no longer valid.
- **<u>**   Offsets a span of text without implying a difference of importance. The default behavior is to underline the text, but this could be accommodated better by using a span tag with the appropriate style.
- **<mark>**   Marks, or highlights, a span of text.
- **<ins>**   Indicates inserted text.
- **<del>**   Indicates deleted text.
- **<small>**   Indicates fine print.
- **<sub>**   Indicates subscript.
- **<sup>**   Indicates superscript.
- **<time>**   Denotes a time of day or a date in the text.
- **<kbd>**   Indicates user input.

Using language elements

You might need to provide content that uses characters of Chinese origin, which are called *kanji*. These characters are used in Chinese, Japanese, and Korean (CJK) languages. To indicate the pronunciation of kanji, you can use small phonetic characters, which are commonly called *ruby* or *furigana*. The term "ruby" has English roots from when printers used this term to refer to small type used for this purpose.

Use the *<ruby>* element to place a notation above or to the right of characters. Use the *<rt>* and *<rp>* elements with the *<ruby>* element to place the notation or to place parentheses around the ruby. Use the *<bdo>* element to define the text direction and use the *<bdi>* element to isolate a block of text to set the text direction.

Working with lists

HTML5 defines various semantic elements that can be used to create ordered, unordered, and descriptive lists. All lists have list items, which are implemented by using the *<li>* element. All lists support nesting of lists. This section describes each of these lists.

Ordered lists

An *ordered list* is a numbered list. Use the *<ol>* element when you want auto-numbering of the list items. The following example shows three favorite fruits.

```
<h3>Favorite Fruit</h3>
<ol>
    <li>Apples</li>
    <li>Oranges</li>
    <li>Grapes</li>
</ol>
```

This list is automatically rendered with numbers beside each fruit list item, as shown in Figure 5-5.

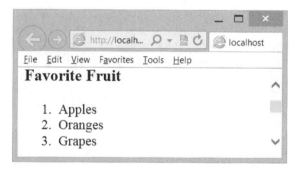

FIGURE 5-5 The ordered list numbering its items automatically

The *<ol>* element supports the following attributes.

- **reversed**   Reverses the number order to be descending instead of ascending
- **start**   Sets the starting number
- **type**   Sets the list type; can be "1", "A", "a", or "I"

The reversed attribute currently does not work in most browsers, but you might find JavaScript libraries, such as *modernizr.js*, that emulate that functionality until the feature is implemented by the browser manufacturer. Even if you set the type to a value such as "A", you still set the start as a number. The following is an example of the type and start attributes, using the favorite fruit list.

```
<h3>Favorite Fruit</h3>
<ol type="A" start="6" >
    <li>Apples</li>
    <li>Oranges</li>
    <li>Grapes</li>
</ol>
```

Figure 5-6 shows the rendered list. The start value of "6" translates to the letter "F" when rendered.

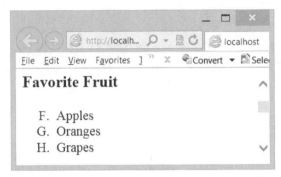

FIGURE 5-6 The ordered list with its type and start attributes set

Unordered lists

An *unordered list* is not auto-numbered. Use the *<ul>* element to create an unordered list of items. When the unordered list is rendered, it produces bullet points before each list item, as shown in the following example that describes the items required to repair a flat tire.

```
<h3>Items required to change a flat tire</h3>
<ul>
    <li>A jack</li>
    <li>A lug wrench with a socket on one end and a pry bar on the other</li>
    <li>A spare tire</li>
</ul>
```

Each item is rendered with a bullet, and where the text wraps to the next line, the text aligns itself properly with the text of the previous line, as shown in Figure 5-7.

FIGURE 5-7 The unordered list rendering each list item as a bullet

Description lists

Use the *<dl>* element to create a description list, which consists of zero or more term-description groupings, also known as name-value or key-value pairs. Each grouping associates one or more terms or names, which are the contents of *<dt>* elements, with one or more descriptions or values, which are the contents of *<dd>* elements, as shown in the following example.

```
<h3>Common Vehicles</h3>
<dl>
    <dt>Boat</dt>
    <dd>A small vehicle propelled on water by oars, sails, or an engine</dd>
    <dt>Car</dt>
    <dd>An automobile</dd>
    <dd>A passenger vehicle designed for operation on ordinary roads
        and typically having four wheels and an engine</dd>
    <dt>Bicycle</dt>
    <dt>Bike</dt>
    <dd>A vehicle with two wheels in tandem, typically propelled by pedals
        connected to the rear wheel by a chain, and having handlebars
        for steering and a saddlelike seat</dd>
</dl>
```

In this example, the boat is associated with a single definition. The car is associated with two definitions. The bicycle and bike are both associated with the same definition. The rendered output is shown in Figure 5-8.

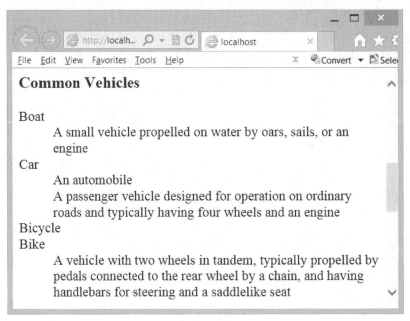

FIGURE 5-8 The definition list with its terms and definitions

Custom lists

You can create custom lists by using the CSS3 styles, and you can use the CSS3 counter and the :before and :after selectors. Consider the following list, which contains nested lists.

```
<ul class="level1">
    <li>Automobiles
    <ul class="level2">
        <li>BMW
            <ul class="level3">
                <li>X1</li>
                <li>X3</li>
                <li>Z4</li>
            </ul>
        </li>
        <li>Chevrolet
            <ul class="level3">
                <li>Cobalt</li>
                <li>Impala</li>
                <li>Volt</li>
            </ul>
        </li>
        <li>Ford
            <ul class="level3">
                <li>Edge</li>
                <li>Focus</li>
                <li>Mustang</li>
            </ul>
        </li>
```

```
        </ul>
    </li>
    <li>Boats
        <ul class="level2">
            <li>Sea Ray</li>
            <li>Cobalt</li>
        </ul>
    </li>
</ul>
```

Figure 5-9 shows the rendered list with the default styles. The bullet shapes change with each level of nesting, and each level of nesting is automatically indented.

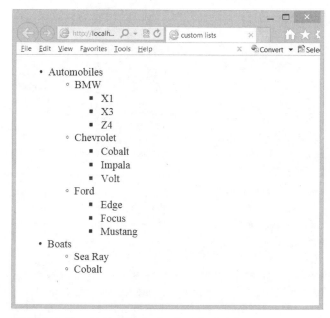

FIGURE 5-9 The rendered output with default styles

In addition to font-related styles and color-related styles, there are also list-related styles that you can alter to change the presentation of your list. In the rendered example, the first-level list-style-type CSS property is set to *disc*, which displays as a filled-in circle. The second-level list-style-type is set to *circle*, and the third-level *list-style-type* is set to *square*. In addition, each of the levels' list-style-position CSS property is set to *outside*, which means that when the text wraps, the first character of the next line will align with the first character of the previous line. If you set the list-style-position to inside, the first character of the next line will align with the bullet symbol of the first line.

In Visual Studio Express 2012 for Web, you can open the CSS file and enter the selector as follows.

```
li {

}
```

After the selector is added, you can right-click the style rule and choose Build Style to display a menu of styles to apply. Clicking List in the Category menu displays the styles that can be applied to a list. Figure 5-10 shows the Modify Style window.

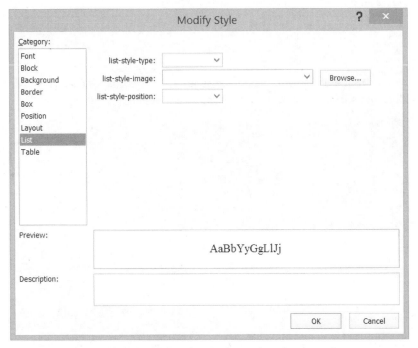

FIGURE 5-10 The Modify Style window showing menu-based style settings

By using the Modify Style window, you can easily override the default setting of the *list-style-type* and *list-style-position*. In addition, you can provide a *list-style-image* when the bullet symbols are not what you want. In this example, set the *list-item-style* to *none* and click OK. The style sheet now contains the modified style rule as follows.

```
li {
 list-style-type: none;
}
```

Try rendering the webpage and note that no bullets are displayed. Try many of the other settings to see how they render.

Instead of using the Modify Style window, you can type the style rules. When you're typing the rules, IntelliSense helps reduce the number of keystrokes. When the IntelliSense menu appears, you can select an item and press the tab key. In the CSS file, insert the following style rules.

```
body {
    counter-reset: section;
}
```

```
ul.level1 > li:before {
    counter-increment: section;
    content: "Section " counter(section) ". ";
    counter-reset: subsection;
}

ul.level2 > li:before {
    counter-increment: subsection;
    content: counter(section) "(" counter(subsection, lower-alpha) ") - ";
}

ul.level1 > li, ul.level2 > li {
    list-style-type: none;
}

ul.level3 > li {
    list-style-type: disc;
}
```

The following is a description of each of the style rules in this example.

- The first style rule resets a user-defined section counter to one when the *<body>* element is styled. The section counter will be set to one only after the page is loaded, but it will be incremented in a different style rule.

- The second style rule is executed when a *<li>* element that is a child of a *<ul>* element with a CSS class of level1 is rendered. It increments the section counter by one. It then inserts the content property before the *<li>* element, which outputs the "Section" string, followed by the value of the section counter and then followed by the ". " string. Finally, the rule resets a user-defined subsection counter to one. This style rule executes twice, before Automobiles and before Boats.

- The third style rule is executed when a *<li>* element that is a child of a *<ul>* element with a CSS class of level2 is rendered. It increments the subsection counter by one. It then inserts the content property before the *<li>* element, which outputs the value of the section counter, followed by the "(" string and then followed by the value of the subsection counter, but this value is converted to lowercase alpha representation. After the subsection is rendered, the ") – " string is rendered. This style rule executes five times.

- The fourth style rule sets the list-style-type to none for level1 and level2 list items.

- The fifth style rule sets the list-style-rule to disc for level3 list items.

The rendered output is shown in Figure 5-11. This should give you a good idea of the capabilities of HTML5 when working with lists.

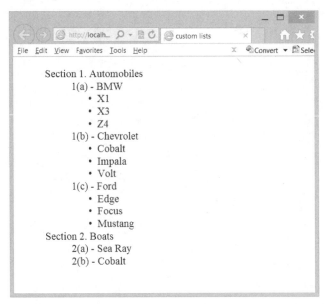

FIGURE 5-11 The rendered custom list

Lesson summary

- Semantic markup provides meaning to HTML elements to aid devices that consume HTML content.

- Nonvisual Desktop Access (NVDA) devices read and process webpages.

- Content that needs to be styled but doesn't clearly fit the meaning of any semantic elements can be styled by wrapping it with a *<div>* or *<span>* element.

- The *<header>* element defines a section that provides a header. The *<footer>* element defines a section that provides a footer. The *<nav>* element defines a section that houses a block of major navigational links. The *<aside>* element defines a section of content that is separate from the content the *<aside>* element is in. The *<section>* element defines part of the whole and is typically named with an *<h1>* to *<h6>* internal element.

- The *<article>* element is a unit of content that can stand on its own and be copied to other locations. A blog post is a good example of an article.

- The Web Accessible Initiative (WAI) specifies the Accessible Rich Internet Applications (ARIA) suite, which is called WAI-ARIA. Use the WAI-ARIA role attribute to provide meaning to elements that are not semantically defined.

- In lieu of the *<b>* element, use the *<strong>* element. In lieu of the *<i>* element, use the *<em>* element.

Lesson review

Answer the following questions to test your knowledge of the information in this lesson. You can find the answers to these questions and explanations of why each answer choice is correct or incorrect in the "Answers" section at the end of this chapter.

1. You are creating a webpage that will display short stories, and you want the stories to be shareable on other sites. Which element should each story be wrapped with?

   A. *<section>*

   B. *<pre>*

   C. *<aside>*

   D. *<article>*

2. You want to indicate an important item in your content text. Which element do you use?

   A. *<b>*

   B. *<em>*

   C. *<strong>*

   D. *<i>*

3. You want to identify the author of webpages on your website by providing the author name and email address in the footer of each page. What is the proper way to do this?

   A. *<address>*<a href="email:author@Contoso.com">*Author Name</a></address>*

   B. *<contact>*<a href="email:author@Contoso.com">*Author Name</a></contact>*

   C. *<author>*<a href="email:author@Contoso.com">*Author Name</a></author>*

   D. *<name>*<a href="email:author@Contoso.com">*Author Name</a></name>*

Lesson 2: Working with tables

Tables are the way to lay out data in your HTML document in rows and columns. A table displays a two-dimensional grid of data. Use the *<table>* element with the *<tr>* element to create table rows and the *<td>* element to create table details, which are better known as table cells. This lesson discusses tables in detail.

After this lesson, you will be able to:

- Create a basic table.
- Add a header and footer to a table.
- Create an irregular table.
- Access column data.
- Apply style rules to table elements.

Estimated lesson time: 30 minutes

Table misuse

HTML tables are powerful and, due to their flexibility, they are often misused. It's important to understand both proper table implementation and where it's inappropriate to implement a table.

Over the years, many developers have used the *<table>* element to create a page layout. Here are some reasons you should not use the *<table>* element to create a page layout.

- The table will not render until the *</table>* tag has been read. Webpages should be written with semantic markup, and the main *<div role="main">* element should be as close to the top of the HTML document as possible. The *<div>* element will render its content as the browser receives it. This enables the user to read the content as it's being loaded into the browser.

- Using a table forces you into a deeply nested HTML structure that is difficult to maintain.

- Using a table confuses accessibility devices.

Remember that using a *<table>* element for anything other than tabular layout of data will be much more difficult to maintain than using *<div>* elements with positioning.

Creating a basic table

You can create a basic table by using the *<table>* element to denote the table. Inside the *<table>* element, you can add a *<tr>* element for each row that you require. Inside each *<tr>* element, add *<td>* elements for each cell that you need. The following is a simple table of vehicle information.

```
<table>
    <tr>
        <td>1957</td>
        <td>Ford</td>
        <td>Thunderbird</td>
    </tr>
    <tr>
        <td>1958</td>
        <td>Chevrolet</td>
        <td>Impala</td>
    </tr>
    <tr>
        <td>2012</td>
        <td>BMW</td>
        <td>Z4</td>
    </tr>
    <tr>
        <td>2003</td>
        <td>Mazda</td>
        <td>Miata</td>
    </tr>
</table>
```

Figure 5-12 shows the rendered output as four rows with three columns in each row. It's not obvious that there are columns in each row, however, and there is no header or footer. You might also want to see a border around all cells to make the table more obvious. This table needs improvement. Would alternating column colors improve it?

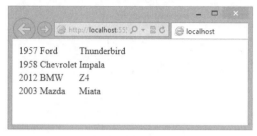

FIGURE 5-12 The rendered table with rows and columns

Adding header cells

Use the *<th>* element instead of the *<td>* element to display a header. The header can be horizontal or vertical. For example, you might want a header across the top to label each column and a header down the left side (in the first column) to label each row. The following is the modified table.

```
<table>
    <tr>
        <th>Vehicle #</th>
        <th>Year</th>
        <th>Make</th>
        <th>Model</th>
    </tr>
    <tr>
        <th>1</th>
        <td>1957</td>
        <td>Ford</td>
        <td>Thunderbird</td>
    </tr>
    <tr>
        <th>2</th>
        <td>1958</td>
        <td>Chevrolet</td>
        <td>Impala</td>
    </tr>
    <tr>
        <th>3</th>
        <td>2012</td>
        <td>BMW</td>
        <td>Z4</td>
    </tr>
    <tr>
        <th>4</th>
        <td>2003</td>
```

```
        <td> Mazda</td>
        <td>Miata</td>
      </tr>
</table>
```

The rendered table is shown in Figure 5-13. This revised table now has horizontal and vertical headers. Notice that the default style of the *<th>* element is bold.

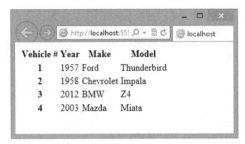

FIGURE 5-13 The revised table with horizontal and vertical headers

Styling the table headers

Now that you have *<th>* elements for the headers, add a style to the *<th>* elements as follows.

```
th {
    background-color: #BDEAFF;
    width: 100px;
}
```

This adds a pale blue background to all the *<th>* elements and sets the width of all columns to 100 pixels. What changes can you make to give the horizontal header and vertical header different styles? The following example can accomplish this task.

```
th {
    background-color: #BDEAFF;
    width: 100px;
}

th:only-of-type {
    background-color: #FFFF99;
}
```

The first style rule sets the color of all *<th>* elements to a pale blue and sets the width to 100 pixels. The second style rule has a higher priority, so it overrides the first style rule and applies a pale yellow color to the vertical header.

Declaring the header, footer, and table body

Most browsers automatically wrap all *<tr>* elements with a *<tbody>* element to indicate the body of the table. What would happen if you had a CSS style selector of `table > tr`? You wouldn't get a match because the browser adds the *<tbody>* element. The selector can be rewritten as `table > tbody > tr` instead, or maybe `tbody > tr` is all you need. It's good practice to define the *<tbody>* element explicitly in every table.

You might also have multiple rows that are to be used as horizontal headers or footers. You can use the *<thead>* element to identify rows that are header rows and use the *<tfoot>* element to identify rows that are footer rows. The following is an example of the addition of the *<thead>*, *<tfoot>*, and *<tbody>* elements.

```
<table>
    <thead>
        <tr>
            <th>Vehicle #</th>
            <th>Year</th>
            <th>Make</th>
            <th>Model</th>
            <th>Price</th>
        </tr>
    </thead>
    <tbody>
        <tr>
            <th>1</th>
            <td>1957</td>
            <td>Ford</td>
            <td>Thunderbird</td>
            <td>14,000</td>
        </tr>
        <tr>
            <th>2</th>
            <td>1958</td>
            <td>Chevrolet</td>
            <td>Impala</td>
            <td>3,000</td>
        </tr>
        <tr>
            <th>3</th>
            <td>2012</td>
            <td>BMW</td>
            <td>Z4</td>
            <td>40,000</td>
        </tr>
        <tr>
            <th>4</th>
            <td>2003</td>
            <td>Mazda</td>
            <td>Miata</td>
            <td>5,000</td>
        </tr>
    </tbody>
    <tfoot>
```

```
        <tr>
            <th>Total:</th>
            <th></th>
            <th></th>
            <th></th>
            <th>62,000</th>
        </tr>
    </tfoot>
</table>
```

In addition to adding structure to the table, you can use the *<thead>*, *<tbody>*, and *<tfoot>* elements to control the styling of the *<th>* elements better. Without these elements, how would you provide a different style to the header and footer? The following style rules provide an example of such styling.

```
thead th {
    background-color: #BDEAFF;
    width: 100px;
}

tbody th {
    background-color: #FFFF99;
}

tfoot th {
    background-color: #C2FE9A;
}

    tfoot th:last-of-type {
        text-align: right;
    }

td {
    text-align: center;
}

    td:last-of-type {
        text-align: right;
    }
```

The rendered table is shown in Figure 5-14. The following is a description of the style rules applied.

- The first style rule applies a blue background color to the header and sets the width of all columns to 100 pixels.

- The second style rule applies a yellow background color to the vertical header.

- The third style rule applies a green background color to the footer.

- The fourth style rule applies right alignment to the price in the footer.

- The fifth style rule centers the text of all table cells.

- The last style rule applies right alignment to the price cells.

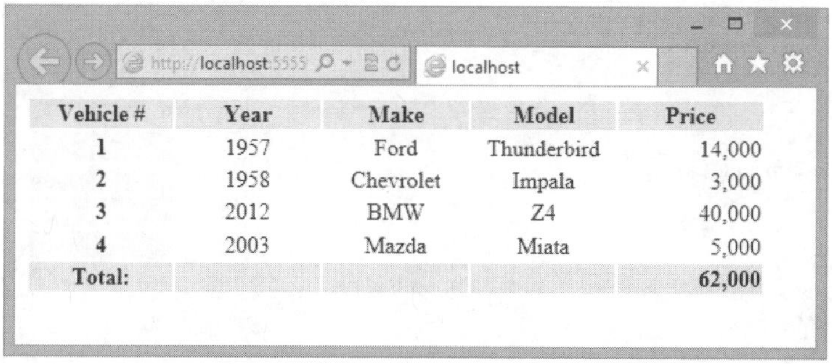

FIGURE 5-14 The styled table

Although you can have a maximum of one *<thead>* element and one *<tfoot>* element, you can have many *<tbody>* elements within a *<table>* element. The benefit of having multiple *<tbody>* elements is that you can group rows to apply styles. You can even display or hide groups of rows by setting the style display property to none (to hide) or by clearing the display property (to show). The following example extends the previous example by using multiple *<tbody>* elements, adding one for Antique Cars and one for Non-Antique Cars.

```
<!DOCTYPE html>
<html xmlns="http://www.w3.org/1999/xhtml">
<head>
    <title>Vehicles</title>
    <link href="Content/vehicles.css" rel="stylesheet" />
    <script src="Scripts/vehicles.js"></script>
</head>
<body>
    <div role="main">
        <button id="showAntique">Antique Cars</button>
        <button id="showNonAntique">Non-Antique Cars</button>
        <table>
            <thead>
                <tr>
                    <th>Vehicle #</th>
                    <th>Year</th>
                    <th>Make</th>
                    <th>Model</th>
                    <th>Price</th>
                </tr>
            </thead>
            <tbody id="antiqueCars">
                <tr>
                    <th>1</th>
                    <td>1957</td>
                    <td>Ford</td>
                    <td>Thunderbird</td>
                    <td>14,000</td>
                </tr>
                <tr>
                    <th>2</th>
                    <td>1958</td>
```

```
                <td>Chevrolet</td>
                <td>Impala</td>
                <td>3,000</td>
            </tr>
        </tbody>
        <tbody id="nonAntiqueCars">
            <tr>
                <th>3</th>
                <td>2012</td>
                <td>BMW</td>
                <td>Z4</td>
                <td>40,000</td>
            </tr>
            <tr>
                <th>4</th>
                <td>2003</td>
                <td>Madza</td>
                <td>Miata</td>
                <td>5,000</td>
            </tr>
        </tbody>
        <tfoot>
            <tr>
                <th>Total:</th>
                <th></th>
                <th></th>
                <th></th>
                <th>62,000</th>
            </tr>
        </tfoot>
    </table>
</div>
</body>
</html>

<script>
    init();
</script>
```

This example shows the complete HTML document, so you can see the inclusion of the CSS file and JavaScript file. The HTML has been extended to include two buttons at the top so you can filter by Antique Cars or Non-Antique Cars. There are two *<tbody>* elements, each having an explicit id of antiqueCars and nonAntiqueCars, respectively, and a *<script>* element at the bottom that initializes the JavaScript, which will attach event handlers to the click event of the buttons. The CSS file is slightly modified from the previous example as follows.

```
thead th {
    background-color: #BDEAFF;
    width: 100px;
}

tbody th {
    background-color: #FFFF99;
```

```
}

tfoot th {
    background-color: #C2FE9A;
}

    tfoot th:last-of-type {
        text-align: right;
    }

td {
    text-align: center;
}

    td:last-of-type {
        text-align: right;
    }

.hidden {
    display: none;
}

.visible {
    display: normal;
}
```

The CSS file now has the .hidden and .visible selectors. These are used to show or hide the *<tbody>* elements, including their contents. The JavaScript file contains the following code.

```
function init() {
    document.getElementById('showAntique').addEventListener('click', showAntiqueCars);
    document.getElementById('showNonAntique').addEventListener('click',
showNonAntiqueCars);
}

function showAntiqueCars() {
    document.getElementById('antiqueCars').className = "visible";
    document.getElementById('nonAntiqueCars').className = "hidden";
}

function showNonAntiqueCars() {
    document.getElementById('antiqueCars').className = "hidden";
    document.getElementById('nonAntiqueCars').className = "visible";
}
```

The JavaScript code contains an init function that is called when the HTML document is loaded. The init function attaches event handlers to the click event of the two buttons. The additional functions set the CSS class to display or hide the *<tbody>* elements.

When the webpage is displayed, all vehicles are displayed. Clicking the Antique Cars button displays the antique cars and hides the non-antique cars. Clicking the Non-Antique Cars button displays the non-antique cars and hides the antique cars.

Creating irregular tables

Tables need to be rectangular to work properly, but you'll often need to present tables that don't contain the same number of cells in each row. In the case of the previous examples, the footer contained the same number of cells as the other rows, but you only need to have two cells, one for "Total:" and one for the total price. You might also want to add a column that indicates Antique Cars versus Non-Antique Cars, but you don't want a cell on every row that says "Antique Car" or "Non-Antique Car". You want to add a single cell that says "Antique Cars" and is the combined height of all Antique Car rows. You want to add a single cell that says "Non-Antique Cars" and is the combined height of all Non-Antique Car rows. Use the *rowspan* or *colspan* attributes on the *<td>* or *<th>* element to solve this problem.

The colspan attribute tells the browser that a *<td>* or *<th>* element should be the size of multiple horizontal cells. In the previous example, where you want the "Total:" text to span the footer row, use <th colspan="4"> as follows.

```
<tfoot>
    <tr>
        <th colspan="4">Total:</th>
        <th>62,000</th>
    </tr>
</tfoot>
```

The default style for the *<th>* element is bold and centered. When "Total:" is displayed, it's centered within the four cells it spans. The CSS style rule is changed to right-align "Total:" as follows.

```
tfoot th {

    background-color: #C2FE9A;

}

    tfoot th:first-of-type {

        text-align: right;

    }

    tfoot th:last-of-type {

        text-align: right;

    }
```

You could just right-align all *<th>* elements in the footer by eliminating the last two style rules in this example and adding the text-align style to the first style rule. The rendered output is shown in Figure 5-15.

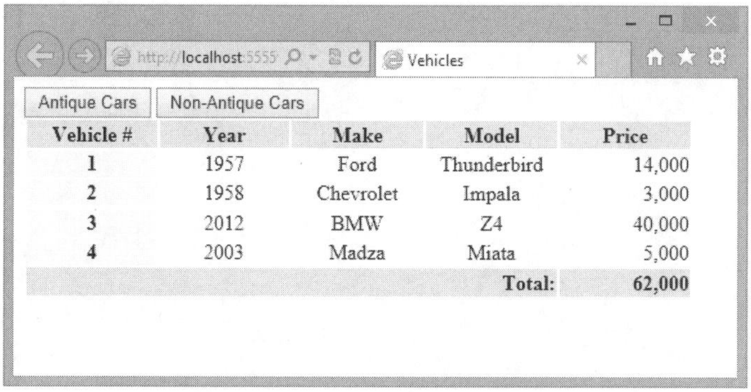

FIGURE 5-15 The rendered page with the footer containing only two cells

The rowspan attribute tells the browser that a *<td>* or *<th>* element should be the size of multiple vertical cells. In the previous example, when you want to add a column with only two cells, use *<td rowspan="n">* where *n* equals the number of rows to span, in this case, 2. Remember that adding a column also requires you to add the column to the header and to modify the colspan attribute in the footer. The following is the modified table.

```
<table>
    <thead>
        <tr>
            <th>Vehicle #</th>
            <th>Category</th>
            <th>Year</th>
            <th>Make</th>
            <th>Model</th>
            <th>Price</th>
        </tr>
    </thead>
    <tbody id="antiqueCars">
        <tr>
            <th>1</th>
            <td rowspan="2">Antique</td>
            <td>1957</td>
            <td>Ford</td>
            <td>Thunderbird</td>
            <td>14,000</td>
        </tr>
        <tr>
            <th>2</th>
            <td>1958</td>
            <td>Chevrolet</td>
            <td>Impala</td>
            <td>3,000</td>
        </tr>
    </tbody>
    <tbody id="nonAntiqueCars">
        <tr>
            <th>3</th>
            <td rowspan="2">Non-Antique</td>
```

```
            <td>2012</td>
            <td>BMW</td>
            <td>Z4</td>
            <td>40,000</td>
        </tr>
        <tr>
            <th>4</th>
            <td>2003</td>
            <td>Mazda</td>
            <td>Miata</td>
            <td>5,000</td>
        </tr>
    </tbody>
    <tfoot>
        <tr>
            <th colspan="5">Total:</th>
            <th>62,000</th>
        </tr>
    </tfoot>
</table>
```

To help illustrate the rowspan and colspan attributes, a black border is added to the table cells. The following is the complete CSS file.

```css
table {
    border: medium solid #000000;
}

thead th {
    background-color: #BDEAFF;
    width: 100px;
}

tbody th {
    background-color: #FFFF99;
}

tfoot th {
    background-color: #C2FE9A;
}

    tfoot th:first-of-type {
        text-align: right;
    }

    tfoot th:last-of-type {
        text-align: right;
    }

td {
    text-align: center;
    border: thin solid #000000;
}

    td:last-of-type {
```

```
            text-align: right;
    }

th {
    border: thin solid #000000;
}

.hidden {
    display: none;
}

.visible {
    display: normal;
}
```

The results are displayed in Figure 5-16.

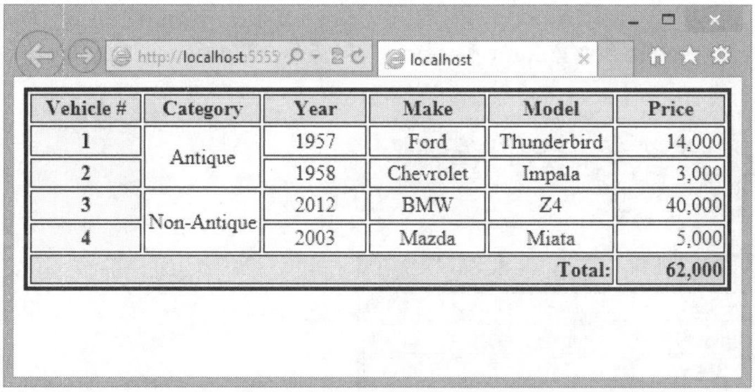

FIGURE 5-16 The rendered page with borders set, clearly showing the rowspan and colspan attributes

Adding a caption to a table

You can use the *<caption>* element to define and associate a caption with a table. The default style of the caption is centered and located above the table. You can use the CSS *text-align* and *caption-side* properties to override the default style. If you use the *<caption>* element, it must be the first element within the *<table>* element.

Styling columns

Styling columns is a common difficulty because tables are row-centric, not column-centric. It's relatively easy to apply a style to a row because you can apply a *<tr>* element to the style, but there isn't a *<tc>* element for a column. Remember that the *<td>* element represents a cell, not a column. Columns are actually created implicitly by creating the cells. Use the *<col-group>* and *<col>* elements to style columns.

The *<colgroup>* element is placed inside the *<table>* element to define columns that can be styled. Remember that styling includes hiding and displaying the columns. Inside the

<colgroup> element, *<col>* elements are added for each column to be styled. The *<col>* element has a *span* attribute that identifies multiple columns that will have the same style.

In the previous examples, the *<colgroup>* and *<col>* elements can provide a style for the vertical headers, but this time, you want to apply a style to the first two columns. You can define the columns as follows.

```
<colgroup>
    <col span="2" class="verticalHeader" />
</colgroup>
```

This example defines the first two columns to have a style of verticalHeader. The vertical-Header class is set to apply a gray background color as follows.

```
.verticalHeader {
    background-color: #C0C0C0;
}
```

In addition, the existing style for the first column has been removed. Figure 5-17 shows the rendered webpage.

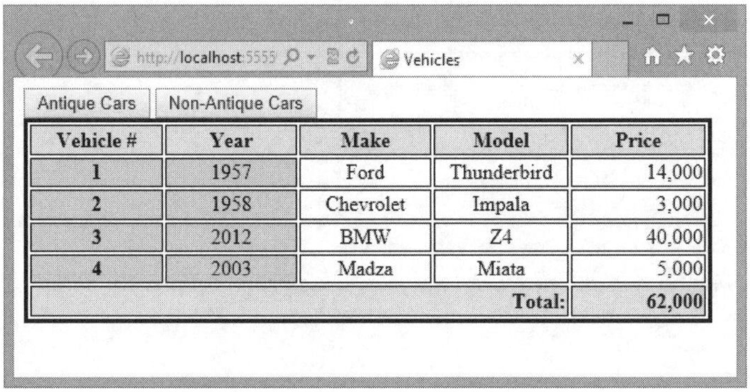

FIGURE 5-17 Using the *<colgroup>* and *<col>* elements to apply a style to multiple columns

Lesson summary

- Refrain from using the *<table>* element for page layout.
- A *<tr>* element creates a table row. A *<td>* element creates a table cell in a table row.
- To identify a header cell, use the *<th>* element instead of using the *<td>* element.
- Use the *<thead>* element to specify table rows that comprise the table header. Use the *<tfoot>* element to specify table rows that comprise the table footer. Use the *<tbody>* element to specify data rows. You can group data rows by specifying many *<tbody>* elements.
- Use the rowspan and colspan attributes on the *<th>* and *<td>* elements to create irregular tables.

- Use the *<caption>* element directly after the *<table>* element to specify a caption for your table.
- Use the *<colgroup>* and *<col>* elements to apply styles to a column.

Lesson review

Answer the following questions to test your knowledge of the information in this lesson. You can find the answers to these questions and explanations of why each answer choice is correct or incorrect in the "Answers" section at the end of this chapter.

1. You are creating a webpage that will be used to display a list of salespeople with their sales statistics for the years of 2010, 2011, and 2012 in two categories: sales of products and sales of services. You want to each of the years to be in the horizontal header, and under each year, you will have a "Products" column and a "Services" column. How will you define the element for year 2011?

   A. *<th>2011</th>*

   B. *<th colspan="2">2011</th>*

   C. *<th span="2">2011</th>*

   D. *<th style="2">2011</th>*

2. You want to provide the ability to display or show columns, but you don't want to add a style or other marking to each *<td>* element. How can you accomplish this?

   A. Add a *<colgroup>* element to the *<table>* element and define each column by using a *<col>* element inside the *<colgroup>* element.

   B. Add an id to each *<td>* element and provide a unique id for each; use the ids in your style sheet rules to obtain the desired style.

   C. Add a *<col>* element to the *<table>* element and define each column by using a *<id>* element inside the *<col>* element.

   D. Add a *<hidden>* element to the *<table>* element and define each column by using a *<col>* element inside the *<hidden>* element.

3. Which element can you add to the *<table>* element to provide a table caption?

   A. *<thead>*

   B. *<colgroup>*

   C. *<caption>*

   D. *<th>*

Practice exercises

If you encounter a problem completing any of these exercises, the completed projects can be installed from the Practice Exercises folder that is provided with the companion content.

Exercise 1: Add a page layout to the calculator project

In this exercise, you apply your knowledge of semantic markup by adding a page layout to the WebCalculator project that you worked on in Chapter 4, "Getting started with CSS3," and then you add style rules to improve the look of the webpage.

This exercise continues with the goal of adding style rules with a minimum of modifications to the default.html file.

1. Start Visual Studio Express 2012 for Web. Click File, choose Open Project, and then select the solution you created in Chapter 4.

2. Select the WebCalculator.sln file and click Open. You can also click File, choose Recent Projects And Solutions, and then select the solution.

    If you didn't complete the exercises in Chapter 4, you can use the solution in the Chapter 5 Exercise 1 Start folder.

3. In the Solution Explorer window, right-click the default.html file and choose Set As Start Page. Press F5 to verify that your home page is displayed.

4. Open the default.html page and wrap the *<div>* element whose id is calculator with a *<div>* element, and then set the id to container.

    This *<div>* element will contain the complete page layout.

5. In the container *<div>* element, insert a *<header>* element containing an *<hgroup>* element with an id of headerText. In the *<hgroup>* element, insert an *<h1>* element containing the text, "Contoso, Ltd." After the *<h1>* element, insert an *<h2>* element containing the text, "Your success equals our success."

    The header should look like the following.

    ```
    <header>
        <hgroup id="headerText">
            <h1>Contoso Ltd.</h1>
            <h2>Your success equals our success</h2>
        </hgroup>
    </header>
    ```

6. After the *<header>* element, insert a *<nav>* element.

    The *<nav>* element typically contains the primary links on the page, but there are no other pages in this site.

7. Insert a dummy link to the home page, which is the current page.

    This will display on the page to give you an idea of what the *<nav>* element is used for. The *<nav>* element should look like the following.

    ```
    <nav>
        <a href="default.html">Home</a>
    </nav>
    ```

8. After the *<nav>* element, wrap the calculator *<div>* element with a *<div>* element whose role is set to main.

The main *<div>* element with the calculator *<div>* element should look like the following.

```
<div role="main">
    <div id="calculator">
        <input id="txtResult" type="text" readonly="readonly" /><br />
        <input id="txtInput" type="text" /><br />
        <button id="btn7">7</button>
        <button id="btn8">8</button>
        <button id="btn9">9</button><br />
        <button id="btn4">4</button>
        <button id="btn5">5</button>
        <button id="btn6">6</button><br />
        <button id="btn1">1</button>
        <button id="btn2">2</button>
        <button id="btn3">3</button><br />
        <button id="btnClear">C</button>
        <button id="btn0">0</button>
        <button id="btnClearEntry">CE</button><br />
        <button id="btnPlus">+</button>
        <button id="btnMinus">-</button>
    </div>
</div>
```

9. After the main *<div>* element, insert an *<aside>* element, which will contain the advertisements. Because there are no advertisements, insert a *<p>* element with the word Advertisements so you can see where the *<aside>* element renders.

    The completed *<aside>* element should look like the following.

```
<aside>
    <p>Advertisements</p>
</aside>
```

10. After the *<aside>* element, insert a *<footer>* element. In the *<footer>* element, add a *<p>* element with the following content: Copyright © 2012, Contoso Ltd., All rights reserved.

    The completed *<footer>* element should look like the following.

```
<footer>
    <p>
        Copyright &copy; 2012, Contoso Ltd., All rights reserved
    </p>
</footer>
```

The following is the complete default.html webpage.

```
<!DOCTYPE html>
<html xmlns="http://www.w3.org/1999/xhtml">
<head>
    <title>Web Calculator</title>
    <link href="Content/default.css" rel="stylesheet" />
    <script type="text/javascript" src="Scripts/CalculatorLibrary.js"></script>
</head>
<body>
    <div id="container">
```

```
        <header>
            <hgroup id="headerText">
                <h1>Contoso Ltd.</h1>
                <h2>Your success equals our success</h2>
            </hgroup>
        </header>
        <nav>
            <a href="default.html">Home</a>
        </nav>
        <div role="main">
            <div id="calculator">
                <input id="txtResult" type="text" readonly="readonly" /><br />
                <input id="txtInput" type="text" /><br />
                <button id="btn7">7</button>
                <button id="btn8">8</button>
                <button id="btn9">9</button><br />
                <button id="btn4">4</button>
                <button id="btn5">5</button>
                <button id="btn6">6</button><br />
                <button id="btn1">1</button>
                <button id="btn2">2</button>
                <button id="btn3">3</button><br />
                <button id="btnClear">C</button>
                <button id="btn0">0</button>
                <button id="btnClearEntry">CE</button><br />
                <button id="btnPlus">+</button>
                <button id="btnMinus">-</button>
            </div>
        </div>
        <aside>
            <p>Advertisements</p>
        </aside>
        <footer>
            <p>
                Copyright &copy; 2012, Contoso Ltd., All rights reserved
            </p>
        </footer>
    </div>
    <script type="text/javascript">
        window.addEventListener('load', initialize, false);
    </script>
</body>
</html>
```

Exercise 2: Add styles to the calculator layout

Now that you have completed the layout container, add and modify styles in the
default.css file.

1. Open the default.css file and, at the top of the file, add a style rule to set the margin
   and padding of all elements to 0 pixels.

   Your style rule should look like the following.

   ```
   * { margin : 0; padding : 0; }
   ```

2. After that style rule, insert another style rule that sets the *<aside>*, *<footer>*, *<header>*, *<hgroup>*, and *<nav>* elements to display as a block to ensure that all browsers render these elements as blocks.

Your style rule should look like the following.

```
aside, footer, header, hgroup, nav {
    display: block;
}
```

The current page background color is a dark blue. This background color needs to be lightened, and the font-family needs to be set to Cambria with a backup font of Times New Roman and final fallback of serif font. The font color needs to be set to match the Contoso standard blue. Your body style rule should be modified to match the following.

```
body {
    background-color: hsl(255, 95%, 95%);
    font-family: Cambria, 'Times New Roman' , serif;
    color: #0068AC;
}
```

3. To add a new folder called Images to the project, right-click the project in the Solution Explorer window. Click Add, choose New Folder, and name the folder **Images**.

4. To add the image from the Resource folder, in the Solution Explorer window, right-click the Images folder that you just added.

5. Click Add, choose Existing Item, and select the ContosoLogo.png file that is located in the Chapter05 Resources folder.

6. After the body style rule, insert a header style rule that sets the height to 100 pixels and set the background image to the ContosoLogo.png file.

7. Set the background-repeat to no-repeat and set the top margin to 10 pixels by adding the header selector with the curly braces, right-clicking in the style rule, and clicking Build Style. When the Modify Style window is displayed, set the properties.

The completed style rule should look like the following.

```
header {
    height: 100px;
    background-image: url('../Images/ContosoLogo.png');
    background-repeat: no-repeat;
    margin-top: 10px;
}
```

8. Add a style rule based on the element id equal to headerText. Set the position to absolute, set the top to 0 pixels, and set the left to 80 pixels, which will locate the header text to the right of the Contoso logo.

9. Set the width to 100 percent and set the margin top to 10 pixels as follows.

```
#headerText {
    position: absolute;
```

```
    top: 0px;
    left: 80px;
    width: 100%;
    margin-top: 10px;
}
```

10. After the headerText style rule, insert a text rule for the *<h1>* element. Add styles to set the font size to 64 pixels and set the line height to 55 pixels as follows.

```
h1 {
    font-size: 64px;
    line-height: 55px;
}
```

11. After the h1 style rule, insert a text rule for the *<h2>* element. Add styles to set the font size to 18 pixels, set the line height to 20 pixels, and set the font style to italic as follows.

```
h2 {
    font-size: 18px;
    line-height: 20px;
    font-style: italic;
}
```

12. After the h2 style rule, create a style rule for the *<nav>* element. Set the styles to float the *<nav>* element to the left, set the width to 20 percent, and set the minimum width to 125 pixels as follows.

```
nav {
    float: left;
    width: 20%;
    min-width:125px;
}
```

13. After the nav style rule, add a style rule for the main *<div>* element. Set the styles to float to the left, beside the *<nav>* element, and set the width to 60 percent as follows.

```
div[role="main"] {
    float:  left;
    width: 60%;
}
```

14. After the main div style rule, add a style rule for the *<aside>* element. Set the styles to float to the left, beside the main *<div>* element, set the width to 20 percent, and set the minimum width to 125 pixels as follows.

```
aside {
    float: left;
    width: 20%;
    min-width:125px;
}
```

15. After the aside style rule, add a style rule for the *<footer>* element. Set the styles to position the footer clear after the *<aside>* element, set the width to 100 percent, set the height to 70 pixels, and set the font size to small as follows.

```
footer {
    clear: both;
    width: 100%;
    height: 70px;
    font-size: small;
}
```

16. After the footer style rule, add a style rule for the *<div>* element whose id is container.

The purpose of this style is to ensure that the float: left styles you've added don't wrap when the browser window is resized to a small size.

17. Set the minimum width to 800 pixels as follows.

```
#container {
    min-width: 800px;
}
```

18. In the existing style rule for the calculator *<div>* element, change the height and width to 400 pixels as follows.

```
#calculator {
    border: solid;
    background-color: hsl(255, 100%, 60%);
    width: 400px;
    height: 400px;
    margin-left: auto;
    margin-right: auto;
    text-align: center;
    padding: 10px;
}
```

19. In the existing style rule for the input button, change the font size to 20 point as follows.

```
input, button {
    font-family: Arial;
    font-size: 20pt;
    border-width: thick;
    border-color: hsl(255, 100%, 100%);
    margin: 5px;
}
```

The following is the completed style sheet for your reference.

```
* { margin : 0; padding : 0; }

aside, footer, header, hgroup, nav {
    display: block;
}
```

```css
body {
    background-color: hsl(255, 95%, 95%);
    font-family: Cambria,'Times New Roman' , serif;
    color: #0068AC;
}

header {
    height: 100px;
    background-image: url('../Images/ContosoLogo.png');
    background-repeat: no-repeat;
    margin-top: 10px;
}

#headerText {
    position: absolute;
    top: 0px;
    left: 80px;
    width: 100%;
    margin-top: 10px;
}

h1 {
    font-size: 64px;
    line-height: 55px;
}

h2 {
    font-size: 18px;
    line-height: 20px;
    font-style: italic;
}

nav {
    float: left;
    width: 20%;
    min-width:125px;
}

div[role="main"] {
    float:  left;
    width: 60%;
}

aside {
    float: left;
    width: 20%;
    min-width:125px;
}

footer {
    clear: both;
    width: 100%;
    height: 70px;
    font-size: small;
```

```css
}

#container {
    min-width: 800px;
}

#calculator {
    border: solid;
    background-color: hsl(255, 100%, 60%);
    width: 400px;
    height: 400px;
    margin-left: auto;
    margin-right: auto;
    text-align: center;
    padding: 10px;
}

input {
    width: 85%;
    height: 7%;
    text-align: right;
    padding: 10px;
    border: inset;
}

button {
    background-color: hsl(255, 50%, 80%);
    width: 25%;
    height: 10%;
    border: outset;
}

    button:hover {
        background-color: hsl(255, 50%, 90%);
    }

    button:active {
        border: inset;
        border-width: thick;
        border-color: hsl(255, 100%, 100%);
        background-color: hsl(255, 50%, 50%);
    }

input, button {
    font-family: Arial;
    font-size: 20pt;
    border-width: thick;
    border-color: hsl(255, 100%, 100%);
    margin: 5px;
}

[readonly] {
    background-color: hsl(255, 50%, 80%);
}
```

20. To see your results, press F5 to start debugging the application.

You should see a nicer-looking calculator interface with a page layout as shown in Figure 5-18.

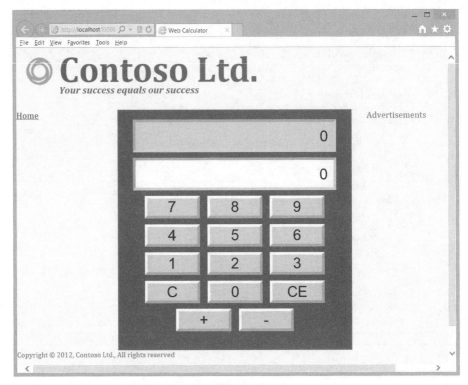

FIGURE 5-18 The web calculator with its page layout

Exercise 3: Cleaning up the web calculator

The calculator's buttons are positioned by keeping them the same size and using *
* elements for each line of buttons. Although the calculator doesn't look too bad, the buttons aren't in their traditional locations. For example, the clear and clear entry buttons are normally at the top, whereas the plus and minus buttons are typically on the right. The goal of this lesson is to reposition the buttons.

In this exercise, you continue with the project from Exercise 2 and modify the default.html file. The elements of the calculator will be positioned by placing them in a table. There will be seven rows and four columns.

1. Open the project from Exercise 2.

If you didn't perform Exercise 2, you can use the project located in the Exercise 2 Start folder.

2. Open the default.html file.

3. Surround the inputs and buttons with a *<table>* element.

4. Remove all *
* elements from the default.html file.

5. Surround the txtResult text box with a table cell that spans four columns. Surround the table cell with a table row.

The table row should look like the following.

```
<tr>
    <td colspan="4">
        <input id="txtResult" type="text" readonly="readonly" />
    </td>
</tr>
```

6. With the txtInput text box, repeat the previous step as follows.

```
<tr>
    <td colspan="4">
        <input id="txtInput" type="text" />
    </td>
</tr>
```

The next table row will have two empty columns, for future buttons, and then a column for the clear entry button and another column for the clear button as follows.

```
<tr>
    <td></td>
    <td></td>
    <td><button id="btnClearEntry">CE</button></td>
    <td><button id="btnClear">C</button></td>
</tr>
```

The next table row will have buttons 7, 8, 9, and the plus button as follows.

```
<tr>
    <td>
        <button id="btn7">7</button></td>
    <td>
        <button id="btn8">8</button></td>
    <td>
        <button id="btn9">9</button></td>
    <td>
        <button id="btnPlus">+</button>
    </td>
</tr>
```

The next table row will have buttons 4, 5, 6, and the minus button as follows.

```
<tr>
    <td>
        <button id="btn4">4</button>
    </td>
    <td>
        <button id="btn5">5</button>
    </td>
    <td>
```

```
            <button id="btn6">6</button>
        </td>
        <td>
            <button id="btnMinus">-</button>
        </td>
    </tr>
```

The next table row will have buttons 1, 2, and 3 and an empty column as follows.

```
<tr>
    <td>
        <button id="btn1">1</button>
    </td>
    <td>
        <button id="btn2">2</button>
    </td>
    <td>
        <button id="btn3">3</button>
    </td>
    <td>
    </td>
</tr>
```

The last table row will have an empty column, the 0 button, and two more empty columns as follows.

```
<tr>
    <td></td>
    <td>
        <button id="btn0">0</button>
    </td>
    <td></td>
    <td></td>
</tr>
```

The following is the completed main *<div>* element.

```
<div role="main">
    <div id="calculator">
        <table>
            <tr>
                <td colspan="4">
                    <input id="txtResult" type="text" readonly="readonly" />
                </td>
            </tr>
            <tr>
                <td colspan="4">
                    <input id="txtInput" type="text" />
                </td>
            </tr>
            <tr>
                <td></td>
                <td></td>
                <td>
                    <button id="btnClearEntry">CE</button>
                </td>
```

```
                <td>
                    <button id="btnClear">C</button>
                </td>
            </tr>
            <tr>
                <td>
                    <button id="btn7">7</button></td>
                <td>
                    <button id="btn8">8</button></td>
                <td>
                    <button id="btn9">9</button></td>
                <td>
                    <button id="btnPlus">+</button>
                </td>
            </tr>
            <tr>
                <td>
                    <button id="btn4">4</button>
                </td>
                <td>
                    <button id="btn5">5</button>
                </td>
                <td>
                    <button id="btn6">6</button>
                </td>
                <td>
                    <button id="btnMinus">-</button>
                </td>
            </tr>

            <tr>
                <td>
                    <button id="btn1">1</button>
                </td>
                <td>
                    <button id="btn2">2</button>
                </td>
                <td>
                    <button id="btn3">3</button>
                </td>
                <td></td>
            </tr>

            <tr>
                <td></td>
                <td>
                    <button id="btn0">0</button>
                </td>
                <td></td>
                <td></td>
            </tr>
        </table>
    </div>
</div>
```

7. Now that the default.html file is completed, modify the style sheet by opening the default.css file and, at the bottom, adding the table selector and setting the width to 100 percent as follows.

```
table {
    width: 100%;
}
```

8. Add a td selector and set the width to 25 percent as follows.

```
td {
    width: 25%;
}
```

9. Locate the existing button selector. Change the width to 90 percent as follows.

```
button {
    background-color: hsl(255, 50%, 80%);
    width: 90%;
    height: 10%;
    border: outset;
}
```

10. Locate the existing input selector. Change the padding to 5 pixels as follows.

```
input {
    width: 85%;
    height: 7%;
    text-align: right;
    padding: 5px;
    border: inset;
}
```

11. Press F5 to run the application.

Figure 5-19 shows the completed calculator.

FIGURE 5-19 The completed calculator

Suggested practice exercises

The following additional exercises are designed to give you more opportunities to practice what you've learned and to help you successfully master the lessons presented in this chapter.

- **Exercise 1**   Learn more about semantic markup by adding additional sections to your webpage.

- **Exercise 2**   Learn more about tables by adding more rows and cells to the table to hold future buttons.

Answers

This section contains the answers to the lesson review questions in this chapter.

Lesson 1

1. **Correct answer: D**

    A. Incorrect: The *<section>* element denotes a part of something.

    B. Incorrect: The *<pre>* element displays preformatted content.

    C. Incorrect: The *<aside>* element displays content that is related to the site.

    D. Correct: An article wraps stand-alone items that can be shared.

2. **Correct answer: C**

    A. Incorrect: You should refrain from using the *<b>* element.

    B. Incorrect: The *<em>* element indicates emphatic stress but not necessarily importance.

    C. Correct: The *<strong>* element indicates importance.

    D. Incorrect: You should refrain from using the *<i>* element.

3. **Correct answer: A**

    A. Correct: The *<address>* element provides contact information for the author of the webpage.

    B. Incorrect: The *<contact>* element is not valid.

    C. Incorrect: The *<author>*element is not valid.

    D. Incorrect: The *<name>* element is not valid.

Lesson 2

1. **Correct answer: B**

    A. Incorrect: The column needs to span two columns.

    B. Correct: The column needs the *colspan*="2" attribute to span the Products and Services columns.

    C. Incorrect: The span attribute is used with the *<col>* element but not with the *<th>* element.

    D. Incorrect: The style attribute cannot be used to cause spanning across two columns.

2. **Correct answer: A**

    A. Correct: You can assign styles to the *<col>* element, which will apply the style to the corresponding table column.

    B. Incorrect: Adding an id to each *<td>* element does not satisfy the criteria.

    C.   **Incorrect:** The *<col>* element must be inside a *<colgroup>* element.

    D.   **Incorrect:** The *<hidden>* element is not valid.

3.   **Correct answer: C**

    A.   **Incorrect:** The *<thead>* element specifies heading rows.

    B.   **Incorrect:** The *<colgroup>* element specifies columns.

    C.   **Correct:** The *<caption>* element adds a caption to the top of a table.

    D.   **Incorrect:** The *<th>* element specifies header cells.

## CHAPTER 6

Essential JavaScript and jQuery

The flexibility of JavaScript is amazing. In the previous chapters, you learned how to add JavaScript code to your webpage to provide dynamic changes to the page when an event is triggered.

One of the biggest difficulties with webpage development is the differences among different browsers, but this book is primarily focused on HTML5, CSS3, and JavaScript (ECMAScript5.1). A completely separate book could be written that deals just with the differences among browsers and browser versions.

In this chapter, you learn how to create objects, which are an important aspect of JavaScript. You use objects to create entities, which are passed to and from the server, and to encapsulate functionality that you want to modularize. You also need to extend objects that others have created.

This chapter also introduces jQuery, the answer to writing browser-compatible code. Although jQuery doesn't solve all browser-compatibility issues, it does solve most of the day-to-day issues that you encounter among browsers. In addition, jQuery is fun and easy to use.

Lessons in this chapter:

Before you begin

To complete this book, you must have some understanding of web development. This chapter requires the hardware and software listed in the "System requirements" section in the book's Introduction.

Lesson 1: Creating JavaScript objects

In JavaScript, everything is an object. Strings, numbers, and functions are all objects. You have learned how to create functions, so you already have exposure to creating objects, as you see in this lesson.

After this lesson, you will be able to:

- Understand basic object-oriented terminology.
- Create JavaScript objects.

Estimated lesson time: 20 minutes

Using object-oriented terminology

In many object-oriented languages, when you want to create objects, you start by creating a *class*, which is a blueprint for an object. Like a blueprint for a house, the blueprint isn't the house; it's the instructions that define the *type* of object that you will be constructing, which is the house. By using a house blueprint, you can create, or *construct*, many houses that are based on the blueprint. Each house is an *object* of type house, also known as an *instance* of the house type.

The developer writes the class, which is then used to construct objects. In a baseball application, you might create a Player (classes are normally capitalized) class that has properties for first and last name, batting average, error count, and so on. When you create your team, you might use the Player class to create nine Player objects, each having its own properties. Each time you construct a Player object, memory is allocated to hold the data for the player, and each piece of data is a property, which has a name and a value.

The three pillars of object-oriented programming are *encapsulation*, *inheritance*, and *polymorphism*. Encapsulation means that you hide all details except those that are required to communicate with your object in order to simplify the object for anyone using the object. Inheritance means that you can create an "is a" relationship between two classes, in which the child class automatically inherits everything that is in the parent class. Polymorphism means that you can execute a function on the parent class, but the behavior changes (morphs) because your child class has a function that overrides the function in the parent class.

The *parent class* is also known as the *base* class, the *super* class, or the *generalized* class. The *child class* is also known as the *derived* class, the *subclass*, or the *specialized* class. Because it's easy to think of actual children inheriting from parents, the terms parent and child are usually used, but you should remember the other terms for these classes to communicate effectively with others about object-oriented programming.

In object-oriented programming, objects can have data implemented as properties and behaviors implemented as methods. A *property* is essentially a variable that is defined on an object and owned by the object. A *method* is a function that is defined on an object and owned by the object.

Understanding the JavaScript object-oriented caveat

JavaScript is a very flexible language. You can create objects, but the relationship between the JavaScript language and class-based, object-oriented programming is not direct. The most glaring example is that there is no *class* keyword in JavaScript. If you're familiar with class-based, object-oriented programming, you'll be struggling to find the "class."

JavaScript is a prototype-based, object-oriented programming language. In JavaScript, everything is an object, and you either create a new object from nothing, or you create an object from a clone of an existing object, known as a *prototype*.

Conceptually, you can simulate class creation by using a function. Class-based, object-oriented purists dislike the idea of a function being used to simulate a class. Keep an open mind as patterns are presented. This lesson should give you what you need to accomplish your tasks.

The problem you typically encounter is finding one correct solution for all scenarios. As you read on, you'll find that achieving proper encapsulation of private data requires you to create copies of the functions that can access the private data for each object instance, which consumes memory. If you don't want to create copies of the method for each object instance, the data needs to be publicly exposed, thus losing the benefits of encapsulation, by which you hide object details that users shouldn't need to see.

The general consensus of this issue of encapsulation versus wasteful memory consumption is that most people would rather expose the data to minimize memory consumption. Try to understand the benefits and drawbacks of each pattern when deciding which option to implement in your scenario.

Using the JavaScript object literal pattern

Probably the simplest way to create an object in JavaScript is to use the object literal syntax. This starts with a set of curly braces to indicate an object. Inside the curly braces is a comma-separated list of name/value pairs to define each property. Object literals create an object from nothing, so these objects contain precisely what you assign to them and nothing more. No prototype object is associated with the created object. The following example demonstrates the creation of two objects that represent vehicles.

```
var car1 = {
    year: 2000,
    make: 'Ford',
    model: 'Fusion',
    getInfo: function () {
        return 'Vehicle: ' + this.year + ' ' + this.make + ' ' + this.model;
    }
};
```

```
var car2 = {
    year: 2010,
    make: 'BMW',
    model: 'Z4',
    getInfo: function () {
        return 'Vehicle: ' + this.year + ' ' + this.make + ' ' + this.model;
    }
};
```

In this example, public properties are created for *year*, *make*, *model*, and *getInfo*. The get-Info property doesn't contain data; it references an anonymous function instead, so getInfo is a method. The method uses the *this* keyword to access the data. Remember that the *this* keyword references the object that owns the code where the *this* keyword is. In this case, the object is being created. If the *this* keyword were omitted, the code would look in the global namespace for *year*, *make*, and *model*.

To test this code, the following QUnit test checks to see whether each object contains the data that is expected.

```
test("Object Literal Test", function () {
    expect(2);
    var expected = 'Vehicle: 2000 Ford Fusion';
    var actual = car1.getInfo();
    equal(actual, expected, 'Expected value: ' + expected +
        ' Actual value: ' + actual);
    var expected = 'Vehicle: 2010 BMW Z4';
    var actual = car2.getInfo();
    equal(actual, expected, 'Expected value: ' + expected +
        ' Actual value: ' + actual);
});
```

This test performs an assertion by using the *car1* variable and then performs another assertion by using the *car2* variable. The successful test is shown in Figure 6-1.

If you want to define an array of items and assign it to a property, you can use square brackets as shown in the following example.

```
var car1 = {
    year: 2000,
    make: 'Ford',
    model: 'Fusion',
    repairs: ['repair1', 'repair2', 'repair3'],
    getInfo: function () {
        return 'Vehicle: ' + this.year + ' ' + this.make + ' ' + this.model;
    }
};
```

Because this is one of the easiest ways to create an object, you'll probably use it to gather data to send to other code. In this example, two instances of a type Object are created, and properties are dynamically added to each instance. This does not create a Vehicle type.

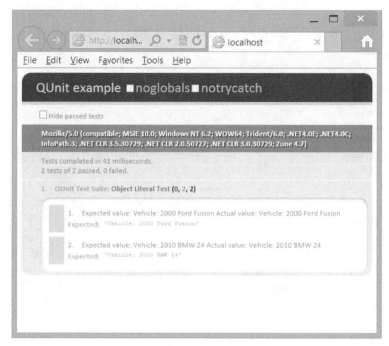

FIGURE 6-1 The JavaScript object literal test

Creating dynamic objects by using the factory pattern

In addition to using the JavaScript literal object syntax, JavaScript has an Object type, and you can use it to create an object programmatically. Object has a prototype object that is cloned when you use the *new* keyword to create a new Object instance. The prototype object has the following inherited methods.

- **constructor**   The function that is called to initialize a new object
- **hasOwnProperty**   Returns a Boolean indicator of whether the current object has the specified property
- **isPrototypeOf**   Returns a Boolean indicator of whether the current object is in the specified object's prototype object chain
- **propertyIsEnumerable**   Returns true if the object can be enumerated in a for...in loop
- **toLocalString**   Converts a date to a string value based on the current local
- **toString**   Returns the string representation of the current object
- **valueOf**   Returns the value of the current object converted to its most meaningful primitive value

After the object is created, you can dynamically add properties to it that hold the data and reference functions. You can wrap this code in a function that returns the object as shown in the following code example.

```
function getVehicle(theYear, theMake, theModel) {
    var vehicle = new Object();
    vehicle.year = theYear;
    vehicle.make = theMake;
    vehicle.model = theModel;
    vehicle.getInfo = function () {
        return 'Vehicle: ' + this.year + ' ' + this.make + ' ' + this.model;
    };
    return vehicle;
}
```

This code takes advantage of JavaScript's dynamic nature to add *year, make, model,* and *getInfo* to the object and then returns the object. Placing this code in a function makes it easy to call the getVehicle function to get a new object. The encapsulation of the code to create an object is commonly referred to as using the *factory pattern*. Can you create multiple instances of vehicle? You can create multiple instances of Object and add properties dynamically to each instance, but the actual type is Object, not vehicle. The following QUnit test demonstrates the creation of multiple instances.

```
test("Create Instances Test Using Factory Pattern", function () {
    expect(2);
    var car1 = getVehicle(2000, 'Ford', 'Fusion');
    var car2 = getVehicle(2010, 'BMW', 'Z4');
    var expected = 'Vehicle: 2000 Ford Fusion';
    var actual = car1.getInfo();
    equal(actual, expected, 'Expected value: ' + expected +
        ' Actual value: ' + actual);
    var expected = 'Vehicle: 2010 BMW Z4';
    var actual = car2.getInfo();
    equal(actual, expected, 'Expected value: ' + expected +
        ' Actual value: ' + actual);
});
```

This might be all you need when you are gathering some data to put into an object structure and pass to some other code or service. Although the getVehicle function encapsulates the object creation, the properties are all public. This can be desirable in some scenarios, but if you want the data to be private, this approach won't work. Like when using the literal object syntax, you might encounter the problem that every vehicle's type is Object, and you might want to create a Vehicle class to have a named Vehicle type.

Creating a class

There is no *class* keyword in JavaScript, but you can simulate a class by starting with a function, which is actually the *constructor function* of the object. Consider the following function.

```
function Vehicle(theYear, theMake, theModel) {
    year = theYear;
```

```
        make = theMake;
        model = theModel;
        getInfo = function () {
            return 'Vehicle: ' + year + ' ' + make + ' ' + model;
        };
    }
```

There are several problems with this code. All the variables are defined without the *var* keyword, so *year*, *make*, *model*, and *getInfo* are automatically defined in the global scope and are accessible from anywhere. The following is a passing QUnit test that initializes Vehicle and calls the getInfo method to retrieve the data.

```
test("Function Test", function () {
    expect(2);
    Vehicle(2000, 'Ford', 'Fusion');
    var expected = 'Vehicle: 2000 Ford Fusion';
    var actual = getInfo();
    equal(actual, expected, 'Expected value: ' + expected +
        ' Actual value: ' + actual);
    expected = 2000;
    actual = year;
    equal(actual, expected, 'Expected value: ' + expected +
        ' Actual value: ' + actual);
});
```

The Vehicle function accepts three parameters and doesn't return anything. Instead, it is setting global variables, and there is no provision for multiple instances. To prove that global variables are being set, the second assertion is checking to see whether there is a global variable named *year* that equals 2,000. This assertion succeeds, which proves that the data is not encapsulated, and there is only one copy of the data. For example, the following QUnit test fails.

```
test("Failing Function Test", function () {
    expect(1);
    Vehicle(2000, 'Ford', 'Fusion');
    Vehicle(2010, 'BMW', 'Z4');
    var expected = 'Vehicle: 2000 Ford Fusion';
    var actual = getInfo();
    equal(actual, expected, 'Expected value: ' + expected +
        ' Actual value: ' + actual);
    expected = 2000;
    actual = year;
    equal(actual, expected, 'Expected value: ' + expected +
        ' Actual value: ' + actual);
});
```

Figure 6-2 shows the failures. The problem is that *year*, *make*, and *model* of the second vehicle replaced *year*, *make*, and *model* of the first vehicle. The variable *getInfo* was also replaced, but instead of holding data, it holds a reference to the function code. The *getInfo* variable's value was replaced with new function code; it just happened to be the same code. Once again, there is no encapsulation.

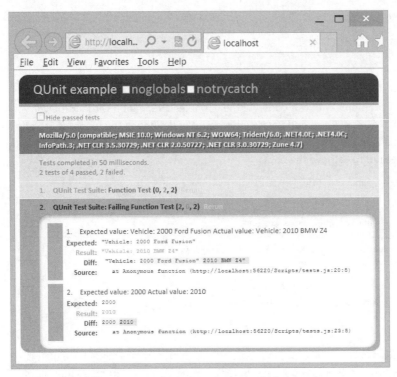

FIGURE 6-2 The failing test assertions after a second vehicle is used

To solve the problem, you want to implement encapsulation. Then you need to create objects, each with its own data. To implement encapsulation, use the *var* keyword for the *year*, *make*, and *model*. This will make these variables private to the function. Notice that the *var* keyword is not used with *getInfo* because the *getInfo* variable needs to be public to be called from outside the object, but you don't want the *getInfo* variable to be global. Assign *getInfo* to the current object by using the *this* keyword. The result is a class that encapsulates the data and exposes *getInfo* to retrieve the data in a controlled way as follows.

```
function Vehicle(theYear, theMake, theModel) {
    var year = theYear;
    var make = theMake;
    var model = theModel;
    this.getInfo = function () {
        return 'Vehicle: ' + year + ' ' + make + ' ' + model;
    };
}
```

> **IMPORTANT   PRIVATE DATA ISN'T SECURE**
>
> In object-oriented programming, private data is not intended to be secure. Private data provides encapsulation so the details can be hidden; the user sees only what is necessary and isn't bogged down in the details.

Remember that the *this* keyword references the object that owns the current code. The way the test is currently written, the *this* keyword references the global object, and *getInfo* will still be a global variable. To solve the problem, the *new* keyword must be used to create an object from this class, as shown in the modified test code.

```
test("Encapsulation Test", function () {
    expect(2);
    var car1 = new Vehicle(2000, 'Ford', 'Fusion');
    var car2 = new Vehicle(2010, 'BMW', 'Z4');
    var expected = 'Vehicle: 2000 Ford Fusion';
    var actual = car1.getInfo();
    equal(actual, expected, 'Expected value: ' + expected +
        ' Actual value: ' + actual);
    expected = 2000;
    actual = year;
    equal(actual, expected, 'Expected value: ' + expected +
        ' Actual value: ' + actual);
});
```

Notice that a new variable is defined, *car1*, and it is assigned the object that is created by using the *new* keyword. After that, another new variable is defined, *car2*, and it is assigned the second Vehicle object created by using the *new* keyword. Two instances of the Vehicle class are being created, which means that two Vehicle objects are being constructed. Each instance has its own data and its own copy of the getInfo method. The getInfo method is public but has access to the private data. A method that is public but has access to private data is called

a *privileged method*.

Figure 6-3 shows the test results. Notice that the first assertion passed, which proves that there are separate object instances, each having its own data. The second assertion failed. The failure message states that the year is undefined, which proves that the year is not directly accessible from the test, which is in the global namespace. Instead, *year*, in addition to *make* and *model*, is encapsulated in the object.

You have now created a class and constructed objects from the class, but there's more to cover in the Vehicle function that is being used as a class. The Vehicle function is known

as a *constructor function*. The *new* keyword created an object and executed the constructor function to initialize the object by creating the *year*, *make*, and *model* private variables and the public *getInfo* variable. Each instance has these four variables, and memory is allocated for them. That's what you want for the data, but is that what you want for the *getInfo* variable that references a function? The answer is that it depends on what you are trying to accomplish with your code.

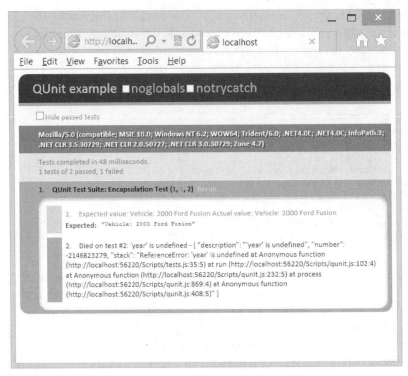

FIGURE 6-3 Successful first assertion and failed second assertion

Consider the following test code that creates two Vehicle objects, but then replaces the code in *getInfo* of the first Vehicle object with different code. Does this replace the code in the second Vehicle object?

```
test("Function Replacement Test", function () {
    expect(2);
    var car1 = new Vehicle(2000, 'Ford', 'Fusion');
    var car2 = new Vehicle(2010, 'BMW', 'Z4');
    car1.getInfo = function () {
        return 'This is a Car';
    };
    var expected = 'This is a Car';
    var actual = car1.getInfo();
    equal(actual, expected, 'Expected value: ' + expected +
        ' Actual value: ' + actual);
    var expected = 'This is a Car';
    var actual = car2.getInfo();
    equal(actual, expected, 'Expected value: ' + expected +
        ' Actual value: ' + actual);
});
```

The test result is shown in Figure 6-4. The first assertion succeeded, which proves that the function was successfully replaced on the first Vehicle object. The second assertion failed, which proves that the second Vehicle object's getInfo function was not replaced. Is that what you expected? Is that what you wanted? You can see that in some scenarios, this behavior is desirable, but in other scenarios, you might have wanted to replace the function across all objects. To do this, you use the *prototype* pattern.

> **NOTE** **ACCESS TO PRIVATE DATA**
>
> In the example, the replacement function cannot access the private data because the replacement is executed externally to the Vehicle.

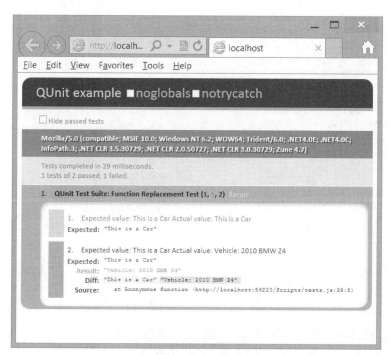

FIGURE 6-4 Successful first assertion, proving that the function was replaced; failed second assertion, proving that the second Vehicle's function was not replaced

Using the prototype property

In JavaScript, everything, including the function, is an Object type, which has a *prototype* property. The prototype itself is an object containing properties and methods that should be available to all instances of the type you're working with. However, this prototype is typically specified externally to the constructor function, so the prototype doesn't have access to private variables. Therefore, you must expose the data for the prototype to work. The following is an example of using the prototype property to create a single getInfo method that is shared across all instances.

```
function Vehicle(theYear, theMake, theModel) {
    this.year = theYear;
```

```
        this.make = theMake;
        this.model = theModel;
}
Vehicle.prototype.getInfo = function () {
        return 'Vehicle: ' + this.year + ' ' + this.make + ' ' + this.model;
}
```

By using this class and the prototype, you can write the following test to ensure that each instance has its own data and that the getInfo function works properly.

```
test("Instance Test Using Prototype", function () {
        expect(2);
        var car1 = new Vehicle(2000, 'Ford', 'Fusion');
        var car2 = new Vehicle(2010, 'BMW', 'Z4');
        var expected = 'Vehicle: 2000 Ford Fusion';
        var actual = car1.getInfo();
        equal(actual, expected, 'Expected value: ' + expected +
                ' Actual value: ' + actual);
        var expected = 'Vehicle: 2010 BMW Z4';
        var actual = car2.getInfo();
        equal(actual, expected, 'Expected value: ' + expected +
                ' Actual value: ' + actual);
});
```

In this test, two instances of the Vehicle class are created, each having different data. The first assertion calls getInfo on *car1* and verifies that the proper result is returned. The second assertion calls getInfo on *car2* and verifies that the proper result is returned. The result is shown in Figure 6-5.

FIGURE 6-5 The modified class using the prototype property to create the getInfo function

Now that you have a functioning class, change the prototype to see whether it can be changed across all instances.

```
test("Instance Test Using Prototype Replace Function", function () {
    expect(2);
    var car1 = new Vehicle(2000, 'Ford', 'Fusion');
    var car2 = new Vehicle(2010, 'BMW', 'Z4');
    Vehicle.prototype.getInfo = function () {
        return 'Car: ' + this.year + ' ' + this.make + ' ' + this.model;
    }
    var expected = 'Car: 2000 Ford Fusion';
    var actual = car1.getInfo();
    equal(actual, expected, 'Expected value: ' + expected +
        ' Actual value: ' + actual);
    var expected = 'Car: 2010 BMW Z4';
    var actual = car2.getInfo();
    equal(actual, expected, 'Expected value: ' + expected +
        ' Actual value: ' + actual);
});
```

This test creates two Vehicle instances and then changes getInfo. Next, the two assertions are modified to check both instances to see whether they are using the updated getInfo. The result is shown in Figure 6-6.

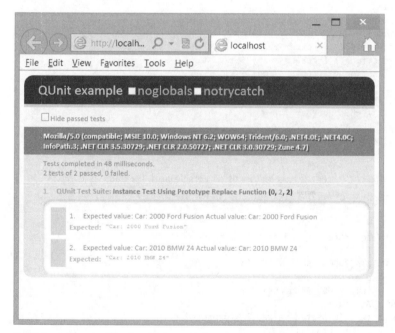

FIGURE 6-6 The modification of the getInfo prototype affected all instances

You might use the prototype property when creating functions that will be shared across all instances, but remember that the prototype is defined externally to the constructor function, so all properties must be public when using the *this* keyword. If you don't need to replace individual instance functions and you don't mind making your data public, the proto-type is efficient.

Debating the prototype/private compromise

You've learned the primary patterns for creating a JavaScript object, but there can be a com-promise in which you can have private data that is readable by creating a method for retriev-ing the data, also known as a *getter*, which has no *setter*, a method for setting the value. This would require you to write a function that is copied for each object, but you should keep the function as small as possible, as shown in the following code example.

```
function Vehicle(theYear, theMake, theModel) {
    var year = theYear;
    var make = theMake;
    var model = theModel;
    this.getYear = function () { return year; };
    this.getMake = function () { return make; };
    this.getModel = function () { return model; };
}
Vehicle.prototype.getInfo = function () {
    return 'Vehicle: ' + this.getYear() +
        ' ' + this.getMake() +
        ' ' + this.getModel();
}
```

The QUnit test for this code creates two instances of Vehicle and, for each assertion, executes the getInfo method of each object and checks for the proper value. The test is as follows.

```
test("Instance Test Using Prototype and getters", function () {
    expect(2);
    var car1 = new Vehicle(2000, 'Ford', 'Fusion');
    var car2 = new Vehicle(2010, 'BMW', 'Z4');
    var expected = 'Vehicle: 2000 Ford Fusion';
    var actual = car1.getInfo();
    equal(actual, expected, 'Expected value: ' + expected +
        ' Actual value: ' + actual);
    var expected = 'Vehicle: 2010 BMW Z4';
    var actual = car2.getInfo();
    equal(actual, expected, 'Expected value: ' + expected +
        ' Actual value: ' + actual);
});
```

This test is successful, so replace the getInfo method and add more tests. The following test code does this.

```
test("Instance Test Using Prototype and getters", function () {
    expect(4);
    var car1 = new Vehicle(2000, 'Ford', 'Fusion');
    var car2 = new Vehicle(2010, 'BMW', 'Z4');
    var expected = 'Vehicle: 2000 Ford Fusion';
    var actual = car1.getInfo();
    equal(actual, expected, 'Expected value: ' + expected +
        ' Actual value: ' + actual);
    var expected = 'Vehicle: 2010 BMW Z4';
    var actual = car2.getInfo();
    equal(actual, expected, 'Expected value: ' + expected +
        ' Actual value: ' + actual);
    Vehicle.prototype.getInfo = function () {
        return 'Car Year: ' + this.getYear()
            + ' Make: ' + this.getMake()
            + ' Model: ' + this.getModel();
    };
    var expected = 'Car Year: 2000 Make: Ford Model: Fusion';
    var actual = car1.getInfo();
    equal(actual, expected, 'Expected value: ' + expected +
        ' Actual value: ' + actual);
    var expected = 'Car Year: 2010 Make: BMW Model: Z4';
    var actual = car2.getInfo();
    equal(actual, expected, 'Expected value: ' + expected +
        ' Actual value: ' + actual);
});
```

The test result is shown in Figure 6-7. You can replace the getInfo method and, because the data is exposed as read-only, it's available to be used in the new method. In addition, the privileged getters are small, which minimizes the amount of memory consumed when each instance has a copy of the method. Remember to create only getter methods as needed and to keep them small and concise.

Quick check

- How can you expose private data as read-only?

Quick check answer

- Add a getter method that retrieves the data but cannot change the data.

FIGURE 6-7 The use of getters to expose read-only data as a good compromise

Implementing namespaces

One problem to watch for is the pollution of the global namespace. As your program gets larger and libraries are added, more entries are added to the global object. How can you minimize this global namespace pollution?

JavaScript doesn't have a namespace keyword, but you can implement the equivalent of a namespace by using techniques that are similar to those used to create objects. Consider the following code sample.

```
var vehicleCount = 5;

var vehicles = new Array();

function Car() { }
function Truck() { }

var repair = {
    description: 'changed spark plugs',
    cost: 100
};
```

This code sample places five entries in the global namespace, and as the application grows, this global namespace pollution also grows. You can implement the namespace pattern to solve the problem. The following example shows the creation of an object that contains the five items from the previous example.

```
var myApp = {};

myApp.vehicleCount = 5;

myApp.vehicles = new Array();

myApp.Car = function () { }
myApp.Truck = function () { }

myApp.repair = {
    description: 'changed spark plugs',
    cost: 100
};
```

In this sample, myApp is the only entry in the global namespace. It represents the name of the application and its root namespace. Notice that object literal syntax is used to create an empty object and assign it to myApp. Everything else is added to the object. Sub-namespaces can also be created and assigned to myApp.

You can see that a namespace was created by creating an object. Although only one entry is made in the global namespace, all the members of myApp are globally accessible. In addition, if you create a namespace for your application, and your application has many JavaScript files, you might want to have logic to create the namespace object only if it hasn't been created. In the following example, the code for myApp is modified to create the namespace object if it doesn't already exist. This code uses the OR operator to create a new object if myApp does not have a value.

```
var myApp = myApp || {};
```

You can use the object techniques already defined in this lesson to make some members of the namespace private and some public. The difference is that the namespace is a single-ton object, so you create a single instance for the namespace. You don't need to worry about functions defined in the constructor function consuming additional memory for each instance because there is only one instance. Here is an example of the use of an *immediately invoked function expression* (IIFE) to create the myApp namespace in which *Car* and *Truck* are public, but *vehicleCount*, *vehicles*, and *repair* are private.

```
(function () {
    this.myApp = this.myApp || {};
    var ns = this.myApp;

    var vehicleCount = 5;
    var vehicles = new Array();

    ns.Car = function () { }
    ns.Truck = function () { }

    var repair = {
        description: 'changed spark plugs',
        cost: 100
    };
}());
```

An *IIFE* (pronounced *iffy*) is an anonymous function expression that has a set of parentheses at the end of it, which indicates that you want to execute the function. The anonymous function expression is wrapped in parentheses to tell the JavaScript interpreter that the function isn't only being defined; it's also being executed when the file is loaded.

In this IIFE, the first line creates the myApp namespace if it doesn't already exist, which represents the singleton object that is used as the namespace. Next, an *ns* variable (for namespace) is created as an alias to the namespace to save typing within the IIFE, so *ns* can be used in place of this.myApp. After that, the private members of the namespace are defined by using the *var* keyword. *Car* and *Truck* are public, so they are prefixed with *ns*.

If you're wondering how you would create a sub-namespace under myApp, the following example shows how you can add a billing namespace under the myApp namespace.

```
(function () {
    this.myApp = this.myApp || {};
    var rootNs = this.myApp;
    rootNs.billing = rootNs.billing || {};
    var ns = rootNs.billing;

    var taxRate = .05;
    ns.Invoice = function () { };
}());
```

This example also implements an IIFE to create the namespace. First, the myApp namespace is created if it doesn't already exist and is assigned to a local *rootNs* variable to save typing inside the namespace. Next, the billing namespace is created and assigned to the local *ns* variable to save typing inside the namespace. Finally, the private taxRate property is defined while the public *Invoice* is defined.

Implementing inheritance

JavaScript provides the ability to implement inheritance, which is useful when you can define the relationship between two objects as an "is a" relationship. For example, an apple is a fruit, an employee is a person, and a piano is an instrument. You look for "is a" relationships because they provide an opportunity to implement code reuse. If you have several types of vehicles, you can create Vehicle with the common vehicle traits defined in it. After Vehicle is created, you can create each vehicle type and inherit from Vehicle so you don't need duplicate code in each vehicle type.

As an example of inheritance, start by defining the base class. Using the Vehicle example, the following is an example of a Vehicle base class.

```
var Vehicle = (function () {
    function Vehicle(year, make, model) {
        this.year = year;
        this.make = make;
        this.model = model;
    }
```

```
    Vehicle.prototype.getInfo = function () {
        return this.year + ' ' + this.make + ' ' + this.model;
    };
    Vehicle.prototype.startEngine = function () {
        return 'Vroom';
    };
    return Vehicle;
})();
```

This class is wrapped in an IIFE. The wrapper encapsulates the function and the Vehicle prototype. There is no attempt to make the data private. The code works as follows.

- When the code is loaded into the browser, the IIFE is immediately invoked.

- A nested function called Vehicle is defined in the IIFE.

- The Vehicle function's prototype defines getInfo and startEngine functions that are on every instance of Vehicle.

- A reference to the Vehicle function is returned, which is assigned to the *Vehicle* variable.

This is a great way to create a class, and all future class examples use this pattern. To create Vehicle objects, you use the *new* keyword with the *Vehicle* variable. The following test creates an instance of Vehicle and tests the getInfo and startEngine methods.

```
test('Vehicle Inheritance Test', function () {
    expect(2);
    var v = new Vehicle(2012, 'Toyota', 'Rav4');
    var actual = v.getInfo();
    var expected = '2012 Toyota Rav4';
        equal(actual, expected, 'Expected value: ' + expected +
            ' Actual value: ' + actual);
    var actual = v.startEngine();
    var expected = 'Vroom';
    equal(actual, expected, 'Expected value: ' + expected +
        ' Actual value: ' + actual);
});
```

Now that you have a Vehicle parent class with three properties and two methods, you can create child classes for Car and Boat that inherit from Vehicle. Start by writing an IIFE but, this time, pass Vehicle into the IIFE as follows.

```
var Car = (function (parent) {

})(Vehicle);
```

Because Vehicle in this example is the *Vehicle* variable, not the Vehicle function, Car needs to be defined after Vehicle. Vehicle is passed into the IIFE and is available inside the IIFE as *parent*. Next, the function for Car can be added inside the IIFE. Inside the function, add any additional properties, such as wheelQuantity, and initialize to four. In the function, call the parent class's constructor for Car to allocate memory slots for the year, make, and model. To call the parent constructor function, use a *call* method that exists on the Function object, which accepts a parameter for the *this* object, and parameters for the parameters on the function being called, as follows.

```
var Car = (function (parent) {
    function Car(year, make, model) {
        parent.call(this, year, make, model);
        this.wheelQuantity = 4;
    }
    return Car;
})(Vehicle);
```

Notice how this example used the *call* method to modify the *this* object; the *this* object is the Car object, so the call to the parent constructor function creates year, make, and model on the Car object. The Function object has another method, *apply,* that does the same thing, but the extra parameters are passed as an array instead of as a comma-delimited list.

Next, the inheritance must be set up. You might think that you've already set up inheritance because the previous example calls the parent class's constructor, and the year, make, and model are created on Car, but getInfo and startEngine were not inherited. The inheritance is accomplished by changing the Car prototype object to be a new Vehicle object. Remember that the prototype is the object that is cloned to create the new object. By default, the prototype is of type Object. After the new Vehicle is assigned to the prototype, the constructor of that Vehicle is changed to be the Car constructor as follows.

```
var Car = (function (parent) {
    Car.prototype = new Vehicle();
    Car.prototype.constructor = Car;
    function Car(year, make, model) {
        parent.call(this, year, make, model);
        this.wheelQuantity = 4;
    }
    return Car;
})(Vehicle);
```

Finally, you can add more methods into Car. In this example, the getInfo method is added, which replaces the Vehicle getInfo method. The new getInfo gets some code reuse by calling the existing getInfo method on the parent Vehicle object's prototype. However, you must use the *call* method and pass the *this* object as follows.

```
var Car = (function (parent) {
    Car.prototype = new Vehicle();
    Car.prototype.constructor = Car;
    function Car(year, make, model) {
        parent.call(this, year, make, model);
        this.wheelQuantity = 4;
    }
    Car.prototype.getInfo = function () {
        return 'Vehicle Type: Car ' + parent.prototype.getInfo.call(this);
    };
    return Car;
})(Vehicle);
```

This completes Car, and Boat is similar except that Boat has a propellerBladeQuantity, which is initialized to three, instead of the wheelQuantity property. In addition, getInfo returns the vehicle type of Boat and calls the Vehicle getInfo method as follows.

```
var Boat = (function (parent) {
    Boat.prototype = new Vehicle();
    Boat.prototype.constructor = Boat;
    function Boat(year, make, model) {
        parent.call(this, year, make, model);
        this.propellerBladeQuantity = 3;
    }
    Boat.prototype.getInfo = function () {
        return 'Vehicle Type: Boat ' + parent.prototype.getInfo.call(this);
    };
    return Boat;
})(Vehicle);
```

In addition to the Vehicle tests already presented, you need to verify the following for the child classes.

- Car and Boat have the inherited year, make, and model properties.

- Car has its wheelQuantity property and it's set.

- Boat has its propellerBladeQuantity and it's set.

- Car and Boat return the proper value from the replaced getInfo method.

- Car and Boat return the proper value from the inherited startEngine method.

The following are the Car and Boat tests.

```
test('Car Inheritance Test', function () {
    expect(6);
    var c = new Car(2012, 'Toyota', 'Rav4');
    var actual = c.year;
    var expected = 2012;
    equal(actual, expected, 'Expected value: ' + expected +
        ' Actual value: ' + actual);
    var actual = c.make;
    var expected = 'Toyota';
    equal(actual, expected, 'Expected value: ' + expected +
        ' Actual value: ' + actual);
    var actual = c.model;
    var expected = 'Rav4';
    equal(actual, expected, 'Expected value: ' + expected +
        ' Actual value: ' + actual);
    var actual = c.wheelQuantity;
    var expected = 4;
    equal(actual, expected, 'Expected value: ' + expected +
        ' Actual value: ' + actual);
    var actual = c.getInfo();
    var expected = 'Vehicle Type: Car 2012 Toyota Rav4';
    equal(actual, expected, 'Expected value: ' + expected +
        ' Actual value: ' + actual);
```

```
        var actual = c.startEngine();
        var expected = 'Vroom';
        equal(actual, expected, 'Expected value: ' + expected +
            ' Actual value: ' + actual);
});

test('Boat Inheritance Test', function () {
    expect(6);
    var b = new Boat(1994, 'Sea Ray', 'Signature 200');
    var actual = b.year;
    var expected = 1994;
    equal(actual, expected, 'Expected value: ' + expected +
        ' Actual value: ' + actual);
    var actual = b.make;
    var expected = 'Sea Ray';
    equal(actual, expected, 'Expected value: ' + expected +
        ' Actual value: ' + actual);
    var actual = b.model;
    var expected = 'Signature 200';
    equal(actual, expected, 'Expected value: ' + expected +
        ' Actual value: ' + actual);
    var actual = b.propellerBladeQuantity;
    var expected = 3;
    equal(actual, expected, 'Expected value: ' + expected +
        ' Actual value: ' + actual);
    var actual = b.getInfo();
    var expected = 'Vehicle Type: Boat 1994 Sea Ray Signature 200';
    equal(actual, expected, 'Expected value: ' + expected +
        ' Actual value: ' + actual);
    var actual = b.startEngine();
    var expected = 'Vroom';
    equal(actual, expected, 'Expected value: ' + expected +
        ' Actual value: ' + actual);
});
```

Figure 6-8 shows the test output. All tests have passed.

FIGURE 6-8 The passing inheritance tests

Lesson summary

- A class is a blueprint for an object in which an object is an instance of a class.
- The three pillars of object-oriented programming are encapsulation, inheritance, and polymorphism.
- The class from which you inherit is called the parent, base, super, or generalized class. The class that is derived from the parent is called the child, derived, sub, or specialized class. You can implement inheritance by replacing the Child class prototype with a new instance of the parent and replacing its constructor with the Child class constructor function.

- JavaScript is a prototype-based, object-oriented programming language. A prototype is the object used to create a new instance.

- The literal pattern can be used to create an object by using curly braces to create the object. The factory pattern can be used to create a dynamic object.

- JavaScript does not have a class keyword, but you can simulate a class by defining a function.

- Creating private members is possible but usually involves creating privileged getter methods that can be memory consuming.

- The *new* keyword constructs an object instance.

- The *function* is an object. The function that simulates a class is called the *constructor function*.

- Namespaces can be created by using an immediately invoked function expression (IIFE).

Lesson review

Answer the following questions to test your knowledge of the information in this lesson. You can find the answers to these questions and explanations of why each answer choice is correct or incorrect in the "Answers" section at the end of this chapter.

1. What is the blueprint for an object called?

   A. property

   B. method

   C. class

   D. event

2. What does JavaScript use as a starting object when constructing a new object?

   A. prototype

   B. property

   C. class

   D. event

3. How is inheritance supported in JavaScript?

   A. You replace the prototype of the child object with a new instance of the parent object and then replace the prototype constructor with the child constructor.

   B. You call the createChild method on the parent object.

   C. You call the setParent method on the child object.

   D. JavaScript does not support inheritance.

Lesson 2: Working with jQuery

This lesson introduces jQuery, which is very well documented at *http://jquery.com*. Subsequent chapters take advantage of jQuery whenever possible to minimize typing and benefit from jQuery's cross browser–compatible helper functions.

> **After this lesson, you will be able to:**
> - Explain the benefits of using jQuery.
> - Use jQuery to select DOM elements.
> - Use jQuery to modify the DOM.
> - Use jQuery to set styles.
>
> **Estimated lesson time: 30 minutes**

Introducing jQuery

jQuery is a library of helper functions that are cross browser–compatible. If you feel comfortable working with JavaScript, you might think that you don't need jQuery, but you do. You can minimize the amount of browser-specific code you must write by using jQuery, an open-source add-in that provides an easy, browser-agnostic means for writing JavaScript.

jQuery is written in JavaScript, so it is JavaScript. You can read the jQuery source code to understand how jQuery works. Probably millions of developers use jQuery. It's easy to use, it's stable, it's fully documented, and it works well with other frameworks. The following is a list of the categories of functionality jQuery provides.

- **Ajax**   Methods that provide synchronous and asynchronous calls to the server
- **Attributes**   Methods that get and set attributes of document object model (DOM) elements
- **Callbacks object**   An object that provides many methods for managing callbacks
- **Core**   Methods that provide core jQuery functionality
- **CSS**   Methods that get and set CSS-related properties
- **Data**   Methods that assist with associating arbitrary data with DOM elements
- **Deferred object**   A chainable object that can register multiple callbacks into call-back queues and relay the success or failure state of any synchronous or asynchronous functions
- **Dimensions**   Helper methods for retrieving and setting DOM element dimensions
- **Effects**   Animation techniques that can be added to your webpage
- **Events**   Methods that provide the ability to register code to execute when the user interacts with the browser

- **Forms**   Methods that provide functionality when working with form controls
- **Offset**   Methods for positioning DOM elements
- **Selectors**   Methods that provide the ability to access DOM elements by using CSS selectors
- **Traversing**   Methods that provide the ability to traverse the DOM
- **Utilities**   Utility methods

This lesson only scratches the surface of jQuery's capabilities, but subsequent lessons use jQuery whenever possible.

Getting started with jQuery

To get started with jQuery, add the jQuery library to your project. In this example, the QUnit testing framework has already been added to an empty web project, and it will demonstrate jQuery capabilities. You can add jQuery by either downloading the library from *http://jQuery .com* or adding the library from NuGet. To add it from NuGet, open your project and, in the Project menu, click Manage NuGet Packages. In the Search Online text box, type **jQuery** and press Enter. You should see a screen that is similar to that shown in Figure 6-9.

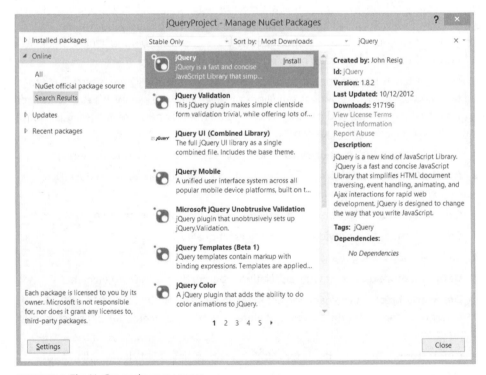

FIGURE 6-9 The NuGet package manager

After locating jQuery, click the Install button. The installation will start and, in a moment, you'll see a green check box on jQuery, indicating that the installation has completed successfully. Click the Close button and look at the Solution Explorer window, as shown in Figure 6-10. If your project didn't have a Scripts folder, a Scripts folder was added. Inside the Scripts folder, you'll find the latest release of jQuery. There is a file for IntelliSense and a complete jQuery library file. Finally, there is a minimized version of jQuery, which is the file you use at production time to minimize bandwidth usage.

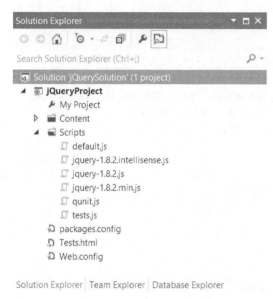

FIGURE 6-10 The completed installation of jQuery

Using jQuery

You're probably still trying to understand what jQuery is and how you benefit from using it, so the first feature to learn is how to use jQuery to locate an element or a group of elements. First, the jQuery library must be referenced on the page on which you will be using it. In this first example, the basic QUnit Test.html file is used, and the jQuery library is added so that the file contains the following HTML.

```html
<!DOCTYPE html>
<html xmlns="http://www.w3.org/1999/xhtml">
<head>
    <title></title>
    <link rel="stylesheet" type="text/css" href="Content/qunit.css" />
    <script type="text/javascript" src="Scripts/qunit.js"></script>
    <script src="Scripts/jquery-1.8.2.js"></script>
    <script type="text/javascript" src="Scripts/default.js"></script>
    <script type="text/javascript" src="Scripts/tests.js"></script>
</head>
<body>
```

```
    <h1 id="qunit-header">QUnit example</h1>
    <h2 id="qunit-banner"></h2>
    <div id="qunit-testrunner-toolbar"></div>
    <h2 id="qunit-userAgent"></h2>
    <ol id="qunit-tests"></ol>
    <div id="qunit-fixture">
        test markup, will be hidden
        <input id="txtInput" type="text"  /><br />
        <input id="txtResult" type="text"  /><br />
    </div>
</body>
</html>
```

In the Solution Explorer window, the Test.html file has been set as the startup page by right-clicking the file and choosing Set As Start Page.

In the default.js file, the following code sets a reference to the *txtInput* and *txtResult* text boxes and then calls the clear function to initialize the two text boxes to '0'.

```
var txtInput;
var txtResult;

function initialize() {
    txtInput = document.getElementById('txtInput');
    txtResult = document.getElementById('txtResult');
    clear();
}

function clear() {
    txtInput.value = '0';
    txtResult.value = '0';
}
```

The tests.js file contains a simple test of the initialize method. When the test is run, the two assertions pass. The following is the tests.js file contents.

```
module('QUnit Test Suite', { setup: function () { initialize(); } });

test("Initialize Test", function () {
    expect(2);
    var expected = '0';
    equal(txtInput.value, expected, 'Expected value: ' + expected +
        ' Actual value: ' + txtInput.value);
    equal(txtResult.value, expected, 'Expected value: ' + expected +
        ' Actual value: ' + txtResult.value);
});
```

Now that the test is passing, change some code to use jQuery. The jQuery library code is in the jQuery namespace, but this namespace also has an alias of $ (dollar sign) and can be used as follows.

```
jQuery.someFeature
$.someFeature
```

You can use either of these names to access the library features, so in the interest of minimizing keystrokes, use the dollar sign. First, change the code inside the initialize function of the default.js file. The code to locate elements can be rewritten to use jQuery and CSS selectors as follows.

```
function initialize() {
    txtInput = $('#txtInput');
    txtResult = $('#txtResult');
    clear();
}
```

This code uses the CSS selector to retrieve the elements that match. In this example, there is only one match for each of the jQuery selectors. The hash (#) symbol indicates that you want to search for the id of the element. When the statement is executed, the *txtInput* variable will contain a jQuery object, which is a wrapper object that contains the results. This is different from the original code, in which the *txtInput* variable contained a direct reference to the DOM element. The wrapper object has an array of elements that match the search criteria or has no elements if there is no match. Even if the query doesn't match any elements, *txtInput* still contains the wrapper object, but no elements would be in the results.

When a breakpoint is added to the code after the two statements are executed, you can debug the code and explore the jQuery wrapper, as shown in Figure 6-11.

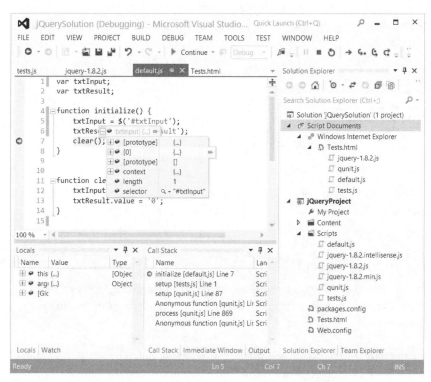

FIGURE 6-11 The jQuery wrapper object for *txtInput* with one element

In Figure 6-11, notice there is an array element (shown as [0]), and the length property is set to 1. This is how you can verify the result of the query. Element 0 is a direct reference to the txtInput DOM element.

When you run the test, it will pass but not for the correct reason; *txtInput* and *txtResult* reference the jQuery wrapper, not the actual DOM element. When the value property is set to '0', a new property is dynamically created on the jQuery object and set to '0'. However, the intent of this query is to set the text box value to '0'. To correct this problem, you can use the *val* method on the jQuery object. The val method gets or sets the value property of a form control that has a value property. The following is the modified test code.

```
module('QUnit Test Suite', { setup: function () { initialize(); } });

test("Initialize Test", function () {
    expect(2);
    var expected = '0';
    equal(txtInput.val(), expected, 'Expected value: ' + expected +
        ' Actual value: ' + txtInput.val());
    equal(txtResult.val(), expected, 'Expected value: ' + expected +
        ' Actual value: ' + txtResult.val());
});
```

After the four changes are made to the test, running the test shows that test assertions fail because value properties on the DOM elements are not being set. To fix the problem, modify the code in the clear function to set the value by using jQuery's val method. The following is the completed code.

```
var txtInput;
var txtResult;

function initialize() {
    txtInput = $('#txtInput');
    txtResult = $('#txtResult');
    clear();
}

function clear() {
    txtInput.val('0');
    txtResult.val('0');
}
```

> **IMPORTANT REFRESH YOUR SCREEN**
> HTML documents and JavaScript files are normally cached by the browser, so you might not see changes you made by just running the webpage. To refresh, press Ctrl+F5 after the screen is displayed.

This code is complete, the tests pass, and the text boxes are populated with '0'. It's important for you to use the jQuery object whenever possible so you can benefit from the cross browser–compatible features that jQuery has. If you need to reference the DOM object from the jQuery wrapper, you can do it as follows.

```
var domElement = $('#txtInput')[0];
```

Don't forget that you can put this code inside a conditional statement that checks the length property to see whether an element exists before attempting to access element 0 of the result.

```
var domElement;
if($('#txtInput').length > 0){
    domElement = $('#txtInput')[0];
}
```

Enabling JavaScript and jQuery IntelliSense

When learning a new language or library, it's always good to have some help to keep you from getting stuck on every statement you write. When you installed jQuery, an IntelliSense file was added, but it is not yet being used. For example, in the default.js file, if you type a jQuery expression that includes a selector and then press the Period key, you would like to see a valid list of available methods and properties. Before setting up IntelliSense, Figure 6-12 shows an example of what you see in the IntelliSense window when you type in a jQuery expression with a selector and press Period.

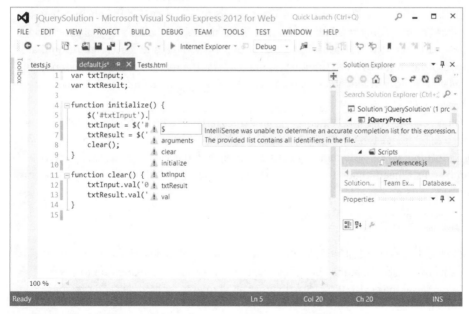

FIGURE 6-12 The IntelliSense window when not properly set up for jQuery

All the IntelliSense suggestions have a yellow warning triangle, and a message is displayed that states, "IntelliSense was unable to determine an accurate completion list for this expression. The provided list contains all identifiers in the file."

To activate IntelliSense, you must set a reference to the jQuery file (not the IntelliSense file) in every JavaScript file that requires IntelliSense. The following is an example of the default.js file with the reference set.

```
/// <reference path="jquery-1.8.2.js" />
var txtInput;
var txtResult;

function initialize() {
    txtInput = $('#txtInput');
    txtResult = $('#txtResult');
    clear();
}

function clear() {
    txtInput.val('0');
    txtResult.val('0');
}
```

This reference was added by just dragging and dropping the jquery-1.8.2.js file to the top of the file. You can imagine that this can become a problem because you add many libraries and have hundreds of JavaScript files in a project. You might also want to benefit from IntelliSense in HTML files. To solve the problem, Microsoft has provided the ability to create a reference list and then just add the reference list to the top of the JavaScript files. You do so by adding a _references.js JavaScript file to your Scripts folder and then referencing that file in your JavaScript files. Even though you need to add the reference to the _references.js file to all your JavaScript files, when you add another library, you need to add it only to the _references.js file.

Why do you need the special name and why does it need to be in the Scripts folder when you need to reference the file explicitly? If you use a file called _references.js that is located in the Scripts folder, you automatically have a reference to this file in your HTML pages, although you still need to add the reference to your JavaScript files. The following is the contents of the _references.js file.

```
/// <reference path="jquery-1.8.2.js" />
/// <reference path="qunit.js" />
```

Visual Studio automatically locates the associated IntelliSense file, if one exists with the same name as the library, in the libraryName.intellisense.js format. In addition to using IntelliSense files if they exist, Visual Studio looks at all referenced libraries and provides default IntelliSense.

```
var txtResult;

function initialize() {
    txtInput = $('#txtInput');
```

```
    txtResult = $('#txtResult');
    clear();
}

function clear() {
    txtInput.val('0');
    txtResult.val('0');
}
```

After adding the reference, if you type a jQuery expression, you activate IntelliSense as soon as you enter the dollar sign and the opening parenthesis, as shown in Figure 6-13.

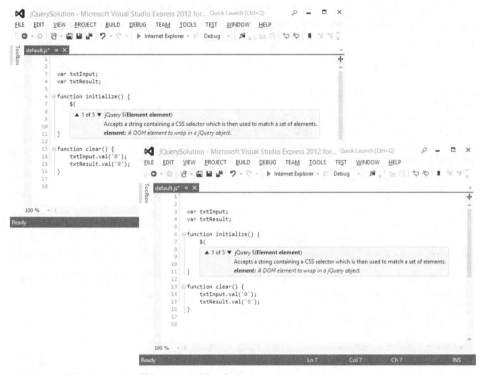

FIGURE 6-13 The jQuery IntelliSense providing help as you type

Notice in Figure 6-13 that after you finish typing the selector and you press Period, you are provided with a valid list of properties and methods for the jQuery wrapper object.

What happens if you are in the clear function and type txtInput and press period? Did IntelliSense make sense? You get an IntelliSense response that is similar to that in Figure 6-12. Simply put, don't activate IntelliSense; *txtInput* and *txtResult* are global variables that can be set to anything anywhere in your application, so Visual Studio can't possibly provide accurate IntelliSense. However, if you try typing **txtInput** and press Period at the bottom of the initialize function, you get proper IntelliSense that's similar to that in Figure 6-13. The difference is that Visual Studio is examining your code and knows that you just assigned a jQuery object to txtInput, so proper IntelliSense can be provided. To take advantage of IntelliSense, the global variables are eliminated, as shown in the following, modified default.js file.

```
function initialize() {
    clear();
}

function clear() {
    $('#txtInput').val('0');
    $('#txtResult').val('0');
}
```

This code is much smaller without the global variables, but the test is now failing because the test still references the global variables. To fix the test, replace the global variable references as follows.

```
module('QUnit Test Suite', { setup: function () { initialize(); } });

test("Initialize Test", function () {
    expect(2);
    var expected = '0';
    equal($('#txtInput').val(), expected, 'Expected value: ' + expected +
        ' Actual value: ' + $('#txtInput').val());
    equal($('#txtResult').val(), expected, 'Expected value: ' + expected +
        ' Actual value: ' + $('#txtResult').val());
});
```

When the test is run, it passes.

 Quick check

- You want to save time when writing JavaScript code. Which library can you use to accomplish this goal?

Quick check answer

- Use the jQuery library.

Creating a jQuery wrapper for a DOM element reference

You've seen how the use of CSS selectors create a jQuery result, which is a wrapper around zero to many DOM elements that match the selector. You can also create a jQuery wrapper from a DOM element reference, as shown in the following examples.

```
var doc = $(document);
var innerText = $(this).text();
```

The first expression wraps the document object and assigns the result to a *doc* variable so you can use jQuery's methods with the document object. The second expression wraps the *this* object, which is a DOM element being passed to an event listener. After wrapping the *this object*, the jQuery *text* method retrieves the inner text of the element and assigns it to an *innerText* variable.

Adding event listeners

In HTML5, you can use the addEventListener function to subscribe to an event. If you want a browser-independent way to add an event listener, you can use the jQuery .on method. There is also a corresponding .off method to remove an event listener. The .on method can be used as follows.

```
$('#btnSubmit').on('click', myFunction);
```

In this example, a button whose id is btnSubmit is located, using jQuery and the .on method to add a call to the user-defined myFunction function to the click event of the button. To remove the event listener, use the same code but replace the .on with .off as follows.

```
$('#btnSubmit').off('click', myFunction);
```

Triggering event handlers

When you need to trigger the event handlers by using code, you'll find that jQuery can help. Probably the most common reason to trigger event handlers by using code is to test your code. Using jQuery's trigger or the triggerHandler method causes the handler code to execute.

The trigger method causes the default behavior of the control to execute, whereas the triggerHandler method does not. For example, executing the trigger method on a submit button causes the submit action to take place in addition to executing your event handler code. Another difference is that the trigger method executes for all elements matched in the jQuery selector, whereas the triggerHandler method executes for only the first element. The following is an example of triggering the event handler code for the click event on a submit button.

```
$('#btnSubmit').triggerHandler('click');
```

Initializing code when the browser is ready

You will often need to execute initialization code after the HTML document is loaded and ready, and jQuery executes with a browser-independent way to execute code when the document is loaded as follows.

```
<script>
    $(document).ready(function () {
        initialize();
    });
</script>
```

It's best to place this at the bottom of your HTML document and call an initialize function that contains all initialization code.

Lesson summary

- Download jQuery from *http://jQuery.com* or install it from the NuGet package manager.
- The jQuery library is in a jQuery namespace and is aliased as a dollar sign ($).
- Use the $(selector) syntax to locate document object model (DOM) elements. The result of $(selector) is a jQuery wrapper object containing zero to many DOM elements that match the selector. You can use the length property to find out whether there are any matches to the selector.
- Use jQuery's val method to get or set the value of a DOM element that has a value property.
- To enable IntelliSense, create a _references.js file in the Scripts folder and add library references to this file. In your JavaScript files, add a reference to the _references.js file.
- Use jQuery's .on and .off methods to add and remove event listeners.
- Use the $(document).ready(function(){ initialize( ); }); expression to add initialization code.

Lesson review

Answer the following questions to test your knowledge of the information in this lesson. You can find the answers to these questions and explanations of why each answer choice is correct or incorrect in the "Answers" section at the end of this chapter.

1. You want to locate all the elements on your webpage that are assigned the CSS class name Hidden. Which jQuery statement can you use?

    A. var hidden = $ ('#Hidden');

    B. var hidden = $ ('.Hidden');

    C. var hidden = $ ('Hidden');

    D. var hidden = $('class=Hidden');

2. You are interested in writing event-driven JavaScript code that will work on most browsers without writing browser-specific code. How can you accomplish this?

    A. Use the jQuery library to help.

    B. Use only JavaScript statements that are the same across all browsers.

    C. Do not use any JavaScript.

    D. It's impossible to write event-driven JavaScript code that is not browser-specific.

3. You are interested in locating all *<p>* elements on your webpage, so your statement is var paragraphs = $('p'). Which line of code would confirm whether at least one element is found?

    A. if(paragraphs.exists)

    B. if(paragraphs==null)

    C. if(paragraphs.length)

    D. if(paragraphs.count > 0)

Practice exercises

If you encounter a problem completing any of these exercises, the completed projects can be installed from the Practice Exercises folder that is provided with the companion content.

Exercise 1: Create a calculator object

In this exercise, you apply your JavaScript object-oriented programming knowledge by modifying the calculator you've been using to have a calculator object in the *calculatorLibrary* namespace and changing JavaScript code to use jQuery when necessary.

1. Start Visual Studio Express 2012 for Web. Click File and choose Open Project. Navigate to the solution you created in Chapter 5, "More HTML," and select the webCalculator.sln file. Click Open.

    If you didn't complete the exercises in Chapter 5, you can use the solution in the Chapter 6 Exercise 1 Start folder.

2. In the Solution Explorer window, right-click the CalculatorTests.html file and choose Set As Start Page. Press F5 to verify that your test runs and passes.

3. In the Solution Explorer window, add jQuery to the project by right-clicking the project node. Choose Manage NuGet Packages. Type **jQuery** in the search online text box and click the search button. Click the Install button on the jQuery result.

4. Add a file to the Scripts folder called _references.js and, in the file, add a reference to jQuery, QUnit, and the CalculatorLibrary.

    Your file should look like the following.

```
/// <reference path="jquery-1.8.2.js" />
/// <reference path="qunit.js" />
/// <reference path="CalculatorLibrary.js" />
```

5. Open the CalculatorLibrary.js file and add a reference to the _references.js file.

6. Create the *calculatorLibrary* namespace by surrounding the existing code in the CalculatorLIbrary.js file with an immediately invoked function expression (IIFE). In the IIFE, create an alias to calculatorNamespace called ns, which will save you from typing the complete namespace while you're in the IIFE.

Your code should look like the following.

```
/// <reference path="_references.js" />

(function () {
    this.calculatorNamespace = this.calculatorNamespace || {};
    var ns = this.calculatorNamespace;

    //existing code here....

})();
```

7. Remove the variables that reference *txtInput* and *txtResult* because jQuery will be used to access these DOM elements as needed.

    The initialize function will remain in the namespace.

8. Surround the numberClick, plusClick, minusClick, clearEntry, and clear functions with an IIFE that is assigned to a Calculator property in calculatorNamespace.

    Your code should look like the following.

```
ns.Calculator = (function () {

    function numberClick() {
        txtInput.value = txtInput.value == '0' ?
            this.innerText : txtInput.value + this.innerText;
    }

    function plusClick() {
        txtResult.value = Number(txtResult.value) + Number(txtInput.value);
        clearEntry();
    }

    function minusClick() {
        txtResult.value = Number(txtResult.value) - Number(txtInput.value);
        clearEntry();
    }

    function clearEntry() {
        txtInput.value = '0';
    }

    function clear() {
        txtInput.value = '0';
        txtResult.value = '0';
    }
}());
```

9. Add a Calculator function inside the IIFE, which will be the constructor function. There is no code for the constructor at this time. At the bottom of the IIFE, add code to return this constructor function. Try this on your own, but if you have a problem, the sample code is shown in step 10.

10. Modify the numberClick, plusClick, minusClick, clearEntry, and clear functions to define these functions on the Calculator prototype.

The CalculatorLibrary.js should look like the following.

```javascript
/// <reference path="_references.js" />

(function () {
    this.calculatorNamespace = this.calculatorNamespace || {};
    var ns = this.calculatorNamespace;

    function initialize() {
        for (var i = 0; i < 10; i++) {
            document.getElementById('btn' + i)
                .addEventListener('click', numberClick, false);
        }
        txtInput = document.getElementById('txtInput');
        txtResult = document.getElementById('txtResult');

        document.getElementById('btnPlus')
            .addEventListener('click', plusClick, false);
        document.getElementById('btnMinus')
            .addEventListener('click', minusClick, false);
        document.getElementById('btnClearEntry')
            .addEventListener('click', clearEntry, false);
        document.getElementById('btnClear')
            .addEventListener('click', clear, false);
        clear();
    }

    ns.Calculator = (function () {

        function Calculator() {
        }

        Calculator.prototype.numberClick = function () {
            txtInput.value = txtInput.value == '0' ?
                this.innerText : txtInput.value + this.innerText;
        };

        Calculator.prototype.plusClick = function () {
            txtResult.value = Number(txtResult.value) + Number(txtInput.value);
            clearEntry();
        };

        Calculator.prototype.minusClick = function () {
            txtResult.value = Number(txtResult.value) - Number(txtInput.value);
            clearEntry();
        };

        Calculator.prototype.clearEntry = function () {
            txtInput.value = '0';
        };

        Calculator.prototype.clear = function () {
```

```
            txtInput.value = '0';
            txtResult.value = '0';
        };

        return Calculator;
    }());

})();
```

11. In the initialize function, create a *calculator* variable and assign a new Calculator object to it. Be sure to use the namespace when creating the new Calculator object.

    The state should look like the following.

    ```
    var calculator = new ns.Calculator();
    ```

12. Convert the loop that adds event listeners to each of the number buttons to a single jQuery statement based on finding all button elements that have an id that starts with btnNumber.

    The statement should look like the following.

    ```
    $('button[id^="btnNumber"]').on('click', calculator.numberClick);
    ```

    To make the code work in this step, change the ids on the number buttons.

13. Open the default.html file and replace the number button ids with btnNumber*X* where *X* is the number on the button.

14. Open the CalculatorTests.html file and replace the number button ids with btnNumber*X* where *X* is the number on the button.

15. In the CalculatorLibrary.js file, locate the initialize function and delete the statements that set *txtInput* and *txtResult*.

16. Convert the code that adds event listeners to btnPlus, btnMinus, btnClearEntry, and btnClear to use jQuery.

    The completed initialize function should look like the following.

    ```
    function initialize() {
        var calculator = new ns.Calculator();
        $('button[id^="btnNumber"]').on('click', calculator.numberClick);
        $('#btnPlus').on('click', calculator.plusClick);
        $('#btnMinus').on('click', calculator.minusClick);
        $('#btnClearEntry').on('click', calculator.clearEntry);
        $('#btnClear').on('click', calculator.clear);
        clear();
    }
    ```

17. Convert the numberClick method to use jQuery.

    You can use the jQuery text method to retrieve the inner text. The completed method should look like the following.

    ```
    Calculator.prototype.numberClick = function () {
        $('#txtInput').val($('#txtInput').val() == '0' ?
    ```

```
        $(this).text() : $('#txtInput').val() + $(this).text());
    };
```

18. Convert the plusClick method to use jQuery.

You must call the clearEntry method, but you can't use the *this* keyword to call
clearEntry because the clicked button is referenced by *this*. Because there is only one
copy of the clearEntry method, and it's on the prototype, call the clearEntry method
from the Calculator prototype. Your code should look like the following.

```
Calculator.prototype.plusClick = function () {
    $('#txtResult').val(Number($('#txtResult').val()) +
        Number($('#txtInput').val()));
    Calculator.prototype.clearEntry();
};
```

19. Convert the minusClick method to use jQuery.

Your code should look like the following.

```
Calculator.prototype.minusClick = function () {
    $('#txtResult').val(Number($('#txtResult').val()) -
        Number($('#txtInput').val()));
    Calculator.prototype.clearEntry();
};
```

20. Convert the clearEntry method and the clear method to use jQuery.

The completed CalculatorLibrary.js file should look like the following.

```
/// <reference path="_references.js" />

(function () {
    this.calculatorNamespace = this.calculatorNamespace || {};
    var ns = this.calculatorNamespace;

    ns.initialize = function () {
        var calculator = new ns.Calculator();
        $('button[id^="btnNumber"]').on('click', calculator.numberClick);
        $('#btnPlus').on('click', calculator.plusClick);
        $('#btnMinus').on('click', calculator.minusClick);
        $('#btnClearEntry').on('click', calculator.clearEntry);
        $('#btnClear').on('click', calculator.clear);
        calculator.clear();
    }

    ns.Calculator = (function () {

        function Calculator() {
        }

        Calculator.prototype.numberClick = function () {
            $('#txtInput').val($('#txtInput').val() == '0' ?
                $(this).text() : $('#txtInput').val() + $(this).text());
        };
```

```
        Calculator.prototype.plusClick = function () {
            $('#txtResult').val(Number($('#txtResult').val()) +
                Number($('#txtInput').val()));
            Calculator.prototype.clearEntry();
        };

        Calculator.prototype.minusClick = function () {
            $('#txtResult').val(Number($('#txtResult').val()) -
                Number($('#txtInput').val()));
            Calculator.prototype.clearEntry();
        };

        Calculator.prototype.clearEntry = function () {
            $('#txtInput').val('0');
        };

        Calculator.prototype.clear = function () {
            $('#txtInput').val('0');
            $('#txtResult').val('0');
        };

        return Calculator;
    }());

})();
```

21. Open the default.html file and add a reference to the jQuery library.

Be sure to add the reference before the reference to the CalculatorLibrary.js file
because that file uses jQuery. Don't forget that you can drag and drop the file to create
the reference. The *<head>* element should look like the following.

```
<head>
    <title>web Calculator</title>
    <link href="Content/default.css" rel="stylesheet" />
    <script src="Scripts/jquery-1.8.2.js"></script>
    <script type="text/javascript" src="Scripts/CalculatorLibrary.js"></script>
</head>
```

22. At the bottom of the default.html file, change the code so that the initialize function in
calculatorNamespace is executed when the document is ready.

The completed default.html file should look like the following.

```
<!DOCTYPE html>
<html xmlns="http://www.w3.org/1999/xhtml">
<head>
    <title>web Calculator</title>
    <link href="Content/default.css" rel="stylesheet" />
    <script src="Scripts/jquery-1.8.2.js"></script>
    <script type="text/javascript" src="Scripts/CalculatorLibrary.js"></script>
</head>
<body>
    <div id="container">
        <header>
            <hgroup id="headerText">
```

```
        <h1>Contoso Ltd.</h1>
        <h2>Your success equals our success</h2>
    </hgroup>
</header>
<nav>
    <a href="default.html">Home</a>
</nav>
<div role="main">
    <div id="calculator">
        <table>
            <tr>
                <td colspan="4">
                    <input id="txtResult" type="text"
                        readonly="readonly" />
                </td>
            </tr>
            <tr>
                <td colspan="4">
                    <input id="txtInput" type="text" />
                </td>
            </tr>
            <tr>
                <td></td>
                <td></td>
                <td>
                    <button id="btnClearEntry">CE</button>
                </td>
                <td>
                    <button id="btnClear">C</button>
                </td>
            </tr>
            <tr>
                <td>
                    <button id="btnNumber7">7</button></td>
                <td>
                    <button id="btnNumber8">8</button></td>
                <td>
                    <button id="btnNumber9">9</button></td>
                <td>
                    <button id="btnPlus">+</button>
                </td>
            </tr>
            <tr>
                <td>
                    <button id="btnNumber4">4</button>
                </td>
                <td>
                    <button id="btnNumber5">5</button>
                </td>
                <td>
                    <button id="btnNumber6">6</button>
                </td>
                <td>
                    <button id="btnMinus">-</button>
                </td>
```

```
                </tr>
                <tr>
                    <td>
                        <button id="btnNumber1">1</button>
                    </td>
                    <td>
                        <button id="btnNumber2">2</button>
                    </td>
                    <td>
                        <button id="btnNumber3">3</button>
                    </td>
                    <td></td>
                </tr>
                <tr>
                    <td></td>
                    <td>
                        <button id="btnNumber0">0</button>
                    </td>
                    <td></td>
                    <td></td>
                </tr>
            </table>
        </div>
    </div>
    <aside>
        <p>Advertisements</p>
    </aside>
    <footer>
        <p>
            Copyright &copy; 2012, Contoso Ltd., All rights reserved
        </p>
    </footer>
</div>
<script type="text/javascript">
    $(document).ready(function () {
        calculatorNamespace.initialize();
    });
</script>
</body>
</html>
```

You must modify the tests to use jQuery.

23. Open the CalculatorTests.html file and add a reference to the jQuery library.

The completed CalculatorTests.html file should look like the following.

```
<!DOCTYPE html>
<html xmlns="http://www.w3.org/1999/xhtml">
<head>
    <title></title>
    <link rel="stylesheet" type="text/css" href="Content/qunit.css" />
    <script type="text/javascript" src="Scripts/qunit.js"></script>
    <script src="Scripts/jquery-1.8.2.js"></script>
    <script type="text/javascript" src="Scripts/CalculatorLibrary.js"></script>
    <script type="text/javascript" src="Scripts/tests.js"></script>
```

```
        </head>
        <body>
            <h1 id="qunit-header">QUnit example</h1>
            <h2 id="qunit-banner"></h2>
            <div id="qunit-testrunner-toolbar"></div>
            <h2 id="qunit-userAgent"></h2>
            <ol id="qunit-tests"></ol>
            <div id="qunit-fixture">
                test markup, will be hidden
                <input id="txtResult" type="text" readonly="readonly" /><br />
                <input id="txtInput" type="text" /><br />
                <button id="btnNumber7">7</button>
                <button id="btnNumber8">8</button>
                <button id="btnNumber9">9</button><br />
                <button id="btnNumber4">4</button>
                <button id="btnNumber5">5</button>
                <button id="btnNumber6">6</button><br />
                <button id="btnNumber1">1</button>
                <button id="btnNumber2">2</button>
                <button id="btnNumber3">3</button><br />
                <button id="btnClear">C</button>
                <button id="btnNumber0">0</button>
                <button id="btnClearEntry">CE</button><br />
                <button id="btnPlus">+</button>
                <button id="btnMinus">-</button>
        </div>
    </body>
    </html>
```

You must modify the tests.js file to use jQuery, calculatorNamespace, and the Calculator object.

24. Open the tests.js file.

25. In the tests.js file, add a reference to the _references.js file and modify the module function to call calculatorLibrary.initialize( ) as follows.

```
/// <reference path="_references.js" />
module('Calculator Test Suite', {
    setup: function () {
        calculatorNamespace.initialize();
    }
});
```

26. Modify the Initialize Test.

You don't need to set *txtInput* and *txtResult* because the initialize method calls the clear method to set these text boxes.

27. Modify the rest of the method to use jQuery and run the test to see it pass.

The completed Initialize Test should look like the following.

```
test("Initialize Test", function () {
    expect(2);
    var expected = '0';
    equal($('#txtInput').val(), expected, 'Expected value: ' + expected +
```

```
                    ' Actual value: ' + $('#txtInput').val());
          equal($('#txtResult').val(), expected, 'Expected value: ' + expected +
                    ' Actual value: ' + $('#txtResult').val());
      });
```

28. Modify the Button Click Test to use jQuery. Run the test to see it pass. Use jQuery's triggerHandler method to test each button.

Your code should look like the following.

```
test("Button Click Test", function () {
    var buttonQuantity = 10;
    expect(buttonQuantity * 2);
    for (var i = 0; i < buttonQuantity; i++) {
        $('#btnNumber' + i).triggerHandler('click');
        var result = $('#txtInput').val()[$('#txtInput').val().length - 1];
        var expected = String(i);
        equal(result, expected, 'Expected value: ' + expected +
            ' Actual value: ' + result);
        var expectedLength = i < 2 ? 1 : i;
        equal($('#txtInput').val().length, expectedLength,
            'Expected string length: ' + expectedLength +
            ' Actual value: ' + $('#txtInput').val().length);
    }
});
```

29. Modify the Add Test to use jQuery. Run the test to see it pass.

Your code should look like the following.

```
test("Add Test", function () {
    expect(2);
    $('#txtInput').val('10');
    $('#txtResult').val('20');
    $('#btnPlus').triggerHandler('click');
    var expected = '30';
    equal($('#txtResult').val(), expected, 'Expected value: ' + expected +
        ' Actual value: ' + $('#txtResult').val());
    expected = '0';
    equal($('#txtInput').val(), expected, 'Expected value: ' + expected +
        ' Actual value: ' + $('#txtInput').val());
});
```

30. Modify the Subtract Test to use jQuery. Run the test to see it pass.

Your code should look like the following.

```
test("Subtract Test", function () {
    expect(2);
    $('#txtInput').val('10');
    $('#txtResult').val('20');
    $('#btnMinus').triggerHandler('click');
    var expected = '10';
    equal($('#txtResult').val(), expected, 'Expected value: ' + expected +
        ' Actual value: ' + $('#txtResult').val());
    expected = '0';
```

```
    equal($('#txtInput').val(), expected, 'Expected value: ' + expected +
        ' Actual value: ' + $('#txtInput').val());
});
```

31. Modify the Clear Entry Test to use jQuery. Run the test to see it pass.

    Your code should look like the following.

    ```
    test("Clear Entry Test", function () {
        expect(1);
        $('#txtInput').val('10');
        $('#btnClearEntry').triggerHandler('click');
        var expected = '0';
        equal($('#txtInput').val(), expected, 'Expected value: ' + expected +
            ' Actual value: ' + $('#txtInput').val());
    });
    ```

32. Modify the Clear Test to use jQuery. Run the test to see it pass.

    Your code should look like the following.

    ```
    test("Clear Test", function () {
        expect(2);
        $('#txtInput').val('10');
        $('#txtResult').val('20');
        $('#btnClear').triggerHandler('click');
        var expected = '0';
        equal($('#txtInput').val(), expected, 'Expected value: ' + expected +
            ' Actual value: ' + $('#txtInput').val());
        equal($('#txtResult').val(), expected, 'Expected value: ' + expected +
            ' Actual value: ' + $('#txtResult').val());
    });
    ```

    At this point, you should be able to run all the tests, and they should all pass.

33. Right-click the default.html file and choose Set As Start Page. To see that your calcula-
    tor still works, press F5 to start debugging the application.

34. Try entering data and clicking the plus and minus signs.

    You might need to refresh your screen, but the calculator should be working.

Suggested practice exercises

The following additional exercises are designed to give you more opportunities to practice
what you've learned and to help you successfully master the lessons presented in this chapter.

- **Exercise 1** Learn more about JavaScript objects by adding more features to the calculator that you created in the practice exercise.

- **Exercise 2** Learn more about jQuery by exploring the jQuery site at
  http://jQuery.com.

Answers

This section contains the answers to the lesson review questions in this chapter.

Lesson 1

1. **Correct answer: C**

    A. **Incorrect:** A property is a variable that's defined on an object.

    B. **Incorrect:** A method is a function that's defined on an object.

    C. **Correct:** A class is a blueprint for an object.

    D. **Incorrect:** An event takes place from external input, usually from user input.

2. **Correct answer: A**

    A. **Correct:** The prototype is the starting object that is cloned when creating a new object.

    B. **Incorrect:** A property is a variable that's defined on an object.

    C. **Incorrect:** A class is a blueprint for an object.

    D. **Incorrect:** An event takes place from external input, usually from user input.

3. **Correct answer: A**

    A. **Correct:** You replace the prototype of the child object with a new instance of the parent object and then replace the prototype constructor with the child constructor.

    B. **Incorrect:** The createChild method is not a valid method.

    C. **Incorrect:** The setParent method is not a valid method.

    D. **Incorrect:** JavaScript does support inheritance by replacing the prototype of the child object with a new instance of the parent object and then replacing the prototype constructor with the child constructor.

Lesson 2

1. **Correct answer: B**

    A. **Incorrect:** The use of the hash (#) symbol in the CSS selector indicates that you want to locate an element based on its id.

    B. **Correct:** The use of the period (.) in the CSS selector indicates that you want to locate the elements that match the CSS class name.

    C. **Incorrect:** Supplying a name for a CSS selector indicates that you want to locate the elements that have that tag name.

    D. **Incorrect:** The var hidden = $('class=Hidden'); syntax is invalid.

2. **Correct answer: A**

   A. Correct: Using jQuery will help you create event-driven, browser-independent code.

   B. Incorrect: The code for creating and subscribing to events is browser-specific.

   C. Incorrect: You need to use JavaScript to write event-driven code.

   D. Incorrect: Use the jQuery library to write browser-independent code.

3. **Correct answer: C**

   A. Incorrect: jQuery does not have an exists property.

   B. Incorrect: Even if no elements are found, jQuery will return a wrapper object.

   C. Correct: If no elements are found, the length property will be 0, which converts to a Boolean false.

   D. Incorrect: jQuery does not have a count property.

## CHAPTER 7

Working with forms

The previous chapters cover much basic information regarding HTML document creation and manipulation. Not explained yet is how to get information back to the server. For this, you need to understand how forms work and how to create them. This chapter provides the information you need to accomplish these tasks.

Lessons in this chapter:

Before you begin

To complete this book, you must have some understanding of web development. This chapter requires the hardware and software listed in the "System requirements" section in the book's Introduction.

Lesson 1: Understanding forms

A form is responsible for collecting data and sending it somewhere. In most cases, the data is sent back to the server for processing. Because server-side processing hasn't been explained yet, you will send the data to an email address instead. This is not a recommended practice; in fact, you should never do this because it exposes your email address to the public. However, this technique provides an intermediate step in helping you understand the browser side of forms before server-side processing is discussed.

To understand how forms work, you need a basic understanding of how HTTP protocol works. This lesson provides the necessary introduction to HTTP protocol and then discusses form implementation.

Understanding web communications

It's important to understand the roles of the server, browser, and HTTP to develop web applications. When web communication occurs, the sequence can be generalized into the following steps:

1. The user browses to a website, which causes the browser to initiate a request for a web server resource.
2. HTTP protocol sends a GET request to the web server.
3. The web server processes the request.
4. The web server sends a response to the web browser, also by using HTTP protocol.
5. The browser processes the response, causing a webpage to display.
6. The user enters data into a form on the webpage and clicks a Submit button that causes the data to be sent back to the web server.
7. HTTP protocol posts the data back to the server.
8. The web server processes the data.
9. The web server sends the response back to the browser through the HTTP protocol.
10. The web browser processes the response, displaying the webpage.

The web server

Web servers originally were responsible for only receiving and handling requests from the browsers through HTTP. The web server handled the request and sent a response back to the web browser, and then the web server closed the connection and released all resources that were involved in the request. Releasing all resources was paramount because the web server needed to handle thousands of requests per minute. The original webpages were simple, static HTML pages. The web environment was considered to be *stateless* because no data was held at the web server between web browser requests, and the connection was closed after the response, as shown in Figure 7-1.

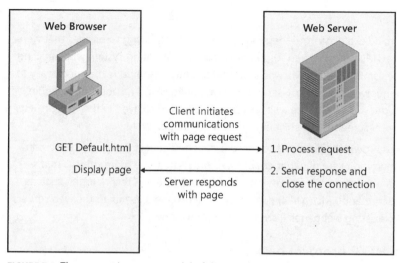

FIGURE 7-1 The request/response model of the stateless model

Web servers now deliver services that go far beyond the original web servers. Now web servers also handle requests for pages that contain code that will execute at the server and respond with the results of code execution, as shown in Figure 7-2. Web servers now hold state (data) between webpage requests, so the developer can connect many pages to form a web application. Most websites are now set up as web applications containing many webpages. The idea of a web server delivering a single page to the web browser and then closing the connection is outdated. Web servers now implement "keep alive" features for connections that make the web servers hold the connections to the web browsers open for a period of time with anticipation of additional page requests from a web browser.

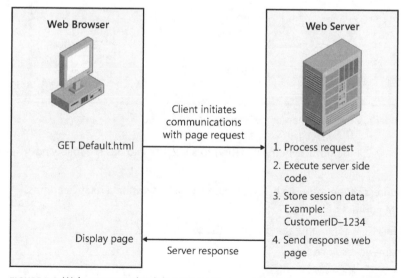

FIGURE 7-2 Web servers maintaining connections and holding state across page requests

The web browser

The web browser provides a platform-independent means of displaying webpages that were written with HTML. HTML was designed to render within any operating system while placing no constraint on the window size. HTML was designed to flow, wrapping text as necessary to fit in the browser window. The web browser also displays images and responds to hyperlinks. When a webpage request is sent to the web server, the result is displayed in the web browser by clearing the browser screen and displaying the new webpage.

Although the web browser's role is just to present data and collect data, new client-side technologies are emerging every day that enable web browsers to be more robust, so it's simpler to develop a webpage while improving the user's experience. Technologies such as Asynchronous JavaScript and XML (AJAX) enable the web browsers to talk to the web servers without clearing the existing webpages from the browser window.

Understanding HTTP protocol basics

HTTP (Hypertext Transfer Protocol) is the protocol of the web. HTTP protocol is a text-based protocol, so text commands are sent to the server. By using a network sniffer program, you can see the commands sent and the responses received. Microsoft Internet Explorer has a built-in network sniffer that is part of the developer tools and that you can access by pressing the F12 function key, which displays the developer tools window. Figure 7-3 shows the developer tools window after capturing some network traffic.

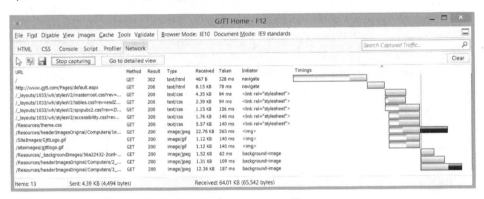

FIGURE 7-3 The developer tools window showing network traffic

This window displays all the traffic when navigating to a website and has the following columns.

- **URL**   The address of the resource being accessed, which might be a relative address or an absolute address

- **Method**   The HTTP command being sent to the server

- **Result**   A numeric result code

- **Type**   The MIME (Multipurpose Internet Mail Extensions) type of the resource being accessed

- **Received** The quantity of bytes transferred
- **Taken** The time taken for the request
- **Initiator** The trigger of the request
- **Timings** A sequential timing chart that conveys a timeline of the requests

When the user types *http://gjtt.com* to navigate to this site, the first entry shows that the result code of the request is 302, which is an indicator of a redirect. In this case, the redirect was to *http://www.gjtt.com/Pages/default.aspx*. There are many HTTP return codes, which are divided into categories based on the first of the three digits in the return code. The following describes the categories of return status codes.

- **1xx** Informational message
- **2xx** Success
- **3xx** Redirect
- **4xx** Client error
- **5xx** Server error

The second request is for the *http://www.gjtt.com/Pages/default.aspx* page, which returns a result code of 200, indicating success. When the resulting HTML is returned from this request, the HTML contains links to style sheets, which are consequently requested by the browser. The HTML also contains images that are requested.

Understanding the HTTP method

The *HTTP method,* which is also known as the *HTTP verb*, represents the command being sent to the server. In Figure 7-3, all requests to the server used the GET method, which is used to request a resource. The following is a list of the valid method values.

- **OPTIONS** A request for information about the communication options available. This method enables the browser to determine the options and requirements associated with a resource without retrieving it.
- **GET** A request to retrieve a resource such as an HTML file or an image file.
- **HEAD** Operates like the GET method except that the server does not return a message body in the response. The HEAD method retrieves metadata about a resource.
- **POST** Request for the server to accept the data being sent from the client to modify existing server data.
- **PUT** Request for the server to accept the data being sent from the client to insert new server data.
- **DELETE** Request for the server to delete a specific resource.
- **TRACE** Invokes a remote, application-layer loopback of the request message, which enables the client to see what the server is receiving. This is typically used for testing or diagnostic information.

- **CONNECT**   Used with a proxy that can switch dynamically to being a tunnel.
- **DEBUG**   Not defined in the HTTP/1.1 specification; starts ASP.NET debugging. Informs Visual Studio 2012 of the process to which the debugger will attach.

When you browse to a webpage, the GET method is used to retrieve the page from the server. If the webpage contains a form for collecting data from the user and the data is submitted to the server, the browser will execute the POST method and pass the data to the server. In Chapter 8, "Websites and services," you see how you can use GET, POST, PUT, and DELETE to perform create, retrieve, update, and delete (CRUD) operations, which you might use when modifying data.

Submitting form data to the web server

You can use the HTML *<form>* element to create a web form that collects data and sends the data to the web server or to another location such as an email address. A typical use of the *<form>* element is as follows.

```
<form method="post" action="getCustomer.aspx" >
    Enter Customer ID:
    <input type="text" name="Id" />
    <input type="submit" value="Get Customer" />
</form>
```

This form prompts the user to enter a customer ID, displays a text box that collects the desired customer ID, and displays a submit button that initiates the sending of data to the web server. The method of the form indicates the HTTP method to use when sending the data to the server. The action is either an absolute or relative URL of the resource that will receive the data.

Sending data when submitting a form

Not all elements can send data when the Submit button is clicked. For simplicity, the elements that can send data upon submission will be referred to as *form submission elements*. There are many new input types with HTML5. If the browser doesn't recognize the input type, it will fall back to treating the input as a text box. The following is a list of the form submission elements available in HTML5.

- **<textarea>**   A multiline text input control. The cols attribute indicates the desired width of the *<textarea>* based on the quantity of columns you want. The *<textarea>* element has a *maxlength* attribute that can be set to constrain the quantity of characters the *<textarea>* will accept. You can also set a *placeholder* attribute to provide a small hint to the user until text is entered. The *wrap* attribute can be set to *soft* or *hard*. Setting to soft (the default) does not insert linefeeds in the posted data. Setting to hard inserts linefeeds based on the cols attribute setting.
- **<select>**   A drop-down list containing *<option>* elements, which are the list items. The *<select>* element has a *multiple* attribute that specifies that you want to allow

multiple selections. The multiple attribute is a Boolean attribute. You can change the *<select>* element from a drop-down list to a list by setting the *size* attribute to the quantity of items that should be displayed as a list. If the size is smaller than the quantity of items in the list, the list displays a scroll bar. The *<option>* element has a *selected* attribute to indicate that the option is selected. The selected attribute is a Boolean attribute. You can use jQuery to locate all selected *<option>* elements by using the following selector.

```
$('option:selected')
```

- **<button>**   A clickable button that can have HTML content, such as an *<img>* element, and can be configured as a submit button by using the *type* attribute, which can be set to *button* (default), *reset*, or *submit*.

- **<input type='button'>**   A clickable button that displays a text prompt.

- **<input type='checkbox'>**   A check box. In addition to having a *value* attribute, the check box has a *checked* attribute that is readable and settable. The checked attribute is a Boolean attribute. You can use jQuery to locate all selected check boxes by using the following selector.

```
$('input[type=checkbox]:checked')
```

- **<input type='color'>**   A color picker.

- **<input type='date'>**   A date-only control (no time).

- **<input type='datetime'>**   A date and time control based on the UTC time zone.

- **<input type='datetime-local'>**   A date and time control (no time zone).

- **<input type='email'>**   An email address field.

- **<input type='file'>**   A file-select field and a Browse button for uploading files.

- **<input type='hidden'>**   A hidden input field. Use the hidden input field when you want to send data that is calculated from JavaScript to the server. The JavaScript code can get and set the value as needed. Never store secrets in this element because this element is intended to be hidden and not intended to be secure. It's very easy to see this element by viewing the webpage source.

- **<input type='image'>**   An image submit button.

- **<input type='month'>**   A month and year control.

- **<input type='number'>**   A numeric field.

- **<input type='password'>**   A password field in which the characters are masked.

- **<input type='radio'>**   An option button. In addition to having a *value* attribute, the option button has a *checked* attribute that is readable and settable. The checked attribute is a Boolean attribute. You can use jQuery to locate all selected option buttons by using the following selector.

```
$('input[type=radio]:checked')
```

- **<input type='range'>** A control for entering a numeric value when the exact value is not important. On newer browsers, this renders as a slider control and is commonly referred to as a slider control. This control has a *value* attribute, which is the current slider value. The *min* attribute is the minimum settable value (default is 0). The *max* attribute is the maximum settable value (default is 100). The *step* attribute defines the granularity of the value, which is the amount of change the value will have as the slider moves (default is 1). The step attribute must be an int unless the *min* value is set to a non-int value.

- **<input type='reset'>** A button that resets all form values to default values; note that this does not send data when the form is submitted.

- **<input type='search'>** A text field for entering a search string.

- **<input type='submit'>** A submit button.

- **<input type='tel'>** A telephone number field.

- **<input type='text'>** A single-line text field whose default width is 20 characters. This is the default if the type attribute is not supplied.

- **<input type='time'>** A control for entering a time (no time zone).

- **<input type='url'>** A URL field.

- **<input type='week'>** A week and year control (no time zone).

Using the *<label>* element

The *<label>* element can be used for labels that help the user identify the form submission element. Consider the following HTML form.

```
<form method="post" action="getCustomer.aspx" >
   Enter Customer ID:
   <input type="text" name="Id" />
   <input type="submit" value="Get Customer" />
</form>
```

In this form, "Enter Customer ID:" can be placed inside a *<label>* element as follows.

```
<form method="post" action="getCustomer.aspx" >
   <label for="Id">Enter Customer ID:</label>
   <input type="text" name="Id" />
   <input type="submit" value="Get Customer" />
</form>
```

When the text is placed in a *<label>* element, the user sees no difference. When the user clicks the label text, the Id element gets the focus. This provides better functionality for mouse users or tablet users. Notice that the label has a *for* attribute, which must contain the id of the element that will receive the focus when the user clicks the text.

Another interesting benefit from using the label is that you can assign style rules to the *<label>* element. The following is a typical style rule for the *<label>* element.

```
label {
    clear: both;
    display: block;
    float: left;
    width: 125px;
}
```

This style displays the *<label>* element as a block instead of inline and clears previous blocks. The style is set to float left and be 125 pixels wide. If you have several inputs, you can line up the inputs vertically by using the *<label>* element and setting its width.

Specifying the parent forms

Previous releases of HTML required the form submission element to be in a form to submit its data. This could become a problem when form submission elements are scattered over a webpage and more than one form is on the page. With HTML5, the form submission elements have a *form* attribute that can be set to the id of one or more *<form>* elements, and the form submission elements no longer need to be inside a *<form>* element. The flexibility of a form submission element belonging to more than one *<form>* element is especially useful. Firefox, Opera, Chrome, and Safari implement the form attribute, but as of this writing, Internet Explorer 10 does not.

Triggering the form submission

Triggering the form submission causes the browser to gather its associated form submission element data and send it to the URI specified in the action attribute of the form, using the form's specified HTTP method. To trigger the submission of a form, you can use any of the following elements.

```
<button type='submit' name='submitButton' >Submit</button>
<input type='submit' name='submitButton' value='Submit' />
<input type='image' src='/images/submit.gif' alt='Submit' />
```

In addition, you can use JavaScript to submit a form by executing jQuery's *submit* method on the form element. Consider the following HTML document that contains a *<form>* element whose id is myForm.

```
<!DOCTYPE html>
<html xmlns="http://www.w3.org/1999/xhtml">
<head>
    <title></title>
    <script src="Scripts/jquery-1.8.2.js"></script>
    <script src="Scripts/default.js"></script>
</head>
<body>
    <form id="myForm">
        Favorite Car:
```

```
        <select name="favoriteCar">
            <option>Ford Fiesta</option>
            <option value="Chevy">Chevrolet</option>
            <option>BMW</option>
        </select><br />
        Comment:
        <input type="text" name="comment" />
    </form>
    <button id="myButton">Click Me</button>
</body>
</html>
```

The form contains a drop-down list of three *<option>* elements. Each *<option>* element has displayed text content. In addition, the *<option>* element can have a *value* attribute. If the value attribute is not set, the value defaults to match the text content. The form also contains a text box for the user to enter a comment. The HTML document has reference to the default.js file that contains the following code.

```
/// <reference path="_references.js" />

$(document).ready(function () {
    $('#myButton').on('click', submitTheForm);
});

function submitTheForm() {
    $('#myForm').submit();
}
```

This code attaches the *submitTheForm* function to the *click* event of the *<button>* element whose id is myButton. The *<button>* element is not inside the form, and its type attribute is not set to *submit*. In this scenario, the *<button>* element is programmed to call the submit-TheForm function, which calls the jQuery submit method to submit the form.

In the example code, the *<form>* element has only an id, so the method attribute will default to GET, and the action attribute will default to the same URL as the page. If the user selects Ford Fiesta, types **This is Bob's car!** in the comment text box, and clicks the button, you'll see the URL change, as shown in Figure 7-4.

FIGURE 7-4 The URL changing when the button is clicked

The URL now includes the QueryString, which is everything after the question mark (?). The QueryString contains the following.

```
favoriteCar=Ford+Fiesta&comment=This+is+Bob%27s+car%21
```

The QueryString is a list of name value pairs that are URI encoded. Spaces become plus signs (+), the apostrophe becomes %27, and the exclamation point becomes %21. The separator between each name and value is the equal sign (=), whereas the separator between each name value pair is the ampersand (&).

 Quick check

- How can you use the URL to send data to the server?

Quick check answer

- Add a question mark (?) to the URL after the webpage name and then include the QueryString.

Serializing the form

If you want to create the same string of URI-encoded name value pairs to use in your code, you can use the jQuery *serialize* method. This method converts the form data to a URI-encoded list of name value pairs. This could be useful when you want to post data programmatically to the server. The serialize method looks like this.

```
var formData = $('#myForm').serialize();
```

If you are working with the URI-encoded data and you want to decode the data, you can use either the decodeURI function to decode a complete URI or the decodeURIComponent function to decode a QueryString. For example, you can use the following code sample to serialize the form data and then decode the data.

```
var formData = $('#myForm').serialize();
var data = decodeURIComponent(formData);
```

Using the autofocus attribute

When an HTML form is displayed, the default focus behavior is that no control has focus. In the past, developers have added JavaScript to set the focus to a specific control when the page is loaded and ready. The following is an example of using jQuery to set the focus to the text box whose name attribute is comment.

```
$(document).ready(function () {
    $('input[name="comment"]').focus();
});
```

HTML5 introduces the autofocus attribute to form controls. The autofocus attribute is a Boolean attribute and can be set for the comment as follows.

```
<input type="text" name="comment" autofocus="autofocus"/>
```

Using data submission constraints

To send data, each form submission element must meet specific constraints as described in the following list.

- The form submission element must have its name attribute set.
- The form submission element must have its value set.
- The form submission element must be defined within a *<form>* element, but HTML5 describes the ability to assign an id to the form and then reference the form's id on a form submission element by using the *form* attribute. This is not supported by Internet Explorer 10 and earlier.
- The form submission element must not be disabled, but it is permissible for the form submission element to be hidden by using a CSS style such as *display: none*.
- If a form has more than one submit button, only the submit button that is activated will submit its value.
- Check boxes must be selected for their value to be sent.
- Option buttons must be selected for their value to be sent.
- The *<select>* elements must have an *<option>* element set to *selected* for its value to be sent.
- File selection fields must have at least one file selected.
- Reset buttons never send data when the form is submitted.
- Object elements must have the *declare* attribute set.

It's interesting to note that a form submission element does not need to have an id for its data to be sent upon submission, and the name attribute does not need to be unique. If you have multiple form submission elements with the same name, they will submit as an array.

Using POST or GET

There are two HTTP methods that can be used to submit the form data back to the web server: GET and POST. When the GET method is used, the *QueryString* containing the data is appended to the URL. The *QueryString* is a collection of URI-encoded key=value statements, separated by ampersand (&) characters, which can be passed to the web server by concatenating a question mark (?) to the end of the URL and then concatenating the QueryString as follows.

```
http://www.contoso.com/getProduct.aspx?productId=123&color=blue
```

In this example, a GET request is made to the web server for a webpage called getProduct .aspx on the root of the website. The file extension of the webpage will not be .html because you need to send the data to a page that supports server-side processing such as an .aspx page. The QueryString contains the data that follows the question mark (?).

An advantage of using the GET verb is that you can see and modify the complete URL and QueryString in the address bar of the web browser as needed. However, depending on the scenario, this could also be a disadvantage. The complete URL and QueryString are easy to save or send as a unit. For example, you can bookmark a webpage containing data that is included in the QueryString.

One disadvantage of using the GET method is that the QueryString is limited in size by the web browser and web server you use. For example, when using Internet Explorer and Internet Information Server (IIS), the limit is 1,024 characters. Another consideration is that you might not want to allow a user to type the URL and QueryString directly into the address bar without navigating through other webpages first.

When you use the POST method to submit data back to the web server, the data is placed in the message body instead of being concatenated to the URL. This makes the data invisible, at least to the typical user. Using the POST method removes the size constraint on the data. You could post megabytes of data; although it will work, sending that much data across the Internet can cause other problems, primarily bandwidth-related, such as timeout errors and performance problems.

The POST method does not allow the user just to type the data into the QueryString because this data is hidden in the message body. For most scenarios, consider using the POST method to send data to the web server.

 Sending data back to the server is often referred to as a *PostBack* to the server when the POST method is used.

Lesson summary

- HTTP protocol is a text-based protocol that sends a method, or verb, to indicate the type of request being made. Common methods are GET and POST. GET is typically used to retrieve a resource; POST is typically used to update a resource.
- Web servers reply to requests and send a three-digit status code in which 1xx is information, 2xx is success, 3xx is redirect, 4xx is client error, and 5xx is server error.
- Data can be submitted to the web server by adding a *<form>* element with form submission elements. Form submission elements are *<textarea>*, *<select>*, *<input>*, and *<button>*.
- Use a *<button type='submit'>*, *<input type='submit'>*, or *<input type='image'>* to submit a form.
- The jQuery serialize function converts form data to a URI-encoded list of name-value pairs.
- The decodeURIComponent can be used to decode a QueryString.
- The autofocus attribute sets the focus when the page is loaded.

Lesson review

Answer the following questions to test your knowledge of the information in this lesson. You can find the answers to these questions and explanations of why each answer choice is correct or incorrect in the "Answers" section at the end of this chapter.

1. You are creating a webpage that will collect data and send it to a server. Which element must you implement to be able to send data to the server?

   A. *<nav>*

   B. *<form>*

   C. *<textarea>*

   D. *<div>*

2. When you retrieve a webpage from the server that contains Customer information, you want to be able to specify the id of the Customer within the URL. What can you use to provide the id?

   A. the PostBack

   B. the QueryString

   C. the domain name

   D. a label

3. You have serialized the form data that has an *<input type="email">* element. You want to deserialize the data to see the email address as entered. Which function can you use?

   A. decodeURIComponent

   B. deserialize

   C. submit

   D. deserializeEmail

Lesson 2: Form validation

When writing a web application, the root of all mishap is user input. If you didn't need to collect data from a user, you would probably have a secure web application, but a web application that collects no data is probably not useful. As soon as you need to collect user data, you open the door to your application, so you need to make sure that user input is secure. To do so, provide input validation at the server. Validation at the server is secure and ensures data integrity.

The problem with input validation at the server is that a round trip has to be made to the server to do the validation, and the time to make the round trip can be annoying to the user. To manage this problem, you can provide input validation at the browser. However, if you provide validation at the browser, you need validation at the server. The problem with validation at the browser is that browser validation is easy for an attacker to bypass. Therefore, you must provide server-side validation for security and client-side validation to minimize the time users must wait to find out that there is an input error. This lesson discusses client-side validation that is available in HTML5.

> **After this lesson, you will be able to:**
> - Understand HTML5 form validation.
> - Apply HTML5 form validation.
>
> **Estimated lesson time: 20 minutes**

Required validation

Probably the simplest type of form validation is the *required* attribute on most form submission elements. The required attribute is a Boolean attribute that requires the user to enter data before submitting to the server. Consider the following form.

```
<form id="myForm">
    Favorite Car:
    <select name="favoriteCar" required="required">
        <option>Ford Fiesta</option>
        <option value="Chevy">Chevrolet</option>
        <option>BMW</option>
    </select><br />
    Comment:
    <input type="text" name="comment" required="required"/><br />
    Email:
    <input type="email" name="email" required="required"/><br />
    <button type="submit" name="submit">Submit</button>
</form>
```

In this form, all the form submission elements have required attributes. When the page is displayed, there is no indication of required fields. If the user immediately clicks the Submit button, the browser cancels the submission, and the result is displayed, as shown in Figure 7-5. The *<select>* element doesn't have the red border because the first option is selected by default.

Browsers display validation errors differently. For example, the message in Chrome and Firefox is, "Please fill out this field," and the message in Chrome is prefixed with an icon. Opera and Internet Explorer have the same message, "This is a required field," but instead of a red border, the background of the message is red. You can provide CSS styles rules to suit your needs.

FIGURE 7-5 The empty required fields with red borders and the required message displayed

One of the reasons HTML5 has new input types for email, URL, date, and so on, is that validation can be automatically applied based on the type. In the previous example, the *<input type="email">* element automatically provides extra validation in an attempt to ensure that a valid email address is entered. The extra validation is different based on the browser. You'll typically find that browsers only look for *@* to be valid, but that might change.

You can also provide a *placeholder* attribute on most form submission elements, which provides a prompt in the field until the user enters the first character. In the past, this required a lot of extra code. The following adds the placeholder to the previous form example.

```
<form id="myForm">
    Favorite Car:
    <select name="favoriteCar" required="required">
        <option>Ford Fiesta</option>
        <option value="Chevy">Chevrolet</option>
        <option>BMW</option>
    </select><br />
    Comment:
    <input type="text" name="comment"
        required="required" placeholder="enter a comment"/><br />
    Email:
    <input type="email" name="email"
        required="required" placeholder="give me your email"/><br />
    <button type="submit" name="submit">Submit</button>
</form>
```

When the form is displayed, the comment and email address display the placeholder text if they are empty. The result is shown in Figure 7-6.

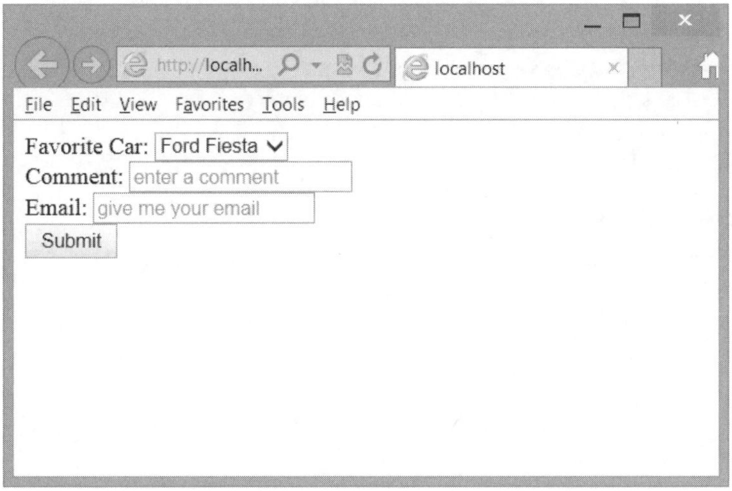

FIGURE 7-6 The placeholder text displayed until user inputs data

Validating URL input

The *<input type="url">* element validates a URL by adding the required attribute and optional placeholder. In addition, you can add the *pattern* attribute to provide a JavaScript regular expression to fine-tune the required input. Consider the following form.

```
<form id="myForm">
  website:
  <input type="url" name="website"
    required="required" pattern="https?://.+" />
    <button type="submit" name="submit">Submit</button>
</form>
```

The pattern states that the URL must start with http. The letter s is followed with a question mark (?), which means that the letter s is optional. After that, the colon and two slashes (://) are required. The period and plus sign combination means that you must provide one to many characters. The last part could be fine-tuned to require at least one period or to set a limit on the number of characters.

When the page is displayed and the user enters abc, validation fails with the message shown in Figure 7-7.

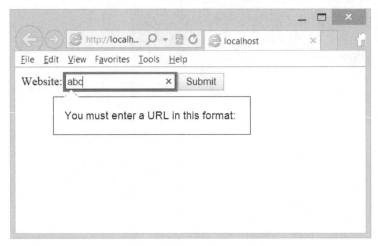

FIGURE 7-7 URL validation fails with incomplete message

The validation message is incomplete. To implement the pattern attribute properly, you must provide a title attribute that gives a hint to the user about what is required. The title will be displayed in the validation failure message. The following is the modified *<form>* element.

```
<form id="myForm">
  website:
  <input type="url" name="website"
      title="http://contoso.com or https://contoso.com"
      required="required" pattern="https?://.+" />
  <button type="submit" name="submit">Submit</button>
</form>
```

After the title attribute is supplied and the user enters invalid data, the new validation error message is displayed, as shown in Figure 7-8.

FIGURE 7-8 The URL validation message with the title supplied

Validating numbers and ranges

Use the *<input type="number">* and *<input type="range">* elements to accept numeric values. Both of these elements accept *min*, *max*, and *step* parameter attributes. The step attribute defaults to one if omitted. Consider the following *<form>* element that contains the number and range inputs.

```
<form id="myForm">
    Current Age:
    <input type="number" name="age"
        min="18" max="99" value="30"
        required="required" /><br />
    Rating:
    <input type="range" name="rating"
        min="1" max="7" value="4" /><br />
    <button type="submit" name="submit">Submit</button>
</form>
```

Figure 7-9 shows the rendered page. The user must enter a value in the number input, but the range input renders as a slider. If you don't include the required attribute on the number input, you can leave the field empty, but if you provide a value, it must be within the min and max value attributes.

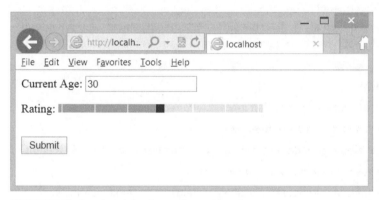

FIGURE 7-9 The rendered number and range inputs

The range input renders differently on different browsers. In addition, Internet Explorer displays a pop-up message as the slider is operated; other browsers currently don't.

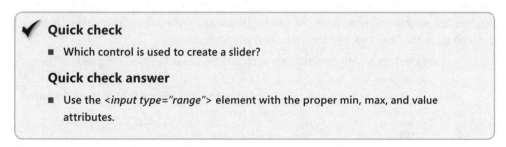

> ✔ **Quick check**
> - Which control is used to create a slider?
>
> **Quick check answer**
> - Use the *<input type="range">* element with the proper min, max, and value attributes.

Styling the validations

You can apply style rules to valid and invalid input by implementing style rules on the :valid, :invalid, :required, and :optional pseudo classes. The following is an example of setting the pseudo classes to control the look of the webpage.

```
:valid {
    border:solid lime;
    font-weight:normal;
  }
:invalid {
    border:solid red;
    font-weight:bold;
  }
:required{
    background-color:Yellow;
  }
:optional{
    background-color:LightGray;
  }
```

The :valid and :invalid pseudo classes are opposites. When the form submission element's value is determined to be invalid, it matches the :invalid selector, and when the form submission element's value is determined to be valid, it matches the :valid selector. If a form submission element has the required attribute, it matches the :required selector, and if the form submission element does not have the required attribute, it matches the :optional selector.

Lesson summary

- Use the *required* attribute to specify that input is required.
- Browsers render validation errors differently.
- The *placeholder* attribute provides prompting text to the user when the field is empty.
- To create a slider, use the *<input type="range">* element.
- You can provide alternate style rules to validation elements by implementing style rules on the :valid, :invalid, :required, and :optional pseudo classes.

Lesson review

Answer the following questions to test your knowledge of the information in this lesson. You can find the answers to these questions and explanations of why each answer choice is correct or incorrect in the "Answers" section at the end of this chapter.

1. You are creating a webpage that prompts for a new user's profile information. The profile page requires the user to provide a user name, and if no user name is provided, the user will not be able to submit the page to the server. Which attribute must be placed on the user name text box to enforce this requirement?

    A. enforced

    B. mandatory

    C. required

    D. user name

2. When you want to send form data to the server to update data in the database, which HTTP method should you specify of the *<form>* element?

    A. POST

    B. GET

    C. CONNECT

    D. SEND

3. If you want to add a slider control to a webpage, which element do you use?

    A. *<input type="slider" name="myslider" />*

    B. *<input type="number" name="myslider" />*

    C. *<input type="submit" name="myslider" />*

    D. *<input type="range" name="myslider" />*

Practice exercises

If you encounter a problem completing any of these exercises, the completed projects can be installed from the Practice Exercises folder that is provided with the companion content.

Exercise 1: Create a Contact Us form

In this exercise, you apply your HTML5 form and form validation knowledge by creating a Contact Us page for the calculator application in the previous chapter. The webpage will prompt the user for first and last name, email address, and nature of the communications. All the fields will be required.

1. Start Visual Studio Express 2012 for Web. Click FILE and choose Open Project. Navigate to the solution you created in Chapter 6, "Essential JavaScript and jQuery." Select the WebCalculator.sln file and click Open.

    If you didn't complete the exercises in Chapter 6, you can use the solution in the Chapter 7 Exercise 1 Start folder.

2. In the Solution Explorer window, right-click the default.html file and choose Set As Start Page. Press F5 to verify that your home page is displayed.

3. In the Solution Explorer window, copy the default.html page to a new HTML file by right-clicking the default.html file and choosing Copy. Right-click the WebCalculator project node and choose Paste.

    This creates a file named *Copy of default.html.*

4. Right-click the new file and choose Rename.

5. Name the new file **ContactUs.html** and press Enter.

6. Open the ContactUs.html page and delete the *<div id="calculator">* element and its content. Delete the *<script>* element that references the CalculatorLibrary.js file and the script block at the bottom that calls the initialize function.

The ContactUs.html page should look like the following.

```
<!DOCTYPE html>
<html xmlns="http://www.w3.org/1999/xhtml">
<head>
    <title>web Calculator</title>
    <link href="Content/default.css" rel="stylesheet" />
    <script src="Scripts/jquery-1.8.2.js"></script>
</head>
<body>
    <div id="container">
        <header>
            <hgroup id="headerText">
                <h1>Contoso Ltd.</h1>
                <h2>Your success equals our success</h2>
            </hgroup>
        </header>
        <nav>
            <a href="default.html">Home</a>
        </nav>
        <div role="main">

        </div>
        <aside>
            <p>Advertisements</p>
        </aside>
        <footer>
            <p>
                Copyright &copy; 2012, Contoso Ltd., All rights reserved
            </p>
        </footer>
    </div>
</body>
</html>
```

7. Change content of the *<title>* element to **Contact Us**.

8. Inside the *<div role="main">* element, add a new *<div>* element and set its id to ContactUs.

9. Inside the new *<div>* element, add a *<form>* element. Set the name of the form to ContactForm. Set the method to GET.

Setting the method to GET enables you to see when the form is actually submitted because you see the form data in the QueryString in the URL. The main content should look like the following.

```
<div id="ContactUs">
    <form name="ContactForm" method="get">

    </form>
</div>
```

10. Add a *<div>* element containing a *<label>* element and an *<input type="text">* element for firstName, lastName, emailAddress, and message. Be sure to assign the id and the name attributes of each form submission element.

The form should look the like the following.

```
<form name="ContactForm" method="get">
    <div>
        <label for="firstName">First Name:</label>
        <input type="text" id="firstName" name="firstName" />
    </div>
    <div>
        <label for="lastName">Last Name:</label>
        <input type="text" id="lastName" name="lastName" />
    </div>
    <div>
        <label for="email">Email Address:</label>
        <input type="text" id="email" name="email" />
    </div>
    <div>
        <label for="message">Message:</label>
        <input type="text" id="message" name="message" />
    </div>
    <div>
        <button type="submit" id="submit" name="submit" >Submit</button>
    </div>
</form>
```

11. Open the default.css file and, at the bottom of the file, add a style rule for the *<label>* element that clears the previous elements and displays as a block that is floated left. Set the width to 125 pixels and set the height to 12 pixels. Set vertical alignment to bottom and padding to 10 pixels.

Your style should look like the following.

```
label {
    clear: both;
    display: block;
    float: left;
    width: 125px;
    height: 12px;
    vertical-align: bottom;
    padding: 10px;
}
```

12. Add another style rule to the bottom of the default.css file for *<input>* elements, but only for *<input>* elements that are inside a *<form>* element. Set the width to 200 pixels. Set the border width to medium and the border color to hsl(255, 100%, 100%). Set the height to 12 pixels and set text alignment to left and vertical alignment to top. Set the font family to Arial and the font size to 12 point.

Your style should look like the following.

```
form input {
    width: 200px;
```

```
        border-width: medium;
        border-color: hsl(255, 100%, 100%);
        height: 12px;
        text-align: left;
        vertical-align: top;
        font-family: Arial;
        font-size: 12pt;
}
```

13. Add another style rule to the bottom of the default.css file for *<button>* elements, but only for *<button>* elements that are inside a *<form>* element. Set the width to 100 pixels. Set the border width to medium and the border color to hsl(255, 100%, 100%). Set the vertical alignment to top. Set the font family to Arial and the font size to 12 point. Set the top and bottom margins to 10 pixels. Set the left and right margins to 50 percent.

Your style should look like the following.

```
form button {
        width: 100px;
        border-width: medium;
        border-color: hsl(255, 100%, 100%);
        vertical-align: top;
        font-family: Arial;
        font-size: 12pt;
        margin-top: 10px;
        margin-right: 50%;
        margin-bottom: 10px;
        margin-left: 50%;
}
```

The last thing you must do is add a hyperlink on the main page that references the ContactUs.html file.

14. Open the default.html file.

15. In the *<nav>* section, add a *
* element and then add the hyperlink to reference the ContactUs.html file.

Your *<nav>* section should look like the following.

```
<nav>
    <a href="default.html">Home</a><br />
    <a href="ContactUs.html">Contact Us</a>
</nav>
```

16. Press F5 to run to run the application. Click the Contact Us link to display the ContactUs.html page. Without entering any data, click the Submit button.

Notice that the URL has changed, and the QueryString is displayed after the page name. Notice also that the name of each element is shown, but there is no data because you clicked the Submit button without entering any data. The URL looks like the following.

```
http://localhost:55506/ContactUs.html?firstName=&lastName=&email=&message=&submit=
```

Figure 7-10 shows the ContactUs.html page. When you see the QueryString, it means that the Submit button worked. Currently, the data isn't being processed at a server. That will come in the next chapter. For now, you want to limit the ability of the Submit button so it doesn't operate until data is entered in all fields.

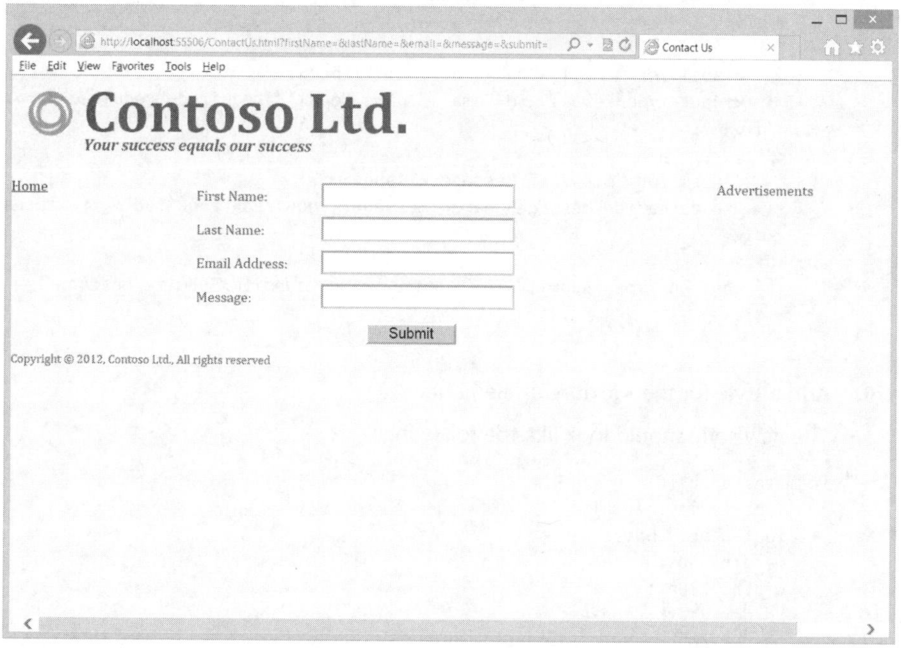

FIGURE 7-10 The ContactUs.html page

Exercise 2: Add validation to the Contact Us form

In this exercise, you continue with the project from Exercise 1 and modify the ContactUs.html file to clean up the webpage and add validation to it.

1. Open the project from Exercise 1.

   If you didn't perform Exercise 1, you can use the project located in the Exercise 2 Start folder.

2. Open the ContactUs.html file.

3. Add the *required* attribute to the firstName, lastName, email, and message fields.

4. Replace the type attribute on the email field with type="email", which will provide added validation of the email address.

5. Change the message to a *<textarea>* element.

   Your completed form should look like the following.

```
<form name="ContactForm" method="get">
    <div>
```

```
        <label for="firstName">First Name:</label>
        <input type="text" id="firstName" name="firstName" required="required"/>
    </div>
    <div>
        <label for="lastName">Last Name:</label>
        <input type="text" id="lastName" name="lastName" required="required"/>
    </div>
    <div>
        <label for="email">Email Address:</label>
        <input type="email" id="email" name="email" required="required"/>
    </div>
    <div>
        <label for="message">Message:</label>
        <textarea id="message" name="message" required="required"></textarea>
    </div>
    <div>
        <button type="submit" id="submit" name="submit">Submit</button>
    </div>
</form>
```

6. Add a style for the *<textarea>* element.

   The new style should look like the following.

```
form textarea {
    font-family: Arial;
    font-size: 20pt;
    margin: 5px;
    width: 210px;
    border-width: medium;
    border-color: hsl(255, 100%, 100%);
    height: 100px;
    text-align: left;
    vertical-align: top;
    font-family: Arial;
    font-size: 12pt;
}
```

7. Press F5 to run the application. Don't enter any data; just click the Submit button.

   If your browser supports validation, you will see the validation errors, as shown in
   Figure 7-11.

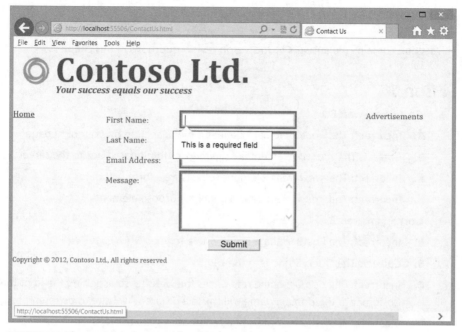

FIGURE 7-11 The completed page with validation error

Notice that after clicking the Submit button, the URL hasn't changed because no attempt was made to send the data to the server. If you enter data in all the fields and click the Submit button, you'll see the QueryString with its data.

Suggested practice exercises

The following additional exercises are designed to give you more opportunities to practice what you've learned and to help you successfully master the lessons presented in this chapter.

- **Exercise 1** Learn more about positioning by adding more *<div>* elements to the webpage to define a header and footer for the page. Use CSS style rules to set the position.

- **Exercise 2** Add more elements to the page and try setting the format by selecting the elements without using an id.

- **Exercise 3** Change the color scheme of the page by using RGB values.

Answers

This section contains the answers to the lesson review questions in this chapter.

Lesson 1

1. **Correct answer: B**

    A. **Incorrect:** The *<nav>* element defines a menu section on your html page.

    B. **Correct:** The *<form>* element is required to submit data back to the server.

    C. **Incorrect:** The *<textarea>* element collects free-form text data.

    D. **Incorrect:** The *<div>* element is a general-purpose element.

2. **Correct answer: B**

    A. **Incorrect:** The PostBack data is not visible to you.

    B. **Correct:** The QueryString is in the URL.

    C. **Incorrect:** The domain name references the website, so assigning the id of the Customer to the domain name will cause a different website to be referenced.

    D. **Incorrect:** A label does not send its content to the server.

3. **Correct answer: A**

    A. **Correct:** The decodeURIComponent function can deserialize the QueryString.

    B. **Incorrect:** Although jQuery has a serialize function, it has no deserialize function.

    C. **Incorrect:** Although jQuery has a submit function, it serializes the form and sends the data to the server.

    D. **Incorrect:** There is no deserializeEmail function.

Lesson 2

1. **Correct answer: C**

    A. **Incorrect:** There is no enforced attribute.

    B. **Incorrect:** There is no mandatory attribute.

    C. **Correct:** The required attribute indicates a required field.

    D. **Incorrect:** There is no user name attribute.

2. **Correct answer: A**

    A. **Correct:** Using the POST method is generally preferred for sending updates to the server.

    B. **Incorrect:** Using the GET method is generally preferred for retrieving data from the server.

    C. **Incorrect:** The CONNECT method is used to establish a tunneled connection.

    D. **Incorrect:** There is no SEND method.

3. **Correct answer: D**

   A. **Incorrect:** There is no slider type.

   B. **Incorrect:** The number type accepts numbers and displays them in a text box.

   C. **Incorrect:** The submit type creates a submit button.

   D. **Correct:** The range type renders as a slider.

CHAPTER 8

Websites and services

The previous chapters have presented many things you can do at the browser, but you can also do things at the server. When using Microsoft technologies, it's typical to create a website by using Visual Studio .NET, which uses ASP.NET or model, view, controller (MVC) technologies that are programmed using Visual Basic .NET or C#. These technologies and languages are outside the scope of this book, but can you learn to create a form without creating a website to process the form?

This book is about HTML5, CSS3, and JavaScript; this chapter covers web services, using JavaScript on the web server, which is possible by using Node.js, a platform built on the Google Chrome JavaScript runtime.

Lessons in this chapter:

Before you begin

To complete this book, you must have some understanding of web development. This chapter requires the hardware and software listed in the "System requirements" section in the book's Introduction.

Lesson 1: Getting started with Node.js

The Node.js platform is built on the Google Chrome JavaScript runtime for easily building fast, scalable network applications. The platform implements an event-driven, non-blocking I/O model and is lightweight and efficient. This platform is perfect for data-intensive, real-time applications that run across distributed devices.

Using Node.js, you can write JavaScript that executes on the back-end server. Node.js interprets and executes your JavaScript by using Google's V8 virtual machine, which is the same runtime environment for JavaScript that Google Chrome uses.

After this lesson, you will be able to:

- Install Node.js.
- Create a Node.js webpage.

Estimated lesson time: 20 minutes

Installing Node.js

To install Node.js on your computer, download the version for your machine from *http://nodejs.org/download/* and run the installer. For typical Windows-based, 64-bit computers at the time of this writing, this is the node-v0.8.14-x64.msi file. The installation requires accepting the licensing agreements. By default, the Node.js files install to the C:\Program Files\nodejs\ folder. You'll find the node.exe file in the installation folder, which is the primary executable for Node.js. You will also find a folder for node modules; this folder contains *npm*, the *node package manager*. You use npm to install modules in Node.js.

The Node.js installer adds the Node.js and npm folder locations to the path environment setting so you can open the command prompt window easily and run the program.

Creating Hello World from Node.js

After the installation completes, you can create your first Node.js website by opening the command prompt and using your favorite text editor. Create a file called HelloWorld.js containing the following.

```
var http = require('http');
http.createServer(function (request, response) {
  response.writeHead(200, {'Content-Type': 'text/plain'});
  response.end('Hello World from Node.js!\n');
  console.log('Handled request');
}).listen(8080, 'localhost');
console.log('Server running at http://localhost:8080/');
```

This is JavaScript! The first line of code states that the *http* module needs to be loaded. The http module is a core built-in, low-level module that is highly optimized for performance.

The next line uses the http module to create a server object. The createServer function accepts a single parameter that is an anonymous function and has request object and response object parameters. Inside the function, you include all the code to run your website or, better yet, to make calls to other functions that handle your website. This example does nothing with the request object, but it uses the response object to write an HTTP header in which 200 means success, and the content type tells the browser that the content is plain text. The next line ends the response with the Hello World message and, finally, a message is sent to the console window, stating that a request was handled.

When the createServer function is executed, a server object is returned. The server object calls the listen function, in which port 8080 is specified as the port to listen on, and the IP address is set to localhost, which is 127.0.0.1. As long as you have an operating network adapter installed on your computer, this web server should start listening for incoming web requests.

The last statement uses the console object to write a message to the screen to let you know that the server is waiting for requests.

After you save this file, run the following from the command prompt to start running your web server.

```
Node HelloWorld.js
```

Leave the command prompt open and open the browser. Navigate to the following URL.

```
http://localhost:8080/
```

When the request is received, a response is sent, and a message is logged to the console window, as shown in Figure 8-1.

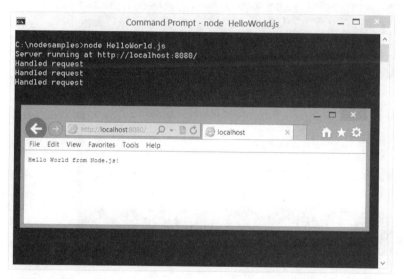

FIGURE 8-1 The running HelloWorld website responding with a message

Congratulations! You have installed Node.js and written your first Node.js website. To stop running, you don't need to close the command prompt window; you can just press Ctrl+C to cancel.

Of course, the next thing you want to do is process the request data to produce a response based on the request. For that, you can require the *url* module, which provides help for parsing the QueryString. The url object has a parse method that accepts the actual URL, and the second parameter is a flag by which passing a value of *true* parses the QueryString. The following code reads the name from the QueryString and creates a personalized response.

```
var http = require('http');
var url = require('url');
http.createServer(function (request, response) {
  var url_parts = url.parse(request.url, true);
  response.writeHead(200, {'Content-Type': 'text/plain'});
  response.end('Hello ' + url_parts.query.name + '!\n');
  console.log('Handled request from ' + url_parts.query.name);
}).listen(8080, 'localhost');
console.log('Server running at http://localhost:8080/');
```

This application was saved to hello_joe.js. Run the application and then launch the browser. Navigate to the following URL.

```
http://localhost:8080/?name=Joe
```

When the request is received, a response is sent, and a message is logged to the console window, as shown in Figure 8-2. Try different names and notice that you get a personalized response.

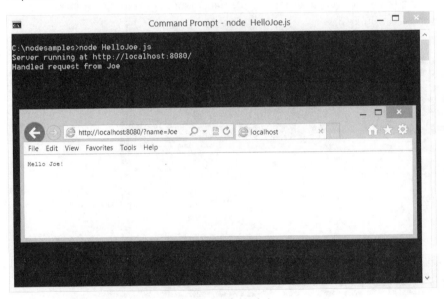

FIGURE 8-2 Creating a personalized response with Node.js

Creating a Node.js module

In the previous examples, you used the require function to load modules, which provide code reuse when adding functionality to Node.js. You can create your own module by wrapping your code in a function and exporting it so it can be called from other code, as follows.

```
var http = require('http');
var url = require('url');

function start(){
```

```
http.createServer(function (request, response) {
  var url_parts = url.parse(request.url, true);
  response.writeHead(200, {'Content-Type': 'text/plain'});
  response.end('Hello ' + url_parts.query.name + '!\n');
  console.log('Handled request from ' + url_parts.query.name);
}).listen(8080, 'localhost');
console.log('Server running at http://localhost:8080/');
}
```

exports.start = start;

In this example, the existing code has been wrapped with a start function. At the bottom of the file, the start function is assigned to a start property on the exports object. The code is saved to a hello.js file, and the module is created.

You use the new module just as you use other modules, by using the require function. Create an index.js file and enter the following code to use your module.

```
var hello = require('./hello.js');
hello.start();
```

In this example, the module name is "./hello.js". Notice that a relative path to the file is used. The require function returns an object that is assigned to the hello variable, and then the start method is executed.

After saving the file, you can run the code by executing the following at the command prompt.

```
node index.js
```

This code works the same as the hello_joe.js code except that this code uses your new module.

Creating a Node.js package

A Node.js *package*, also known as an *application*, is a collection of modules with a manifest that describes the package and its dependencies and can be publicly and privately published for you and others to use. After you publish your package, you can use the node package manager (npm) to install a package. The package can be installed in a single application you're creating or globally for use with many applications.

In this example, a call_counter.js module will be created, which will produce a console message whenever its count_call function is executed. A simple_math.js module will be created, which will contain an add function and a subtract function. An advanced_math.js module will be created, which will contain multiply, divide, and Fibonacci functions. All the math functions will be usable by other applications, but the call counter will remain private to the package, so that each math function will call the count_call function. Although all these functions could be placed in a single module, this example demonstrates the use of multiple modules.

These modules will be packaged so they can be published. After the package is published, you and others can install the package and use it in other applications.

The following is a typical folder structure for creating a package. You start by creating a root folder for your package.

```
\packageName
    \bin
        main.js
    \lib
        module1.js
        module2.js
    package.json
    README.md
```

Inside the package root folder, you have a package.json file, which is the manifest file. You also need a README.md file containing enough help to get the user started. In addition, you need a *bin* folder and a *lib* folder. The bin folder contains the entry point to your package; the lib folder contains the modules.

In this example, the package root folder is created at C:\node_samples\math_example; math_example is the package name.

In the lib folder, the first module is created, called call_counter.js, which has the following code.

```
var internal_call_counter=0;

function count_call(){
    ++internal_call_counter;
    console.log('You have made ' + internal_call_counter + ' calls!');
}

module.exports = count_call;
```

It looks like the *internal_call_counter* variable and the count_call function are polluting the global namespace, but this module code will be wrapped so that neither will be in the global namespace. You can define what is available when a user uses the require('call_counter') function by assigning something to module.exports. In this case, the only exported function is count_call, but you can specify multiple functions by wrapping them in an object, as you'll see in the simple_math.js and advanced_math.js modules.

The next module created in the lib folder is simple_math.js, which has the following code.

```
var call_counter = require('./call_counter');

function add(x, y){
    call_counter();
    return x + y;
}

function subtract(x, y){
    call_counter();
    return x - y;
}
```

```
module.exports = {
    addition: add,
    subtraction: subtract
}
```

In the simple_math.js file, the require function references the call_counter.js module. The use of the './call_counter' syntax indicates that this is a local module in the current folder as opposed to a package. The reference is assigned to the *call_counter* variable. The add and subtract functions call the *call_counter* variable, which references the count_call function. This module exports two functions, so an object is created to provide access to these functions. In this case, the addition method references the add function, whereas the subtraction method references the subtract function. It's more typical for the method name to be the same as the function name, but this example demonstrates that they can be different.

The next module created in the lib folder is advanced_math.js, which has the following code.

```
var call_counter = require('./call_counter');

function multiply(x, y){
    call_counter();
    return x * y;
}

function divide(x, y){
    call_counter();
    return x / y;
}

function fibo(count) {
    call_counter();
    return private_fibo(count)
}

function private_fibo(count, counter, first, second) {
    if (count == 0) return 0;
    if (counter == undefined) {
        counter = 1
        first = 1;
        second = 2;
    }
    result = first + second;
    if (counter == count) return result;
    private_fibo(count, ++counter, second, result)
    return result;
}

module.exports = {
    multiplication: multiply,
    division: divide,
    fibonacci : fibo
}
```

In the advanced_math.js file, the require function also references the call_counter.js module. The multiply, divide, and fibo functions call the *call_counter* variable, which references the count_call function. The advanced_math.js module exports three functions, so an object is created to provide access to these functions.

The fibo function calls the private_fibo function, a recursive function that calls itself until the count and counter are equal. The private_fibo function is not exported, so it will be accessible only from the fibo function that is exported.

Creating an aggregate module

After the modules are created, you might want to expose a single object with the items that are exported across all the modules. Exposing a single object makes it easier for your package users to access the features of your package. This is the entry point module, which is an aggregate of the other modules in your package.

In the bin folder, create a main.js module that contains the following code.

```
var path = require('path');
var fs = require('fs');
var lib = path.join(path.dirname(fs.realpathSync(__filename)), '../lib');
var simple = require(lib + '/simple_math.js');
var advanced = require(lib + '/advanced_math.js');
module.exports = {
        addition: simple.addition,
        subtraction: simple.subtraction,
        multiplication: advanced.multiplication,
        division: advanced.division,
        fibonacci: advanced.fibonacci
}
```

This module first references two built-in node.js packages, *path* and *fs*. These packages are helpers that get the path to the lib folder. Next, references to simple_math.js and advanced_math.js are created using this path to the lib. The call_counter.js module is not referenced because the package uses it but does not expose it. Finally, module.exports is assigned an object in which the functions that were exposed on simple_math.js and advanced_math.js are now exported by the package.

Creating the README.md file

The README.md file contains enough help to get the user started with your package. The file extension of .md denotes a *Markdown* file. A *Markdown file* is a simple way of providing formatting on a text document so it can be displayed nicely as text or in a browser. A quick search on the web for markdown language will yield numerous articles and free Markdown editors, such as MarkdownPad, as shown in Figure 8-3. The contents of the README.md file are as follows.

```
math_example package
====================
```

The following functions are available in the math_example package.
- **addition** Adds two numbers and returns the result.
- **subtraction** Subtracts the second number from the first and returns the result.
- **multiplication** Multiplies two numbers and returns the result.
- **division** Divides the first number by the second number and returns the result.
- **fibonacci** Applies the fibonacci sequence count times and returns the result.

The formatting is very readable. When it's rendered to HTML, it's also very readable, as shown in the live view window in Figure 8-3.

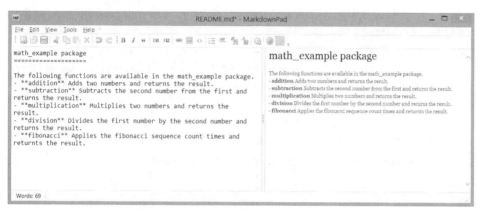

FIGURE 8-3 Editing the README.md file using MarkdownPad

Creating the package.json file

The package.json file is the manifest for your package. This file contains the metadata that describes your package. You can create this file manually, but an easier way to create the file is to type the following command.

```
npm init
```

When you run this command, it leads you through a series of prompts, and then the file is created for you. You can always edit the file later if needed.

As the file extension implies, this file is written in JSON, which is JavaScript Object Notation. The following is the package.json file for math_example.

```
{
  "name": "math_example",
  "version": "0.0.0",
  "description": "An example of creating a package",
  "main": "bin/main.js",
  "scripts": {
    "test": "echo \"Error: no test specified\" && exit 1"
  },
  "repository": "",
  "keywords": [
    "math",
    "example",
```

```
      "addition",
      "subtraction",
      "multiplication",
      "division",
      "fibonacci"
    ],
    "author": "Glenn Johnson",
    "license": "BSD"
}
```

You can provide test scripts in your package so users can install your package and run the tests on their computers.

You can specify a *git* repository URL. Git is one of the best source control managers, and if you're not using any kind of source control, this might be a good time to learn about git at *http://git-scm.com/*. If your package has dependencies, they would also be listed in the package.json file.

Publishing the package

You now have a package with a folder structure that looks like the following.

```
\packageName
    \bin
        main.js
    \lib
        advanced_math.js
        call_counter.js
        simple_math.js
    package.json
    README.md
```

Publishing a package makes the package available to all users for use in their applications. You use npm to publish to the npm registry, and then you use npm to search for packages and install your package.

Before you can publish a node.js package, you must create an account by which to publish all your packages. Use npm to create the account by executing the following command.

```
npm adduser
```

Follow the prompts for a user name (lowercase), password, and email address. After you've entered all the required information, npm contacts registry.npmjs.org to create your account. Validation of account currently is not required, so anyone can create an account and put bad code into the registry; therefore, when you install an unknown package from the npm registry, *beware*!

Now that you have an account, you can publish to the npm registry. Open the command prompt window and change from your current directory to the root directory of the package, where the package.json file is located. Enter the following command to publish the package.

```
npm publish
```

You see npm sending HTTP GET and PUT methods until the publishing is complete. If you have no errors, the package should be published and immediately available for everyone to use.

Installing and using the package

Now that your package is published, you can install it and use it. You can install the package globally, or you can install it locally to the application you're creating. Installing the package globally gives all applications the same version of the package so that when you update the global package with a new version, all applications get the new version. If you install the package locally to the application, you reinstall the package for each application. You can update the package for one application, and you don't need to worry about updating the package for all applications. The global option is typically more appealing to most people, but often you don't want to be forced into regression testing for all applications when you update the package. This choice is about having control to update when needed versus the convenience of updating all at once.

In this example, a new application, math_user, is created, so this folder is created under the node_samples folder.

To install the package locally, use the command prompt window to navigate to the folder that contains your application and enter the following command.

```
npm install math_example
```

This creates a node_modules subdirectory; in the folder that contains your application is a folder for the installed package with all its files.

To install the package globally, type the following command.

```
npm install -g math_example
```

Figure 8-4 shows the screen after executing this command. The last line shows the folder location in which the package was installed.

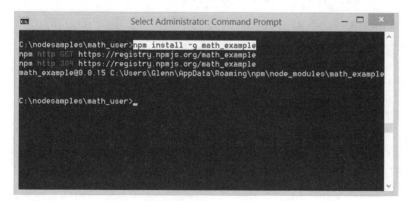

FIGURE 8-4 The successful global package install

After the package is globally installed, create a link to the global install from each application that will use the global package. To accomplish this, navigate to the root folder of your application and enter the following command.

```
npm link math_example
```

In this example, the command was executed in the math_user folder. After the command is executed, you see that a folder called node_modules exists. If you navigate to that folder and look at the contents of the directory, you'll see that a math_example junction exists, as shown in Figure 8-5.

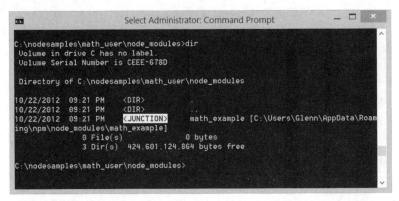

FIGURE 8-5 The npm link command showing a junction to the global install

A junction is a route to the global install. It behaves like a folder. You can change from the node_modules folder to that folder by using the *cd math_example* command, and you can change back to the node_modules folder by using the *cd ..* command.

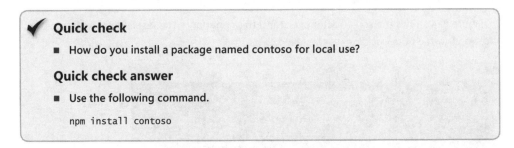

✔ Quick check

■ How do you install a package named contoso for local use?

Quick check answer

■ Use the following command.

```
npm install contoso
```

Now that you have installed the math_example package, write some code that accesses the math_example package. In the math_user folder, create a JavaScript file called main.js and enter the following code.

```
var math_example = require('math_example');

var result = 0;

console.log();
result = math_example.addition(5,10);
```

```
console.log('addition(5,10) = ' + result);


console.log();
result = math_example.subtraction(50,10);
console.log('subtraction(50,10) = ' + result);

console.log();
result = math_example.multiplication(3,7);
console.log('multiplication(3,7) = ' + result);

console.log();
result = math_example.division(27,3);
console.log('division(27,3) = ' + result);

console.log();
result = math_example.fibonacci(3);
console.log('fibonacci(3) = ' + result);


console.log('done');
```

This code sets a reference to the math_example package. The code executes a small test of each of the exported functions. Run the code by executing the following command.

```
node main
```

The result is shown in Figure 8-6. Each function returns a result, and then the result is displayed.

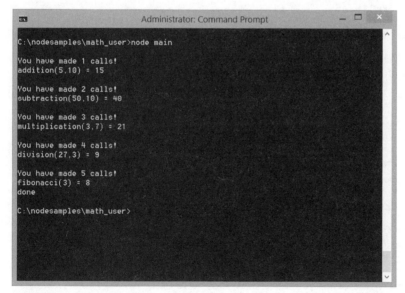

FIGURE 8-6 The result of executing node main

Uninstalling a package

Uninstall a local package by executing the following command from the root folder of the application.

```
npm uninstall math_example
```

To uninstall a global package, execute the following command.

```
npm uninstall -g math_example
```

Fast forward to express

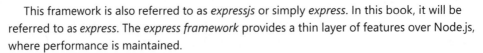

Although it is relatively easy to create a Hello module with Node.js, much more work is necessary if you intend to create a complete web framework. For example, when a request is received at the server for a resource such as a webpage or a web service, you typically need to route the request to get the proper resource. You might also want to implement sessions to hold data between each request. What about authentication? It doesn't make sense for you to create this framework when you can install a more streamlined framework. The *express web application framework for node.js* is available at *http://expressjs.com/*. You can install express by using the previously mentioned npm install command, or you can read the next section to learn how to install express from a dependency list.

This framework is also referred to as *expressjs* or simply *express*. In this book, it will be referred to as *express*. The *express framework* provides a thin layer of features over Node.js, where performance is maintained.

Starting with express

To begin using express, you must install Node.js first, and then you create a folder for your web application. In this example, the folder is the following.

```
C:\node_samples\HelloExpress
```

Next, you set up a dependency on express, so you need the current version number of express. Execute the following command to get the version information.

```
npm info express version
```

At the time of this writing, the version is 3.0.0. You need this version number when you add the dependency to the package.json file.

To create the package.json file in the HelloExpress folder, navigate to that folder, execute the following command, and follow the prompts.

```
npm init
```

The following is the completed package.json.

```
{
  "name": "HelloExpress",
```

```
  "version": "0.0.0",
  "description": "A simple Web site",
  "main": "index.js",
  "scripts": {
    "test": "echo \"Error: no test specified\" && exit 1"
  },
  "repository": "",
  "author": "Glenn Johnson",
  "license": "BSD"
}
```

Open the file with a text editor and add the dependency to express as follows.

```
{
  "name": "HelloExpress",
  "version": "0.0.0",
  "description": "A simple Web site",
  "main": "index.js",
  "scripts": {
    "test": "echo \"Error: no test specified\" && exit 1"
  },
  "repository": "",
  "author": "Glenn Johnson",
  "license": "BSD",
  "private": true,
  "dependencies": {
    "express": "3.0.0"
  }
}
```

The version number could have been set to "3.x" to retrieve the latest of version 3, and private is set to true, which indicates that this application will be used only locally. If you don't supply the private indicator, you might get a message from your firewall provider stating that the website is running with limited functionality.

Now that you have the dependency to express configured, you can use npm to install all dependencies by executing the following command.

```
npm install
```

This installs express and all its dependencies into the node_modules folder. You can verify that express is installed by executing the following command.

```
npm ls
```

This command provides a list of packages installed for this application. You see that express is installed, but many other packages are also installed, as shown in Figure 8-7.

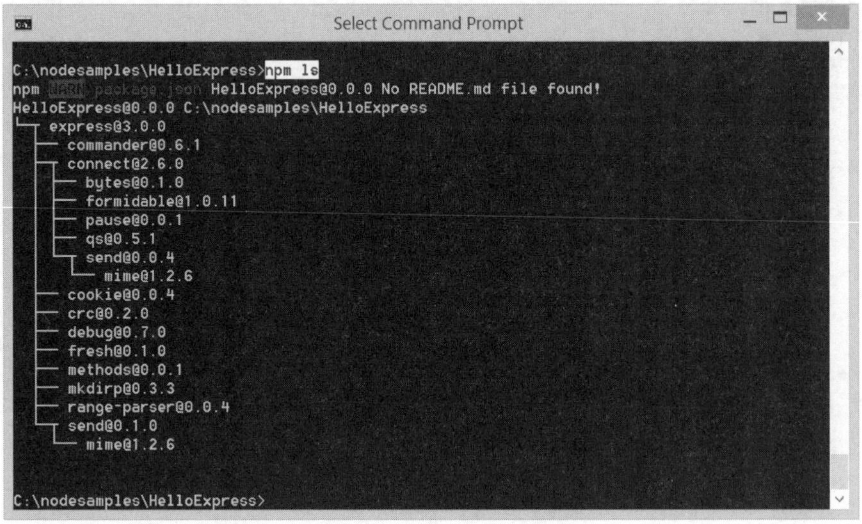

FIGURE 8-7 Installing express, which also installs its dependencies

Using Visual Studio 2012 Express for Web

You can use Visual Studio 2012 Express for Web as your editor and file manager for a Node.js folder structure by opening Visual Studio 2012 Express for Web, clicking File, and choosing Open Web Site. Select the HelloExpress folder and click Open. Visual Studio opens the folder structure for your use. If you click the Save All button, you find that Visual Studio creates a solution file (.sln) that contains the settings, so you can easily use the .sln file to reopen the solution.

You can continue to use your favorite text editor to work with the Node.js files, and you still must keep a command prompt window open to run the Node.js application.

Creating a Hello web application with express

You have now installed express, so create a web application. In the HelloExpress folder, create an app.js file and add the following to the file.

```
var express = require('express');
var app = express();
```

This code sets a reference to the express package that you installed and then creates an express application object and assigns it to the app variable. This object provides many time-saving features rather than creating everything from the beginning in Node.js.

Express provides the ability to define routes by using app.*Method*() syntax, in which *Method* is the HTTP method, or verb. The following code is added to the app.js file, which defines a route that matches a request by using the GET method and relative URL of "/". Upon match, the code is programmed to deliver a Hello World message to the user.

```
app.get('/', function(request, response){
  response.send('Hello World');
});
```

The request and response objects are the same objects that Node.js provides. The last bit of code to add is the statements that are required to listen for a request as follows.

```
var port = 8080;
app.listen(port);
console.log('Listening on port: ' + port);
```

Your completed app.js file should look like the following.

```
var express = require('express');
var app = express();

app.get('/', function (request, response) {
    response.send('Hello World');
});

var port = 8080;
app.listen(port);
console.log('Listening on port: ' + port);
```

Save and run the following command to start the web server.

```
node app
```

When the application is started, you see a message stating that the application is listening on port 8080. Open the browser and enter the following URL.

```
http://localhost:8080/
```

This request is routed to the function that handles the request, and Hello World is sent to the response, as shown in Figure 8-8.

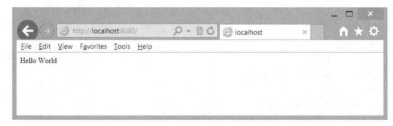

FIGURE 8-8 The express application responding to a page request

Adding a webpage to the application

Instead of writing JavaScript to render every page, you can create HTML pages that can be retrieved automatically with a minimum of code. In the app.js file, replace the app.get statement with the following.

```
app.use(express.static(__dirname + '/public'));
```

This statement starts with app.use, which mounts a path from which to serve files. In the app.use function, express.static specifies the location of static files. In this case, you need to create a *public* folder within your application.

After creating the public folder, create an HTML file in the public folder called HelloForm. html containing the following.

```
<!DOCTYPE html>
<html xmlns="http://www.w3.org/1999/xhtml">
<head>
    <title></title>
</head>
<body>
    <form method="get" action="/SubmitHello">
        Enter Name: <input type="text" name="userName" />
        <input type="submit" value="Submit" />
    </form>
</body>
</html>
```

This HTML file contains a *<form>* element, and its method attribute is set to GET, whereas the action attribute is set to /SubmitHello. This means that you need a resource called / SubmitHello at the server that can handle the data passed to the server in the QueryString.

In the app.js file, add the following code after the app.use statement.

```
app.get('/SubmitHello', function (request, response) {
    response.writeHead(200, { 'Content-Type': 'text/html' });
    response.write('Hello ' + request.query.userName + '!<br />');
    response.end('Have a great day!');
    console.log('Handled request from ' + request.query.userName);
});
```

This code is similar to the original app.get statement except that the SubmitHello resource is specified, and the QueryString is accessible by using request.query. The following is the completed app.js file.

```
var express = require('express');
var app = express();

app.use(express.static(__dirname + '/public'));

app.get('/SubmitHello', function (request, response) {
    response.writeHead(200, { 'Content-Type': 'text/html' });
    response.write('Hello ' + request.query.userName + '!<br />');
    response.end('Have a great day!');
    console.log('Handled request from ' + request.query.userName);
});

var port = 8080;
app.listen(port);
console.log('Listening on port: ' + port);
```

The response has a writeHead method to write headers. There is also a write method to write HTML to the browser. Finally, you can use the end method to send the last bit of HTML to the browser and close the connection.

In the command prompt window, run the application by executing the following command.

```
node app
```

After the application is running, open the browser and enter the following URL.

```
http://localhost:8080/HelloForm.html
```

You see the webpage, as shown in Figure 8-9.

FIGURE 8-9 The HelloForm.html webpage retrieved

Entering a name in the text box and clicking the Submit button presents the form data to the server. The QueryString is processed, and the result is displayed, as shown in Figure 8-10.

FIGURE 8-10 The result displayed

In this example, when you click the Submit button, the URL changes to the following.

```
http://localhost:8080/SubmitHello?userName=Glenn
```

The routing in the app.js file matches the resource of SubmitHello and then executes the code associated with the resource. In the code, userName is retrieved from the QueryString.

Did you notice that the URL to get the HelloForm.html page was the following?

```
http://localhost:8080/HelloForm.html
```

You didn't need to provide the word "public" in the URL because the app.use function didn't specify a resource folder for the URL. The app.use specified the location of the files only, so the URL path is the root of the website (\). You can specify the URL path explicitly by inserting the path in front of the original argument, as shown in the following example.

```
app.use('/forms', express.static(__dirname + '/public'));
```

After making this change, run the application again. This time, enter the following URL in the browser.

```
http://localhost:8080/Forms/HelloForm.html
```

If you try the original URL, you might still see the form because it's cached. If so, refresh your browser screen, and you no longer can retrieve the HelloForm.html from the original URL.

Parsing posted form data

The previous examples demonstrated the ability to use Node.js to serve a webpage and process the QueryString data by using the GET method, but in the previous chapter, you learned that in addition to being able to attach data to the URL through the QueryString, you can put data in the message body by using the POST method.

In this section, you learn to process the postback data by using a *formidable* package. This package provides helper methods that simplify posted data retrieval.

Copy the HelloForm.html file to a new file called HelloPost.html in the same public folder. Modify the HTML in the HelloPost.html by changing the *<form>* element's method attribute to *post* and changing the action attribute to *SubmitHelloPost*. The completed HelloPost.html file should look like the following.

```
<!DOCTYPE html>
<html xmlns="http://www.w3.org/1999/xhtml">
<head>
    <title></title>
</head>
<body>
    <form method="post" action="/SubmitHelloPost">
        Enter Name: <input type="text" name="userName" />
        <input type="submit" value="Submit" />
    </form>
</body>
</html>
```

Because the method attribute is set to POST, the processing of the data is different, which is why a new action is provided. In the meantime, the existing HTML page continues to operate.

In the command prompt window, execute the following npm command to retrieve information about the formidable package.

```
npm info formidable
```

At the time of this writing, the latest version is 1.0.10, but you can also use a wild card to specify the version in the package.json file in which you must specify this dependency. The following is the modified package.json file.

```
{
  "name": "HelloExpress",
  "version": "0.0.0",
  "description": "A simple Web site",
  "main": "index.js",
  "scripts": {
    "test": "echo \"Error: no test specified\" && exit 1"
  },
  "repository": "",
  "author": "Glenn Johnson",
  "license": "BSD",
  "private": true,
  "dependencies": {
    "formidable": "1.x",
    "express": "3.0.0"
  }
}
```

The addition of formidable version 1.x retrieves the latest release of version 1.

In the command prompt window, install the formidable package by entering the following npm command.

```
npm install
```

This command reads the package.json file and installs the dependent packages. You now have the formidable package installed locally, so update the app.js file to process post-back data. At the top of the app.js file, add the following code to reference the formidable package.

```
var formidable = require('formidable');
```

Next, process the posted data. Instead of adding an app.get function call, add an app.post function call. In the call, you must create an instance of the formidable package's IncomingForm object and assign it to a *form* variable. You then must use the *form* variable fields and display a message to the user. The completed app.js file with the app.post function should look like the following.

```
var express = require('express');
var app = express();
var formidable = require('formidable');

app.use('/forms', express.static(__dirname + '/public'));

app.post('/SubmitHelloPost', function (request, response) {
```

```
        if (request.method.toLowerCase() == 'post') {
            // parse form data
            var form = new formidable.IncomingForm();
            form.parse(request, function (err, fields) {
                response.writeHead(200, { 'Content-Type': 'text/html' });
                response.write('Hello ' + fields.userName + '!<br />');
                response.end('Have a POST great day!');
                console.log('Handled request from ' + fields.userName);
            });
        }
});

app.get('/SubmitHello', function (request, response) {
    response.writeHead(200, { 'Content-Type': 'text/html' });
    response.write('Hello ' + request.query.userName + '!<br />');
    response.end('Have a great day!');
    console.log('Handled request from ' + request.query.userName);
});

var port = 8080;
app.listen(port);
console.log('Listening on port: ' + port);
```

Run the application and then enter the following in the browser URL.

```
http://localhost:8080/Forms/HelloPost.html
```

Enter a name in the text box and click Submit. You should see the result displayed in the browser window, as shown in Figure 8-11.

FIGURE 8-11 The posted form data processed and displayed

There is no QueryString, and the URL clearly shows that the posted data was sent to the SubmitHelloPost. In earlier examples, the GET method was used to show you how it works. Remember that you should always send data back to the server by using the POST method.

Lesson summary

- Node.js provides a server-side way of creating websites that are JavaScript-based.
- A module is a shareable file that promotes reuse.
- A package is a shareable set of modules that promote reuse and is published for you and others to use.
- Use node package manager (npm) to manage packages.
- Use the express package to create a website easily.

Lesson review

Answer the following questions to test your knowledge of the information in this lesson. You can find the answers to these questions and explanations of why each answer choice is correct or incorrect in the "Answers" section at the end of this chapter.

1. What can you publish by using npm?
    A. A JavaScript file
    B. A module
    C. A JavaScript class
    D. A package

2. What scoping can a package have? (Choose all that apply.)
    A. Local
    B. Grouped
    C. Named
    D. Global

3. Why would you install the express package?
    A. Simplify website creation
    B. Provide session management
    C. Simplify retrieval of static content
    D. All of the above

Lesson 2: Working with web services

In the previous lesson, you saw how you can create a website that can serve webpages and provide HTML responses to requests. One problem with the website scenario is that posting form data causes a response that repaints the page with the HTML result. If the HTML response looks like the existing page, you waste bandwidth and resources to repaint the page.

Web services provide the ability to send data to the server and receive data back from the server without requiring a repaint of the browser screen. There are various types of web services, and this lesson helps you understand them. You also use Node.js to create a web service.

To send requests to a web service from your webpage, you will be using AJAX, which stands for Asynchronous JavaScript and XML. Using AJAX, you can write JavaScript that asynchronously calls the server and processes the result. While this is happening, the user's screen doesn't lock up or freeze while waiting for the call to the server to complete.

> **After this lesson, you will be able to:**
> - Explain the difference between websites and web services.
> - Understand the differences between web service types.
> - Create a Node.js web service.
> - Use AJAX to call a web service.
>
> **Estimated lesson time: 30 minutes**

Introducing web services

A web service provides communications between a web server and a client. The client can be a web browser, another web service, a cell phone, or any machine that can communicate with the web service. A client needs the ability to assemble a request, send the request to the web service, and then receive the response and parse it.

As web services become more pervasive, developers can create applications by just piecing together web services. This is known as creating *mashups*.

There are two major classes of web services. The first is called Representational State Transfer (REST), in which the primary purpose of the service is to manipulate web resources by using a uniform set of stateless operations. The second is arbitrary web services, in which the service might expose an arbitrary set of operations. An example implementation of REST web service is called WEB API; an example of an arbitrary set of operations is the Microsoft Windows Communication Foundation (WCF).

Understanding Representational State Transfer (REST)

REST attempts to use the standard operations of HTTP (or similar protocols) by mapping create, retrieve, update, and delete (CRUD) operations to HTTP methods so that GET retrieves data or performs an operation that does not change server-side data. POST updates data but can retrieve data when complex parameter values need to be sent to the server. PUT inserts new data, and DELETE deletes data. REST focuses on interacting with stateless resources rather than on messages or operations. Clean URLs are tightly associated with the REST concept. Because the method infers a verb, the URL should describe the entity as a noun. Here are some examples of REST URLs.

- **Retrieve customer number five**   The number five is part of the URL and not part of the QueryString. The routing mechanism in the server would need to parse this correctly. Because this is retrieving data, the HTTP method would be set to GET. You can POST to this location to update or DELETE to this URL to delete the customer.

  ```
  http://localhost:8080/Customer/5
  ```

- **Retrieve vehicle with a Vehicle Identification Number (VIN) of ABC123**   The VIN is in the QueryString. Once again, the HTTP method is set to GET.

  ```
  http://localhost:8080/Vehicle?VIN=ABC123
  ```

- **Retrieve all orders**   The HTTP method is set to GET, and there is no parameter. A PUT to this URL adds an order.

  ```
  http://localhost:8080/Orders
  ```

- **Insert customer**   The HTTP method is set to PUT, and the postback data is in the request body, so you don't see the data in the URL or QueryString. The following is the URL and the postback data.

  ```
  http://localhost:8080/Customers
  name=ACME&Address=123+Bumblebee+Lane
  ```

To work around the problem when many firewalls don't allow PUT and DELETE methods, you can specify a verb in your QueryString or postback data. You should not change the URL to contain the method because that breaks the RESTful interface, which specifies that the URL must be a reference to an entity or entity collection. Here are a couple of examples of placing the verb in the data.

- **Delete vehicle with a Vehicle Identification Number (VIN) of ABC123**   The VIN is in the QueryString. The HTTP method is set to GET to get past the firewall.

  ```
  http://localhost:8080/Vehicle?verb=DELETE&VIN=ABC123
  ```

- **Insert customer**   The HTTP method is set to POST, and the postback data is in the request body, so you don't see the data in the URL or QueryString. The verb is set to PUT in the data. The following is the URL and the postback data.

  ```
  http://localhost:8080/Customers
  varb=PUT&name=ACME&Address=123+Bumblebee+Lane
  ```

You can implement security by using HTTPS protocol to encrypt the communications and basic authentication to require a user name and password to access resources.

The biggest benefits of using REST are that it is easy to connect to; it is lightweight and thin, so it doesn't consume many resources; and it is fast. In addition, REST does not need to use verbose XML when sending and receiving data. Many developers prefer to send data to the server as name=value pairs that are URI encoded (same as sending form data through POST or GET). When receiving data from the server, developers typically like to use JSON (JavaScript Object Notation) due to its compact size.

One of the biggest drawbacks to using REST is that some browsers support only GET and POST methods, whereas many firewalls allow passage of only GET and POST methods. Because of this problem, many developers create APIs that are similar to REST (are *RESTful*) when compatibility is maintained with browsers and firewalls and only GET and POST are used.

Understanding arbitrary web services

Arbitrary web services are also known as big web services. Arbitrary web services such as Windows Communication Foundation (WCF) don't attempt to map aspects of the protocol to operations because the exposed operations might be more arbitrary than providing simple REST operations. Arbitrary web services are more focused on the ability to offer more functionality such as message routing and various means of security that can provide partial message encryption and various forms of authentication.

Arbitrary web services typically have an interface format that enables the client to read and parse the information. This information enables the client to make calls to the web service immediately. One of the more common API formats is Web Services Description Language (WSDL), by which a WSDL document that fully describes the exposed operations can be retrieved from the web service.

Arbitrary web services require the client to assemble a request, or message, by using a specially formatted XML message called a Simple Object Access Protocol (SOAP) message. The web service is not required to communicate over HTTP protocol, and it's quite common to use HTTP protocol or for the web service to strip away the HTTP protocol layer and just use TCP protocol for better performance.

Creating a RESTful web service by using Node.js

The following describes creating a RESTful web service by using Node.js to expose the math_example package that was created in Lesson 1 as a RESTful service. In this example, GET, POST, PUT, and DELETE demonstrate that they can be used. In a real application, math operations would typically use the GET method on a Math entity, and the operation would be passed as a data parameter. For example, the following would be a more appropriate RESTful implementation of performing addition of two numbers.

```
http://localhost:8080/Math?operation=addition&x=10&y=45
```

In this example, a math_service folder is created under the node_samples folder, and the following package.json file is created.

```json
{
  "name": "math_service",
  "version": "0.0.0",
  "description": "A simple Web service",
  "main": "index.js",
  "scripts": {
    "test": "echo \"Error: no test specified\" && exit 1"
  },
  "repository": "",
  "author": "Glenn Johnson",
  "license": "BSD",
  "private": true,
  "dependencies": {
    "formidable": "1.x",
    "express": "3.0.0",
    "math_example": "0.x"
  }
}
```

In this example, there are three dependencies. After you create this file and save it, you can open a command prompt window, navigate to the math_service folder, and execute the following command to install the dependencies from npm.

```
npm install
```

After the installation completes, you can use these packages. In the math_service folder, create an app.js file and add references to these packages as follows.

```js
var express = require('express');
var app = express();
var formidable = require('formidable');
var math = require('math_example');
```

After setting up the package references, create a public folder under the math_service folder and use the app object to mount the public folder as the root of the website. The public folder will house webpages. The code should look like the following.

```js
app.use(express.static(__dirname + '/public'));
```

In this example, the operations will be part of the URL, so the addition operation is created by adding the following code.

```js
app.get('/addition', function (request, response) {
    var x = Number(request.query.x),
        y = Number(request.query.y),
        result = math.addition(x, y);

    response.writeHead(200, { 'Content-Type': 'application/json' });
    response.end('{ "result": ' + result + '}');
    console.log('Handled addition request for x=' + x + ' : y=' + y);
});
```

The addition operation uses the GET method as signified by the app.get function call. This creates a route by which a GET request that matches addition executes the code block. In the code block, three variables (*x*, *y*, and *result*) are declared and initialized. The *x* and *y* parameters are retrieved from the QueryString and converted to numbers. Next, the result is populated by executing the addition method on the math object with *x* and *y*. Finally, the response object is used to write the status code in which 200 is a success, and the content type is set to return a JSON result. The response object is then used to write the JSON object.

In this example, the JSON object is represented by curly braces. One property is called result, and its value is set to the result of the addition method call.

At the end of the file, add the following code to start the web service.

```
var port = 8080;
app.listen(port);
console.log('Listening on port: ' + port);
```

After saving the app.js file, you can start the web service by executing the following command.

```
node app
```

To test this, you can use the browser, but depending on the browser you use, you might need to click through several prompts to view the results. Here is the URL.

```
http://localhost:8080/addition?x=5&y=10
```

When you finally see the result, it should look like the following.

```
{ "result": 15}
```

The code in this example is similar to the code on the math_user website; however, that site returned HTML, albeit crude HTML, whereas this example returned a JSON object. This is your web service, but how can you call it from a webpage and use the return object? This is when AJAX comes into play.

Using AJAX to call a web service

Use AJAX to create asynchronous calls to web services. AJAX *is* JavaScript. You can think of it as being advanced JavaScript. Instead of designing a submit button to post the data back to the server and then watching the screen be repainted, JavaScript calls back to the server and processes the result without causing a complete repaint of the screen.

Create and consider the following Math.html webpage that is created in the public folder of math_service.

```
<!DOCTYPE html>
<html xmlns="http://www.w3.org/1999/xhtml">
<head>
    <title></title>
    <script type="text/javascript" src="/scripts/jquery-1.8.2.min.js"></script>
    <script type="text/javascript" src="/scripts/default.js"></script>
```

```
    </head>
    <body>
        <form id="mathForm">
            Enter X:<input type="text" id="x" /><br />
            Enter Y:<input type="text" id="y" /><br />
            Result: <span id="result"></span><br />
            <button id="btnAdd" type="button">Add</button>
        </form>
    </body>
</html>
```

Under the public folder, create a scripts folder and a default.js JavaScript file to contain your code. Add the jQuery library to this folder. You can get the jQuery library from *http://jquery.com* if you don't already have it.

The Math.html file contains the basic HTML user interface elements needed to collect data from the user and display a result. In this example, the *<form>* element isn't needed because the form will never be submitted. The *<form>* element is used only as a means of grouping the form controls. If the form will be used to submit data to the server, the name attributes of the form submission elements must be set. In this example, JavaScript and jQuery will be used to access these elements and make the AJAX call.

Using XMLHttpRequest

The primary object that makes an AJAX call is XMLHttpRequest. As the name implies, this object certainly can be used to send and receive XML data, but it can also be used to send and receive other data. In its simplest form, you can use this object as follows.

```
var xmlhttp=new XMLHttpRequest();
xmlhttp.open("GET","/addition?x=5&y=10",false);
xmlhttp.send();
var xmlDoc=xmlhttp.responseXML;
```

The first line creates a new XMLHttpRequest object and assigns it to the *xmlhttp* variable. The next line sets up the request to use the GET method with a relative URL of /addition and QueryString of x=5&y=10. The last parameter (false) indicates whether the operation is to be performed asynchronously when false means that operation is synchronous. The open method does not communicate to the server; it just sets up the request. The xmlhttp. send method call communicates to the server. Because the communication in this example is synchronous, JavaScript execution will not advance to the next line of code until the communication is completed. The next line sets the *xmlDoc* variable to the xmlhttp.responseXML property. From there, you can parse the XML as part of processing the results.

In the math web service, the result is not XML; it's JSON, so the last line of code needs to change. In addition to having a responseXML property, the XMLHttpRequest object has a response property that is a string. The response string needs to be converted to an object, and the JSON.parse method can accomplish the task. In addition, the URL must be pieced together by taking the values from text boxes to build this QueryString. The following code can be added to the default.js file to make the AJAX call.

```
$(document).ready(function () {
    $('#btnAdd').on('click', addNumbers)
});

function addNumbers() {
    var x = document.getElementById('x').value;
    var y = document.getElementById('y').value;
    var result = document.getElementById('result');
    var xmlhttp = new XMLHttpRequest();
    xmlhttp.open("GET", "/addition?x=" + x + "&y=" + y , false);
    xmlhttp.send();
    var jsonObject = JSON.parse(xmlhttp.response);
    result.innerHTML = jsonObject.result;
}
```

The first part of this code uses jQuery and adds the subscription to the btnAdd button after the document is ready. This causes the addNumbers function to execute when the button is clicked.

The addNumbers function doesn't use jQuery yet. First, the *x* and *y* values are extracted from the *<input>* elements. The *result* variable is set to reference the *<span>* element whose id is result. The XMLHttpRequest object is created, and then the open method is executed with a constructed QueryString. The send method is executed, and the response is parsed to create an object. Finally, the innerHTML for the result *<span>* element is populated with the result property value from the server. To test this page, first execute the following command to start the web service.

```
node app
```

After the web service is running, open the browser and enter the following URL.

```
http://localhost:8080/Math.html
```

Enter values in *X* and *Y* and click the Add button. You should see the result as shown in Figure 8-12.

FIGURE 8-12 The AJAX call displaying the proper result

Now that the code is operational, you might want to execute the AJAX call asynchronously. You can do this by locating the open method call and changing the false to true. However, because that setting causes a thread to be created and the send method to be called, the code won't wait for the result to be returned. Instead, the program continues to the next line of code, where it attempts to process the result even though the result might not have arrived from the server. To handle the asynchronous call, you must subscribe to the *onready-statechange* event, which is triggered whenever the state of XMLHttpRequest changes. If the ready state changes to 4, the call has completed, but you must also test the HTTP status code to ensure that no error has occurred by verifying that the return code is 200. The following is the modified addNumber function that correctly handles the asynchronous call.

```
function addNumbers() {
    var x = document.getElementById('x').value;
    var y = document.getElementById('y').value;
    var result = document.getElementById('result');
    var xmlhttp = new XMLHttpRequest();
    xmlhttp.onreadystatechange = function () {
        if (xmlhttp.readyState == 4 && xmlhttp.status == 200) {
            var jsonObject = JSON.parse(xmlhttp.response);
            result.innerHTML = jsonObject.result;
        }
    }
    xmlhttp.open("GET", "/addition?x=" + x + "&y=" + y , true);
    xmlhttp.send();
}
```

You might be wondering what the number 4 means. The following is a list of the readyState codes.

- **0 Uninitialized**   The open method has not been called yet.
- **1 Loading**   The send method has not been called yet.
- **2 Loaded**   The send method has been called; headers and status are available.
- **3 Interactive**   Downloading; the response properties hold the partial data.
- **4 Completed**   All operations are finished.

As these values show, you need to subscribe to the onreadystatechange event before you call the open method.

Handling progress

If the server provides progress events, you can subscribe to the progress event at the browser. You can add an event listener to subscribe to the progress event and execute code each time the event is triggered, as shown in the following code.

```
function addNumbers() {
    var x = document.getElementById('x').value;
    var y = document.getElementById('y').value;
    var result = document.getElementById('result');
    var xmlhttp = new XMLHttpRequest();
    xmlhttp.onreadystatechange = function () {
```

```
        if (xmlhttp.readyState == 4 && xmlhttp.status == 200) {
            var jsonObject = JSON.parse(xmlhttp.response);
            result.innerHTML = jsonObject.result;
        }
    }
    xmlhttp.addEventListener("progress", updateProgress, false);
    xmlhttp.open("GET", "/addition?x=" + x + "&y=" + y , true);
    xmlhttp.send();
}

function updateProgress(evt) {
    if (evt.lengthComputable) {
        var percentComplete = evt.loaded / evt.total;
        //display percenComplete
    } else {
        // Need total size to compute progress
    }
}
```

The server must provide a value for both the loaded property and the total property for this to work properly. The progress event might be most useful when loading a large amount of data to the browser or loading a large file.

Handling errors

If an error occurs, the HTTP status code will be something other than 200. You can also subscribe to the error and abort events, as shown in the following code example.

```
function addNumbers() {
    var x = document.getElementById('x').value;
    var y = document.getElementById('y').value;
    var result = document.getElementById('result');
    var xmlhttp = new XMLHttpRequest();
    xmlhttp.onreadystatechange = function () {
        if (xmlhttp.readyState == 4 && xmlhttp.status == 200) {
            var jsonObject = JSON.parse(xmlhttp.response);
            result.innerHTML = jsonObject.result;
        }
    }
    xmlhttp.addEventListener("progress", updateProgress, false);
    xmlhttp.addEventListener("error", failed, false);
    xmlhttp.addEventListener("abort", canceled, false);

    xmlhttp.open("GET", "/addition?x=" + x + "&y=" + y , true);
    xmlhttp.send();
}

function transferFailed(evt) {
  alert("An error occurred");
}

function canceled(evt) {
  alert("canceled by the user");
}
```

Now that you know about the XMLHttpRequest object, be aware that browsers might implement this object differently. Therefore, rather than write a large amount of code to deal with differences, use one of the jQuery wrappers for XMLHttpRequest.

Using jQuery XMLHttpRequest wrappers

You can use jQuery to simplify AJAX calls and be browser independent. The jQuery methods can be executed synchronously or asynchronously. The following is a list of the available jQuery methods; remember that the jQuery object is aliased to the dollar sign ($) to save typing so many characters. Where there is no dollar sign, the method can be executed on jQuery objects that are referenced with a selector.

- **$.ajax()**   Low-level interface to perform an AJAX request

- **.ajaxComplete()**   Global AJAX event handler to register a handler to be called when AJAX requests complete

- **.ajaxError()**   Global AJAX event handler to register a handler to be called when AJAX requests complete with an error

- **$.ajaxPrefilter()**   Low-level interface that handles custom AJAX options before each request is sent and before $.ajax() processes the requests

- **.ajaxSend()**   Global AJAX event handler that you use to attach a function to be executed before an AJAX request is sent

- **$.ajaxSetup()**   Low-level interface that sets default values for future AJAX requests

- **.ajaxStart()**   Global AJAX event handler to register a handler to be called when the first AJAX request begins

- **.ajaxStop()**   Global AJAX event handler to register a handler to be called when all AJAX requests have completed

- **.ajaxSuccess()**   Global AJAX event handler to attach a function to be executed whenever an AJAX request completes successfully

- **$.get()**   Shorthand method to load data from the server by using an HTTP GET request

- **$.getJSON()**   Shorthand method to load JSON-encoded data from the server by using a GET HTTP request

- **$.getScript()**   Shorthand method to load a JavaScript file from the server by using a GET HTTP request and then execute it

- **.load()**   Shorthand method to load data from the server and place the returned HTML in the matched element

- **$.param()**   Helper method to create a serialized representation of an array or object, suitable for use in a URL query string or an AJAX request

- **$.post()**   Shorthand method to load data from the server by using an HTTP POST request

- **.serialize()** Helper method to encode a set of form elements as a string for submission

- **.serializeArray()** Helper method to encode a set of form elements as an array of names and values

Some of these methods are discussed in later chapters, but you can get more information at *http://jquery.com.*

The $.ajax() method is a wrapper for the XMLHttpRequest object that provides a browser-independent way to write your AJAX call. The $.ajax() method accepts an object parameter that contains all the settings for the AJAX call. The following code example is a replacement for the addNumber function.

```
function addNumbers() {
    var x = $('#x').val();
    var y = $('#y').val();
    var data = { "x": x, "y": y };
    $.ajax({
        url: '/addition',
        data: data,
        type: 'GET',
        cache: false,
        dataType: 'json',
        success: function (data) {
            $('#result').html(data.result);
        }
    });
}
```

In this example, jQuery retrieves the values of *x* and *y*. A data variable object is then created to hold *x* and *y*. The $.ajax() call is executed next; it takes an object argument with all the settings for the call. In this example, the object is created inline. The url property is set, and the data is set to the data object created in the previous statement. The type property is the HTTP method, which supports GET, POST, PUT, and DELETE, but remember that many firewalls block PUT and DELETE. The cache property is set to false to indicate that the result should not be cached. The dataType property defines the type of data you expect to receive from the server and can be set to 'json', 'xml', 'html', 'script', 'jsonp', or 'text'.

> *NOTE* **CROSS-DOMAIN ACCESS BY USING JSONP**
> Using JSONP provides cross-domain access to an existing JSON API by wrapping a JSON payload in a function call. This is considered obsolete; the replacement is to use cross-origin resource sharing (CORS). CORS is described later in this lesson.

The last property, success, is set to a function to execute when the call returns successful. This could be a function name that contains the code or, as shown in the example, this could be an anonymous function with the code. This code runs asynchronously like the previous XMLHttpRequest code.

You can use a more concise way to write this code with the $.get() method instead or, better yet, use the $.getJSON() method, as shown in the following example.

```
function addNumbers() {
    var x = $('#x').val();
    var y = $('#y').val();
    var data = { "x": x, "y": y };
    $.getJSON('/addition', data, function (data) {
            $('#result').html(data.result);
    });
}
```

The size of the addNumbers function has dropped substantially! This is a good time to implement the other math functions. For the implementation of the other functions, the HTML page has buttons added as follows.

```
<!DOCTYPE html>
<html xmlns="http://www.w3.org/1999/xhtml">
<head>
    <title></title>
    <script type="text/javascript" src="/scripts/jquery-1.8.2.min.js"></script>
    <script type="text/javascript" src="/scripts/default.js"></script>
</head>
<body>
    <form id="mathForm">
        Enter X:<input type="text" id="x" /><br />
        Enter Y:<input type="text" id="y" /><br />
        Result: <span id="result"></span><br />
        <button id="btnAdd" type="button">Add</button>
        <button id="btnSubtract" type="button">Subtract</button>
        <button id="btnMultiplication" type="button">Multiplication</button>
        <button id="btnDivision" type="button">Division</button>
    </form>
</body>
</html>
```

At the top of the default.js file, code is added to subscribe to the button click events for the new buttons, as shown in the following code example.

```
$(document).ready(function () {
    $('#btnAdd').on('click', addNumbers)
    $('#btnSubtract').on('click', subtractNumbers)
    $('#btnMultiplication').on('click', multiplyNumbers)
    $('#btnDivision').on('click', divideNumbers)
});
```

For the subtractNumbers function, you can use the $.post() method where the HTTP POST method is required. For the multiplyNumbers function where the HTTP PUT method will be used, and for the divideNumbers function where an HTTP DELETE method will be used, the $.ajax() method will be called. The following code example demonstrates these functions, but they won't work until the app.js file is updated to accept these calls.

```
function subtractNumbers() {
    var x = $('#x').val();
```

```
        var y = $('#y').val();
        var data = { "x": x, "y": y };
        $.post('/subtraction', data, function (data) {
                $('#result').html(data.result);
            }, 'json');
    }

    function multiplyNumbers() {
        var x = $('#x').val();
        var y = $('#y').val();
        var data = { "x": x, "y": y };
        $.ajax({
            url: '/multiply',
            data: data,
            type: 'PUT',
            dataType: 'json',
            cache: false,
            success: function (data) {
                $('#result').html(data.result);
            }
        });
    }

    function divideNumbers() {
        var x = $('#x').val();
        var y = $('#y').val();
        var data = { "x": x, "y": y };
        $.ajax({
            url: '/divide',
            data: data,
            type: 'DELETE',
            dataType: 'json',
            cache: false,
            success: function (data) {
                $('#result').html(data.result);
            }
        });
    }
```

The following is the completed app.js file that shows the routing for the subtraction, multiply, and divide requests.

```
var express = require('express');
var app = express();
var formidable = require('formidable');
var math = require('math_example');

app.use(express.static(__dirname + '/public'));

app.get('/addition', function (request, response) {
    var x = Number(request.query.x),
        y = Number(request.query.y),
        result = math.addition(x, y);

    response.writeHead(200, { 'Content-Type': 'application/json' });
```

```
            response.end('{ "result": ' + result + '}');
            console.log('Handled addition request for x=' + x + ' : y=' + y);
    });

    app.post('/subtraction', function (request, response) {
        var form = new formidable.IncomingForm();
        form.parse(request, function (err, fields) {
            var x = Number(fields.x),
                y = Number(fields.y),
                result = math.subtraction(x, y);
            response.writeHead(200, { 'Content-Type': 'application/json' });
            response.end('{ "result": ' + result + '}');
            console.log('Handled subtraction request for x=' + x + ' : y=' + y);
        });
    });

    app.put('/multiply', function (request, response) {
        var form = new formidable.IncomingForm();
        form.parse(request, function (err, fields) {
            var x = Number(fields.x),
                y = Number(fields.y),
                result = math.multiplication(x, y);
            response.writeHead(200, { 'Content-Type': 'application/json' });
            response.end('{ "result": ' + result + '}');
            console.log('Handled multiplication request for x=' + x + ' : y=' + y);
        });
    });

    app.delete('/divide', function (request, response) {
        var form = new formidable.IncomingForm();
        form.parse(request, function (err, fields) {
            var x = Number(fields.x),
                y = Number(fields.y),
                result = math.division(x, y);
            response.writeHead(200, { 'Content-Type': 'application/json' });
            response.end('{ "result": ' + result + '}');
            console.log('Handled division request for x=' + x + ' : y=' + y);
        });
    });

var port = 8080;
app.listen(port);
console.log('Listening on port: ' + port);
```

Using jQuery promises

You can see that jQuery simplifies the AJAX calls. All these functions execute the same code when successful, and you might want to refactor this code to call a common function. You might also be working with a large application that calls addNumbers from multiple functions, but you want different code to execute on success. There is no code to deal with errors. You also might want to execute cleanup code regardless of whether the AJAX call is successful or failed. Most important, you might want to execute another AJAX call after the first AJAX call is successful. You can use promises to accomplish this.

When you use jQuery to execute an AJAX call, a promise object is returned. Think of a promise as being a promise to do work. The promise object enables you to register a callback method to execute when the AJAX call is successful, has failed, is progressing, and has completed. The promise object has the following methods that you can use to register called functions.

- **always()** Add handlers to be called when the AJAX call has completed, regardless of whether it was successful
- **done()** Add handlers to be called when the AJAX call is successful
- **fail()** Add handlers to be called when the AJAX call has failed
- **progress()** Add handlers to be called when the AJAX call generates progress notifications

The following code demonstrates the refactoring of the addNumbers function to use the promise that's returned from the AJAX call.

```
function addNumbers() {
    var data = getFormData();
    serverAddition(data).done(displayResult);
}

function getFormData() {
    var x = $('#x').val();
    var y = $('#y').val();
    return { "x": x, "y": y };
}

function serverAddition(data) {
    return $.getJSON('/addition', data);
}

function displayResult(serverData) {
    $('#result').html(serverData.result);
}
```

So what happened here? It looks like the code grew in size, and in some respects, it did, but the code got cleaner, too. The serverAddition function handles the AJAX call to the server but does not attempt to handle the results. Instead, the serverAddition function returns a promise object, and the caller can decide how to handle the result.

The addNumbers function is responsible for collecting the data to pass to the serverAddition function and deciding how to process the result. To collect the data, a call is made to the getFormData function that collects the data and creates an object that can be used for the AJAX call. The data object is passed to the serverAddition function. The returned promise is used by chaining a call to the done method. The done method requires a function parameter, which can be an anonymous function as in the previous examples, or you can pass the name of a function as in the example where the displayResult function is specified. Creating a specific function enables the other functions to call the displayResult function, which helps promote code reuse. The following is the default.js file after refactoring the other functions.

```
$(document).ready(function () {
    $('#btnAdd').on('click', addNumbers)
    $('#btnSubtract').on('click', subtractNumbers)
    $('#btnMultiplication').on('click', multiplyNumbers)
    $('#btnDivision').on('click', divideNumbers)
});

function addNumbers() {
    var data = getFormData();
    serverAddition(data).done(displayResult);
}

function getFormData() {
    var x = $('#x').val();
    var y = $('#y').val();
    return { "x": x, "y": y };
}

function serverAddition(data) {
    return $.getJSON('/addition', data);
}

function displayResult(serverData) {
    $('#result').html(serverData.result);
}

function subtractNumbers() {
    var data = getFormData();
    serverSubtraction(data).done(displayResult);
}

function serverSubtraction(data) {
    return $.post('/subtraction', data, 'json');
}

function multiplyNumbers() {
    var data = getFormData();
    serverMultiplication(data).done(displayResult);
}

function serverMultiplication(data) {
    return $.ajax({
                url: '/multiply',
                data: data,
                type: 'PUT',
                dataType: 'json',
                cache: false
            });
}

function divideNumbers() {
    var data = getFormData();
    serverDivision(data).done(displayResult);
}
```

```
function serverDivision(data) {
    return $.ajax({
                url: '/divide',
                data: data,
                type: 'DELETE',
                dataType: 'json',
                cache: false
        });
}
```

If you display the webpage and enter numbers for *x* and *y*, you should see proper return values until you try to divide by zero. In JavaScript, dividing by zero doesn't throw an exception; it returns infinity. The conversion to a JSON object will, however, throw a parse error, so no value is displayed.

To solve this problem, a displayError function is added, and the promise's fail method is used to subscribe to the failure of the AJAX call, as shown in the following code example.

```
function divideNumbers() {
    var data = getFormData();
    serverDivision(data).done(displayResult).fail(displayError);
}

function displayError(serverData, error) {
    var value = 'No result';
    if ('result' in serverData) value = serverData.result;
    $('#result').html(value + ' - ' + error);
}
```

The fail method is chained to the serverDivision call after the done method call. In addition, the displayError function determines whether serverData has a result property by using the *in* keyword. If the result property exists, its value will be displayed. This function has a second parameter, called error, that identifies the source of the error. Both of these items are concatenated and displayed.

Cross-origin resource sharing

In the previous examples, the Math.html webpage came from the same website that contained the web service, and the URL for the web service requests was a relative URL on the site. If the Math.html page had AJAX called, and it contained URLs to access web services on other websites, the AJAX call would fail because this represents a potential cross-site scripting (XSS) attack. There are ways to allow cross-site AJAX calls, the most common of which is *cross-origin resource sharing (CORS)*. CORS is a browser specification that defines ways for a web server to allow its resources to be accessed by a webpage from a different domain. CORS provides a compromise by which you can configure access across domains instead of allowing everyone access or denying everyone access.

You implement CORS on the web server by sending the Access-Control-Allow-Origin header when the web service is accessed. Here is an example of the header.

```
Access-Control-Allow-Origin: *
```

This example allows anyone to access the web service, but that could open the site for XSS attacks from malicious websites. It's generally preferred to list the allowed sites explicitly, as follows.

```
Access-Control-Allow-Origin: http://contoso.com:8080 http://www.adventure-works.com/
```

 Quick check

- You have a web service that provides read-only access to data. You want to expose this web service so it can be called from any other website. What header would you return?

Quick check answer

- Use the following header.

```
Access-Control-Allow-Origin: *
```

Lesson summary

- Web services provide the ability to send data to the server and receive data back from the server without requiring a repaint of the browser screen.

- AJAX, which stands for Asynchronous JavaScript and XML, enables you to write JavaScript that asynchronously calls the server and processes the result.

- Piecing multiple web services together to create an application is called a mashup.

- Representational State Transfer (REST) is implemented by manipulating web resources, using a uniform set of stateless operations. REST attempts to use the standard operations of HTTP (or similar protocols) by mapping *CRUD* (create, retrieve, update, and delete) operations to HTTP methods.

- Arbitrary web services expose an arbitrary set of operations and are known as big web services. They typically use specially formatted XML messages called SOAP (Simple Object Access Protocol) messages. The primary object that makes an AJAX call is XMLHttpRequest.

- You can use jQuery to create browser-independent asynchronous calls to the server. JQuery has a promise object you can use to register functions to execute when the AJAX call is progressing, is successful, has failed, or has completed. A promise object is returned from all AJAX calls.

- Cross-origin resource sharing (CORS) can be implemented at the server to allow browsers to make calls to the web service from other domains.

Lesson review

Answer the following questions to test your knowledge of the information in this lesson. You can find the answers to these questions and explanations of why each answer choice is correct or incorrect in the "Answers" section at the end of this chapter.

1. You want to create a REST service for your internal web service and use the HTTP verbs that match CRUD operations. You know the browser your users will be using is compatible, and the firewall will not be a problem. What are the HTTP verbs that match with CRUD (in order)?

   A. CREATE, POST, GET, DELETE

   B. GET, RETRIEVE, UPDATE, DELETE

   C. PUT, GET, POST, DELETE

   D. POST, GET, UPDATE, DELETE

2. What is the primary object used to make an asynchronous AJAX call that returns a JSON result?

   A. XMLHttpRequest

   B. AjaxRequest

   C. JsonResponse

   D. AjaxAsync

3. You want to use jQuery to make an AJAX call that will use the HTTP POST method. Which jQuery method can you use?

   A. $.post()

   B. $.getJSON()

   C. $.get()

   D. $.param()

Practice exercises

If you encounter a problem completing any of these exercises, the completed projects can be installed from the Practice Exercises folder that is provided with the companion content.

Exercise 1: Create a website to receive data

In this exercise, you apply your website, web service, and Node.js knowledge by creating a website that receives postback data from the ContactUs.html page of the WebCalculator project that you modified in the previous chapter. You create the website in a folder separate from your WebCalculator solution and then copy the WebCalculator project to a subdirectory of the website. In this scenario, Node.js can still serve pages from the WebCalculator project. From the Node.js perspective, all the files are in its website, but you can still open the WebCalculator solution in Visual Studio as needed.

1. If you haven't done so yet, install Node.js from *http://nodejs.org/*.

2. Open the command prompt window.

3. Create a folder for the new website.

   This requires you to navigate to the location and then create the folder. For example, the following commands navigate to the Practice Exercises folder on the root of the C drive, create a new ContosoWeb folder, and then navigate to the new folder.

   ```
   C:
   cd \Practice Exercises
   md ContosoWeb
   cd ContosoWeb
   ```

4. In the Resources folder, find the WebCalculator solution. Copy the solution and paste it into the ContosoWeb folder.

5. In the ContosoWeb folder, create a package.json file by typing the following command.

   ```
   npm init
   ```

   This command starts the wizard. Enter the following.

   - name: ContosoWeb
   - version: 0.0.0
   - description: Contoso Web Site
   - main: index.js
   - keywords: Contoso, WebCalculator
   - author: *your name*
   - license: BSD

6. Open the package.json file and add a dependency on the express and formidable packages, as shown in the following modified package.json file.

   ```
   {
     "name": "ContosoWeb",
     "version": "0.0.0",
     "description": "Contoso Web Site",
     "main": "index.js",
     "scripts": {
       "test": "echo \"Error: no test specified\" && exit 1"
     },
     "repository": "",
     "keywords": [
       "Contoso",
       "WebCalculator"
     ],
     "author": "Glenn Johnson",
     "license": "BSD",
     "dependencies": {
   ```

```
    "formidable": "1.x",
    "express": "3.0.0"
  }
}
```

7. Install the dependent packages by typing the following command.

```
npm install
```

8. Open Visual Studio Express 2012 for Web. Click File and choose Open Web Site; select the ContosoWeb folder.

9. In the Contoso website folder, create an index.js file and add a reference to the express and formidable packages as follows.

```
var express = require('express');
var app = express();
var formidable = require('formidable');
```

10. Add a statement to map static requests to the WebSolution/WebCalculator folder as follows.

```
app.use(express.static(__dirname + '/WebCalculatorSolution/WebCalculator'));
```

11. Add code to redirect the user to the default.html page if the URL does not include a file name, as follows.

```
app.get('/', function (request, response) {
    response.redirect('default.html');
});
```

12. Add code to listen on port 8080 and log a message to the console stating this. The index.js file should look like the following.

```
var express = require('express');
var app = express();
var formidable = require('formidable');

app.use(express.static(__dirname + '/WebCalculatorSolution/WebCalculator'));

app.get('/', function (request, response) {
    response.redirect('default.html');
});


var port = 8080;
app.listen(port);
console.log('Listening on port: ' + port);
```

13. Test your work by running the website and using the following command in the command prompt window.

```
node index
```

14. If you see a pop-up prompt stating that Windows Firewall has blocked some features, as shown in Figure 8-13, make sure both check boxes are selected and click the Allow Access button to continue.

FIGURE 8-13 Accepting both options when prompted

15. After starting the website, open the web browser and type **http://localhost:8080** to see the Contoso home page.

Be sure to clear the cache for the page by pressing Ctrl+F5. You should see the Contoso home page and be able to click the link for the ContactUs page to see that page.

16. Modify the index.js file so that a POST to /ContactMessage returns a thank you message to the customer and logs a small message to the console window as follows.

```
app.post('/ContactMessage', function (request, response) {
    var form = new formidable.IncomingForm();
    form.parse(request, function (err, fields) {
        var lastName = fields.lastName,
            firstName = fields.firstName,
            email =  fields.email,
            message = fields.message;

        response.writeHead(200, { 'Content-Type': 'text/html' });
        response.write('Thank you, ' + firstName + ' ' + lastName + '<br/>');
        response.write('We will contact you at ' + email + '<br/>');
        response.end('Your message: ' + message + '<br />');
        console.log('Handled request for ' + firstName + ' ' + lastName);
    });
});
```

17. In Visual Studio, open the ContactUs.html page and change the *<form>* element to POST to the /ContactMessage URL.

The modified *<form>* element should look like the following.

```
<form name="ContactForm" method="post" action="/ContactMessage">
```

18. Stop and start the website and then open the browser and navigate to the ContactUs. html page. Be sure to refresh the cache by pressing Ctrl+F5.

19. Enter data into the form and click the Submit button.

You should see the response in the browser window, as shown in Figure 8-14.

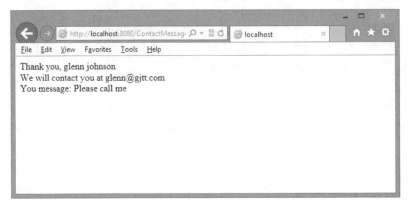

FIGURE 8-14 The processed form

Wouldn't it be nice to put the message on the page without repainting the page?

Exercise 2: Create a web service to receive data

In this exercise, you modify the existing website from Exercise 1 by adding a web service to accept the data and return a response that is displayed on the ContactUs.html page.

1. Stop running Node.js if it's running.

2. Open the index.js file. Create a copy of the app.post() function that you created in Exercise 1. Modify the copy so that it will be the web service and accessible by using the /ContactService-relative URL. Modify the code so that a JSON object is returned with a result property that contains the same message that was on the webpage response from Exercise 1. Modify the message logged to the console so that you can tell the difference between handling a page postback and a web service post.

The completed index.js file should look like the following.

```
var express = require('express');
var app = express();
var formidable = require('formidable');

app.use(express.static(__dirname + '/WebCalculatorSolution/WebCalculator'));

app.get('/', function (request, response) {
    response.redirect('default.html');
```

```
    });

    app.post('/ContactMessage', function (request, response) {
        var form = new formidable.IncomingForm();
        form.parse(request, function (err, fields) {
            var lastName = fields.lastName,
                firstName = fields.firstName,
                email =   fields.email,
                message = fields.message;

            response.writeHead(200, { 'Content-Type': 'text/html' });
            response.write('Thank you, ' + firstName + ' ' + lastName + '<br/>');
            response.write('We will contact you at ' + email + '<br/>');
            response.end('You message: ' + message + '<br />');
            console.log('Handled request for ' + firstName + ' ' + lastName);
        });
    });

    app.post('/ContactService', function (request, response) {
        var form = new formidable.IncomingForm();
        form.parse(request, function (err, fields) {
            var lastName = fields.lastName,
                firstName = fields.firstName,
                email = fields.email,
                message = fields.message,
                result = 'Thank you, ' + firstName + ' ' + lastName + '<br/>'
                        + 'We will contact you at ' + email + '<br/>'
                        + 'You message: ' + message + '<br />';

            response.writeHead(200, { 'Content-Type': 'application/json' });
            response.end('{ "result": "' + result + '"}');
            console.log('Handled service request for ' + firstName + ' ' + lastName);
        });
    });

    var port = 8080;
    app.listen(port);
    console.log('Listening on port: ' + port);
```

3. Using Visual Studio, locate the scripts folder that contains the Calculator library.js file. Right-click the scripts folder and add a new JavaScript file called ContactUs.js.

4. Open the ContactUs.html file and add *<script>* elements for jQuery and the new ContactUs.js file.

5. Change the type attribute of the submit button from submit to button.

6. Add a *<div>* element after the end of the *<form>* element and set its id to result.

   The following is the completed ContactUs.html page.

```
<!DOCTYPE html>
<html xmlns="http://www.w3.org/1999/xhtml">
<head>
    <title>Contact Us</title>
    <link href="Content/default.css" rel="stylesheet" />
```

```html
        <script src="Scripts/jquery-1.8.2.js"></script>
        <script src="Scripts/ContactUs.js"></script>
    </head>
    <body>
        <div id="container">
            <header>
                <hgroup id="headerText">
                    <h1>Contoso Ltd.</h1>
                    <h2>Your success equals our success</h2>
                </hgroup>
            </header>
            <nav>
                <a href="default.html">Home</a>
            </nav>
            <div role="main">
                <div id="ContactUs">
                    <form name="ContactForm" method="post" action="/ContactMessage">
                        <div>
                            <label for="firstName">First Name:</label>
                            <input type="text" id="firstName" name="firstName"
                                required="required" />
                        </div>
                        <div>
                            <label for="lastName">Last Name:</label>
                            <input type="text" id="lastName" name="lastName"
                                required="required" />
                        </div>
                        <div>
                            <label for="email">Email Address:</label>
                            <input type="email" id="email" name="email"
                                required="required" />
                        </div>
                        <div>
                            <label for="message">Message:</label>
                            <textarea id="message" name="message"
                                required="required"></textarea>
                        </div>
                        <div>
                            <button type="button" id="submit"
                                name="submit">Submit</button>
                        </div>
                    </form>
                    <div id="result"></div>
                </div>
            </div>
            <aside>
                <p>Advertisements</p>
            </aside>
            <footer>
                <p>
                    Copyright &copy; 2012, Contoso Ltd., All rights reserved
                </p>
            </footer>
        </div>
    </body>
</html>
```

7. In the ContactUs.js file, add a callServer function that uses jQuery to make an AJAX call that posts the data to the /ContactService URL and puts the result into the <div id="result"> element.

Your code should look like the following.

```
function callServer() {
    var data = $('#ContactForm').serialize();
    $.post('/ContactService', data, function (returnObject) {
        $('#result').html(returnObject.result);
    },'json');
}
```

8. In the ContactUs.js file, add a reference to jQuery and add a $(document).ready() function with a call to subscribe to the click event of the submit button so that clicking the submit button executes the callServer function.

The completed ContactUs.js file should look like the following.

```
/// <reference path="jquery-1.8.2.js" />

$(document).ready(function () {
    $('#submit').on('click', callServer);
});

function callServer() {
    var data = $('form[name="ContactForm"]').serialize();
    $.post('/ContactService', data, function (returnObject) {
        $('#result').html(returnObject.result);
    }, 'json');
}
```

9. Stop and start ContosoWeb.

10. In the browser, navigate to the ContactUs.html page.

11. Press Ctrl+F5 to ensure that you have the latest version of the file.

12. Enter data in the form and click the Submit button.

Instead of seeing a new page, you should see the result on the same page, as shown in Figure 8-15.

FIGURE 8-15 The submitted form displaying a message on the same page

Suggested practice exercises

The following additional exercises are designed to give you more opportunities to practice what you've learned and to help you successfully master the lessons presented in this chapter.

- **Exercise 1**   Learn more about Node.js by creating a web service that has more functionality.
- **Exercise 2**   Learn more about web services by creating a web service in Visual Studio .NET using your choice of .NET language.

Answers

This section contains the answers to the lesson review questions in this chapter.

Lesson 1

1. **Correct answer: D**

    A. **Incorrect:** You can't publish a JavaScript file by itself because you need to include a manifest, which is the package.json file.

    B. **Incorrect:** A module is a file, and you can't publish a module by itself because you need to include a manifest, which is the package.json file.

    C. **Incorrect:** A file or module can contain classes, but the manifest, which is the package.json file, is required.

    D. **Correct:** The package contains a package.json manifest and the modules you want to publish.

2. **Correct answers: A and D**

    A. **Correct:** A package can be installed locally.

    B. **Incorrect:** Grouped is not a valid scope.

    C. **Incorrect:** Named is not a valid scope.

    D. **Correct:** A package can be installed globally.

3. **Correct answer: D**

    A. **Incorrect:** The express package, also known as expressjs, simplifies website creation but does more.

    B. **Incorrect:** The express package provides session management but does more.

    C. **Incorrect:** The express package simplifies retrieval of static content but does more.

    D. **Correct:** The express package simplifies website creation, provides session management, and simplifies retrieval of static content.

Lesson 2

1. **Correct answer: C**

    A. **Incorrect:** CREATE is not an HTTP method.

    B. **Incorrect:** RETRIEVE and UPDATE are not HTTP methods.

    C. **Correct:** PUT is for create, GET is for retrieve, POST is for update, and DELETE is for delete.

    D. **Incorrect:** UPDATE is not an HTTP method.

2. **Correct answer: A**

    A.   **Correct:** XMLHttpRequest is used to make AJAX calls.

    B.   **Incorrect:** AjaxRequest is not a valid object.

    C.   **Incorrect:** JsonResponse is not valid object.

    D.   **Incorrect:** AjaxAsync is not a valid object.

3. **Correct answer: A**

    A.   **Correct:** $.post() is used to POST.

    B.   **Incorrect:** $.getJSON() uses the HTTP GET method.

    C.   **Incorrect:** $.get() uses the HTTP GET method.

    D.   **Incorrect:** $.param() sets parameters and does not call the server.

CHAPTER 9

Asynchronous operations

Have you ever run an application and had the screen freeze when you clicked a button? You waited until its operation completed, and then the application started working again. Have you seen this behavior on webpages? You know that the problem is due to long-running operations, but shouldn't there be a better way to write this code?

The answer to these questions is to implement long-running operations as asynchronous operations because these operations are currently synchronous operations. Synchronous code has one sequential execution path, and when the long-running code is executing, nothing else can be accomplished. What's needed is another execution path so that the long-running code can execute on one execution path while the user interface is responsive on another execution path; this is what asynchronous operations do.

This chapter explores asynchronous operations, using jQuery and web workers.

Lessons in this chapter:

Before you begin

To complete this book, you must have some understanding of web development. This chapter requires the hardware and software listed in the "System requirements" section in the book's Introduction.

Lesson 1: Asynchronous operations using jQuery and WinJS

An *asynchronous operation* is executed on a thread that is different from the main thread, a *thread* being a separate execution path. The previous chapter provided a brief introduction to asynchronous programming when executing AJAX calls to the server. In addition to jQuery's support for using AJAX calls, you might want to perform local asynchronous calls for operations that are time consuming. For example, if you are performing animations by using jQuery, you'll find that jQuery animations are performed asynchronously.

This lesson focuses on jQuery's deferred and promise objects for controlling execution of asynchronous execution.

After this lesson, you will be able to:

- Describe asynchrony, using jQuery.
- Implement asynchronous operations by using the promise object.

Estimated lesson time: 20 minutes

Using a promise object

 The pattern for working with asynchrony is to use a promise object. The *promise* (also known as a *future* or *deferred*) object provides a mechanism to schedule work to be done on a value that might not yet be computed. The promise object can be in one of three states: pending, resolved, or rejected. It starts in the pending state, moves to either resolved or rejected, and then does not change. The benefit is that it enables you to write non-blocking logic that executes asynchronously without having to write a lot of synchronization and plumbing code.

CommonJS, which defines a specification for using JavaScript everywhere, defines the Promise/A specification that many JavaScript technologies implement. The promise object is implemented in WinJS and jQuery. After you understand the concept of a promise object, you'll find that it's easy to implement using any technology.

Consider the following synchronous code example that uses the XMLHttpRequest object to make an AJAX call.

```
function fetchAjaxSync(url) {
  var xhr = new XMLHttpRequest();
  xhr.open(url, "GET", false);
  xhr.send();
  if (xhr.status == 200) {
    return xhr;
  }
  throw new Error(xhr.statusText);
}
```

In this example, passing a value of *false* to the open method causes the code to run synchronously. When the send method is called, the program waits until the result is available and then proceeds to the next line of code, where the returned status is checked to determine whether an error occurred. In this example, the result can just be returned to the caller that is waiting for the operation to complete. It's as though the caller is pulling the result from the fetchAjaxSync function.

The code block is compact, easy to read, and simple. In this example, the AJAX call takes 30 seconds to complete, and other code cannot run. The result is that the screen appears to lock up until the AJAX call has completed. This is the case for providing an asynchronous programming model. The following code illustrates the rewrite.

```
function fetchAjaxAsync(url, callback, errorCallback) {
  var xhr = new XMLHttpRequest();
  xhr.onreadystatechange = function() {
    if (xhr.readyState == 4) {
      if (xhr.status == 200) {
        processResult();
      }
      else {
        errorCallback(new Error(xhr.statusText));
      }
    }
  }
  xhr.open(url, "GET", true);
  xhr.send();
}
```

In this example, passing a *true* value to the open method indicates that asynchrony is best. In addition, the onreadystatechanged event is assigned a function that executes whenever the XMLHttpRequest object changes state. When the state has a value of *4*, the operation is complete and the status is checked for an error. Because this is an asynchronous operation, the program doesn't wait when it calls the send method. Instead, the program proceeds to the next line and exits the fetchAjaxAsync function. When the result is available, a call to the processResult function is made, and the result is passed. It's as though the asynchronous call is pushing the result to the code that will process it.

This code block is certainly larger than the synchronous code block. It's also a bit harder to read, but the benefit is that there is no blocking, so the program remains fast and fluid.

When you have code that needs to chain several asynchronous calls, so each call must complete before the next call starts, you want to create an asynchronous call to a sequence of calls. This gets difficult quickly. Currently, the fetchAjaxAsync function is somewhat generic; you pass in the parameters and get a result. However, if you want to chain additional calls, you might need to modify this code to make it more specific to the task you're trying to accomplish. The promise object helps solve these problems and allows operations to chain easily.

Creating jQuery promise objects by using $.Deferred()

You can create a promise object by using the $.Deferred method. It seems a bit strange that the method name is not called $.Promise(), but $.Deferred() returns a deferred object that wraps the promise object with the functionality to control the promise object, as shown in Figure 9-1. The creator of the promise object controls the state of it by calling one of the methods on the deferred object. The methods that end with "with" pass data to the promise object's subscribers. The creator of the deferred object can execute the promise method on the deferred object to get the promise object, which is read-only. Code that references the promise object can subscribe to state changes on that object but cannot modify its state. For example, calling the done method on the promise object enables you to pass a function containing code that executes when the promise object is resolved (completed).

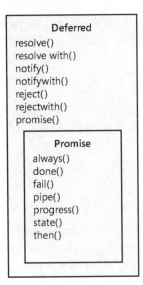

```
        Deferred
resolve()
resolve with()
notify()
notifywith()
reject()
rejectwith()
promise()

          Promise
    always()
    done()
    fail()
    pipe()
    progress()
    state()
    then()
```

FIGURE 9-1 The Deferred and Promise objects

The following is an example of using the $.Deferred() method to set a timeout that a user can subscribe to by using the methods on the promise object.

```
function timeoutAsync(milliseconds) {
    var deferred = $.Deferred();
    setTimeout(function () { deferred.resolve(); }, milliseconds);
    return deferred.promise();
}
```

In this code example, the function name ends with Async as a convention to help the developer understand that an asynchronous call is being made in this function. A deferred object is created by using the $.Deferred method and assigned to the deferred variable. Next, the JavaScript global function setTimeout is called, which has a function parameter and a timeout milliseconds parameter. The function parameter contains the code to execute when the timer expires. No application-specific code is in the function. Instead, the resolve method is called on the deferred object to indicate the completion of the timer. Calling the resolve method on the deferred object changes the state of the promise object to resolved and executes all code that was attached to the promise object by using the done method. In addition to the resolve method, you can call the reject method to indicate a failure of the asynchronous function. The following is an example of the use of the timeoutAsync function.

```
function abcAsync() {
    var promise = timeoutAsync(2000);
    promise.done(function () { alert('done!') });
    return promise;
}
```

In this example, the function name also ends with Async to indicate that it's asynchronous. It's important to keep this convention and always return a promise object that the called function can use to add more code to execute on completion or that the caller can use to check the state of the promise. The timeoutAsync function is called, which performs the time-out action but doesn't execute application-specific code. Next, the application-specific code is added to the promise object by calling the done method on the promise object and passing the code. When you subscribe to the promise object by using the done method, your code is executed upon successful completion (resolved, not rejected). Finally, the promise object is returned to the caller.

When this code is executed, there is a two-second delay, and then a pop-up is displayed with the message, "done!"

You can call the done method multiple times to add more code to be executed upon successful completion. The order in which you add the code is how the code will execute. In addition, the code is guaranteed to execute only once because you cannot change the state after it's been changed to resolved or failed.

Handling failure

You can execute code upon failure of the asynchronous call by subscribing to the promise object and using the fail method. The following example demonstrates the use of the fail method to execute code upon failure, which is the rejected state.

```
function abcAsync() {
    var promise = timeoutAsync(2000);
    promise.done(function () { alert('done!') });
    promise.fail(function () { alert('failed!') });
    return promise;
}
```

Handling completion cleanup

In addition to subscribing to success or failure, you can add code to execute when the asynchronous call has completed, regardless of success or failure. Subscribe to the promise object by using the always method. The following example demonstrates the use of the always method.

```
function abcAsync() {
    var promise = timeoutAsync(2000);
    promise.always(function () { alert('always!') });
    promise.done(function () { alert('done!') });
    promise.fail(function () { alert('failed!') });
    return promise;
}
```

Behind the scenes is a done collection of functions and a failed collection of functions. One of the collections of functions is executed upon the change from pending to either resolved or rejected. When you use the always method to add code to execute upon completion, your function is added to the done and failed collections. In this example, you see the "always!" message before the "done!" or "failed!" message because the always subscription is before the others. If the always subscription is the last subscription, it will execute last.

Subscribing to a completed promise object

It's useful to know that you can subscribe to the promise object even after it's been resolved. This immediately executes the function you pass to the done method. Consider the following example in which two promise objects are used to chain actions together, and the completion of secondPromise adds a function to firstPromise, which has already completed.

```
function abcAsync() {
    var firstPromise = timeoutAsync(2000);
    firstPromise.done(function () {
        var secondPromise = timeoutAsync(3000);
        secondPromise.done(function () {
            firstPromise.done(function () { alert('done!') });
        });
    });
    return firstPromise;
}
```

In this example, after 2 seconds, the firstPromise object completes, which starts a new timeout, thus creating the secondPromise object. After 3 seconds (5 seconds from the start of the function), the secondPromise object completes, which adds a function to the firstPromise object. Because the firstPromise object has already completed, the function is executed immediately. Existing subscriptions are not re-executed because the subscriber functions are guaranteed to execute only once.

Chaining promises by using the pipe method

There is a problem with the previous code example in that abcAsync is returning the first-Promise object. That is a problem because the abcAsync object should return a promise object that indicates the completion of all code within the function. In this case, when first-Promise is complete, code is still executing that's represented by the secondPromise object. It would be conceptually correct to try to return the secondPromise object, but the second-Promise object isn't even created for 2 seconds.

Did you also notice that chaining the second asynchronous operation required you to nest the second operation inside the successful completion code of the first asynchronous operation? When you need to chain three, four, or more operations, you can get caught up in nesting several levels and creating unmanageable code, as the following example demonstrates.

```
function abcAsync() {
    var firstPromise = timeoutAsync(2000);
    firstPromise.done(function () {
        var secondPromise = timeoutAsync(3000);
        secondPromise.done(function () {
            var thirdPromise = timeoutAsync(1000);
```

```
        thirdPromise.done(function () {
            var fourthPromise = timeoutAsync(1234);
            fourthPromise.done(function () {
                firstPromise.done(function () { alert('done!') });
            });
        });
    });
    return firstPromise;
}
```

To solve the problem, implement chaining by using the pipe function on the promise object. The following code is a rewrite of the previous example by using the pipe function to eliminate nesting.

```
function abcAsync() {
    var firstPromise = timeoutAsync(2000);
    var secondPromise = firstPromise.pipe(function () {
        return timeoutAsync(3000);
    });
    var thirdPromise = secondPromise.pipe(function () {
        return timeoutAsync(1000);
    });
    var fourthPromise = thirdPromise.pipe(function () {
        return timeoutAsync(1234);
    });
    fourthPromise.done(function () {
        firstPromise.done(function () { alert('done!') });
    });
    return fourthPromise;
}
```

In this example, the fourthPromise object is correctly returned so the caller can know when all code is completed. The calling function can also call the done, fail, or always methods on the returned promise object to add code to execute upon completion.

In the nested example is a 6-second delay before the fourthPromise object is created. Even if the *fourthPromise* variable were in scope, this would be a problem for the calling code that might want to subscribe to the returned promise object immediately, which will be null.

The pipe method immediately creates a promise object that can be subscribed to and properly returned to the caller. This is interesting because timeoutAsync(1234) still isn't called for 6 seconds, and that call was creating the fourthPromise object. The pipe method created a proxy object and returned it, but after 6 seconds, the call to timeoutAsync(1234) created a promise object, which was then attached to the original proxy object.

There's more to this story, however. If the first asynchronous call fails, the failure is automatically passed to the piped promise object in the chain. You don't require extra code to deal with this. You can subscribe to the fail of the fourthPromise object, and you will automatically be notified if any asynchronous call in the chain failed.

Quick check

- You want to chain several asynchronous calls together. Which promise method will you use?

Quick check answer

- Use the pipe method on the promise object.

Parallel execution using $.when().then()

The previous examples exhibited chained operations by which each operation waits for the previous operation to complete before starting. For example, the previous example took 7.234 seconds to complete. Sometimes this is necessary, but you might want to run the operations simultaneously. If you execute each operation in parallel, how can you know that all four operations completed?

You can use the $.when() method to indicate completion of multiple asynchronous operations. The $.when() method is non-blocking, so it's usually used with a deferred object. In the following example, the previous example is rewritten to run all four operations in parallel.

```
function abcAsync() {
    var deferred = $.Deferred();
    var firstPromise = timeoutAsync(2000);
    var secondPromise = timeoutAsync(3000);
    var thirdPromise = timeoutAsync(1000);
    var fourthPromise = timeoutAsync(1234);
    $.when(firstPromise, secondPromise, thirdPromise, fourthPromise)
        .then(function () { alert('done!'); deferred.resolve(); },
            function () { deferred.reject(); });
    return deferred.promise();
}
```

The $.when() method accepts promise parameters and monitors for all to complete. If a parameter is not a promise object, it is immediately considered to be completed. The $.when() method creates its own promise that is passed to the then() method, which first accepts a function to be executed upon success and then accepts a function to be executed upon failure. Not shown here is that the then() method also accepts a third function parameter to be executed when the progress changes.

Updating progress

The deferred object can also notify its promise object when progress has changed. It does this by executing the notify method of the deferred object when you want to update the progress.

The promise object has a progress method that accepts a function called when the notify method is executed.

The following example is a rewrite of the previous example; the deferred object notifies its subscribers of progress change.

```
function abcAsync() {
    var deferred = $.Deferred();
    var count = 0;
    var firstPromise = timeoutAsync(2000);
    var secondPromise = timeoutAsync(3000);
    var thirdPromise = timeoutAsync(1000);
    var fourthPromise = timeoutAsync(1234);
    firstPromise.always(function () { deferred.notify( ++count); });
    secondPromise.always(function () { deferred.notify(++count); });
    thirdPromise.always(function () { deferred.notify(++count); });
    fourthPromise.always(function () { deferred.notify(++count); });
    $.when(firstPromise, secondPromise, thirdPromise, fourthPromise)
        .then(function () { alert('done!'); deferred.resolve(); },
              function () { deferred.reject(); });
    return deferred.promise();
}
```

In this example, the *count* variable is initialized to zero, and then, upon completion of each asynchronous call, the *count* variable is incremented. The following code calls the abcAsync function and displays the progress.

```
function runAbcAsync() {
    var promise = abcAsync();
    promise.progress(function (msg) { alert(msg); });
    return promise;
}
```

In this example, as the progress is updated, a pop-up is displayed with the numeric value. The asynchronous calls can complete in any order.

Conditional asynchronous calls

Sometimes, you need to make an asynchronous call conditionally. In the case of chained operations in which a middle operation is conditionally executed, you need a way to splice in (or out) the operation. Consider the following example, in which the third asynchronous operation is conditionally executed.

```
function abcAsync(includeThird) {
    var firstPromise = timeoutAsync(2000);
    var secondPromise = firstPromise.pipe(function () {
        return timeoutAsync(3000);
    });
    var thirdPromise = includeThird ? secondPromise.pipe(function () {
        return timeoutAsync(1000);
    }) : secondPromise;
    var fourthPromise = thirdPromise.pipe(function () {
        return timeoutAsync(1234);
    });
    fourthPromise.done(function () {
        firstPromise.done(function () { alert('done!') });
```

```
    });
    return fourthPromise;
}
```

In this example, the *includeThird* variable is passed into the abcAsync function and is used to determine whether the third asynchronous function should be called. If *includeThird* is false, the *thirdPromise* variable still needs to be assigned a promise to chain the fourth asynchronous call, so secondPromise is assigned directly to the *thirdPromise* variable. This maintains the chain of operations.

When making parallel asynchronous calls, conditionally calling the third operation is done differently, as shown in the following example.

```
function abcAsync(includeThird) {
    var deferred = $.Deferred();
    var firstPromise = timeoutAsync(2000);
    var secondPromise = timeoutAsync(3000);
    var thirdPromise =  includeThird ? timeoutAsync(1000) : $.when();
    var fourthPromise = timeoutAsync(1234);
    $.when(firstPromise, secondPromise, thirdPromise, fourthPromise)
        .then(function () { alert('done!'); deferred.resolve(); },
             function () { deferred.reject(); });
    return deferred.promise();
}
```

In this example, if *includeThird* is true, the third asynchronous call is executed and assigned to the *thirdPromise* variable. If *includeThird* is false, $.when() is assigned to the *thirdPromise* variable. Remember that $.when() is used at the bottom of the function to indicate that all asynchronous operations have completed, which creates a new promise that is passed to the then() method. If you call $.when() with no parameters, a new promise object is created with its status set to resolved.

> **NOTE   USE THE $.when() METHOD**
>
> When you need to create a promise object whose state is resolved, use the $.when() method.

Lesson summary

- The deferred object is a wrapper for the promise object. The deferred object provides control of the promise object, which is read-only.
- The promise object has the done, fail, always, and progress methods that accept a function parameter, which enables you to subscribe to state change. The then() method on the promise object enables you to subscribe to done, fail, and progress.
- The subscription functions execute a maximum of one time.
- The state method can be used to get the current state of the promise object.
- The promise object's pipe method chains asynchronous operations.

- The deferred object's resolve and resolvewith methods indicate successful completion. The deferred object's reject and rejectwith methods indicate a failed operation. The deferred object's notify and notifywith methods update the progress.

- The name of all functions that perform asynchronous calls should end with Async, and these functions should always return a promise object.

- Use the $.when() method to monitor the completion of many parallel asynchronous calls. Use the $.when() method with no parameters to create a resolved promise object.

- Chained and parallel asynchronous operations automatically pass failure and progress to the end of the chain.

Lesson review

Answer the following questions to test your knowledge of the information in this lesson. You can find the answers to these questions and explanations of why each answer choice is correct or incorrect in the "Answers" section at the end of this chapter.

1. Which method chains asynchronous operations?
   - **A.** pipe()
   - **B.** done()
   - **C.** resolve()
   - **D.** always()

2. Which method creates a resolved promise object?
   - **A.** resolve()
   - **B.** done()
   - **C.** $.when()
   - **D.** $.Deferred().

3. Which method do you call to subscribe to the successful completion of an asynchronous operation?
   - **A.** done
   - **B.** always
   - **C.** complete
   - **D.** success

4. Which method do you call on the deferred object to indicate a change in progress?
   - **A.** progress
   - **B.** notify
   - **C.** done
   - **D.** resolve

Lesson 2: Working with web workers

Another way to perform asynchronous operations is to use web workers. Web workers are useful for execution of a script file in a background task. The worker can send messages to the spawning task by posting messages to an event handler specified by the creator. Messages can be any object that can be serialized. The worker thread doesn't block the user interface thread, so the UI remains fast and fluid.

> **After this lesson, you will be able to:**
>
> - Describe web workers.
> - Implement asynchronous operations by using the web worker.
>
> **Estimated lesson time: 20 minutes**

Web worker details

Web workers' state is isolated from the webpage. When messages are posted to and from the web worker, the message object is serialized. This creates a copy of the message, so the web worker and the creator never reference the same object. Web workers also lack synchronization locks, critical sections, semaphores, or mutexes. They don't have access to the document object model (DOM), so if you need to access the DOM, the web worker must post a message back to the creator, and the creator must process the message and access the DOM as needed.

It's common to start a web worker, which creates its own event loop and waits for further input. This is similar to a service, which starts and waits for input and doesn't terminate after processing input.

Consider the following HTML page that accepts input and has a button that sends the input to a web worker. The web worker responds once for each character in the message sent, returning the uppercase of the letter.

```html
<!DOCTYPE html>
<html xmlns="http://www.w3.org/1999/xhtml">
<head>
    <title></title>
    <script src="Scripts/jquery-1.8.2.js"></script>
    <script src="default.js"></script>
</head>
<body>
    <input type="text" id="message" value="Enter message here" /><br />
    <button id="btnSend" type="button">Send Message</button><br />
    <div id="result"></div>
</body>
</html>
```

This HTML page has a reference to jQuery and a default.js file. The default.js file has code to create a new web worker by calling the Worker() constructor and passing the URI of a script to execute. You can receive notifications from the web worker by setting the onmessage and the onerror properties to an event handler function, as shown in the following example.

```
/// <reference path="Scripts/jquery-1.8.2.js" />
var worker = new Worker('myWork.js');
worker.onmessage = function (e) {
    $('#result').append(e.data + '<br />');
}
worker.onerror = function (e) {
    $('#result').append('Error: ' + e.data + '<br />');
}

$('document').ready(function () {
    $('#btnSend').on('click', function () {
        worker.postMessage($('#message').val());
    });
});
```

The web worker code is in the myWork.js file. This example also shows the subscription to btnSend, which retrieves the value from the message and posts the message to the worker. The myWork.js file contains the following code.

```
self.onmessage = function (e) {
    for (c in e.data) {
        postMessage(e.data[c].toUpperCase());
    }
}
```

This code subscribes to the onmessage event. In this example, when a message is received from the creator, this code loops through each character, converts it to uppercase, and sends the uppercased character back to the creator.

You can stop a web worker by calling the worker.terminate() method from the creator or calling the close() method inside the worker itself.

 Quick check

- You want to perform an asynchronous operation in your browser code. Which object can you use?

Quick check answer

- Use the worker object.

Lesson summary

- A web worker provides asynchronous code execution.
- Communication to and from the web worker is accomplished by using the postMessage method.

- The postMessage method accepts a serializable object.
- The web worker does not have access to DOM elements.

Lesson review

Answer the following questions to test your knowledge of the information in this lesson. You can find the answers to these questions and explanations of why each answer choice is correct or incorrect in the "Answers" section at the end of this chapter.

1. In the web worker code, you want the asynchronous code to update the DOM. Which method can you use?

   A. updateDom().

   B. workerUpdate().

   C. dom().

   D. You cannot update the DOM from within the asynchronous code.

2. Which object can be used when the web worker and the creator need to reference the same object?

   A. Mutex.

   B. Semaphore.

   C. Closure.

   D. The web worker and the creator cannot reference the same object.

Practice exercises

If you encounter a problem completing any of these exercises, the completed projects can be installed from the Practice Exercises folder that is provided with the companion content.

Exercise 1: Implement asynchronous code execution

In this exercise, you practice your asynchronous code execution skills by creating a web application that uses the promise object to perform animations when displaying a message.

The implementation of the custom message box starts with a *<div>* element that covers the screen so a user cannot click anywhere else on the screen when the message box is displayed. The cover has transparency so the user can still see the screen.

Over the cover is a completely transparent *<div>* element for the overall message box. This *<div>* element also covers the screen. This is required to center the message content. Nested inside the message box is another *<div>* element that holds the message content, which is centered by setting the left and right margins to auto on the message content.

You can animate the message box display and use promise objects to sequence the animations.

1. Start Visual Studio. Click File and choose New Project. Navigate to Installed | Templates | Visual Basic or Visual C# | ASP.NET Empty Web Application.

2. Set the name of your application to **AnimationExample**.

3. Select a location for your application.

4. Set the solution name to **AnimationExampleSolution**.

5. Be sure to keep the Create Directory For Solution check box selected.

6. Click OK to create your new project.

   When the application is created, you will have an empty project.

7. To add a home page, right-click the AnimationExample project in the Solution Explorer window, choose Add, select HTML Page, and name it **default.html**.

8. To set it as the start page, right-click the new default.html page in Solution Explorer and click Set As Start Page.

9. Add a reference to jQuery by right-clicking the project node. Click Manage NuGet Packages. Type **jQuery** in the search text box. Click the Install button on the jQuery result.

10. In the Solution Explorer window, right-click the Scripts folder and add a JavaScript file called default.js.

11. In the Solution Explorer window, right-click the AnimationExample project, choose Add, select New Folder, and name it **Content**. In the Content folder, add a default.css style sheet file.

12. In the default.html file, reference the default.css, jquery-1.8.2.js, and default.js files by dragging the files from the Solution Explorer window and dropping them after the *<title>* element.

    Remember that you should use the version of jQuery that you installed using the NuGet Package Manager. Your *<head>* element should look like the following.

```
<head>
    <title></title>
    <link href="Content/default.css" rel="stylesheet" />
    <script src="Scripts/jquery-1.8.2.js"></script>
    <script src="Scripts/default.js"></script>
</head>
```

13. Add a *<div>* element that covers the screen with its id attribute set to cover.

14. Add a *<div>* element that displays the message and sets its id attribute to messageBox. The *<body>* element should look like the following.

```
<body>
    <div id="cover">
    </div>
    <div id="messageBox">
    </div>
</body>
```

15. Add a *<div>* element inside the messageBox *<div>* element and set its id attribute to messageContent.

16. Add a *<div>* element inside the messageContent *<div>* element and set its id to message.

The *<body>* element should look like the following.

```
<body>
    <div id="cover">
    </div>
    <div id="messageBox">
        <div id="messageContent">
            <div id="message"> </div>
        </div>
    </div>
</body>
```

17. After the message *<div>* element, add a <br /> element and then add a *<button>* element, which will be used to test the custom message box, and set its id attribute to btnShowMessage.

Your default.html page should look like the following.

```
<!DOCTYPE html>
<html xmlns="http://www.w3.org/1999/xhtml">
<head>
    <title></title>
    <link href="Content/default.css" rel="stylesheet" />
    <script src="Scripts/jquery-1.8.2.js"></script>
    <script src="Scripts/default.js"></script>
</head>
<body>
    <div id="cover">
    </div>
    <div id="messageBox">
        <div id="messageContent">
            <div id="message"> </div>
            <br />
            <button type="button" id="messageOk">OK</button>
        </div>
    </div>
    <button type="button" id="btnShowMessage">Show Message</button>
</body>
</html>
```

18. In the default.css file, add a style rule for the cover element.

This element will not be displayed by default. Its size should be the entire screen. Its Z-Index should be higher than anything on the page except the cover that is set in the next step. Its background color should be set to black. Your style should look like the following.

```
#cover {
    display: none;
```

```
        position: absolute;
        background-color: black;
        z-index:100;
        top: 0px;
        left: 0px;
        width: 100%;
        height: 100%;
    }
```

19. Add a style rule for the messageBox element.

    This element will not be displayed by default. Its size should be the entire screen. Its
    Z-Index should be higher than anything on the page, including the cover that you just
    set. Your style should look like the following.

```
#messageBox {
    display: none;
    position: absolute;
    top: 0px;
    left: 0px;
    width: 100%;
    height: 100%;
    z-index: 101;
}
```

20. Add a style rule for the messageContent element.

    This element will not be displayed by default. Its size should be 30 percent wide and
    30 percent tall. It will be centered by setting the left and right margins to auto. Its
    top margin will be 100 pixels from the top. Its border style will be set to solid, and its
    border width will be set to 1 pixel. Its padding will be set to 10 pixels. Your style should
    look like the following.

```
#messageContent {
    border-style: solid;
    border-width: 1px;
    display: none;
    position: relative;
    margin: 100px auto auto auto;
    background-color: yellow;
    width: 30%;
    height: 30%;
    padding: 10px;
}
```

21. In the default.js file, add a reference to the jQuery library. Add a *milliseconds* variable
    by which to set the duration of the animations and set it to 1,000. Add an *opacity* vari-
    able by which to set the opacity of the cover and set it to 0.5, as shown in the following
    code example.

```
/// <reference path="jquery-1.8.2.js" />

var milliseconds = 1000;
var opacity = 0.5;
```

22. To provide an animated fade-in of the cover element, create a displayCoverAsync function and add code to fade to the value of the previously defined opacity value. Return the promise object as follows.

```
function displayCoverAsync() {
    return $('#cover').fadeTo(milliseconds, opacity).promise();
}
```

23. To set the message and provide an animated slide down from the top of the screen of the message content, add a showMessageContentAsync function. In the function, add code to set the HTML of the message element, add code to show the messageBox element, and, finally, add code to slide the messageContent element down from the top, using the *millisecond* variable as the duration, as follows.

```
function showMessageContentAsync(message) {
    $('#message').html(message);
    $('#messageBox').show();
    return $('#messageContent').slideDown(milliseconds).promise();
}
```

24. Add a showMessageAsync function that has a message parameter.

This function will call the displayCoverAsync and set a *coverPromise* variable to the returned promise object.

25. Add code that calls showMessageContentAsync after the displayCoverAsync has completed. Return a promise that identifies the completion of all asynchronous calls in the function.

Your code should look like the following.

```
function showMessageAsync(message) {
    var coverPromise = displayCoverAsync();
    var messagePromise = coverPromise.pipe(function () {
        return showMessageContentAsync(message);
    });
    return messagePromise;
}
```

26. When btnShowMessage is clicked, it will show a message using the current time. Add a getTime function that returns the current time. Add a displayTimeAsync function that creates a message by calling the getTime function and then calls the showMessageAsync function.

Your code should look like the following.

```
function displayTimeAsync() {
    var message = 'The time is now ' + getTime();
    return showMessageAsync(message);
}

function getTime() {
    var dateTime = new Date();
    var hours = dateTime.getHours();
    var minutes = dateTime.getMinutes();
```

```
        return hours + ':' + (minutes < 10 ? '0' + minutes : minutes);
    }
```

27. Add code that executes when the document is ready.

This code will subscribe to the click event of the btnShowMessage button and call the displayTimeAsync function, as follows.

```
$(document).ready(function () {
    $('#btnShowMessage').click(displayTimeAsync);
});
```

28. Press F5 to run the application. Click the Show Message button.

You should see the animated cover that fades in, and then you should see the message window slide down from the top of the screen. The final screen is shown in Figure 9-2.

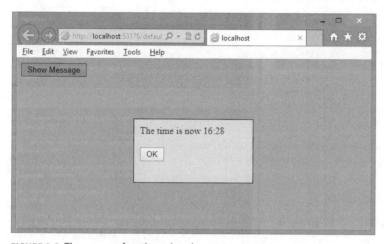

FIGURE 9-2 The screen after the animation stops

Notice that although the Show Message button is still visible, you can't click it now because the cover is over the button. Furthermore, the OK button isn't programmed to close the message window. When you click the OK button, the message window should slide back up and disappear, and the cover should fade out. The Show Message button should be clickable.

29. Stop running the application.

30. Add a hideMessageContentAsync function. In the function, add code to slide the messageContent element up to the top of the screen. Assign the created promise to a new *promise* variable and add code to hide the messageBox element. Add code to return the promise, as follows.

```
function hideMessageContentAsync(message) {
    var promise = $('#messageContent').slideUp(milliseconds).promise();
    promise.done(function () { $('#messageBox').hide(); });
    return promise;
}
```

31. Add a hideCoverAsync function. In the function, add code to fade out the cover element and return the promise object, as follows.

```
function hideCoverAsync() {
    return $('#cover').fadeOut(milliseconds).promise();
}
```

32. Add a hideMessageAsync function that calls the hideMessageContentAsync function and assigns the returned promise to a *messagePromise* variable. Add code to call the hideCoverAsync function when *messagePromise* has completed and assign the returned promise to a *coverPromise* variable. Return *coverPromise* as shown in the following code example.

```
function hideMessageAsync() {
    var messagePromise = hideMessageContentAsync();
    var coverPromise = messagePromise.pipe(function () {
        return hideCoverAsync();
    });
    return coverPromise;
}
```

33. Modify the existing document-ready code to subscribe to the click event of the messageOk button and call the hideMessageAsync function as follows.

```
$(document).ready(function () {
    $('#btnShowMessage').click(displayTimeAsync);
    $('#messageOk').click(hideMessageAsync);
});
```

34. Run the application.

    When you click the Show Message button, the animated message is displayed. When you click the OK button, the message is removed from the screen by sliding up to the top of the screen, and then the cover fades out.

Suggested practice exercises

The following additional exercises are designed to give you more opportunities to practice what you've learned and to help you successfully master the lessons presented in this chapter.

- **Exercise 1**   Learn more about asynchronous operations by writing more code that makes asynchronous calls to web services.

- **Exercise 2**   Learn more about web workers by writing an application that has a web worker that performs client-side code.

Answers

This section contains the answers to the lesson review questions in this chapter.

Lesson 1

1. **Correct answer: A**

   A. **Correct:** Use the pipe method to chain asynchronous operations because it provides access to progress, failure, success, and complete.

   B. **Incorrect:** The done method executes code when completed but does not provide access to failure, progress, and complete.

   C. **Incorrect:** The resolve method indicates success but is not used for chaining.

   D. **Incorrect:** The always method executes on completion regardless of success or failure. This method does not provide access to progress, success, or failure.

2. **Correct answer: C**

   A. **Incorrect:** The resolve method resolves an existing promise object, but it doesn't create a new resolved promise object.

   B. **Incorrect:** The done method executes code upon success of a promise object, but it does not create a resolved promise object.

   C. **Correct:** The $.when() method creates a resolved promise object.

   D. **Incorrect:** The $.Deferred() method creates an unresolved promise object.

3. **Correct answer: A**

   A. **Correct:** The done method executes code upon successful completion.

   B. **Incorrect:** The alway method executes code regardless of success or failure.

   C. **Incorrect:** The complete method does not exist.

   D. **Incorrect:** The success method does not exist.

4. **Correct answer: B**

   A. **Incorrect:** The progress method executes code when progress has changed; it does not to indicate a change in progress.

   B. **Correct:** The notify method indicates a change in progress.

   C. **Incorrect:** The done method executes code when completed but does not indicate a change in progress.

   D. **Incorrect:** The resolve method indicates success, not a change in progress.

Lesson 2

1. **Correct answer: D**

   A. **Incorrect:** There is no updateDom() method.

   B. **Incorrect:** There is no workerUpdate() method.

   C. **Incorrect:** There is no dom() method.

   D. **Correct:** The web worker cannot modify the DOM.

2. **Correct answer: D**

   A. **Incorrect:** There is no JavaScript Mutex object.

   B. **Incorrect:** There is no JavaScript Semaphore object.

   C. **Incorrect:** There is no JavaScript Closure object.

   D. **Correct:** The web worker cannot access the same object, and objects passed to the web worker from the creator are serialized to produce a copy of the object the web worker will access.

## CHAPTER 10

WebSocket communications

This book has covered AJAX and web services, which provide a means to communicate to the server from the browser client. This chapter is about initiating communications from the browser to the server or from the server to the browser. If the server can send messages to the browser, the browser doesn't need to poll the server for status information.

An example of two-way communications is a chat room application by which the server can notify many browsers that a message was received from a browser. Many games send data to a server, and the server controls data being sent back to the clients. Another example is when you initiate an asynchronous operation at the server, and the server provides status update messages to the browser. This chapter explores bidirectional communications, using WebSocket.

Lesson in this chapter:

- Lesson 1: Communicating by using WebSocket **415**

Before you begin

To complete this book, you must have some understanding of web development. This chapter requires the hardware and software listed in the "System requirements" section in the book's Introduction.

Lesson 1: Communicating by using WebSocket

The WebSocket protocol is a web technology that provides full-duplex communications over a single TCP connection. The WebSocket application programming interface (API) is currently in working draft status by the World Wide Web Consortium (W3C), but the WebSocket protocol has been standardized by the Internet Engineering Task Force (IETF) as RFC 6455.

WebSocket replaces the *long polling* concept. With long polling, the client sends a request to the server, and if the server has information with which to respond, it responds. If the server doesn't have information with which to respond, the server keeps the connection open and doesn't respond until it has data. When the client receives the data, it sends another request to the server, and the sequence repeats itself. The benefit of long polling is that the client is waiting for data, and the server has an open connection. When data is ready, it's sent immediately, which results in decreased latency. One problem with this concept is that connections can time out, which requires the creation of a new connection.

> **After this lesson, you will be able to:**
> - Describe the WebSocket protocol.
> - Describe and implement the WebSocket object.
>
> **Estimated lesson time: 20 minutes**

Understanding the WebSocket protocol

The WebSocket protocol provides a standardized way for the server to send content to the browser without being solicited by the client and to allow messages to be passed back and forth while keeping the connection open. A two-way (bidirectional), ongoing conversation can take place between a browser and the server.

The WebSocket protocol is designed to be implemented in web browsers and web servers, but any client or server application can use it. The protocol is an independent, TCP-based protocol. Its only relationship to HTTP is that its handshake is interpreted by HTTP servers as a request to switch to WebSocket protocol. Each frame of WebSocket protocol has only 2 bytes of overhead, and there are no headers. The light weight of the WebSocket protocol enables more interaction between a browser and a website. This performance makes the WebSocket protocol an easy choice for communicating when it's necessary to deliver live content and create real-time games.

Defining the WebSocket API

The W3C is responsible for defining the WebSocket API; as mentioned, the API is in working draft status at the time of this writing. This means that the W3C could make many more changes before the API becomes a recommendation. However, the latest versions of Internet Explorer, Google Chrome, Firefox, Opera, and Safari support WebSocket.

At the heart of the WebSocket API is the WebSocket object, which is defined on the window object. You can easily test whether this object exists to determine whether the browser supports WebSocket. The WebSocket object contains the following members.

- **WebSocket constructor** A method that requires a URL argument and can optionally accept additional parameters to define the sub-protocol that you'll use, such as *chat* or *rpc*. The client and the server are typically matched to use the same protocol.
- **close** A method that closes WebSocket.
- **send** A method that sends data to the server.

- **binaryType**   A property that indicates the binary data format the onmessage event receives.

- **bufferedAmount**   A property containing the number of data bytes queued using the send method.

- **extensions**   A property that indicates the extensions the server selected.

- **onclose**   An event property that's called when the socket is closed.

- **onerror**   An event property that''s called when there is an error.

- **onmessage**   An event property that's called when a message is received.

- **onopen**   An event property that's called when WebSocket establishes a connection.

- **protocol**   A property that indicates the protocol that the server selected.

- **readyState**   A property that indicates the state of the WebSocket connection.

- **url**   A property that indicates the current URL of the WebSocket object.

Implementing the WebSocket object

WebSocket protocol communications typically use TCP port number 80, so environments that block non-standard Internet connections by using a firewall will still pass WebSocket packets.

In the following example, a webpage is created that calls the WebSocket.org echo server, which will return the message passed to it. Consider the following webpage that contains a text box for entering a message and a button to send the message to a server; all output is appended to the *<div>* element whose id is divOutput.

```
<!DOCTYPE html>
<html xmlns="http://www.w3.org/1999/xhtml">
<head>
    <title></title>
    <script src="Scripts/jquery-1.8.2.js"></script>
    <script src="Scripts/default.js"></script>
</head>
<body>
    <h2>WebSocket Test</h2>
    Enter Message: <input type="text" id="txtMessage" />
    <button type="button" id="btnSend">Send</button><br />
    <div id="divOutput"></div>
</body>
</html>
```

Whereas an HTTP URL begins with http:// or https:// for secure HTTP, the WebSocket URL begins with ws:// or wss:// for secure WebSocket protocol. In the browser code, you create a WebSocket object and configure the onopen, onmessage, onerror, and onclose events. Call the send method to send a message, and the onmessage event triggers if there is a response. The default.js file contains the following.

```
/// <reference path="_references.js" />
var wsUri = 'ws://echo.websocket.org/';
```

```
var webSocket;

$(document).ready(function () {
    if (checkSupported()) {
        connect();
        $('#btnSend').click(doSend);
    }
});

function writeOutput(message) {
    var output = $("#divOutput");
    output.html(output.html() + '<br />' + message);
}

function checkSupported() {
    if (window.WebSocket) {
        writeOutput('WebSockets supported!');
        return true;
    }
    else {
        writeOutput('WebSockets NOT supported');
        $('#btnSend').attr('disabled', 'disabled');
        return false;
    }
}

function connect() {
    webSocket = new WebSocket(wsUri);
    webSocket.onopen = function (evt) { onOpen(evt) };
    webSocket.onclose = function (evt) { onClose(evt) };
    webSocket.onmessage = function (evt) { onMessage(evt) };
    webSocket.onerror = function (evt) { onError(evt) };
}

function doSend() {
    if (webSocket.readyState != webSocket.OPEN)
    {
        writeOutput("NOT OPEN: " + $('#txtMessage').val());
        return;
    }
    writeOutput("SENT: " + $('#txtMessage').val());
    webSocket.send($('#txtMessage').val());
}

function onOpen(evt) {
    writeOutput("CONNECTED");
}

function onClose(evt) {
    writeOutput("DISCONNECTED");
}

function onMessage(evt) {
    writeOutput('RESPONSE: ' + evt.data);
}
```

```
function onError(evt) {
    writeOutput('ERROR: ' + evt.data);
}
```

In this example, wsUri is set to the WebSocket.org echo server, which echoes messages sent to it. The ready function calls the checkSupported function to see whether WebSocket is supported. This is accomplished by checking whether the window object has a WebSocket object. If WebSocket is supported, the connect function is called.

The connect function instantiates WebSocket. The constructor accepts a URI argument. Creating the WebSocket object automatically initiates communications to the URI to attempt to open the connection asynchronously. The connect function also subscribes to the onopen, onclose, onmessage, and onerror events. It's important to subscribe to these events immediately because the connection might open quickly, and you want to ensure that you are subscribed to the onopen event as soon as possible so you don't miss the event.

 Quick check

■ Can you create a WebSocket object and call the open method when you want to open a WebSocket connection?

Quick check answer

■ No, there is no open method on the WebSocket object. When you instantiate the WebSocket object, it automatically attempts to open asynchronously.

The doSend function sends a message to the server. Before sending the message, this function checks the readyState property of the WebSocket object. The readyState property contains one of the following values.

■ **CONNECTING = 0**   Connection is not yet open.
■ **OPEN = 1**   Connection is open and ready to communicate.
■ **CLOSING = 2**   Connection is in the process of closing.
■ **CLOSED = 3**   Connection is closed or couldn't be opened.

The readyState property will be set to one of the numeric values, but you can use the constants as shown in the doSend function that tests for webSocket.OPEN. If WebSocket is not open, a message is displayed, and the function returns without sending. If WebSocket is open, a message is displayed, and the message is sent using the send method.

When a message is received from the server, the onMessage function is called, and the event object is passed. The data property of the event object contains the message.

When an error is received, the onError function is called, and the event object is passed. An error can come from the server or be generated when either the client cannot connect to the server or the connection is timed out. Depending on the error, the event object might pass the cause on the data property. You might also find that the data property is undefined, especially in a timeout scenario.

When the webpage is displayed using Internet Explorer 10, a message is displayed stating, WebSockets Supported! The CONNECTED message is displayed when the connection is open. If a message is entered and the Send button is clicked, the message is sent to the server, and the response is displayed, as shown in Figure 10-1.

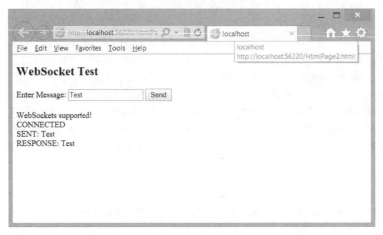

FIGURE 10-1 The completed WebSocket test page

Dealing with timeouts

One of the problems you might encounter is that the server might time out your connection after a period of inactivity. You might also have firewalls between your browser and the server that can time out your connection. In many cases, an error is triggered without an associated message. You can identify timeout errors by not triggering any activity for up to 20 minutes. You might see that you consistently get timeouts after only 30 seconds. Although it's relatively new, the W3C draft for WebSocket does not address timeouts.

One way of dealing with timeouts is to send an empty message to the server periodically. The completed default.js file provides an example of periodically sending an empty message, as follows.

```
/// <reference path="_references.js" />

var wsUri = 'ws://echo.websocket.org/';
var webSocket;
var timerId = 0;

$(document).ready(function () {
    if (checkSupported()) {
        connect();
        $('#btnSend').click(doSend);
    }
});
```

```
function writeOutput(message) {
    var output = $("#divOutput");
    output.html(output.html() + '<br />' + message);
}

function checkSupported() {
    if (window.WebSocket) {
        writeOutput('WebSockets supported!');
        return true;
    }
    else {
        writeOutput('WebSockets NOT supported');
        $('#btnSend').attr('disabled', 'disabled');
        return false;
    }
}

function connect() {
    webSocket = new WebSocket(wsUri);
    webSocket.onopen = function (evt) { onOpen(evt) };
    webSocket.onclose = function (evt) { onClose(evt) };
    webSocket.onmessage = function (evt) { onMessage(evt) };
    webSocket.onerror = function (evt) { onError(evt) };
}

function keepAlive() {
    var timeout = 15000;
    if (webSocket.readyState == webSocket.OPEN) {
        webSocket.send('');
    }
    timerId = setTimeout(keepAlive, timeout);
}

function cancelKeepAlive() {
    if (timerId) {
        cancelTimeout(timerId);
    }
}

function doSend() {
    if (webSocket.readyState != webSocket.OPEN)
    {
        writeOutput("NOT OPEN: " + $('#txtMessage').val());
        return;
    }
    writeOutput("SENT: " + $('#txtMessage').val());
    webSocket.send($('#txtMessage').val());
}

function onOpen(evt) {
    writeOutput("CONNECTED");
    keepAlive();
}
```

```
function onClose(evt) {
    cancelKeepAlive();
    writeOutput("DISCONNECTED");
}

function onMessage(evt) {
    writeOutput('RESPONSE: ' + evt.data);
}

function onError(evt) {
    writeOutput('ERROR: ' + evt.data);
}
```

In this example, the bold code was added. At the top is the declaration of the timerId.
A keepAlive function has been added that sends an empty message every 15 seconds. The
keepAlive function is called when the onOpen function is executed and is recursive; it doesn't
stop until the timer is cancelled by using the timerId. A cancelKeepAlive function has been
added to cancel the looping of the keepAlive function, and it's called when the onClose function is called.

Handling connection disconnects

In addition to providing the keepAlive capability, you might also need to deal with connections that close due to network errors. This can require you to call the connect function from
within the onClose function. Depending on your application, this could cause problems at
the server when the server doesn't recognize that the new connection belongs to an existing
client. Your application might need to handle this by forcing the client to send an identification message. Keep in mind that the messages are in the format that you dictate, so you can
define your own messaging strategy for your application.

Dealing with web farms

 Sometimes, when pushing your WebSocket application to production, you need your application to run in a *web farm*, when multiple servers handle incoming requests. These requests
are typically load balanced to provide the best performance. How can you have an open connection to a server and still have load balancing?

When there are multiple web servers, you can implement sticky servers, by which the client
continuously goes to the same server it originally went to. This takes care of the open connection problem. You can share state across multiple web servers by using one of the many products that handle this problem, such as Redis (remote dictionary service) and the Microsoft
App Fabric Caching Service.

Just remember to test your web farm environment early for compatibility and problems
because you will surely need to adjust for this environment.

Using WebSocket libraries

Dealing with timeouts, dropped connections, incompatible browsers, and web farms can be a daunting task. Wouldn't it be much better to have a library that can handle this task for you in a consistent manner? It turns out that there are libraries to help you, but you need to understand that these are client and server libraries; you use the library at the client and server. The following is a short list of libraries that can help solve some of these problems. Because WebSocket is not yet a recommendation, and these are relatively new products, this list should get you started, but do some web searching for the latest releases of these and other products.

SignalR

SignalR is a Microsoft library for ASP.NET developers. It is meant to be implemented on an ASP.NET website, using a .NET language such as C# or Visual Basic. The client code is still JavaScript, however.

SignalR simplifies the addition of real-time web functionality to your applications. It uses WebSocket when it's available but gracefully falls back to techniques such as long polling when WebSocket is not available. The best part is that you don't need to change your code for this transition. You might have clients that support WebSocket and clients that don't; the clients work well together even if they don't support WebSocket.

SignalR also provides connection events to which you can subscribe for connection management. SignalR is so easy to use that you should consider this if you are working on an ASP.NET website. SignalR can also work on the Windows Azure cloud. You must provide state management for SignalR to share data between servers, but it is doable.

Socket.IO

Socket.IO is a WebSocket library created by Guillermo Rauch, CTO and cofounder of LearnBoost; developer and inventor of Socket.IO, Engine.IO, and codestre.am; JSConf.ar curator; open-source enthusiast; and blogger.

Socket.IO has a client-side and server-side library; the client side uses JavaScript, and the server side is JavaScript for use with Node.js. It uses feature detection to decide whether the connection will be established with WebSocket, AJAX long polling, or Flash polling, which is yet another way to implement polling but requires Flash at the browser.

The Socket.IO library is easy to use and is used in the exercises to create a chat server.

Lesson summary

- The WebSocket protocol provides a standardized way for the server to send content to the browser without being solicited by the client, and it allows messages to be passed back and forth while keeping the connection open.
- The WebSocket object contains methods to send data and close the connection.
- The WebSocket object contains the following events: onclose, onmessage, onerror, and onopen.
- You can check the readyState property on the WebSocket object to obtain the state of the connection.
- Use ws:// for WebSocket protocol or wss:// for secure WebSocket protocol.
- Timeouts, dropped connections, web farm implementations, and browser incompatibility are problems you must resolve when implementing WebSocket.

Lesson review

Answer the following questions to test your knowledge of the information in this lesson. You can find the answers to these questions and explanations of why each answer choice is correct or incorrect in the "Answers" section at the end of this chapter.

1. When working with the WebSocket object, which event can be used to retrieve the data that was received from the server?
   A. onopen
   B. onclose
   C. onmessage
   D. onerror

2. Which library would you use if you are creating a Node.js website and want to write browser-independent code that uses WebSocket?
   A. SignalR
   B. Socket.IO
   C. FarmSockets
   D. AgnosticSocket

3. You want to ensure that the WebSocket connection is not disconnected as a result of inactivity. How can you accomplish this?

    A. Add code to the onclose event to reopen the connection when it's closed.

    B. Add code to send an empty message periodically before the connection is closed.

    C. Set the keepAlive property on the WebSocket object to true.

    D. Create a new WebSocket object each time you send a message.

Practice exercises

If you encounter a problem completing any of these exercises, the completed projects can be installed from the Practice Exercises folder that is provided with the companion content.

Exercise 1: Create a chat server

In this exercise, you apply your WebSocket knowledge by creating a chat server web application. Although you won't use the WebSocket object directly, you will use the Socket.IO library, which provides a WebSocket wrapper that simplifies client and server communications.

In this exercise, you create the chat server. You won't be able to test this server effectively until you complete Exercise 2, in which you create the HTML page.

1. If you haven't done so yet, install Node.js from *http://nodejs.org/*.

2. Open the command prompt window.

3. Create a folder for the new website.

You must navigate to the location and then create the folder. For example, the following commands navigate to the node_samples folder on the root of the C drive, create a new chat_service folder, and then navigate to the new folder.

```
C:
cd \node_samples
md chat_service
cd chat_service
```

4. In the chat_service folder, create a package.json file by typing the following command.

```
npm init
```

This command starts the wizard. Enter the following. (Press Enter to accept default values for fields not shown.)

- Name: chat_service
- Version: 0.0.0
- Description: A simple chat service
- Entry Point: app.js

- Author: *your name*
- License: BSD

5. Open the package.json file and add a dependency on the express and formidable packages as shown in the following modified package.json file.

```
{
  "name": "chat_service",
  "version": "0.0.0",
  "description": "A simple chat service",
  "main": "app.js",
  "scripts": {
    "test": "echo \"Error: no test specified\" && exit 1"
  },
  "repository": "",
  "author": "Glenn Johnson",
  "license": "BSD",
  "private": true,
  "dependencies": {
    "express": "3.0.x",
    "socket.io": "0.9.x"
  }
}
```

6. Install the dependent packages by typing the following command.

```
npm install
```

7. Open Visual Studio Express 2012 for Web. Click File and choose Open Web Site; select the chat_service folder.

8. In the chat_service website folder, create an app.js file and add a reference to the express, http, and socket.io packages. Call the listen method as follows.

```
var express = require('express')
  , app = express()
  , http = require('http')
  , server = http.createServer(app)
  , io = require('socket.io').listen(server);
```

In this code, you are using the http object to create a server based on the express object. After that, you are using the socket.io object to call the listen method and passing the server object to indicate the server that will be listening.

9. In the Solution Explorer window, right-click the chat_service node, click Add, and choose New Folder. Name the folder **public**.

10. In the app.js file, add a statement to map static requests to the /public folder as follows.

```
app.use(express.static(__dirname + '/public'));
```

11. Add a statement to map a request for the root to the index.html file (to be created in Exercise 2) as follows.

```
app.get('/', function (req, res) {
  res.sendfile(__dirname + '/public/index.html');
});
```

The index.html file is the main chat page.

12. Add code to redirect the user to the default.html page if the URL does not include a file name, as follows.

```
app.get('/', function (request, response) {
    response.redirect('default.html');
});
```

13. Add a statement to create a *usernames* variable and initialize it as an empty object, as follows.

```
var usernames = {};
```

14. Add code to subscribe to the socket.io events as follows.

```
io.sockets.on('connection', function (socket) {
    socket.on('sendchat', function (data) {
       io.sockets.emit('updatechat', socket.username, data);
    });

    socket.on('adduser', function(username){
       socket.username = username;
       usernames[username] = username;
       socket.emit('updatechat', 'SERVER', 'you have connected');
       socket.broadcast.emit('updatechat', 'SERVER'
           , username + ' has connected');
       io.sockets.emit('updateusers', usernames);
    });

    socket.on('disconnect', function(){
       delete usernames[socket.username];
       io.sockets.emit('updateusers', usernames);
       socket.broadcast.emit('updatechat', 'SERVER'
           , socket.username + ' has disconnected');
    });
});
```

The first line of this code subscribes to the connection event and executes an anonymous function. The anonymous function code accepts a socket parameter, which is the object that represents the newly created user connection. Inside the anonymous function, subscriptions are created to the sendchat, adduser, and disconnect events. The sendchat and adduser events are developer-defined.

The sendchat event is triggered when a message is received from a chat client. This code uses the io.sockets object to broadcast the message to all chat clients.

The adduser event is triggered after the client makes a connection. It adds the username to the usernames collection and then uses the socket object to call the updatechat event on the current client to indicate to the user that the connection is successful. The socket.broadcast object sends a message indicating that the current client is connected. This message is broadcast to all clients except the current client. Finally, the io.sockets.emit event broadcasts an updated user list to all clients.

The disconnect event deletes the user from the usernames list and broadcasts the usernames to all clients. The socket.broadcast object broadcasts a disconnect message to all clients except the current client.

15. Add code to listen on port 8080 and log a message to the console stating this.

The app.js file should look like the following.

```
var express = require('express')
  , app = express()
  , http = require('http')
  , server = http.createServer(app)
  , io = require('socket.io').listen(server);

app.use(express.static(__dirname + '/public'));
app.get('/', function (req, res) {
  res.sendfile(__dirname + '/public/index.html');
});

var usernames = {};

io.sockets.on('connection', function (socket) {
    socket.on('sendchat', function (data) {
        io.sockets.emit('updatechat', socket.username, data);
    });

    socket.on('adduser', function(username){
        socket.username = username;
        usernames[username] = username;
        socket.emit('updatechat', 'SERVER', 'you have connected');
        socket.broadcast.emit('updatechat', 'SERVER'
            , username + ' has connected');
        io.sockets.emit('updateusers', usernames);
    });

    socket.on('disconnect', function(){
        delete usernames[socket.username];
        io.sockets.emit('updateusers', usernames);
        socket.broadcast.emit('updatechat', 'SERVER'
            , socket.username + ' has disconnected');
    });
});

var port = 8080;
server.listen(port);
console.log('Listening on port: ' + port);
```

16. Test your work by running the website, using the following command in the command prompt window.

```
node app.js
```

You should see the listening message, as shown in Figure 10-2.

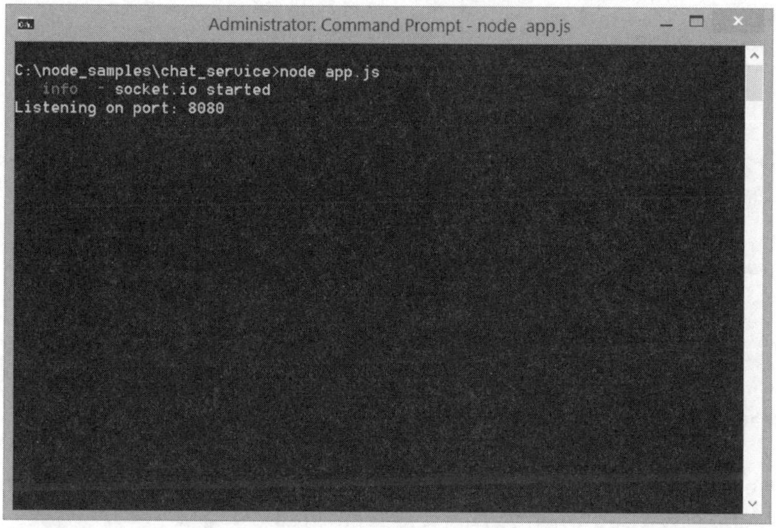

FIGURE 10-2 The running chat service

Exercise 2: Create the chat client

In this exercise, you continue with the chat service from Exercise 1 and add the chat client code. When you're finished with this exercise, you will have a functional chat application.

1. Open the client website, which is different from Exercise 1. Open Visual Studio Express 2012 for Web. Click File, choose Open Web Site, and select the public folder under the chat_service.

2. In the Solution Explorer window, right-click the public node, choose Add, and then select HTML Page. Name the file **Index.html** and click OK.

3. In the Solution Explorer window, right-click the public node. Click Add, choose Style Sheet, and name the file **default.css**. Click OK.

4. In the Solution Explorer window, right-click the public node, choose Add, select New Folder, name the folder **Scripts**, and click OK.

5. In the Solution Explorer window, right-click the Scripts folder, choose Add, select JavaScript File, name the file **default.js**, and click OK.

6. Add the jQuery library by right-clicking the public node. Choose Manage NuGet Packages, select Online, and type **jQuery** in the search box.

You should see jQuery, as shown in Figure 10-3.

7. Click Install to install jQuery.

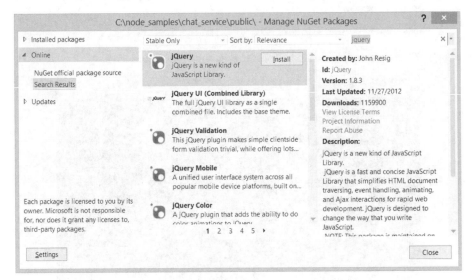

FIGURE 10-3 The NuGet Window with jQuery selected

Add the socket.io client files. These files were automatically downloaded to your computer during Exercise 1 when you executed npm install.

8. In the Solution Explorer window, right-click the Scripts folder, choose Add, and select Existing Item. Navigate to the chat_service folder and then to the node_modules\socket.io\node_modules\socket.io-client\dist folder.

9. In the file type drop-down list, select All Files (*.*) and then select the four files that are now showing in the folder, as shown in Figure 10-4.

FIGURE 10-4 The socket.io client files that need to be added to the website

Now that you have all the files you need, it's time to add your code.

10. In the Index.html file, add references to the default style sheet, jquery, socket.io.js, and default.js file.

The *<head>* element should look like the following.

```html
<head>
    <title></title>
    <link href="default.css" rel="stylesheet" />
    <script src="scripts/jquery-1.8.3.js"></script>
    <script src="scripts/socket.io.js"></script>
    <script src="scripts/default.js"></script>
</head>
```

11. In the *<body>* element, add a *<div>* element for the user list and a *<div>* element for the conversation.

The *<body>* element should contain the following.

```html
<div class="userContainer" >
    <h2>Users</h2>
    <div id="users"></div>
</div>
<div class="conversationContainer">
    <input id="data"  />
    <input type="button" id="datasend" value="send" />
    <div id="conversation"></div>
</div>
```

12. Open the default.css file and add the following style rules.

```css
.userContainer {
    float: left;
    width: 200px;
    border-right: 1px solid black;
    height: 300px;
    padding: 10px;
    overflow: auto;
}

.conversationContainer {
    float: left;
    width: 400px;
    height: 300px;
    overflow: auto;
    padding: 10px;
}

#data {
    width: 250px;
}
```

13. Open the default.js file. To get IntelliSense, from the Solution Explorer window, drag the *jquery-1.8.3.js* file and drop it at the top of the default.js file to add a reference to the jQuery library as follows.

```
/// <reference path="jquery-1.8.3.js" />
```

14. Declare a *socket* variable. Subscribe to the ready event of the document. In this code, use the io object to connect to the chat service and assign the result to the *socket* variable.

15. Subscribe to the connect, updatechat, and updateusers events of the socket.

16. Finally, subscribe to the click event of the datasend button and the keypress event of the data text box, as follows.

```
var socket;

$(document).ready(function () {
    socket = io.connect('http://localhost:8080');
    socket.on('connect', addUser);
    socket.on('updatechat', processMessage);
    socket.on('updateusers', updateUserList);
    $('#datasend').click(sendMessage);
    $('#data').keypress(processEnterPress);
});
```

This code is subscribing to the events, which execute functions that are not yet created. You add these functions next.

17. Add the addUser function, which calls the emit method on the socket to call the adduser method on the chat server.

The result of the pop-up prompt for the username is also passed. The addUser function should look like the following.

```
function addUser() {
    socket.emit('adduser', prompt("What's your name?"));
}
```

18. Add the processMessage function.

This function is called when the chat service sends a message. The username and data are passed to this function.

19. Use jQuery to create a jQuery object with the response and insert the message after the conversation <*div*> element.

The processMessage function should look like the following.

```
function processMessage(username, data) {
    $('<b>' + username + ':</b> ' + data + '<br />')
        .insertAfter($('#conversation'));
}
```

20. Add the updateUserList function.

This function is called when the chat service sends an updated user list.

21. Add code to clear the existing user list and repopulate the list.

The updateUserList function should look like the following.

```
function updateUserList(data) {
    $('#users').empty();
    $.each(data, function (key, value) {
        $('#users').append('<div>' + key + '</div>');
    });
}
```

22. Add the sendMessage function.

This function is called to send a message to the chat service. The sendMessage function should look like the following.

```
function sendMessage() {
    var message = $('#data').val();
    $('#data').val('');
    socket.emit('sendchat', message);
    $('#data').focus();
}
```

23. Add the processEnterPress function.

This function is called when the user presses the Enter key. The processEnterPress function should look like the following.

```
function processEnterPress(e) {
    if (e.which == 13) {
        e.preventDefault();
        $(this).blur();
        $('#datasend').focus().click();
    }
}
```

24. Review the code.

The completed default.js file is as follows.

```
/// <reference path="jquery-1.8.2.js" />
var socket;

$(document).ready(function () {
    socket = io.connect('http://localhost:8080');
    socket.on('connect', addUser);
    socket.on('updatechat', processMessage);
    socket.on('updateusers', updateUserList);
    $('#datasend').click(sendMessage);
    $('#data').keypress(processEnterPress);
});
```

```
function addUser() {
    socket.emit('adduser', prompt("What's your name?"));
}

function processMessage(username, data) {
    $('<b>' + username + ':</b> ' + data + '<br />')
        .insertAfter($('#conversation'));
}

function updateUserList(data) {
    $('#users').empty();
    $.each(data, function (key, value) {
        $('#users').append('<div>' + key + '</div>');
    });
}

function sendMessage() {
    var message = $('#data').val();
    $('#data').val('');
    socket.emit('sendchat', message);
    $('#data').focus();
}

function processEnterPress(e) {
    if (e.which == 13) {
        e.preventDefault();
        $(this).blur();
        $('#datasend').focus().click();
    }
}
```

25. To start chat_service, open a command prompt window. Navigate to the chat_service folder. Type the following command.

```
node app.js
```

26. Open a browser.

27. Navigate to *http://localhost:8080*, where you should see the chat page.

You should get a pop-up prompt for your username.

28. Enter a name and click OK.

29. Open another browser window and repeat the previous step.

As you type your message, you should see it displayed in both windows, as shown in Figure 10-5.

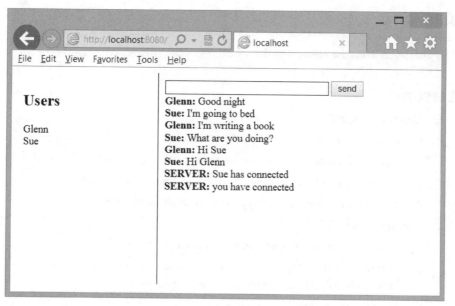

FIGURE 10-5 The chat client in action

Suggested practice exercises

The following additional exercises are designed to give you more opportunities to practice what you've learned and to help you successfully master the lessons presented in this chapter.

- **Exercise 1** Learn more about WebSocket by writing more code that implements the WebSocket object directly.

- **Exercise 2** Learn more about WebSocket by writing a sketch application by which multiple users can draw shapes on a common drawing surface.

Answers

This section contains the answers to the lesson review questions in this chapter.

Lesson 1

1. **Correct answer: C**

    A. **Incorrect:** The onopen event is triggered when the connection is opened.

    B. **Incorrect:** The onclose event is triggered when the connection is closed.

    C. **Correct:** The onmessage event is triggered when data is received.

    D. **Incorrect:** The onerror event is triggered when an error is thrown.

2. **Correct answer: B**

    A. **Incorrect:** SignalR does not work with Node.js websites.

    B. **Correct:** The Socket.IO library works with Node.js to provide a browser-independent library for WebSocket communications.

    C. **Incorrect:** FarmSockets does not exist.

    D. **Incorrect:** AgnosticSocket does not exist.

3. **Correct answer: B**

    A. **Incorrect:** If you wait until the connection is closed, you will need to create a new WebSocket object.

    B. **Correct:** You can add code to send empty messages periodically.

    C. **Incorrect:** There is no keepAlive property on the WebSocket object.

    D. **Incorrect:** If you create a new WebSocket object each time you send a message, the server will think that new browsers are communicating with it.

## CHAPTER 11

HTML5 supports multimedia

One of the most popular features of HTML5 is its support for multimedia. In the past, you needed to load a plug-in to play video or audio. Probably the most popular multimedia plug-in is Flash. This chapter examines the HTML5 support for playing audio and video.

Lessons in this chapter:

Before you begin

To complete this book, you must have some understanding of web development. This chapter requires the hardware and software listed in the "System requirements" section in the book's Introduction.

Lesson 1: Playing video

The World Wide Web Consortium (W3C) introduced the video element for the purpose of playing videos and movies. The intent was to offer a standard way to play video on the web without requiring plug-ins. This goal has been circumvented by lack of agreement about which video formats should be supported in web browsers.

Currently, the W3C does not specify which video formats browsers should support. Browsers can decide which format they want to support, so the developer must provide formats that are available across most browsers.

After this lesson, you will be able to:
- Describe the common video formats available on the Internet.
- Implement the *<video>* element.

Estimated lesson time: 20 minutes

Video formats

The W3C is trying to come up with a video format that can be specified for all browsers to support as a minimum. Having a minimum of one format that is common across browsers would simplify the developer's job as long as the format provided good compression and quality and was royalty free. There are many formats; the following list describes the most popular formats.

- **Ogg/Theora (.ogv extension)**   At one point, W3C specified the Ogg/Theora format, which appears to be a format that is royalty free without patent issues. Then the W3C removed the Ogg/Theora from the specifications because of the possibility of litigation. This format is supported by the Firefox, Chrome, and Opera browsers.

- **WebM/VP8 (.webm extension)**   Google acquired the WebM/VP8 format when it bought On2 Technology. According to Google officials, WebM works well on even lower-power devices, including netbooks and handhelds. WebM will be available under a royalty-free Berkeley Software Distribution (BSD) open-source license. The WebM/VP8 video format is supported by the Firefox, Chrome, Opera, and Android browsers. In addition, Internet Explorer 9+ will support this format when the VP8 codec is installed. The current release of the VP8 codec is available here: *https://tools.google .com/dlpage/webmmf/*.

- **MPEG-4/H.264 (.mp4 extension)**   This format is an evolution of previous formats that was intended to create a standard capable of providing good video quality at substantially lower bit rates than previous standards. The MPEG-4/H.264 format has patented technologies, but MPEG LA, which is a private organization in charge of administrating the patents, announced that the H.264-encoded Internet video that is free to end users will never be charged royalties. MPEG-4/H.264 is supported by the Internet Explorer, Chrome, and Safari browsers, but Chrome has announced its intent to remove support for MPEG-4/H.264 in the near future.

MPEG-4/H.264 is the most common format for most video-editing software. It also provides the best performance when comparing data-stream size to picture quality, although the difference is not great enough to make a decision based solely on performance. Many existing mobile devices have MPEG-4/H.264 hardware decoders, which provide better performance, and there are too many of these mobile devices to ignore. The result is that it could take a long time for browser makers and the W3C to agree on a single format for the web.

Implementing the *<video>* element

The *<video>* element is used to play video. The following is a sample implementation of the *<video>* element.

```
<video width="320" height="240" controls="controls">
    <source src="movie.mp4" />
    You need a browser that supports HTML5!
</video>
```

In this example, the *<video>* element size is set to 320 pixels by 240 pixels. The controls attribute provides controls to start and stop the video, to view and set the video cursor location, and to maximize and restore the video size on the screen. The *<video>* element contains a *<source>* element that describes the video source as .mp4. The *<video>* element also contains text that is displayed on browsers that don't support the *<video>* element.

Setting the source

The *<source>* element specifies a video source. At a minimum, you need to set the src attribute to the URL of the video. You should also include more than one *<source>* element to provide many sources so the browser can choose the most appropriate video codec. In the following example, the same movie has been rendered for each of the three most popular formats.

```
<video controls="controls" height="480">
    <source src="eagle.webm" type='video/webm; codecs="vorbis, vp8"' />
    <source src="eagle.ogv" type='video/ogg; codecs="theora, vorbis"' />
    <source src="eagle.mp4" type='video/mp4; codecs="avc1.42E01E, mp4a.40.2"' />
</video>
```

When the developer provides multiple formats, the browser can choose the format it can use to display the video, which provides the most compatible experience to users. The position of the *<source>* elements is important because a browser starts looking at the top and stops when it finds a file that it can display. The recommended order is to start with the .webm file because it's royalty free and open source, and it's becoming more popular. Next, use the .ogv file because it is also royalty free, but the quality is not as good as the .webm file. Finally, use the .mp4 format for browsers that don't support .webm or .ogv files.

The type attribute includes both the MIME type and the codecs. Although the type attribute isn't usually required, the browser can use it to help choose the proper video file to display.

The availability of multiple video files requires the developer to transcode videos to multiple formats. You can find web utilities at such websites as Firefogg.org that transcode a video from one format to another, as shown in Figure 11-1.

To use the Firefogg website, you must be running Firefox and have installed the Firefogg plug-in. This plain website produces good-quality transcoded videos.

If you prefer to use an application that you can download and install on your computer, you might like the Miro Video Converter. This is a stand-alone utility that enables you to convert one file type to another. The Miro Video Converter is shown in Figure 11-2.

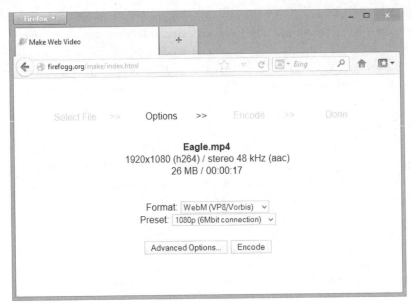

FIGURE 11-1 The Firefogg screen prompting for .webm or .ogv file type

FIGURE 11-2 The Miro Video Converter

You might find that the Miro Video Converter produces low-quality videos. It seems as though the .ogv files are very choppy, and the site doesn't offer many conversion options.

Configuring the *<video>* element

The *<video>* element can be configured to provide the behavior you need for your webpage. The following is the list of attributes you can use to configure the *<video>* element to suit your needs.

- **autoplay**   Specifies that video starts playing immediately.
- **controls**   Specifies that the play/pause button, video cursor, and maximize be displayed.
- **height**   Indicates the height in pixels of the rendered *<video>* element.
- **loop**   Specifies that the video will repeat when it has reached the end of its stream.
- **muted**   Specifies that the audio is silent.
- **poster**   Specifies that the URL of an image is to be shown when the video is not playing.
- **preload**   Specifies how the video should be loaded when the page loads. It can be set to auto, metadata, or none. The auto setting starts loading the video when the page loads. The metadata setting loads only the metadata, and the none setting doesn't load anything.
- **src**   Specifies the URL of the video.
- **width**   Indicates the width in pixels of the rendered *<video>* element.

 Quick check

- You want an image to be displayed when the video is not running. Which property should you set to the URL of an image to be displayed?

Quick check answer

- Set the poster property to the URL of an image.

Accessing tracks

The W3C has developed a new standard, called WebVTT (Web Video Text Tracks), that provides the ability to display captions on the video; all browsers implementing the *<track>* element will support it. The WebVTT file format is simple and easily readable by browsers and developers. It's based on a popular subtitling format called SubRip Text (SRT). If you already have your content in SRT format, converters are available on the web to convert to the WebVTT format.

A less-used standard called Timed Text Markup Language (TTML) is an XML-based format that is more verbose than WebVTT. TTML is outside the scope of this book.

Using the WebVTT format

WebVTT format is very simple. The file starts with a declaration of the WebVTT file, a line is skipped, and a cue is defined. The cue is composed of a timespan on the first line, and the caption follows on the next line or lines. After that, a new line separator is provided, and the next cue is defined. The following is a WebVTT file.

```
WEBVTT FILE

00:00:07.500 --> 00:00:08.750
He's fidgety.

00:00:09.000 --> 00:00:12.000
There he goes!!!
```

You can include comments by using the word NOTE followed by a space or a new line, as shown in the following example.

```
WEBVTT FILE

00:00:07.500 --> 00:00:08.750
He's fidgety.

NOTE I think the timing should be adjusted to span to the end of the video
00:00:09.000 --> 00:00:12.000
There he goes!!!
```

The WebVTT format is evolving and provides for other features that are not currently supported on most browsers. One such feature is the ability to put an ID on a cue so you can assign a CSS format to the cue. You can also add elements within the caption and provide CSS styles for the elements.

Adding support for WebVTT to IIS Express

If you try to use WebVTT files on a website that is hosted by IIS Express, you might find that IIS Express won't serve a .vtt file because it serves only known file types. You can add support for .vtt files by executing the following commands.

```
cd "C:\Program Files\IIS Express"
appcmd set config /section:staticContent /+[fileExtension='.vtt',mimeType='text/vtt']
```

When you enter the second command, you should get a message stating that the changes were applied.

Lesson summary

- The *<video>* element is new in HTML5.
- The most common video formats for the web are .ogg/Theora, WebM/VP8, and MPEG-4/H.264.
- When implementing the *<video>* element, at a minimum you must provide a video source.

- It's best to provide multiple video sources to be compatible with most browsers.
- Use the autoplay attribute to start playing immediately.
- Use the poster attribute to specify an image to display when not playing the video.
- You can provide captions in WebVTT or TTML format.

Lesson review

Answer the following questions to test your knowledge of the information in this lesson. You can find the answers to these questions and explanations of why each answer choice is correct or incorrect in the "Answers" section at the end of this chapter.

1. You want to include a video on your webpage that has an .avi file extension. If you supply the codec information, what will be displayed in browsers that support the *<video>* element but don't have the codec?

   A. The browser will show the *<video>* element, but will not play the video.

   B. The browser will automatically download the codec and play the video.

   C. The browser will display the contents of the *<video>* element.

   D. The browser will automatically download a version of the browser that supports the codec.

2. You don't want to supply an .ogg video because you find that the .ogg format is choppy and low quality. What other video formats can you include to be compatible with most browsers? (Choose all that apply.)

   A. .webm

   B. .avi

   C. .mpg

   D. .mp4

   E. .mjpg

3. The W3C standardized using which format for video?

   A. .webm

   B. .avi

   C. .mpg

   D. .mp4

   E. No standard has been selected.

Lesson 2: Playing audio

The W3C introduced the *<audio>* element for the purpose of playing music and sounds. Like the introduction of the *<video>* element, the intent was to offer a standard way to play multimedia on the web without requiring plug-ins.

Much of the content in this lesson is similar to that of the *<video>* element; they both inherit from the HTMLMediaElement. The most notable difference is that the *<video>* element consumes more screen space to display video.

> **After this lesson, you will be able to:**
> - Describe the common audio formats available on the Internet.
> - Implement the *<audio>* element.
>
> **Estimated lesson time: 20 minutes**

Audio formats

The W3C does not specify which audio formats browsers should support, but the battle over formats is not as competitive as for the video formats. The W3C is trying to decide on an audio format that can be specified for all browsers to support as a minimum. There are many audio formats, but the following are the most common.

- **Ogg/Vorbis (.oga, .ogg extention)**   This format appears to be royalty free without patent issues. It's supported by the Firefox, Chrome, and Opera browsers and has a MIME type of audio/ogg and a codec of vorbis.

- **MP3 (.mp3 extension)**   This format is pervasive because it's a common format for much of the music media. It's supported by the Safari, Chrome, and Internet Explorer browsers and has a MIME type of audio/mpeg and a codec of .mp3.

- **MP4 (.mp4, .mp4a, .aac extension)**   This format is primarily used by Apple. In spite of this format's high quality AAC or AAC+ codec, the MP3 format is still more prevalent. This format is supported on the Internet Explorer and Safari browsers and has a MIME type of audio/mp4; mp4a.40.5 is the codec value.

- **WAV (.wav extension)**   This format is also pervasive and is usually used for audio fragments, or snippets, such as ring tones and sounds. It's supported by the Firefox, Chrome, and Opera browsers and has a MIME type of audio/wav and a codec of 1 (the number one).

The *<audio>* element

The *<audio>* element is used to play audio. The following is a sample implementation of the *<audio>* element.

```
<audio controls="controls">
    <source src="song.mp3" />
    You need a browser that supports HTML5!
</audio>
```

In this example, the *<audio>* element is configured with the controls attribute, which provides controls to start and stop the audio, to view and set the audio cursor location, and to set the volume. The *<audio>* element contains a *<source>* element that describes the audio source as .mp3. The *<audio>* element also contains text that is displayed on browsers that don't support the *<audio>* element.

One characteristic of audio is that the developer might play multiple audio files at the same time. Although this is common in games, most browsers can't handle playing multiple audio files at the same time.

Setting the source

The *<source>* element specifies an audio source. At a minimum, you need to set the src attribute to the URL of the audio. You should also include more than one *<source>* element to provide many sources so the browser can choose the most appropriate audio codec. In the following example, the same sound has been rendered for each of the three most popular formats.

```
<audio id="audio" controls="controls">
    <source src="media/kittycat.oga" type='audio/ogg; codecs="vorbis"' />
    <source src="media/kittycat.wav" type='audio/wav; codecs="1"' />
    <source src="media/kittycat.mp3" type='audio/mpeg; codecs="mp3"' />
</audio>
```

By providing multiple formats, the browser can choose the format that displays the audio, which provides the most compatible experience to users. As mentioned earlier, the position of the *<source>* elements is important because a browser starts looking at the top and stops when it finds a file it can display. The recommended order is to start with the .oga file because it's royalty free, open source, and becoming more popular for the web. Next, use the .wav file, because it is also quite popular. Finally, use the .mp3 for browsers that don't support .oga and .wav files.

The type attribute includes both the MIME type and the codecs. Although the type attribute isn't usually required, the browser can use it to help choose the proper audio file to display.

Configuring the *<audio>* element

The *<audio>* element can be configured to provide the behavior you need for your webpage. The following is the list of attributes you can use to configure the *<audio>* element to suit your needs.

- **autoplay**   Specifies that audio starts playing immediately.
- **controls**   Specifies that the play/pause button, audio cursor, and maximize are displayed.
- **loop**   Specifies that the audio repeats when it has reached the end of its stream.

- **preload**   Specifies how the audio should be loaded when the page loads. It can be set to auto, metadata, or none. The auto setting starts loading the audio when the page loads. The metadata setting loads only the metadata, and the none setting doesn't load anything.
- **src**   Specifies the URL of the audio.

 Quick check

- You want to repeat the audio continuously when it completes. Which attribute must you set?

Quick check answer

- Set the loop attribute as follows.

```
<audio loop='loop'>
```

Lesson summary

- The *<audio>* element is new in HTML5.
- The most common audio formats for the web are .ogg/Vorbis, .mp3, and .wav.
- When implementing the *<audio>* element, at a minimum you must provide an audio source.
- It's best to provide multiple audio sources to be compatible with most browsers.
- Use the autoplay attribute to start playing immediately.

Lesson review

Answer the following questions to test your knowledge of the information in this lesson. You can find the answers to these questions and explanations of why each answer choice is correct or incorrect in the "Answers" section at the end of this chapter.

1. You want to supply an audio file using a format that is compatible with the Internet Explorer, Safari, and Chrome browsers. Which audio formats can you include to be compatible with most browsers? (Choose all that apply.)

   A. .mp4

   B. .wav

   C. .mp3

   D. .oga

2. You don't want to supply an .mp3 format because you are concerned about potentially paying royalties. What other audio formats can you include to be compatible with most browsers? (Choose all that apply.)

A.   .mp4

B.   .wav

C.   .h264

D.   .oga

Lesson 3: Using the HTMLMediaElement object

The *<audio>* and *<video>* elements inherit from an HTMLMediaElement object, so they inherit the properties, methods, and events that are defined on the HTMLMediaElement object.

After this lesson, you will be able to:

- Describe the HTMLMediaElement object.
- Subscribe to the HTMLMediaElement events.
- Control media.

Estimated lesson time: 20 minutes

Understanding the HTMLMediaElement methods

You can use the members of the HTMLMediaElement object to control the video and audio playback. You can also get notifications of status changes. The following is a list of the *<video>* element methods.

- **addTextTrack()**   Adds a new text track to the audio or video
- **canPlayType()**   Determines whether the browser can play the specified audio or video type
- **load()**   Reloads the audio or video
- **play()**   Plays the audio or video
- **pause()**   Pauses the currently playing audio or video

Using HTMLMediaElement properties

In addition to the methods that enable you to control playback, you can use many properties to view or set the state of the *<audio>* or *<video>* element. The following is a list of all the properties.

- **audioTracks**   Gets a reference to the AudioTrackList object that has the available audio tracks
- **autoplay**   Sets or gets the indicator that determines whether the audio or video should start playing when it's loaded

- **buffered**   Gets a reference to the TimeRanges object that represents the buffered parts of the audio or video
- **controller**   Gets a reference to the MediaController object representing the current media controller of the audio or video
- **controls**   Sets or gets the indicator that determines whether the audio or video should display playback controls to the user
- **crossOrigin**   Sets or gets the CORS settings of the audio or video
- **currentSrc**   Gets the URL of the current audio or video
- **currentTime**   Sets or gets the current playback position in seconds
- **defaultMuted**   Sets or gets the indicator that determines whether the audio or video is muted by default
- **defaultPlaybackRate**   Sets or gets the default speed of the audio or video playback
- **duration**   Gets the length in seconds of the current audio or video
- **ended**   Gets the indicator that determines whether the playback of the audio or video has ended
- **error**   Gets a reference to a MediaError object representing the error state of the audio or video
- **loop**   Sets or gets an indicator that determines whether the audio or video should automatically restart when it reaches the end of the stream
- **mediaGroup**   Sets or gets the group to which the audio or video belongs, which is used to link multiple audio or video elements
- **muted**   Sets or gets an indicator that determines whether the audio or video is muted
- **networkState**   Gets a reference to the current network state of the audio or video
- **paused**   Sets or gets an indicator that determines whether the audio or video is paused
- **playbackRate**   Sets or gets the speed of the audio or video playback
- **played**   Gets a reference to a TimeRanges object that represents the played parts of the audio or video
- **preload**   Sets or gets an indicator that determines whether the audio or video should be loaded when the page loads
- **readyState**   Gets an indicator of the current ready state of the audio or video
- **seekable**   Gets a reference to a TimeRanges object that represents the seekable parts of the audio or video
- **seeking**   Gets an indicator that determines whether the user is currently seeking in the audio or video
- **src**   Sets or gets the current source of the audio or video
- **startDate**   Gets a Date object representing the current time offset

- **textTracks**   Gets a reference to a TextTrackList object that represents the available text tracks
- **videoTracks**   Gets a reference to a VideoTrackList object that represents the available video tracks
- **volume**   Sets or gets the volume of the audio or video

Subscribing to HTMLMediaElement events

In addition to the methods and properties of HTMLMediaElement, the following is a list of the events that you can subscribe to.

- **onabort**   Triggers on abort
- **oncanplay**   Triggers when a file has been buffered enough to start playing
- **oncanplaythrough**   Triggers when a file can be played all the way to the end without pausing for buffering
- **ondurationchange**   Triggers when the length of the media changes
- **onemptied**   Triggers when an error occurs and the file is suddenly unavailable
- **onended**   Triggers when the media has reached the end of the stream
- **onerror**   Triggers when an error occurs as the file is being loaded
- **onloadeddata**   Triggers when media data is loaded
- **onloadedmetadata**   Triggers when metadata such as duration and dimensions are loaded
- **onloadstart**   Triggers when the file begins to load but before anything is actually loaded
- **onpause**   Triggers when the media is paused
- **onplay**   Triggers when the media starts playing
- **onplaying**   Triggers when the media actually has started playing
- **onprogress**   Triggers when the browser is retrieving the media
- **onratechange**   Triggers each time the playback rate changes
- **onreadystatechange**   Triggers each time the ready state changes
- **onseeked**   Triggers to indicate that seeking has ended
- **onseeking**   Triggers to indicate that seeking is active
- **onstalled**   Triggers when the browser is unable to retrieve the media
- **onsuspend**   Triggers when media retrieval stops prior to being completely loaded
- **ontimeupdate**   Triggers when the playing position has changed
- **onvolumechange**   Triggers each time the volume or mute is changed
- **onwaiting**   Triggers when the media has paused but is expected to resume

Using media control

Given that HTMLMediaElement has many methods, properties, and events, you can provide custom controls for the media or a custom means to start and stop the media playback. The following is a small example of using the methods, properties, and events. Consider the following HTML document.

```
<!DOCTYPE html>
<html xmlns="http://www.w3.org/1999/xhtml">
<head>
    <title></title>
    <link href="default.css" rel="stylesheet" />
    <script src="Scripts/jquery-1.8.3.js"></script>
    <script src="Scripts/default.js"></script>
</head>
<body>
    <video id="media" height="480">
        <source src="eagle.webm" type='video/webm; codecs="vorbis, vp8"' />
        <source src="eagle.ogv" type='video/ogg; codecs="theora, vorbis"' />
        <source src="eagle.mp4" type='video/mp4; codecs="avc1.42E01E, mp4a.40.2"' />
        <track id="englishtrack" kind="subtitles" src="captions.vtt"
            srclang="en" label="English" default="" />
    </video>
    <br />
    <button type="button" id="play">Play</button>
</body>
</html>
```

This document contains a reference to the jQuery library and the default.js file. It also contains a *<video>* element whose id attribute is set to media, and the controls attribute is not set. There are *<source>* elements for the .webm, .ogv, and .mp4 video files. A caption file is in WebVTT format. Under the *<video>* element is a *<button>* element whose id is set to play.

Because the controls attribute is not set, the *<video>* element doesn't display the built-in controls such as play/pause, the position indicator, and the full-screen button. Sometimes, you might not want to allow the user to maximize the video, so turning off the controls is appropriate. If so, you must provide your own play/pause button, as shown in the following default.js file.

```
/// <reference path="jquery-1.8.3.js" />
$(document).ready(function () {
    $('#play').on('click', playStop);
    $('#media').on('play', function () { $('#play').html('Pause'); });
    $('#media').on('pause', function () { $('#play').html('Play'); });
});

function playStop() {
    var media = $('#media')[0];
    if (media.paused) {
        media.play();
    }
    else {
        media.pause();
```

```
        }
}
```

In the default.js file, the document ready method is added with the code to subscribe to the events. The click event on the play button executes the playStop function. The playStop function gets a reference to the media element and then uses the paused property to determine whether to play or pause the video by executing the play or pause method.

When the play button is pressed, the text on the play button changes from Play to Pause because the play event is triggered on the media element. When the play button is pressed again, the play button text changes from Pause to Play because the pause event is triggered on the play button. This is accomplished by subscribing to the play and pause events in the document ready function.

Lesson summary

- The *<video>* and *<audio>* elements inherit from the HTMLMediaElement object.
- Use the play() method to start playing the media and the pause() method to pause the playing media.
- The paused property can be used to determine whether the media is playing.
- The onplay and the onpause events can be subscribed to and provide notifications when the media is played or paused.

Lesson review

Answer the following questions to test your knowledge of the information in this lesson. You can find the answers to these questions and explanations of why each answer choice is correct or incorrect in the "Answers" section at the end of this chapter.

1. The *<video>* and *<audio>* elements inherit from which object?

   A. HTMLMediaElement

   B. MediaElement

   C. MultiMediaElement

   D. the Multimedia object

2. If you want your media to repeat continuously, which property would you set to true?

   A. preload

   B. readyState

   C. seekable

   D. loop

3. You want to trigger some code when the media is loaded. Which event should you subscribe to?

   A. onstalled

   B. onseeked

    C. onplay

    D. onloadeddata

Practice exercises

If you encounter a problem completing any of these exercises, the completed projects can be installed from the Practice Exercises folder that is provided with the companion content.

Exercise 1: Create a webpage that displays video

In this exercise, you apply your knowledge of the *<video>* element by creating a web application that displays video.

At Contoso Ltd., you have been asked to create a prototype webpage that displays video using the *<video>* element. The webpage needs to display video to the Firefox, Internet Explorer, and Chrome browsers at a minimum, but you want to reach as many browsers as possible.

You know that you need to convert your .mp4 file to other formats, but you also want to identify the file type the browser used so you can determine the file types that provide the most browser coverage.

1. Start Visual Studio Express 2012 for Web. Create an ASP.NET Empty Web Application project and name it **MultimediaPrototype**.

2. Add a new folder, **Media**, to the project.

3. Add the Eagle video files. Right-click the Media folder, choose Add, and select Existing Item. Locate the Resource folder and select the three Eagle video files.

4. Add an HTML file to the project. Name it **VideoPage.html**.

5. Add a CSS file to the project. Name it **default.css**.

6. Add a new folder, **Scripts**, to the project.

7. Right-click the Scripts folder and add a new JavaScript default.js file.

8. Add a reference to the jQuery library by right-clicking the project node; choose Manage NuGet Packages. Click Online and type **jQuery** in the search criteria. When the jQuery library displays, click the Install button.

9. In the VideoPage.html file, add a reference to the default.css, jQuery library, and default.js files.

10. Title your page **Video Prototype**.

    Your HTML page should look like the following.

```
<!DOCTYPE html>
<html xmlns="http://www.w3.org/1999/xhtml">
<head>
    <title>Video Prototype</title>
    <link href="default.css" rel="stylesheet" />
```

```
        <script src="Scripts/jquery-1.8.3.js"></script>
        <script src="Scripts/default.js"></script>
    </head>
    <body>

    </body>
</html>
```

11. In the *<body>* element, add a *<div>* element whose id is container.

12. In the container, add a *<video>* element whose id is media. Add the controls attribute to display the basic video controls. After the *<video>* element, add a break, and then add a *<span>* element whose id is message.

    Your container should look like the following.

```
<div id="container">
    <video id="media" controls="controls">

    </video>
    <br />
    <span id='message'></span>
</div>
```

13. In the *<video>* element, add sources for each of the Eagle video files. Be sure that the first video file is the .webm file, following by the .ogv file, followed by the .mp4 file.

14. After the *<source>* elements are added, add a message stating that the user needs an HTML5 browser.

    Your *<video>* element should look like the following.

```
<video id="media" controls="controls">
  <source src="media/eagle.webm" type='video/webm; codecs="vorbis, vp8"' />
  <source src="media/eagle.ogv" type='video/ogg; codecs="theora, vorbis"' />
  <source src="media/eagle.mp4" type='video/mp4; codecs="avc1.42E01E, mp4a.40.2"'
/>
  You need an HTML5 compatible browser.
</video>
```

15. In the default.css file, set the background color of the *<body>* element to a very light yellow.

16. Add a style rule for the container. This style should set the background color to light blue, set the border to groove, set the width to 900 pixels, and set the height to 600 pixels. Set the left and right margins to auto. Set the text-align to center and set the padding to 20 pixels.

    The completed default.css file should look like the following.

```
body {
    background-color: #FFFFCC;
}

#container {
    background-color: #99CCFF;
```

```
    border-style: groove;
    width: 900px;
    height: 600px;
    margin-right: auto;
    margin-left: auto;
    text-align:center;
    padding: 20px;
}
```

17. To know which source was selected by the browser (although this will be apparent when you play the video), add code to the default.js file to display the current source when the video is played.

Your code should look like the following.

```
/// <reference path="jquery-1.8.3.js" />
$(document).ready(function () {
    $('#media').on('play', function () {
        $('#message').html($('#media')[0].currentSrc);
    });
});
```

18. In Solution Explorer, right-click the VideoPage.html file and choose Set As Start Page.

19. Test your work by running the website by pressing F5.

You should see the VideoPage.html page as shown in Figure 11-3.

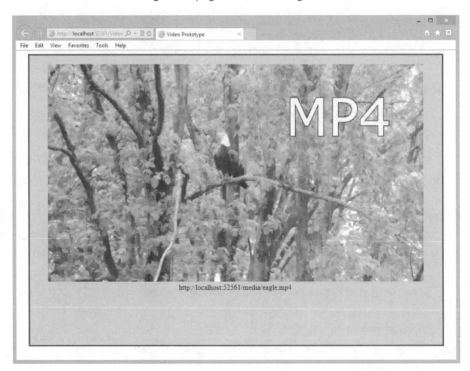

FIGURE 11-3 The running video page

Suggested practice exercises

The following additional exercises are designed to give you more opportunities to practice what you've learned and to help you successfully master the lessons presented in this chapter.

- **Exercise 1**   Learn more about video and audio by creating a web application that offers the ability to play from a list of files.

- **Exercise 2**   Learn more about video and audio by writing a web application that uses many of the properties, methods, and events of the *<video>* and *<audio>* elements.

Answers

This section contains the answers to the lesson review questions in this chapter.

Lesson 1

1. **Correct answer: A**

   A. **Correct:** The browser must support the codec that is specified but does not attempt to download the specified codec automatically.

   B. **Incorrect:** The browser does not attempt to download codecs automatically.

   C. **Incorrect:** The browser only displays the contents of the *<video>* element if the browser doesn't support the *<video>* element.

   D. **Incorrect:** The browser does not attempt to download a browser that is compatible.

2. **Correct answers: A and D**

   A. **Correct:** The .webm format is becoming popular on the latest browsers.

   B. **Incorrect:** The .avi format is not compatible with most browsers.

   C. **Incorrect:** The .mpg format is not compatible with most browsers.

   D. **Correct:** The .mp4 format is compatible with Safari and Internet Explorer.

   E. **Incorrect:** The .mjpg format is not compatible with most browsers.

3. **Correct answer: E**

   A. **Incorrect:** The .webm format is becoming popular but has not been selected as a standard.

   B. **Incorrect:** The .avi format is not compatible with most browsers.

   C. **Incorrect:** The .mpg format is not compatible with most browsers.

   D. **Incorrect:** The .mp4 format is compatible with Safari and Internet Explorer but has not been selected as a standard.

   E. **Correct:** The W3C has not selected a standard format.

Lesson 2

1. **Correct answer: C**

   A. **Incorrect:** .The .mp4 format is not compatible with Chrome.

   B. **Incorrect:** The .wav format is not compatible with Internet Explorer.

   C. **Correct:** The .mp3 format is compatible with Internet Explorer, Safari, and Chrome.

   D. **Incorrect:** The .oga format is not compatible with Internet Explorer.

2. **Correct answers: A, B, and D**

    A. Correct: The .mp4 format is becoming popular on the latest browsers.

    B. Correct: The .wav format is compatible with most browsers.

    C. Incorrect: The .h264 format is a video format.

    D. Correct: The .oga format is compatible with most browsers.

Lesson 3

1. **Correct answer: A**

    A. Correct: The *<video>* and *<audio>* elements inherit from the HTMLMediaElement object.

    B. Incorrect: The MediaElement object does not exist.

    C. Incorrect: The MultiMediaElement object does not exist.

    D. Incorrect: The Multimedia object does not exist.

2. **Correct answer: D**

    A. Incorrect: The preload property is used to indicate whether you want to preload the data.

    B. Incorrect: The readyState property is used to identify the current state of the media.

    C. Incorrect: The seekable property is used to indicate whether the media can be seeked.

    D. Correct: The loop property is used to indicate that you want to repeat the media continuously when it reaches its end of stream.

3. **Correct answer: D**

    A. Incorrect: The onstalled event triggers when the browser is unable to retrieve the media.

    B. Incorrect: The onseeked event triggers when seeking has ended, after you perform a seek operation.

    C. Incorrect: The onplay event triggers when the media starts playing.

    D. Correct: The onloadeddata event triggers when the media is loaded.

## CHAPTER 12

Drawing with HTML5

In the past, the most common method for drawing on a webpage was by using Adobe Flash. As the quest to create browsers that don't require plug-ins to display multimedia continues, a large gap in functionality has been filled with the ability to draw in HTML5 by using the *<canvas>* element and to create and display Scalable Vector Graphics (SVG) by using the *<svg>* element.

Although Adobe Flash still provides more functionality than the *<canvas>* element, you might find that the *<canvas>* element is all you need and that you don't need to add a third-party product to your application.

SVG is a language by which to define two-dimensional graphics in XML, and the XML can be rendered by the browser by using the *<svg>* element. Although you could learn SVG and write SVG graphics, you will likely use an image editor to create SVG images and then use them in your web application. The benefit is that the images are scalable.

This chapter presents the *<canvas>* element and demonstrates drawing on the canvas. This is not an all-inclusive tutorial on this element, however; its power could easily fill its own book. The chapter then presents the *<svg>* element from an implementation perspective rather than from a drawing perspective.

Lessons in this chapter:

Before you begin

To complete this book, you must have some understanding of web development. This chapter requires the hardware and software listed in the "System requirements" section in the book's Introduction.

Lesson 1: Drawing by using the *<canvas>* element

The only significant attributes that the *<canvas>* element has are the height and width attributes. The content that you place in the *<canvas>* element is displayed if the browser doesn't support the canvas element. The following is an example of a simple implementation of this element, informing the user that a browser that supports HTML5 is required. This content is displayed only if the browser doesn't support the *<canvas>* element.

```
<canvas id="myCanvas" width="800" height="600">
    You need a browser that supports HTML5!
</canvas>
```

For the subsequent examples, the following style is applied to the *<canvas>* element because it is invisible by default.

```
canvas {
    border: 1px solid black;
}
```

> **After this lesson, you will be able to:**
> - Describe the *<canvas>* element.
> - Configure the drawing state.
> - Draw with paths.
> - Draw text and images.
>
> **Estimated lesson time: 20 minutes**

The *<canvas>* element reference

The *<canvas>* element exposes an abundance of functionality through its canvas context, which is accessible using JavaScript. This element provides the following members.

- **height**   Property that sets or gets the height of the canvas
- **width**   Property that sets or gets the width of the canvas
- **getContext()**   Method that accepts a parameter of 2d and returns a CanvasRenderingContext2D object that represents the canvas context
- **toDataUrl()**   Method that creates a URL that can be used with an element that requires an image URL, such as the *<img>* element

CanvasRenderingContext2D context object reference

The *<canvas>* element is simply a graphics container; the context object that is returned from the getContext method is used to draw on the canvas. The following is a list of the context object's members. Many of these methods and properties are used in this lesson.

- **addColorStop()** Method to set the colors and stop positions in a gradient object
- **arc()** Method to create an arc/curve
- **arcTo()** Method to create an arc/curve between two tangents
- **beginPath()** Method to start a path or reset the current path
- **bezierCurveTo()** Method to create a cubic Bézier curve
- **clearRect()** Method to clear a given rectangle
- **clip()** Method to clip a region of any shape and size from the original canvas
- **closePath()** Method to create a path from the current point back to the starting point
- **createImageData()** Method to create a new, blank ImageData object
- **createLinearGradient()** Method to create a linear gradient
- **createPattern()** Method to repeat a specified element in a specified direction
- **createRadialGradient()** Method to create a radial/circular gradient
- **data** Property that gets an ImageData object that contains the image data
- **drawImage()** Method to draw an image, canvas, or video onto the canvas
- **fill()** Method to fill the drawing path
- **fillRect()** Method to draw a filled rectangle
- **fillStyle** Property that sets or gets the color, gradient, or pattern used to fill the drawing
- **fillText()** Method to draw filled text on the canvas
- **font** Property that sets or gets the font properties for text content
- **getImageData()** Method to get an ImageData object that copies the pixel data for the specified rectangle on a canvas
- **globalAlpha** Property that sets or gets the current alpha or transparency value of the drawing
- **globalCompositeOperation** Property that sets or gets how a new image is drawn onto an existing image
- **isPointInPath()** Method that returns true if the specified point is in the current path
- **lineCap** Property that sets or gets the style of the end caps for a line
- **lineJoin** Property that sets or gets the type of corner to create when two lines meet
- **lineTo()** Method that adds a new point and creates a line from that point to the last specified point in the canvas
- **lineWidth** Property that sets or gets the current line width
- **measureText()** Method that gets an object that contains the width of the specified text
- **miterLimit** Property that sets or gets the maximum miter length

- **moveTo()**   Method that moves the path to the specified point in the canvas without creating a line
- **putImageData()**   Method that puts the image data from a specified ImageData object back onto the canvas
- **quadraticCurveTo()**   Method that creates a quadratic Bézier curve
- **rect()**   Method that creates a rectangle
- **restore()**   Method that pops the previously saved context state from the stack
- **rotate()**   Method that rotates the current drawing
- **save()**   Method that pushes the state of the current context onto a stack
- **scale()**   Method that scales the current drawing bigger or smaller
- **setTransform()**   Method that resets the current transform to the identity matrix and then calls the transform() method
- **shadowBlur**   Property that sets or gets the blur level setting to use for shadows
- **shadowColor**   Property that sets or gets the color setting to use for shadows
- **shadowOffsetX**   Property that sets or gets the horizontal distance setting of the shadow from the shape
- **shadowOffsetY**   Property that sets or gets the vertical distance setting of the shadow from the shape
- **stroke()**   Method to draw the path you have defined
- **strokeRect()**   Method to draw a rectangle without fill
- **strokeStyle**   Property that sets or gets the color, gradient, or pattern used for strokes
- **strokeText()**   Method that draws text on the canvas without fill
- **textAlign**   Property that sets or gets the alignment setting for text content
- **textBaseline**   Property that sets or gets the text baseline setting used when drawing text
- **transform()**   Method that replaces the transformation matrix setting for the drawing
- **translate()**   Method that remaps the (0, 0) position on the canvas

Implementing the canvas

When working with the canvas object, you must get a reference to the canvas context. This can be accomplished by using the getContext method, which accepts a parameter. Currently, the only value for the parameter is 2d when using Internet Explorer, but Firefox and Chrome support an experimental-webgl parameter, which supports three-dimensional drawing. Expect to see this technology evolve over time.

This lesson focuses on the more mature 2d parameter, which returns a CanvasRenderingContext2D object. This object will be referred to as the *context* object. The following example demonstrates the creation of the context object.

```
$(document).ready(function () {
    drawSomething();
});

function drawSomething() {
    var canvas = document.getElementById('myCanvas');
    var ctx = canvas.getContext('2d');
    ctx.fillRect(10, 50, 100, 200);
}
```

In this example, canvas is a reference to the *<canvas>* element whose id is myCanvas. After that, ctx is set to reference the context object, with which you can start drawing. The coordinates of the drawing surface are represented as x, y where 0, 0 is the upper-left corner of the canvas.

 Quick check

- What is the proper parameter to pass to the getContext method on the canvas to create two-dimensional drawings?

Quick check answer

- 2d

Drawing rectangles

The methods for creating rectangles accept four parameters. The first two parameters are the x and y locations of the upper-left corner of the rectangle. The last two parameters represent the width and height of the rectangle. You can create rectangles by using one of the following methods.

- **clearRect(x, y, w, h)** Clear the specified rectangular area.
- **fillRect(x, y, w, h)** Draw a filled rectangular area.
- **strokeRect(x, y, w, h)** Draw an unfilled rectangular area.

The following code example demonstrates the use of these methods to create rectangles.

```
$(document).ready(function () {
    drawSomething();
});

function drawSomething() {
    var canvas = document.getElementById('myCanvas')
        , ctx = canvas.getContext('2d')
        , offset = 15
        , clearOffset = 30
        , pushDownOffset = 10
        , height = 50
        , width = 100
        , count = 4
```

```
                    , i = 0;

    for (i = 0; i < count; i++) {
        ctx.fillRect(i * (offset + width) + offset, offset, width, height);
        ctx.clearRect(i * (offset + width) + (clearOffset / 2) + offset,
            offset + (clearOffset / 2) + pushDownOffset,
            width - clearOffset, height - clearOffset)
        ctx.strokeRect(i * (offset + width) + offset,
            (2 * offset) + height, width, height);
    }
}
```

In this example, the fillRect method is used to create four filled rectangles. Each of the rectangles is spaced horizontally by the offset amount. Next, the clearRect method is used to clear a rectangular area that is inside the filled-in area created by the fillRect method. Finally, the strokeRect method is used to create a second row of rectangles, but these rectangles are not filled in. The result is shown in Figure 12-1.

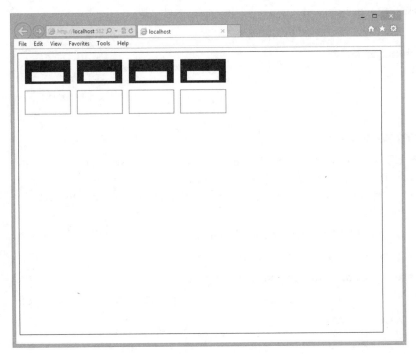

FIGURE 12-1 Drawing rectangles on the canvas

You can see that the drawing on the canvas does indeed require knowledge of JavaScript and the canvas context object.

Configuring the drawing state

In the previous example, what is the fill color when calling fillRect? What is the line thickness and color when calling strokeRect? The canvas context has properties that you can set before you call any of the drawing methods. After you change a property, the new value is used for subsequent drawing statements.

Setting fillStyle

Use the fillStyle property to specify how you want to fill shapes. You can set fillStyle to one of the following values.

- **CSS color**   Creates a solid color fill based on a valid CSS color value such as black, red, or #00FF00. The following is an example of setting fillStyle by using a *CSS color* value.

```
function drawUsingCssColor() {
    var canvas = document.getElementById('myCanvas')
        , ctx = canvas.getContext('2d')
        , offset = 10
        , size = 50;

    ctx.fillStyle = "red";
    ctx.fillRect(offset + (0 * (offset + size)), offset, size, size);
    ctx.fillRect(offset + (1 * (offset + size)), offset, size, size);

    ctx.fillStyle = "#00FF00";
    ctx.fillRect(offset + (2 * (offset + size)), offset, size, size);
    ctx.fillRect(offset + (3 * (offset + size)), offset, size, size);

    ctx.fillStyle = "rgba(0, 0, 255, 0.25)";
    ctx.fillRect(offset + (4 * (offset + size)), offset, size, size);
    ctx.fillRect(offset + (5 * (offset + size)), offset, size, size);
}
```

In this example, fillStyle is set to "red", and two rectangles are created. Next, fillStyle is set to green, using "#00FF00", and two rectangles are created. Finally, fillStyle is set to blue with opacity of 25 percent, using "rgba(0,0,255,0.25)", and two rectangles are created. The results are shown in Figure 12-2.

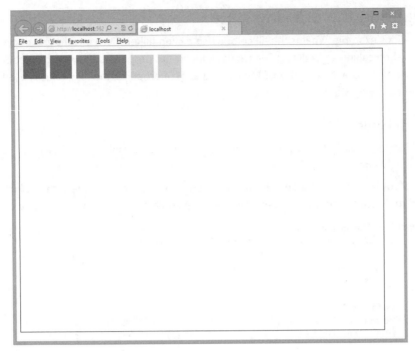

FIGURE 12-2 The rendered rectangles, using *CSS color* values

- **Gradient** A CanvasGradient object that is created by the context's createLinearGradient or createRadialGradient method to create a gradient fill.

The createLinearGradient method accepts the x and y values of two points that are used to create a linear gradient, for example, createLinearGradient(x0, y0, x1, y1).

The createRadialGradient accepts the x and y center and the radius of two circles, for example, createRadialGradient(x0, y0, r0, x1, y1, r1).

After the gradient object is created, call its addColorStop method to specify that a color is set at a location on the gradient. The addColorStop function takes two parameters; the first parameter is the location, which is a value between 0 and 1 where 0 is the beginning of the gradient and 1 is the end of the gradient, and the second parameter is the color value.

The following is an example of setting fillStyle, using a gradient value.

```
function drawGradient() {
    var canvas = document.getElementById('myCanvas')
        , ctx = canvas.getContext('2d')
        , x0 = 0
        , y0 = 0
        , r0 = 0
        , x1 = 200
        , y1 = 0
        , r1 = 100
        , width = 300
```

```
          , height = 50
          , offset = 10;

          gradient = ctx.createLinearGradient(x0, y0, x1, y1);
          addColorStops(gradient);
          ctx.fillStyle = gradient;
          ctx.fillRect(10, 0 * (height + offset), width, height);
          ctx.fillRect(100, 1 * (height + offset), width, height);

          y1 = 300;
          gradient = ctx.createLinearGradient(x0, y0, x1, y1);
          addColorStops(gradient);
          ctx.fillStyle = gradient;
          ctx.fillRect(10, 2 * (height + offset), width, height);
          ctx.fillRect(100, 3 * (height + offset), width, height);

          x0 = x1 = width / 2;
          y0 = y1 = 4 * (height + offset) + (height / 2);
          gradient = ctx.createRadialGradient(x0, y0, r0, x1, y1, r1);
          addColorStops(gradient);
          ctx.fillStyle = gradient;
          ctx.fillRect(10, 4 * (height + offset), width, height);
          ctx.fillRect(100, 5 * (height + offset), width, height);

          y0 = 5 * (height + offset) + (height / 2);
          y1 = y0 + 100;
          gradient = ctx.createRadialGradient(x0, y0, r0, x1, y1, r1);
          addColorStops(gradient);
          ctx.fillStyle = gradient;
          ctx.fillRect(10, 6 * (height + offset), width, height);
          ctx.fillRect(100, 7 * (height + offset), width, height);
}

function addColorStops(gradient) {
     gradient.addColorStop("0", "magenta");
     gradient.addColorStop(".25", "blue");
     gradient.addColorStop(".50", "green");
     gradient.addColorStop(".75", "yellow");
     gradient.addColorStop("1.0", "red");
}
```

When this example code is executed, it produces the result shown in Figure 12-3.

FIGURE 12-3 Creating and assigning gradients to the fillStyle property

This example code displays two rectangles for each test, in which the second rectangle is offset from the first rectangle, so you can see how the gradient is rendered relative to the canvas, not to the rectangle.

The first pair of rectangles demonstrates a horizontal linear gradient when y0 and y1 are equal.

The second pair of rectangles shows what happens when y1 is different from y0. In this example, if you draw a line from x0, y0 to x1, y1, the line will be angled downward. The gradient is rendered along this line and displays as a diagonal linear gradient.

The third pair of rectangles illustrates the radial gradient when x0=x1 and y0=y1, but r0 is set to zero when r1 is set to 100. Because both points are the same, the radial gradient is circular. Because r0 is zero, the gradient starts in the center. The gradient ends at r1, which is set to 100.

The last pair of rectangles shows what happens when the two points are not the same. In this case, x0 and x1 are the same, but y0 and y1 are different, which produces a non-circular gradient.

- **Pattern**   A CanvasPattern object that is created by using the context's createPattern method and creates a pattern fill. The createPattern method takes an image parameter and a direction parameter. The image is a reference to an *<img>* element, and the direction is a string containing no-repeat, repeat-x, repeat-y, or repeat.

Figure 12-4 shows a small image with a rectangle and a circle. This image has a transparent background, and there is no border around the edge of the image.

FIGURE 12-4 Image used to create a repeating pattern

By using the image in Figure 12-4, the following code creates a pattern that is assigned to the fillStyle property.

```
function drawPattern() {
    var canvas = document.getElementById('myCanvas')
        , ctx = canvas.getContext('2d');

    // create new image object to use as pattern
    var img = new Image();
    img.src = 'images/pattern.gif';
    img.onload = function () {
        // create pattern
        var ptrn = ctx.createPattern(img, 'repeat');
        ctx.fillStyle = ptrn;
        ctx.fillRect(0, 0, 400, 400);
    }
}
```

In this example, instead of creating an *<img>* element, the image is dynamically created, and its source (src) is set to the pattern.gif file. Next, the onload event of the image is subscribed to that creates the pattern on the canvas after the pattern.gif file is loaded. The result is shown in Figure 12-5.

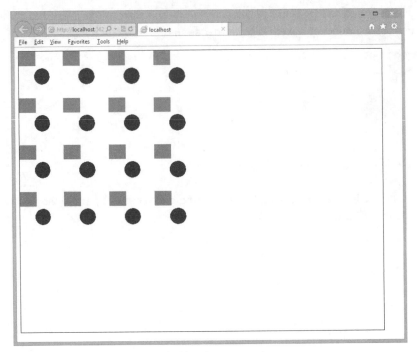

FIGURE 12-5 The pattern repeated within the rectangular area

Setting lineWidth

The lineWidth property specifies the thickness of any line you draw. The following code example draws rectangles by using different lineWidth settings.

```
function drawLineWidth() {
    var canvas = document.getElementById('myCanvas')
        , ctx = canvas.getContext('2d')
        , offset = 40
        , width = 5
        , height = 5
        , lineWidth = 1
        , i = 0
        , centerX = canvas.width / 2
        , centerY = canvas.height / 2;

    for (i = 1; i < 15; i++) {
        ctx.lineWidth = i;
        ctx.strokeRect(centerX - (width / 2) - (i * offset / 2),
            centerY - (height / 2) - (i * offset / 2),
            width + (i * offset), height + (i * offset));
    }
}
```

In this example, lineWidth is changed on each iteration of the for loop; the drawn rectangle starts small and gets larger with each iteration. The result is shown in Figure 12-6.

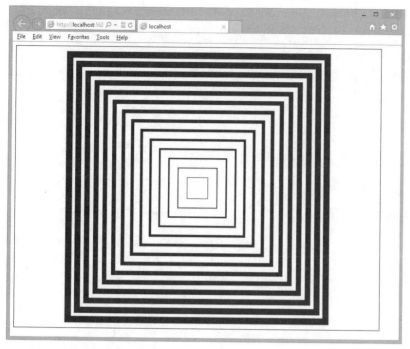

FIGURE 12-6 The lineWidth, increased on each iteration of the for loop

Setting lineJoin

The lineJoin property specifies the way lines that join each other are drawn. You can set the lineJoin property to round, bevel, or miter. The default value is miter. The difference between these settings is most noticeable with thicker lines.

The following code demonstrates the creation of three rectangles that have different lineJoin settings.

```
function drawLineJoin() {
    var canvas = document.getElementById('myCanvas')
        , ctx = canvas.getContext('2d');
    ctx.lineWidth = 20;

    ctx.lineJoin = 'round';
    ctx.strokeRect(20, 20, 50, 50);

    ctx.lineJoin = 'bevel';
    ctx.strokeRect(100, 100, 50, 50);

    ctx.lineJoin = 'miter';
    ctx.strokeRect(180, 180, 50, 50);
}
```

In this example, the first rectangle's lineJoin property is set to round. This produces a rectangle with rounded corners. The second rectangle's lineJoin property is set to bevel, which produces a rectangle with beveled corners. Finally, the third rectangle's lineJoin property is set to miter, which produces a rectangle with mitered, or pointy, corners. The result is shown in Figure 12-7.

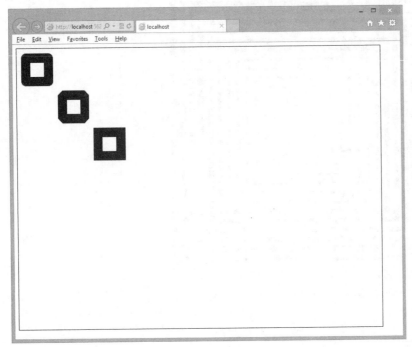

FIGURE 12-7 The lineJoin property specifying the look of the corners

Setting strokeStyle

The strokeStyle property specifies the way you want to draw lines. This setting is the same as the fillStyle property described earlier. See the "Setting fillStyle" section for more information regarding the valid settings. The following is an example of the strokeStyle property.

```
function drawGradientStroke() {
    var canvas = document.getElementById('myCanvas')
        , ctx = canvas.getContext('2d')
        , x0 = 0
        , y0 = 0
        , r0 = 0
        , x1 = 200
        , y1 = 0
        , r1 = 100
        , width = 300
        , height = 40
        , offset = 25;

    ctx.lineWidth = 15;
    gradient = ctx.createLinearGradient(x0, y0, x1, y1);
```

```
    addColorStops(gradient);
    ctx.strokeStyle = gradient;
    ctx.strokeRect(10, 0 * (height + offset), width, height);
    ctx.strokeRect(100, 1 * (height + offset), width, height);

    y1 = 300;
    gradient = ctx.createLinearGradient(x0, y0, x1, y1);
    addColorStops(gradient);

    ctx.strokeStyle = gradient;
    ctx.strokeRect(10, 2 * (height + offset), width, height);
    ctx.strokeRect(100, 3 * (height + offset), width, height);

    x0 = x1 = width / 2;
    y0 = y1 = 4 * (height + offset) + (height / 2);
    gradient = ctx.createRadialGradient(x0, y0, r0, x1, y1, r1);
    addColorStops(gradient);
    ctx.strokeStyle = gradient;
    ctx.strokeRect(10, 4 * (height + offset), width, height);
    ctx.strokeRect(100, 5 * (height + offset), width, height);

    y0 = 5 * (height + offset) + (height / 2);
    y1 = y0 + 100;
    gradient = ctx.createRadialGradient(x0, y0, r0, x1, y1, r1);
    addColorStops(gradient);
    ctx.strokeStyle = gradient;
    ctx.strokeRect(10, 6 * (height + offset), width, height);
    ctx.strokeRect(100, 7 * (height + offset), width, height);

}
```

This example is a modified version of the drawGradient function that was presented as an example of the fillStyle property. The addColorStops function is also defined in that example. The result is shown in Figure 12-8.

FIGURE 12-8 The strokeStyle property, which accepts the same values as fillStyle

Saving and restoring the drawing state

It is possible to save all the context object properties to a stack, which is a last-in, first-out (LIFO) collection. This does not save the actual canvas; just the settings are saved. The save method saves the current settings, and the restore method restores the settings. The following example shows the save and restore methods.

```
function saveRestore() {
    var canvas = document.getElementById('myCanvas')
        , ctx = canvas.getContext('2d');
    ctx.lineWidth = 20;
    ctx.strokeStyle = "green";
    ctx.lineJoin = 'round';
    ctx.strokeRect(20, 20, 50, 50);
    ctx.save();

    ctx.lineWidth = 10;
    ctx.strokeStyle = "red";
    ctx.lineJoin = 'bevel';
    ctx.strokeRect(100, 100, 50, 50);

    ctx.restore();
    ctx.strokeRect(180, 180, 50, 50);
}
```

In this example, the lineWidth, strokeStyle, and lineJoin properties are set, and a rectangle is drawn. The save method is called to save the settings. The settings are modified, and a new rectangle is drawn with the new settings. Finally, the restore method is called, which pops (gets and removes) the settings from the stack, and a rectangle is drawn. This rectangle has the same property settings as the first rectangle. The result is shown in Figure 12-9.

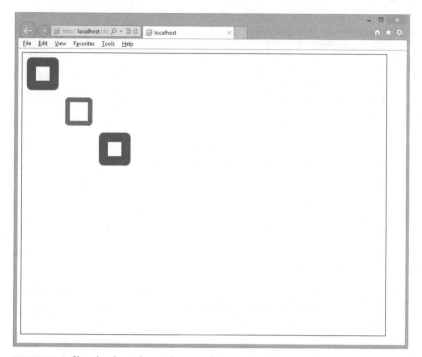

FIGURE 12-9 Showing how the settings can be saved and restored

You can save many times to create a stack of settings and then restore many times to empty the stack.

Drawing by using paths

A path is a set of lines that are used to draw shapes. Each line is called a *sub-path*. Each sub-path has a start and an end, and the end of one sub-path is typically where the next sub-path starts. The collection of sub-paths makes a shape.

The sequence for creating a shape is as follows.

1. Start a path by calling the beginPath method.
2. Go to the starting position by calling the moveTo method.
3. Draw sub-paths calling methods such as lineTo and rect.
4. End the path by optionally calling the closePath method.
5. Render the filled shape or outlined shape by calling fill or stroke methods, respectively.

The examples that follow have a simple webpage with a *<canvas>* element and references to canvasPath.css, canvasPath.js, and jquery-1.8.2.js files as follows.

```
<!DOCTYPE html>
<html xmlns="http://www.w3.org/1999/xhtml">
<head>
    <title></title>
    <link href="Content/canvasPath.css" rel="stylesheet" />
    <script src="Scripts/jquery-1.8.2.js"></script>
    <script src="Scripts/canvasPath.js"></script>
</head>
<body>
    <canvas id="myCanvas" width="800" height="600">
        You need a browser that supports HTML5!
    </canvas>
</body>
</html>
```

The canvasPath.js file is presented in each example. The canvasPath.css file contains the following style rule.

```
canvas {
    border: 1px solid black;
}
```

Drawing lines

The easiest path to create is one composed of lines. This is accomplished by using the lineTo method, which accepts x and y parameters. The following is an example of using lines to create shapes that have a yellow outline and green fill.

```
$(document).ready(function () {
    drawLine();
});

function drawLine(){
    var canvas = document.getElementById('myCanvas')
    , ctx = canvas.getContext('2d');

    ctx.fillStyle = 'green';
    ctx.strokeStyle = 'yellow';
    ctx.lineWidth = 10;

    ctx.beginPath();
    ctx.moveTo(100, 250);
    ctx.lineTo(150, 350);
    ctx.lineTo( 50, 350);
    ctx.closePath();
    ctx.fill();

    ctx.beginPath();
    ctx.moveTo(150, 250);
    ctx.lineTo(250, 250);
    ctx.lineTo(200, 350);
```

```
    ctx.closePath();
    ctx.fill();
    ctx.stroke();

    ctx.beginPath();
    ctx.moveTo(300, 250);
    ctx.lineTo(350, 350);
    ctx.lineTo(250, 350);
    ctx.fill();
    ctx.stroke();

    ctx.beginPath();
    ctx.moveTo(500, 250);
    ctx.lineTo(500, 350);
    ctx.moveTo(450, 300);
    ctx.lineTo(550, 300)
    ctx.fill();
    ctx.stroke();

}
```

This example draws four shapes. The rendered output is shown in Figure 12-10.

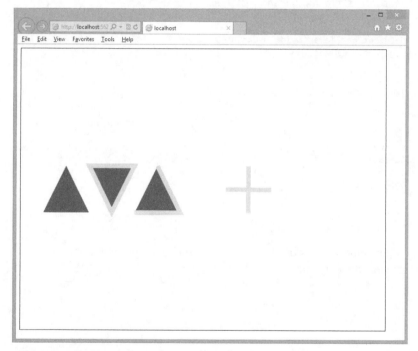

FIGURE 12-10 Rendered shapes that are drawn by using the lineTo method

The first shape is a triangle. It's created by drawing two lines and then calling the closePath method, which draws a line from the end back to the start. The fill method is called to fill the triangle with green. There is no outline because the stroke method was not called.

The second shape is also a triangle and is drawn like the first triangle, but the stroke method is called after the fill method is called. The stroke method creates the yellow outline.

The third shape is also a triangle, but this code doesn't call the closePath method. In this example, the fill method implicitly calculates the fill area, but because the closePath method is not called, there is no line from the end to the start; therefore, no outline is rendered from the end to the start.

The fourth shape is a plus sign. This demonstrates the use of the moveTo method to create a line that doesn't start where the previous line ended. The stroke method creates the lines, but the fill method doesn't render anything.

Drawing rectangles

You can add rectangles to your path by calling the rect method. Keep in mind that if all you need to do is draw a rectangle, you can use the fillRect and the strokeRect methods, discussed earlier in this lesson.

The rect method is useful when you are defining a complex shape. Instead of adding many lineTo calls to draw a rectangle, you just call the rect method. The following is an example of creating a shape that consists of a triangle and rectangle.

```
function drawRect() {
    var canvas = document.getElementById('myCanvas')
    , ctx = canvas.getContext('2d');

    ctx.fillStyle = 'green';
    ctx.strokeStyle = 'yellow';
    ctx.lineWidth = 10;

    ctx.beginPath();
    ctx.moveTo(100, 300);
    ctx.lineTo(150, 250);
    ctx.lineTo(200, 300);
    ctx.rect(100, 300, 100, 100);
    ctx.fill();
    ctx.stroke();
}
```

The rendered output is shown in Figure 12-11. Notice in the rendered output that the triangle and the rectangle are outlined.

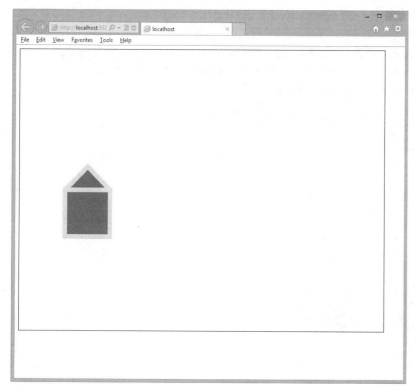

FIGURE 12-11 The rendered output, using lineTo and rect methods

 Quick check

- What are the four parameters of the rect method?

Quick check answer

- The first and second parameters are the x and y coordinates of the upper-left corner of the rectangle. The third parameter is the width, and the fourth parameter is the height.

Ordering the fill and the stroke method calls

You might be wondering whether there is a difference between calling fill and then stroke versus calling stroke and then fill. There is a difference, but before the difference is displayed, you need to understand how the stroke is rendered.

When stroke is called, the outline is created using the current lineWidth property. Half of lineWidth is outside the shape, and half is inside the shape. The part of the outline that is inside the shape overwrites the fill if the stroke method is called after the fill method.

However, if the fill method is called after the stroke method, the fill overwrites the stroke that is inside the fill area.

Consider the following example that draws two shapes, each consisting of a triangle and a rectangle. The difference is the order in which the fill method and the stroke method are called. The rendered output is shown in Figure 12-12.

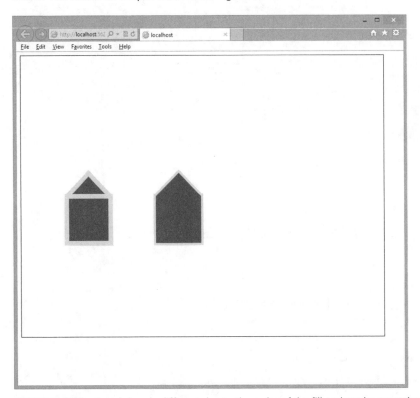

FIGURE 12-12 Rendered shapes, different due to the order of the fill and stroke execution

```
function drawRect() {
    var canvas = document.getElementById('myCanvas')
    , ctx = canvas.getContext('2d');

    ctx.fillStyle = 'green';
    ctx.strokeStyle = 'yellow';
    ctx.lineWidth = 10;

    ctx.beginPath();
    ctx.moveTo(100, 300);
    ctx.lineTo(150, 250);
    ctx.lineTo(200, 300);
    ctx.rect(100, 300, 100, 100);
    ctx.fill();
    ctx.stroke();

    ctx.beginPath();
```

```
    ctx.moveTo(300, 300);
    ctx.lineTo(350, 250);
    ctx.lineTo(400, 300);
    ctx.rect(300, 300, 100, 100);
    ctx.stroke();
    ctx.fill();
}
```

The rendered output of the outline of the second shape is narrow compared to the outline of the first shape, and the second shape does not have the horizontal line of the triangle. These differences result from the fill method being called after the stroke method, so the fill color overwrites any previous color.

Drawing arcs by using the arcTo method

In addition to drawing straight lines, you can draw curved lines by using the arc and the arcTo methods on the context object.

The arcTo method accepts an x1 and a y1 coordinate that define a point through which the arc lines must pass, followed by an x2 and a y2 coordinate that define the endpoint, followed by the radius of the arc. Although only two points are provided as parameters, a third point (x0, y0) is the starting point of the arc. The third point is the ending point of the previous sub-path.

Drawing an arc by using the arcTo method can be confusing. To understand how arcTo works, perform the following steps.

1. On a piece of paper, draw a line through (x0, y0) and (x1, y1).

2. Draw a line through (x1, y1) and (x2, y2).

3. On a separate piece of paper, draw a circle of radius r and cut it out.

4. Place the circle on the paper that has the two lines and slide the circle up between the line that contains (x0, y0) and the line that contains (x2, y2) until it just touches both lines. The two points where the circle touches the lines are called tangent points, where t1 is closest to (x0, y0), and t2 is closest to (x2, y2).

5. Draw a line from point (x0, y0) to the first tangent point on the line from (x0, y0) to (x1, y1).

6. Draw an arc from that tangent point to the other tangent point on the line from (x1, y1) to (x2, y2) along the circumference of the circle.

7. The endpoint of arcTo is the second tangent point on the line from (x1, y1) to (x2, y2).

Figure 12-13 shows two examples of the arcTo implementation.

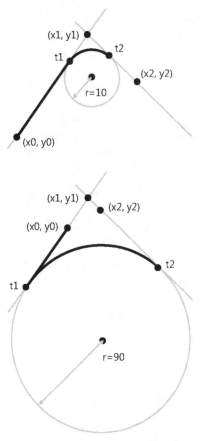

FIGURE 12-13 The arcTo method producing unexpected results if you don't understand how it works

In the first example, the radius of the circle is small, so the circle is slid up past x0, y0 and x2, y2 until it touches the lines. In this example, t1 is between x0, y0 and x1, y1, whereas t2 is between x1, y1 and x2, y2. There is some distance between x0, y0 and t1, so this arc starts as a straight line until it reaches t1. At t1, the curve starts until it reaches t2, where the arc ends.

In the second example, the radius is much larger, so the circle is slid up until it touches the lines, but this time, t1 is outside x0, y1, and t2 is outside x2, y2. There is still some distance between (x0, y0) and t1, so a straight line is drawn between the two points. At t1, the curve starts until it reaches t2, where the arc ends.

Consider the following code example that draws two lines and then creates an arc by using the arcTo method.

```
function drawArcTo() {
    var canvas = document.getElementById('myCanvas')
    , ctx = canvas.getContext('2d');

    ctx.strokeStyle = 'gray';
```

```
    ctx.lineWidth = 1;
    ctx.beginPath();
    ctx.moveTo(300, 200);
    ctx.lineTo(400, 500);
    ctx.lineTo(600, 300);
    ctx.stroke();

    ctx.strokeStyle = 'black';
    ctx.lineWidth = 5;
    ctx.beginPath();
    ctx.moveTo(300, 200);
    ctx.arcTo(400, 500, 600, 300, 50);
    ctx.stroke();
}
```

In this example, the lines are drawn to depict the lines from the previous example. The lines are gray, and lineWidth is set to 1. The arc is drawn by using the arcTo method. This starting point is 300, 200, the second point is 400, 500, and the last point is 600, 300. The radius is set to 50. The rendered output is shown in Figure 12-14.

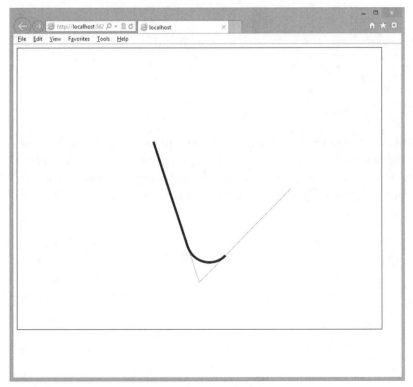

FIGURE 12-14 The rendered arc when the radius is set to 50

Because the starting point is always the ending point of the previous sub-path (or, in this case, the moveTo location), the stroke continues from that point until it reaches the first tangent, and then the curve starts until it reaches the second tangent, and then the arc is finished.

In this code example, the points stay the same, but the radius is changed from 50 to 300 as follows.

```
function drawArcTo() {
    var canvas = document.getElementById('myCanvas')
    , ctx = canvas.getContext('2d');

    ctx.strokeStyle = 'gray';
    ctx.lineWidth = 1;

    ctx.beginPath();
    ctx.moveTo(300, 200);
    ctx.lineTo(400, 500);
    ctx.lineTo(600, 300);
    ctx.stroke();

    ctx.strokeStyle = 'black';
    ctx.lineWidth = 5;

    ctx.beginPath();
    ctx.moveTo(300, 200);
    ctx.arcTo(400, 500, 600, 300, 300);
    ctx.stroke();
}
```

The result is shown in Figure 12-15. The radius of the circle has a profound impact on the rendered arc. In addition, because the circle is slid into the angle that's formed by the line x0, y0 is on and the line x2, y2 is on, you can't possibly create an arc that is greater than 180 degrees because the circle will always touch these lines to create tangents t1 and t2 before the arc reaches 180 degrees.

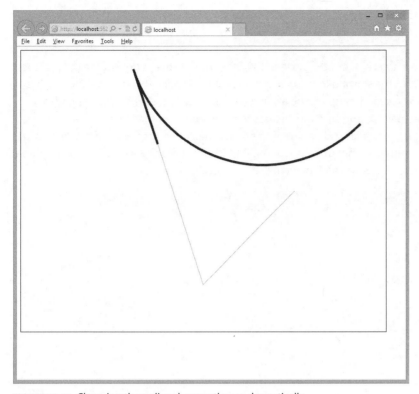

FIGURE 12-15 Changing the radius changes the arc dramatically

Drawing arcs by using the arc method

The arc method is much simpler to use than the arcTo method. The arc method can be used to draw a circle or any part of a circle. This is different from the behavior of the arcTo method, which cannot draw more than half a circle and might produce lines with the arc in an effort to continue a path without breaking the stroke.

The arc method accepts x and y coordinates as the center of the circle used to draw the arc, followed by the radius of the circle that the arc will use, followed by the starting angle and the ending angle. You can add a direction parameter that indicates the direction of the arc. The following example code shows how to create a circle by using the arc method.

```
function drawArc() {
    var canvas = document.getElementById('myCanvas')
    , ctx = canvas.getContext('2d');

    ctx.strokeStyle = 'blue';
    ctx.fillStyle = 'yellow';
    ctx.lineWidth = 5;

    ctx.beginPath();
    ctx.arc(400, 300, 100, 0, 2 * Math.PI);
```

```
    ctx.fill();
    ctx.stroke();
}
```

In this example, the center of the circle is 400, 300, which is the middle of the canvas. The radius is set to 100. The starting location must be a value between 0 and 6.283185, which is 2 * PI. The ending location must also be a value between 0 and 6.283185. The values 0 and 6.283185 can be used to represent the farthest right-side point of the circle. The value of 3.14159 (PI) is the farthest left-side point of the circle. The uppermost point of the circle is 1.5 * PI, while the lowermost point of the circle is .5 * PI. The rendered canvas is shown in Figure 12-16. The rendered circle has a blue outline and yellow fill.

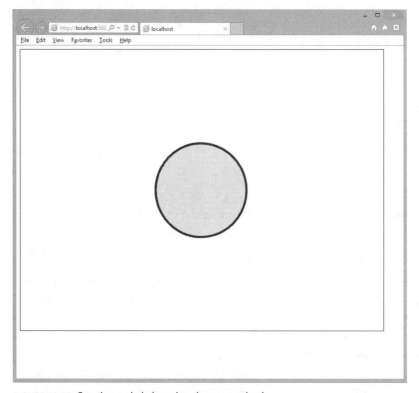

FIGURE 12-16 Creating a circle by using the arc method

To draw an arc that represents part of the circle, you need valid start and end locations, and you need to consider the optional direction parameter. By default, the stroke is rendered clockwise, which means that the direction is set to false. Consider the following example, in which you provide a start location of 0 and an end location of 1.5 * PI.

```
function drawArc() {
    var canvas = document.getElementById('myCanvas')
    , ctx = canvas.getContext('2d');
```

```
    ctx.strokeStyle = 'blue';
    ctx.fillStyle = 'yellow';
    ctx.lineWidth = 5;

    ctx.beginPath();
    ctx.arc(400, 300, 100, 0, 1.5 * Math.PI);
    ctx.fill();
    ctx.stroke();
}
```

The rendered arc is shown in Figure 12-17, which shows that three-quarters of the circle is rendered. Is that what you wanted or expected? If you want to render only the quarter of the circle that is missing, you have two possible solutions.

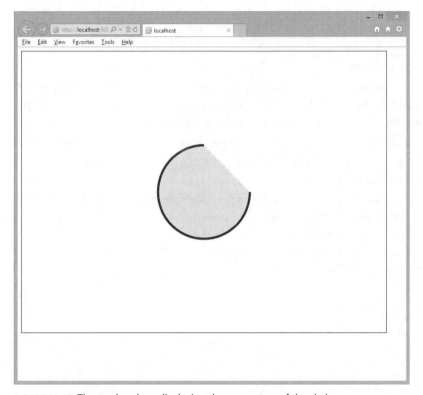

FIGURE 12-17 The rendered arc displaying three-quarters of the circle

One solution is to set the start location to 1.5 * Math.PI and the end location to 0. Because the rendering renders the stroke clockwise, the arc will start rendering at the uppermost point of the circle and stop at the rightmost point of the circle.

The other solution is to leave the start at 0 and the end at 1.5 * Math.PI but add the optional direction parameter, passing in a value of *true*. This causes the stroke rendering to go counterclockwise, which renders the quarter circle.

Drawing text

You can also draw text on the canvas by using the fillText or strokeText method. Support for drawing text is somewhat basic. Both methods require you to pass the text to be drawn as the first parameter, followed by x and y coordinates that specify where the text is drawn. The exact meaning of the coordinate depends on the value of the textAlign and textBaseline properties, but the default is that the coordinate is at the lower-left corner of the text that's drawn. You can also provide a parameter to indicate the maximum width of the text to be drawn.

In addition to the methods, the following properties can be set to control the look of the rendered text.

- **font**   Sets the font style, size, and family, delimited by spaces. The style can be normal, italic, or bold. The size can be a CSS size. The family represents the font family, which can be a generic font family, such as serif or sans serif, or a specific font family, such as Arial or Courier.

- **textAlign**   Sets the horizontal alignment of the text in relation to the coordinate that is passed into the fillText or strokeText method. Can be start, end, left, right, or center. Note that start and left are the same, and end and right are the same.

- **textBaseline**   Sets the vertical alignment of the text in relation to the coordinate that is passed into the fillText or strokeText method. Can be top, hanging, middle, alphabetic, ideographic, or bottom.

The following example code draws a line across the canvas, through its center point (400, 300). After that, "Hello" is drawn using the coordinate of 400, 300.

```
function drawText() {
    var canvas = document.getElementById('myCanvas')
    , ctx = canvas.getContext('2d');

    ctx.strokeStyle = 'magenta';
    ctx.fillStyle = 'yellow';
    ctx.lineWidth = 2;
    ctx.font = "bold 100pt TimesNewRoman";

    ctx.beginPath();
    ctx.moveTo(100, 300);
    ctx.lineTo(700, 300);
    ctx.stroke();

    ctx.strokeStyle = 'blue';
    ctx.fillText("Hello", 400, 300);
    ctx.strokeText("Hello", 400, 300);
}
```

The line is drawn as its own path, and then the stroke color is changed to blue, but there is no need to start a new path because fillText and strokeText create their own path. The fillText method automatically fills the text without requiring a call to the fill method. The strokeText automatically outlines the text; in this case, this text overlies the rendered fillText. The result is shown in Figure 12-18.

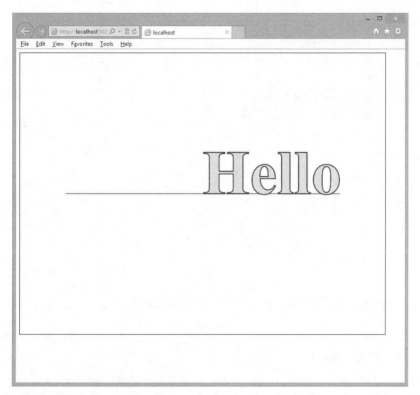

FIGURE 12-18 The rendered Hello message showing that the coordinate is at the lower left of the text

The provided coordinate of 400, 300 is at the lower left of the rendered text, which means that the default value of the textAlign property is start or left, and the default value of the textBaseline is bottom. If you change the textAlign property to center and change the text-Baseline to middle, the text will be centered horizontally and vertically within the canvas, as shown in Figure 12-19.

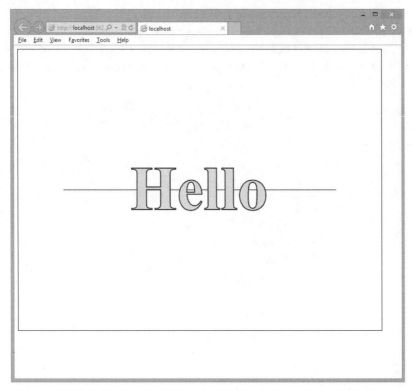

FIGURE 12-19 Changing the textAlign and the textBaseline to center the text within the canvas

Drawing with images

In addition to drawing the many shapes this lesson has covered, you might want to place images on the canvas. You can do this by drawing the image on the canvas, using the drawImage method of the context object.

The drawImage method can accept either three or five arguments. The first argument is the source of the image, which can be an *<img>* or *<video>* element or another *<canvas>* element. When the *<video>* element is used, a snapshot of the frame that is currently displayed is used as the image. When passing three arguments to the drawImage method, the second and third arguments are the x and y coordinates of the upper-left corner of the image. You can also create the *<img>* element in your JavaScript, which is great for when the presentation of the image might be conditional and you don't want to waste time loading the image unless it's required. The following code example demonstrates the creation of the *<img>* element dynamically, loading it with a photo of an iceboat. When the image is loaded, the drawImage method is called, and the image is passed in as the first argument.

```
function drawImage() {
    var canvas = document.getElementById('myCanvas')
        , ctx = canvas.getContext('2d');
```

```
    var img = new Image();
    img.src = "images/IceBoat.jpg";
    img.onload = function () {
        ctx.drawImage(img, 0, 0);
    }
}
```

The results are shown in Figure 12-20. The image is drawn at its native width and height. If the image is larger than the canvas, it's clipped. This image is 538 pixels wide and 718 pixels tall. Because the canvas is 800 pixels wide and 600 pixels tall, the bottom of this image is clipped.

FIGURE 12-20 The drawn image placed in the upper-left corner of the canvas

You might need to control the size of the drawn image. Specify this with two more arguments when calling the drawImage method, the width and the height. In the following example, the width is set to 300, and the height is set to 400.

```
function drawImage() {
    var canvas = document.getElementById('myCanvas')
        , ctx = canvas.getContext('2d');
    var img = new Image();
    img.src = "images/IceBoat.jpg";
    img.onload = function () {
```

```
        ctx.drawImage(img, 0, 0, 300, 400);
    }
}
```

The result is shown in Figure 12-21. When providing the height and width, you should try to maintain the proportions of the image to keep the image from being skewed to look very skinny or very fat.

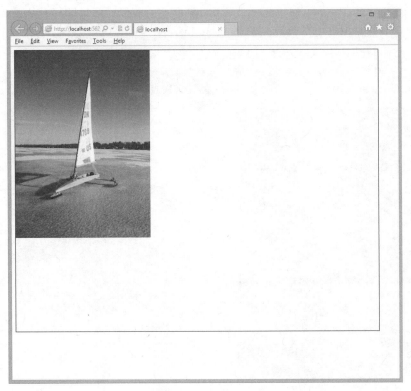

FIGURE 12-21 The image drawn with a reduced size so it fits within the canvas

Keep in mind that you can draw your image and then overlay other shapes as necessary. The following code demonstrates this by annotating the image.

```
function drawImage() {
    var canvas = document.getElementById('myCanvas')
        , ctx = canvas.getContext('2d');
    var img = new Image();
    img.src = "images/IceBoat.jpg";
    img.onload = function () {
        ctx.font = 'bold 24pt Arial';

        ctx.drawImage(img, 175, 0, 450, 600);

        ctx.strokeStyle = 'black';
        ctx.lineWidth = 2;
```

```
ctx.beginPath();
ctx.moveTo(405, 180);
ctx.lineTo(325, 180);
ctx.stroke();
ctx.strokeStyle = 'white';
ctx.lineWidth = 1;
ctx.textAlign = 'right';
ctx.textBaseline = 'middle';
ctx.fillText('Mast', 325, 180);
ctx.strokeText('Mast', 325, 180);

ctx.strokeStyle = 'black';
ctx.lineWidth = 2;
ctx.beginPath();
ctx.moveTo(420, 220);
ctx.lineTo(525, 220);
ctx.stroke();
ctx.strokeStyle = 'white';
ctx.lineWidth = 1;
ctx.textAlign = 'left';
ctx.textBaseline = 'middle';
ctx.fillText('Sail', 525, 220);
ctx.strokeText('Sail', 525, 220);

ctx.strokeStyle = 'black';
ctx.lineWidth = 2;
ctx.beginPath();
ctx.moveTo(420, 360);
ctx.lineTo(500, 360);
ctx.stroke();
ctx.strokeStyle = 'white';
ctx.lineWidth = 1;
ctx.textAlign = 'left';
ctx.textBaseline = 'middle';
ctx.fillText('Boom', 500, 360);
ctx.strokeText('Boom', 500, 360);
    }
}
```

The result is shown in Figure 12-22.

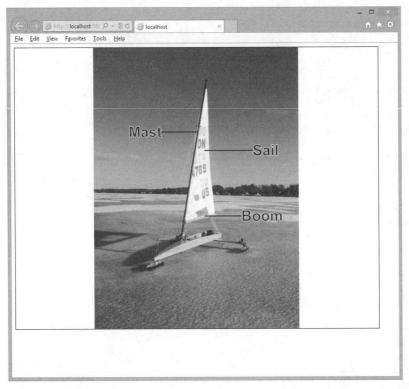

FIGURE 12-22 The annotated image showing that you can mix images and shapes on the canvas

Lesson summary

- The *<canvas>* element is new in HTML5 and provides a drawing context that is accessible using JavaScript.
- Use the getContext method on the *<canvas>* element to get a reference to the context object.
- Use the fillRect and strokeRect methods to draw rectangles.
- Methods that start with *fill* are used to fill the shape with the value of the fillStyle property. The fillStyle property can be set to a color, gradient, or pattern.
- Methods that begin with *stroke* create an outline of the shape with the value of the strokeStyle property. The strokeStyle property can be set to a color, gradient, or pattern.
- The context object's properties can be pushed onto a stack by using the save method or popped from the stack by using the restore method.
- Use paths to create complex shapes using lines, rectangles, and arcs.
- Use the fillText and strokeText methods to draw text on the canvas. Use the drawImage method to draw images on the canvas.

Lesson review

Answer the following questions to test your knowledge of the information in this lesson. You can find the answers to these questions and explanations of why each answer choice is correct or incorrect in the "Answers" section at the end of this chapter.

1. Which code example can be used to draw a rectangle on a *<canvas>* element that has an id of myCanvas?

   A. var canvas = document.getElementById('myCanvas');
   var ctx = canvas.getContext();
   ctx.rectangle(10, 10, 50, 75);

   B. var canvas = document.getElementById('myCanvas');
   canvas.rectangle(10, 10, 50, 75);

   C. var canvas = document.getElementById('myCanvas');
   var ctx = canvas.getContext('2d');
   ctx.fillRect(10, 10, 50, 75);

   D. var canvas = document.getElementById('myCanvas');
   var ctx = canvas.getContext();
   ctx.fillRect(10, 10, 50, 75);

2. You want to draw an arc that is approximately three-quarters of a circle. Which method is the easiest to use to accomplish this task?

   A. arcTo()

   B. arc()

   C. circle()

   D. dot()

Lesson 2: Using scalable vector graphics

What is scalable vector graphics (SVG), and why would you want to use it? These are common questions, especially as everyone becomes aware of SVG due to its inclusion in HTML5. In Lesson 1, "Drawing by using the *<canvas>* element," you learned to draw on a *<canvas>* element, using JavaScript. Although you might have used shape-specific methods such as fillRect or arc, the rendering on the canvas is done in a bitmapped manner, meaning that pixels are commanded to display, and after the shape rendered, the canvas is left with bitmapped results. In other words, the canvas does not store the fact that you created a rectangle. If the drawing surface is scaled larger, the canvas only has the pixels to work with, so the result is a blocky, or pixelated, version of the graphic.

SVG is different from the canvas; with SVG, the commands are stored in a manner that enables them to be re-executed. If the size of the drawing surface changes, the commands can be scaled and re-executed for the new drawing to create a new image, based on the SVG commands. The result is that you see a crisp image regardless of the scale.

Even though SVG renders much better than the canvas, it takes time to scale and re-execute the commands, so performance is not as good. The canvas is preferable when performance is more important.

SVG is XML-based, and you can embed SVG in your HTML page by using the *<svg>* element. The content of the *<svg>* element contains the XML-based commands that make the drawing. The *<svg>* element, plus its content, is part of the document object model (DOM), so all of the *<svg>* element and its children are accessible from JavaScript. Events can also be attached to any of the elements. However, you don't want to write all the XML that's required to create a complex drawing. It's typically best to use an SVG editor to create the drawing and then embed the drawing into your webpage.

In this lesson, you learn how to use the *<svg>* element to embed a drawing in an HTML page to display simple graphics. In addition, you learn how to use the *<img>* element to display .svg files.

> **After this lesson, you will be able to:**
> - Describe the *<svg>* element.
> - Implement the *<svg>* element.
> - Display SVG files using the *<img>* element.
>
> **Estimated lesson time: 20 minutes**

Using the *<svg>* element

The *<svg>* element is a container for the XML-based commands. Using it in your HTML page enables you to embed your drawing directly into the page. The following is an example of a basic *<svg>* element.

```
<svg width="500" height="300" xmlns="http://www.w3.org/2000/svg">
</svg>
```

In this example, the width and height are set, and the XML namespace is defined to indicate that this is an SVG drawing.

Creating a path

A path is a sequence of commands that create a complex shape. Use the *<path>* element, which has id, fill, and d attributes, to create a path. The fill attribute is passed the color with which you want to fill the path. The d attribute is for the *<path>* element's data, which is populated with the commands and typically starts with a command to move to the point at which the drawing of the shape begins. The command to move is *m* or *M*. When the lowercase command is used, it indicates that the coordinates are relative. When the uppercase command is used, it indicates that the coordinates are absolute.

The following is a list of commands that can be used in a path.

- **M or m**   Move to a specified coordinate.
- **L or l**   Draw a line from the current location to the coordinate specified.
- **H or h**   Draw a horizontal line from the current location to the new *x* value specified on the same horizontal plane.
- **V or v**   Draw a vertical line from the current location to the new *y* value specified on the same vertical plane.
- **A or a**   Parameters are *rx, ry, x-axis-rotation, large-arc, sweep, x, and y*. This command draws an elliptical arc from the current point to the specified coordinate of *x, y* with x-radius *rx* and y-radius *ry*. The ellipse is rotated *x-axis-rotation* degrees. If the arc is less than 180 degrees, *large-arc* is zero; else it is one. If the arc is greater than 180 degrees, the *large-arc* is set to 1. If the arc is drawn in the positive direction, the *sweep* is set to 1; else the *sweep* is set to zero.
- **Q or q**   Parameters are *x1, y1, x, and y*. This command draws a quadratic Bézier curve from the current location to the coordinate specified as x, y by using the control point specified as x1, y1.
- **T or t**   Draw a quadratic Bézier curve from the current point to the coordinate specified, using the previous Q command's control point.
- **C or c**   Parameters are *x1, y1, x2, y2, x, and y*. This command draws a cubic Bézier curve from the current point to the x, y coordinate specified by using control point x1, y1 for the beginning of the curve and control point x2, y2 for the end of the curve.
- **S or s**   Parameters are *x2, y2, x, and y*. This command draws a cubic Bézier curve from the current point to the x, y coordinate specified by using the control point from the previous C command for the beginning of the curve and control point x2, y2 for the end of the curve.
- **Z or z**   Close the path from the current position to the beginning of the path.

The following example draws a car body by using a path that moves to 267, 76 and draws lines by using the l (lowercase L) command.

```
<path d="m267 76 l-21 -4 -144 0 -90 47 0 54 11 11 23 0 15 -30 15 -10 30 0 15 10
               15 30 220 0 15 -30 15 -10 30 0 15 10 15 30 l25 0 7 -7 -13 -38
               -20 -10 -95 -15 z" fill="blue" id="carBody"/>
```

In this example, the lowercase L was not repeating for each line command, which demonstrates that you can specify the command once, provide parameters, provide parameters again, and so on. The path ends with the lowercase Z command, which closes the path. The fill color is set to blue, and the id attribute is set to carBody.

Here are two more paths, which create the front and rear windows of the car.

```
<path d="m65 105 l40 -25 65 0 0 34 -112 0 z" fill="white" id="rearWindow" />
<path d="m300 105 l-40 -25 -78 0 0 34 122 0 z" fill="white" id="frontWindow" />
```

These paths have a fill color of white. The result in Figure 12-23 shows the rendered car body with its windows.

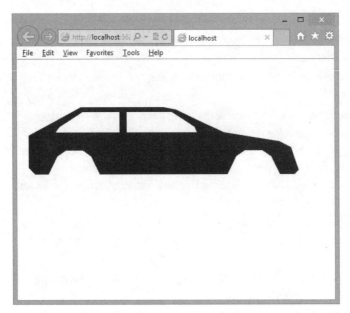

FIGURE 12-23 The *<path>* element that is used to create a car body with windows

Drawing circles

You can add circles to an SVG drawing by using the *<circle>* element, which has r, cx, cy, fill, and id attributes. The r attribute sets the circle radius. The cx and cy attributes set the circle center coordinate. The fill attribute sets the color of the circle. The following example adds two wheels to the vehicle body created in the previous example.

```
<circle r="35" cy="185" cx="90" fill="black" id="rearWheel" />
<circle r="35" cy="185" cx="400" fill="black" id="frontWheel" />
```

The completed *<svg>* element is as follows.

```
<svg width="500" height="300" xmlns="http://www.w3.org/2000/svg">
    <path d="m267 76 l-21 -4 -144 0 -90 47 0 54 11 11 23 0 15 -30 15 -10 30 0
                 15 10 15 30 220 0 15 -30 15 -10 30 0 15 10 15 30 125 0 7 -7
                 -13 -38 -20 -10 -95 -15 z" fill="blue" id="carBody" />
    <path d="m65 105 l40 -25 65 0 0 34 -112 0 z" fill="white" id="rearWindow" />
    <path d="m300 105 l-40 -25 -78 0 0 34 122 0 z" fill="white" id="frontWindow" />
    <circle r="35" cy="185" cx="90" fill="black" id="rearWheel" />
    <circle r="35" cy="185" cx="400" fill="black" id="frontWheel" />
</svg>
```

The completed car is shown in Figure 12-24.

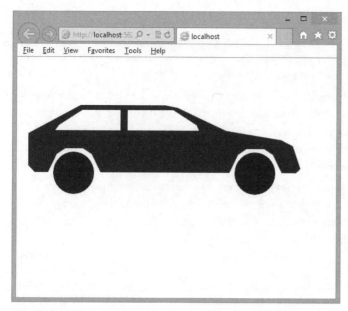

FIGURE 12-24 The rendered car using *<path>* and *<circle>* elements

Displaying SVG files by using the *<img>* element

You have just seen how you can create SVG images by writing the XML yourself, but you can use any of the SVG editors, such as svg-edit, which is a browser-based application, available at *http://code.google.com/p/svg-edit/*.

If you use an SVG editor, you typically want to externalize the SVG into its own file to make it easier to work on the drawing rather than embedding the drawing in your HTML page in an *<svg>* element. You can do this by using the *<img>* element and setting the source to the location of the .svg file. In the following example, the *<svg>* element is cut from the HTML page and pasted into a new file called car.svg. In the HTML page, an *<img>* element is added with a reference to the car.svg file.

```
<!DOCTYPE html>
<html xmlns="http://www.w3.org/1999/xhtml">
<head>
    <title></title>
    <link href="Content/svg.css" rel="stylesheet" />
</head>

<body>
    <img src="images/car.svg" />
</body>
</html>
```

When you display the HTML page, the car is displayed. If you try to resize the page, the image won't resize because the settings need to be changed.

Making the SVG scalable

The SVG file currently has the contents from the *<svg>* element, but you need to make some changes to make the image scale. First, change the height and width setting to 100 percent and then add a viewBox attribute to the *<svg>* element.

The viewBox attribute describes the part of the canvas you want the viewer to see. Even though the drawing covers the entire computer screen, the figure on your drawing might only exist in a small part of the drawing. The viewBox attribute enables you to tell the parser to zoom in on that part to eliminate the extra white space. Set viewBox to get the proper zoom capabilities when you resize your HTML page.

The viewBox attribute has four parameters: the minimum x coordinate, the minimum y coordinate, the width, and the height. This enables you to describe the rectangular area to be displayed. In this example, some white space at the top and bottom of the drawing will be cropped, so the following is the viewBox attribute setting.

```
viewBox="0 50 500 175"
```

This setting crops 50 pixels from the top and limits the viewing height to 175 pixels. The original width of the drawing was 500 pixels, and there isn't a lot of white space on the sides, so it is left as is. The following is the content of the .svg file after the changes are made.

```
<svg width="100%" height="100%" xmlns="http://www.w3.org/2000/svg"
    viewBox="0 50 500 175" >
  <path d="m267 76 l-21 -4 -144 0 -90 47 0 54 11 11 23 0 15 -30 15 -10 30 0
      15 10 15 30 220 0 15 -30 15 -10 30 0 15 10 15 30 125 0 7 -7
      -13 -38 -20 -10 -95 -15 z" fill="blue" id="carBody" />
  <path d="m65 105 140 -25 65 0 0 34 -112 0 z" fill="white" id="rearWindow" />
  <path d="m300 105 l-40 -25 -78 0 0 34 122 0 z" fill="white" id="frontWindow" />
  <circle r="35" cy="185" cx="90" fill="black" id="rearWheel" />
  <circle r="35" cy="185" cx="400" fill="black" id="frontWheel" />
</svg>
```

In the svg.css file, the following style rule has been added to resize the *<img>* element automatically when the HTML page is resized.

```
img {
    width: 100%;
}
```

Display the HTML page. You might need to refresh the page to see the change. The *<img>* element is now the size of the HTML page, and resizing the page resizes the *<img>* element, as shown in Figure 12-25.

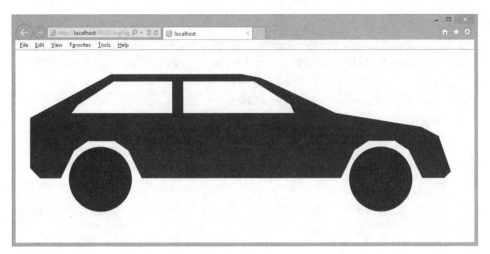

FIGURE 12-25 The *<img>* element automatically resizing the *<svg>* element when the HTML page is resized

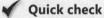 **Quick check**

- What is the purpose of the viewBox attribute?

Quick check answer

- The viewBox attribute describes the part of the drawing that you want the user to see.

Lesson summary

- The *<svg>* element is used to create and display scalable vector graphics (SVG).

- SVG is XML-based, and the contents of the *<svg>* element contain the commands that compose the drawing in XML format. The *<svg>* element can be placed in an .svg file.

- Use the *<path>* element to create complex shapes. The path contains a list of commands to create a shape. Each command is represented as an uppercase or lowercase letter. Uppercase indicates that the coordinates are absolute; lowercase indicates that the coordinates are relative. The *<circle>* element is used to draw a circle. To include an external .svg file on an HTML page, use the *<img>* element and set the src element to the location of the .svg file.

- To make the *<svg>* element automatically scale when the HTML page is resized, set the height and width attributes on the *<svg>* element to 100 percent and add a viewBox attribute that describes the view area of the drawing. Finally, add a style rule to your *<img>* element that sets its width to 100 percent.

Lesson review

Answer the following questions to test your knowledge of the information in this lesson. You can find the answers to these questions and explanations of why each answer choice is correct or incorrect in the "Answers" section at the end of this chapter.

1. The content of the *<svg>* element is in which format?

   A. SGML

   B. HTML

   C. XHMTL

   D. XML

2. On the *<svg>* element, what attribute provides a window into the drawing and enables zoom capabilities?

   A. zoom

   B. window

   C. viewBox

   D. zoomWindow

Practice exercises

If you encounter a problem completing any of these exercises, the completed projects can be installed from the Practice Exercises folder that is provided with the companion content.

Exercise 1: Create a webpage by using a canvas

In this exercise, you apply your knowledge of the *<canvas>* element by creating a web application that enables you to take snapshots of a video as it plays.

1. Start Visual Studio Express 2012 for Web. Create an ASP.NET Empty Web Application project called **CanvasSnapshooter**.

2. After the project is created, add a new folder, called **Media,** to the project.

3. Add the IceBoat.mp4 video file. Right-click the Media folder, choose Add, and select Existing Item. Locate the Resource folder and select the IceBoat.mp4 video file.

4. Add an HTML file to the project. Name the file **CanvasPage.html**.

5. Add a CSS file to the project. Name the file **default.css**.

6. Add a new folder, called **Scripts,** to the project.

7. Right-click the Scripts folder and add a new JavaScript file, called **default.js**.

8. Add a reference to the jQuery library by right-clicking the project node. Choose Manage NuGet Packages. Click Online and type **jQuery** in the search criteria. When the jQuery library is displayed, click the Install button.

9. In the CanvasPage.html file, add a reference to the default.css, jQuery library, and default.js files.

10. Add the title **Canvas Snapshooter** to your page. Your HTML page should look like the following.

```
<!DOCTYPE html>
<html xmlns="http://www.w3.org/1999/xhtml">
<head>
    <title>Canvas Snapshooter</title>
    <link href="default.css" rel="stylesheet" />
    <script src="Scripts/jquery-1.8.3.js"></script>
    <script src="Scripts/default.js"></script>
</head>
<body>

</body>
</html>
```

11. In the *<body>* element, add a *<video>* element whose id is myVideo. Set the src attribute to the IceBoat.mp4 file. Add the controls attribute to display the basic video controls. Set the width attribute to 360 and set the height attribute to 240. Inside the *<video>* element, add a message for incompatible browsers. After the *<video>* element, add a break.

12. Add a *<button>* element whose id is btnSnapshot. After the *<button>* element, add a break.

13. Add a *<canvas>* element whose id is myCanvas. Set the width attribute to 360 and set the height attribute to 240. Inside the *<canvas>* element, add a message for incompatible browsers. Your HTML page should look like the following.

```
<!DOCTYPE html>
<html xmlns="http://www.w3.org/1999/xhtml">
<head>
    <title></title>
    <link href="default.css" rel="stylesheet" />
    <script src="Scripts/jquery-1.8.3.js"></script>
    <script src="Scripts/default.js"></script>
</head>
<body>
    <video id="myVideo" src="media/IceBoat.mp4" controls="controls"
        width="360" height="240">
        You need a browser that supports HTML5 video!
    </video>
    <br />
    <button id="btnSnapshot" type="button">Snapshot</button>
    <br />
    <canvas id="myCanvas" width="360" height="240">
        You need a browser that supports HTML5 canvas!
    </canvas>
</body>
</html>
```

14. In the default.css file, set the border on the canvas as follows.

```css
canvas {
    border: 1px solid black;
}
```

15. In the default.js file, add the document ready function. In the document ready function, subscribe to the click event of the button. When the button is clicked, call a new function, drawVideoFrame. Your code should look like the following.

```javascript
$(document).ready(function () {
    $('#btnSnapshot').on('click', drawVideoFrame);
});
```

16. Add the drawVideoFrame function. In this function, add code to get a reference to the canvas. Add code to get a reference to the video element. Add code to call the getContext method on the canvas and, using the context object, call the drawImage method with the video. Your code should look like the following.

```javascript
function drawVideoFrame() {
    var canvas = document.getElementById('myCanvas');
    var video = document.getElementById('myVideo');
    canvas.getContext('2d').drawImage(video, 0, 0, 360, 240);
}
```

17. In Solution Explorer, right-click the CanvasPage.html file and choose Set As Start Page.

18. Test your work by pressing F5 to run the website. You should see the VideoPage.html page as shown in Figure 12-26.

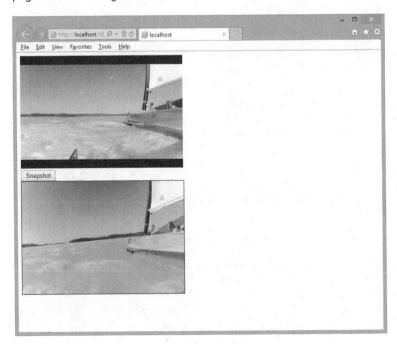

FIGURE 12-26 The running canvas snapshooter page

Suggested practice exercises

The following additional exercises are designed to give you more opportunities to practice what you've learned and to help you successfully master the lessons presented in this chapter.

- **Exercise 1**   Learn more about the *<canvas>* element by creating a simple game such as tic-tac-toe that gives the ability to play the game.

- **Exercise 2**   Learn more about the *<svg>*element by writing a web application that provides the ability to display .svg files on your disk.

Answers

This section contains the answers to the lesson review questions in this chapter.

Lesson 1

1. **Correct answer: C**

   A. **Incorrect:** The getContext method requires the 2d parameter, and there is no rectangle method on the context object.

   B. **Incorrect:** To draw on the canvas, you need to execute the getContext method to get a reference to a context object, and there is no rectangle method on the canvas object.

   C. **Correct:** This is the correct code, in which a reference to a context object is obtained by calling the getContext method with the 2d parameter.

   D. **Incorrect:** The getContext method requires the 2d parameter.

2. **Correct answer: B**

   A. **Incorrect:** The arcTo method typically draws a line and an arc. Although it could accomplish the task, it would be very difficult in comparison to the arc method.

   B. **Correct:** Using the arc method is the easiest way to accomplish this task.

   C. **Incorrect:** The circle method does not exist.

   D. **Incorrect:** The dot method does not exist.

Lesson 2

1. **Correct answer: D**

   A. **Incorrect:** HTML is derived from SGML, but the *<svg>* element is XML-based.

   B. **Incorrect:** HTML is used for webpages, but the *<svg>* element is XML-based.

   C. **Incorrect:** XHTML is used for webpages, but the *<svg>* element is XML-based.

   D. **Correct:** The *<svg>* element is XML-based.

2. **Correct answer: C**

   A. **Incorrect:** The zoom attribute does not exist.

   B. **Incorrect:** The window attribute does not exist.

   C. **Correct:** The viewBox attribute provides a window into the drawing and enables zoom capabilities.

   D. **Incorrect:** The zoomWindow attribute does not exist.

CHAPTER 13

Drag and drop

Prior to HTML5, the ability to drag and drop operations was possible with some browsers but wasn't compatible across different browsers. You typically implemented drag and drop by using a third-party library such as jQuery. Drag and drop is a first-class citizen of HTML5, which is the first step toward having a compatible implementation across browsers. You might still use jQuery for other functionality, but it's not required for drag and drop.

This chapter shows you how to drag and drop from one location to another on the webpage and then how to to drag and drop files.

Lessons in this chapter:

Before you begin

To complete this book, you must have some understanding of web development. This chapter requires the hardware and software listed in the "System requirements" section in the book's Introduction.

Lesson 1: Dragging and dropping

Making drag and drop part of HTML5 means that you can get browser compatibility and browser integration and, as you'll see in Lesson 2, "Dragging and dropping files," you can achieve integration with the operating system.

After this lesson, you will be able to:
- Describe HTML5 drag and drop.
- Implement drag and drop using HTML5.

Estimated lesson time: 20 minutes

To illustrate the drag and drop technique, consider the following HTML page, which defines a large square with three squares inside it.

```
<!DOCTYPE html>
<html xmlns="http://www.w3.org/1999/xhtml">
<head>
    <title></title>
    <link href="MicroScramble.css" rel="stylesheet" />
    <script src="Scripts/jquery-1.8.3.js"></script>
    <script src="Scripts/MicroScramble.js"></script>
</head>
<body>
    <div id="container">
        <div id="hole1" class="hole"><div id="item1" class="item">1</div></div>
        <div id="hole2" class="hole"><div id="item2" class="item">2</div></div>
        <div id="hole3" class="hole"><div id="item3" class="item">3</div></div>
        <div id="hole4" class="hole"></div>
    </div>
</body>
</html>
```

This HTML document contains a *<div>* element whose id is called container. Inside the container are four *<div>* elements that are holes that can contain an item. The first three holes are populated with an item.

The HTML document contains a reference to the MicroScramble.css style sheet, which contains the following style rules.

```
#container {
    border: solid;
    width: 332px;
    height: 332px;
    margin-right: auto;
    margin-left: auto;
}

.hole {
    background-color: black;
    border: solid;
    width: 160px;
    height: 160px;
    float: left;
}

.item {
    font-size: 128px;
    font-family: Arial, Helvetica, sans-serif;
    width: 140px;
    height: 140px;
    background-color: #C0C0C0;
    color: #FFFFFF;
    text-align: center;
    -webkit-user-select: none;
    -khtml-user-select: none;
    -moz-user-select: none;
```

```
    -ms-user-select: none;
    user-select: none;
}
```

The first style rule is for the container, which has a solid border, and the height and width settings form a square. The setting of the margin-left and margin-right to auto results in the container being centered.

The next style rule is for the holes. Each hole is a black square. The last style rule is for the items. An item is a gray square with a number in it. The number is centered and displays in a large font. Note that the last part of the style rule sets the user-select property to none and that there are several entries, based on the browser manufacturer. This property is set to none to keep the user from swiping across the item by mistake and selecting the text, which is the number. Figure 13-1 shows the rendered webpage.

FIGURE 13-1 The initial HTML page ready for drag and drop functionality

Dragging

To specify to the browser that an element can be dragged, use the draggable attribute, which has three valid values: *true*, *false*, and *auto*. For most browsers, the auto setting is the default, which means that the browser decides whether the element should be draggable. For example, the *<img>* element is usually draggable by default, but a *<div>* element is not draggable by default. In this sample HTML document, the item is a *<div>* element, and it's not draggable by default. After adding the draggable attribute, the container looks like the following.

```
<div id="container">
    <div id="hole1" class="hole">
        <div id="item1" draggable="true" class="item">1</div>
```

```
        </div>
        <div id="hole2" class="hole">
            <div id="item2" draggable="true" class="item">2</div>
        </div>
        <div id="hole3" class="hole">
            <div id="item3" draggable="true" class="item">3</div>
        </div>
        <div id="hole4" class="hole"></div>
</div>
```

After adding the draggable attribute to the items, you can drag them, as shown in Figure 13-2.

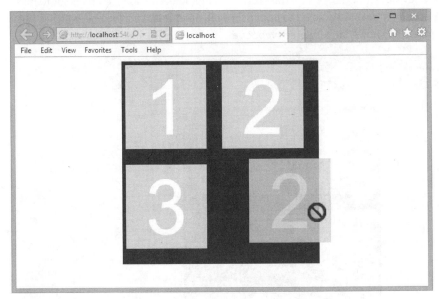

FIGURE 13-2 The added draggable attribute, allowing the item to be dragged

You can drag an item, but the item contains the *no-entry* symbol to indicate that the item cannot be dropped.

Understanding drag events

When dragging and dropping, there are events that are based on the dragged element, and there are events that are based on the drop target. Using these events, you should be able to customize the drag and drop operation as needed. The following events are based on the dragged element.

- **dragstart** Triggers when the drag is started
- **drag** Triggers continuously as the element is being dragged
- **dragend** Triggers when the drag is finished

The following code is placed in the MicroScramble.js file and shows the use of the drag-start and dragend events to change the style of the item being dragged until the dragging ends.

```
/// <reference path="jquery-1.8.3.js" />
var $draggedItem;

$(document).ready(function () {
    $('.item').on('dragstart', dragging);
    $('.item').on('dragend', draggingEnded);
});
function dragging(e) {
    $(e.target).addClass('dragging');
    $draggedItem = $(e.target);
}

function draggingEnded(e) {
    $(e.target).removeClass('dragging');
}
```

This example uses the document ready function in jQuery to subscribe to the dragstart and dragend events on all elements that have the CSS class item assigned. The dragging function adds the dragging CSS class when the dragging starts and then sets the $draggedItem with the value of the item being dragged. The draggingEnded function removes the dragging CSS class.

In the MicroScramble.css file, the dragging CSS rule is defined as follows.

```
.dragging {
    background-color: yellow;
}
```

In this example, the background of the dragged item changes to yellow until the dragging stops.

Dropping

After dragging, the drop must be made operational. The following events are based on the drop target.

- **dragenter** Triggers when the drag enters a drop zone
- **dragover** Triggers continuously as the element is dragged over the drop zone
- **dragleave** Triggers when the dragged item leaves a drop zone
- **drop** Triggers when the dragged item is dropped

The dragenter and dragover events default to rejecting dragged items, which is why you can't currently drop an item. You can enable dropping by cancelling the default action on these events.

The drop event removes the dropped item from the document object model (DOM) and then adds it back to the DOM at the drop zone location. The following code subscribes to the dragenter, dragover, and drop events.

```
/// <reference path="jquery-1.8.3.js" />

var $draggedItem;

$(document).ready(function () {
    $('.item').on('dragstart', dragging);
    $('.item').on('dragend', draggingEnded);
    $('.hole').on('dragenter', preventDefault);
    $('.hole').on('dragover', preventDefault);
    $('.hole').on('drop', dropItem);
});

function dragging(e) {
    $(e.target).addClass('dragging');
    $draggedItem = $(e.target);
}

function draggingEnded(e) {
    $(e.target).removeClass('dragging');
}

function preventDefault(e) {
    e.preventDefault();
}

function dropItem(e) {
    var hole = $(e.target);
    if (hole.hasClass('hole') && hole.children().length == 0) {
        $draggedItem.detach();
        $draggedItem.appendTo($(e.target));
    }
}
```

In this example, the document ready function has added statements to subscribe to dragenter, dragover, and drop. Notice that dragenter and dragover call the same preventDefault function, which prevents the rejection of the dragged items.

The drop event calls the dropItem function. In dropItem, a jQuery object is created from e.target, which is the drop target, and is assigned to a *hole* variable. The if statement checks whether the drop target has the hole CSS class. This is necessary because you might drop something on top of an item instead of on a hole. When the item is in a hole, the drop event bubbles up and executes the drop event on the hole. If the drop target is a hole, the code checks whether there are children; if there is a child, this hole already has an item, and you shouldn't be able to drop. If the drop target is a hole with no children, jQuery detaches the dragged item from the DOM and then appends draggedItem to the drop target. Figure 13-3 shows the item when it is being dragged and when it is dropped.

Quick check

- Which two events' default operations must be prevented to allow the drop event to operate?

Quick check answer

- The dragenter and dragover events

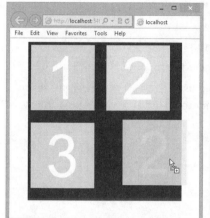

FIGURE 13-3 The item being dragged and the item after being dropped

Using the DataTransfer object

The previous example demonstrates a complete drag and drop operation, but you can also use the DataTransfer object to pass data from the dragstart event to the drop event. By using the DataTransfer object, you don't need to create a global variable to reference the item being dragged. Using the DataTransfer object also empowers you to pass any data to the drop event as long as it can be represented as a string or URL. The DragStart object is referenced as a dataTransfer property on the dragstart event.

> **NOTE USING THE DATATRANSFER OBJECT WITH JQUERY**
>
> If you're using jQuery to bind events, the dataTransfer property will be missing, but it can be added by adding the following statement to the document ready function.
>
> ```
> jQuery.event.props.push('dataTransfer');
> ```
>
> jQuery creates a wrapper object that resembles the original event and copies only the data from the original object that jQuery needs. This statement tells jQuery to look for the dataTransfer property on the original object and, if it exists, to copy it to the jQuery wrapper.

You can pass data to the drop event by using the dataTransfer property. The DataTransfer object has the following members.

- **clearData()**   Method that clears the data in the DataTransfer object.
- **dropeffect**   Property that gets or sets the type of drag and drop operation and the cursor type. It can be set to copy, link, move, or none.
- **effectAllowed**   Property that gets or sets the allowed operations on the source element.
- **files**   Property that gets a file list of the files being dragged.
- **getData()**   Method that gets the data in the DataTransfer object.
- **setData()**   Method that sets the data in the DataTransfer object.
- **types**   Property that gets a string list of types being sent.

In the following example, the HTML document has an unordered list of cars, from which you can drag and drop any of the cars to a different unordered list of favorite cars as follows.

```
<!DOCTYPE html>
<html xmlns="http://www.w3.org/1999/xhtml">
<head>
    <title></title>
    <script src="Scripts/jquery-1.8.3.js"></script>
    <script src="Scripts/CarList.js"></script>
</head>
<body>
    <p>What cars do you like?</p>
    <ul id="carList">
        <li draggable="true" data-value="car,Chevrolet">Chevrolet</li>
        <li draggable="true" data-value="car,Ford">Ford</li>
        <li draggable="true" data-value="car,BMW">BMW</li>
    </ul>
    <p>Drop your favorite cars below:</p>
    <ul  id="favoriteCars" style="min-height:100px;background-color:yellow;">
    </ul>
</body>
</html>
```

There is no CSS file to make the page or the drag and drop operation look neat, but an inline style is applied to favoriteCars so the user can see a drop area. Each of the cars is drag-gable and uses data attributes to provide data that will be collected when the dragging starts and then passed to the drop event. The JavaScript file is similar to the previous example, which was used to move numbers, but this time, the data is passed to the drop event by using the DataTransfer object as follows.

```
/// <reference path="jquery-1.8.3.js" />

$(document).ready(function () {
    jQuery.event.props.push('dataTransfer');
    $('#carList').on('dragstart', dragging);
    $('#favoriteCars').on('dragenter', preventDefault);
    $('#favoriteCars').on('dragover', preventDefault);
```

```
        $('#favoriteCars').on('drop', dropItem);
});

function dragging(e) {
    var val = e.target.getAttribute('data-value');
    e.dataTransfer.setData('text', val);
    e.dataTransfer.effectAllowed = 'copy';
}
function preventDefault(e) {
    e.preventDefault();
}

function dropItem(e) {
    var data = e.dataTransfer.getData('text').split(',');
    if (data[0] == 'car') {
        var li = document.createElement('li');
        li.textContent = data[1];
        e.target.appendChild(li);
    }
}
```

In the document ready function, the dataTransfer property is pushed to the collection of properties that needs to be copied to the jQuery wrapper. The dragging function is called when the dragging starts. It collects the data from the data-value attribute and assigns it to the DataTransfer object. The effectAllowed property is set to *copy*, which changes the mouse pointer to a pointer with a plus sign under it. If the setting were set to *move*, the mouse pointer would be a pointer with a small box under it. If the effectAllowed property were set to *link*, the mouse pointer would be a pointer with a shortcut symbol under it.

The dropItem function is called from the drop event. The DataTransfer object is also available on the drop event through the dataTransfer property. The data is retrieved, split into an array, and assigned to the data variable. Next, the first element is tested to see whether it is a car. If so, a new list item is created, and the car make, which is in data[1], is assigned to the textContent property of the list item. Finally, the list item is appended to the drop element.

Figure 13-4 shows the finished screen after a car has been dragged and dropped to the favorite car list.

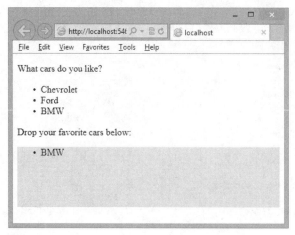

FIGURE 13-4 Completed drag and drop with list items

Lesson summary

- The drag and drop functionality in HTML5 will be consistent and compatible across browsers.
- The draggable attribute must be set to true and added to each element that needs to be draggable.
- The dragstart and dragend events can be used to change the style of the element being dragged.
- The dragenter and dragover events must be coded to prevent the default operation and enable dropping.
- The drop event triggers when the item is dropped on a drop target.
- The DataTransfer object is used to pass data between the dragstart event and the drop event.

Lesson review

Answer the following questions to test your knowledge of the information in this lesson. You can find the answers to these questions and explanations of why each answer choice is correct or incorrect in the "Answers" section at the end of this chapter.

1. Which of the following events trigger continuously during a drag and drop operation? (Choose all that apply.)

   A. dragstart

   B. drag

   C. dragend

   D. dragenter

    E. dragover

    F. dragleave

    G. drop

2. Which of the following events are associated with the item being dragged? (Choose all that apply.)

    A. dragstart

    B. drag

    C. dragend

    D. dragenter

    E. dragover

    F. dragleave

    G. drop

3. Using the DataTransfer object, what kind of data can you pass to the drop event?

    A. Any valid string, number, date/time, or Boolean value

    B. Any URL that is within the same domain as the webpage

    C. Any JSON object

    D. Any object that can be represented as a string or URL

Lesson 2: Dragging and dropping files

You can drag and drop files by using the File application programming interface (API), which is also part of HTML5. The File API provides indirect access to files in a tightly controlled manner.

After this lesson, you will be able to:

- Describe HTML5 drag and drop operating system integration.
- Implement file drag and drop using HTML5.

Estimated lesson time: 20 minutes

Using the FileList and File objects

When dropping a file, the DataTransfer object returns a FileList object, which is a collection of File objects that were dropped. The File object has the following properties.

- **name** Property that gets the file name and extension without a path
- **type** Property that gets the MIME type of the file
- **size** Property that gets the file size in bytes

The following HTML document has a *<div>* element onto which files can be dropped and a *<table>* element that is populated with information about the dropped files.

```html
<!DOCTYPE html>
<html xmlns="http://www.w3.org/1999/xhtml">
<head>
    <title></title>
    <link href="FileDragAndDrop.css" rel="stylesheet" />
    <script src="Scripts/jquery-1.8.3.js"></script>
    <script src="Scripts/FileDragAndDrop.js"></script>
</head>
<body>
    <div id="target">
        <p>Drag and drop files here...</p>
    </div>
    <table id="fileInfo"></table>
</body>
</html>
```

The FileDragAndDrop.css file contains style rules to size the drag and drop target. This file also contains style rules to format the file information table as follows.

```css
#target {
    border: solid;
    height: 150px;
    width: 500px;
    background-color: yellow;
    text-align: center;
}

#fileInfo {
    width: 500px;
}

table, th, td {
    border-collapse: collapse;
    border: 1px solid black;
}

th, td {
    padding: 5px;
}
```

Figure 13-5 shows the webpage. There is no JavaScript yet, so you might think that you can't drag and drop any files here, but there is a default behavior for files that are dragged and dropped. If you drop a file anywhere on the webpage, the file opens in another window. For example, if you drag and drop a movie onto the webpage, the movie will start playing in a new window.

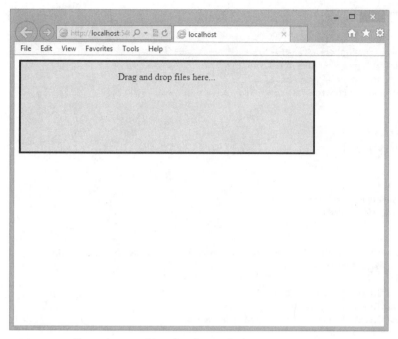

FIGURE 13-5 The webpage with style rules applied

To process the dropped files and display the file information in a table below the drop box, the following JavaScript is added to the FileDragAndDrop.js file.

```
/// <reference path="jquery-1.8.3.js" />

$(document).ready(function () {
    jQuery.event.props.push('dataTransfer');
    $('#target').on('dragenter', preventDefault);
    $('#target').on('dragover', preventDefault);
});

function preventDefault(e) {
    e.preventDefault();
}
```

In the document ready function, jQuery is set up to expose the DataTransfer object. The dragenter and dragover events are then programmed to prevent the default operation that prevents dropping. When the drop event is added, the dragged file can be dropped.

Next, the drop event is subscribed to, which calls the dropItem function. The dropItem function retrieves the files collection from the DataTransfer object. The content in the file information table is overwritten with the header, which also clears any existing information that was in the table. Finally, a for loop is used to loop over the files and add a row of information to the file information table for each file. The following is the completed JavaScript file.

```
/// <reference path="jquery-1.8.3.js" />

$(document).ready(function () {
    jQuery.event.props.push('dataTransfer');
    $('#target').on('dragenter', preventDefault);
    $('#target').on('dragover', preventDefault);
    $('#target').on('drop', dropItem);
});

function preventDefault(e) {
    e.preventDefault();
}

function dropItem(e) {
    var files = e.dataTransfer.files
        , $table = $('#fileInfo')
        , i = 0;
    $table.html(
        '<thead><tr><th>Name</th><th>Type</th><th>Size</th></tr></thead>');
    for (i = 0; i < files.length; i++) {
        $('<tr><td>'
            + files[i].name + '</td><td>'
            + files[i].type + '</td><td>'
            + files[i].size + '</td></tr>').appendTo($table);
    }
    preventDefault(e);
}
```

Figure 13-6 shows the webpage after several files were dragged and dropped. The file information table is populated and displayed. The first column contains the file names (without a path) of the dropped files. The second column contains the file's MIME type if the type can be derived. The last column contains the file size in bytes.

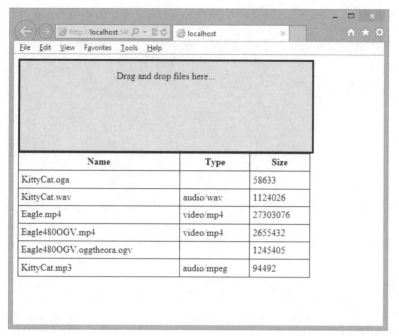

Name	Type	Size
KittyCat.oga		58633
KittyCat.wav	audio/wav	1124026
Eagle.mp4	video/mp4	27303076
Eagle480OGV.mp4	video/mp4	2655432
Eagle480OGV.oggtheora.ogv		1245405
KittyCat.mp3	audio/mpeg	94492

FILE 13-6 The completed webpage after files were dragged and dropped

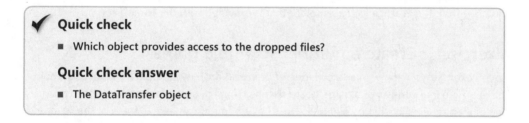

Quick check

- Which object provides access to the dropped files?

Quick check answer

- The DataTransfer object

Lesson summary

- The File object provides the name, type, and size properties.
- To enable dropping of files, the dragenter and dragover events must be programmed to prevent the default behavior that prevents dropping.
- The DataTransfer object provides access to the list of dropped files.
- The drop event provides access to the DataTransfer object.

Lesson review

Answer the following questions to test your knowledge of the information in this lesson. You can find the answers to these questions and explanations of why each answer choice is correct or incorrect in the "Answers" section at the end of this chapter.

1. To which events do you need to subscribe to program file drag and drop? (Choose all that apply.)

    A. dragstart

    B. drag

    C. dragend

    D. dragenter

    E. dragover

    F. dragleave

    G. drop

2. Which of the following is not a property on the File object?

    A. name

    B. path

    C. type

    D. size

Practice exercises

If you encounter a problem completing any of these exercises, the completed projects can be installed from the Practice Exercises folder that is provided with the companion content.

Exercise 1: Create a number scramble game

In this exercise, you apply your knowledge of drag and drop by creating a number scramble game. The game consists of a game board that has four rows and four columns, thus providing sixteen squares in which a sliding tile that has a number can exist. Fifteen of the squares are occupied by numbered tiles. This leaves one empty square that can be used to move tiles. The object is to arrange the tiles in numeric order by dragging tiles to the empty space after they have been scrambled. The only tiles that can be dragged to the empty space are tiles horizontally or vertically adjacent to the empty space.

In Exercise 1, you create the game board and the tiles by creating the webpage, the CSS file, and the first part of the JavaScript file. In Exercise 2, "Add drag and drop to the game," you add the drag and drop functionality.

1. Start Visual Studio Express 2012 for Web. Create an ASP.NET Empty Web Application project called **NumberScramble**.

2. Add an HTML file to the project. Name the file **default.html**.

3. Add a CSS file to the project. Name the file **default.css**.

4. Add a new folder called **Scripts** to the project.

5. Right-click the Scripts folder and add a new JavaScript file called **default.js**.

6. Add a reference to the jQuery library by right-clicking the project node and choosing Manage NuGet Packages. Click Online and type **jQuery** in the search criteria. When the jQuery library is displayed, click the Install button.

7. In the default.html file, add a reference to the default.css, jQuery library, and default.js files.

8. Add the title **Number Scramble** to your page.

   Your HTML page should look like the following.

```
<!DOCTYPE html>
<html xmlns="http://www.w3.org/1999/xhtml">
<head>
    <title>Number Scramble</title>
    <link href="default.css" rel="stylesheet" />
    <script src="Scripts/jquery-1.8.3.js"></script>
    <script src="Scripts/default.js"></script>
</head>
<body>

</body>
</html>
```

9. In the *<body>* element, add a *<div>* element whose id is message. In the *<div>* element, add the default message, **Refresh to scramble**.

10. After the message *<div>* element, add another *<div>* element whose id is gameBoard.

    The content of the game board is populated from the JavaScript. Your completed default.html should look like the following.

```
<!DOCTYPE html>
<html xmlns="http://www.w3.org/1999/xhtml">
<head>
    <title>Number Scramble</title>
    <link href="default.css" rel="stylesheet" />
    <script src="Scripts/jquery-1.8.3.js"></script>
    <script src="Scripts/default.js"></script>
</head>
<body>
    <div id="message">
        Refresh to scramble.
    </div>
    <div id="gameBoard">

    </div>
</body>
</html>
```

11. In the default.css file, add the following style rules for the game board, the message, and the squares and tiles that are to be created programmatically.

```
body {
    font-family: Arial, Helvetica, sans-serif;
}
```

```
#gameBoard {
    width: 345px;
    height: 345px;
    margin-right: auto;
    margin-left: auto;
}

#message {
    background-color: black;
    font-size: 36px;
    color: lime;
    text-align: center;
    width: 345px;
    height: 80px;
    margin-right: auto;
    margin-left: auto;
}

.tile {
    font-size: 64px;
    width: 80px;
    height: 80px;
    background-color: gray;
    color: white;
    text-align: center;
}

.square {
    background-color: black;
    border: solid;
    width: 80px;
    height: 80px;
    float: left;
}

.dragged {
    background-color: red;
}
```

12. In the default.js file, add a reference to the jQuery library. Declare a *squareCount* variable and set it to 16. Declare an *emptySquare* variable as follows.

```
/// <reference path="jquery-1.8.3.js" />

var squareCount = 16
var emptySquare;
```

13. In the default.js file, add the document ready function. In the document ready function, add a statement to instruct jQuery to copy the dataTransfer property to its event wrapper when the event has this property. Add a call to a createBoard function and add a call to an addTiles function.

These functions are created next. Your code should look like the following.

```
/// <reference path="jquery-1.8.3.js" />

var squareCount = 16
var emptySquare;

$(document).ready(function () {
    jQuery.event.props.push('dataTransfer');
    createBoard();
    addTiles();
});
```

14. Under the document ready function, add a createBoard function. In this function, add a for loop that loops while the *loop* variable is less than the *squareCount* variable. In the for loop, use jQuery to create a *<div>* element whose id is square plus the value of the *loop* variable. Add a data-square attribute and assign the *loop* variable's value. Add the class attribute and assign the square class. Append the newly created square to the game board.

Your code should look like the following.

```
function createBoard() {
    for (var i = 0; i < squareCount; i++) {
        var $square = $('<div id="square' + i + '" data-square="'
            + i +'"  class="square"></div>');
        $square.appendTo($('#gameBoard'));
    }
}
```

15. Under the createBoard function, add an addTiles function. In this function, add a statement to assign the value of the *squareCount* variable minus one to the *emptySquare* variable. Add a for loop that loops while the *loop* variable is less than the *emptySquare* value. In the for loop, use jQuery to get a reference to the square that corresponds to the *loop* variable. Use jQuery to create a *<div>* element whose id is tile plus the value of the *loop* variable. Add a draggable attribute and set its value to *true*. Add the class attribute and assign the tile class. In the content of this *<div>* element, put the value of the *loop* variable plus one. Append the newly created tile to the corresponding square.

Your code should look like the following.

```
function addTiles() {
    emptySquare = squareCount - 1;
    for (var i = 0; i < emptySquare; i++) {
        var $square = $('#square' + i);
        var $tile = $('<div draggable="true" id="tile' + i
            + '" class="tile">' + (i + 1) + '</div>');
        $tile.appendTo($square);
    }
}
```

16. In Solution Explorer, right-click the default.html file and choose Set As Start Page.

17. Test your work by pressing F5 to run the website. You should see the default.html page as shown in Figure 13-7.

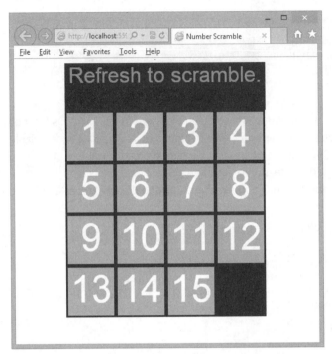

FIGURE 13-7 The rendered number scramble page

At this point, you have the default message and the rendered game board with the tiles. There is no drag and drop functionality, and the numbers don't scramble.

Exercise 2: Add drag and drop to the game

In this exercise, you apply your knowledge of drag and drop by adding code to the number scramble game you created in Exercise 1, "Create a number scramble game," to support drag and drop functionality.

1. Start Visual Studio Express 2012 for Web. Open the NumberScramble project.

2. In the default.js file, add the following code to the document ready function to subscribe to the dragstart, dragend, dragenter, dragover, and drop events.

```
$(document).ready(function () {
    jQuery.event.props.push('dataTransfer');
    createBoard();
    addTiles();
    $('#gameBoard').on('dragstart', dragStarted);
    $('#gameBoard').on('dragend', dragEnded);
    $('#gameBoard').on('dragenter', preventDefault);
```

```
$('#gameBoard').on('dragover', preventDefault);
$('#gameBoard').on('drop', drop);
});
```

3. At the bottom of the default.js file, add the dragStarted function that takes an e event parameter. In this function, create a *$tile* variable that is a jQuery wrapper for e.target. Use $tile to add the dragged CSS class to the tile. Declare a *sourceLocation* variable and assign to it the value of the data-square attribute from the tile's parent (the square).

   The sourceLocation is the square number the tile is in.

4. Assign the string value of sourceLocation to the DataTransfer object and set the effectAllowed property to move. Your code should look like the following.

```
function dragStarted(e) {
    var $tile = $(e.target)
    $tile.addClass('dragged');
    var sourceLocation = $tile.parent().data('square');
    e.dataTransfer.setData('text', sourceLocation.toString());
    e.dataTransfer.effectAllowed = 'move';
}
```

5. After the dragStarted function, add a dragEnded function. In this function, use jQuery to remove the dragged CSS class from the tile.

   Your code should look like the following.

```
function dragEnded(e) {
    $(e.target).removeClass('dragged');
}
```

6. Under the dragEnded function, add a preventDefault function that takes an e event parameter. In this function, add a statement to call the preventDefault method on e.

   Your code should look like the following.

```
function preventDefault(e) {
    e.preventDefault();
}
```

7. Under the preventDefault function, add a drop function that takes an e event parameter. In this function, add a statement to create a jQuery wrapper for e.target and assign it to a *$square* variable. Add an if statement to verify that the target of the drop is a square by checking to see whether *$square* has the CSS class called square. If so, use jQuery to add code that reads the data-square attribute $square and place the value in a *destinationLocation* variable. Compare the value of *emptySquare* with the value of the destination location and, if they are not equal, exit the drop function by using a return statement.

8. Add code to get the data from the DataTransfer object. Assign it to a *sourceLocation* variable and then call the moveTile function that you create next, passing the *sourceLocation* variable.

Your code should look like the following.

```
function drop(e) {
    var $square= $(e.target);
    if ($square.hasClass('square')) {
        var destinationLocation = $square.data('square');
        if (emptySquare != destinationLocation) return;
        var sourceLocation = Number(e.dataTransfer.getData('text'));
        moveTile(sourceLocation);
    }
}
```

9. Under the drop function, add a moveTile function that takes the sourceLocation parameter. In this function, add a statement to create a *distance* variable that is set to the sourceLocation parameter minus the *emptySquare* value.

10. Add a statement to make the distance a positive value if it's negative. Compare the distance to 1 or 4, in which the value of 1 indicates a drop from a horizontally adjacent square, and a value of 4 indicates a drop from a vertically adjacent square. If the distance is equal to 1 or 4, call the swapTileAndEmptySquare function with the sourceLocation parameter.

Your code should look like the following.

```
function moveTile(sourceLocation) {
    var distance = sourceLocation - emptySquare;
    if (distance < 0) distance = -(distance);
    if (distance == 1 || distance == 4) {
        swapTileAndEmptySquare(sourceLocation);
    }
}
```

11. Under the moveTile function, add a swapTileAndEmptySquare function that takes the sourceLocation parameter. In this function, use jQuery to retrieve the tile from the tile at the sourceLocation parameter and assign the value to a *$draggedItem* variable. Use jQuery to detach the dragged item from the document object model (DOM). Create a *$target* variable and assign the square at the emptySquare location. Use jQuery to append the dragged item to the target.

12. Assign sourceLocation to emptySquare.

The following is the complete default.js file.

```
/// <reference path="jquery-1.8.3.js" />

var squareCount = 16;
var emptySquare;

$(document).ready(function () {
    jQuery.event.props.push('dataTransfer');
    createBoard();
    addTiles();
    $('#gameBoard').on('dragstart', dragStarted);
    $('#gameBoard').on('dragend', dragEnded);
```

```javascript
    $('#gameBoard').on('dragenter', preventDefault);
    $('#gameBoard').on('dragover', preventDefault);
    $('#gameBoard').on('drop', drop);
});

function createBoard() {
    for (var i = 0; i < squareCount; i++) {
        var $square = $('<div id="square' + i + '" data-square="' + i
            + '" class="square"></div>');
        $square.appendTo($('#gameBoard'));
    }
}

function addTiles() {
    emptySquare = squareCount - 1;
    for (var i = 0; i < emptySquare; i++) {
        var $square = $('#square' + i);
        var $tile = $('<div draggable="true" id="tile' + i
            + '" class="tile">' + (i + 1) + '</div>');
        $tile.appendTo($square);
    }
}

function dragStarted(e) {
    var $tile = $(e.target)
    $tile.addClass('dragged');
    var sourceLocation = $tile.parent().data('square');
    e.dataTransfer.setData('text', sourceLocation.toString());
    e.dataTransfer.effectAllowed = 'move';
}

function dragEnded(e) {
    $(e.target).removeClass('dragged');
}

function preventDefault(e) {
    e.preventDefault();
}

function drop(e) {
    var $square = $(e.target);
    if ($square.hasClass('square')) {
        var destinationLocation = $square.data('square');
        if (emptySquare != destinationLocation) return;
        var sourceLocation = Number(e.dataTransfer.getData('text'));
        moveTile(sourceLocation);
    }
}

function moveTile(sourceLocation) {
    var distance = sourceLocation - emptySquare;
    if (distance < 0) distance = -(distance);
    if (distance == 1 || distance == 4) {
        swapTileAndEmptySquare(sourceLocation);
    }
```

```
    }

    function swapTileAndEmptySquare(sourceLocation) {
        var $draggedItem = $('#square' + sourceLocation).children();
        $draggedItem.detach();
        var $target = $('#square' + emptySquare);
        $draggedItem.appendTo($target);
        emptySquare = sourceLocation;
    }
```

13. Test your work by pressing F5 to run the website.

    You should be able to move the tiles by dragging and dropping a tile to the empty
    space. The default.html page after moving some tiles is shown in Figure 13-8.

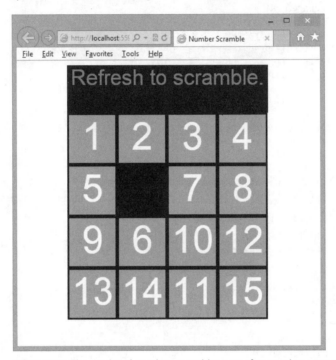

FIGURE 13-8 The rendered number scramble page after moving some tiles

Exercise 3: Add scramble and winner check

In this exercise, you apply your knowledge of drag and drop by adding code to the number
scramble game you created in Exercise 2 to scramble the tiles when the page is rendered and
check for a winner after each drag and drop.

1. Start Visual Studio Express 2012 for Web. Open the NumberScramble project.

2. In the default.js file, add the following code to the document ready function to call a
   scramble function that you create next.

```
$(document).ready(function () {
    jQuery.event.props.push('dataTransfer');
    createBoard();
    addTiles();
    $('#gameBoard').on('dragstart', dragStarted);
    $('#gameBoard').on('dragend', dragEnded);
    $('#gameBoard').on('dragenter', preventDefault);
    $('#gameBoard').on('dragover', preventDefault);
    $('#gameBoard').on('drop', drop);
    scramble();
});
```

3. At the bottom of the default.js file, add the following scramble function.

```
function scramble() {
    for (var i = 0; i < 128; i++) {
        var random = Math.random()
        var sourceLocation;
        if (random < 0.5) {
            var column = emptySquare % 4
            if (column == 0 || (random < 0.25 && column != 3)) {
                sourceLocation = emptySquare + 1;
            }
            else {
                sourceLocation = emptySquare - 1;
            }
        }
        else {
            var row = Math.floor(emptySquare / 4)
            if (row == 0 || (random < 0.75 && row != 3)) {
                sourceLocation = emptySquare + 4;
            }
            else {
                sourceLocation = emptySquare - 4;
            }
        }
        swapTileAndEmptySquare(sourceLocation);
    }
}
```

The scramble function executes a loop of 128 random movements to scramble the
tiles. Each time the loop executes, a new random number is created, and, based on its
value, an adjacent tile is moved to the empty square.

4. In the drop function, add code to call the checkForWinner function that you create
next.

Your code should look like the following.

```
function drop(e) {
    var $square = $(e.target);
    if ($square.hasClass('square')) {
        var destinationLocation = $square.data('square');
        if (emptySquare != destinationLocation) return;
        var sourceLocation = Number(e.dataTransfer.getData('text'));
        moveTile(sourceLocation);
```

```
        checkForWinner();
    }
}
```

5. At the bottom of the default.js file, add a checkForWinner function. In this function, add a statement to check that the empty square is at the lower-right corner. Add a loop to retrieve each tile and check its parent square to see whether the tile is in the correct square. If not, exit the checkForWinner function by using a return statement. If you make it to the bottom of the function, change the message to "Winner!"

Your code should look like the following.

```
function checkForWinner() {
    if (emptySquare != squareCount - 1) return;
    for (var i = 0; i < emptySquare; i++) {
        if ($('#tile' + i).parent().attr('id') != 'square' + i) return;
    }
    $('#message').html('Winner!');
}
```

The following is the completed default.js file.

```
/// <reference path="jquery-1.8.3.js" />

var squareCount = 16
var emptySquare;

$(document).ready(function () {
    jQuery.event.props.push('dataTransfer');
    createBoard();
    addTiles();
    $('#gameBoard').on('dragstart', dragStarted);
    $('#gameBoard').on('dragend', dragEnded);
    $('#gameBoard').on('dragenter', preventDefault);
    $('#gameBoard').on('dragover', preventDefault);
    $('#gameBoard').on('drop', drop);
    scramble();
});

function createBoard() {
    for (var i = 0; i < squareCount; i++) {
        var $square = $('<div id="square' + i + '" data-square="' + i
            + '" class="square"></div>');
        $square.appendTo($('#gameBoard'));
    }
}

function addTiles() {
    emptySquare = squareCount - 1;
    for (var i = 0; i < emptySquare; i++) {
        var $square = $('#square' + i);
        var $tile = $('<div draggable="true" id="tile' + i
            + '" class="tile">' + (i + 1) + '</div>');
        $tile.appendTo($square);
    }
}
```

```
function dragStarted(e) {
    var $tile = $(e.target)
    $tile.addClass('dragged');
    var sourceLocation = $tile.parent().data('square');
    e.dataTransfer.setData('text', sourceLocation.toString());
    e.dataTransfer.effectAllowed = 'move';
}

function dragEnded(e) {
    $(e.target).removeClass('dragged');
}

function preventDefault(e) {
    e.preventDefault();
}

function drop(e) {
    var $square = $(e.target);
    if ($square.hasClass('square')) {
        var destinationLocation = $square.data('square');
        if (emptySquare != destinationLocation) return;
        var sourceLocation = Number(e.dataTransfer.getData('text'));
        moveTile(sourceLocation);
        checkForWinner();
    }
}

function moveTile(sourceLocation) {
    var distance = sourceLocation - emptySquare;
    if (distance < 0) distance = -(distance);
    if (distance == 1 || distance == 4) {
        swapTileAndEmptySquare(sourceLocation);
    }
}

function swapTileAndEmptySquare(sourceLocation) {
    var $draggedItem = $('#square' + sourceLocation).children();
    $draggedItem.detach();
    var $target = $('#square' + emptySquare);
    $draggedItem.appendTo($target);
    emptySquare = sourceLocation;
}

function scramble() {
    for (var i = 0; i < 128; i++) {
        var random = Math.random()
        var sourceLocation;
        if (random < 0.5) {
            var column = emptySquare % 4
            if (column == 0 || (random < 0.25 && column != 3)) {
                sourceLocation = emptySquare + 1;
            }
            else {
                sourceLocation = emptySquare - 1;
            }
```

```
        }
        else {
            var row = Math.floor(emptySquare / 4)
            if (row == 0 || (random < 0.75 && row != 3)) {
                sourceLocation = emptySquare + 4;
            }
            else {
                sourceLocation = emptySquare - 4;
            }
        }
        swapTileAndEmptySquare(sourceLocation);
    }
}

function checkForWinner() {
    if (emptySquare != squareCount - 1) return;
    for (var i = 0; i < emptySquare; i++) {
        if ($('#tile' + i).parent().attr('id') != 'square' + i) return;
    }
    $('#message').html('Winner!');
}
```

6. Test your work by pressing F5 to run the website.

When the page is displayed, the tiles should be scrambled. You should be able to move the tiles by dragging and dropping a tile to the empty space. When you have finished sorting the tiles, you should see the winning message as shown in Figure 13-9.

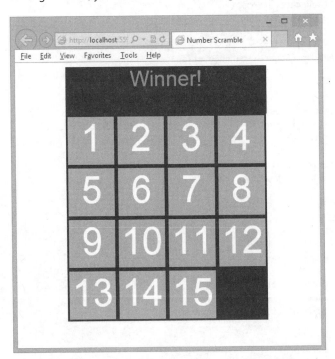

FIGURE 13-9 The rendered number scramble page after winning

Suggested practice exercises

The following additional exercises are designed to give you more opportunities to practice what you've learned and to help you successfully master the lessons presented in this chapter.

- **Exercise 1** Learn more about drag and drop by creating an application that enables the user to make selections by dragging and dropping options.

- **Exercise 2** Learn more about dragging and dropping files by creating an application that enables the user to select drag and drop image files that you render on the page.

Answers

This section contains the answers to the lesson review questions in this chapter.

Lesson 1

1. Correct answers: B and E

    A. **Incorrect:** The dragstart event triggers only when you start a drag operation.

    B. **Correct:** The drag event triggers many times while you drag an item.

    C. **Incorrect:** The dragend event triggers only when you end a drag operation.

    D. **Incorrect:** The dragenter event triggers only when you enter a drop target.

    E. **Correct:** The dragover event triggers continuously as you drag an item over a drop target.

    F. **Incorrect:** The dragleave event triggers only when you leave a drop target.

    G. **Incorrect:** The drop event triggers only when you drop the item being dragged.

2. Correct answers: A, B, and C

    A. **Correct:** The dragstart event triggers in association with the drag item.

    B. **Correct:** The drag event triggers in association with the drag item.

    C. **Correct:** The dragend event triggers in association with the drag item.

    D. **Incorrect:** The dragenter event triggers in association with the drop target.

    E. **Incorrect:** The dragover event triggers in association with the drop target.

    F. **Incorrect:** The dragleave event triggers in association with the drop target.

    G. **Incorrect:** The drop event triggers in association with the drop target.

3. Correct answer: D

    A. **Incorrect:** Although these data types can be passed, you can pass any object that can be represented as a string or URL.

    B. **Incorrect:** Although URLs can be passed, you can pass any object that can be represented as a string or URL.

    C. **Incorrect:** Although these data types can be passed, you can pass any object that can be represented as a string or URL.

    D. **Correct:** You can pass any object that can be represented as a string or URL.

Lesson 2

1. Correct answers: D, E, and G

   A. **Incorrect:** No dragstart event is associated with dragging files.

   B. **Incorrect:** No drag event is associated with dragging files.

   C. **Incorrect:** No dragend is associated with dragging files.

   D. **Correct:** The dragenter event triggers when you enter a drop target, and its default operation must be prevented.

   E. **Correct:** The dragover event triggers continuously as you drag over a drop target, and its default operation must be prevented.

   F. **Incorrect:** The dragleave triggers only when you leave a drop target, and it is not required for dropping files.

   G. **Correct:** The drop event triggers only when you drop the item on a drop target, and it is required to process the dropped files.

2. Correct answer: B

   A. **Incorrect:** The name property exists on the File object.

   B. **Correct:** The path property does not exist on the File object.

   C. **Incorrect:** The type property exists on the File object.

   D. **Incorrect:** The size property exists on the File object.

## CHAPTER 14

Making your HTML location-aware

The Geolocation application programming interface (API) provides an interface with device location information such as latitude and longitude; you can use the Geolocation API to make your applications location-aware. Imagine creating an application that enables the user to enter favorite information, such as where to drink coffee or shop for computers. As the user gets close to a favorite place such as a coffee shop or a computer store, the device displays a map with the location. Maybe the coffee shop could provide incentives to motivate the user to stop by for a quick cup of coffee.

The API is generic enough to interface with many underlying location information sources such as the Global Positioning System (GPS) and locations inferred from network signals such as IP address, radio frequency identification (RFID), Wi-Fi and Bluetooth MAC addresses, and cellular IDs and from user input. No guarantee is given that the API returns the device's actual location, and the accuracy can vary widely. Increasingly, mobile devices are shipped with GPS in addition to accelerometer and compass. These sensors can provide great accuracy to the Geolocation API.

The Geolocation API is being standardized by the Geolocation Working Group, which is separate from the HTML5 Working Group. Therefore, the Geolocation API is not part of HTML5, although support for geolocation is being added to browsers in parallel with HTML5.

The API is designed to enable both one-shot position requests and repeated position updates. Lesson 1, "Basic positioning," covers one-shot queries; Lesson 2, "Monitored positioning," covers repeated position updates.

Lessons in this chapter:

Before you begin

To complete this book, you must have some understanding of web development. This chapter requires the hardware and software listed in the "System requirements" section in the book's Introduction.

Lesson 1: Basic positioning

The Geolocation object is accessible by using the *navigator.geolocation global* variable. Most browsers support the Geolocation API, and the following code can be used to determine whether the user's browser provides support.

```
function supportsGeolocation() {
    return 'geolocation' in navigator;
}
```

This code checks whether a geolocation property is on the object that's referenced by the *navigator global* variable. If the property exists, it will reference a Geolocation object.

After this lesson, you will be able to:

■ Understand the Geolocation object.

■ Retrieve the current position.

■ Handle positioning errors.

Estimated lesson time: 20 minutes

Geolocation object reference

The Geolocation object has a simple API with the following methods.

■ **getCurrentPosition()**   Method that accepts a success callback, an error callback, and options array and calls the success callback with the current position

■ **watchPosition()**   Method that accepts a success callback, an error callback, and options array and continuously calls the success callback with the current position

■ **clearWatch()**   Method that stops continuous calling that was started by using the watchPosition method

Notice that the getCurrentPosition and watchPosition methods have the same parameters. The Position object has the following properties.

■ **coords**   Gets a Coordinates object that contains information about the current position.

- **timestamp** Gets the time that the Coordinates object was created. The format for the timestamp is milliseconds since the start of the Unix Epoch and can be converted to a regular date and time by using the following code.

```
var dateTime = new Date(timeStamp).toLocaleString();
```

By focusing on the coords property that gets a Coordinates object, the Coordinates object contains the following information about the current location.

- **latitude** Gets the latitude in decimal degrees
- **longitude** Gets the longitude in decimal degrees
- **altitude** Gets the height in meters
- **accuracy** Gets the accuracy of the coordinates in meters
- **altitudeAccuracy** Gets the accuracy of the altitude in meters
- **heading** Gets the direction of travel in degrees
- **speed** Gets the speed of travel in meters/second

The device hardware is the determining factor regarding the properties returned. For example, with a GPS, most properties are populated, but if location is determined by using your IP address, you might be missing altitude, heading, and speed-related information.

Retrieving the current position

It is easy to retrieve the current position by using the Geolocation object's getCurrentPosition method. At a minimum, you need to pass a callback method to receive a Position object, which has coords and timestamp properties. For the subsequent examples, consider the following webpage.

```
<!DOCTYPE html>
<html xmlns="http://www.w3.org/1999/xhtml">
<head>
    <title></title>
    <link href="GeoLocation.css" rel="stylesheet" />
    <script src="Scripts/jquery-1.8.3.js"></script>
    <script src="Scripts/GeoLocation.js"></script>
</head>
<body>
    <div id="message">
    </div>
</body>
</html>
```

The webpage has a reference to the Geolocation.css style sheet that is currently empty, the jQuery library, and the Geolocation.js JavaScript file, which is currently empty. The *<body>* element contains only a *<div>* element whose id is message.

The following code example demonstrates a simple call to the getCurrentPosition method.

```
/// <reference path="jquery-1.8.3.js" />
```

```
$(document).ready(function () {
    getLocation();
});

function supportsGeolocation() {
    return 'geolocation' in navigator;
}

function showMessage(message) {
    $('#message').html(message);
}

function getLocation() {
    if (supportsGeolocation()) {
        navigator.geolocation.getCurrentPosition(showPosition);
    }
    else {
        showMessage("Geolocation is not supported by this browser.");
    }
}

function showPosition(position) {
    var datetime = new Date(position.timestamp).toLocaleString();
    showMessage("Latitude: " + position.coords.latitude + "<br />"
            + "Longitude: " + position.coords.longitude + "<br />"
            + "Timestamp: " + datetime);
}
```

The document ready function calls the getLocation function. In the getLocation function an if statement determines whether it should attempt to call the getCurrentPosition method by calling the supportsGeolocation function. The supportsGeolocation function checks whether the *navigator global* variable has a geolocation property.

When the getCurrentPosition method is called, the showPosition function is passed. The showPosition function is called when the position information has been successfully obtained. When the showPosition function is called, it's passed a Position object that contains a coords and timestamp property. Figure 14-1 shows the rendered result.

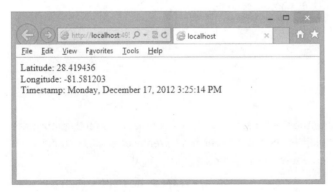

FIGURE 14-1 The rendered current position and converted timestamp

Handling errors

You must handle errors when calling methods on the Geolocation object. You handle errors by adding another callback parameter to the call so that the first parameter is the success callback, and the second parameter is the error callback.

The following code demonstrates the use of the error callback when calling the getCurrentPosition method.

```javascript
/// <reference path="jquery-1.8.3.js" />

$(document).ready(function () {
        getLocation();
});

function supportsGeolocation() {
    return 'geolocation' in navigator;
}

function showMessage(message) {
    $('#message').html(message);
}

function getLocation() {
    if (supportsGeolocation()) {
        navigator.geolocation.getCurrentPosition(showPosition, showError);
    }
    else {
        showMessage("Geolocation is not supported by this browser.");
    }
}

function showPosition(position) {
    var datetime = new Date(position.timestamp).toLocaleString();
    showMessage("Latitude: " + position.coords.latitude + "<br />"
            + "Longitude: " + position.coords.longitude + "<br />"
            + "Timestamp: " + datetime);
}

function showError(error) {
    switch (error.code) {
        case error.PERMISSION_DENIED:
            showMessge("User denied Geolocation access request.");
            break;
        case error.POSITION_UNAVAILABLE:
            showMessage("Location information unavailable.");
            break;
        case error.TIMEOUT:
            showMessage("Get user location request timed out.");
            break;
        case error.UNKNOWN_ERROR:
            showMessage("An unknown error occurred.");
            break;
    }
}
```

In this example, the showError function is called if there is an error when calling the getCurrentPosition method. An error object is passed to the showError function. This example attempts to determine the cause of the error and display a meaningful message.

Addressing privacy

If a webpage can get your current position, is that an invasion on your privacy? Yes, and you will receive a prompt that says, "*DomainName* wants to track your physical location." At that point, you can decide whether you want your location to be retrieved once, all the time, or not at all. Figure 14-2 shows the prompt.

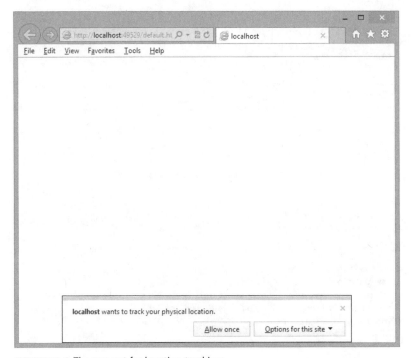

FIGURE 14-2 The request for location tracking

Specifying options

The third parameter that you can pass to the getCurrentPosition method is the options, which is a PositionOptions object that provides you with the following optional properties.

- **enableHighAccuracy**   This specifies that the best possible result is requested even if it takes more time. Default is false.

- **timeout**   This specifies the timeout in milliseconds that the browser will wait for a response. Default is -1, which means there is no timeout.

- **maximumAge**   Specifies that a cached location is acceptable as long as it's no older that the specified milliseconds. Default is 0, which means that a cached location is not used.

The following is an example of passing the options to the getCurrentPosition method.

```
function getLocation() {
    if (supportsGeolocation()) {
        var options = {
            enableHighAccuracy: true,
            timeout: 3000,
            maximumAge: 20000
        };
        navigator.geolocation.getCurrentPosition(showPosition, showError, options);
    }
    else {
        showMessage("Geolocation is not supported by this browser.");
    }
}
```

> ✔ **Quick check**
> - What must you do to prevent sites from retrieving your location without your knowledge?
>
> **Quick check answer**
> - When you visit a site that requests your location, a pop-up is displayed, and you must grant permission explicitly to the site before your location can be retrieved. Be careful about selecting Always Allow because it's easy to forget that you selected it.

Lesson summary

- The Geolocation API provides an interface with device location information.
- Depending on the location source, you can receive latitude, longitude, altitude, heading, speed, and accuracy information.
- The Geolocation API is accessible by using the geolocation property on the *navigator* global variable.
- The Geolocation object has a getCurrentPosition method that is a one-time call to get the current location.
- The getCurrentPosition method takes a success callback, an error callback, and an options parameter.

Lesson review

Answer the following questions to test your knowledge of the information in this lesson. You can find the answers to these questions and explanations of why each answer choice is correct or incorrect in the "Answers" section at the end of this chapter.

1. Which method gets your current location once from the Geolocation object?

   A. watchPosition()

   B. watchLocation()

   C. getCurrentPosition()

   D. getCurrentLocation()

2. Which of the following is not a valid parameter on the getCurrentPosition method?

   A. Error callback function

   B. Position options object

   C. Success callback function

   D. Use GPS only

Lesson 2: Monitored positioning

If you were writing an application that plotted your current location on a map, it would be more efficient to let the Geolocation API tell you when the location changes than to write code that continues to poll for the current location. That's the focus of this lesson.

> **After this lesson, you will be able to:**
> - Use the Geolocation object to watch the current position.
> - Calculate the distance between two sample points.
>
> **Estimated lesson time: 20 minutes**

Where are you now? How about now?

You can use the Geolocation object's watchPosition method to retrieve continuous position updates. This method takes the same parameters as the getCurrentPosition method. The difference is that when you call the watchPosition once, it continues calling the success function until you call the clearWatch method to stop monitoring your position.

The watchPosition method returns an id, which is passed to the clearWatch method to end the monitoring. In this example, the webpage is modified with the addition of a button to start location monitoring and another button to end location monitoring, as follows.

```
<!DOCTYPE html>
<html xmlns="http://www.w3.org/1999/xhtml">
```

```
<head>
    <title></title>
    <link href="GeoLocation.css" rel="stylesheet" />
    <script src="Scripts/jquery-1.8.3.js"></script>
    <script src="Scripts/GeoLocation.js"></script>
</head>
<body>
    <div id="message">
    </div>
    <button id="startMonitoring">Start Monitoring</button>
    <button id="stopMonitoring">Stop Monitoring</button>
</body>
</html>
```

With the added buttons and the change to use the watchPosition method, the following is the updated JavaScript; the notable changes are in bold.

```
/// <reference path="jquery-1.8.3.js" />

var watchId = 0;

$(document).ready(function () {
    $('#startMonitoring').on('click', getLocation);
    $('#stopMonitoring').on('click', endWatch);
});

function supportsGeolocation() {
    return 'geolocation' in navigator;
}

function showMessage(message) {
    $('#message').html(message);
}

function getLocation() {
    if (supportsGeolocation()) {
        var options = {
            enableHighAccuracy: true
        };
        watchId = navigator.geolocation.watchPosition(showPosition, showError, options);
    }
    else {
        showMessage("Geolocation is not supported by this browser.");
    }
}

function endWatch() {
    if (watchId != 0) {
        navigator.geolocation.clearWatch(watchId);
        watchId = 0;
        showMessage("Monitoring ended.");
    }
}

function showPosition(position) {
```

```
            var datetime = new Date(position.timestamp).toLocaleString();
            showMessage("Latitude: " + position.coords.latitude + "<br />"
                    + "Longitude: " + position.coords.longitude + "<br />"
                    + "Timestamp: " + datetime);
    }

    function showError(error) {
        switch (error.code) {
            case error.PERMISSION_DENIED:
                showMessge("User denied Geolocation access request.");
                break;
            case error.POSITION_UNAVAILABLE:
                showMessage("Location information unavailable.");
                break;
            case error.TIMEOUT:
                showMessage("Get user location request timed out.");
                break;
            case error.UNKNOWN_ERROR:
                showMessage("An unknown error occurred.");
                break;
        }
    }
```

This code doesn't require many changes to get the benefit of continuous monitoring. The big change is the addition of the endWatch function that uses the *watchId global* variable to stop location monitoring.

Calculating distance between samples

When you're continuously monitoring the user's location, you might want to calculate the distance between samples.

Calculating the distance traveled is relatively easy if you are traveling over a flat plane. Because people are traveling over the earth, you need to use spherical geometry to calculate the distance traveled. There are several formulas for this calculation, based primarily on accuracy. In addition, all calculations are based on the earth being perfectly round with no hills and valleys.

This example shows implementation of the haversine formula to calculate the distance. This formula is a bit more complex than other formulas, such as the spherical law of cosines, but it provides better accuracy. The following is a getDistance function using the haversine formula.

```
function getDistance(lat1, lon1, lat2, lon2) {
    var earthRadius = 3959; //miles
    var latRadians = getRadians(lat2 - lat1);
    var lonRadians = getRadians(lon2 - lon1);
    var a = Math.sin(latRadians / 2) * Math.sin(latRadians / 2) +
            Math.cos(getRadians(lat1)) * Math.cos(getRadians(lat2)) *
            Math.sin(lonRadians / 2) * Math.sin(lonRadians / 2);
    var c = 2 * Math.atan2(Math.sqrt(a), Math.sqrt(1 - a));
    var distance = earthRadius * c;
```

```
    return distance;
}

function getRadians (latlongDistance) {
    return latlongDistance * Math.PI / 180;
}
```

 Quick check

- Which method monitors your location?

Quick check answer

- The watchPosition method

Lesson summary

- The watchPosition method monitors your location and takes the same parameters as the getCurrentPosition method.
- The watchPosition method returns an id that is used when you want to stop monitoring.
- The clearWatch method stops monitoring.
- The clearWatch method requires a watch id.

Lesson review

Answer the following questions to test your knowledge of the information in this lesson. You can find the answers to these questions and explanations of why each answer choice is correct or incorrect in the "Answers" section at the end of this chapter.

1. Which method continuously monitors your current location from the Geolocation object?

   A. watchPosition()

   B. watchLocation()

   C. getCurrentPosition()

   D. getCurrentLocation()

2. Which of the following formulas can you use to calculate the distance between two samples?

   A. haversine

   B. Pythagorean theorem

   C. quadratic

   D. hyperbolic

Practice exercises

If you encounter a problem completing any of these exercises, the completed projects can be installed from the Practice Exercises folder that is provided with the companion content.

Exercise 1: Map your current positions

In this exercise, you apply your knowledge of the Geolocation API by creating a web application that retrieves your current location and displays a map with your location. This exercise uses the Google Maps API because you don't need an account to use it, but you can also use the Bing maps API. The Bing API is different and *requires* you to get a developer account, but it's easy to implement.

1. Start Visual Studio Express 2012 for Web. Create an ASP.NET Empty Web Application project called **PositionMapper**.

2. Add an HTML file to the project. Name the file **default.html**.

3. Add a CSS file to the project. Name the file **default.css**.

4. Add a folder called **Scripts** to the project.

5. Right-click the Scripts folder and add a new JavaScript file called **default.js**.

6. Add a reference to the jQuery library by right-clicking the project node. Choose Manage NuGet Packages. Click Online and type **jQuery** in the search criteria. When the jQuery library is displayed, click the Install button.

7. In the default.html file, add a reference to the default.css, jQuery library, and default.js files.

8. Above the jQuery reference, add the following reference to the Google Maps API.

   ```
   <script src="http://maps.google.com/maps/api/js?sensor=false"></script>
   ```

9. Add a title called **Position Mapper** to your page.

   Your HTML page should look like the following.

   ```
   <!DOCTYPE html>
   <html xmlns="http://www.w3.org/1999/xhtml">
   <head>
       <title>Position Mapper</title>
       <link href="default.css" rel="stylesheet" />
       <script src="http://maps.google.com/maps/api/js?sensor=false"></script>
       <script src="Scripts/jquery-1.8.3.js"></script>
       <script src="Scripts/default.js"></script>
   </head>
   <body>

   </body>
   </html>
   ```

10. In the *<body>* element, add a *<div>* element whose id is map.

11. Under the *<div>* element, add another *<div>* element whose id is message.

Your HTML page should look like the following.

```
<!DOCTYPE html>
<html xmlns="http://www.w3.org/1999/xhtml">
<head>
    <title>Position Mapper</title>
    <link href="default.css" rel="stylesheet" />
    <script src="http://maps.google.com/maps/api/js?sensor=false"></script>
    <script src="Scripts/jquery-1.8.3.js"></script>
    <script src="Scripts/default.js"></script>
</head>
<body>
    <div id="map"></div>
    <div id="message"></div>
</body>
</html>
```

12. In the default.css files, add the following style rules to center and size the map and message.

```
#map {
    width: 800px;
    height: 600px;
    margin-right: auto;
    margin-left: auto;
    border: solid;
}

#message {
    width: 800px;
    height: 50px;
    margin-right: auto;
    margin-left: auto;
    border: solid;
}
```

13. In the default.js file, add the document ready function. In the document ready function, call the getLocation function that you create in the next step.

Your code should look like the following.

```
$(document).ready(function () {
    getLocation();
});
```

14. Add the following code for the getLocation, supportsGeolocation, showMessage, and showError functions.

This is the same code that was covered in Lesson 1.

```
function getLocation() {
    if (supportsGeolocation()) {
        watchId = navigator.geolocation.getCurrentPosition(showPosition
                    , showError);
    }
    else {
```

```
            showMessage("Geolocation is not supported by this browser.");
        }
    }

    function supportsGeolocation() {
        return 'geolocation' in navigator;
    }

    function showMessage(message) {
        $('#message').html(message);
    }

    function showError(error) {
        switch (error.code) {
            case error.PERMISSION_DENIED:
                showMessage("User denied Geolocation access request.");
                break;
            case error.POSITION_UNAVAILABLE:
                showMessage("Location information unavailable.");
                break;
            case error.TIMEOUT:
                showMessage("Get user location request timed out.");
                break;
            case error.UNKNOWN_ERROR:
                showMessage("An unknown error occurred.");
                break;
        }
    }
```

15. Add the showPosition function that is called when the getCurrentPosition function call is successful.

```
    function showPosition(position) {
        var mapcanvas = document.getElementById('map');
        var coords = new google.maps.LatLng(position.coords.latitude
                        , position.coords.longitude);
        var options = {
            zoom: 13,
            center: coords,
            mapTypeControl: false,
            navigationControlOptions: {
                style: google.maps.NavigationControlStyle.SMALL
            },
            mapTypeId: google.maps.MapTypeId.ROADMAP
        };
        var map = new google.maps.Map(mapcanvas, options);
        var marker = new google.maps.Marker({
            position: coords,
            map: map,
            title: "You are here!"
        });
    }
```

This is where the mapping takes place. The first line gets a reference to the *<div>* element for the map and assigns it to the *mapcanvas* variable. The second statement uses the Google API to create a coordinate object based on latitude and longitude, and it's assigned to the *coords* variable. The next statement creates an object with the map settings and assigns it to the *options* variable. The Map method in the Google API is called, which renders the map in the *mapcanvas* variable and returns a reference to the map. Finally, the Google API is used to create a marker with the current location.

16. In Solution Explorer, right-click the default.html file and choose Set As Start Page.

17. Test your work by pressing F5 to run the website.

    You should see the default.html page as shown in Figure 14-3.

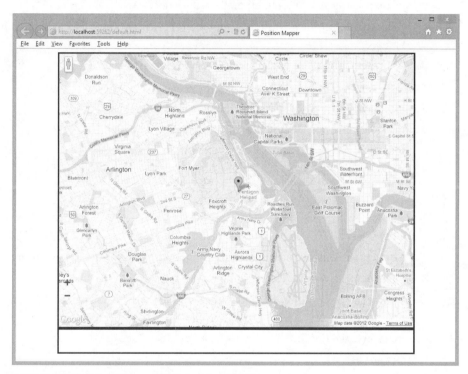

FIGURE 14-3 The Google map with the current location

Suggested practice exercises

The following additional exercises are designed to give you more opportunities to practice what you've learned and to help you successfully master the lessons presented in this chapter.

- **Exercise 1**   Learn more about positioning by creating an application that retrieves the user's current location to help find nearby locations such as gas stations or restaurants.

- **Exercise 2**   Learn more about monitored positioning by writing an application that monitors your position and displays a trail of your travels on a map.

Answers

This section contains the answers to the lesson review questions in this chapter.

Lesson 1

1. **Correct answer: C**

    A. **Incorrect:** The watchPosition() method continuously returns the current location.

    B. **Incorrect:** The watchLocation() method does not exist.

    C. **Correct:** The getCurrentPosition() method retrieves the current location a single time.

    D. **Incorrect:** The getCurrentLocation() method does not exist.

2. **Correct answer: D**

    A. **Incorrect:** The error callback function is a valid paramete.

    B. **Incorrect:** The position options object is a valid parameter.

    C. **Incorrect:** The success callback function is a valid parameter.

    D. **Correct:** The use GPS only parameter is not valid.

Lesson 2

1. **Correct answer: A**

    A. **Correct:** The watchPosition() method continuously returns the current location.

    B. **Incorrect:** The watchLocation() method does not exist.

    C. **Incorrect:** The getCurrentPosition() method retrieves the current location a single time.

    D. **Incorrect:** The getCurrentLocation() method does not exist.

2. **Correct answer: A**

    A. **Correct:** The haversine formula calculates spherical distance.

    B. **Incorrect:** You use the Pythagorean theorem to calculate the hypotenuse of a right triangle.

    C. **Incorrect:** You use the quadratic formula to solve $ax^2 + bx + c = 0$ for x.

    D. **Incorrect:** Hyperbolic functions are analogs of the ordinary trigonometric, or circular, functions.

## CHAPTER 15

Local data with web storage

So far, you've learned how to take advantage of a wide array of tools to produce applications that are aesthetically appealing, responsive, and fast. However, your primary means of data storage has been confined to sending information back to the server, which requires the application to wait for a round-trip to occur.

To minimize the cost of relying entirely on server-side persistence, most modern browsers now support web storage (also known as DOM storage), a relatively new feature that enables storing small amounts of user data on the client machine.

This chapter begins with an overview of the two storage mechanisms (localStorage and sessionStorage) and how they can make dramatic improvements in how user data is retained. The chapter then examines how the use of storage events can combat complex problems such as race conditions.

Lessons in this chapter:

Before you begin

To complete this book, you must have some understanding of web development. This chapter requires the hardware and software listed in the "System requirements" section in the book's Introduction. Specifically, you need a browser (such as Internet Explorer 8 or a newer version) that can accommodate web storage.

Lesson 1: Introducing web storage

Most web applications rely on some method of data storage, which usually involves a server-side solution such as a SQL Server database. However, in many scenarios, that might be excessive, and the ability to store simple, non-sensitive data in your browser would easily meet your needs.

After this lesson, you will be able to:

- Understand web storage.

- Implement the localStorage object.

Estimated lesson time: 20 minutes

Understanding cookies

For years, storing data in the browser could be accomplished by using HTTP cookies, which have provided a convenient way to store small bits of information. Today, cookies are used mostly for storing basic user profile information. The following is an example of how cookies are used.

```javascript
// setting the cookie value
function setCookie(cookieName, cookieValue, expirationDays) {
    var expirationDate = new Date();
    expirationDate.setDate(expirationDate.getDate() + expirationDays);
    cookieValue = cookieValue + "; expires=" + expirationDate.toUTCString();
    document.cookie = cookieName + "=" + cookieValue;
}

// retrieving the cookie value
function getCookie(cookieName)
{
    var cookies = document.cookie.split(";");

    for (var i = 0; i < cookies.length; i++) {
      var cookie = cookies[i];
      var index = cookie.indexOf("=");
      var key = cookie.substr(0, index);
      var val = cookie.substr(index + 1);

      if (key == cookieName)
        return val;
    }
}

// usage
setCookie('firstName', 'Glenn', 1);
var firstName = getCookie('firstName');
```

Using the jQuery cookie plug-in

The example demonstrates that working with cookies isn't complicated, but the interface for doing so leaves much to be desired. To simplify working with cookies, you can use the jQuery. Cookie plug-in available at *https://github.com/carhartl/jquery-cookie*. Here is the modified code example when using the jQuery plug-in.

```
$.cookie('firstName', 'Glenn');
var firstName = $.cookie('firstName');
```

This example shows that the plug-in provides a much simpler interface.

Working with cookie limitations

Cookies will continue to be an effective tool for the foreseeable future, but they have some drawbacks.

- **Capacity limitations**   Cookies are limited to about 4 KB of data, which is not large, although you can create more than 30 cookies per site. (The actual maximum limit depends on which browsers you are targeting; the average is between 30 and 50.)

- **Overhead**   Every cookie is sent with each HTTP request/response made, regardless of whether the values are needed. This is often true even for requests for static content (such images, css files, and js files), which can create heavier-than-necessary HTTP messages.

Alternatives to cookies prior to HTML5

Because the limitations of cookies were so high, demand was great for more powerful storage capabilities. Some creative alternatives were developed within a few of the more popular plug-ins.

- **Flash Player**   Adobe Flash Player plug-in was one of the earliest to offer a reliable storage mechanism through its Local Shared Objects function. It comes with the ability to store much more data than cookies and gives the user the ability to increase or limit the amount of space allowed for each site. Another extremely useful feature of Local Shared Objects is its ability to be written by one browser and read by others. For example, if a user creates a to-do list on a website by using Internet Explorer, that list can later be accessed by Flash Player running within Firefox.

- **User Data**   Internet Explorer has supported an application programming interface (API), referred to as User Data, since version 5. It provides the ability to store up to 1 MB of information in the form of a key/value pair. Although not as robust as the HTML5 storage offerings, it can still be a good alternative for applications that are meant to be Internet Explorer–specific and are required to work in earlier versions such as Internet Explorer 6 or Internet Explorer 7.

- **Google Gears**   A solution that was ahead of its time was Google Gears, which several high-volume web utilities used, such as YouTube and Gmail. In 2010, however, Google announced that it is no longer developing new features for Gears. Instead, Google's efforts are turned to building on the HTML5 web standards.

- **Java Applets**   Another popular open-source solution was Java Applets, which was another cross browser–friendly way to store information. However, like Flash Player and Gears, its usage is dropping dramatically in favor of HTML5 alternatives.

Looking beyond plug-ins

Although the features within these plug-ins provided great answers to the storage problem, they came with limitations that restricted their usefulness.

- **Plug-in required**   The first hurdle is that the user must not only have the plug-in installed but also often have the correct plug-in version.

- **User blocking**   Because of security and performance concerns, many users install tools such as Flash blockers, which can require a user to click to enable the plug-in or even block the plug-in entirely.

- **Corporate users**   In some organizations, employees are prohibited from installing third-party plug-ins to avoid potential security vulnerabilities.

- **Vendor-specific**   The biggest drawback to each plug-in option is that it relies on individual vendors for support and development. If that vendor decides to discontinue or reduce support, you might have to find another solution quickly.

Understanding HTML5 storage

Existing solutions leave a lot to be desired; HTML5 breaks new ground with several innovative tools. Each is unique and carries its own set of pros and cons, which this chapter discusses individually.

- **Web storage**   Easily the simplest new form of storage, web storage provides a way to store key/value pairs of data in a manner that rivals cookies in ease of use. In the next section, you see that it's currently the most widely supported option.

- **Web SQL database**   For more complex applications, this might be a good alternative to web storage. It provides the power of a full relational database, including support for SQL commands, transactions, and performance tuning. Unfortunately, its support is extremely limited, and it might be left behind in favor of other options.

- **IndexedDB**   This tool appears to be a strong candidate for the solution to complex storage requirements in the future. As a non-relational (NoSQL) database, it provides simplicity that's similar to web storage while still accommodating common needs such as indexing and transactions.

- **Filesystem API**   This tool is useful for storing larger data types such as text files, images, and movies. However, it suffers from a lack of adoption by many of today's modern browsers. As of this writing, it's primarily supported in Chrome only.

Considering security

Although the four storage types have many differences, they also have some striking similarities beyond all being vehicles for storing data on the client's machine.

One property they all have in common is that the data being stored is tied to the URL (or, more specifically, the origin), which ensures that data can't be accessed by other sites.

Therefore, the same host, port, and protocol (for example, HTTP versus HTTPS) must be provided before a webpage can access data written by another page.

Given data storage that was created using the URL *http://www.example.com/area1 /page1.html*, consider whether each of the following URLs can access that data storage.

- **http://www.otherexample.com/area1/page1.html**   No, different domains
- **http://store.example.com/area1/page1.html**   No, different hosts
- **http://example.com/area1/page1.html**   No, different hosts
- **https://www.example.com/area1/page1.html**   No, different protocol
- **http://www.example.com:8080/area1/page1.html**   No, different ports
- **http://www.example.com/area1/page2.html**   Yes
- **http://www.example.com/area2/page1.html**   Yes

The strict association to the origin is an important consideration when developing sites that may be hosted on a shared domain. In most cases, it would be better practice to avoid using web storage entirely if your site will live within a shared domain in the future, because any sub-site within the domain would be able to access your data.

Using browser support

Many HTML5 features have different levels of implementation and compatibility by the different browser manufacturers, and this is especially true when working with the different storage options. By far, the most universally supported storage option is web storage. The following is a summary of browser support.

- **Web storage**
  - **Supported**   Internet Explorer (v8.0 and newer versions), Firefox (v15.0+), Chrome (v22.0+), Safari (v5.1+), Safari Mobile (v3.2+), Blackberry (v7.0+), Android (v2.1+), Opera (v12.0+)
  - **Not supported**   Opera Mobile
- **Web SQL**
  - **Supported**   Chrome (v22.0+), Safari (v5.1+), Safari Mobile (v3.2+), Blackberry (v7.0+), Android (v2.1+), Opera (v12.0+)
  - **Not supported**   Internet Explorer, Firefox, Opera Mobile
- **IndexedDB**
  - **Supported**   Internet Explorer (v10.0 and newer versions), Firefox (v15.0+), Chrome (v23.0+), Blackberry (v10.0+)
  - **Not supported**   Safari, Safari Mobile, Android, Opera, Opera Mobile
- **FileSystem API**
  - **Supported**   Chrome (v22.0+), Blackberry (v10.0+)
  - **Not supported**   Internet Explorer, Firefox, Safari, Safari Mobile, Android, Opera, Opera Mobile

This chapter examines the two types of web storage: localStorage and sessionStorage. Chapter 16, "Offline web applications," examines the remaining three storage options in more depth.

Exploring localStorage

The *localStorage* global variable is a Storage object. One of the greatest strengths of *localStorage* is its simple API for reading and writing key/value pairs of strings. Because it's essentially a NoSQL store, it's easy to use by nature.

Using the *localStorage* object reference

The following is a list of methods and attributes available on the Storage object as it pertains to *localStorage*.

- **setItem(key, value)** Method that stores a value by using the associated key. The following is an example of how you can store the value of a text box in *localStorage*. The syntax for setting a value is the same for a new key as for overwriting an existing value.

  ```
  localStorage.setItem('firstName', $('#firstName').val());
  And since it's treated like many other JavaScript dictionaries, you could also set
  values using other common syntaxes.
  localStorage['firstName'] = $('#firstName').val();
  or
  localStorage.firstName = $('#firstName').val();
  ```

- **getItem(key)** Method of retrieving a value by using the associated key. The following example retrieves the value for the 'firstName' key. If an entry with the specified key does not exist, null will be returned.

  ```
  var firstName = localStorage.getItem('firstName');
  And like setItem, you also have the ability to use other syntaxes to retrieve
  values from the dictionary.
  var firstName = localStorage['firstName'];
  or
  var firstName = localStorage.firstName;
  ```

- **removeItem(key)** Method to remove a value from *localStorage* by using the associated key. The following example removes the entry with the given key. However, it does nothing if the key is not present in the collection.

  ```
  localStorage.removeItem('firstName');
  ```

- **clear()** Method to remove all items from storage. If no entries are present, it does nothing. The following is an example of clearing the *localStorage* object.

  ```
  localStorage.clear();
  ```

- **length** Property that gets the number of entries currently being stored. The following example demonstrates the use of the length property.

  ```
  var itemCount = localStorage.length;
  ```

- **key(index)** Method that finds a key at a given index. The World Wide Web Consortium (W3C) indicates that if an attempt is made to access a key by using an index that is out of the range of the collection, null should be returned. However, some browsers will throw an exception if an out-of-range index is used, so it's recommended to check the length before indexing keys.

```
var key = localStorage.key(1);
```

Very high browser support

Another benefit of *localStorage*, as seen in the previous section, is that *localStorage*, in addition to *sessionStorage*, is well supported in modern browsers. In fact, it's the only one of the four storage options that is consistently supported across desktop and mobile browsers.

Determining whether the user's browser supports web storage

Although most browsers support web storage, it's still a good idea to verify that it's available in case the user is running an older browser version. If it's not available, you could experience a null reference exception the first time an attempt is made to access *localStorage* or *sessionStorage*. There are several ways to check availability; the following is one example.

```
function isWebStorageSupported() {
    return 'localStorage' in window;
}

if (isWebStorageSupported()) {
    localStorage.setItem('firstName', $('#firstName').val());
}
```

The popular JavaScript library, Modernizr, comes with a method that could do this check for you.

```
if (Modernizr.localstorage) {
    localStorage.setItem('firstName', $('#firstName').val());
}
```

Amount of data that can be kept in web storage

The *localStorage* object provides much more space than was available with older tools. Modern browsers support a minimum of 5 MB of data, which is substantially more than is allowed through cookies (which are limited to 4 KB each).

> *NOTE* **STORAGE CAPACITY**
>
> The 5 MB limit is currently recommended by the W3C, but it's ultimately up to the browser vendors to determine how much they will allow. Currently, Internet Explorer supports a 10 MB limit.

Reaching the storage limit

If the storage limit is reached, or if the user manually turns off storage capabilities, a QuotaExceededError exception is thrown. The following is an example of how you can use a try/catch block to keep your application from failing if that happens.

```
try{
    localStorage.setItem('firstName', $('#firstName').val());
}
catch(e) {
    // degrade gracefully
}
```

Storing complex objects

Currently, only string values can be stored in web storage, but sometimes you might need to store more interesting items such as arrays or JavaScript objects. To accomplish this, you can take advantage of some of the available JavaScript Object Notation (JSON) utility methods.

The following example creates a JSON object and uses the stringify() method to convert the value to a string that can then be placed in web storage.

```
var person = { firstName: 'Glenn', lastName: 'Johnson' };
localStorage.setItem('glenn', JSON.stringify(person));
```

You can then use the parse() method to deserialize a new instance of the object from the string representation that was stored in the previous example.

```
var person = JSON.parse(localStorage.getItem('glenn'));
```

Don't forget that a potential drawback to cookies is that they are always included in web requests and responses, even if you don't use them. The situation when using web storage is the opposite; its values are never automatically passed to the server. You can do this yourself by including values in an AJAX call or by using JavaScript to copy the values into posted form elements.

Using short-term persistence with *sessionStorage*

In the previous section, you learned how to use *localStorage*, which, like cookies, is designed to retain data across multiple sessions. However, if you want to purge stored information, you must use the removeItem() or clear() method.

In addition to *localStorage*, you can use *sessionStorage*; it is also a Storage object, so the same methods and properties exist. The difference is that *sessionStorage* retains data for a single session only. After the user closes the browser window, records stored are automatically cleared. This is an important advantage because only a limited amount of space is available.

At their core, both *localStorage* and *sessionStorage* are firmly dedicated to their respective browsing contexts. Because that context for *localStorage* includes other tabs and windows within the same URL base, its data is shared among all open instances. In contrast, *sessionStorage* has a context that, by design, is extremely confined. It's limited to a single browser tab or window. Its data cannot be passed from one tab to the next. However, the data can be shared among any *<iframe>* elements that exist on the page.

 Quick check

- What object type are *localStorage* and *sessionStorage*?

Quick check answer

- They are Storage objects.

Anticipating potential performance pitfalls

Web storage doesn't come without a few drawbacks. This section covers some of the pitfalls of using *localStorage* and *sessionStorage*.

Synchronously reading and writing to the hard drive

One of the biggest issues with the Storage object that is used with *localStorage* and *sessionStorage* is that it operates synchronously, which can block the page from rendering while read/writes occur. The synchronous read/writes are even more costly because they are committed directly to the client's hard drive. By itself, that might not be a cause for concern, but the following activities can make these interactions annoyingly slow for the user.

- Indexing services on the client machine
- Scanning for viruses
- Writing larger amounts of data

Although the amount of time it usually takes to perform these actions is typically too small to notice, they could lock the browser from rendering while it's reading and writing values to the hard disk. With that in mind, it's a good idea to use web storage for very small amounts of data and use alternative methods for larger items.

> **NOTE** **WHY NOT USE WEB WORKERS TO READ/WRITE ASYNCHRONOUSLY?**
>
> Web storage is not available within web workers. If you need to write a value while in web workers, you must use the postMessage() method to notify the parent thread and allow it to perform the work instead.

Anticipating slow search capabilities

Because web storage does not have indexing features, searching large data sets can be time consuming. This usually involves iterating over each item in the list to find items that match the search criteria.

No transaction support

Another benefit of other storage options that is missing from web storage is support for transactions. Although difficulties are unlikely in the majority of applications, applications using web storage can run into problems if a user is modifying the same value in localStorage within multiple open browser tabs. The result would be a race condition in which the second tab immediately overwrites the value inserted by the first tab.

 Quick check

- You would like to store the user's name after he authenticates on your site, but he will need to authenticate again on his next visit, at which time you would reload his information (including name). Which storage mechanism should you use?

Quick check answer

- *sessionStorage.* Although you could use *localStorage* to store the user's name, it would be held permanently. Placing it in *sessionStorage* would purge it automatically after the window is closed.

Lesson summary

- Web storage provides you with an easy method for storing key/value pairs of data without relying on a server.
- With nearly universal support across current desktop and mobile browsers, web storage is the most supported form of offline data storage.
- Web storage comes in two forms, which have the same methods.
  - **localStorage**   Shares data across all windows and tabs within the same origin.
  - **sessionStorage**   Data is sandboxed to only the current tab or window and is cleared when closed.
- Reads/writes to web storage can be performed only synchronously.
- Web storage does not support advanced features such as transactions or indexing.
- Only storage for string values is currently supported within web storage, but storage for more complex objects can be achieved by using the JSON.stringify() and JSON.parse() utility methods.

Lesson review

Answer the following questions to test your knowledge of the information in this lesson. You can find the answers to these questions and explanations of why each answer choice is correct or incorrect in the "Answers" section at the end of this chapter.

1. Which of the following URLs can access data stored on *http://www.example.com/lesson1/page1.html*?

    A. *http://www2.example.com/lesson1/page1.html*

    B. *http://www.example.com:8081/lesson1/page1.html*

    C. *https://www.example.com/lesson1/page1.html*

    D. *http://www.example.com/lesson2/page1.html*

    E. *http://example.com/lesson1/page1.html*

2. What is the web storage limit currently recommended by the World Wide Web Consortium (W3C)?

    A. 4 KB

    B. 5 MB

    C. 500 MB

    D. 10 MB

3. What is the correct syntax for removing all values existing in *localStorage*?

    A. localStorage.clear();

    B. localStorage.removeAll();

    C. localStorage.abandon();

    D. localStorage.reset();

4. Which of the following storage mechanisms has the highest level of cross-browser support?

    A. Web storage

    B. Web SQL

    C. IndexDB

    D. FileSystem API

5. Which of the following features does web storage support?

    A. Indexing

    B. Transactions

    C. Asynchronous read/write

    D. Simple key/value pair storage

Lesson 2: Handling storage events

One of the biggest challenges you'll face when working with web storage is keeping everything in sync when a user has multiple tabs or browser instances open at the same time. For example, browser tab one might have displayed a value it retrieved from *localStorage* just before that entry was updated in browser tab two. In this scenario, tab one doesn't know that the value it displayed has just become stale.

To solve this problem, web storage has a storage event that is raised whenever an entry is added, updated, or removed. You can subscribe to this event within your application to provide notification when something has changed and inform you of specific details about those changes. These events work in both *localStorage* and *sessionStorage*.

After this lesson, you will be able to:

- Understand the StorageEvent object.
- Implement the event handling on the localStorage object.

Estimated lesson time: 20 minutes

Sending notifications only to other windows

The W3C recommends that events not be received in the tab (or window) that made the change when working with storage events. This makes sense because the intent is to allow other windows to respond when a storage value changes. However, some browsers (such as later versions of Internet Explorer) have implemented storage events in a way that allows the source window to receive the notification, too. It is only safe to rely on this implementation if your application will target those browsers specifically.

Using the StorageEvent object reference

Subscribers to the storage event receive a StorageEvent object containing detailed information about what has changed. The following is a list of properties included on the StorageEvent object.

- **key**   Gets the key of the record that was added, updated, or removed; will be null or empty if the event was triggered by the clear() method
- **oldValue**   Gets the initial value if the entry was updated or removed; will be null or empty if a new item was added or the clear() method was invoked
- **newValue**   Gets the new value for new and updated entries; will be null or empty if the event was triggered by either the removeItem() or clear() methods
- **url**   Gets the URL of the page on which the storage action was made
- **storageArea**   Gets a reference to either the window's *localStorage* or *sessionStorage* object, depending on which was changed

Many browsers initially began supporting storage events without fully implementing the properties of the StorageEvent interface specification, so some older browsers might trigger storage events, but the properties outlined here might be null or empty.

Bubbling and canceling events

Unlike some other types of events, the storage event cannot be canceled from within a callback; it's simply a means for informing subscribers when a change occurs. It also does not bubble up like other events.

Subscribing to events

To begin listening for event notifications, add an event handler to the storage event as follows.

```
function respondToChange(e) {
    alert(e.newValue);
}
window.addEventListener('storage', respondToChange, false);
```

To trigger this event, perform an operation like the following in a new tab within the same site.

```
localStorage.setItem('name', 'Glenn');
```

Considering Internet Explorer 8 performance with storage events

Storage events are only partially supported in Internet Explorer 8, so if you need to support that specific browser version, consider these factors.

- Only the url property is implemented on the StorageEvent object. The rest of the properties will return null.

- The storage event itself is not triggered on the window object as it is in browsers that are more current; instead, it is triggered on the document object.

- The addEventListener() method is not available, but you can use the attachEvent() method.

The following example subscribes to storage changes while safeguarding against when Internet Explorer 8 might be used.

```
if (window.addEventListener) { // check for IE8
    window.addEventListener('storage', respondToChange, false);
} else {
    document.attachEvent('onstorage', respondToChange);
}
```

Binding to storage events by using jQuery

An alternative method to using addEventListener() for your subscriptions is to use the event-binding features jQuery provides. You have to update your respondToChange() method because it will now return a different event that actually wraps the raw event you were working with in the previous example.

```
function respondToChange(e) {
```

```
        alert(e.originalEvent.newValue);
}

$(window).on('storage', respondToChange);

if ('onstorage' in document) // bind to document for IE8
    $(document).on('storage', respondToChange);
```

Using events with *sessionStorage*

In the previous lesson, you learned that browser context dictates when data can be shared.
Because the context for *localStorage* includes other tabs and windows, notifications are
passed to each open instance. However, *sessionStorage* gains little benefit from events
because its context includes the active tab only. Current browsers have included *<iframe>*
elements within that context definition, so it is possible to pass notifications to and from them
if necessary.

Lesson summary

- Other tabs and windows can subscribe to storage events to receive notifications when
  a change occurs to *localStorage*.
- The StorageEvent object passed to subscribers contains detailed information regarding
  what changes were made.
- Because *sessionStorage* data is not shared beyond the current tab or window, others
  will not receive notifications when a change occurs.
- Storage events cannot be canceled and do not bubble up.

Lesson review

Answer the following questions to test your knowledge of the information in this lesson. You
can find the answers to these questions and explanations of why each answer choice is correct
or incorrect in the "Answers" section at the end of this chapter.

1. Which of the following is not a property of the StorageEvent object?

   A. oldValue

   B. key

   C. changeType

   D. storageArea

2. If you modify a value stored in *sessionStorage*, which of the following could receive
   notifications of the change (if subscribed)?

   A. Another tab opened to a page on the same domain

   B. A second browser window open to the same page

C. An iframe on the same page whose source is within the same domain

D. The operating system that is hosting the browser

3. Which of the following is the correct way to cancel a storage event?

A. event.returnValue = false;

B. event.preventDefault();

C. event.stopPropagation();

D. Storage events cannot be canceled after they are triggered.

Practice exercises

If you encounter a problem completing any of these exercises, the completed projects can be installed from the Practice Exercises folder that is provided with the companion content.

Exercise 1: Create a contact book by using *localStorage*

In this exercise, you practice working with web storage by creating a simple contact list that is persisted as an array in *localStorage*. The page will display the complete contact list within a grid and use a form for adding and editing contacts. The website itself will consist of a single page; no server-side logic is needed. The HTML and CSS code is already complete, so your focus is on adding the JavaScript needed to make it work.

1. Open Visual Studio Express 2012 for Web. Click File and choose Open Project. Navigate to the ContactBook folder under the Exercise1Start folder. Select ContactBook.sln and click Open.

2. Review the starting default.html file.

   This file has a reference to the default.css file, the jQuery file, and the ContactsLibrary.js file. In the *<body>* element is a contacts table and a form that includes fields for first name, last name, email, and phone number of the contact as follows.

```
<!DOCTYPE html>
<html xmlns="http://www.w3.org/1999/xhtml">
<head>
    <title>Contact Book</title>
    <link href="Content/default.css" rel="stylesheet" />
    <script src="Scripts/jquery-1.8.3.min.js"></script>
    <script src="Scripts/ContactsLibrary.js"></script>
</head>
<body>
    <div id="container">
        <header>
            <hgroup id="headerText">
                <h1>Contacts</h1>
            </hgroup>
        </header>
        <div role="main">
```

```
        <table id="contacts">
            <thead>
                <tr>
                    <th>Email</th>
                    <th>Name</th>
                    <th></th>
                </tr>
            </thead>
            <tbody>
            </tbody>
        </table>

        <div id="editContact">
            <h2 id="currentAction"></h2>
            <div>
                <label for="firstName">First Name:</label>
                <input type="text" id="firstName" name="firstName" />
            </div>
            <div>
                <label for="lastName">Last Name:</label>
                <input type="text" id="lastName" name="lastName" />
            </div>
            <div>
                <label for="email">Email Address:</label>
                <input type="email" id="email" name="email" />
            </div>
            <div>
                <label for="phoneNumber">Phone Number:</label>
                <input type="text" id="phoneNumber" name="phoneNumber" />
            </div>
            <div class="buttons">
                <button id="btnSave" name="save">Save</button>
            </div>
        </div>
    </div>
  </div>
</body>
</html>
```

3. Review the default.css file.

This file starts by resetting the margin, padding, font size, and font family of all elements. The semantic markup elements are set as blocks, and then the body element is formatted. Specific formatting is applied to produce an attractive webpage. The following is the default.css file.

```
* {
    margin: 0;
    padding: 0;
    font-size: 12px;
    font-family: Arial;
}

aside, footer, header, hgroup, nav {
    display: block;
```

```
    }

    body {
        color: #776E65;
        padding: 10px;
    }

    header {
        height: 20px;
        background-repeat: no-repeat;
        margin-top: 10px;
    }

    #headerText {
        position: absolute;
        top: 0px;
        width: 100%;
    }

    h1 {
        font-size: 24px;
    }

    div[role="main"] {
        float: left;
        width: 60%;
    }

    #editContact {
        background: none repeat scroll 0 0 #F8F8F8;
        border: 1px solid #E1E1E1;
        width: 400px;
        margin-top: 20px;
    }

    #editContact h2 {
        padding-left: 10px;
        margin-top: 10px;
        font-size: 18px;
        width: 200px;
    }

    #editContact div {
        width: 350px;
        padding: 10px;
    }

    #editContact div.buttons {
        text-align: center;
    }

    #editContact label {
        width: 150px;
        height: 12px;
        vertical-align: bottom;
```

```
        clear: left;
        display: block;
        float:left;
    }

    #editContact input {
        width: 150px;
        padding: 2px;
    }

    button {
        width: 200px;
        margin-top: 10px;
    }

    #contacts {
        width: 400px;
        border: 1px solid #E1E1E1;
        margin: 0px;
        padding: 0px;
    }

    #contacts thead {
        background-color: #e1e1e1;
        color: #7C756D;
        font-weight: bold;
        text-align: left;
    }

    #contacts tbody tr:nth-child(even) {
        background-color: #eee;
    }

    #contacts th {
        border-color: #7C756D;
        border-style: none none solid;
        border-width: 0 0 1px;
    }

    #contacts th, #contacts td {
        margin: 0px;
        padding: 5px 10px;
    }
```

4. Open and review the ContactsLibrary.js file.

   This file has a reference to the jQuery library. Following that is a document ready function that calls the initialize function in the contactsNamespace. Under the document ready function is the contactsNamespace, which contains a *currentRecord* variable and the initialize property, which is assigned an empty function. The ContactsLibrary.js file is as follows.

   ```
   /// <reference path="jquery-1.8.3.js" />

   $(document).ready(function () {
   ```

```
        contactsNamespace.initialize();
    });

    (function () {
        this.contactsNamespace = this.contactsNamespace || {};
        var ns = this.contactsNamespace;
        var currentRecord;

        ns.initialize = function () {

        };

    })();
```

5. To add code to the ContactsLibrary.js file, add a retrieveFromStorage method that pulls the contact list from *localStorage*.

   The contact list will be stored as an array of JSON Contact objects, but remember that *localStorage* supports only storage of string values, so you must parse the result as an array. You must also handle occasions when the contacts might not yet exist in storage. Your code should look like the following.

```
    (function () {
        this.contactsNamespace = this.contactsNamespace || {};
        var ns = this.contactsNamespace;
        var currentRecord;

        ns.initialize = function () {

        };

        function retrieveFromStorage() {
            var contactsJSON = localStorage.getItem('contacts');
            return contactsJSON ? JSON.parse(contactsJSON) : [];
        }
    })();
```

6. Populate the grid by iterating through the results array and creating a row for each record. Within each row, include three cells: the email address, the full name, and an edit link that will include a data-key attribute to hold the contact's index within the array.

7. If the array is empty, display a "No records available" message. Add a publicly available display method that pulls items from storage and passes them to a private bindToGrid method.

   Your code should look like the following.

```
    ns.display = function () {
        var results = retrieveFromStorage();
        bindToGrid(results);
    };

    function bindToGrid(results) {
```

```
        var html = '';
        for (var i = 0; i < results.length; i++) {
            var contact = results[i];
            html += '<tr><td>' + contact.email + '</td>';
            html += '<td>' + contact.firstName + ' ' + contact.lastName + '</td>';
            html += '<td><a class="edit" href="javascript:void(0)" data-key='
                    + i + '>Edit</a></td></tr>';
        }
        html = html || '<tr><td colspan="3">No records available</td></tr>';
        $('#contacts tbody').html(html);
    }
```

You created the edit link for each row; now you create the methods needed to display the details for the selected row.

Because the method is invoked by clicking the link, you can get the index of the item by inspecting the data-key attribute on the *this* object.

8. Use the index to find the corresponding item in the contacts array and then store the index and contact object within the currentRecord field.

You will call a displayCurrentRecord method, which you create in the next step. Your code should look like the following.

```
ns.loadContact = function () {
    var key = parseInt($(this).attr('data-key'));
    var results = retrieveFromStorage();
    $('#currentAction').html('Edit Contact');
    currentRecord = { key: key, contact: results[key] }
    displayCurrentRecord();
};
```

9. Add the displayCurrentRecord method, which populates the form fields with contact information as follows.

```
function displayCurrentRecord() {
    var contact = currentRecord.contact;
    $('#firstName').val(contact.firstName);
    $('#lastName').val(contact.lastName);
    $('#email').val(contact.email);
    $('#phoneNumber').val(contact.phoneNumber);
}
```

10. In the bindToGrid method that you created earlier, add the following line to the end of the method.

This binds the click event of the Edit links to the loadContact method.

```
$('#contacts a.edit').on('click', ns.loadContact);
```

11. Update the display method to instantiate an empty default currentRecord object that is used to add a contact as follows.

```
ns.display = function () {
    $('#currentAction').html('Add Contact');
    currentRecord = { key: null, contact: {} };
```

```
    displayCurrentRecord();
    var results = retrieveFromStorage();
    bindToGrid(results);
};
```

12. Add the public save method. In this method, create a *contact* variable and assign the contact property of currentRecord. Retrieve each of the field values from the form and assign them to the contact object as follows.

```
ns.save = function () {
    var contact = currentRecord.contact;
    contact.firstName = $('#firstName').val();
    contact.lastName = $('#lastName').val();
    contact.email = $('#email').val();
    contact.phoneNumber = $('#phoneNumber').val();
};
```

13. Add logic to the end of the save method that either adds the contact to the array if it's a new contact or updates the contact if it already exists. Convert the object to a JSON string and store it in *localStorage*. Update the page by calling the display method.

The completed save method is as follows.

```
ns.save = function () {
    var contact = currentRecord.contact;
    contact.firstName = $('#firstName').val();
    contact.lastName = $('#lastName').val();
    contact.email = $('#email').val();
    contact.phoneNumber = $('#phoneNumber').val();

    var results = retrieveFromStorage();

    if (currentRecord.key != null) {
        results[currentRecord.key] = contact;
    }
    else {
        results.push(contact);
    }

    localStorage.setItem('contacts', JSON.stringify(results));
    ns.display();
};
```

14. Update the initialize method to bind the save button and invoke the display() method.

```
ns.initialize = function () {
    $('#btnSave').on('click', ns.save);
    ns.display();
};
```

Your JavaScript file should look like the following.

```
/// <reference path="jquery-1.8.3.js" />

$(document).ready(function () {
    contactsNamespace.initialize();
```

```
});
(function () {
    this.contactsNamespace = this.contactsNamespace || {};
    var ns = this.contactsNamespace;
    var currentRecord;

    ns.initialize = function () {
        $('#btnSave').on('click', ns.save);
        ns.display();
    };

    function retrieveFromStorage() {
        var contactsJSON = localStorage.getItem('contacts');
        return contactsJSON ? JSON.parse(contactsJSON) : [];
    }

    ns.display = function () {
        $('#currentAction').html('Add Contact');
        currentRecord = { key: null, contact: {} };
        displayCurrentRecord();

        var results = retrieveFromStorage();
        bindToGrid(results);
    };

    function bindToGrid(results) {
        var html = '';

        for (var i = 0; i < results.length; i++) {
            var contact = results[i];
            html += '<tr><td>' + contact.email + '</td>';
            html += '<td>' + contact.firstName + ' ' + contact.lastName + '</td>';
            html += '<td><a class="edit" href="javascript:void(0)" data-key='
                        + i + '>Edit</a></td></tr>';
        }
        html = html || '<tr><td colspan="3">No records available</td></tr>';
        $('#contacts tbody').html(html);
        $('#contacts a.edit').on('click', ns.loadContact);
    }

    ns.loadContact = function () {
        var key = parseInt($(this).attr('data-key'));
        var results = retrieveFromStorage();
        $('#currentAction').html('Edit Contact');
        currentRecord = { key: key, contact: results[key] }
        displayCurrentRecord();
    };

    function displayCurrentRecord() {
        var contact = currentRecord.contact;
        $('#firstName').val(contact.firstName);
        $('#lastName').val(contact.lastName);
        $('#email').val(contact.email);
        $('#phoneNumber').val(contact.phoneNumber);
    }
```

```
ns.save = function () {
    var contact = currentRecord.contact;
    contact.firstName = $('#firstName').val();
    contact.lastName = $('#lastName').val();
    contact.email = $('#email').val();
    contact.phoneNumber = $('#phoneNumber').val();

    var results = retrieveFromStorage();

    if (currentRecord.key != null) {
        results[currentRecord.key] = contact;
    }
    else {
        results.push(contact);
    }

    localStorage.setItem('contacts', JSON.stringify(results));
    ns.display();
};

})();
```

15. In the Solution Explorer window, right-click the default.html file and choose Set As Start Page.

16. Run the website and start adding contacts. Try closing the browser and rerunning the website to see the persisted contacts.

Figure 15-1 shows the completed webpage with a fictitious contact added.

FIGURE 15-1 The completed contact book

Suggested practice exercises

The following additional exercises are designed to give you more opportunities to practice what you've learned and to help you successfully master the lessons presented in this chapter.

- **Exercise 1** Modify the contact list to use *sessionStorage* instead of *localStorage*. Notice that your list is cleared after the browser window is closed.

- **Exercise 2** Subscribe to the storage event and display an alert message each time a value is updated. Test this by using a second browser tab.

Answers

This section contains the answers to the lesson review questions in this chapter.

Lesson 1

1. **Correct answer: D**

    A. **Incorrect:** The use of a different host (www2 instead of www) disallows this URL from access.

    B. **Incorrect:** The port number must match the origin port nmber.

    C. **Incorrect:** Matching protocols must be used. In this answer, https is used rather than http.

    D. **Correct:** Because this example uses the same origin, it will have access to the same data storage space.

    E. **Incorrect:** This example does not have a matching host and would not be allowed access.

2. **Correct answer: B**

    A. **Incorrect:** The cookie value limit is 4 KB.

    B. **Correct:** The recommended limit is 5 MB, although the browser vendor can determine the respective limits.

    C. **Incorrect:** If websites could store 500 MB of data on the client machine, drastic performance degradation would result.

    D. **Incorrect:** Internet Explorer supports 10 MB, but that's not the recommended limit.

3. **Correct answer: A**

    A. **Correct:** The clear() method removes all existing key/value pairs existing for the origin.

    B. **Incorrect:** The removeAll() method does not exist.

    C. **Incorrect:** The abandon() method does not exist.

    D. **Incorrect:** The reset() method does not exist.

4. **Correct answer: A**

    A. **Correct:** Nearly all modern browsers support web storage (*localStorage* and *sessionStorage*).

    B. **Incorrect:** Some popular browsers (namely Chrome and Safari) support Web SQL, but neither Internet Explorer nor Firefox supports it yet.

    C. **Incorrect:** Although IndexDB seems to be gaining support ahead of Web SQL, it is yet to be adopted by Safari or some of the major mobile browsers.

    D. **Incorrect:** With only Chrome as its strongest supporter, FileSystem API is the least adoption option.

5. **Correct answer: D**

   A. **Incorrect:** Web storage does not support indexing.

   B. **Incorrect:** Web storage does not support transactions.

   C. **Incorrect:** Web storage does not support asynchronous processing.

   D. **Correct:** The simple key/value pair storage's easy-to-use interface is perhaps the best feature of web storage.

Lesson 2

1. **Correct answer: C**

   A. **Incorrect:** Storage events have an oldValue property that contains original values when an entry is updated or removed.

   B. **Incorrect:** Storage events have a key property that contains the name of the entry being added, updated, or deleted.

   C. **Correct:** There is no property on storage events called changeType.

   D. **Incorrect:** Storage events have a storageArea property that contains either the *localStorage* or *sessionStorage* collection that was changed.

2. **Correct answer: C**

   A. **Incorrect:** Session storage events do not go beyond the active tab; other tabs would not be notified when changes occur.

   B. **Incorrect:** Session storage events do not reach outside their current window.

   C. **Correct:** In this case, an iframe could receive change notifications.

   D. **Incorrect:** Session storage events do not go beyond the active tab; the operating system would not be notified when changes occur.

3. **Correct answer: D**

   A. **Incorrect:** The event.returnValue = false; method is a fairly common way to cancel many events after they start, but storage events cannot be canceled.

   B. **Incorrect:** The event.preventDefault(); method is another way to cancel many types of events, but storage events cannot be canceled.

   C. **Incorrect:** Storage events do not bubble up, so the event.stopPropagation(); method would have no effect.

   D. **Correct:** Storage events cannot be canceled after they have been triggered.

## CHAPTER 16

Offline web applications

In the preceding chapter, you learned about the most widely used offline solution, web storage, but it's not always the best tool for the job. At times, you might need more advanced features such as true asynchronous support, indexing for faster searching, or transactions. Those features are available in the other offline storage mechanisms.

This chapter begins by looking at one option that provides all the power of a relational database, Web SQL. An alternative that's more of an object database, IndexedDB (Indexed Database), is covered next; it gives you the power of indexing and transactions without the need to set up a formal relational structure. Although both those solutions are good for typical data concerns, neither is designed for storage of files (such as images, text files, XML, or even movies). For that need, this chapter discusses the FileSystem API. Last, you see how you can make an entire website offline-friendly with very little effort by using the offline application HTTP cache.

As each tool is reviewed, pay attention to the levels of support within today's modern browsers because this is an important consideration when deciding whether to adopt the tool for your next application.

Lessons in this chapter:

Before you begin

To complete this book, you must have some understanding of web development. This chapter requires the hardware and software listed in the "System requirements" section in the book's Introduction. Because no current browser supports all offline features, some of the examples require different browsers if you want to follow along on your own equipment.

Lesson 1: Working with Web SQL

Web SQL is arguably one of the most powerful options available to you. It provides a full relational database that includes many of the features you've come to enjoy from the server-side database offerings.

Most current implementations are built on SQLite, which is one of the most widely used lightweight database engines. It's an open-source solution with a vibrant community backing it.

> **After this lesson, you will be able to:**
> - Describe the use of Web SQL.
> - Implement transactions using Web SQL.
>
> **Estimated lesson time: 20 minutes**

Considering the questionable longevity of Web SQL

Before starting with Web SQL, be aware that the World Wide Web Consortium (W3C) has stated that Web SQL is no longer on its recommendation track. In 2010, the W3C Web Applications Working Group announced that it does not intend to maintain the specification.

> *NOTE* **DISCONTINUED SUPPORT**
>
> For further details regarding the W3C's decision to discontinue support of the Web SQL specifications, please see its explanation at *http://dev.w3.org/html5/webdatabase/*.

What this means for Web SQL depends on the browser you're targeting. Although the specification is no longer being maintained, some browsers have continued their support. (See Chapter 15 for a complete list.) Therefore, Web SQL might be a viable option if you're building specifically for a platform such as iOS for iPad or iPhone. Another common use is in Google Chrome extensions. If you're building a browser-agnostic application, consider one of the other offline storage solutions.

If you do plan on developing with Web SQL, it might be a good idea to remember what alternatives are available (such as IndexedDB) and what level of effort might be needed if other browser vendors decide to move away from it in the future.

Creating and opening the database

In the following sections, examine the syntax used to create or open a database, start a transaction, and execute a SQL command. Most of these commands should look very familiar if you've used other relational databases.

To start communication with a database, use the openDatabase method, which returns a Database object. If you attempt to open a database that doesn't exist, it will be automatically created for you, so you won't need to execute any extra steps for new databases. The following are the openDatabase parameters.

- **name**   The database name, which is case-sensitive. Most characters are allowed; even an empty string is considered valid.

- **version**   Expected version of the database. If an empty string is passed, it's implied that whatever version currently exists is fine.

- **displayName**   Descriptive name of the database.

- **estimatedSize**   Estimated size required for the database. The typical default value is 5 MB; the browser might prompt the user for permission, depending on the size you specify.

- **creationCallback**   If the database does not yet exist and is being created, this callback will be invoked. It is optional and not needed for the database to be created and versioned correctly.

In the following example, a database named Library is created with an estimated size of 5 MB. It returns a Database object that supports transactional operations.

```
var db = openDatabase('Library', '1.0', 'My library', 5 * 1024 * 1024);
```

If you're familiar with traditional database connections, you might be expecting a need to close a connection. With Web SQL, however, that's automatically handled, so you don't have to close the connection manually.

Performing schema updates

As your application grows, your data requirements change. You might need to add new tables, drop existing ones, or even change particular columns. The Database object provides the following hooks for making those changes.

- **version**   Property that gets the current schema version

- **changeVersion**   Method for performing schema changes between one version and the next

The changeVersion method contains the following arguments.

- **oldVersion**   Schema version you are migrating from

- **newVersion**   Schema version you are migrating to

- **callback**   Callback method containing schema changes such as adding and dropping tables

- **errorCallback**   Optional; callback method is invoked if an error occurs while the transaction is being processed

- **successCallback**   Optional; callback method is invoked if all statements successfully execute within the transaction

Adding a table

You can add an authors table to the Library database created earlier. You need a callback method that accepts a transaction object, which executes the CREATE TABLE script. The transaction object allows multiple actions within it, and it automatically rolls back all changes if any fail. For now, this example keeps the idea simple by adding just one table.

```
function migrateDB(transaction) {
    transaction.executeSql("CREATE TABLE IF NOT EXISTS authors(" +
                "id INTEGER PRIMARY KEY AUTOINCREMENT, " +
                "firstName TEXT, "+
                "lastName TEXT, " +
                "dateCreated TIMESTAMP DEFAULT(datetime('now', 'localtime')))");
}
function onError(error) {
    alert("Error code: " + error.code + " Message: " + error.message);
}
function onSuccess() {
    alert("Migration complete!");
}

var db = openDatabase('Library', '1.0', 'My library', 5 * 1024 * 1024);
db.changeVersion('1.0' , '2.0', migrateDB, onError, onSuccess);
```

Later in the chapter, you can read the version property of the Database object to determine the schema version with which you are working. Note that version updates are applied asynchronously, so if the following line was placed immediately after the db.changeVersion() call in the preceding code, it would still display 1.0 because the alert() method would fire before the migrations had a chance to complete.

```
alert("Current schema: " + db.version);
```

Now that the migration has been applied, you have a new table in your database with the following columns.

- **id**   Table identifier; new records are automatically assigned an id that is one greater than the id of the last record added.
- **firstName**   Text field for storing a person's first name.
- **lastName**   Text field for storing a person's last name.
- **dateCreated**   Time stamp; when a record is first created, this column defaults to the current time with the help of the SQLite datetime method. Instead of using its default mode of GMT, you can indicate that it should use the local time zone.

Using transactions

Now that you have a schema in place, you can use transactions to execute SQL statements. To do this, the Database object provides the following two methods.

- **transaction**   Starts a new transaction that executes SQL statements; allows both read and write commands

- **readTransaction**   Works similarly to the transaction method but allows read commands only

Both methods accept the same three parameters.

- **callback**   Callback method containing the individual commands that are to be executed as part of the transaction
- **errorCallback**   Optional callback method invoked if an error occurs while the transaction is being processed
- **successCallback**   Optional callback method invoked if all statements successfully execute within the transaction

The callback method will receive a transaction object that includes an executeSql method for performing data changes. It has the following parameters.

- **sqlStatement**   The SQL statement string to be executed.
- **arguments**   Array of object parameters to be used by the SQL command.
- **callback**   Optional callback method invoked after the command is executed. When data is retrieved, this method includes the collection of selected rows.
- **errorCallback**   Optional callback method invoked if an error occurs while the statement is being executed.

In the next section, you see how you can use transactions to execute some of the most commonly used SQL commands.

Inserting a new record

Now that you have a database and table in place, add a new record. Like creating a new table, do this by using the executeSql method on the transaction instance.

```
var db = openDatabase('Library', '2.0', 'My library', 5 * 1024 * 1024);

db.transaction(function(t){
    t.executeSql("INSERT INTO authors(firstName, lastName) "
        + " VALUES('Daniel', 'Defoe')");
});
```

However, in general, it's a good idea to use SQL parameters when working with dynamic SQL. The preceding statement can be rewritten to take advantage of an optional second parameter on the executeSql method, which accepts an array of field values. Note the use of question marks to indicate that the value will be populated from the array being passed in.

```
var firstName = 'Daniel';
var lastName = 'Defoe';
db.transaction(function(t){
    t.executeSql("INSERT INTO authors(firstName, lastName) VALUES(?, ?)"
                , [firstName, lastName]);
});
```

You can go a step further by adding a callback to the executeSql method, which enables you to capture the Id of the newly created row.

```
function itemInserted(transaction, results) {
    alert("Id: " + results.insertId);
}


var firstName = 'Daniel';
var lastName = 'Defoe';
db.transaction(function(t){
    t.executeSql("INSERT INTO authors(firstName, lastName) VALUES(?, ?)"
                 , [firstName, lastName]
                 , itemInserted);
});
```

Updating an existing record

In the following example, the lastName of the author, which has an id of 1, is updated. Besides the SQL syntax differences, it's very similar to the code used for adding a new record.

```
var db = openDatabase('Library', '2.0', 'My library', 5 * 1024 * 1024);
var authorId = 1;
var lastName = 'Smith';
db.transaction(function(t){
    t.executeSql("UPDATE authors SET lastName = ? WHERE id = ?"
                 , [lastName, authorId]);
});
```

Deleting a record

Removing records is also fairly straightforward. The following example deletes the author record with an id of 1.

```
var db = openDatabase('Library', '2.0', 'My library', 5 * 1024 * 1024);
var authorId = 1;
db.transaction(function(t){
    t.executeSql("DELETE FROM authors WHERE id = ?", [authorId]);
});
```

Reading values from the database

Now that you know how to add data to the database, you can read and display those records back to the user. Create a simple SELECT statement to read all values from the authors table. When executeSql is called this time, a callback method is passed that accepts a transaction object and a resultset containing the rows returned from the SQL statement.

As the displayResults method iterates through the rows, it formats the person's name in a list item and adds it to an unordered list with an id of items. To access the individual column values within the row, use dot notation, which reads each as a property on the object.

```
function displayResults(transaction, results) {
    for (var i = 0; i < results.rows.length; i++) {
        var item = results.rows.item(i);
        $('#items').append('<li>' + item.firstName + " " + item.lastName + '</li>');
    }
}
```

```
var db = openDatabase('Library', '2.0', 'My library', 5 * 1024 * 1024);
db.transaction(function(t){
    t.executeSql("SELECT * FROM authors", [], displayResults)
});
```

Because you are only retrieving data, you just as easily could have used the
readTransaction method instead of the transaction method.

```
db.readTransaction(function(t){
    t.executeSql("SELECT * FROM authors", [], displayResults)
});
```

 Quick check

■ The following statement has a syntax error in the second step of the transaction
  in this migration script (misspelled CREATE as CRATE). What do you expect will
  happen because of this migration script?

```
function migrateDB(transaction) {
    transaction.executeSql("CREATE TABLE authors(firstName TEXT)");
    transaction.executeSql("CRATE TABLE books(title TEXT)");
}

var db = openDatabase('Library', '1.0', 'My library', 5 * 1024 * 1024);
db.changeVersion('1.0' , '2.0', migrateDB)
```

Quick check answer

■ Neither table will be created.

Filtering results

You rarely want to read every row from a database table; most of the time, you need to limit
those results to specific criteria. Because current implementations are based on SQLite, you
have all the power of a mature database engine to help you.

For example, you can add a WHERE clause to return only records with a specific lastName
value, as follows.

```
var db = openDatabase('Library', '2.0', 'My library', 5 * 1024 * 1024);
var lastName = 'Defoe';
db.transaction(function(t){
    t.executeSql("SELECT * FROM authors WHERE lastName = ?", [lastName], displayResults)
});
```

You might like to find all authors whose last name starts with the letter D. To do so, use the
LIKE keyword along with the '%' wildcard.

```
var lastName = 'D%';
db.transaction(function(t){
    t.executeSql("SELECT * FROM authors WHERE lastName LIKE ?", [lastName],
```

```
displayResults)
});
```

Using JOIN commands

Web SQL includes support for traditional JOIN statements (such as INNER JOIN and LEFT JOIN), which can be used to include columns from multiple tables within a single SELECT statement.

Assume you added a books table to your library database and would now like to modify your earlier query to include the title of each book in the results.

```
var db = openDatabase('Library', '2.0', 'My library', 5 * 1024 * 1024);
var lastName = 'D%';
db.transaction(function(t){
    t.executeSql("SELECT a.firstName, a.lastName, b.title " +
                "FROM authors a " +
                "INNER JOIN books b ON a.id = b.authorId " +
                "WHERE a.lastName like ?"
                , [lastName]
                , displayResults)
});
```

Aggregating functions

Another useful feature of Web SQL is the ability to group results, which enables the use of more advanced functions such as COUNT(x), MIN(x), MAX(x), and SUM(x) within your SELECT statements. For example, the following is a new query that finds the number of books written by each author.

```
db.transaction(function(t){
    t.executeSql("SELECT a.firstName, a.lastName, COUNT(b.id) AS numOfBooks " +
                "FROM authors a " +
                "INNER JOIN books b ON a.id = b.authorId " +
                "GROUP BY a.id"
                , []
                , displayResults)
});
```

Lesson summary

- The World Wide Web Consortium (W3C) has stated that the Web SQL specification is no longer on its recommendation track. It may still be used when targeting specific platforms that have continued support, but other options such as IndexedDB and web storage should be considered when possible.

- Current browser implementations are based on SQLite, which gives you all the power of a full relational database.

- Database communication is started by calling the openDatabase() command. If the database does not exist, it will be created automatically.

- Schema migration support is available by using the changeVersion() method.

- Web SQL supports a common SQL syntax for create, retrieve, update, and delete (CRUD) operations.

- If one statement in a transaction fails, all actions are rolled back.

Lesson review

Answer the following questions to test your knowledge of the information in this lesson. You can find the answers to these questions and explanations of why each answer choice is correct or incorrect in the "Answers" section at the end of this chapter.

1. Which of the following would be a good candidate for Web SQL?

   A. Mobile applications built specifically for Safari on the iOS platform

   B. Mobile applications built for any mobile device

   C. Public-facing web applications

   D. Mobile applications built specifically for Internet Explorer

2. You need to create a new database. Which of the following commands should you use?

   A. var db = createDatabase('mydb', '1.0', 'My database', 5 * 1024 * 1024);

   B. var db = new Database('mydb');

   C. var db = initDatabase('mydb', '1.0', 'My database', 5 * 1024 * 1024);

   D. var db = openDatabase('mydb', '1.0', 'My database', 5 * 1024 * 1024);

3. Which of the following will correctly insert a new record, using values passed in as SQL arguments to an executeSql() call?

   A. t.executeSql("INSERT INTO books(title) VALUES(?)", ["A Tale of Two Cities"]);

   B. t.executeSql("INSERT INTO books(title) VALUES([0])", ["A Tale of Two Cities"]);

   C. t.executeSql("INSERT INTO books(title) VALUES([1])", ["A Tale of Two Cities"]);

   D. t.executeSql("INSERT INTO books(title) VALUES({0})", ["A Tale of Two Cities"]);

Lesson 2: Working with IndexedDB

So far, you've seen two extremes for client-side data storage. Web storage provides a simple key/value persistence model but lacks some of the features that are important when working with a database. The other extreme, Web SQL, provides many of the features associated with a fully functional relational database but brings with it all the manual work required for setting up and maintaining the persistence structure.

IndexedDB provides a compromise between the two alternatives. It's a key/value database in which values can range from simple strings to complex object structures. To provide for fast retrieval and searching, it includes an easy way to create indexes for each of your object stores. Much like Web SQL, interfacing with the database is transaction-based and requires minimal effort.

Because the W3C announced that it will not continue development of the Web SQL specification, IndexedDB has gained even more support. Although it's not yet supported by every major browser, it does have wider adoption than Web SQL.

After this lesson, you will be able to:

- Describe the use of IndexedDB.
- Understand the use of object stores.
- Implement transactions using Web SQL.

Estimated lesson time: 40 minutes

Using browser-specific code

To work with IndexedDB, you need to use methods that might contain browser-specific prefixes because of the continuing development of the specification. To make your examples cross browser–friendly, include the following fix at the top of your scripts to avoid the need to put browser-specific logic in each of your methods. All subsequent examples will be based on this code.

```
window.indexedDB = window.indexedDB || window.mozIndexedDB
      || window.webkitIndexedDB || window.msIndexedDB;
window.IDBTransaction = window.IDBTransaction || window.webkitIDBTransaction;
window.IDBCursor = window.IDBCursor || window.webkitIDBCursor;
window.IDBKeyRange = window.IDBKeyRange || window.webkitIDBKeyRange;
```

Creating and opening the database

The first step in working with IndexedDB is to create and open a database. You need to access the browser's indexedDB object, which, in the previous example, was assigned to a consistent variable.

```
var indexedDB = window.indexedDB;
```

This *indexedDB* variable is an IDBFactory object that provides access to your databases through the open method, which has the following parameters.

- **name**   The name of the object store
- **version**   Optional; the version of the object store

This method returns an IDBRequest object and begins an asynchronous process of opening a connection. The IDBRequest object includes an onsuccess event that can be subscribed to, which provides notification when the connection is ready for use. It also includes an onerror event that can notify your application if an error occurs during an attempt to connect. The following example shows the open method.

```
var indexedDB = window.indexedDB;
var openRequest = indexedDB.open('Library', 1);
var db;

openRequest.onsuccess = function(response) {
    db = openRequest.result;
};

openRequest.onerror = function (response) {
    alert("Error code: " + response.target.errorCode);
};
```

In this example, the open method is called, and, within the onsuccess event handler, the *db* variable is assigned a reference to the database object for later use.

Using object stores

In standard relational databases, tables are created that are defined by rigid schemas. Each table contains a set of columns, each of which has a name and a data type. This doesn't allow for much flexibility because it requires a lot of work when schema changes are needed. Therefore, instead of these table structures, IndexedDB uses spaces called object stores, which are key/value storage areas.

Understanding versioning

Before creating a new object store, you need to understand how IndexedDB handles versioning.

```
var openRequest = indexedDB.open('Library', 1);
```

In this call to open a database connection, a version number is passed as the second parameter. The request object received contains an onupgradeneeded event that will be triggered if the version requested doesn't match the current version of the existing database. It will also be triggered if the database does not yet exist. The onupgradeneeded event will be fired before the onsuccess event.

The onupgradeneeded event is defined by the latest API specification. Earlier versions handled versioning by a setVersion method on the database object. If you're targeting older browser versions, make sure to use the appropriate versioning method.

Within the onupgradeneeded event handler, use the createObjectStore method to allocate a new storage area. This method requires an object store name and an object containing any extra parameters to use in configuring the store.

Using the keypath property

One important property of the parameter object is the keypath. Its purpose is to specify which property on the value object should be used as the key. This key is then used as the primary index for stored instances. If the property specified by the keypath does not exist on the value object, you must use a key generator such as autoIncrement, which creates auto-incrementing numeric keys for you as follows.

```
var openRequest = indexedDB.open('Library', 1);
openRequest.onupgradeneeded = function(response) {
    response.currentTarget.result.createObjectStore("authors",
{ keypath: 'id', autoIncrement: true });
};
```

In this example, a new object store called "authors" is created. Notice that you are not required to identify the properties explicitly or even identify the type of object that will be stored. However, this example allows IndexedDB to create the keys by setting the autoIncrement property to true. You just as easily could specify a field on the value object as the key. You could use the following code example if each author had an email that you would like to use as the key.

```
response.currentTarget.result.createObjectStore("authors", { keypath: 'email' });
```

Adding indexes

Although the key will be the primary index for object stores, you can specify other indexes. This can provide a performance boost if properties other than the key might be commonly used in sorting or filtering. To do so, use the createIndex method on the object store, which has the following parameters.

- **name**   The index name.
- **keyPath**   Specifies the property on the value object for which the index will be created.
- **optionalParameters**   Optional parameter that can contain an object with properties used for advanced index settings. Currently, IndexedDB supports two advanced settings. The first is 'unique', which when true adds a constraint to the property that prohibits two records from having the same value. The second property that can be set is 'multiEntry', which indicates how the index should behave when the keyPath is an array. If set to true, an index entry is created for each value in the array. If set to false, a single index entry is created for the array as a whole.

The following demonstrates the use of the createIndex method on the object store to a new, non-unique index for the lastName property of the authors object store.

```
var openRequest = indexedDB.open('Library', 2);
openRequest.onupgradeneeded = function(response) {
    var store = response.currentTarget.transaction.objectStore("authors");
    store.createIndex('lastName', 'lastName', { unique: false });
};
```

The createIndex method is called during a database migration, within the onupgradeneeded event handler, to ensure that the index is created when the version is updated.

Removing indexes

If you decide that an index is no longer needed, you can remove it by creating a database migration that uses the object store's deleteIndex() method, as shown in the following example code.

```
var openRequest = indexedDB.open('Library', 3);
openRequest.onupgradeneeded = function(response) {
    var store = response.currentTarget.transaction.objectStore("authors");
    store.deleteIndex('lastName');
};
```

Removing object stores

As you probably guessed, the steps to remove an object store are very similar to the steps for creating one. You create a new migration that uses the database's deleteObjectStore() method as follows.

```
var openRequest = indexedDB.open('Library', 4);
openRequest.onupgradeneeded = function(response) {
    response.currentTarget.result.deleteObjectStore("authors");
};
```

Using transactions

When your object stores are in place, you must use the IDBTransaction object to add or remove objects. An IDBTransaction object, which is a transaction, is created by using the transaction method of the database object and takes the following parameters.

- **objectStoreNames**   Specifies the object stores with which the transaction will work. If only one object store is needed, the parameter can be a single string. If multiple object stores are needed, pass an array of strings. The following is an example of opening a transaction for a single object store.

  ```
  var trans = db.transaction('authors');
  ```

  Here is an example of opening a transaction for multiple object stores.

  ```
  var trans = db.transaction(['authors', 'books']);
  ```

- **mode**   Optional when possible values are *readonly* and *readwrite*. If not specified, the transaction will be defaulted to *readonly*. If left in readonly mode, multiple transactions can be run concurrently. The following is an example of a transaction being opened in readonly mode.

```
var trans = db.transaction('authors', 'readonly');
```

Example of a transaction being opened in readwrite mode.

```
var trans = db.transaction('authors', 'readwrite');
```

Inserting a new record

After a transaction instance has been created, you can use it to add a new record. To do so, you must first find the object store to which you would like to add the record. Call the add method of the object store, which will insert the record asynchronously. The add method returns a request instance in which you can subscribe to an onsuccess event that provides notification when the operation is completed. You can then use the request.result property to obtain the auto-generated id for the new record. You can also subscribe to the onerror event if the operation fails, as shown in the following example.

```
var openRequest = indexedDB.open('Library', 1);
var db;

openRequest.onsuccess = function(response) {
    db = openRequest.result;
    addAuthor();
};

function addAuthor() {
    var trans = db.transaction('authors', 'readwrite');
    var authors = trans.objectStore("authors");
    var request = authors.add({firstName: 'Daniel', lastName: 'Defoe'});
    request.onsuccess = function(response) {
        alert('New record id: ' + request.result);
    };

    request.onerror = function(response) {  // display error };
}
```

Updating an existing record

Modifying existing objects is similar to adding a record, but instead of the add method, you use the put method of the object store. Actually, you could use the put method for both adding and updating values. The add method, however, can be used for new records only. An exception is thrown if the add method is called using a key that already exists. The following code demonstrates the use of the put method.

```
var openRequest = indexedDB.open('Library', 1);
var db;

openRequest.onsuccess = function(response) {
    db = openRequest.result;
    updateAuthor();
};
```

```
function updateAuthor() {
    var trans = db.transaction('authors', 'readwrite');
    var authors = trans.objectStore("authors");
    var request = authors.put({firstName: 'Bob', lastName: 'Defoe'}, 1);
    request.onsuccess = function(response) {
        alert('Updated record id: ' + request.result);
    };

    request.onerror = function(response) {  // display error };
}
```

The preceding example updates the first and last names of the author record with a key of 1.

Deleting a record

To remove a stored object, you only need to know its key value, which is passed to the delete method of the object store.

```
function deleteAuthor() {
    var trans = db.transaction('authors', 'readwrite');
    var authors = trans.objectStore("authors");
    var request = authors.delete(1);

    request.onsuccess = function(response) {  // success! };
    request.onerror = function(response) {  // display error };
}
```

Retrieving a record

Several methods are available for finding existing records. If you need to find a specific record, use the get method of the object store. The only parameter needed to pass to the method is the key of the object being retrieved. Like other operations, this needs to be done within a transaction. In the following example, the transaction mode is set to *readonly*.

```
var openRequest = indexedDB.open('Library', 1);
var db;

openRequest.onsuccess = function(response) {
    db = openRequest.result;
    getAuthor();
};

function getAuthor() {
    var trans = db.transaction('authors', 'readonly');
    var authors = trans.objectStore("authors");
    var request = authors.get(1);

    request.onsuccess = function(response) {
        var author = response.target.result;
        alert('Last name: ' + author.lastName);
    };
```

```
    request.onerror = function(response) {  // display error };
}
```

Understanding cursors

The other approach to finding records is by using cursors. A cursor can be opened by calling the object store's openCursor method, which returns a request object and accepts the following parameters.

- **range**   This parameter allows you to provide a key range to limit records included in the results.

- **direction**   By default, cursors are executed in ascending order. To change the order to descending, use IDBCursor.PREV.

The following is a simple example that iterates through all records held in the authors object store.

```
var openRequest = indexedDB.open('Library', 1);
var db;

openRequest.onsuccess = function(response) {
    db = openRequest.result;
    findAuthors();
};

function findAuthors() {
    var trans = db.transaction('authors', 'readonly');
    var authors = trans.objectStore("authors");
    var request = authors.openCursor();

    request.onsuccess = function(response) {
       var cursor = response.target.result;

       if (!cursor) {
           alert('No records found.');
           return;
       }

       alert('Id: ' + cursor.key + ' Last name: ' + cursor.value.lastName);
       cursor.continue();
    };

    request.onerror = function(response) {  // display error };
}
```

The cursor itself is on the result property of the response of the onsuccess event handler. If no records are found, the onsuccess event will still fire, but the result will be undefined (or null). If records are found, the cursor's value property will contain the current record. To continue iterating, invoke the cursor's continue method, which will trigger the onsuccess event handler again, this time with the next record in the results. When it reaches the end of the collection, the onsuccess event will have a null cursor.

Indexing cursors

Cursors can also be created by using an index of an object store. A standard cursor, like the one in the previous example, can be created by using the openCursor method and will return the entire object associated to the index value. However, if you only need the corresponding keys and not the full object, you can use the openKeyCursor method instead.

The following is a modified version of the findAuthors method, which creates a cursor against the lastName index instead of going directly against the object store. The sort order is specified as IDBCursor.PREV, so the authors result is sorted by the last name in descending order.

```
function findAuthors() {
    var trans = db.transaction('authors', 'readonly');
    var authors = trans.objectStore('authors');
    var index = authors.index('lastName');
    var request = index.openCursor(null, IDBCursor.PREV);

    request.onsuccess = function(response) {
        var cursor = response.target.result;

        if (!cursor) {
            alert('No records found.');
            return;
        }

        alert('Index value (lastName): ' + cursor.key
            + ' First name: ' + cursor.value.firstName);
        cursor.continue();
    };

    request.onerror = function(response) {  // display error };
}
```

Applying key range limits

Most of the time, just a subset of an object store is needed instead of the entire contents. To limit the results, pass an *IDBKeyRange* value as the first parameter to the openCursor method. The following is a list of the various range methods available through the IDBKeyRange object.

- **bound** The most flexible range type is the bound method, by which you specify upper and lower limits and specify whether the outer bounds should be included in the results. The bound range method accepts the following parameters.
  - **lower** Specifies the lower bound of the range.
  - **upper** Specifies the upper bound of the range.

- **lowerOpen** Optional; can be true or false. If true, the lower end of the range is considered bounded, so the lower bound won't be included in the results. If false, it's considered unbounded, and the lower bound will be included in the results.

- **upperOpen** Optional; can be true or false. If true, the upper bound won't be included in the results. If false, it will be included.

For example, consider an index on the lastName property on the authors object store. Following are some results in scenarios when ranges are applied against that index.

authors content: Daniel Defoe, Herman Melville, Mark Twain, Jules Verne

```
index.openCursor(IDBKeyRange.bound('Defoe', 'Verne', false, false));
```

results: Daniel Defoe, Herman Melville, Mark Twain, Jules Verne

```
index.openCursor(IDBKeyRange.bound('Defoe', 'Verne', false, true));
```

results: Daniel Defoe, Herman Melville, Mark Twain

```
index.openCursor(IDBKeyRange.bound('Defoe', 'Verne', true, false));
```

results: Herman Melville, Mark Twain, Jules Verne

```
index.openCursor(IDBKeyRange.bound('Defoe', 'Verne', true, true));
```

results: Herman Melville, Mark Twain

- **upperBound** The upperBound method enables you to limit only the upper side of the range. The following are parameters of the upperBound method.

  - **upper** Specifies the upper bound of the range.

  - **upperOpen** Optional; can be true or false. If true, the upper bound won't be included in the results. If false, it will be included.

authors content: Daniel Defoe, Herman Melville, Mark Twain, Jules Verne

```
index.openCursor(IDBKeyRange.upperBound('Verne', false));
```

results: Daniel Defoe, Herman Melville, Mark Twain, Jules Verne

```
index.openCursor(IDBKeyRange.upperBound('Verne', true));
```

results: Daniel Defoe, Herman Melville, Mark Twain

- **lowerBound** The lowerBound method enables you to limit only the lower end of the range. The following are parameters of the lowerBound method.

  - **lower** Specifies the lower bound of the range.

  - **lowerOpen** Optional; can be true or false. If true, the lower bound won't be included in the results. If false, it will be included.

authors content: Daniel Defoe, Herman Melville, Mark Twain, Jules Verne

```
index.openCursor(IDBKeyRange.lowerBound('Defoe', false));
```

results: Daniel Defoe, Herman Melville, Mark Twain, Jules Verne

```
index.openCursor(IDBKeyRange.lowerBound('Defoe', true));
```

results: Herman Melville, Mark Twain, Jules Verne

- **only** You can restrict to a specific key value rather than to a range by using the only method. The following is a parameter of the only method.

  - **value** The specific key value against which to match.

  authors content: Daniel Defoe, Herman Melville, Mark Twain, Jules Verne

  ```
  index.openCursor(IDBKeyRange.only('Twain'));
  ```

  results: Mark Twain

Dropping a database

The IDBFactory object that is referenced by the indexedDB object contains a deleteDatabase method that removes an existing database. This method takes a name parameter and returns a request object immediately while asynchronously attempting to drop the database, as shown in the following example.

```
var dropRequest = indexedDB.deleteDatabase('Library');
dropRequest.onsuccess = function(response) {  // success! };
dropRequest.onerror = function (response) { // display error };
```

If the database doesn't exist, no action is taken. If another connection to the database is open, a blocked event will be fired by the request object.

Lesson summary

- IndexedDB is a key-based object database available in most current browsers.
- Databases contain object stores, which are somewhat equivalent to table structures in a relational database.
- Each object store has a designated key path that identifies its key.
- Instead of a property on the object value, a key can be created through a key generator such as autoIncrement, which creates a distinct numeric identifier as new records are added.
- Indexes can be created for properties other than the key that might be commonly used for sorting or filtering.
- All operations are performed through transactions, which can be read-only or read/write. Read-only operations can run concurrently.
- An object store's add method can be used only for adding new records, but its put method can be used for new or existing records. Its delete method removes records.
- Cursors find records in an object store and can be created on either the object store itself or one of its indexes.

Lesson review

Answer the following questions to test your knowledge of the information in this lesson. You can find the answers to these questions and explanations of why each answer choice is correct or incorrect in the "Answers" section at the end of this chapter.

1. Which of the following features is not supported by IndexedDB?

   A. Transactions

   B. Cursors

   C. Indexed

   D. SQL

2. What is the correct method for creating a transaction that will add a new record?

   A. var trans = db.transaction('authors', 'readonly');

   B. var trans = db.transaction('authors', 'readwrite');

   C. var trans = db.transaction('authors');

   D. var trans = db.createTransaction('authors','readwrite');

3. Which object store method retrieves a record by its key value?

   A. get(key)

   B. find(key)

   C. single(key)

   D. first(key)

Lesson 3: Working with the FileSystem API

So far, you've seen several ways to store user data within the browser, and although you could use solutions such as data URIs to store larger bits of information (images, text files, and so on), none is really designed for that type of use and would certainly lead to high performance costs.

HTML5 has a solution: the FileSystem API. By using the FileSystem API, you can create directories and files within a sandboxed location on the user's file system, and this opens the door to a number of new capabilities that were previously limited to desktop applications.

In this lesson, you learn how to use the FileSystem API to perform common tasks such as creating and reading files. Although the lesson does not cover every available feature, you should gain a high-level understanding of what this technology offers.

Assessing browser support

As of this writing, the only major browser supporting the FileSystem API is Chrome, so you might want to have it installed if you want to follow along with the examples. It is not known if other browsers are planning to add support in the future.

Because of its limited browser support, the most common applications to take advantage of the FileSystem API are those targeting Chrome, such as Chrome extensions.

Opening the file system

The JavaScript window object contains a method for making requests to open communication with the file system. Depending on the version of Chrome you have installed, this can be either window.requestFileSystem() or window.webkitRequestFileSystem(). To make the following examples as compatible as possible, the following snippet is at the top of the subsequent scripts.

```
window.requestFileSystem  = window.requestFileSystem ||
    window.webkitRequestFileSystem;
```

The requestFileSystem method operates asynchronously and includes success and error callbacks that provide notification that the application can begin reading and writing files. The following parameters are accepted.

- **type**   This parameter specifies whether the file system should be temporary or permanent. If temporary, you pass TEMPORARY as the argument, and the browser automatically removes the files as it needs space. If you pass PERSISTENT, files are removed only when requested by the application or user.

- **size**   This parameter is an estimation of the size (in bytes) that the application will need.

- **successCallback**   If the request for a file system is successful, this callback is invoked and includes a FileSystem object as an argument.

- **errorCallback**   If the request fails, this callback is invoked and includes a FileError argument. The error includes a code that indicates why the failure occurred, such as exceeding quota or discovering security issues.

Creating and opening a file

To create a file, you must first have a DirectoryEntry object so you have an allocated place in which to put the file. The FileSystem argument passed to successCallback includes a special DirectoryEntry as a property named root, which points to the root of the file system reserved specifically for the application (origin). Later in this lesson, you learn how to create a subdirectory under root. For now, you create a new file in this location.

A DirectoryEntry object has a getFile method that can both create new files and read those that already exist. The following are the parameters of the getFile method.

- **path** Path to the file being requested. Both relative and absolute paths can be used.

- **options** Allows for two flags, create and exclusive, that indicate how the file should be opened. If the file doesn't exist, create must be set to true or an error will be thrown. If both create and exclusive are set to true, an attempt will be made to create the file but will throw an error if the file already exists.

- **successCallback** If the file is successfully created or opened, this callback will be invoked with a FileEntry argument.

- **errorCallback** If the request fails, this callback will be invoked and will include a FileError argument.

The following example creates a new temporary file called "example.txt" in the root directory.

```
window.requestFileSystem(TEMPORARY, 5 * 1024 * 1024, getFile, handleError);

function getFile(fileSystem) {
    fileSystem.root.getFile("example.txt", { create: true }, fileOpened, handleError);
}

function fileOpened(fileEntry) {
    alert("File opened!");
}

function handleError(error) {
    alert(error.code);
}
```

Writing to a file

When you have access to a FileEntry object, you can create a FileWriter, which persists data to the opened file. This is done by using its write method, which accepts a binary large object (BLOB) data parameter.

In the following example, the fileOpened method in the previous example is modified to create a new FileWriter and write a line of text to the opened document. Notice that in the writeToFile method, you must assign the onwriteend and onerror callbacks before performing the write action.

```
window.requestFileSystem(TEMPORARY, 5 * 1024 * 1024, getFile, handleError);

function getFile(fileSystem) {
    fileSystem.root.getFile("example.txt", { create: true }, fileOpened, handleError);
}

function fileOpened(fileEntry) {
    fileEntry.createWriter(writeToFile, handleError);
}

function writeToFile(fileWriter) {
    fileWriter.onwriteend = function() { alert('Success'); };
    fileWriter.onerror = function() { alert('Failed'); };
    fileWriter.write(new Blob(['Hello world'], {type: 'text/plain'}));
}

function handleError(error) {
    alert(error.code);
}
```

If you were opening an existing file and wanted to append new data at the end of the file, you would use the seek method to point the cursor to the end of the file as follows.

```
function writeToFile(fileWriter) {
    fileWriter.onwriteend = function() { alert('Success'); };
    fileWriter.onerror = function() { alert('Failed'); };
    fileWriter.seek(fileWriter.length);
    fileWriter.write(new Blob(['Hello world'], {type: 'text/plain'}));
}
```

Reading a file

The FileEntry object also has a file method, which makes it return a File object. After you have a reference to a File object, you can read it by using the FileReader object. Similar to FileWriter, you must set your onloadend and onerror callbacks before making a read attempt.

The following example uses the readAsText method to read the contents of the file and store it in a string that can then be accessed in the *this.result* value within the onloadend callback.

```
window.requestFileSystem(TEMPORARY, 5 * 1024 * 1024, getFile, handleError);

function getFile(fileSystem) {
    fileSystem.root.getFile("example.txt", { create: true }, fileOpened, handleError);
}

function fileOpened(fileEntry) {
    fileEntry.file(readFile, handleError);
}

function readFile(file) {
    var fileReader = new FileReader();
    fileReader.onloadend = function() { alert(this.result); };
```

```
        fileReader.onerror = function() { alert('Failed'); };
        fileReader.readAsText(file);
    }

    function handleError(error) {
        alert(error.code);
    }
```

In addition to the readAsText method, the FileReader object contains the readArrayBuffer and readAsDataURL methods for reading content types other than text.

Deleting a file

The last file operation covered in this section is deleting a file. Like the other operations, this requires a FileEntry object. Because the FileEntry object inherits from the Entry object, it has a remove method to remove itself from the file system. It accepts both a successCallback call and an onError callback, as demonstrated in the following example.

```
window.requestFileSystem(TEMPORARY, 5 * 1024 * 1024, getFile, handleError);

function getFile(fileSystem) {
    fileSystem.root.getFile("example.txt", { create: true }, fileOpened, handleError);
}

function fileOpened(fileEntry) {
    fileEntry.remove(fileRemoved, handleError);
}

function fileRemoved() {
    alert('Success');
}

function handleError(error) {
    alert(error.code);
}
```

Creating and opening a directory

Working with directories within the FileSystem API is very similar to working with files. For example, to open or create a file, use the getFile method. To do the same with a directory, use the getDirectory method.

The following example creates a new directory called "Chapter16". If it's created successfully, its full path is displayed.

```
window.requestFileSystem(TEMPORARY, 5 * 1024 * 1024, getDirectory, handleError);

function getDirectory(fileSystem) {
    fileSystem.root.getDirectory("Chapter16", { create: true },
        directoryOpened, handleError);
}
```

```
function directoryOpened(directoryEntry) {
    alert(directoryEntry.fullPath); // will display "/Chapter16"
}

function handleError(error) {
    alert(error.code);
}
```

Writing a file to a directory

You learned to add a file to the root directory of your application's file system. The following example writes the file to a new subdirectory.

```
window.requestFileSystem(TEMPORARY, 5 * 1024 * 1024, getDirectory, handleError);

function getDirectory(fileSystem) {
    fileSystem.root.getDirectory("Chapter16", { create: true },
        directoryOpened, handleError);
}

function directoryOpened(directoryEntry) {
    directoryEntry.getFile("example.txt", { create: true }, fileOpened, handleError);
}

function fileOpened(fileEntry) {
    fileEntry.createWriter(writeToFile, handleError);
}

function writeToFile(fileWriter) {
    fileWriter.onwriteend = function() { alert('Success'); };
    fileWriter.onerror = function() { alert('Failed'); };
    fileWriter.seek(fileWriter.length);
    fileWriter.write(new Blob(['Hello world'], {type: 'text/plain'}));
}

function handleError(error) {
    alert(error.code);
}
```

Deleting a directory

The DirectoryEntry object also inherits from the Entry object, which provides a remove method for deleting itself from the file system. However, this method can be used for empty directories only. An error is thrown if the directory contains other subdirectories or files.

```
window.requestFileSystem(TEMPORARY, 5 * 1024 * 1024, getDirectory, handleError);

function getDirectory(fileSystem) {
    fileSystem.root.getDirectory("Chapter16", { create: true },
        directoryOpened, handleError);
}
```

```
function directoryOpened(directoryEntry) {
    directoryEntry.remove(directoryRemoved, handleError);
}

function directoryRemoved() {
    alert('Success');
}

function handleError(error) {
    alert(error.code);
}
```

To delete a directory forcefully, along with any contents under it in subdirectories and files, use the removeRecursively method as follows.

```
function directoryOpened(directoryEntry) {
    directoryEntry.removeRecursively(directoryRemoved, handleError);
}
```

Lesson summary

- You can use the File System API to store binary files on the client's file system.
- Chrome is currently the only major browser supporting File System API.
- Communication with the file system is initiated through the requestFileSystem method available on the window object.
- File systems can be created by using two modes. The first, TEMPORARY, allows the browser to remove the files automatically if space is needed. Only the application or user can delete contents if the second mode, PERSISTENT, is used.
- Files are created and opened by using the getFile method on the DirectoryEntry object.
- A FileWriter is used to write and append to a file.
- The FileReader class contains the following methods for reading the contents of a file: readAsText, readArrayBuffer, and readAsDataURL.
- A file can be removed by calling the FileEntry remove method.

Lesson review

Answer the following questions to test your knowledge of the information in this lesson. You can find the answers to these questions and explanations of why each answer choice is correct or incorrect in the "Answers" section at the end of this chapter.

1. Which of the following methods should you use when storing files that are relatively unimportant and can be removed if the browser is low in available space?

   A. window.requestFileSystem(LOW, 5 * 1024 * 1024, getDirectory, handleError);

   B. window.requestFileSystem(PERSISTENT, 5 * 1024 * 1024, getDirectory, handleError);

    C. window.requestFileSystem(SIMPLE, 5 * 1024 * 1024, getDirectory, handleError);

    D. window.requestFileSystem(TEMPORARY, 5 * 1024 * 1024, getDirectory, handleError);

2. Which of the following allows FileWriter to append data to the end of the file?

    A. fileWriter.seek(fileWriter.length);

    B. fileWriter.seek(fileWriter.end);

    C. fileWriter.moveLast()

    D. fileWriter.moveToEnd();

3. Which of the following removes a directory that contains existing files?

    A. directoryEntry.remove(directoryRemoved, handleError);

    B. directoryEntry.removeRecursively(directoryRemoved, handleError);

    C. directoryEntry.removeAll(directoryRemoved, handleError);

    D. directoryEntry.remove(directoryRemoved, ALL, handleError)

Lesson 4: Working with the offline application HTTP cache

You've learned about several features that provide the opportunity to store key/value pairs, structured data elements, objects, and files. However, none of them alone enables your application to operate offline easily. Suppose you have a dynamic web application that gets all its data from a local IndexedDB instance, but you still need to retrieve items such as CSS files, JavaScript files, images, and the web page itself. To a degree, you already have this feature through the browser cache, but it's always been somewhat unreliable and could not truly operate without a network connection.

HTML5 delivers an improvement to caching with the application cache, which introduces the ability to configure how files are cached by including a manifest file. Within this file is a list of resources to include and exclude from cache and alternate file designations to serve in some cases.

The application cache works behind the scenes to keep the local cache up to date as the manifest file is updated. If you lose Internet connection and the browser is taken offline, it will automatically switch to serve local files.

After this lesson, you will be able to:

- Understand the offline application HTTP cache.
- Implement the offline application HTTP cache.

Estimated lesson time: 20 minutes

Browser support

The application cache is now supported in the latest version of all major browsers. Internet Explorer is the latest to add support with the release of Internet Explorer 10. It's also supported in most mobile browsers, which can make it very useful when cellular data services aren't available.

The cache manifest file

The application cache hinges on the existence of a manifest file in your web application. The key to being served correctly is to use the text/cache-manifest content type in the HTTP response. The file itself can reside anywhere on your web server, such as /home/manifest" or "/manifest.appcache. If you choose to use a static file reference, you might need to configure the MIME type in Internet Information Server (IIS) first or add a mimeMap element to your application's web.config file as follows.

```
<system.webServer>
    <staticContent>
        <mimeMap fileExtension=".appcache" mimeType="text/cache-manifest" />
    </staticContent>
</system.webServer>
```

To include the manifest file in your application, it must be referenced by using the manifest attribute on the page's <html> element as follows.

```
<!DOCTYPE html>
<html manifest="manifest.appcache ">
```

This example references the manifest file by using a relative URL, but you can use an absolute URL as long as it's part of the same origin, as follows.

```
<html manifest="http://www.example.com/manifest.appcache ">
```

Understanding structure

You've learned how to reference a manifest file and that it must be served with the text/cache-manifest content type. The following is what a sample manifest file looks like.

```
CACHE MANIFEST
# version 1.0

# Explicit cache declarations
CACHE:
/Content/Styles/Site.css
http://ajax.aspnetcdn.com/ajax/jQuery/jquery-1.8.0.js

# The following should not be cached
NETWORK:
/Login/
/API/

# Alternative files
```

```
FALLBACK:
/Content/Images/Products/ /Content/Images/offline.jpg
```

There are some important things to point out in this example. First, the top line of the file must always be the CACHE MANIFEST statement. Comment lines begin with a # symbol and will be ignored by the browser. Empty lines are also ignored. The file has the following three sections within it.

- **CACHE** This section contains any items that you want to cache explicitly. The URLs within it can be fully qualified or relative to the location of the manifest file. You can also list these files directly under the CACHE MANIFEST header.

- **NETWORK** This section contains white-listed URLs that require a connection. These files will not be included in the cache, so they will not be available when offline. In the sample, the /API/ section of the site is specified because this area contains services that can only function when a network connection is available.

- **FALLBACK** The last section enables you to specify substitute files that you might not want cached for whatever reason but would like something to be used in their place. The URL on the left side is substituted by the one on the right. In this example, all images in the Products directory should be replaced by a default offline.jpg image.

Updating the cache

When a change is made to the manifest file, the browser is triggered to download every file listed within it. It does this asynchronously behind the scenes, so it won't block the rendering of the page being displayed.

After the browser caches resources listed in the manifest file, those files are held until one of the following occurs.

- The manifest file is updated.
- The user manually clears the cache.
- The cache is updated through a developer-created script.

A change to a resource itself doesn't trigger it to be automatically updated within the cache, so it can be very easy for the cache become stale. A common practice is to include a version number or timestamp as a comment line that is updated with each deployment of the web application as follows.

```
CACHE MANIFEST
# version 1.0
```

 Quick check

- When do you use the FALLBACK section of a manifest file?

Quick check answer

- Use the FALLBACK section to specify substitutions for resources in offline mode.

Understanding events

In general, the application cache process occurs silently, but the window.applicationCache object enables you to inject some custom functionality into that workflow.

As the browser executes each step in the cache process, it fires a series of events on the applicationCache object. The following is a summary of those events.

- **checking**   This is always the first triggered within the sequence of events. It indicates that the browser is checking whether the manifest file has been updated or needs to be downloaded for the first time.

- **noupdate**   If it's determined that the manifest file hasn't changed, the noupdate event will be triggered. No other events will fire afterward.

- **downloading**   If the browser determines that the file has changed or will be downloaded for the first time, this event will be fired as the new files are being downloaded.

- **progress**   As the new files are being downloaded, this event will fire. It will include a total attribute reflecting the number of files to be downloaded. It will also include a loaded attribute to indicate the number of files that have been downloaded thus far.

- **cached**   This event fires after all files have been downloaded for the first time.

- **updateReady**   If an existing cache has been updated, this event will fire to inform you that all files have been downloaded.

- **obsolete**   The obsolete event will fire if the request for the manifest file results in a 404 or 410 result. Contents of the cache will be deleted.

- **error**   Building the cache can fail for a number of reasons, such as an invalid resource URL listed in the manifest. If the process fails, the error event will fire.

The applicationCache object includes an update() method that can be used to start the caching process programmatically, as follows.

```
window.applicationCache.update();
```

After the new cache has been downloaded and the updateReady event has fired, you can call the swapCache method to replace the old cache with the new, as follows.

```
window.applicationCache.addEventListener('updateready',

function(){ window.applicationCache.swapCache(); }, false );
```

Lesson summary

- The application cache incorporates a manifest file that can be customized for how your application operates when in an offline state.

- The first line of a manifest file must contain the CACHE MANIFEST statement.

- URLs can be explicitly included in the cache by adding them to the CACHE section of the file, or they can be added directly underneath the CACHE MANIFEST statement.

- Items that can operate only when a network connection is present should be listed in the NETWORK section of the manifest file.

- The FALLBACK section of the manifest file provides a place to designate file substitutions when in offline mode.

- It's a good idea to include a version number in the manifest file. Cached items are not automatically updated when changed on the server.

- Various events are available on the window.applicationCache object that provide notification so your application can react to cache changes.

Lesson review

Answer the following questions to test your knowledge of the information in this lesson. You can find the answers to these questions and explanations of why each answer choice is correct or incorrect in the "Answers" section at the end of this chapter.

1. Which of the following is a valid statement for the first line of a manifest file?

   A. CACHE

   B. CACHE MANIFEST

   C. CACHE-MANIFEST

   D. CACHE-ALWAYS

2. Which event is fired after an existing cache has been updated with new resources?

   A. downloading

   B. cached

   C. updateReady

   D. completed

Practice exercises

If you encounter a problem completing any of these exercises, the completed projects can be installed from the Practice Exercises folder that is provided with the companion content.

Exercise 1: Modify a contact book to use IndexedDB

In the previous chapter's exercise, you created a contact book that is stored in *localStorage*. In this exercise, you modify that website to use IndexedDB. If you haven't finished the practice exercise in Chapter 15, "Local data with web storage," the Practice Exercises for this chapter include a Visual Studio solution that's ready for you to use. If you're using Internet Explorer, you must have version 10 installed.

1. Open Visual Studio Express 2012 for Web. Click File and choose Open Project. Select the ContactBook folder in the Exercise1Start folder and then select the ContactBook.sln file; click Open.

2. The names of the IndexedDB variables with which you'll need to work vary across different browsers. Handle those differences by adding the following to the top of the ContactsLibrary.js file.

```
window.indexedDB = window.indexedDB || window.mozIndexedDB ||
            window.webkitIndexedDB || window.msIndexedDB;
window.IDBTransaction = window.IDBTransaction || window.webkitIDBTransaction;
window.IDBCursor = window.IDBCursor || window.webkitIDBCursor;
```

3. Prepare to add a database instance that's accessible to all methods in the namespace by adding a *db* variable at the start of the immediately invoked function expression (IIFE) function.

```
this.contactsNamespace = this.contactsNamespace || {};
var ns = this.contactsNamespace;
var db;
var currentRecord;
```

4. Within the initialize method, create the contacts object store and open the database connection. Instead of just relying on an item's index within the total resultset, allow IndexedDB to create an auto-incremented key as follows.

```
ns.initialize = function () {
    $('#btnSave').on('click', ns.save);
    var request = indexedDB.open('Chapter16', 1);

    request.onupgradeneeded = function (response) {
        var options = { keypath: 'id', autoIncrement: true };
        response.currentTarget.result.createObjectStore("contacts", options);
    };

    request.onsuccess = function (response) {
        db = request.result;
        ns.display();
    };
};
```

5. Convert the remaining methods in the order in which they appear in the JavaScript file, starting with the save method. Within it, start a readwrite transaction against the contacts store. If updating an existing record, use the put method. If adding a new record, use the add method.

Notice that this occurs asynchronously.

```
ns.save = function () {
    var contact = currentRecord.contact;
    contact.firstName = $('#firstName').val();
    contact.lastName = $('#lastName').val();
    contact.email = $('#email').val();
    contact.phoneNumber = $('#phoneNumber').val();

    var trans = db.transaction('contacts', 'readwrite');
    var contacts = trans.objectStore("contacts");
    var request = currentRecord.key != null
```

```
                    ? contacts.put(contact, currentRecord.key)
                    : contacts.add(contact);
        request.onsuccess = function (response) {
            ns.display();
        };
    };
};
```

Loading the list of contacts requires the use of a cursor to iterate through and build an array of results. In the previous chapter, the *results* variable was a simple array of contact records. In contrast, this code creates an array of objects that contain the object's key and the contact instance. After the cursor moves past the end of the data set, its result object will be null.

6. At the result object's null point, call the bindToGrid method as follows.

```
ns.display = function () {
    $('#currentAction').html('Add Contact');
    currentRecord = { key: null, contact: {} };
    displayCurrentRecord();

    var trans = db.transaction('contacts', 'readonly');
    var request = trans.objectStore("contacts").openCursor();
    var results = [];

    request.onsuccess = function (response) {
        var cursor = response.target.result;

        if (!cursor) {
            bindToGrid(results);
            return;
        }

        results.push({ key: cursor.key, contact: cursor.value });
        cursor.continue();
    };
};
```

7. The loadContact method can now be changed to use the object store's get method to find the selected record by its key, as follows.

```
ns.loadContact = function () {
    var key = parseInt($(this).attr('data-key'));
    var trans = db.transaction('contacts', 'readonly');
    var store = trans.objectStore("contacts");
    var request = store.get(key);

    request.onsuccess = function (response) {
        $('#currentAction').html('Edit Contact');
        currentRecord = { key: key, contact: response.target.result }
        displayCurrentRecord();
    };
};
```

No changes are needed within the displayCurrentRecord method.

Because the results array that's passed to the bindToGrid method contains objects that are slightly more complex, the for loop needs some modifications. Remember that the data key is now the object's primary key instead of just its index. Your bindToGrid method should look like the following.

```
function bindToGrid(results) {
    var html = '';

    for (var i = 0; i < results.length; i++) {
        var key = results[i].key;
        var contact = results[i].contact;
        html += '<tr><td>' + contact.email + '</td>';
        html += '<td>' + contact.firstName + ' ' + contact.lastName + '</td>';
        html += '<td><a class="edit" href="javascript:void(0)" data-key='
            + key + '>Edit</a></td></tr>';
    }

    html = html || '<tr><td colspan="3">No records available</td></tr>';
    $('#contacts tbody').html(html);
    $('#contacts a.edit').on('click', ns.loadContact);
}
```

When you finish, the final JavaScript file should be similar to the following.

```
/// <reference path="jquery-1.8.3.js" />

window.indexedDB = window.indexedDB || window.mozIndexedDB || window.
webkitIndexedDB || window.msIndexedDB;
window.IDBTransaction = window.IDBTransaction || window.webkitIDBTransaction;
window.IDBCursor = window.IDBCursor || window.webkitIDBCursor;


$(document).ready(function () {
    contactsNamespace.initialize();
});

(function () {
    this.contactsNamespace = this.contactsNamespace || {};
    var ns = this.contactsNamespace;
    var db;
    var currentRecord;

    ns.initialize = function () {
        $('#btnSave').on('click', ns.save);
        var request = indexedDB.open('Chapter16', 1);

        request.onupgradeneeded = function (response) {
            var options = { keypath: 'id', autoIncrement: true };
            response.currentTarget.result.createObjectStore("contacts", options);
        };

        request.onsuccess = function (response) {
            db = request.result;
            ns.display();
        };
```

```
    };

    function retrieveFromStorage() {
        var contactsJSON = localStorage.getItem('contacts');
        return contactsJSON ? JSON.parse(contactsJSON) : [];
    }

    ns.display = function () {
        $('#currentAction').html('Add Contact');
        currentRecord = { key: null, contact: {} };
        displayCurrentRecord();

        var trans = db.transaction('contacts', 'readonly');
        var request = trans.objectStore("contacts").openCursor();
        var results = [];

        request.onsuccess = function (response) {
            var cursor = response.target.result;

            if (!cursor) {
                bindToGrid(results);
                return;
            }

            results.push({ key: cursor.key, contact: cursor.value });
            cursor.continue();
        };
    }

    function bindToGrid(results) {
        var html = '';

        for (var i = 0; i < results.length; i++) {
            var key = results[i].key;
            var contact = results[i].contact;
            html += '<tr><td>' + contact.email + '</td>';
            html += '<td>' + contact.firstName + ' ' + contact.lastName + '</td>';
            html += '<td><a class="edit" href="javascript:void(0)" data-key=' +
key + '>Edit</a></td></tr>';
        }

        html = html || '<tr><td colspan="3">No records available</td></tr>';
        $('#contacts tbody').html(html);
        $('#contacts a.edit').on('click', ns.loadContact);
    }

    ns.loadContact = function () {
        var key = parseInt($(this).attr('data-key'));
        var trans = db.transaction('contacts', 'readonly');
        var store = trans.objectStore("contacts");
        var request = store.get(key);

        request.onsuccess = function (response) {
            $('#currentAction').html('Edit Contact');
            currentRecord = { key: key, contact: response.target.result }
```

```
                    displayCurrentRecord();
            };
        };


        function displayCurrentRecord() {
            var contact = currentRecord.contact;
            $('#firstName').val(contact.firstName);
            $('#lastName').val(contact.lastName);
            $('#email').val(contact.email);
            $('#phoneNumber').val(contact.phoneNumber);
        }

        ns.save = function () {
            var contact = currentRecord.contact;
            contact.firstName = $('#firstName').val();
            contact.lastName = $('#lastName').val();
            contact.email = $('#email').val();
            contact.phoneNumber = $('#phoneNumber').val();

            var trans = db.transaction('contacts', 'readwrite');
            var contacts = trans.objectStore("contacts");
            var request = currentRecord.key != null
                        ? contacts.put(contact, currentRecord.key)
                        : contacts.add(contact);
            request.onsuccess = function (response) {
                ns.display();
            };
        };


    })();
```

8. In the Solution Explorer window, right-click the default.html file and choose Set As Start Page.

9. Run the website and start adding contacts. Try closing the browser and re-running the website to see the persisted contacts.

    The website behaves the same way as in the previous chapter.

Suggested practice exercises

The following additional exercises are designed to give you more opportunities to practice what you've learned and to help you successfully master the lessons presented in this chapter.

- **Exercise 1**   Add the ability to delete items from the contact book application.
- **Exercise 2**   Convert the contact book application to use Web SQL instead of IndexedDB. Make sure you use a browser that supports Web SQL, such as Chrome or Safari.

Answers

This section contains the answers to the lesson review questions in this chapter.

Lesson 1

1. **Correct answer: A**

    A. **Correct:** Because iOS web applications can target Safari's mobile browser specifically, you can be sure that Web SQL will be available.

    B. **Incorrect:** Not all mobile browsers support Web SQL and therefore should be avoided.

    C. **Incorrect:** Not all desktop browsers support Web SQL and therefore should be avoided.

    D. **Incorrect:** Internet Explorer does not support Web SQL.

2. **Correct answer: D**

    A. **Incorrect:** A createDatabase() command does not exist in Web SQL.

    B. **Incorrect:** A new database cannot be created by instantiating an instance of the Database class.

    C. **Incorrect:** An initDatabase() command does not exist in Web SQL.

    D. **Correct:** The openDatabase() command is used for both new and existing databases.

3. **Correct answer: A**

    A. **Correct:** The question mark is used as a placeholder for SQL arguments being passed in.

    B. **Incorrect:** No syntax is available for accessing arguments by a zero-based index.

    C. **Incorrect:** No syntax is available for accessing arguments by a one-based index.

    D. **Incorrect:** This form of placeholder is commonly used for string.Format() method calls in C# but is not valid for Web SQL.

Lesson 2

1. **Correct answer: D**

    A. **Incorrect:** Transactions are supported by IndexedDB.

    B. **Incorrect:** Cursors are supported by IndexedDB.

    C. **Incorrect:** Indexes are supported by IndexedDB.

    D. **Correct:** The SQL syntax is not supported by IndexedDB.

2. **Correct answer: B**

   A. **Incorrect:** An exception is thrown if a write action such as adding a new record is performed by using a transaction in readonly mode.

   B. **Correct:** Transactions must be in readwrite mode to add a new record.

   C. **Incorrect:** If a transaction mode isn't specified, it will default to readonly mode. This would cause an exception to be thrown if an attempt to add a new record is made.

   D. **Incorrect:** There is no createTransaction function.

3. **Correct answer: A**

   A. **Correct:** The get() method finds a specific value by using its key.

   B. **Incorrect:** Object stores do not have a find() method.

   C. **Incorrect:** Object stores do not have a single() method.

   D. **Incorrect:** Object stores do not have a first() method.

Lesson 3

1. **Correct answer: D**

   A. **Incorrect:** LOW is not a valid file system mode.

   B. **Incorrect:** Using PERSISTENT mode only will not allow the browser to remove files if it begins running low in space.

   C. **Incorrect:** SIMPLE is not a valid file system mode.

   D. **Correct:** Using TEMPORARY mode allows the browser to remove files as space is needed.

2. **Correct answer: A**

   A. **Correct:** The seek() method moves the cursor to the given location, which in this case will be the end of the file because you're passing in the entire file length.

   B. **Incorrect:** To find the end of the file, you should use the length property.

   C. **Incorrect:** The FileWriter class does not contain a moveLast() method.

   D. **Incorrect:** The FileWriter class does not contain a moveToEnd() method.

3. **Correct answer: B**

   A. **Incorrect:** The remove method can be used only for directories that are empty. If a file or subdirectory exists within a directorty, an error will be thrown.

   B. **Correct:** The removeRecursively() method removes the directory and all files and subdirectories below it.

   C. **Incorrect:** The DirectoryEntry class does not have a removeAll() method.

   D. **Incorrect:** The DirectoryEntry class does not have a remove() method.

Lesson 4

1. **Correct answer: B**

   A. Incorrect: CACHE is not a valid statement for the first line of a manifest file.

   B. Correct: The CACHE MANIFEST statement must appear at the top of every manifest file.

   C. Incorrect: CACHE-MANIFEST is not a valid statement for the first line of a manifest file.

   D. Incorrect: CACHE-ALWAYS is not a valid statement for the first line of a manifest file.

2. **Correct answer: C**

   A. Incorrect: The downloading event is fired as the browser is downloading new content.

   B. Incorrect: The cached event is fired for newly created caches only.

   C. Correct: The updateReady event tells you when a cache is updated with new resources.

   D. Incorrect: The applicationCache object does not have an available completed event.

Index

Symbols

&& (and) operator, 70–71, 84
+ (addition) operator, 67–68, 70
& (ampersand), 41, 322
* (asterisk) symbol, 147, 155
\\ (backslash) character, 69
^ (caret) symbol, 156
: (colon), 150, 327
© (copyright), 41
/ (division) operator, 67–68, 70
$ (dollar sign), 72–73, 157, 288
" (double quotes), 41, 69
/ (forward slash) character, 337
> (greater-than sign), 41, 148
(hash) symbol
   id selectors and, 146
   internal hyperlinks and, 46
   jQuery support, 289
   in manifest file, 609
   in RGB values, 166
< (less-than sign), 41
* (multiplication) operator, 67–68, 70
! (not) logical operator, 70–71
|| (or) logical operator, 70–71
!=== operator, 84
=== operator, 84
() (parentheses), 68–69
. (period) symbol, 146, 327
+ (plus sign), 67–69, 151, 327
? (question mark), 322, 327
® (registered trademark), 41

; (semicolon), 71, 139
' (single quotes), 69
- (subtraction) operator, 67–69
~ (tilde) character, 152
_ (underscore), 45, 72–73

A

<a> element
   data-linktype attribute, 157–158
   described, 32
   <dfn> element and, 218
   href attribute, 46, 153–157
   target attribute, 46–47
   working with hyperlinks, 46–47
<abbr> element, 32, 214–215, 218
abort event, 119
absolute position (*<div>* element), 182–186
.acc file extension, 444
Access-Control-Allow-Origin header, 380–381
Accessibility window (IE), 159
Accessible Rich Internet Applications (ARIA), 212
accesskey global attribute, 37
<acronym> element, 214
:active pseudo class, 149
addEventListener() function, 115, 295, 567
addition (+) operator, 67–68, 70
<address> element, 32, 215
adjacent selectors, 151–152
Adobe Flash Player, 557

G

H

I

K

L

M

N

O

embedding content from, 50–52
limitations of, 558
plus sign (+), 67–69, 151, 327
PNG file type, 48
polymorphism, 262
popstate event, 117
Position object
  coords property, 540–541
  timestamp property, 541
PositionOptions object
  described, 544
  enableHighAccuracy property, 544
  maximumAge property, 545
  timeout property, 544
POST method (HTTP), 315–316, 322–323, 365–366
poster attribute (*<video>* element), 441
<pre> element, 34, 217
precedence order
  for element styles, 160–161
  for operators, 68–69
preformatted content, displaying, 217
preload attribute
  <audio> element, 446
  <video> element, 441
preventDefault() function, 512
primitive values, 67
private data
  JavaScript objects and, 268–271
  prototype pattern and, 274–276
privileged methods, 269
<progress> element, 34
progress event, 120, 371, 610
Promise/A specification, 394
promise object (jQuery)
  always() method, 378, 397–399
  asynchronous operations and, 394–395
  chaining promises, 398–400
  conditional calls, 401–402
  creating, 395–397
  Deferred() method, 395–397

described, 377–380, 394–395
done() method, 378, 398–399
fail() method, 378, 397, 399
handling completion cleanup, 397–398
handling failure, 397
parallel execution and, 400
pipe() method, 398–400
progress() method, 378, 400–401
subscribing to completed, 398
then() method, 400, 402
timeouts, 396–397
updating progress, 400–401
when() method, 400, 402
prompt() function, 76–77
properties. *See also* CSS properties
  array, 109–110
  described, 109, 262–263
Properties window, 7, 11
prototype pattern, 271, 274–276
prototype property, 271–274
prototypes, 263
pseudo-class selectors, 148–149
pseudo classes, 148–149, 330
pseudo-element selectors, 148–150
pseudo elements, 149–150
pt measurement unit, 175
publisher-subscriber design pattern, 114
publishing packages, 350–351
PUT method (HTTP), 315–316
px measurement unit, 174

Q

<q> element
  annotating content, 215–216
  cite attribute, 215
  described, 34
QueryString
  form submissions and, 320–323
  Node.js and, 343, 359–360

W

X

About the author

GLENN JOHNSON is a professional trainer, consultant, and developer whose experience spans the past 25 years. As a consultant and developer, he has worked on many large projects, mostly in the insurance industry. Glenn's strengths are with Microsoft products such as ASP.NET, Model-View-Controller (MVC), Silverlight, Windows Presentation Foundation (WPF), Windows Communication Foundation (WCF), and Microsoft SQL Server using C#, Visual Basic, and T-SQL. This is yet another of many .NET books that Glenn has authored. He also develops courseware for and teaches classes in many countries on HTML5, JavaScript, Microsoft MVC, Microsoft ASP.NET, Visual Basic .NET, C#, and the .NET Framework.

Glenn holds the following Microsoft certifications: MCT, MCPD, MCTS, MCAD, MCSD, MCDBA, MCP + Site Building, MCSE + Internet, MCP + Internet, and MCSE. You can find Glenn's website at *http://GJTT.com*.

Training Guide: Programming in HTML5 with JavaScript and CSS3 and Exam 70-480

This book is designed to help build and advance your job-role expertise. In addition, it covers some of the topics and skills related to Microsoft Certification Exam 70-480 and might be useful as a complementary study resource.

Note: This book is not designed to cover all exam topics; see the following chart. If you are preparing for the exam, use additional materials to help bolster your readiness, in conjunction with real-world experience.

EXAM OBJECTIVES/SKILLS	SEE TOPIC-RELATED COVERAGE HERE
IMPLEMENT AND MANIPULATE DOCUMENT STRUCTURES AND OBJECTS	
Create the document structure.	Chapters 2 and 5
Write code that interacts with UI controls.	Chapters 3, 7, 11, 12, and 13
Apply styling to HTML elements programmatically.	Chapter 4
Implement HTML5 APIs.	Chapters 10, 14, 15, and 16
Establish the scope of objects and variables.	Chapters 3 and 6
Create and implement objects and methods.	Chapter 6
IMPLEMENT PROGRAM FLOW	
Implement program flow.	Chapter 3 and 6
Raise and handle an event.	Chapter 3 and 6
Implement exception handling.	Chapter 3
Implement a callback.	Chapter 3, 6, 8, and 9
Create a web worker process.	Chapter 9
ACCESS AND SECURE DATA	
Validate user input by using HTML5 elements.	Chapter 7
Validate user input by using JavaScript.	Chapter 7
Consume data.	Chapter 8
Serialize, deserialize, and transmit data.	Chapter 7

USE CSS3 IN APPLICATIONS

Style HTML text properties.	Chapter 4
Style HTML box properties.	Chapter 4
Create a flexible content layout.	Chapter 4
Create an animated and adaptive UI.	Chapter 4
Find elements by using CSS selectors and jQuery.	Chapter 4 and 6
Structure a CSS file by using CSS selectors.	Chapter 4

For complete information about Exam 70-480, visit *http://www.microsoft.com/learning/en/us /exam.aspx?ID=70-480*. In addition, for more information about Microsoft certifications, visit *http://www.microsoft.com/learning*.

What do you think of this book?

We want to hear from you!
To participate in a brief online survey, please visit:

microsoft.com/learning/booksurvey

Tell us how well this book meets your needs—what works effectively, and what we can do better. Your feedback will help us continually improve our books and learning resources for you.

Thank you in advance for your input!